Karen Bro

SPAIN

Charming Inns & Itineraries

Written by
CYNTHIA SAUVAGE and CLARE BROWN

Illustrations by Barbara Tapp
Cover Painting by Jann Pollard

Karen Brown's Guides, San Mateo, California

Karen Brown Titles

Austria: Charming Inns & Itineraries

California: Charming Inns & Itineraries

England: Charming Bed & Breakfasts

England, Wales & Scotland: Charming Hotels & Itineraries

France: Charming Bed & Breakfasts

France: Charming Inns & Itineraries

Germany: Charming Inns & Itineraries

Ireland: Charming Inns & Itineraries

Italy: Charming Bed & Breakfasts

Italy: Charming Inns & Itineraries

Portugal: Charming Inns & Itineraries

Spain: Charming Inns & Itineraries

Switzerland: Charming Inns & Itineraries

Dedicated
to
Cyndi & David
and their sons
Michael & Evan

The painting on the front cover is the Alhambra Palace, Granada

Editors: Clare Brown, Karen Brown, June Brown, Kim Brown Holmsen, Iris Sandilands.

Illustrations: Barbara Tapp; Cover painting: Jann Pollard.

Maps: Susanne Lau Alloway—Greenleaf Design & Graphics; Back cover photo: William H. Brown.

Copyright © 1985, 1986, 1988, 1992, 1993, 1995, 1996, 1997, 1998, 1999 by Karen Brown's Guides.

This book or parts thereof may not be reproduced in any form without obtaining written permission from the publisher: Karen Brown's Guides, P.O. Box 70, San Mateo, CA 94401, USA, email: karen@karenbrown.com.

Distributed by Fodor's Travel Publications, Inc., 201 East 50th Street, New York, NY 10022, USA.

Distributed in the United Kingdom by Random House UK, 20 Vauxhall Bridge Road, London, SW1V 2SA, phone: 44 171 973 9000, fax: 44 171 840 8408.

Distributed in Australia by Random House Australia, 20 Alfred Street, Milsons Point, Sydney NSW 2061, Australia, phone: 61 2 9954 9966, fax: 61 2 9954 4562.

Distributed in New Zealand by Random House New Zealand, 18 Poland Road, Glenfield, Auckland, New Zealand, phone: 64 9 444 7197, fax: 64 9 444 7524.

Distributed in South Africa by Random House South Africa, Endulani, East Wing, 5A Jubilee Road, Parktown 2193, South Africa, phone: 27 11 484 3538, fax: 27 11 484 6180.

A catalog record for this book is available from the British Library.

Library of Congress Cataloging-in-Publication Data

Sauvage, Cynthia, 1955-
    Karen Brown's Spain : charming inns & itineraries / written by
  Cynthia Sauvage and Clare Brown ; illustrations by Barbara Tapp ;
  cover painting by Jann Pollard.
      p.   cm. -- (Karen Brown's country inn series)
    Includes index.
    ISBN 0-930328-82-5
    1. Hotels--Spain--Guidebooks. 2. Spain--Guidebooks. I. Brown,
  Clare.   II. Title.   III. Series.
  TX907.5.S7S28   1999
  647. 9446' 01--dc21   98-6799
                                              CIP

Contents

INTRODUCTION

Introduction   1
About This Guide   2
About Spain   3–23
About Itineraries   24–34
About Hotels   35–44

ITINERARIES

Overview of Itineraries   45
Moorish Memories   46–62
Pilgrimage to Santiago   63–76
Treasures off the Beaten Track   77–90
Cradle of the Conquistadors   91–106
Old Castile and the Cantabrian Coast   107–124
The Costa Brava and Beyond   125–134
Andalusian Adventures   135–144
Madrid and More   145–156
Seville Highlights   157–162
Barcelona Highlights   163–168

HOTEL DESCRIPTIONS

Hotels Listed Alphabetically by Town   169–290

MAPS

Maps   291–300

RESERVATION LETTER

Reservation Letter in Spanish and English   301

INDEX

Hotels, Towns, Sightseeing   302–315

Introduction

Once you fall under Spain's magical spell, there will be no breaking free, nor any urge to do so—only the desire to return, again and again. However, many seasoned travelers never experience its enchantment, since Spain is considered somewhat "off the beaten path." Outside the major cities, you quickly find yourself away from hoards of tourists and happily immersed in the magic of places that haven't changed for hundreds of years. You will be entranced by the beauty of the landscape, the rich selection of places to see, the diversity of the culture, and the warmth of welcome. We are constantly amazed that more people have not yet discovered Spain's many wonders and hope our guide will entice you to visit. You too will become addicted to its boundless charms.

About This Guide

Our goal in writing this guide is to share with you the most charming, historic hotels in Spain and to provide itineraries that will lead you to them by the most scenic and interesting routes. This book is designed for the traveler looking for a guide to more than the capital city and a handful of highlights, for the visitor who wants to add a little out of the ordinary to his agenda. We do not claim to be objective reporters—that sort of treatment is available anywhere—but subjective, on-site raconteurs. We have definite biases toward hotels with romantic ambiance, from charming stone farmhouses tucked in the mountains to sumptuous castles overlooking the sea. We believe that your choice of accommodation helps to weave the tapestry of your trip. The locations you select to spend the night can enhance your memories immeasurably. If you follow our itineraries (each one of which we have traveled personally) and trust in our hotel recommendations (every one of which we have visited personally), you will be assured of Spain's best lodgings while discovering the country's most intriguing destinations.

This book is divided into four parts. First, the *Introduction* gives a general overview of Spain. The second section, *Itineraries*, outlines itineraries throughout Spain to help you plan where to go and what to see. The third section, *Hotel Descriptions*, is our recommended selection of hotels in all price ranges with a description, an illustration, and pertinent information provided on each one. The fourth section, *Maps*, pinpoints the location of each of the recommended hotels.

About Spain

Spain is a country with something for everyone: from the birthplace of Don Juan to the birthplace of Hernán Cortés, Conquistador of Mexico, from the tomb of St. James the Apostle to the tomb of El Cid, Spain's medieval epic hero. You can visit the plains traversed by Don Quixote in search of "wrongs to right" and can admire the quixotic architectural achievements of Antonio Gaudí. You can drive the highest road in Europe and visit the largest wildlife refuge. You can see the youthful work of Picasso and the mature work of Salvador Dalí. To cap it all off, there are great beaches, spectacular mountains, stunning gorges, beautiful landscapes, fine dining, and, above all—a warm, welcoming people. Following are some facts about Spain, listed alphabetically.

BANKS

Generally, banks in Spain are open from 9 am to 1:30 pm, sometimes 2 pm, Monday through Friday. Some banks (most frequently in larger towns) maintain similar business hours on Saturday. Many, but not all, exchange foreign currency: look for a *Cambio* (exchange) sign outside the bank. Often your hotel or the local tourist office will exchange your dollars, though usually at a slightly less-favorable rate than at the bank.

CLIMATE

There are three distinct climates in Spain, dividing the country in thirds from north to south. The northern area is subject to the moderating Atlantic currents and has a relatively good climate for most of the year—too cold to swim in winter, but seldom bitterly cold either; summer is warm, but never extremely hot. The central plateau is cut off from those moderating currents and has what the Spanish call *nueve meses de invierno y tres de infierno* (nine months of winter and three of hell). The southern third of the country has a more Mediterranean climate: relatively warm, though with damp winters, and often brutal heat in midsummer, which is slightly alleviated along the coastal areas by sea breezes. If you venture to some of Spain's exotic islands, you will find still other climates. In fact, on some of the Canary Islands (just off the coast of Africa), it is so dry that sometimes it doesn't rain for the entire year.

CLOTHING

Standards of formality can be generalized: In the most elegant city restaurants, dresses and coats and ties are common, though only occasionally required. Skimpy summer attire, though common in resort areas, might make you feel conspicuous elsewhere. When visiting Spain's magnificent cathedrals, it is respectful to dress conservatively.

CURRENT–VOLTAGE

You will need a transformer plus an adapter if you plan to take an American-made electrical appliance. Even if the appliance is dual-voltage, as many of them are these days, you'll still need an adapter plug. The voltage is usually 220, but in a few places 110 is used. Occasionally a 110 outlet is provided in the hotel bathroom, but these should be used only for small appliances such as electric razors, since they usually can't handle things like hair dryers. Be sure to check with the manager if the outlet is not clearly marked.

DRIVING

CAR RENTAL: This guide is the perfect companion for the traveler who wants to experience Spain by car. Most of the major car rental agencies maintain offices in cities throughout Spain. It is usually possible to pick up a car in one city and drop it off in another, although sometimes a surcharge is made.

DRIVER'S LICENSE: You will need to have a valid driver's license from your home country.

GASOLINE: Gasoline is relatively expensive (perhaps double the USA price) and should be considered in your budget if you plan to drive extensively. Gasoline is available in any small town and at frequent intervals along the freeways. Diesel (called *gasoil* or *gasoleo* in Spain) is considerably less costly. With a little common sense, you should have no trouble finding fuel. Many of the major gas stations accept credit cards—if so, most display a sign with the credit card emblems.

ROADS: Roads in Spain run the gamut from superb freeways to barely two-lane country roads (and, as you might expect, our countryside itineraries find you more often on the latter). Travel on the freeways is swift, but as a rule-of-thumb, calculate that you will average only about 50–60 kilometers per hour on the country roads. However, the leisurely pace allows you time to enjoy your surroundings as you drive. The personality of the country does not lend itself to an accelerated pace, nor do the itineraries.

There is order to the Spanish road numbers. A (A6, for example) indicates freeways. N plus a Roman numeral (NIV) indicates major national highways that radiate like spokes from Madrid. N with an Arabic numeral (N403) indicates minor national highways that connect the major ones. C (C321) indicates regional roads, and two letters (which are the first two letters in the name of the province, e.g., TO1234 for Toledo) indicate provincial roads. Their size and the speed possible is usually correspondingly lower as you go down the list from freeways to provincial roads. Roads are constantly being upgraded, so you will encounter many pleasant surprises—a road that looks of questionable quality on a map might turn out to be wider than expected and freshly re-tarred.

Some of the longer freeways are toll roads and every so often require that you pass through a toll booth. When you enter the highway, usually you will be given a ticket with the point of entry marked and will pay according to the number of kilometers accrued when you leave the highway. If you don't know Spanish, look for the amount due on the lighted sign at the booth. While these freeways are excellent and generally uncrowded, the tolls take their "toll" on your wallet if you drive all day on them. Wherever there are freeways, there are also parallel non-toll highways, but you can expect them to double the driving time between two points. Most of the toll stations will take a credit card. This is a great convenience—just one quick swish of your card through their computer and you are on your way.

SEAT BELTS: The use of seat belts is mandatory in Spain, and the law is strongly enforced both in cities and in the countryside, so get into the habit of buckling up when you get into the car.

TRAFFIC: This is never a problem on the freeways. However, on smaller roads it can be ferocious. If you're trying to cover a lot of ground in a given day, we suggest that you try to drive during siesta time—between 1 and 4 pm—when many trucks and buses stop for lunch. In the large cities, unfamiliarity combined with traffic, parking problems, and the fact that almost no two streets are parallel, make driving a trial for all but the bravest of souls. Our preference is to leave the car in the hotel parking lot (or one recommended by the hotel) and take cabs or walk around the cities. Underground public parking areas are common and are designated by a rectangular blue sign with a large white "P." In Madrid and Barcelona try the excellent subway systems (called the Metro and marked with signs bearing a large "M"). If you're stopping to visit a town along an itinerary route, we suggest you park on or near a main square (for easy recall), then venture on by foot into those streets that were never designed with cars in mind. It is not uncommon for parking areas on central streets and plazas to be *vigilados* (overseen) by an attendant, usually wearing something resembling a uniform. He may direct you to a free spot and will approach you after you park—a small tip is appropriate.

ECONOMY

Though long known as a travel bargain, since its entry into the European Union (EU) Spain has made appreciable progress toward bringing the cost of its commodities (including tourist facilities) closer to the level of other EEC members. Tourism accounts for a large share of foreign income, with the number of tourists entering each year exceeding the native population of over 38 million. Fortunately, they don't all arrive at the same time—the vast majority of visitors comes in July and August.

ENGLISH

We suggest you tuck in your suitcase a Spanish phrase book (Berlitz has an excellent one). In the large hotels in the major cities, you will probably never use it, but elsewhere you might find situations where English is not spoken. Most hotels and paradors have someone on the staff who speaks English, but he/she is not always available. When this happens, just pull out your trusty phrase book and point—Spaniards are friendly and you'll eventually make yourself understood (and probably learn some Spanish while you're at it). If you make advance reservations, be sure to take your letters of confirmation and/or vouchers with you: it will save a lot of pointing.

FESTIVALS AND FOLKLORE

By far the six most internationally renowned Spanish festivals are *Semana Santa* (Holy Week), which is celebrated throughout the country; the *Feria* in Seville (the week leading up to Easter and the second week after it, respectively); the *Festival of San Fermín* in Pamplona, which features the running of the bulls (the second week of July); the *Fallas* in Valencia (the middle of March); the *Festival of St. James* in Santiago (the last two weeks of July); and *Carnival* in Cadiz (the week in which Ash Wednesday falls).

In addition, every Spanish town has its patron saint, and every saint its day of honor, so there are as many festivals as there are Spanish towns. If you know where you want to go ahead of time, write to the Tourist Office of Spain or the *Oficina de Turismo* (Tourist Office) in the town(s) you plan to visit for a list of festival dates so that you might arrange your visit to coincide with one or several of these colorful events. Be forewarned, however, that hotel space will be at a premium and room rates are almost always more expensive during festival time.

FOOD AND DRINK

Today, Spanish cuisine is approaching the international European standard. The government rates restaurants from one to five forks: however, its rating system is based on such matters as the number of choices on the menu and the wine cellar rather than the quality of the food, so it can be misleading. For instance, in order to receive three or more forks, the headwaiter must speak, and the menu must be translated into, several languages (which often makes for amusing reading)—an achievement that does not reflect upon the dishes served. A modest-appearing and reasonably priced restaurant will often offer good, regional fare.

A very important aspect of dining in Spain is to acclimate yourself to the national time schedule. Breakfast is at the same time as at home. The main meal, however, is almost exclusively eaten at around 2 pm. Most restaurants open around 1 pm and close about 4 pm and it is during this period that they offer their main menu that can be expected to have almost everything on it. They open again at about 8:30 or 9 pm for dinner, which is normally a light meal and is served until 10 or 11 pm, and, often, even midnight. Traditionally, restaurants have a reduced menu in the evening, although it seems that nowadays more and more establishments are offering the same fare at night as at midday, as Spain becomes increasingly "Europeanized," a process which is taking place rapidly and, logically enough, from north to south in the country. In Catalonia and the Basque country, you'll find that restaurants close earlier—a fact that astounds even many

Spaniards. Restaurants that cater to tourists—such as the parador dining rooms—are the most flexible and will normally offer a full menu in the evening. We feel it is most comfortable to adjust to the Spanish schedule if possible. You may find the service less than perfect if you take a table at a busy restaurant at 2 pm and order only a sandwich, and you may be disappointed if you expect to have a five-course dinner in the evening. Between the *tapas* (munchies) available at all bars at almost all times, and the numerous *cafeterias* where small, quick meals can be had at any hour, you won't starve.

By far the most common type of food on the Spanish menu is the wide variety of seafood. Many of these are totally unknown to most Americans (even where the menu is translated, it doesn't necessarily help). Items such as *angulas* (baby eels), numerous varieties of squid (*calamares*) and octopus (*pulpo*), and shellfish are best viewed as an adventure. You will find many of them excellent and should definitely experiment. Organ meats—such as brains and sweetbreads—are also common and, prepared in many different ways, can be delicious.

If there is any dish more common than seafood, it is the *tortilla española* (Spanish omelet) which is made with eggs and potatoes. It will be found on almost every menu as an appetizer or as a main course for the evening meal. It is also often available as a sandwich (*bocadillo*).

There are a few things you should note about the names of eating and drinking establishments. A *bar* is seldom what we call by that name. It is usually a place where everything from coffee to alcohol is served and is frequented by patrons of all ages. Continental breakfast is served there too, as are pastries and other desserts. Bars often also serve simple sandwiches. A *café* is about the same thing, and indeed, these places are often called *café-bar*—these are the spots that often have tables outside when the weather permits. A *cafeteria* offers a modest but complete menu and relatively fast service. This seldom involves self-service, but provides a less elaborate setting for a meal than the typical restaurant.

Wine is ubiquitous. In the large fancy restaurants a good selection of imported wines is usually available along with the extensive wines of Spain. In smaller restaurants the list is mostly Spanish, which is often a rich selection indeed, and fun to sample. Probably the best wines come from the Rioja region around Logroño. These are followed by those of the Valdepeñas area of La Mancha, which are slightly more astringent. But there are many other smaller wine-producing regions, some of which we'll point out in the itineraries. If you have no particular favorite, you'll rarely go wrong by requesting the *vino de la casa*, often a wine bottled especially for the restaurant, or else a *vino regional* (regional wine), either *tinto* (red), *blanco* (white), or *rosado* (rose), according to your preference.

Sangría is a national favorite, made from red wine mixed with fresh fruit and liqueur, with infinite variations on that theme, and served over ice. It's a great thirst-quencher and, even if it doesn't appear on the menu, any place will happily drum up a passable *sangría*.

If there is a more common drink than wine in Spain, it is coffee. Spanish coffee is usually served as what we call espresso in the United States. It is thus a small cup of very strong brew to which most people add a considerable amount of sugar. Here are some of the common terms used in ordering: *café solo*—a demitasse of espresso; *café solo doble*—a double portion of the same; *café con leche*—the same coffee with an equal amount of warm milk added to it; *café cortado*—espresso with just a splash of milk added.

Beer is another favorite, and is always good, sometimes excellent, especially on hot days in a shady plaza. Asking for *una cerveza* will get you a bottle of regional beer or a draught (*cerveza de barril*). *Una caña* will get you a small glass of draught, and the request for *un tanque* will result in a large glass of the refreshing brew.

Another very common beverage ordered in Spanish restaurants is, believe it or not, water: the bottled kind. Though there is nothing wrong with *agua natural* (tap water), *agua mineral* (mineral water) is popular in either *litro* or *medio litro* (liter or half-liter) sizes. It may also be ordered *con* or *sin gas* (with or without carbonation). You'll notice that Spaniards often dilute their wine with it.

Once you leave the large cities and tourist-frequented restaurants, you'll find that menus are poorly translated, or not translated at all. The following list includes some of the terms of traditional specialties to be found on most Spanish menus:

Desayuno (breakfast): This may be a Continental breakfast, consisting of *pan* (bread) and/or *pan dulce* (sweet rolls) along with *café* (coffee), *te* (tea), *leche* (milk), or *chocolate* (hot chocolate). Many hotels (and all the paradors) offer elaborate buffet breakfasts that include various fruits, cereals, breads, yogurts, cheeses, and meats plus sometimes extras such as *huevos* (eggs)—either *revueltos* (scrambled), *fritos* (fried sunny side up), *pasados por agua* (boiled), *poche* (poached), or in a *tortilla* (omelet).

Comida (lunch): This is the main meal of the day for most Spaniards and is taken around 2 pm. It normally consists of several courses: *entremeses* (appetizers), *sopas* (soup, usually of the thick variety), *carnes* (meat dishes), *pescados y mariscos* (fish and shellfish), *postres* (desserts), and, of course, *vino*. No one orders all these courses—three is most common.

Merienda (afternoon snack): This is taken around 6 pm by many people and may consist of any kind of light food. The most common are *pasteles* (pie or cake, not usually as good as they) and churros (deep-fried dough, somewhat like a stick-shaped donut) along with coffee or chocolate.

Tapas (hors d'oeuvres): This is as much a social tradition as a kind of food and is a feature of after-work bar hopping. Since the variety of *tapas* is apparently infinite, a good method is to search out a bar where they are on display so you can point to what you want. Also available at this time (8 to 10 pm, more or less) are *raciónes* (orders, approximately) which are the same things, but in larger portions (a ración will be a plateful of meatballs, for example, whereas a *tapa* will be just a couple).

Cena (supper): This meal has traditionally been taken in Spain after 10 pm and has been a light meal (one course of the same kinds of things as at lunch). Due to Spain's increasing contact with the rest of Europe in the last decade, customs are changing somewhat. Especially in the larger cities and along the French border, you'll find people eating earlier and restaurants offering a more complete menu at night. Most of the paradors and hotels begin serving the evening meal anywhere from 8 to 9 pm.

Aceite (olive oil): About the only kind of oil used to cook with in Spain and used in many, many dishes.

Carne (meat): *Ternera* (technically veal, but really closer to what we call beef) comes in *chuletas* (veal chop, but similar to a T-bone steak if it's thick), *solomillo* (sirloin), *entrecot* (ribeye), *filete* (thinly sliced and pan fried), and *asada* (roasted). *Cerdo* (pork) and *pollo* (chicken) are also commonly found on menus. In central Spain *cochinillo asado* (roast suckling pig) is a common specialty.

Ensalada mixta (tossed green salad): Besides lettuce, this usually contains any or all of the following: olives, tomato, onion, tuna, hard-boiled egg. But remember that there is only one salad dressing in the entire country: *vinagre* (vinegar) and *aceite* (olive oil).

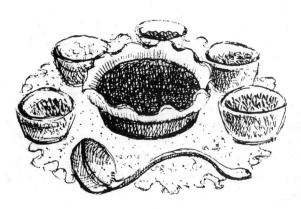

Gazpacho: Another justifiably famous Spanish dish, this is a cold tomato-based soup with various spices and olive oil, and garnished with bits of bread, bacon, green onions, celery, crumbled egg, etc. You are usually given a choice of garnishes at the table. Gazpacho is one of Spain's Moorish legacies, and has multiple variations even though it is usually called *gazpacho Andaluz*, which is the most popular kind. One common variation in the south is *gazpacho de almendras* (almonds), which is white and has thinly sliced almonds floating on top and raisins in it, but tastes pretty much like the regular kind. The soup is an absolutely wonderful cooler if you've been out in the summer heat seeing sights all morning.

Jamön serrano (cured ham, similar to prosciutto): A favorite of most Spaniards as a *tapa, a bocadillo,* or as an added ingredient to another meat dish. There are many varieties and qualities and you'll see them hanging from the ceiling in bars with little cups to catch the juice so it doesn't fall on the customers. *Pata negra* (literally "black foot," a darker variety) is considered the best.

Paella: Probably Spain's best-known dish, it has as many variations as there are Spanish chefs. Based on saffron-flavored rice and olive oil, it may contain any kind of fish, shellfish, chicken, sausage, green peas, beans, bell peppers, or any combination of these. Because it is complicated to make, it may be offered for a minimum of two people and the menu may warn you that there will be a 20- to 30-minute wait if you order it. Connoisseurs will tell you not to order it in the evening because it will be left over from lunch; but, in our experience, better restaurants make it fresh to order.

Pescados y mariscos (fish and shellfish): *Rape* (angler fish), *merluza* (hake), *mero* and *ubina* (sea bass), *lenguado* (sole), and *trucha* (trout) are the common fish varieties. *Pez Espada* (swordfish, also called *aguja* and *emperador*) is often offered thickly sliced like steak and can be superb. *Gambas* (shrimp), *langosta* (a small variety of lobster), *langostino* (large prawns), *almejas* (clams), and *mejillones* (mussels) are common shellfish. In the northern part of Spain there are also *vieiras* (scallops), *centollo* (spider crab), and *changurro* (sizzling crab casserole). A *zarzuela* is a commonly offered fish stew and has the usual infinite number of variations. Although not native to Spain, salmon is popular and frequently found on the menu.

Preparation: Many of the terms describing preparation are relatively meaningless because they simply refer to the origin—*a la Bilbaína*, for example, means Bilbao style, but it never seems to mean the same thing twice. A few terms which are reliable: *al ajillo* (sautéed in garlic), *a la plancha* (grilled), *al pil pil* (sautéed with garlic and olive oil, often with hot pepper), *frito* (fried), *cocido* (stewed), *a la brasa* or *a la parrilla* (charcoal broiled), *en brocheta* (skewered), *al horno* (baked in the oven), and *asado* (roasted).

GEOGRAPHY

Few people realize that Spain, tucked away on the Iberian peninsula, is actually one of Europe's largest countries (second only to France). Also surprisingly, Spain boasts one of the highest average elevations in all of Europe (second only to Switzerland). To continue its accolades, Spain has the highest capital in all of Europe—Madrid. Plus Spain is tops in other areas: her rich, red soil is perfect for growing olives (Spain leads the world in production) and her gentle hills are conducive to the production of grapes (Spain has more land planted in wine grapes than anywhere else in the world).

GOVERNMENT

The current government of Spain (dating from 1975 when Franco died) is a constitutional monarchy similar to Great Britain. The monarchy is hereditary and is balanced by a parliament (called the Cortés). The president is elected in somewhat the same fashion as the British prime minister. The traditional regions, such as Catalonia and Andalusia, which grew up during the Middle Ages, have been granted a degree of self control that might be compared to the powers held by the states in the United States. Strong regionalist identification has always been, and still is, characteristic of Spanish politics.

HISTORY

EARLY PERIOD: Traces of cave-dwelling prehistoric man—Neolithic, Megalithic, and Magdalenian—have been discovered all over the peninsula. Around the 6th century B.C. the area was widely inhabited by the Celts from the north and the Iberians from Africa. The Phoenicians, the Greeks, and especially the Carthaginians founded ports at Cadiz (1100 B.C.), Málaga, Huelva, and Ampurias (north of Barcelona). As a result of the Second Punic War (2nd century B.C.), the peninsula became a Roman colony.

ROMAN PERIOD: Hispania was the most heavily colonized of all Rome's dominions and, thus, the basis for modern Spanish culture. Its language, legal system, and religion all spring from that 600-year period. A number of Roman emperors were born in Spain of either Roman or Hispanic parents, and Julius Caesar himself served there and learned the art of bullfighting. When the entire Roman Empire was overrun by the Germanic tribes from the north, Spain suffered the same fate.

VISIGOTH PERIOD: By the 5th century A.D. the Visigoths had subdued the peninsula almost completely (the Basque area was an exception) and had adopted Roman Catholicism as their own. Their feudalistic system saw the origin of the traditional Spanish regions as kingdoms were combined and divided over the next centuries. Their political system involved a monarch who served at the pleasure of the feudal lords and was thus subject to considerable instability as the kaleidoscope of dynastic unions changed constantly. This characteristic strife provided the opportunity, in 711, for the Moors (Islamic Africans) to invade and sweep across the peninsula from south to north in the space of two decades.

MOORISH PERIOD: The Moors were tolerant people and allowed a diversity of religions to co-exist. At that point in history they represented the highest level of civilization in the western world and contributed greatly to Spanish culture—still evident today in Spanish architecture, painting, philosophy, and science. Córdoba, by the 10th century, was perhaps the most advanced city in Europe. Nevertheless, the Spanish Christians regrouped in the inaccessible mountains of Asturias to launch a crusade to retake their country from Moslem domination, an endeavor that was to last almost eight centuries.

RECONQUEST PERIOD: Legend has it that a Christian leader named Pelayo set up the Kingdom of Asturias after the first defeat of the Moors at Covadonga in 718. The Christians finally established their capital at León in 914. Under their control were Asturias and part of Burgos. The remains of St. James the Apostle were discovered in Galicia, and he became the patron saint of the Reconquest, as well as an object of devotion for millions of pilgrims who made the difficult journey along The Way of St. James (through France and across northern Spain) to venerate the holy remains. The pilgrimage to Santiago de Compostela is still made, albeit by more modern means. By the 11th century, as the frontier between the territories of the Christians and the Moors moved slowly southward, it became fortified with castles and, through various marriages and intrigues, the Kingdom of Castille (the name comes from "castle") had come into existence. During approximately the same period, the Basques began their own process of reconquest that included Catalonia and the eastern coastal areas. During this period border battles were constant, both between the Christian kingdoms themselves, and between the Christians and the Moors.

By 1248 the Castilian campaign had recaptured most of southern Spain from the Moors, including Seville, conquered by Ferdinand III (later to become known as St. Ferdinand). Castile, now united with León, included most of the western half and the south of the peninsula, except for Portugal, which had been established as a separate kingdom in the 11th century.

Meanwhile, the monarchs of Aragón had become supreme on the east side of the peninsula (not to mention in Sicily and Naples) and, when united with Catalonia, ruled from southern France to Valencia. The scene was now set for the transcendental step which would lead to the creation of the modern Spanish nation: the marriage of the heir to the Aragonese throne, Ferdinand V, to the heir to the throne of Castile, Isabella I, thenceforth known as *Los Reyes Católicos* (The Catholic Monarchs).

MODERN PERIOD: Ferdinand (who was a model prince in Machiavelli's famous work of that name) and Isabella spent most of their reign strengthening the monarchy and expanding their dominions, including financing the expedition of Columbus. Their daughter, Juana (the Mad), was too handicapped to rule and so her son Charles was elevated to the throne when Ferdinand died. Charles' father was Phillip the Fair of the Hapsburgs, the family who were in control of the Holy Roman Empire which included half of Europe and most of the western hemisphere, so Charles also gained the title of Emperor Charles V. His son, Phillip, to whom he abdicated the crown in 1556, soon added Portugal to his domain. Portugal held an empire of its own, including Brazil in the New World and Mozambique in Africa, as well as several high-powered trading enclaves in Asia. By the end of the 16th century, Spain's dominions literally ringed the world.

The 17th century saw, however, a serious decline in the monarchy with first Phillip III, then Phillip IV, then Charles II showing a decreasing capacity to rule wisely and an increasing desire to live licentiously on the vast income from their New World mineral riches. During this century, Portugal and many of the European territories were lost. When Charles II died in 1700 without an heir, the Bourbons of France took the throne because Charles's sister had married into that royal family. (The current king, Juan Carlos, is a Bourbon.) The series of Bourbons who ruled during the 18th century— Phillip V, Charles III, Charles IV, and Ferdinand VII—proved to be only marginally better than the Hapsburgs who preceded them, so Spain's holdings continued to dwindle, culminating in the loss of all the American possessions by 1825 (except the Caribbean islands and the Philippines). In 1808, Napoleon seduced the decadent Ferdinand VII with the good life in France, meanwhile installing his own brother on the Spanish throne. The Spaniards reacted swiftly, starting on the *dos de mayo* (the second of May) of the same year, and, with the help of the British (for the first and only time in history), soon regained the crown for Ferdinand. The scene was set for continuing conflict when Ferdinand's brother, Don Carlos, at the head of Basque and Navarrese extremists, disputed Ferdinand's claim to the throne.

The 19th century was thus characterized by three so-called "Carlist Wars" of succession and, in 1898, the Spanish-American War. The Bourbons did manage to hold the throne, but lost the remaining territory of the Empire (Cuba, Puerto Rico, Santo Domingo, and the Philippines). This loss gave rise to widespread intellectual speculation on the causes of Spain's decline by the so-called Generation of 1898.

The early years of the 20th century saw the rise of new populist ideas and continuing labor unrest. In 1923, General Miguel Primo de Rivera established a dictatorship with Alfonso XIII's support. The unrest continued, however, especially in Catalonia. In 1931 the King was forced to abdicate and go into exile by the Republican (essentially socialist) party, which, in the same year, proclaimed the government to be Republican. In 1936 the elections were won by the socialist forces and José Antonio Primo de Rivera, Miguel's son, was head of a rightist revolutionary party. In the same year the revolutionaries began an all-out civil war in the south under the direction of General Francisco Franco. Soon afterward, Germany joined the rebels (Hitler was planning to conquer Europe and used Spain as a testing ground for his weapons), whereas the Republicans were supported by the Soviet Union (allegedly in exchange for some 50 metric tons of gold reserves) and the International Brigade. American volunteers served in the Abraham Lincoln Brigade. Ernest Hemingway covered the war as a journalist and later immortalized the brutality of it in *For Whom The Bell Tolls*. By 1939, the Franco forces had won the war, over a million Spaniards had died, and another half-million were in exile.

As a means of gaining Hitler's support, Spain had promised to remain neutral in any wars he engaged in, and was thus not directly involved in World War II. After the war Spain found itself somewhat of an outcast in international circles because of its neutrality and generally perceived sympathy to Germany. It finally became a member of the United Nations in 1955 and returned to active diplomatic involvement, but with limited success due to the authoritarian regime headed by *El Caudillo* (The Chief), Generalísimo Francisco Franco.

In providing for his succession, Franco proclaimed that Spain was a monarchy and Juan Carlos (born in 1938), grandson of Alfonso XIII, would be the future king. When Franco died in 1975, the young king was installed and the process of creating a constitution began. The document was approved in 1978 and orderly elections have occurred since that time. The death of Franco did not signify the disappearance of rightist sentiment, however, and, as late as 1981, the right-wing military attempted a coup. Juan Carlos reacted swiftly to put it down and thus reassured the world that he was a firmly democratic ruler.

PLAZAS

It may be helpful to understand the general layout of most of the cities and towns of Spain. The "heart" of most of them is the main plaza, often referred to as the *Plaza Mayor*. Some larger cities like Madrid have a central plaza in the old quarter plus others in the more recently constructed sections of town. Small towns usually have just one main plaza in the center of the old quarter, the vicinity you probably most want to visit. The main plaza is frequently the most lively area of the city and is often surrounded by shops and outdoor cafés. This will typically be the site of the cathedral and other historic buildings and the area where the ancient custom of the *paseo* or evening stroll takes place. Plazas serve as excellent orientation points. There is usually parking either in the plaza itself or in a nearby garage which makes a good place to park your car since it will be easy to find and you are in the heart of the sightseeing area.

REGIONS AND PROVINCES

Spain is divided into regions, each of which has its own personality and distinct flavor. The landscape changes constantly and as you move from one region to another, you feel as if you are visiting totally different countries. The regions are further divided into provinces. On the last line of each hotel's description, we indicate the region where it is located while the province is shown in the hotel's address. The provinces are extremely important since there are many towns with identical names, so you need to know in which province your hotel is located in order not to get lost. Note: In the map section is a map showing the regions.

SIESTA

Except for restaurants, almost every place of business closes for two to three hours in the day, sometime between 1 and 5 pm. This includes all but the largest tourist attractions (e.g., the Prado), most stores (El Corte Inglés department store is an exception), and offices. (Banks don't reopen to the public in the afternoon.) So, about the only activities in which to engage during the siesta are dining, drowsing, or driving. You will most likely find "Spanish time" easy to adapt to.

TELEPHONES

Telephone calls made from your hotel room can be exceedingly expensive if you charge the call to your hotel bill. The easiest and least expensive method to call the USA is to use a calling card.

TIPPING

As everywhere, tipping is not a simple matter on which to give advice. Most restaurants and hotels include *servicio* in the bill, but a small tip is appropriate when the service is good, especially in restaurants frequented by tourists. "Small" means different things to different people, but certainly should not exceed 5%. In informal bars and cafeterias no tip is expected.

TOURIST OFFICES OF SPAIN

The Spanish tourist offices are a rich source for information about Spain. You can write in advance of your holiday for information. Their contacts are as follows:

A toll-free information number for the USA is (888) 657-7246 (website: www.okspain.org).

USA: Tourist Office of Spain, Water Tower Place, Suite 915 East, 845 North Michigan Avenue, Chicago, IL 60611, USA, tel: (312) 642-1992, fax: (312) 642-9817.

USA: Tourist Office of Spain, 8383 Wilshire Boulevard, Suite 956, Beverly Hills, CA 90211, USA, tel: (323) 658-7188, fax: (323) 658-1061.

USA: Tourist Office of Spain, 1221 Brickell Avenue, Miami, FL 33131, USA, tel: (305) 358-1992, fax: (305) 358-8223.

USA: Tourist Office of Spain, 666 Fifth Avenue, 35th Floor, New York, NY 10103, USA, tel: (212) 265-8822, fax: (212) 265-8864.

CANADA: Tourist Office of Spain, 2 Bloor Street West, Suite 3402, Toronto, Ontario, M4W 3EZ, Canada, tel: (416) 961-3131, fax: (416) 961-1992.

ENGLAND: Spanish Tourist Office, 57–58 St. James's Street, London SW1A 1LD, England, tel: (0171) 486-8077, fax: (0171) 629-4257.

SPAIN: Tourist Office of Spain, Princesa 1, Edif. Torre de Madrid, 28008 Madrid, Spain. Open 9 am to 6 pm Mondays through Fridays, and 9 am to 2 pm on Saturdays.

The Tourist Offices of Spain can provide you with general information or, at your request, specific information about towns, regions, and festivals. Local tourist offices (*oficina de turismo*) are found in most small towns throughout the country—they are well marked and usually located in the heart of the town or city. They offer an incomparable on-site resource, furnishing town maps and details on local and regional highlights that you might otherwise miss. Those in the regional capitals are especially well equipped to provide you with colorful and informative brochures on the surrounding area. Make the local *oficina de turismo* your first stop at each destination.

TRAINS

The Spanish National Railways (called RENFE) has an extensive network of trains throughout the country with various rail passes, round-trip fares, and special rates available for children and seniors. Trains connect almost every city in Spain. In addition to the normal trains, there are others that offer exceptionally fast, convenient service. One of these is a bullet train called the *AVE* that runs several times a day between Madrid and Seville with one stop en route in Córdoba. This once cumbersome journey now takes a mere two hours and forty minutes. The *AVE* is air conditioned, offers a choice of first- or second-class seating, and has cafeteria service. Another bullet train is the *Talgo 200*, which connects Madrid and Málaga. The train journey between these two popular cities used to take seven hours, but with the super-fast *Talgo 200*, the time is cut to under five hours. Both the *AVE* and the *Talgo 200* are sold in the USA by VE Tours, tel: (800) 222-8383, fax: (305) 477-4220, e-mail: vetours@internetmci.com. The telephone number for the RENFE office in Madrid is (91) 527.48.99, the fax number is (91) 528.99.98.

Also available are the *Estrella,* night trains with first- and second-class accommodation, sleeping compartments (berths or couchettes), and sometimes a restaurant or cafeteria service (depending upon the route and time of departure). For long-distance routes, the *Train-Hotel* offers a new dimension in train travel, providing top quality and comfort. These "traveling hotels" cover routes from Barcelona to Milan, Zurich, Paris, and Seville, and from Madrid to Paris, offering *Gran Clase* accommodation, superb restaurant service, and often such extras as individual videos in the carriages, private telephones, and personal attendants. Most rail tickets (except for the *Talgo 200* and the *AVE* trains) can be purchased in the USA through Rail Europe—tel: (800) 848-7245. Call to see if they can assist you with the train of your choice.

ANDALUSIAN EXPRESS: Spain's answer to the famous Orient Express is called the Andalusian Express (*Al-Andalus Expreso*). From the beginning of April to the end of October, this luxurious *belle-époque* train travels weekly on a six-night package. Starting in Madrid or Seville, passengers spend five nights aboard the train which travels through a landscape of olive groves and white towns, ending the trip in Seville or Madrid. A night in Madrid or Seville before the journey completes the package. This meticulously restored train from the 1920s has thirteen cars including two sumptuous dining cars, two bars (one resembles a London club, the other a chic European bistro), five richly paneled sleeping cars (each with six deluxe double cabins and two luxury suites), and two shower cars (with twenty showers, each with its own private dressing room). All of the cabins have their own washbasin (suites also have private toilet and shower). This train is expensive, but offers a nostalgic journey that combines sightseeing excursions along with your meals and accommodations. Reservations for the Andalusian Express can be made in the United States through Marketing Ahead—tel: (800) 223-1356, fax: (212) 686-0271. In Europe reservations can be made through Iberrail in Madrid—tel: (91) 57.15.815, fax: (91) 57.16.056.

About Itineraries

The itineraries section of this guide features itineraries covering most of Spain. They may be taken in whole or in part, or strung together for a longer journey. Each of the itineraries highlights a different region of the country, and they are of different lengths, enabling you to find one or more to suit your individual taste and schedule. They are designed to accommodate customization.

HOW TO FIND YOUR WAY

ITINERARY MAPS: Accompanying each itinerary is a map showing the routing and places of interest along the way. These are an artist's renderings and are not meant to replace a good commercial map. Before departure, it is truly vital to purchase detailed maps showing highway numbers, expressways, alternate routes, and distances. There are many maps you can buy covering the whole of Spain, but these are not precise enough. Michelin has seven regional maps of Spain that are exceptionally reliable and tie in with the Michelin *Green Guide* for Spain (an excellent source for more detail on sights, museums, and places of interest). Because many of the places we recommend are off the beaten path, you will have difficulty finding them on most maps. However, the Michelin regional maps are so detailed and have such an extensive index, that you can pinpoint each place to stay and highlight your customized itinerary before you ever leave home.

We have intentionally not specified how many nights to stay at each destination—your personality and time restraints will dictate what is best for you. We strongly suggest concentrating your time in fewer locations in order to relax, unpack, and savor the atmosphere and novelty of the spot. We recommend choosing a few hotels that most appeal to you and using them as hubs from which to explore the surrounding regions.

If you're new to Spain and planning a trip there, we hope that upon reading through the itineraries and hotel descriptions, you'll get a feel for which places merit the most time and which can be done justice with an overnight stay. In other words, this guide should be a reference and not a prescription for your personalized trip. In each destination in the itinerary we have recommendations of places to stay. Look in the itinerary section to study the details of each hotel to make your selection. As you study the itinerary maps, note that there are stars locating hotels near the recommended overnight destinations. If you love staying in the countryside, look for stars representing hotels outside of the larger cities and consider "commuting" (you usually will find the price more of a bargain).

FAVORITE PLACES

As you read through our itineraries, you might become muddled as to choices. All of Spain is enchanting—filled with towns that brim with the romance of yesteryear. To assist you, we have described some of our favorite places. Many of these are so well known that they are probably already on your schedule to see, but others are gems that we were surprised to discover. The following list of "favorites" is very subjective— destinations that we think outstanding. Most of these are also featured in our individual itineraries. In the back of the guide (in the *Hotel Descriptions* section) you can find hotel accommodations in all of the following places:

ARCOS DE LA FRONTERA (Andalusia): Arcos de la Frontera is one of the many charming towns dotting the hills that rise from the Costa del Sol. Its setting is very special—the indisputably beautiful town is set on a rocky promontory with cliffs dropping down to the Guadalete river. The town has narrow, sloping streets lined by whitewashed houses, a magnificent cathedral, and several charming places to stay.

ÁVILA (Castilla y León): Ávila cannot help being on every list of special places. Located conveniently close to Madrid, the town is one of the best preserved in Spain. Try to approach from the west where you get the most impressive first impact of the town—you will be astounded by the perfection of the 12th-century crenelated walls punctuated by mighty stone towers surrounding the city. These medieval fortifications are without a doubt some of the finest remaining in Europe. Within the town are a maze of narrow streets and a splendid cathedral that must not be missed.

BARCELONA (Catalonia): Barcelona, the second largest city in Spain, is on the Mediterranean coast, not far from the French border. We have a complete chapter devoted to this delightful city (see *Barcelona Highlights* on pages 163–168).

CARMONA (Andalusia): Carmona is located just a short drive east of Seville and makes a delightful day's excursion, or overnight. The walled town crowns a small hill that rises out of the vast plains of the Guadalquivir. The main entrance is on the lower level through the old Moorish gates, leading to a maze of narrow streets which twist up the hill. Although there are several churches to peek into, the main attraction is the town itself. In its former glory, Carmona was obviously a town of great wealth—the streets are lined with 17th- and 18th-century palaces built by nobility.

CHINCHÓN (Madrid): Chinchón is just a tiny town, about an hour's drive south of Madrid. Being close to a major city makes Chinchón even more special—it's a surprise to find such a quaint, unspoiled town nearby. The fascinating feature of Chinchón is its Plaza Mayor, a real gem. The vast plaza is enclosed on all sides by picturesque three-storied, whitewashed houses with rustic red-tiled roofs. A double row of wooden balconies stretch out from the upper two stories, forming a perfect perch for watching the bullfights. Yes, bullfights: during the season, the plaza is completely sealed and transforms into a picturesque bullring.

CUENCA (Castilla-La Mancha): Cuenca is only about a two-hour drive southeast of Madrid, yet is not as well known as many of Spain's towns that, in our estimation, are not nearly as spectacular. If time allows, definitely include Cuenca—and plan to stay for several days because there is so much to see in the area: the dramatic castle at Belmonte, the Romanesque church in Arcas, the fanciful rock formations in *La Ciudad Encantada* (The Enchanted City), and the Roman amphitheater at Segóbriga. But Cuenca itself is the highlight. The town is perched high on the top of a rock formation that drops straight down to the River Huécar. Clinging impossibly to the cliffs are the *casas colgadas* (hanging houses) whose wooden balconies stretch out over open air. Narrow streets and steep stairways make walking an adventure. Spanning the deep gorge carved by the river, a narrow walking bridge connects the old town with the cathedral (now housing a parador) on the other side of the chasm.

GRANADA (Andalusia): Granada is instantly a favorite of all who visit. When you see the mountain setting, it is easy to understand why this was the last stronghold of the Moors. From its lofty perch, the Alhambra, a fairy tale of palaces built around courtyards filled with flowers, fruit trees, tranquil pools, and beautiful fountains, dominates the newer city. The interior walls are covered with tiny colorful tiles creating intricate patterns that are enhanced by slender columns, graceful arches, and fancy plasterwork. Obviously the Moors were great romantics—all the senses are rewarded from the fragrance of the gardens to the soothing melody of the fountains. As you meander through the enchanting inner courtyards, it is easy to imagine the women of the harem peeking out undetected from their hiding places behind the lacy plaster designs. You must not rush your time here.

GUADALUPE (Extremadura): Guadalupe was a marvelous surprise to us. We knew about its Franciscan monastery where pilgrims have come since the 14th century to worship the Black Virgin of Guadalupe, but we did not expect to find a town of such utter charm. Many of Spain's medieval towns are stunning in their central core, but modern civilization has crept right to their periphery. Not so with Guadalupe: the town exemplifies great architectural purity and there is nothing new to jar the senses.

Monastery of Guadalupe

HONDARRIBIA (Pays Basque): Hondarribia—on some maps named Fuenterrabía—is a picturesque coastal town in northern Spain almost on the border of France. Our preference always gravitates towards towns that are unspoiled and Hondarribia certainly fits the bill. Although close to traffic-congested San Sebastián, Hondarribia maintains the quiet ambiance of a small medieval town. It is located on a gentle hill overlooking a sparkling blue bay lined with modern holiday condominiums and dotted with colorful yachts. Yet within the walled town itself, time stops still. Starting at the lower gates, the streets lead up the hill, terminating in a large plaza with one side opening to a belvedere overlooking the bay. Another side of the plaza is faced by one of Spain's most special paradors, El Emperador, while the other two are lined by brilliantly colored houses with wooden balconies—quite unlike anything you expect to see in Spain.

Convento de San Marcos, León

LEÓN (Castilla y León): León—once the capital of Castilla y León—is a fascinating city dating back to the 10th century, just begging to be explored. Narrow streets spread like a maze in every direction, leading to quaint squares accented by colorful fountains. León's most outstanding sight is its gorgeous 13th-century Gothic-style cathedral with 125 splendid stained-glass windows that must not be missed. Another superb edifice is the *Antiguo Convento de San Marcos* (Monastery of St. Mark), one part of which unbelievably houses one of Spain's most spectacular paradors. If overnighting in León, you must stay here where you have the chance to step into living history.

MADRID (Madrid): Madrid needs no introduction. Spain's capital, located right in the center of the country, is usually the first stop for every tourist coming to Spain. Although a large city, it is a beautiful one, filled with parks and fountains and some of the finest museums in the world. Definitely not to be missed. We have a complete chapter devoted to this wonderful city (see *Madrid and More* on pages 145–156).

MÉRIDA (Extremadura): Mérida is a must if you have even the slightest interest in archaeology. The Roman ruins here are astounding and conveniently grouped together so you can wander from one to the other. Especially awesome is the theater built by Agrippa, the son-in-law of the Emperor Augustus. A semi-circle of tiered stone bleachers faces onto a huge stage backed by a two-storied gallery held up by slender columns interspersed with marble statues. Just across the street from the park where the ruins are located is a stunning museum—a modern edifice of admirable design with a massive arched brick ceiling pierced by skylights that set off to perfection the many Roman artifacts displayed within.

PEDRAZA DE LA SIERRA (Castilla y León): Pedraza de la Sierra became an instant favorite. We could not help pondering why it is not better known (and almost felt reluctant to share its enchantment and perhaps spoil its laid-back perfection). Obviously it is popular with Madridians who flock here on weekends to escape the heat of the city, dine in Pedraza's charming restaurants, and overnight in her pretty hotels. Weekends are busy, but if you go midweek, you will find a quiet, enchanting walled village built upon a small knoll with views out over the countryside in every direction. Walls encircle the lower part of the hill and a castle crowns the summit. The Plaza Mayor is a gem—almost like a stage setting with picturesque houses with wide balconies facing the square. The narrow side streets are lined with medieval houses, many with family crests above the stone doorways. Completely lacking are tacky tourist shops: instead you find pretty, small boutiques selling quality merchandise.

PICOS DE EUROPA (Asturias): Picos de Europa is a range of mountains just before you reach the coast going north from Madrid. What most people relate to when they think of Spain's mountains are the Pyrenees, but for sheer drama, in our estimation, they don't compare with the Picos de Europa. A national park has been set aside to protect these magnificent peaks and provide a paradise for those who want to enjoy nature at its finest. The jagged limestone mountains thrust straight up into the sky, a majestic spectacle reminiscent of the mighty Dolomites in Italy. Lush meadows enhanced by sparkling mountain streams complete the picture of perfection. This is a paradise for those who love hiking, mountain climbing, horseback riding, or fishing.

RONDA (Andalusia): Ronda is tucked high in the hills up a winding road from the Costa del Sol. A rich Arabic and Christian heritage has left its mark on the town that is filled with palatial houses. It was in Ronda that bullfighting first began, and even today bullfights are still held in the colorful bullring. However, it is the setting that makes Ronda stand out from many of the other white villages of Andalusia—the town is split by a deep gorge spanned by an incredibly high, 18th-century arched stone bridge.

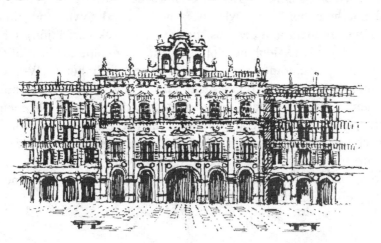

Plaza Mayor
Salamanca

Introduction–About Itineraries

SALAMANCA (Galicia): Salamanca is one of our favorite cities in all of Spain. If you are anywhere close, you must visit it and stay long enough to relish its many wonders. We had not expected to be so enraptured since a university town is not usually so special—but Salamanca is. The Tormes river flows below the city with roads leading up from the riverbanks to meet at the top of the hill in the Plaza Mayor. And what a plaza this is! The plaza is an architectural masterpiece built in the 18th century by Philip V and there is no prettier in all of Spain. It is enclosed by three-storied buildings built of a pastel ochre-colored stone whose ground levels are fronted by a series of identical arches that form a dazzling arcade all around the square. Although the highlight, the Plaza Mayor is not all that Salamanca has to offer. The beautiful old city is filled with buildings of merit, all within walking range. Start at the river and follow San Pablo up to the Plaza Mayor, then loop back down to the river by the Rua Mayor. Be sure to include the characterful buildings of the university, the *catedral nueva* (new cathedral), the *catedral viejo* (old cathedral), the *Casa de las Conchas* (House of Shells), and the *Convento de San Esteban* (St. Stephen's Monastery).

SANTIAGO DE COMPOSTELA (Galicia): Santiago de Compostela is a highlight of Spain and well worth a detour if you are anywhere in the northwestern part of the country. According to legend, Saint James's grave was found by simple shepherds guided to the site by a field of stars and his remains reside in a shrine in Santiago's magnificent cathedral. Since the 11th century the city has been the destination of millions of pilgrims who have made the perilous journey by foot across Europe to worship at the shrine. The first travel guide ever written was printed to help these pilgrims along their way and, to ease their journey, hospices sprang up along the route, several of which are now paradors featured in this book. Santiago's cathedral faces onto a stunning plaza, still bustling with pilgrims. Facing onto the same plaza is one of the original hospices, now housing one of Spain's most deluxe hotels, Los Reyes Católicos.

SANTILLANA DEL MAR (Cantabria): Santillana del Mar is a charming small town in the north of Spain. There is nothing of great tourist value to draw you here—no magnificent cathedrals or museums. Rather, it is the town itself that is the magnet. It is amazing that a town could remain so untouched—the whole town is like a living museum and as you wander along the charming streets, it is as if you have stepped back in time. There are no modern buildings, no hint of the 20th century. Stone mansions, many with the noble owner's crest above the door, line the narrow lanes. Just 2 kilometers away are the famous Altamira Caves with their incredible prehistoric drawings. These are almost impossible to visit for the average tourist, but in the vicinity there are many other similar caves open to the public.

Hotel Alfonso XIII, Seville

SEVILLE (Andalusia): Hands down, Seville is our favorite major city in Spain. It really has all the ingredients to make it special: a lovely setting, a manageable size for walking, a romantic old quarter, beautiful buildings, many parks, friendly people, good shopping, great restaurants, and excellent hotels. For more in-depth information on Seville, see our itinerary *Seville Highlights*, pages 157–162.

Castle at Sigüenza

SIGÜENZA (Guadalajara): Sigüenza is a small village northeast of Madrid, tucked into the barren, rocky landscape. This picture-perfect town of pretty pastel-colored houses roofed with thick rustic tiles seems a world away from modern civilization, yet it is less than a two-hour drive from Madrid. As always, there is the Plaza Mayor in the center of town, and also a lovely 12th-century cathedral which is well worth a visit (be sure to see the exquisite statue of Martín Vázquez de Arce, squire to Isabella the Catholic). The houses in Sigüenza climb in tiers up the hillside to an imposing castle that has been converted into a dramatic parador.

SOS DEL REY CATÓLICO (Aragón): Sos del Rey Católico is one of the most charming towns in Aragón. This is an area of many desolate, windswept, rocky hills, often crowned by a ghost town piercing the sky. I don't know why so many of these walled towns were deserted, but a few have survived, including the delightful Sos del Rey Católico. The town is named for the Ferdinand the Catholic who was born here in 1452 and went on to unite Spain. Be sure to wear sturdy walking shoes for the town is built on a hill that is laced with cobbled streets and walkways that always seem to go straight up or down.

TOLEDO (Castilla-La Mancha): Toledo is justifiably popular: hardly any tourist visits Madrid without taking a side trip to Toledo. Most come for the day, but to enjoy the town to its fullest, try to spend the night so that you can settle in after the bus loads of tourists have left. The site itself is worth a journey—Toledo huddles on a plateau that rises steeply above the River Tagus which forms a steep ravine looping around the city. Within its mighty walls, Toledo is a virtual museum. Don't miss the spectacular Gothic cathedral with paintings by El Greco, Van Dyck, and Goya or the Church of Santo Tomé where El Greco's best work, the *Burial of Count Orgaz* is displayed. Also see the Alcázar, a huge 13th-century fortress converted by Charles V into a royal palace.

Bell Tower of San Martín, Trujillo

TRUJILLO (Extremadura): Trujillo is closely linked with the conquest of America since many of the explorers who ventured to the New World were born here. Most famous of these is Francisco Pizarro, the conqueror of Peru, whose impressive statue stands in the Plaza Mayor—there is an identical statue in Lima. The Plaza Mayor is especially interesting, with a distinct personality distinguishing it from those in many other towns. Its shape is irregular and the ground slopes so that the buildings border it on various levels. Be sure to take the trail up the hill to the 10th-century fortress which hovers above the town. Although the fortress is mostly in ruins, the vistas are lovely.

About Hotels

There still exist in Spain numerous places where you may find yourselves the only English-speaking guests in the castle. Yes, *castle*! Private proprietors, as well as the government, have created some of the most romantic hotels in all of Europe in historical sites such as castles, palaces, convents, and monasteries—many found in locations boasting some of the most spectacular sights in all of Europe.

In the *Hotel Descriptions* section of this guide is a selection of hotels that we consider to be the most charming in Spain. A detailed description, an illustration, and pertinent information are provided on each one. Some are large and posh, offering every amenity and a price to match; others small and cozy (often with correspondingly smaller prices), providing only the important amenities such as private baths, personality, and gracious personnel. Our choices were not governed by room rate, but rather by romantic ambiance, location, and warmth of welcome. We have visited every hotel that appears in the book, and our selection covers a wide price range—tailored to fit every budget.

Sometimes we could not find an ideal hotel in an important sightseeing location where we felt it important to have a place to recommend. In such situations we have chosen for you what we consider to be the best place to stay in the area. We try to be consistently candid and honest in our appraisals. We feel that if you know what to expect, you won't be disappointed.

HOW TO FIND YOUR HOTEL

MAPS SHOWING HOTEL LOCATIONS: In the Maps section (the last section of this book) there is a key map of the whole of Spain plus seven regional maps showing each recommended hotel's position. In order to find which of our regional maps highlights the town where your hotel is located, the pertinent map number is shown on the *top line* of each hotel's description. To further ease the task of spotting the town, we divided the hotel location maps into a grid of four parts. The upper left segment is designated "a," the upper right segment "b," the lower left segment "c," and the lower right segment "d." As an example: Salamanca is located on Map 6 in the upper left segment of the map, so the *top line* of the hotel's description will read "Map: 6a."

SUGGESTED MAPS: As mentioned previously, our maps give you only a broad concept of where the hotels are located. You **must** buy detailed regional maps before leaving home. Because they are exceptionally accurate, have excellent indexes, and are readily available, we use Michelin maps as a cross reference. On the last line of each hotel's description, we also indicate the number of the Michelin map on which the town where your hotel is located can be found. If you can't find the maps you need, your local bookstore can order them for you. Please buy them! They will make planning your vacation so much easier and finding your hotels so much less stressful. Note: When you are looking in the map index for hotel locations, be aware that many towns in Spain have identical names. It is imperative to be sure that the town is in the proper province.

PARADORS

The Spanish government operates a system of hotels called *paradors* (literally "stopping places") which are widely acknowledged to constitute the most outstanding bargain in the country for quality received. The first paradors were created in 1928 in an effort to encourage tourists to those areas of Spain lacking adequate hotel facilities. Over the years, the number of paradors has grown tremendously as new ones have been added (periodically others are taken temporarily "off the market" while closed for renovation). A few of the paradors are situated in starkly modern buildings with no concession to an old-world theme; others are of new construction but built in a creative regional style. However, the great majority of paradors are imaginatively installed in remodeled historic buildings. Numerous paradors are simply stunning and in breathtaking locations such as the Parador San Francisco in Granada—imagine staying in a 15th-century convent literally **within** the Alhambra grounds, just steps from its fabulous palaces and gardens!

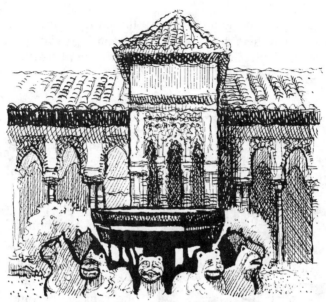
Lion's Court, Alhambra, Granada

The paradors are not privately owned so do not expect the proprietor to be at the front desk to greet you warmly. The management is very professional and the quality of service dependable. The mood of each parador seems to reflect the talents of the individual in charge. The excellence of some of the paradors shows that there are indeed some extremely capable managers in the group—some of the best are women. Also, the amenities vary between the paradors: almost all that we visited had hair dryers, many had small refrigerators in the room, and some even had bathrobes and turn-down service

While you could travel throughout Spain staying practically only in paradors, we also recommend a variety of other charming hotel accommodations. In the hotel section, we give in-depth descriptions of our favorite paradors, along with many other choices of exceptional places to stay. We have not included every parador in Spain in this book, although we have visited almost all of them. Sometimes we have rejected a parador because we have other hotels in the area that we think offer more charm. However, even though we have not featured them in our guide, you cannot go wrong staying at any of the paradors—for a complete list, contact one of the Spanish tourist offices in your area (see Tourist Offices of Spain on pages 21–22).

All paradors have good to excellent dining rooms serving regional culinary specialties from a set menu or *a la carte*. Local wines are also featured. They do not specialize in light fare, however, so be prepared to eat substantially. If you follow the Spanish tradition of taking your big meal at midday, paradors provide good stopping places en route. If you don't feel up to two large meals a day, at most paradors (and hotels) you can frequently purchase a sandwich or snack at the bar. The set menu for lunch or dinner usually features a three-course meal. Food-wise, another bonus is that all of the paradors serve a generous buffet breakfast with an attractively displayed assortment of meats, cheeses, breads, fruits, juices, yogurts, and even sometimes egg dishes. Breakfast is not included in the tarrif.

Another advantage in staying at a parador is that there are almost always signs that lead you from the edge of the town (sometimes even from the freeway) to the parador. This may sound like a minor advantage, but it can save time and frustration.

Not only are stunning new paradors being opened (such as the sensational Parador de Ronda), but the "old timers" are radically improving. Although we love them dearly, we must admit that the decor in many of the paradors that have been around for a long time is, to put it kindly, a bit bland, with a great sameness to the furnishings. But, happily, all that is rapidly changing. Previously, the paradors had to take the furniture sent to them by upper management but a new policy allows the use of private enterprise, and what a difference it is making! As each parador takes its turn for renovation, the most talented interior designers in the country are being hired to plan the decor. The recently refurbished properties are emerging as real beauties—rivaling the finest private hotels in Spain.

Also the quality of the paradors' brochures has been constantly improving. Although it will be a gradual change as more brochures are printed, the latest goal is to have not only a photo of the hotel, but also a wealth of pertinent information: a map giving its location, city tours, excursions available, and cultural and natural places of interest to visit in the area.

In addition to being an overall good value, paradors offer some extremely appealing rates for travel off season. These special rates (which are not available at every parador) are most frequently offered mid-week and usually begin the first of November and last until the end of June. The exact dates and qualifications vary at each parador. Another terrific value (if you are over 60 years old) is the senior rates that give a whopping discount—35% discount for the first and second nights and 50% discount for the third night on. These senior rates are offered only off season, and at some hotels are valid only mid-week—the rules vary with each parador. So, if you are traveling off season (frequently the nicest time to travel anyway), be **sure** to ask if there are any discounts available. Important note: These special room rates are offered only when booked directly with the parador or with the Paradores de Turismo central reservation office in Madrid.

PARADOR RESERVATIONS—PARADORES DE TURISMO: Although you can contact each parador individually, the response to your letter or fax is sometimes slow, and if you call, some of the paradors do not always have a person who is fluent in English available to answer the telephone. Therefore, it is more efficient to contact Paradores de Turismo's central reservation office (*central de reservas*) in Madrid where you can make reservations at any parador in the network without a booking fee. You can write, call, or fax for reservations. If you telephone, the travel consultants, who speak English, can often advise you immediately of availability, and will follow up with a written confirmation (office hours are 9:30 am to 1:30 pm and 3:30 to 5:30 pm, Monday through Thursday—on Fridays the office is open only from 9:30 am to 1:30 pm). A deposit can be made on your credit card to guarantee your arrival. For further information contact: Paradores de Turismo, Central de Reservas, C/Requena, 3, 28013 Madrid, Spain, tel: (91) 51.66.666, fax: (91) 51.66.657.

PARADOR RESERVATIONS—MARKETING AHEAD: If you live in the United States reservations for all the paradors (plus many of the other hotels featured in this guide) can be booked with Marketing Ahead, the Paradores de Turismo's representative in New York. This is a most convenient way to make a reservation. You can call or fax to reserve any of the paradors and there is no surcharge or service fee. Reservations are confirmed within 48 hours and a $50 deposit (per hotel) is collected; then reservations are prepaid 30 days prior to departure from the USA. The prepayment is for the room, tax and breakfast. The rate in dollars is only guaranteed once the prepayment has been made. Vouchers showing proof of payment will be mailed to you. For further information contact Marketing Ahead, 433 Fifth Avenue, 6th Floor, New York, NY 10016, tel: (800) 223-1356, fax: (212) 686-0271.

RATES

Although prices in Spain are playing catch-up with much of the rest of Western Europe, especially in the most popular tourist destinations, there remain many delightful hotel possibilities, reasonable enough to allow you the pleasure of indulging yourself.

The rates hotels charge are regulated by the Spanish government, with inflation causing periodic upward adjustments in prices (usually at the beginning of the year). Most hotels have an intricate system of rates, which vary according to season, local special events, and additional features such as sitting rooms, balconies, and views. Prices quoted in this book reflect the range of rates for a double room for two people in the high season. We state whether the rate includes breakfast and the 7% IVA (tax). Suites are often available for an additional cost. May through June and September through October are lovely times to travel and frequently offer slightly lower rates than July and August, which are the two hottest months in most of Spain. If you can travel in early spring, late fall, or winter, you can often realize substantial savings. Many hotels also have rates for *media pensión* or *pensión completa* which mean breakfast and either one or two meals, respectively. These are often an excellent value and should be investigated where convenient. Children are welcome virtually everywhere in Spain, and frequently there are special rates for those under 14 years old.

Breakfast in all the paradors (and at many of the hotels) is a bountiful buffet where you can have all you want to eat. If you are in the habit of sleeping late, breakfast might appease your hunger until dinner—allowing you to skip lunch. However, if you are on a tight budget, you might consider skipping breakfast and instead stopping for a cup of coffee and a pastry at one of the bars along the way. This will be much less expensive. However, before you decline breakfast, be sure it can be broken down separately on your bill—in a few places it must be included.

RESERVATIONS

When making your reservations be sure to identify yourself as a "Karen Brown Traveler." We hear over and over again that the people who use are guides are such wonderful guests. The hotels appreciate your visit, value their inclusion in our guide, and frequently tell us they take special care of our readers.

Whether or not to reserve ahead is not a question with a simple answer: it depends upon the flexibility in your timetable and your temperament. It also depends to a large extent on the season in which you are traveling. For example, during the peak season, all hotel space is at a premium and a super star (such as the Parador San Francisco in Granada) frequently mandates reservations six to eight months in advance. Other popular hotels with limited rooms are similarly booked, especially those located in towns of particular touristic interest. Prudent travelers make arrangements months in advance to secure desirable accommodations during a local festival. On the other hand, throughout much of the year, space can be obtained in most places with a day's notice, or less. For those who prefer the comfort of knowing where you are going to lay your head each night, following are various ways of making reservations:

E-MAIL: This is our preferred way of making a hotel reservation. If the hotel/posada has an e-mail address, we have included it in the listing. (Always spell out the month as the Spanish reverse the American month/day numbering system.)

FAX: If you have access to a fax, this is an efficient way to contact a hotel. The method of faxing is the same as telephoning—dial the international access code (011), followed by the country code for Spain (34), followed by the local telephone number. Be sure to specify your arrival and departure dates and what type of room(s) you want. And, of course, include your fax number for their response. In the back of the book (immediately after the map section) there is a reservation request letter written in Spanish with an English translation. You can photocopy this to use for either your faxes or letters to Spain. When you receive a reply, send the deposit requested (if any) and ask for confirmation of receipt. Some hotels will take a credit card guarantee or offer to hold the room until a certain time of the day instead of a requiring a deposit. (See e-mail section about dates.)

LETTER: If you start early, you can write to the hotels directly for your reservations. Because the mail to Spain tends to be slow, especially outside the large cities, you should allow six weeks for a reply. (See e-mail section about dates, and fax secton for letter in Spanish.)

TELEPHONE: A convenient method of making reservations is to call (although you might not always find someone at the other end of the phone who speaks English). The advantage is you can have your answer immediately (though you should still request written confirmation), or if space is not available, you can look right away for an alternative. Remember that Spain is six hours ahead of New York for most of the year, so time your call accordingly. (See e-mail section about dates, and fax section for dialing directions.)

PAYMENT BY CREDIT CARDS

Most hotels and many restaurants in Spain accept plastic payment. All paradors accept all major cards. In the *Hotel Descriptions* section we indicate which hotels accept cards with the following abbreviations: AX—American Express, MC—MasterCard, VS—Visa, or simply, all major. Some hotels accept a credit card to guarantee a reservation, but do not accept final payment by credit card.

RESPONSIBILITY

Our goal in this guide is to outline itineraries in regions that we consider of prime interest to our readers and to recommend hotels that we think are outstanding. All of the hotels featured have been visited and selected solely on their merits. Our judgments are made on charm, setting, cleanliness, and, above all, the warmth of welcome. However, sometimes hotels do not maintain their standards. If you find a hotel is not as we have indicated, please let us know, and accept our sincere apologies—we are sorry when hotels have changed and are no longer as we describe them. The rates given are those quoted to us by the hotel for the year of 1999. These rates are not guaranteed, but rather given as a guideline. **Be sure** to ask at the time of booking the exact price for the room, and what it includes (such as breakfast, tax, etc.). We are in no way affiliated with any of the hotels or hotel representatives mentioned in this book, and cannot be responsible for any reservations made nor money sent as deposits or prepayments.

Overview of Itineraries

Moorish Memories

Pilgrimage to Santiago

Treasures Off the Beaten Track

Cradle of the Conquistadors

*Old Castile and the
Cantabrian Coast*

The Costa Brava and Beyond

Andalusian Adventures

Madrid and More

Seville & Barcelona Highlights

Don Quixote and Sancho Panza

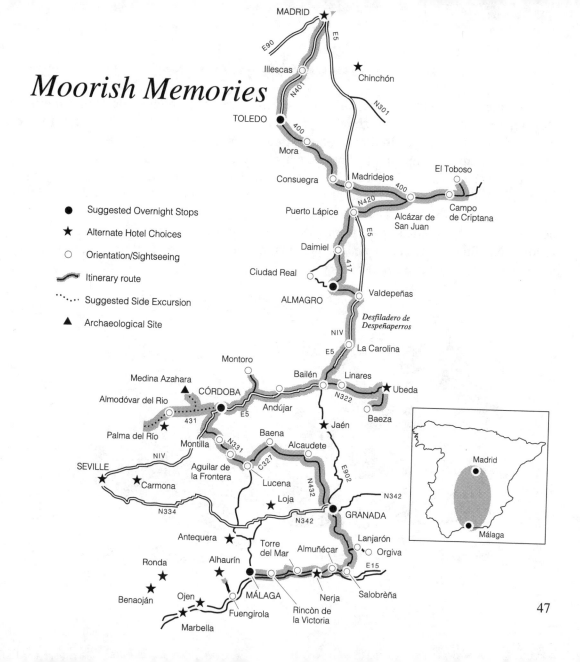

Moorish Memories

MADRID ★

E90   E5

Illescas
Chinchón ★
N401

N301

TOLEDO ●
400
Mora
El Toboso

Consuegra   Madridejos   Campo
400   de Criptana

N420   Alcázar de
Puerto Lápice   San Juan

● Suggested Overnight Stops
E5
★ Alternate Hotel Choices
Daimiel
○ Orientation/Sightseeing
417
Itinerary route   Ciudad Real
Valdepeñas
········ Suggested Side Excursion   ALMAGRO

▲ Archaeological Site   *Desfiladero de
Despeñaperros*

NIV
E5   La Carolina

Montoro
Bailén   Linares

Medina Azahara ▲ CÓRDOBA   Ubeda ★
N322
Almodóvar del Rio   Andújar
E5   Baeza
431
Palma del Río ★   Jaén ★
Montilla   Baena
N331   Alcaudete
SEVILLE   C327
NIV   Aguilar de   N432
Carmona ★   la Frontera   Lucena   E902

Loja ★
N342
N334   GRANADA ●

Antequera ★   Lanjarón
N342   ○
Torre   Almuñécar   Orgiva
Ronda ★   Alhaurín ★   del Mar
Ojen   Nerja ★   Salobrèña
Benaoján ★   MÁLAGA   E15
Marbella   Fuengirola   Rincòn de
la Victoria

Madrid ●

Málaga ●

47

Moorish Memories

The culture of contemporary Spain is a rich mixture of its prehistoric Celtic-Iberian, Roman, Visigothic, and Moorish heritage. When the last of the Moors (Moslems) were expelled from Granada in 1492, after almost 800 years of war known as the Reconquest, the modern nation of Spain was born. Each of the cultures left its mark; however, and nowhere is the variety of modern Spain more evident than in the area covered by this itinerary: from cosmopolitan Madrid to the glamorous Costa del Sol, playground of the jet set. You visit historic Toledo, capital of Visigothic Spain from the 6th to the 8th centuries and of Christian Spain from 1085 to the mid-16th century. Chosen home of the renowned painter, El Greco, Toledo is perhaps the most Spanish of all Spanish towns and a veritable open-air museum of history

Windmills in Don Quixote Country

Next you traverse the plains and pass the windmills of La Mancha, wandering ground of Don Quixote, to Córdoba—capital of Moorish Spain and, in the 10th century, second in wealth and luxury only to Baghdad. Córdoba still recalls the glory of the Moslem empire on the peninsula. Next you visit the Moors' last stronghold, Granada, where the most spectacular architectural monument of that culture, the Alhambra, towers majestically over the city. This itinerary ends on the sunny beaches of the Costa del Sol (Coast of the Sun), where European royalty and Hollywood stars moor their yachts.

Your route passes many kilometers of olive groves and vineyards and winds through small towns spilling down mountainsides under the remains of ancient castles. Be sure to sample the regional wines (Valdepeñas), the delicious cold gazpacho soup (there is nothing so refreshing on a hot day), and the varied seafood specialties.

ORIGINATING CITY　　　MADRID

Whether before or after your stay in Spain's capital city, a journey to her southern cities, steeped in Moorish heritage and graced with Mudéjar mementos, should not be missed. So, when you are ready to leave the hustle and bustle of Madrid, head south to follow in the footsteps of Don Quixote and the warriors who reclaimed Spain for the Christians.

DESTINATION I　　　TOLEDO

Take N401 south from Madrid to **Toledo**, passing through the medieval town of **Illescas**. Fortified Toledo is lovely to come upon, and you may wish to take a turn around the walled city (bear right just before entering the Bisagra gate) when you first arrive. When you witness the incredible views of the city from the hillside across the River Tagus, you understand what inspired El Greco's famous painting, *View of Toledo* (now in the Prado).

Puente de San Martin, Toledo

There is a modern parador on a hill outside town with a stunning view of Toledo from across the river. But our preference is to be right in the heart of the city where our favorite place to stay, the **Hostal del Cardenal**, former summer residence of Cardinal Lorenzana (Archbishop of Toledo in the 18th century), is built into the walls themselves. It is easy to find as it is located just 91 meters from the Puerta de Bisagra, one of Toledo's main medieval gates. Besides the romance of its historical setting, the convenience of its location, and lovely accommodations, the Hostal del Cardenal also boasts one of the finest restaurants in town, so you will definitely want to enjoy a leisurely *al fresco comida* on the garden patio (roast pig and lamb are the specialties) after exploring the town.

Be prepared for wall to wall tourists as you tour the abundance of sights in Toledo. When the capital was moved to Madrid in the 16th century, Toledo remained the center of the Catholic hierarchy in Spain and the cathedral (13th to 15th centuries) reminds you of the great cathedrals of France, but is even more richly adorned. In **Santo Tomé** church you can view El Greco's famous *Burial of the Count of Orgaz* in its original setting (the sixth figure from the left is said to be a self-portrait of the artist) and the **El Greco House and Museum,** which lends an idea of how he lived. Also noteworthy is the startling Mudéjar decoration of the **El Tránsito** and **Santa María la Blanca** synagogues. The **Santa Cruz Museum**, with its fine 16th- and 17th-century art, includes 22 works by El Greco. But above all, roaming the ancient, winding streets of the city, pausing for refreshment in a pretty town square (such as the Plaza de Zocodover), soaking up the essence of Spanish history, and sitting on the terrace of the parador bar to watch the city turn golden in the setting sun, are the highlights of Toledo's offerings.

Toledo is loaded with souvenir shops and is famous for its swords and knives—you find both decorative and real ones in all shapes, sizes, and prices—and for its damascene-ware: gold, silver, and copper filigree inlaid in black steel.

DESTINATION II   ALMAGRO

Leave Toledo on C400. You are soon in **La Mancha** (from *manxa*, an Arabic word meaning parched earth), the land of Cervantes' Don Quixote, famous for its wine, cheese (*queso manchego*), windmills, saffron, olive trees, and ceramics. Above Consuegra, you pass the romantic sight of a ruined 12th-century castle surrounded by 13 windmills. (The best picture-taking spot is after you leave the town to the east.) Between here and Madridejos look for *alfares,* the pottery studios for which this area is known.

If you are a Cervantes (or a *Man of La Mancha*) fan, you should take the short side trip (about 50 fairly fast kilometers each way) east from Madridejos on C400 toward the wine-trade town of Alcázar de San Juan which you bypass continuing east to reach **Campo de Criptana** where, it is claimed, Don Quixote had his tryst with the windmills. A few kilometers farther east brings you to the **Criptana Hermitage** at the junction of N420 and TO104 and another splendid view of the countryside dotted with windmills.

About 15 kilometers northeast is **El Toboso**. Just southeast of the church in the center of town is a reproduction of the home of the peerless Dulcinea, reluctant recipient of the knight-errant's undying love. The house supposedly belonged to Ana Martínez whom Cervantes renamed Dulcinea (*dulce* = sweet + Ana). You will enjoy touring the house which contains 17th-century furniture and an intriguing antique olive-oil press on the patio in the back. Across the street from the church is a collection of over 300 editions of the novel in everything from Japanese to Gaelic. A number of interesting facsimiles and signed and illuminated editions are housed there, too. If you know some Spanish, you see that there are signs which are quotations from the novel all around town pointing the way to the church.

Return to **Alcázar de San Juan** and from there head for Puerto Lapice, where you can follow the signs to the delightful **Venta del Quijote**—a well-restored example of the type of inn where Don Quixote was dubbed knight. The Venta has a charming restaurant and bar, as well as some cute little shops. Continuing southwest, you pass through the fertile plains of the **Campo de Calatrava** on the way to Daimiel. Take C417 south to the lovely town of **Almagro**, once the main stronghold of the knights of the military Order of Calatrava who battled the Moors during the Reconquest.

Almagro's unique, oblong Plaza Mayor is surrounded by wooden houses, and the restored 16th-century **Corral de Comedias** (in the southeast corner) is where the plays of the Spanish Golden Age were performed. It is similar in style and epoch (as were the plays) to the Elizabethan theaters of Shakespeare's time. You will enjoy exploring the town's cobbled streets and alleyways with their marvelous whitewashed houses, sculptured doorways, and shops selling the renowned, locally tatted lace. A number of other historic buildings are in the process of restoration.

Our hotel recommendation is the graceful **Parador de Almagro**, installed in a 16th-century convent, whose Moorish arches, patios, and musical fountains will prepare you for tomorrow's entrance into the delights of Andalusia. The building is mostly new, but

Parador de Almagro, Almagro

the manager says he has trouble convincing people of that because of the incredible attention to detail in the re-creation of the original.

As a side trip from Almagro, visit the wine center of Valdepeñas, a short drive to the east. As you leave Almagro, you are likely to see women outside their homes bent over their work of lace-making. After a short drive through vine-laden flatland, you arrive in **Valdepeñas**, which has made a name for itself with its good light table wine. Wine-harvest festivals are held here in September. Valdepeñas has a charming central plaza, and the Victory Monument hill north of the town on NIV offers a splendid panorama of vine-covered plains. Another worthwhile side trip from Almagro is 21 kilometers southwest where, outside the town of **Calzada de Calatrava**, are the fascinating ruins of the 13th-century castle of **Calatrava la Nueva**.

When you are ready to leave Almagro, rejoin NIV and head south, climbing gradually into the pine-forested Sierra Morena until, at the **Despeñaperros Gorge** (*despeña perros* means throwing off of the dogs, i.e., Moors), you officially enter **Andalusia**. The Andalusians are fond of saying that this is where Europe ends and Africa begins. This is not a total exaggeration—Andalusia has a markedly different culture and a much stronger Moorish tradition than the rest of Spain.

You pass through La Carolina before coming to Bailen, where you head east on N322 through Linares to **Ubeda**. Recaptured from the Moors in 1234, it once served as an important base in the Reconquest campaign. The heart of all Spanish towns is the plaza, and Ubeda's striking oblong **Plaza Vázquez de Molina** was designed for lingering, lined with palaces and mansions with classic Renaissance façades, grills, and balconies and the beautiful El Salvador chapel. You can also spot the remains of old town walls and towers around town. Ubeda's elegant parador (on the plaza in a 16th-century palace) offers an imaginative lunch menu, if the time is appropriate.

From Ubeda it's a short drive to captivating **Baeza**, the seat of a bishop during the Visigothic period and a prominent border town between Andalusia and La Mancha during the Reconquest. Golden seignorial mansions testify to its importance as a Moorish capital before 1227, when it became the first Andalusian town to be reconquered. Make time to drop by the tourist office in the enchanting Plaza de los Leones, pick up a town map, and wander on foot from there to visit this open-air museum of architecture, from Romanesque through Renaissance.

Return to Bailen, then head west toward Córdoba. You pass **Andújar**, with a pretty little plaza dominated by an ochre-colored Gothic church and an arched Roman bridge across the Guadalquivir. You are in the major olive-producing region of Spain now, and drive by seemingly unending, symmetrical rows of olive trees (*olivos*). After passing Villa del Rio, on the left bank of the river is the fortified town of **Montoro** just off the main road to the north. This was an important stronghold during the Moorish period, and you may wish to take time to wander across the 14th-century bridge to the old town and explore its picturesque Andalusian streets. The remaining 55 kilometers to Córdoba passes through a sea of olive trees parted occasionally by cotton fields.

Córdoba was the most opulent of the Moorish cities in Spain and boasted a university to which scholars from all over Europe came to study in the 11th and 12th centuries, when it was the largest city in Europe. Most of the former opulence is gone, but the city preserves one of the architectural marvels of that period, the **Mosque** (*Mezquita*). A vast square of apparently endless red-and-white-striped arches, with a second level above the first to provide a feeling of openness, it is a fantastic example of Moslem construction. The only discordant note is the 16th-century cathedral carved out of the middle of it. Even though the Emperor Charles V had approved the idea, he is said to have lamented "the destruction of something unique to build something commonplace" when he saw the result.

Just northwest of the Mosque is the old **Jewish Quarter** (*Barrio de la Judería*), a virtual maze of twisting streets, modern and ancient shops, and colorful bars and cafés, often punctuated at night by the intricate rhythms of spontaneous flamenco dancing. Don't miss the **Street of Flowers** (Passage des Fleurs), a favorite of tourists because of its profusion of potted flowers dotting the dazzling whitewashed walls of the houses lining the narrow street. This area should not be entered by car. Even on foot, it is very easy to lose your sense of direction in the tiny streets as each one begins to look like the rest. This is especially true if you allow darkness to catch you—which you should let happen if possible, since the area takes on a very different, magical aspect when lit by its quaint lanterns.

Córdoba is such a popular destination that it sometimes seems that every person who comes to Spain stops here. Unfortunately there are numerous shops selling rather tacky souvenirs that have grown up to service this tourist trade. Nevertheless, the town has much character and the setting and old-world ambiance are noteworthy.

Our recommendation for lodging in Córdoba is the **Hotel Albucasis**. If you are looking for deluxe accommodations, this two-star hotel might not fit your needs, but it is one of our favorites because of its quiet central courtyard, friendly owner-management, spotlessly clean rooms, and super location in the heart of the Jewish Quarter. Although it is only a few short blocks from the Mosque, you will need a map to find your way since this fascinating section of Córdoba is a maze of twisting streets. Although the hotel has a parking garage available, it is almost impossible to drive to the hotel without help, so we suggest parking your car somewhere close to the Mosque, then finding the hotel on foot and asking for help.

Hotel Albucasis, Córdoba

If time permits, a side trip to **Medina Azahara** (watch for signs off C431 west of town) would prove interesting. In 936, Moorish King Abdu'r Rahman III began construction of an immense palace on three terraces (mosque, gardens, then the Alcázar at the top) of a hillside outside Córdoba, and named it after his favorite wife, Azahara. It took decades to complete the sophisticated project, and it was sacked and destroyed by Berbers shortly thereafter. But today, thanks to careful excavation and restoration, the delightful palace can be more than just imagined. Not far east on C431 is the tiny town of **Almodóvar del Rio**, above which floats one of the most stunning castles in the region.

Today head south out of town on NIV to follow the Wine Road (*Ruta del Vino*) on a journey to Granada at the foot of the Sierra Nevada. At Cuesta del Espino bear southeast through **Fernan Nuñez** and Montemayor—with 18th- and 14th-century castles, respectively—to **Montilla**, an ancient town perched on two hills. A short time later **Aguilar de la Frontera** appears, an old hilltop town, whose whitewashed, octagonal plaza of San José is particularly charming. Before turning northeast to **Cabra** you see **Monturque**, with fragments of its ancient town walls, and **Lucena**, a center of the Andalusian wine trade (in whose ruined Alcázar, Boabdil, last Moorish king in Spain, was once held prisoner). Near Cabra are the ruins of the **Castillo de los Condes** and **San Juan Bautista church**, one of the oldest in Andalusia.

Continue northeast on a beautifully scenic stretch of road to **Baena**, tiered gracefully on a hillside. In the upper, walled part of town are some wonderful Renaissance mansions. From here you can look forward to a lovely, if not speedy, drive through **Alcaudete**, dominated by a ruined castle, and **Alcala La Real**, overseen by the **Fort of La Mota**, before reaching **Granada**.

Granada fell to the Moors in 711. After Córdoba was recaptured by the Christians in the 13th century, Granada provided refuge for its Moslem residents under whom it flourished until, in 1492, the city was recaptured by Ferdinand and Isabella, marking the official end to almost eight centuries of Moorish presence in Spain.

All of our hotel recommendations are within walking distance of and share the park-like hill with the Alhambra—the only place to be. The **Parador San Francisco** is stunning, but securing a room is almost impossible unless you start planning far in advance. Also deluxe and with great Moorish ambiance is the **Alhambra Palace Hotel**, with its delicate arches, colorful mosaics, and magnificent city views. For a budget selection, the **Hotel America** has the prime location in town, just steps from the entrance to the citadel.

Alhambra Palace, Granada

If you are ready to jump right into sightseeing, the place to see in Granada (indeed, one of THE places to see in the world), the **Alhambra** with its **Generalife Gardens**, is within easy walking distance. Alhambra comes from the Arabic words for "Red Fort" and, though it is red, its somewhat plain exterior belies the richness and elegance of its interior. After your visit to this magical place, we are sure you will agree with the poet Francisco de Icaza who, after experiencing the Alhambra, then seeing a blind beggar, wrote: *Dale limosna mujer, que no hay en la vida nada como la pena de ser ciego en Granada*, meaning "Give him alms, woman, for there is no greater tragedy in life than to be blind in Granada." Look carefully to see a plaque with this inscription set into the Torre de la Vela on the palace grounds.

Most of the Moorish part (the **Alcázar**) dates from the 14th century, and the palace of the Emperor Charles V, one of the finest Renaissance structures in Spain, was designed and begun in the 16th century. It now houses a museum of pieces from the Alcázar and a fine-arts collection of religious painting and sculpture.

The magnificent tile-and-plaster geometric decoration is an expression of Moslem art at its zenith. The stunning patios and gardens with their perfectly symmetrical design will dazzle you as you stroll through the various halls and chambers. Equally appealing are the cool, green gardens of the Generalife, the summer palace. Countless fountains—now, as then, moved by gravity only—surrounded by sumptuous flower gardens, orange trees, and cypresses testify to a desert culture's appreciation of water.

Several spots on the north side of the grounds offer splendid views of the old Moorish quarter (the Albaicín) across the River Darro, as well as of the city of Granada. The same is true of the towers of the Alcazaba (fortress), which is the oldest part of the complex.

Try to schedule a nocturnal visit to the Alhambra grounds. Some nights it is totally illuminated and others only partially (ask at the hotel for the current schedule). Either way, the experience is unforgettable and dramatically different from a daytime visit. Also, inside the grounds are two good dining spots located in hotels: the Parador de San Francisco and the Hotel America.

But your visit to Granada should not end here. The **cathedral**, in the center of town, with its adjoining Royal Chapel (*Capilla Real*) was ordered built by the Catholic monarchs Ferdinand and Isabella for their final resting place and their tombs have been there since it was finished in 1521. Subsequently, their daughter, Juana the Mad, and her husband, Phillip the Fair, plus Juana's son, Prince Miguel, were buried here. Juana's other son was Emperor Charles V of the Holy Roman Empire and King of Spain in the 16th century.

The **Alcaicería** (the old silk market) around the cathedral is now a tourist area full of souvenir shops. At its west end is Granada's most attractive plaza, Bibarrambla. It is a marvelous place to sit with a cold Spanish beer—*una caña* (cahnya) is a glass and *un* *tanque* (tahnkay) is a mug—and watch the Granadinos (including the many gypsies who live nearby) go about their daily business. For the Granadinos, as for all Spaniards, this includes plaza-sitting, and for the gypsies includes begging from the plaza-sitters.

The old **Albaicín quarter** retains much of its former flavor. For an unbelievable view of the Alhambra and Generalife, try the terrace of the **Church of Saint Nicholas** in the Albaicín at sunset, and do not forget your camera. Though it is something of a walk, we do not recommend that you try to drive into the Albaicín's maze of tiny streets (although an experienced Granadino cabbie can manage it). Beyond the Albaicín to the east is the gypsy cave-dwelling area called **Sacromonte**, famous for its gypsy dancing and infamous as a tourist trap.

If time permits and you like mountain scenery, you should definitely take the 60-kilometer round trip to the peaks of the **Sierra Nevada** southeast of the city. An excellent road (at its highest levels, the highest in Europe) winds its way to the winter-sports area of Solynieve (sun and snow) in the shadow of the two highest mountains on the Iberian Peninsula, the **Cerro de Mulhacen** (3,480 meters) and the **Pico de Veleta** (3,428 meters). (There is a 37-kilometer road that ascends to the summit of Mulhacen and down the other side to Prado Llano, but it is open only in early fall.)

DESTINATION V   MÁLAGA

Leave Granada on N323, which runs south to the coast through the wild terrain of the **Alpujarras**—the mountains to which the Moors fled, and from which they launched their futile attempts to retake Granada. After about 15 kilometers, you pass over the **Puerto del Suspiro del Moro** (Pass of the Moor's Sigh) where, it is said, Boabdil, the last of Granada's Moorish kings, wept as he turned to take a last look at his beloved Granada upon his leave-taking. The contrast in scenery on the Motril road is breathtaking: green valleys, rows of olive and almond trees, and the towering, snow-capped peaks of the Sierra Nevada.

If you get an early start, this scenic detour is well worth the hour or so it adds to the journey: About 40 kilometers from Granada, turn left on C333 and continue to **Lanjarón**, a lovely small spa with mineral springs in a gorgeous mountain setting with a ruined castle perched on a shelf above it. The water is supposed to cure various ailments and is bottled and distributed nationally—if you order mineral water with your meals, you have probably tried it already. Continue on C333 to **Orgiva** at the edge of the Alpujarras. This is the area the Moors occupied for more than a century after Granada fell to the Catholic monarchs. In this picturesque little mountain village you find fine views of the Alpujarras, the Sierra Nevada, and the smaller Sierra de la Contraviesa to the south. Leave Orgiva on C333 toward the south and turn right after 3 kilometers on L451. Thirteen scenic kilometers later, you arrive back at N323 which you follow to the coastal highway N340.

Turn right and you soon have the pleasure of coming upon **Salobrèña**, a picturesque, white-walled village crowning a rocky promontory surrounded by a waving sea of green sugar cane. These *pueblos blancos* (white towns) are typical of the warmer areas of Andalusia and you see several as you drive along. Park at the edge of the town and stroll up to its partially restored Alcázar to enjoy the splendid view of the surrounding countryside and the Mediterranean.

As you head west from Salobreña, there are numerous lookout points with fabulous views of the sea and the beautiful coastline. The road winds along the coast through the small seaside resort of **Almuñécar**, with its ruined Castillo de San Miguel. A bit farther on, near the village of Maro, are the impressive **Nerja Caves** (*Cuevas de Nerja*), definitely worth a visit—vast stalactitic caves with prehistoric paintings and evidence of habitation since Paleolithic times. Its archaeological revelations (including parts of Cro-Magnon human skulls) can be seen at the small museum nearby. The caves are efficiently run and offer a cool break from driving. Continuing west, you reach the resort and fishing port of **Nerja**, known for the Balcón (balcony) de Europa, a terrace-promenade with wonderful views rising high above the sea near the center of the charming little town.

Before reaching the final destination, you pass through the seaside port of **Torre del Mar**, with its pretty lighthouse, and the village of **Rincon de La Victoria**, where another, smaller cave (Cueva del Tesoro) with prehistoric drawings can be visited in a park above town. Unlike the Nerja caves, this one was formed by underground water and presents a quite different impression. The area is popular with local Malagueños for weekend beach excursions. Follow the coast road and you arrive in **Málaga**, the birthplace of Pablo Picasso, the provincial capital and one of the oldest Mediterranean ports.

A prime place to stay in Málaga is the **Parador de Gibralfaro**, which reopened in the summer of 1995 after being closed for several years while it underwent a massive renovation that included adding more guestrooms and a complete face lift by Spain's top interior designers. It boasts excellent views of the city and the sea from its perch on top of the hill. Nearby are the ruins of the Moorish **Castillo de Gibralfaro** with beautiful gardens. There are numerous accommodation options along this strip of the Costa del Sol. The **Parador de Golf** (on the sea just west of Málaga) offers an excellent beach and golf facilities. Look in the hotel description section in the back of the guide and see what appeals to you in **Mijas**, **Alhaurín**, **Ronda**, **Ojen**, **Marbella**, and **Benaoján**—all are within easy driving distance and offer accommodation to suit any fancy.

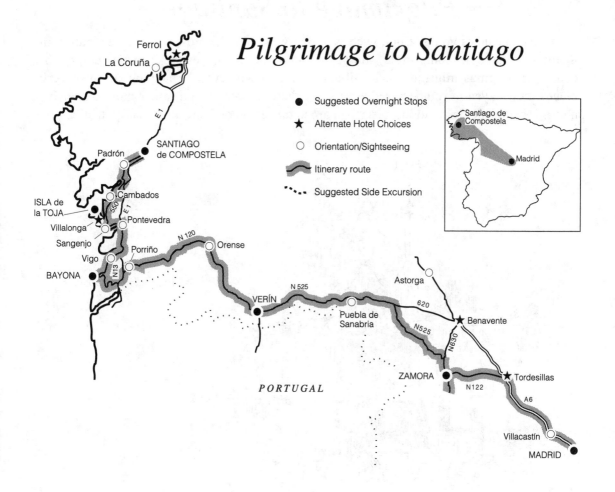

Pilgrimage to Santiago

Ferrol
La Coruña

Legend:
- ● Suggested Overnight Stops
- ★ Alternate Hotel Choices
- ○ Orientation/Sightseeing
- Itinerary route
- ····· Suggested Side Excursion

SANTIAGO de COMPOSTELA

Santiago de Compostela
Madrid

Padrón

ISLA de la TOJA
Cambados
Pontevedra
Villalonga
Sangenjo
Vigo
Porriño
Orense
BAYONA
N 120
N 525
VERÍN
Astorga
Puebla de Sanabria
620
Benavente
N 525
N 630
ZAMORA
Tordesillas
PORTUGAL
N 122
A6
Villacastín
MADRID

E 1
360
E 1
N13

63

Pilgrimage to Santiago

This itinerary takes you to a hallowed spot that was once the most popular destination in Spain—Santiago de Compostela, site of the tomb of Saint James the Apostle and goal of countless religious pilgrims for a millennium. You will even be staying in one of the places they stayed in (modernized a bit since then, of course, and rather more expensive now). Most of the destinations described are in the region of Galicia: basically, that part of

Cathedral
Santiago de Compostela

Spain directly north of Portugal (the provinces of Lugo, Pontevedra, La Coruña, and Orense). It was at one time part of Portugal but, as a result of some royal intrigues, was separated from that kingdom in 1128. Although everyone speaks Spanish, Galicia has its own special language (somewhat of a mixture of Portuguese and Spanish). Because of this, you will notice some spelling variations in town names, depending on whether the Galician or the Castilian spelling is used. The area is separated from the rest of the country by several mountain ranges. Perhaps for that reason, Galicia seems to have kept its face turned to the sea and has developed a strong seafaring tradition and economy. It is also the region that has maintained the strongest Celtic influence since the Celts invaded the peninsula around 3,000 years ago. Galician folk music still has the sound of bagpipes—called here the *gaita*—and the name Galicia is from the same root as Gaul and Wales. Galician cuisine, like that of Portugal, puts a lot of emphasis on cod (*bacalao*) prepared in many ways. *Empanadas* (folded meat or fish pies) are a typical dish, as is *lacón con grelos*, consisting of smoked pork shoulder and turnip greens. Shellfish are also commonly available: be sure to try *vieira* (scallops), a regional specialty prepared in many delicious ways.

ORIGINATING CITY MADRID

This itinerary begins in **Madrid**, a most convenient starting point, and a city worthy of a visit time and again. Be sure to spend a few days enjoying the many museums (the exhibits are constantly changing), taking advantage of fine dining, and, if the weather is pleasant, don't miss a stroll through the beautiful **Buen Retiro Park** before heading off to northwestern Spain. This part of the country is too often foregone by the visitor who views it as relatively inaccessible, and has time only for the more well-known tourist attractions. But this region has its share of the best sights in the country and a flavor all its own. Note: For more in-depth suggestions on sightseeing in and around Madrid, see our chapter titled *Madrid and More*, pages 145–156.

Leave Madrid heading northwest on the A6 freeway until it turns into NVI, on which you continue north toward the first destination. After a few kilometers you pass **Arevalo,** one of the oldest towns in Castile, in whose 14th-century castle Isabella spent her early years. She was born in nearby **Madrigal de Las Altas Torres** whose lovely Plaza de la Villa is typical of Spain, dominated by the Church of Saint Martin's two Mudéjar towers. The **Convent of Saint Francis** was founded by the saint himself in 1214. If church architecture is your interest, you should see the beautiful **Our Lady of the Lugareta Nunnery** 2 kilometers south of town. It constitutes one of the major Romanesque structures in Spain.

Next you come to **Medina del Campo,** historically a very important Castilian market town, but now not really worth a stop. However, the historic market town of **Tordesillas,** where you cross the Duero, one of Spain's major rivers, does make an interesting stop. Juana the Mad (Ferdinand and Isabella's daughter) locked herself away in the **Santa Clara Convent** here for 44 years after the death of her husband, Phillip the Fair, in 1506. The convent has a beautiful patio, and the nearby church has a fabulous artesonado ceiling which you should not miss. This is also the place where the Spanish and Portuguese signed a treaty in 1494 that divided the world between them. Setting a line some 1,620 kilometers west of the Cape Verde Islands, it resulted in Spain's ownership of all of America except Brazil.

From Tordesillas turn west through the small fortified town of **Toro**—picturesquely situated above the Duero and well known for its wines—then to **Zamora,** where we suggest you overnight at the **Parador "Condes de Alba y Aliste"** overlooking a pretty, untouristy, small plaza. The parador boasts fantastic tapestries, coats of arms, and suits of armor, and has one of the prettiest interior patios in Spain, overlooked by an arcaded stone gallery. The Parador "Condes de Alba y Aliste" makes a perfect base for exploring the narrow, picturesque streets of the old quarter of Zamora.

Parador "Condes de Alba y Aliste," Zamora

Zamora, which figured prominently in *El Cid*, has been a point of contention between various warring factions since the time of the Visigoths. Castile and Portugal battled for possession of the strategic town and it was occupied by first one and then the other in the heyday of the struggle. The fortified town seems to be wall-to-wall churches, but if you can see only one, visit the impressive 12th-century **cathedral**, whose tower dome, ringed by arched windows, should not be missed, and whose museum has a stunning collection of 15th- and 16th-century Flemish tapestries. The town, with its many beautifully preserved Romanesque monuments, is a great place for simply strolling and poking down narrow streets and alleyways. Its wealth of beautiful mansions and quaint little plazas add greatly to the charm and atmosphere.

When you are ready to continue the pilgrimage, head north out of Zamora, then bear left after a bit on N525, which takes you through the **Sierra de la Culebra** (snake) National Reserve. At **Mombuey** watch for the lovely 13th-century church—now a national monument. Several mountain ranges converge in the area you pass through, forming a gloriously scenic setting. Rustic stone houses with slate roofs and iron or wood balconies are characteristic of this region.

The landscape grows increasingly rugged as you near **Puebla de Sanabria**. If time allows, stop to see this fine example of a small Castilian hill town that dominates the countryside. Visit the plaza at the tiptop of town, ranking among the most remarkable we have seen. It perfectly preserves a medieval atmosphere, flanked by hunkering whitewashed houses, the old city hall with its wooden gallery, and a reddish 12th-century granite church. The plaza can be reached by car by crossing the river and bearing left, or, for the hardier among you, on foot from the east side. Either way you will love the atmosphere and panoramic views from the top.

We also highly recommend an especially scenic side trip, less than 20 kilometers, to the gorgeous mountain-lake area to the northwest of Puebla de Sanabria. The big, blue lake is over 915 meters above sea level and surrounded by craggy, green mountains and dotted with small towns. This is an ideal spot for a picnic outing—you can rent paddle boats (*patines*) if you are feeling adventurous, taking along one of the good local wines for company. **Ribadelago**, at the far end of the lake (bear left at the fork), is a new town built in the late '50s when floods destroyed the existing town. It has swimming areas and pretty views, combining to make a refreshing interlude. If you bear right at the fork, you will climb to the high mountain town of **San Martin de Castaneda**, whose wonderful 11th-century church overlooks cultivated hillsides dropping to the lake.

Our recommended destination for tonight is the **Parador Monterrey**, a convenient breaking point from Zamora to the coast. Drive through the rather drab city of **Verín** and, as you leave town, you spot on a hill to your right a castle and a small road marked with the parador sign. Weave up the hill and you find your night's lodging, not in the castle, but in the hotel constructed below it. Ask for a room (such as 107) with a romantic view of the castle.

DESTINATION III   BAYONA

DEVIATION NOTE: If you are planning to head for Portugal, there are two ways to go about it. The first is to head south from Verín on C532 to the border crossing and to Chaves in Portugal. The other, more common route, is to follow this itinerary as far as Porriño and head south on N550 to the Spanish border town of Tuy. This brings you to the scenic coast of Portugal.

Continuing west from Verín, you pass over numerous viaducts with splendid views of the surrounding countryside. The earth changes from red to white before your eyes, and the hillsides are sprinkled with granite-colored towns. At the 915-meter pass of **Portillo de la Canda**, you officially enter Galicia, characterized by rocky landscape and its equally rocky buildings constructed from the native stone. Continue on toward Orense, passing between green hillsides dotted with red-roofed stone houses.

The provincial capital of **Orense**, famed for its sulfur springs, has an enchanting old quarter with twisting, stepped streets overhung by old houses, and delightfully punctuated with picturesque plazas. This was an important capital of the pre-Visigoth Suevi in the 6th and 7th centuries. An old bridge (near the newer one) across the Miño was constructed on the foundations of the Roman bridge in the 13th century. Take time out to stop here to see the Plaza Mayor and its Romanesque Bishop's palace. Park in one of the plazas and walk around the old quarter to visit the shops.

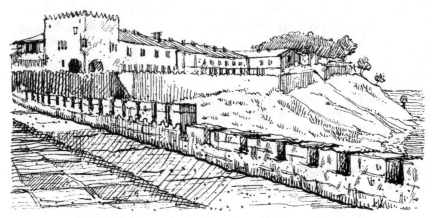

Parador Conde de Gondomar, Bayona

Continue in the direction of Vigo, passing through the beautiful **Miño Valley** (legend has it that gold existed here, thus the name of Orense from the Spanish *oro*, meaning gold). The highway borders landscape carpeted with vineyards and parallels the river Miño as far as Ventosela. When you reach the industrial city of Porriào, turn east on PO331 and continue through Gondomar and A Ramallosa. The road is narrow and winding, but the slow going gives you time to enjoy the incredibly lush forest, interspersed with some spectacular views over the valleys below. At A Ramallosa you turn left and, after a few kilometers, you come to a bridge (paralleling an ancient Roman bridge on your left) leading into **Bayona**, whose former inhabitants were the first to hear the news of the discovery of the New World when the *Pinta* put in here in 1493 (the *Santa María* sought refuge in Lisbon after a storm). Subsequently, it continued to be a major port for the many gold- and silver-laden ships that followed thereafter from America. Thoughts such as these will not seem at all out of place as you stroll on the perfectly preserved seaside battlements which encircle the **Parador Conde de Gondomar**, your suggested resting spot for tonight on this heavenly peninsula.

Since you are staying in the castle, which is the premier tourist attraction in town (non-guests of the parador pay for visiting privileges), you do not have to go far to explore the site or enjoy the little inlet beach at the foot of the drive. The castle ramparts are 3 kilometers in length and parts of them date from the 2nd century B.C. (other parts are as recent as the 17th century). The walk around them affords bird's-eye views of the

crashing sea, the picturesque fishing port, and the coastline stretching into the horizon. If you crave more, however, you can venture out to see Bayona's 12th-century collegiate church or drive the 30 kilometers down the coast to the Portuguese border. About halfway you pass the little fishing village of **Oya**. At the end of the road is the port of **La Guardia**.

DESTINATION IV   ISLA DE LA TOJA

If time is at a premium, from Bayona follow the quickest route back to the freeway and drive north to the pearl of this itinerary, Santiago de Compostela, but, if you are in no hurry and would like to dawdle along the way, we suggest a stop at Isla de la Toja to give you yet another insight into this region of Spain. If this is your choice, drive from Bayona along the craggy coast to **Vigo**, situated on the **Ría de Vigo** (*ría* means inlet or estuary) and the most important fishing port in Spain. In the 15th and 16th centuries English buccaneers preyed upon Spanish galleons returning here from the rich Spanish colonies—Sir Francis Drake the most famous among them. You pass some nice beaches south of Vigo, notably **Alcabre**, **Samil**, and **Canido**. Though Vigo has become quite industrial, it has managed nonetheless to retain old-world charm. It surrounds Castro hill, topped with two castles (and a restaurant appropriately called El Castillo), from which there are extensive views of the city and the bay. Driving in the city is a challenge, particularly as you near the old quarter. Probably the best approach is to drive to the port area, park your car, and walk up into the old quarter. You find interesting shops and ancient houses in a maze of stone-paved streets in the Berbes fishermen's quarter, which has been declared a national historical monument.

If you are a seafood fan, you will be delighted with the dozens of colorful bars and cafés offering everything from full meals to *tapas* featuring the day's catch. Speaking of the day's catch, you will find it in unbelievable variety in the busy fish market (you can find it by the smell) between the Berbes area and the port.

From Vigo head north on the freeway to **Pontevedra**. Signs lead you through town (if you follow them carefully) and out again on the road to **Isla de la Toja** (*A Toxa* in Galician). You now take a scenic drive along the coast through small resort areas, the inevitable condominium complexes, and quaint fishing villages. There are many beaches along here, but they are a few hundred meters off the road. After you round the tip of the peninsula, you come upon the beautiful 6-kilometer-long **La Lanzada**, a gorgeous beach with pale sand and cool, clear water which you will find difficult to resist. And you need not forego this splendid beach for long, for your hotel is nearby. You soon cross a pretty stone bridge with tall stone lamp-posts which connects the idyllic, pine-covered little island of La Toja with the mainland. Here stay in the turn-of-the-century **Gran Hotel**. This large, old-fashioned hotel will satisfy just about your every whim—from gambling in the casino to dining in true splendor, your indoor time will be catered to in style. Outdoors, there is golf, a splendid pool, and tennis, or you can walk, drive, or ride a rented bike to La Lanzada, where you can enjoy exploring the immense expanse of sandy beach, or perhaps consider renting horses for a morning ride.

From Isla de la Toja, continue your pilgrimage on to Santiago de Compostela. Cross the bridge, turn left, and soon you come to **Cambados**, whose colorful little Plaza de Fefiñanes is lined with old stone mansions—a good spot to stretch your legs and take some pictures.

Farther on you join N550 (note the change in letter) and arrive in legendary **Padrón** where, tradition has it, the boat carrying Saint James's remains put in, and in whose parish church you can see the mooring stone upon which the saint's body was placed after the boat docked. The town was formerly called Ilia Flavia, but *padrón* is the word for commemorative stone, hence the name change.

Heading north from Padrón you soon arrive in **Santiago de Compostela**, one of Spain's most famous cities. Justifiably touted as one of the finest hotels on the continent, the **Hostal de Los Reyes Católicos** was built, at the order of Ferdinand and Isabella, as a hospice for the pilgrims who made the arduous journey to this sanctified spot. Today it lacks nothing to help the modern pilgrim thoroughly enjoy and fondly remember his stay here, surrounded by antiques and catered to in medieval splendor. Its location on the main plaza makes it a little difficult to reach by car: you come into the plaza from the north, on the east side of the hotel, and drive down a street with a barrier seemingly prohibiting your entry. Enter anyway (slowly), turn right, and you are in front of the hotel.

According to legend, Saint James (in Spanish, Santiago or Sant Yago) the Apostle came to Galicia and spent seven years preaching there. After he was beheaded in Jerusalem, his disciples brought his remains back to Spain by boat, mooring in Padrón and, after some difficulty, he was finally buried. Seven centuries later, in the year 813, mysterious stars appeared in the sky above his grave and led the Bishop Teodomiro to the spot. The traditional explanation for the name Compostela is that it comes from the Latin *Campus Stellae* or field of stars. The city that grew up around the area was named Santiago de Compostela, and Saint James became the patron saint of all Spain. From that time pilgrimages began, and continue—although not quite so massive as in those times—to the present day. Most pilgrims from Europe took the Way of Saint James through modern-day Vitoria, Burgos, and León. Another route, considered dangerous because of highwaymen, ran closer to the northern coast. As many as two million pilgrims per year made the exhausting journey in the Middle Ages.

The magnificent **Plaza de España** (also called the Plaza del Obradoiro) is bordered on the north by your hotel, on the east by the baroque cathedral, on the south by the Romanesque College of San Jerónimo, and on the west by the neoclassical city hall. The plaza is without a doubt one of the most majestic in Spain.

The **cathedral** dates from the 11th to 13th centuries and was built on the site of Saint James's tomb (and several earlier churches). An unusual feature of the building is the existence of plazas on all sides, which allow encompassing views—of the cathedral from the plazas and vice versa. There is a breathtaking panorama over the red-tiled Santiago rooftops from the upper floor of the cathedral. Be sure to take a stroll around the cathedral through the Plaza Inmaculada (north), the Plaza de la Quintana (east), and the beautiful Plaza de las Platerías (Silversmiths) on the south side. Probably the most impressive artistic element of the cathedral is the Pórtico de la Gloria, just inside the main entrance, where millions of pilgrims have touched the central pillar upon their arrival. A thousand years of loving touches have left the stone worn and smooth. You will discover your hand will fit naturally into a favorite spot on the pillar where millions have touched it before you.

There is often a line of devout pilgrims waiting to enter the cathedral. You will also notice a few modern-day pilgrims throughout Spain walking to Santiago along the Way of Saint James—following the same roads that have been trod by millions before them. As might be imagined, the journey used to be a treacherous one with bandits and various fiefdoms at war along the route. Pilgrims wore a hat adorned with three scallop shells and carried a tall staff. These symbols identified them as pilgrims on a religious journey and was supposed to guarantee them safe passage through dangerous lands. The pilgrims today usually carry a tall staff and frequently wear a badge of scallop shells.

Santiago has one of the most industrious *tunas* we have ever encountered. The tradition of the *tuna* dates from the Middle Ages when university students from a single college— such as the medical school—would form a musical group and frequent bars and

Los Reyes Católicos, Santiago de Compostela

restaurants singing for their supper. They are characterized by their black medieval costumes consisting of hose, bloomers, and capes (each colorful ribbon hanging from their cloaks supposedly comes from a female admirer). You find *tunas* in many of the larger cities of Spain, especially in the tourist areas. Today they are more often just strolling musicians who entertain in restaurants and plazas for contributions. The group in Santiago, however, has elaborated the tradition to the point where they not only sing in the plaza but afterwards go around individually, offering their own records and tapes for sale. You are not likely to escape being approached to buy a memento of the experience.

As for the rest of Santiago, most of it can be seen by walking straight out of your hotel, across the plaza, and (on Calle del Franco) into the streets to the south. While Spaniards seem to be able to navigate the streets in an automobile, we strongly recommend that you leave yours in the underground parking lot of the Reyes Católicos (for a fee per day) and hoof it around the old city. Marvelous old buildings, many small plazas, shops of all kinds, and numerous restaurants and cafés line the narrow streets, which should be explored at leisure for a taste of northern-Spanish atmosphere. If you continue about 400 meters down Calle del Franco, you come to the Paseo de la Herradura, where a calm time can be spent wandering on the wooded hill and enjoying the views back to the city.

SIDE TRIPS: If you need an excuse to extend your stay in the Hostal de los Reyes Católicos, there are some interesting side trips from Santiago.

If quaint fishing villages and gorgeous scenery appeal, get some bread, some smooth Galician San Simön cheese, and some slightly sparkling, white ribeiro wine and head west on C543 to **Noya**, turning north on C550 to explore the coastal road along the *rías*.

If more history of the Way of Saint James intrigues you, drive east on C547 to **Arzua**, then on to **Mellid**—both stops on the medieval pilgrims' route.

If large cities attract you, the major city in Galicia, **La Coruña**, is only an hour away via the A9 freeway. This was Generalísimo Franco's home town, and, understandably, became an important industrial center during his regime.

Treasures off the Beaten Track

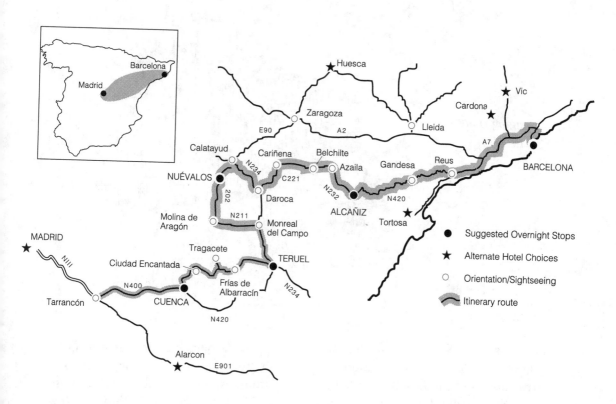

Treasures off the Beaten Track

Hanging Houses
Cuenca

This itinerary starts off in New Castile, traverses Aragón and winds up in Barcelona, the sophisticated, seaside capital of Catalonia. Most of the route, as its name suggests, takes you to areas not so commonly frequented by foreign tourists, and should appeal to those of you who are anxious for a more intimate taste of Spain. It heads east through New Castile, which holds in store the beautifully rugged Cuenca Range and Cuenca, one of Spain's most enchanting medieval towns, famous for its "hanging houses." Then the route continues on to Aragón with its small, earth-colored, hidden villages nestled in gorgeous, scenic mountain valleys or in the midst of olive groves and vineyards. It is easy to understand why these are considered some of the most ancient settlements in the country: the medieval and Moorish past is evident at every turn.

Starting in the 11th century, Aragón began to expand its dominions. Within three centuries, it included parts of southern France, Catalonia, Navarre, and all of southeastern Spain, Sicily, and Naples. Thus, when Ferdinand II of Aragón married Isabella I of Castile (which included the eastern half of Spain) in 1464, the modern nation state was born. No longer so extensive, the old kingdom is now characterized mostly by agricultural activity. The final stop, Barcelona, provides considerable contrast: it is Spain's second largest city and one as glamorous and worldly as any in Europe.

ORIGINATING CITY   MADRID

Almost all tourists fly into or out of Madrid when visiting Spain. After a few days enjoying this lovely city, many then drive on to Barcelona, another of Spain's jewels. It is possible to take a freeway most of the way from Madrid to Barcelona—possible but not very interesting. This itinerary outlines a much more engaging way to make the journey from Spain's largest to its second-largest city. By following this route you enjoy some fabulous sights that are truly "off the beaten track." Note: for more in-depth suggestions on sightseeing in and around Madrid, see our chapter titled *Madrid and More* on pages 145–156.

DESTINATION I   CUENCA

Make your way to the southeast side of Madrid and head out of town on the A3 freeway (which becomes NIII when you leave the city). Continue through Arganda del Rey, then wind through lovely scenery to **Tarrancón**, a little country town with a Gothic church and a mansion built by Queen María Cristina. As you drive, you get a strong feel for one of Spain's major geographical features, the central meseta, or plateau. The drive east between here and Cuenca is one of the loveliest in Spain—through pretty rolling hills of wheat and sunflowers contrasting with pale, golden hay fields.

Posada de San José, Cuenca

Cuenca was originally constructed on the top of the cliff. This is the part known today as the old town, the area of most interest to the visitor. The best way to reach this district is to turn sharply right just after you cross the river as you head into town. The road climbs steeply and enters a small plaza through a massive stone gate. Park here and explore this engaging town by foot.

Ask directions to the hanging houses *(casas colgadas)*, seemingly perched in midair at the edge of the cliff. Inside one of these ancient structures, in impressive and tasteful surroundings, is Spain's most important **Museum of Abstract Art**. The extensive collection of Spanish masters is a must to visit. Also situated in one of the old, cliff-top houses is the restaurant **Meson Casas Colgadas**. If it is not mealtime, you still might want to stop for a cool drink and to savor the views over the ravine. Be sure to save some time for a leisurely walk through the picturesque streets and alleys of this old quarter, and to sit in the lively plaza to soak up the typical Spanish flavor of the town.

The Gothic **cathedral**, parts of which date from the 13th century, is a national monument: be sure to go in to see the elaborate interior. The treasury is also worth a visit—among other works of art, there are two paintings by El Greco.

We recommend two choices of accommodation: if you choose the **Posada de San José**, it is just a short walk from the plaza. As you face the cathedral, look for signs to your left marking the way to your hotel (if you don't see the signs, ask someone). The posada is easy to miss. As you tread the cobbled lane, look for a massive doorway on your right, adorned by a niche with a statue of San José—this is the entrance to the hotel. The Posada de San José is not a deluxe hotel, but ideally situated in the heart of Cuenca with the added advantage of breathtaking views across the gorge to the dramatic Convento de San Pablo, perched on the rocky cliffs opposite your hotel. In the evening, when the convent is softly illuminated, the vista is even more romantic. You can easily walk to the picturesque convent by taking the suspension bridge that links the two sides of the gorge. If you prefer a fancier hotel than the Posada do San José, our other highly recommended place to stay is actually in the **Convento de San Pablo**, which, following meticulous restoration, has become one of the latest historical buildings to be added to the chain of paradors.

Convento de San Pablo, Cuenca

When you are ready to leave, head north on CU921 through the Júcar river ravine (Hoz). Take the turnoff toward Valdecabras for a gorgeous drive through rugged mountain terrain to the **Ciudad Encantada** (Enchanted City). This eerie scene has been created by wind and water erosion which has separated large rock formations from their surrounding mass and carved them into shapes which resemble (with a bit of imagination) buildings, animals, and monsters. You buy your ticket from the booth and follow a well-marked footpath for about an hour through the interesting rock formations. The tour makes a cool and refreshing break from driving.

Continue on the same road, passing through Una and La Toba, at the end of a lovely turquoise reservoir surrounded by green pines. Follow the meandering Júcar river, then the signs to Teruel, climbing through the Puerto de El Cubillo Pass in the **Montes Universales**. This scenery is wonderful, with pine trees lining the narrow road and the sharp gray mountain crests in the distance.

By descending the other side of the pass, you come to a large monument on your left. This area is where the Tagus river begins its long journey to the Atlantic through Toledo and Lisbon in Portugal. It is amazing to see that this important river's origin is a tiny spring flowing out from under a pile of rocks. Continue winding amidst marvelous scenery with expansive views of the valley below until you arrive at the little town of Royuelo where you bear left and then turn right on TE903 for the 7-kilometer drive to the spectacularly situated little mountain town of **Albarracín**. Designated a historical monument by the national government, this whimsical town looks as if it were carved into the living rock below the ruined castle whose towers reach toward the sky.

Albarracín is a medieval gem with narrow, twisting, cobblestoned streets (almost exclusively pedestrian) and ancient brick, stone, and wooden houses whose roofs practically touch each other over the tiniest alleyways. The atmosphere cannot have changed much over the past several hundred years. The handsome **cathedral**, with its collection of 16th-century Brussels tapestries, is interesting to visit, and it is fun to explore the numerous ceramics shops selling their locally made wares. Since you are only a 30-minute drive from the next destination, you should have leisure time to explore this little Aragonese town: if time is short, do not fail to make the excursion from Teruel.

A short distance south of Albarracín are some **Paleolithic caves** with prehistoric paintings. You can get near only one of them by car and to visit the others requires considerable walking, a visit that might best be done as a side trip from Teruel, since it takes half a day. Follow the signs leading to the Pinturas Rupestres. (You see signs as you approach for Cueva del Navazo.) A little rock-climbing brings you to the shallow caves protected by an iron grating. Inside are paintings of hunters and bulls. The other caves are farther along the same increasingly impassable road, but we do not recommend you attempt to proceed by car.

A pretty easterly drive takes you to **Teruel**, surrounded by the gorges of the Río Turia. (Soon after leaving Albarracín, glance up to your left for the dramatic sight of ancient castle ruins crowning a rocky vantage point.) Our hotel recommendation, the **Parador de Teruel**, is located on the left just before you enter Teruel. The parador is restful and comfortable, providing the best accommodations available from which to base your explorations of this region, rich in history and archaeology, and of Teruel, rich in Mudéjar monuments.

Besides its remarkable natural setting, Teruel is noteworthy for the dominance of its Mudéjar architecture. Mudéjar is the style created by the Moors who continued to live in Christian-dominated areas even after they were reconquered. The Moors remained in Teruel a particularly long time, hence the prevalence of the style here. The five Mudéjar towers spread around town are truly of special interest: they are detached belfries with obviously Oriental ornamentation. Two of the delicate structures grace the entrance to the old town.

Parador de Teruel, Teruel

The 13th-century **cathedral** has an artesonado ceiling of intricately carved wood, with numerous other Mudéjar motifs in the sculptured plaster and in the domed ceilings. The tile decoration is of the same style. One of the five towers is the belfry for the cathedral.

Next to **Saint Peter's church** (which has another of the towers as a belfry) is the funerary chapel of the "**Lovers of Teruel**." The legend of Isabel and Juan Diego, who lived in the 13th century and who died of grief at being unable to marry because of her father's disapproval, has inspired numerous famous literary works, the best-known by the 19th-century romantic dramatist Hartzenbusch (thus the name of the street). They were buried in a single grave and their remains are on display here in a glass coffin topped by a recent alabaster relief of the lovers reaching out to touch hands. To visit the chapel, ring at a nearby door (indicated by a sign) and someone will come down to open it for you. (Tip a couple of hundred pesetas.)

Just east is the triangular Plaza del Torico (baby bull), a popular gathering place with a tiny statue of, logically enough, a baby bull in the center.

When you are ready to move on, travel north on what must be one of Spain's best country roads towards the tidy farming center of **Monreal del Campo**, at the foot of the Sierra Menera, and bear left by the impressive, tiny fortified town of **Pozuel del Campo** with its crumbling walls and huge, imposing church. Continue to **Molina de Aragón**, an ancient, pre-Moorish village, once a hotly disputed strong point between warring Aragón and Castile. Perched above the town is a dramatic, red-tinged fortress surrounded by extensive crumbling walls and several restored towers, of which one, the 11th-century Torre de Aragón, is a national monument. This fortress was one of several, including Sigüenza and Alarcón, which served as a second line of Christian defense during the Reconquest.

Turn north in Monreal del Campo, first along a flat road through farmland, then on a more scenic drive through rugged countryside toward Nuévalos, a little south of which you encounter your hotel, the **Monasterio de Piedra**, just across the Piedra river. Remember the size of this river as you cross it because it will amaze you when you see what it does in the nature park ahead. Your first view of the monastery is of the lengthy, sturdy old walls around the grounds, which you follow to the entrance. The 12th-century Cistercian Monasterio de Piedra is situated, thanks to the River Piedra, in a green oasis surrounded by red, arid countryside. Your room is a former monk's cell, but a 12th-century monk would hardly recognize it. Most rooms have a sunny balcony with views of the wooded countryside.

Besides the hotel part of the monastery, there are other interesting remains attached to it and on the surrounding grounds. The 12th-century keep (Torre del Homenaje) is an excellent example of Romanesque-Byzantine-style construction. Off the beautiful cloister is a fascinating old kitchen and, next to it, the large monastery dining hall. On the other side of the cloister is the old church, which has not been restored.

Hotel Monasterio de Piedra, Nuévalos

The hotel is situated next to the **Monasterio de Piedra Park,** the lush park watered by the river which flows through the grounds in capricious ways, forming waterfalls and pools of great beauty. Be sure to visit the series of waterfalls La Caprichosa (the whimsical lady) and the 52-meter Cola de Caballo (horse's tail)—you can see both from a vista point and from underneath in the Iris Grotto. In contrast to the rushing cascades, the lake properly carries the name of Mirror Lake, a truly spectacular natural sight. Buy a ticket at the entrance and follow the arrows for an unforgettable stroll.

While at the monastery, drive to the pretty little town of **Nuévalos**, sitting in a valley surrounded by the deep-red hills. Another worthwhile side trip for scenery lovers is to the spa of **Jaraba**, reached by going south to the tiny village of Campillo de Aragón and turning right on Z452. You have a 12-kilometer drive through a red, green, and gold patchwork quilt of fields as you go over the Campillo Pass, then you descend into steep canyons lined with dark-red cliffs. This is a dramatic excursion.

DESTINATION IV ALCAÑIZ

Leave this gorgeous setting by heading northeast to Calatayud. Today you drive through alternately dusty gray plateaus and deep-red earth planted with fruit trees, vines, and olives, along with occasional hay and wheat fields. **Calatayud** is built up against a hillside, crowned by the minaret of an old mosque and the ruins of the Moorish **Kalat-Ayub** (Castle of Ayub). You might want to stop for a closer inspection of the Mudéjar tower sitting impressively atop its rocky ridge above the hillside covered with tiny houses. You can see the castle on the mountain well before you reach the town, but it blends in so well with the stone ridge that you may not notice unless you are watching.

From here drive southeast, passing the dramatic ruins of a castle near the little village of Maluenda, then drive through **Velilla**, **Fuentes de Jiloca**, and **Montón**, all picturesque towns on hilltops overlooking the lush Jiloca river valley. As you leave Montón, notice that vines are beginning to replace fruit trees on the red landscape.

Turn right on N330 to reach the town of **Daroca**. This beautifully situated medieval town is still enclosed by crumbling 13th-century walls with 114 towers. Park near the first gate you come to and take time to stroll along the Calle Mayor and visit Saint Mary's church and the Plaza Mayor.

Back on N330, drive northeast over the winding **Puerto de Paniza Pass**. As you descend from the pass, you come to **Cariñena**, a little walled town famous for its wine.

Head east on the C221 driving through seemingly endless vineyards on the undulating, reddish-brown hills. A short drive brings you to **Fuendetodos**, the birthplace of Francisco de Goya y Lucientes, one of Spain's greatest artists. It is definitely worth a short stop to see the simple house where he lived. The house is furnished with 18th-century pieces in an effort to re-create the way it must have looked when Goya lived there. You can even see the room where he was born. Signs direct you to Goya's house and there is no admission charge, but a donation (perhaps 100 pesetas per person) is appropriate.

Continue east, through scrubby hills occasionally alternating with lush green vineyards, to **Belchite**, which was extensively destroyed during the Civil War (1936–39). The rebuilt town stands next to the ruins of the former one, a grim monument to the horror of that conflict. The old town soon appears on the right as you leave: an eerie moonscape of bombed-out buildings, houses, and church.

A short drive farther, after a stretch of fairly flat pasture land, lies Azaila, where you turn south on N232 to **Híjar**, another beautiful, small hilltop town overlooking the Martin river from behind its ruined walls. The terrain around the town changes to reflect the ravines carved by the river. From Híjar it is a short drive across flat farmland to **Alcañiz**.

As you enter town, you see the impressive cathedral ahead and, above on the right, dominating the town, your hotel, the **Parador de la Concordia**, itself a national historic monument. Part of the 12th-century castle was converted to a palace in the 18th century, and that part now houses the parador. Behind the palace remain some of the original castle buildings, dating from the 12th and 13th centuries. The tower, chapel, and cloister can also be visited.

Alcañiz is a delightful little town in the middle of an olive- and almond-growing region. The Plaza Mayor is flanked by the town hall with a Renaissance façade, the arcaded 15th-century Lonja (trade hall), and the highly elaborate baroque façade of the colossal Saint Mary's collegiate church. Due to its relative isolation, the town has maintained a serene, medieval atmosphere.

Parador de la Concordia, Alcañiz

DESTINATION V   BARCELONA

Head southeast on N420 and N232 and take N420 east towards Tarragona where the roads separate. As you leave Alcañiz, you see the olive trees slowly give way to vines on the rolling hillsides. About 8 kilometers past Calaceite, at Caseres, you officially enter Catalonia. Since Catalonians speak (in addition to Spanish) their own language, Catalan, you find a number of words spelled differently from the way you may be used to (e.g., river is *riu* instead of *río*).

Gandesa, rebuilt since it suffered severe destruction during the Civil War and thus a relatively modern town, is at the end of a pretty drive. After crossing one of Spain's most important rivers, the Ebro, at Mora de Ebro, you arrive at the new town, from where the best view of the old quarter, built right up to the river's edge on the opposite bank, is presented. Now the grape dominates completely as you enter the rich wine-growing valley around Falset. The vast vine-clad hills are dotted with tiny villages that seem to float above the vineyards on their little hillocks. Look back as you leave Falset, for there is an enchanting view of the town.

The highway follows a winding downward course through a number of passes to Reus, the birthplace of architect Antonio Gaudí and also known for its wool-weaving. The town is now mostly industrial and not particularly appealing to tourists. Just past Reus join the A7 freeway for a short drive into Barcelona. **Barcelona** has a rich selection of places to stay—look in the back of the book in the *Hotel Descriptions* section to see what suits your fancy. Note: For more in-depth suggestions on sightseeing in and around Barcelona, see our chapter titled *Barcelona Highlights* on pages 163–167.

Hotel Gran Vía, Barcelona

Treasures off the Beaten Track

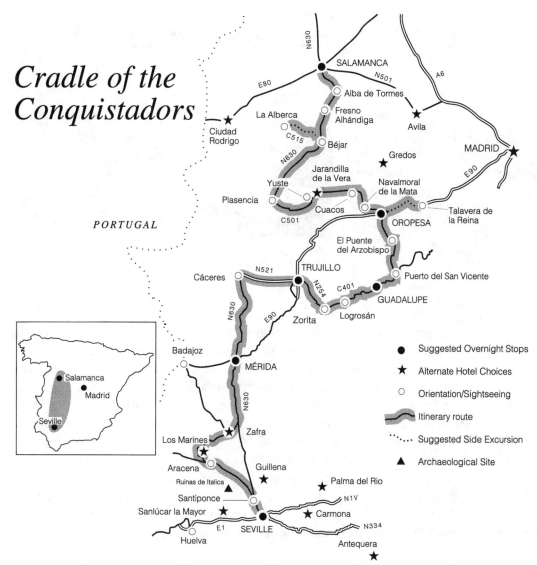

Cradle of the Conquistadors

PORTUGAL

N630

SALAMANCA

E80

N501

A6

Ciudad Rodrigo

La Alberca

Alba de Tormes

Fresno Alhándiga

Avila

C515

N630

Béjar

Gredos

MADRID

Yuste

Jarandilla de la Vera

Navalmoral de la Mata

E90

Plasencia

Cuacos

OROPESA

Talavera de la Reina

C501

El Puente del Arzobispo

Cáceres

N521

TRUJILLO

Puerto del San Vicente

N630

E90

N254

C401

GUADALUPE

Zorita

Logrosán

Badajoz

MÉRIDA

N630

Zafra

Los Marines

Aracena

Guillena

Palma del Rio

Ruinas de Italica

Santiponce

N1V

Sanlúcar la Mayor

Carmona

Huelva

E1

SEVILLE

N334

Antequera

Salamanca
Madrid
Seville

● Suggested Overnight Stops

★ Alternate Hotel Choices

○ Orientation/Sightseeing

Itinerary route

····· Suggested Side Excursion

▲ Archaeological Site

91

Cradle of the Conquistadors

Guadalupe

Most of this itinerary finds you in Extremadura—an area of Spain less frequented by tourists, which is part of its appeal. The name *Extremadura* originated during the Reconquest period and translates as "land beyond the river Duero" (which runs across the country from Soria to Valladolid to Zamora). Historically somewhat at the periphery of national life, and less privileged economically, the area was rich in young men eager to seek their fortunes in the New World, as the name of this itinerary suggests. Some famous Extremadurans you may recognize are Hernán Cortés, conqueror of Mexico; Francisco Pizarro, conqueror of Peru; Orellano, explorer of the Amazon; and Balboa, discoverer of the Pacific Ocean. Indeed, since the explorations were sponsored by Queen Isabella of Castile, which included Extremadura, only Castilians were given the opportunity to make the journey to the New World during the 16th century. The area is still resplendent with fine old mansions built with the treasures found in Mexico and Peru.

Typical cuisine of Extremadura includes one of our favorite Spanish specialties: raw-cured ham (*jamón serrano*), as well as lamb stew (*caldereta de cordero*), fried breadcrumbs with bacon (*migas*), and numerous game dishes such as pheasant (*faisán*) and partridge (*perdiz*). The major local wine is a simple white called Almendralejo.

The last destination brings you into Old Castile and the enchanting medieval university city of Salamanca.

ORIGINATING CITY   SEVILLE

It is never easy to leave Seville, Spain's most romantic city, but, if you fall under its spell, you will be back. However, Spain offers many additional enchantments and much more of it remains to be seen, so set your sights north. Note: for more in-depth suggestions on sightseeing in Seville, see our chapter titled *Seville Highlights*, pages 157–162.

DESTINATION I   MÉRIDA

Leave Seville heading west across the bridge and turn north toward Mérida. After about 24 kilometers look for N433 which takes you northwest to the little hill town of Aracena, a popular escape from the heat of the Andalusian summer. The **Sierra de Aracena**, the western part of the Sierra Morena, is known for copper and pyrite production, as well as the justifiably famous and delicious *jamón serrano*, which must be sampled—especially if you are a prosciutto-lover. It is a ubiquitous and favorite *tapa* throughout the country, and you will have more than likely seen the hams hanging from the ceiling of many a Spanish bar. (Enjoy it while you are here, but do not try to take any home with you, as you will not be allowed through US customs with it.)

About halfway between Seville and Aracena is the dazzling white town of **Castillo de las Guardas** nestled against a green mountainside. As the drive approaches the pretty town of **Aracena**, the air gets cooler, the earth redder, and the hills are covered with cork trees. Aracena is tiered up a hillside, dramatically crowned with the 13th-century church of the Knights Templar and the 12th-century ruins of a Moorish fort with a beautiful brick mosque tower. Directly beneath the castle, within the hill itself, is the **Gruta de las Maravillas** (Cave of Marvels), hollowed out by underground rivers and an amazing sight to behold. Limpid pools and rivers and an underground lake reflect magnificent and multicolored stalactites and stalagmites. The guided visit takes about 45 minutes, but you may have to wait for a group to form for the tour: if so, wile away the time in the quaint shops around the entrance to the cave that offer a surprisingly good-quality selection of regional ceramic ware.

Continue west on N433 for 16 kilometers and turn right on N435 to **Zafra**. Zafra preserves one of the most impressive fortified palaces in the region, now the **Parador de Safra** (see the hotel listing), on one of the prettiest little plazas in the area. Actually the former palace of the Duke of Feria, it was the residence of Hernán Cortés just before he embarked for the New World. Its conversion to a parador has not spoiled it in the least, and it's worth a short visit to see the fabulous chapel and the other faithfully restored public rooms. Leave Zafra on N435 and you have quite a fast drive to today's destination—**Mérida**, caretaker of the richest Roman remains in Spain.

You find Roman antiquities among those decorating your next hotel suggestion, the **Parador Vía de La Plata**, elegantly installed in an old convent that was built on the site of a Roman temple at the top of town. It has also seen duty as a hospital for the plague victims of 1729, and briefly as a jail. The combination of authentic Roman, Arabic, and Spanish architectural features (most discovered on the site) within the hotel make it unique, indeed, and interesting to explore. The parador fronts onto a plaza where it is practically impossible to park, but you will gratefully discover that the hotel has provided parking in back, next to its pretty Mudéjar gardens, as well as an underground parking garage.

Parador Vía de La Plata, Mérida

Founded in 25 B.C., the Roman town of Emerita Augusta, now Mérida, was so well situated at the junction of major Roman roads that it was soon made the capital of Lusitania. Outstanding Roman remains dot the city: bridges, temples, a racecourse, two aqueducts, an arena, and a theater—all attesting to Mérida's historical importance under Roman occupation. If your time is limited, you must not miss the **Roman Arena** (built in the 1st century B.C. with a seating capacity of 14,000) and next to it, the **Roman Theater** (built by Agrippa in the 1st century B.C. with a seating capacity of over 5,000). The astounding theater alone, with its double-columned stage, is worth a detour to Mérida. (If you are here in late June or early July, check at the hotel to see if the Classical Theater Festival is offering live performances.) Just across the road from the arena and theater is a stunning modern museum that you must not miss, **Museo Nacional de Arte Romano**. In this spectacular brick-vaulted, sky-lit building many Roman artifacts and panels of mosaics are displayed. Be sure to also see the **Casa Romana del**

Anfiteatro (1st century A.D. with mosaics and water pipes) and the **Alcazaba** at the city end of the Roman bridge (built by the Moors in the 9th century). If your time and archaeological knowledge are limited, you might want to arrange for a guide who can take you to all the interesting places more efficiently than you can do it on your own. Inquire at your hotel, the Teatro Romano, or the tourist office for information. A few blocks southeast of the parador, you find the **Plaza de España**, Mérida's main center of activity. It is a wonderful place to sit with a drink at one of the outdoor cafés and watch the world go by.

Mérida, Roman Theater

Cradle of the Conquistadors

Today's route includes a visit to one of the most fascinating cities of the region and ends up in another. Head north out of Mérida toward **Cáceres**. Shortly before reaching the golden city, keep your eyes open for some terrific castle ruins on your right. Soon after is Cáceres, the second largest city in Extremadura and a national monument.

Although surrounded by a congested, not-too-attractive, modern city, the totally walled-in section called **Old Cáceres** (Barrio Monumental) has abundant medieval atmosphere. Cáceres was hotly disputed during civil wars between Castile, León, and Extremadura, which explains its extraordinary fortifications. Incredibly well-preserved, the walls are mostly of Moorish construction, although they were built on and incorporated bits of previous Roman walls. Tradition has it that the most glorious of the military orders in Spain, the Knights of Saint James (Santiago) was founded here and for centuries Cáceres was renowned for the number of knights in residence. Many of the mansions were built in the 16th century with money brought back by the conquistadors from the American colonies.

A few hours wandering along the winding, stepped streets and visiting a museum or two richly reward the effort. You can park in the Plaza del General Mola (also known as the Plaza Mayor) where the main entrance gate sits. To the right of the largest of the dozen remaining wall towers (called the Bujaco tower), you enter through the Arco de la Estrella (Star Arch). The many handsome family mansions testify to the austere mood of the 15th and 16th centuries. None has much decoration save the family escutcheons that are mounted above the doors—silent testimony to the nobility of the residents.

As you walk along the narrow streets, which often lead into small, light-filled plazas, do not forget to look up at the church towers where you often see storks nesting precariously above the rooftops. The important thing, though, is to sample the ambiance of this truly medieval Spanish city.

When you are ready to move on, head east on N521 to the most famous cradle of conquistadors, **Trujillo**, a charming city, still pure in its medieval atmosphere which is uncontaminated by modern construction. Its most famous sons were the Pizarro brothers, ingenious and tumultuous conquerors of the Inca Empire in Peru in the middle of the 16th century. The quantities of gold and silver mined there and shipped home in just 50 years created chaos in the economy of all of Europe.

Parador de Trujillo, Trujillo

Our hotel suggestion is the **Parador de Trujillo**, which is installed in the former Convent of Santa Clara. Opened in 1985, it occupies a building dating back 400 years. Its former residents were cloistered nuns who now occupy a smaller convent nearby. Because they sold sweets as a means of support, to the right of the entrance to the parador you see a *torno*, a sort of revolving shelf, which allowed them to send the product out and bring the money in while obviating visual contact with the customer.

Trujillo also boasts a number of splendid mansions constructed with the booty of the travelers to the Americas. Most of the old quarter centers around the spectacularly beautiful Plaza Mayor where there is a large statue of **Pizarro**. The irregular shape and different levels of the plaza make it one of the most charming and appealing in the country. On the plaza, among the many monumental buildings, is the **Palace of Hernando Pizarro**. The mansions here were built a bit later than those of Cáceres and thus are not quite so austere. The **Church of Santa María la Mayor**, a block off the plaza, contains a pantheon of several of Trujillo's illustrious sons. The winding, stone streets around the plaza impart an unusual degree of charm and tranquillity, inviting you to linger and wander around town.

Before leaving Trujillo, stroll up the hill to see the partially-in-ruins castle which towers over the town. There is a pretty little chapel, lovely views, and always a refreshing breeze.

DESTINATION III   GUADALUPE

From Trujillo take C524 south through beautiful countryside which in spring displays a carpet of green laced with flowers and dotted with cork trees. For accommodations along this route, the **Finca Santa Marta** makes an excellent choice (details are given in the hotel descriptions at the back of the book under Trujillo). Turn in left at the tidy little town of Zorita toward Logrosán, and soon begin to climb into the gray ridges of the Guadalupe mountains. A drive of 20 kilometers, through mountainous landscape changing from gray to green, takes you over Puerto Llano pass (unmarked) and exposes some fabulous panoramas of the fertile valleys below. Be on the lookout for the town of **Guadalupe**, because your first glimpse of the tiny white village will take your breath away. Crowned by a golden fortified monastery—which also happens to be one of our suggestions for where to spend the night—it nestles in the shadow of its ancient ramparts.

The Virgin Mary is supposed to have appeared to a humble cattle-herder in this vicinity in 1300 and to have indicated where he should dig to unearth her image. When the pastor arrived home, he discovered his son had died, so he immediately invoked the aid of the Virgin and the boy revived. He and his friends dug where she had indicated and discovered the famous black image in a cave. They then built a small sanctuary for her on the spot. In the 14th century, Alfonso XI had a Hieronymite monastery built there after his victory over the Moors at the Battle of Salado, which he attributed to the **Virgin of Guadalupe**. The monastery has been a popular pilgrimage destination ever since, and the Virgin of Guadalupe has come to be one of the most important religious figures in Spain and Spanish America. Columbus named one of the islands in the Caribbean (now French) after her because he had signed the agreement authorizing his expedition in Guadalupe. When he returned from his voyage with six American Indians, they were baptized here. A short time later, the Virgin appeared again to a Mexican peasant and she became the patron saint of Mexico.

In 1972, the resident Franciscan order officially established an hospedería (hotel) in the monastery's Gothic cloister (though the monastery has sheltered visiting pilgrims and religious dignitaries for ages). It is a hotel, the **Hospedería El Real Monasterio**, through which you actually need a guided tour. This remarkable hotel, filled with antiques of all kinds, is a marvelous lodging choice. Our other highly recommended accommodation in Guadalupe is the **Parador de Guadalupe**, which was built in the 14th century as a hospital and resting place to shelter the pilgrims coming to worship the Virgin of Guadalupe.

Parador de Guadalupe, Guadalupe

When you tour the monastery, be sure to see the Camarín, with the image of the Virgin and her 30,000-jewel headdress, the Moorish Cloister with its two stories of graceful arches, and the church with its Zurbarán paintings and many other objects of art. The positively charming main plaza in Guadalupe has an ancient stone fountain at its center and old mansions huddled around it. Take time to just sit and watch the world go by from this vantage point. As for shopping, this is an area known for ceramics, and Guadalupe is no exception. A local specialty is worked copper and brass.

El Real Monasterio, Guadalupe

DESTINATION IV   OROPESA

If you enjoy ceramics and embroidery, note that this region is the national font for their manufacture (it used to be that you knew where tiles had been made by the colors used), so you might want to do a little shopping along your route today. Even if not, you will enjoy seeing the locals working at their ancient crafts. Return to C401 and turn left toward Puerto de San Vicente pass (follow the signs to Talavera de La Reina). The rocky crests of the Sierra de Guadalupe become sharply pronounced on the approach to the pass. As you drive through the tiny villages beyond, you are likely to spot women sitting outside their homes embroidering (if it is summer). Bear left to **La Estrella** and **El Puente**

del Arzobispo, a traditional ceramics center with many shops. The graceful old hump-backed bridge that takes you across the River Tagus (Tajo) dates from the 14th century. You see a beautiful hermitage on your right as you leave town. From here it is a quick hop to **Oropesa** and your marvelous hotel, the Parador de Oropesa Toledo.

Parador de Oropesa, Oropesa

Installed in a 15th-century castle-palace, the **Parador de Oropesa** was the birthplace of **Don Francisco de Toledo**, one of the early Viceroys of Peru. In addition, the management proudly boasts a dining room that is a cut above the normally fine parador standard. They host a Spanish cooking school here for culinary afficionados and have a small classroom next to the kitchen.

The quiet village, spilling down the hillside below the castle, is noted for its embroidery, and has retained a captivating medieval flavor and numbers of handsome noble homes. You find many opportunities to buy local products both here and in nearby Lagartera. You are treated to some panoramic views of the valley of the Tagus and the Gredos mountain range.

Just east of Oropesa is the ancient ceramics center of **Talavera de la Reina**, where there are many ceramic shops and factories. If you are still scouting for ceramics, your needs are sure to be satisfied here. The best shops are near the west end of town on the road from Oropesa. (Talavera was traditionally known for its blue tile, while Puente del Arzobispo was recognized by its green tile, but this distinction is no longer strictly observed.) Another interesting stop is the **Santa María del Prado** sanctuary at the other end of town. Situated in a park, the sanctuary, park benches, and fountains are all decorated with ceramic tiles, some from the 17th century.

DESTINATION V   SALAMANCA

When you are ready to depart from Oropesa, go west NV E90 to Navalmoral de la Mata where you turn north on CC 904 for a pretty drive through rich green tobacco fields dotted with drying sheds to **Jarandilla de la Vera**, overlooking the Vera plain. You might stop for lunch in the 15th-century castle that houses the **Parador Carlos V** and, upon closer inspection, you will discover it to be complete with towers and drawbridge. It was once owned by the Count of Oropesa, and is where Emperor Charles V resided in 1556 while waiting for his apartments to be completed at the monastery of Yuste, just west of town on C501. **Yuste** is famous as the last retreat of Charles V. Mentally and physically burned out after more than three decades at the head of the world's greatest empire, this is where he died in 1558. You can visit his small palace and share the view he loved of the surrounding countryside. It is easy to imagine the serenity he must have found in this solitude near the end of his otherwise stormy life.

Go on to Plasencia from Yuste, turning north on N630. If you have time, we heartily recommend a detour to **La Alberca**, northwest on C515 beyond Bejar. This tiny, isolated town has preserved its historic charm to an unusual degree, and the sight of its picturesque stone houses overhung with timbered balconies richly rewards the effort.

Back on N630, bear right at Fresno Alhandiga onto SA120 to **Alba de Tormes**, dominated by the 16th-century Torre de la Armería, the only remnant of a former castle of the Dukes of Alba—among the greatest land barons of their time. This small town is one of the most popular pilgrimage destinations in Spain because Santa Teresa of Ávila, important church reformist and mystic, founded a convent and died here over 400 years ago. In the **Carmelite Convent** you can visit the cell where she died and view her relics in a coffer beneath the altar. Her small, ornate coffin is in a place of honor above the high altar. And before leaving town, you should peek into the beautiful Mudéjar-Romanesque **Church of Saint John** on the central plaza.

Cross the River Tormes and head northwest to **Salamanca**, a picture-perfect Castilian town so special in appearance and rich in history that it is now a national monument. We have two recommendations for places to stay. One is the small, elegant, family-owned **Hotel Rector**, conveniently located near the river within walking distance of all the major sights. This intimate, friendly hotel offers some of the finest accommodations in Spain.

Hotel Rector, Salamanca

If your budget doesn't stretch to staying at the Hotel Rector, our other choice, the **Hotel Don Juan**, offers simple, attractive rooms and a superb location just off the Plaza Mayor.

After getting settled, put on your most comfortable shoes and walk to the **Plaza Mayor**, in our opinion the most exquisite plaza in all of Spain. Be sure to set time aside to linger in the very large golden, arcaded plaza with its symmetrical arches and many enticing outdoor cafés. One reason for its beauty is that it was built as a whole in the 18th century and is thus highly integrated in design.

Hotel Don Juan, Salamanca

Next pay a visit to the 12th-century **Saint Martin's Church**. Not far from here, down the Rua Mayor, you find the **Casa de las Conchas** (conch shells), a 15th-century mansion whose entire façade is covered with carved stone shells, with the motif repeated in the grillwork and elsewhere. At the next corner is the Plaza de Anaya, and beyond on the left are the **"New" Cathedral** (16th century), and the **"Old" Cathedral** (12th century). The former is Gothic, the latter Romanesque with an apparently Byzantine dome—quite unusual in Western Europe. Both are good examples of their periods and contain many worthy treasures.

Across from the Plaza de Anaya and the cathedrals is the back of the university. Go around to the opposite side to discover the **Patio de las Escuelas** (Patio of the Schools). Salamanca's major claim to fame is its **University**, the first in Spain, founded in 1218 by Alfonso IX de León. By 1254, when Alfonso X "the Wise" established the Law School,

Salamanca was declared one of the world's four great universities (along with Paris, Bologna, and Oxford). Columbus lectured here, as did San Juan de la Cruz and Antonio de Nebrija. Fray Luis de León, one of Spain's greatest lyric poets, was a faculty member here when he was imprisoned for heresy by the Spanish Inquisition. After five years in prison, he was released and returned to his classroom (which you can still visit). His first words back were *"Dicebamus hesterna die..."*:*"*As we were saying yesterday..." In the 20th century Miguel de Unamuno taught here and served as rector. Not to be missed is the patio itself with the statue of Fray Luis, and the entrance to the university, perhaps the premier example of Plateresque art in Spain. Finished in 1529, it serves as an elaborate façade for the basic Gothic edifice. If you look carefully, you can find a small frog carved into the doorway. A student pointed it out to us on our last visit, and neither she nor we have the slightest idea why it is there nor what the artist must have had in mind when he included this incongruous subject.

As you continue back down to the river, you see the **Puente Romano** with its 26 arches: the nearest half are actually from the 1st century, the others are later reconstructions. On the bridge you discover the stone bull which played a devilish part in the original picaresque novel *Lazarillo de Tormes*.

Cradle of the Conquistadors

Old Castile and the Cantabrian Coast

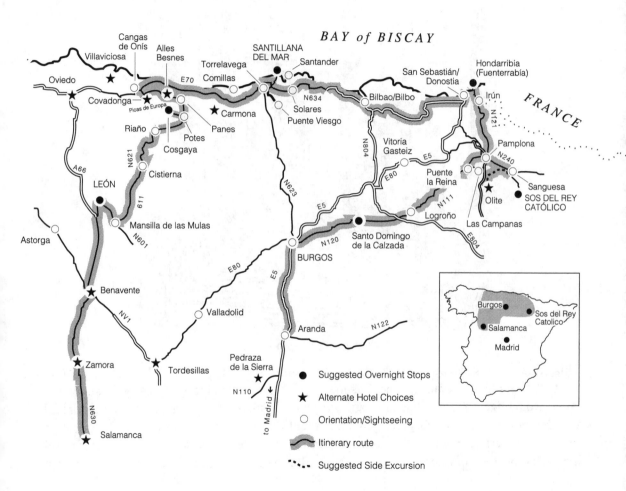

BAY of BISCAY

Villaviciosa
Cangas de Onís
Alles
Besnes
Torrelavega
SANTILLANA DEL MAR
Santander
San Sebastián/ Donostia
Hondarribia (Fuenterrabía)
Oviedo
Comillas
E70
Covadonga
Picos de Europa
Carmona
N634
Solares
Puente Viesgo
Bilbao/Bilbo
Irún
FRANCE
N121
Riaño
Panes
Potes
Cosgaya
Vitoria Gasteiz
Pamplona
N621
N804
N240
Cistierna
A66
611
E5
Puente la Reina
Sanguesa
Olite
SOS DEL REY CATÓLICO
LEÓN
N623
N111
Las Campanas
Astorga
Mansila de las Mulas
N601
E5
Logroño
N804
E80
Santo Domingo de la Calzada
Benavente
N120
BURGOS
NV1
Valladolid
E5
Aranda
N122
Zamora
Tordesillas
Pedraza de la Sierra
N110
to Madrid
N630
Salamanca

● Suggested Overnight Stops

★ Alternate Hotel Choices

○ Orientation/Sightseeing

〰 Itinerary route

···· Suggested Side Excursion

Burgos
Sos del Rey Catolico
Salamanca
Madrid

Old Castile and the Cantabrian Coast

Sos del Rey Católico

This itinerary takes you through the north-central section of Spain. Beginning in Old Castile, it includes Asturias, the Basque region, then Navarre (originally Basque, but later "Romanized"), and back to Castile. It features some of the best-preserved medieval villages in the country and gives you an authentic taste of the Spain of the 11th through the 15th centuries, in addition to amazing you with some of the most spectacular natural landscape on the continent. This is an area filled with ancient cities, even more ancient caves, seaside resorts which are favorites of Spaniards on their summer vacations (because of the cooler climate), and, in the Basque region, Spain's premier cuisine. (The Costa Brava runs a close second.) Along the way, you will enjoy some of Europe's best hotels and some of Spain's finest scenery.

The coastal areas of Asturias and the Basque provinces were the only areas to escape Moorish occupation, and it was from there that the Reconquest (led by the legendary Pelayo) began in 718. The region similarly resisted Roman domination and thus retains the most remarkable prehistoric sites to be found in Spain. Castile traces its beginnings to the 9th century when the Christians built fortress-castles to establish and hold their frontier against the Moslems. Soon it was joined with the kingdom of León, and became the major power in the Reconquest, and ultimately in the creation of the modern nation. The Spanish language is still called *Castellano*, after Castile. Geographically, the itinerary includes the high central *meseta*, or large mesa, the spectacular Cantabrian mountain range, and the coast along the Cantabrian Sea.

ORIGINATING CITY   SALAMANCA

After allowing yourself ample time to sit in the Plaza Mayor and absorb the ambiance of the old university city of Salamanca, head north into the older part of Old Castile: the traditional Spain of castles and earth-colored towns in the vast meseta.

DESTINATION I   LEÓN

Leave Salamanca heading north to **Zamora**, on the bank of the Duero river. Visit the **cathedral** on the main plaza and take a peek inside the marvelous **Parador de Zamora** parador across the square. It is magnificently installed in the 15th-century palace of the Counts of Alba and Aliste, and the public rooms are decorated with beautiful tapestries, coats of arms, and suits of armor.

Continue north, following the signs for **León** as you bypass Benavente. This 70-kilometer drive is relatively uneventful, but the destination is worth the distance. Upon arriving in León, look for your hotel on the left just after crossing the Bernesga River.

Hostal San Marcos, León

The **Hostal San Marcos** is a pure delight—a luxury parador in a former 16th-century monastery with period furniture. This world-class hotel occupies a massive stone building with a fantastic Plateresque façade—itself one of the main tourist attractions in the city. As is often the case, you are staying in one of the major sights in town—the **Convento de San Marcos**, with its interesting archaeological museum and justifiably famous 11th-century ivory Carrizo crucifix. The adjoining church and, of course, the public rooms of the hotel itself are extremely impressive.

León, now a busy provincial capital, was the heart of the ancient kingdom of the same name and the center of Christian Spain in the early days of the Reconquest. As the Christians drove the Moors ever farther south, León was united with Castile and thereafter began to lose its power and importance.

León is a great pedestrian town so procure a map of the city from the hotel desk and head for the **Cathedral Santa María de la Regla**, one of the country's outstanding Gothic edifices, and an important stop on the Way of Saint James pilgrimage route. It features some of the most fabulous stained-glass windows in all of Europe (hope for a sunny day), which should not be missed. There are 125 windows of every period since the 13th century, said to total some 1,800 square meters of glass. If you are lucky enough to be there when the choir is practicing, you will have a thrilling experience. North of the cathedral are portions of the old city walls. South of it is the medieval quarter of the city and the small, colorful Plaza Mayor overhung by ancient buildings, mixed with new shops.

DESTINATION II   COSGAYA

Upon departure from the Hostal San Marcos, take N601 in the direction of Valladolid. In the middle of the little town of Mansilla de las Mulas follow the sign pointing to the left to Villomar and the Picos de Europa and you find yourself on a flat, straight road paralleling the Esla river through numerous quaint little villages. The first glimpse of the sharp, gray **Picos de Europa** (European Peaks) into which you will soon be climbing appears and beckons as you leave the town of Cubillas de Rueda.

The Picos de Europa are indeed spectacular. They rise to almost 2,743 meters within 25 kilometers of the coast and provide stark, desert-like landscapes that contrast vividly with the humid lowland zone. Sheer cliffs broken only by huge slabs of jutting granite pierce the sky. The Torre de Cerredo is the highest peak at 2,648 meters. The entire range, rivaling the Dolomites in dramatic mountain splendor, occupies some 1,330 square

Picos de Europa

kilometers of northern Spain. This region is a haven for mountain climbing and has very controlled policies on hunting and fishing. Inquire in any of the numerous guide centers in the towns for information about these activities.

In Cistierna take the N621, following signs to Riaño, and start your ascent into one of the most scenic natural landscapes in Europe. From Riaño continue on the N621 for about 50 kilometers to Potes. At Potes turn left (west) and follow the Deva river as it winds its way through the valley to **Cosgaya**. Here you find the **Hotel del Oso**, a hotel that is not old, but brims with the charm and comfort of a meticulously run, small hotel. Settle here for a few days to savor the natural beauty of the magnificent region. On one day's excursion, continue west from Cosgaya to the end of the road and have lunch at the dramatic Parador Fuente Dé and take the cable car to the top of the mountain. Note: If

Hotel del Oso, Cosgaya

accommodation at Hotel del Oso is not available, study our other hotel suggestions on Map 2. There are several excellent choices of places to stay in this area.

HOTEL DEL OSO DESTINATION III   SANTILLANA DEL MAR

When you leave Cosgaya, return to Potes and continue north on N621 to Panes, then turn left and follow C6312 west in the direction of **Cangas de Onís**. This scenic drive follows the crystal-clear Cares river. Along this stretch of road are numerous picturesque mountain villages. No apartment blocks around here: the architecture is strictly local. Old stone houses with red-tile roofs and wooden balconies, usually hung with drying garlic, are the typical sight. About 23 kilometers after leaving Panes, you come to **Arenas de Cabrales**, noted for its blue cheese. Cabrales cheese is made in these mountains from a mixture of cow's, goat's, and ewe's milk. If you want to sample some, watch for the signs found all along here for *queso de Cabrales*. The cheese can also be found in other towns of the area. It has become so popular, however, that "counterfeit" cheese has begun to appear, causing its real manufacturers to put an official seal on the genuine article. You probably will not run into the false cheese here, since this is its place of origin.

Horreos (Grain storage sheds)

In this region you will also notice many *horreos*, or grain-storage sheds, raised above the ground outside the farmhouses. These *horreos*, supported on pillars of rock, are especially colorful when viewed with the Picos de Europa in the background.

Leaving Arenas de Cabrales, continue west for about 26 kilometers until you see a road heading south marked to **Covadonga**. On the approach to the town is a breathtaking view on the right of the Romanesque-style **Basilica of Our Lady of the Battles**, built in the late 19th century. This tiny town is touristy but its setting is spectacular. Tourists also come to visit the **Santa Cueva**, a shrine tucked into a cave in the mountain, dedicated to the Virgin of Battles. It is the legendary place where Pelayo initiated the Reconquest of Spain from the Moslems in 718. The religious war raged on and off until 1492. Inside is the famous image of the **Virgin of Covadonga**, patron saint of Asturias, along with the sarcophagi of Pelayo and several of his relatives. In the treasury are the many gifts presented to the Virgin. Beneath the cave is a small pool, with a spring on one side, where you see visitors to the shrine collecting "holy" water.

If you are faint of heart, read no further. The area's main attraction is reached by a very steep, incredibly narrow, one-way road uphill from Covadonga. About 7 kilometers along is the **Mirador de la Reina** (overlook) with views of the **Sierra de Covalierda** and the sea. If you persevere about 5 kilometers farther, you come to **Lago Enol** and **Lago Ercina**, crystal-blue mountain lakes in a spellbinding setting in the **Montana de Covadonga** nature reserve. Though the road is tortuous, it is worth every twist and turn. You pass through green fields strewn with boulders before you reach the icy lakes. At a point called, logically enough, **Entre Dos Lagos** (Between Two Lakes), both lakes are visible from the top of a hill. This would make a fantastic spot to settle for an afternoon (or a whole day) for a picnic.

From Covadonga, return by the same road and join again the C6312 where you turn left to **Cangas de Onís**. As you cross the river, be sure to look to your left to see the picture-perfect 13th-century, humpbacked Roman bridge.

After Cangas de Onís you soon come to the N634 where you turn right in the direction of Santander. After Unquera you start to see signs announcing the availability of *corbatas*. While this word normally means neckties, in this case it refers to a small pastry folded to resemble a necktie, a specialty of this area. Sample them here or in Santillana del Mar.

A brief, scenic drive beyond Unquera brings you to **San Vicente de la Barquera**, a fishing village where the ocean appears for the first time. You are now on the beautiful Cantabrian coast of Spain. It is a picturesque spot with boats in the harbor and outdoor cafés along the waterfront—inviting if you need a break. At La Revilla turn left on the small road C6316 for the short hop through the green Cantabrian countryside to **Comillas**, a quaint old resort perched above the sea, which was the summer home of the Spanish royal court in the 19th century. It has a pretty beach and some handsome old homes. The large structure overlooking the sea is a seminary.

The road now turns slightly inland, through still more beautiful landscapes. As you drive through the village of **Orena**, you will be charmed by the little church and cemetery on the hillside overlooking the sea. Shortly afterward you reach enchanting and historic **Santillana del Mar**, with hunkering stone mansions bearing coats of arms, recalling the lifestyle of Spain's former nobility.

Parador Gil Blas, Santillana del Mar

Our first choice to stay is the 400-year-old **Parador Gil Blas**. It is ideally located in the heart of this perfectly preserved medieval jewel. If the parador is not available, we also recommend the **Hotel Altamira** (which is just around the corner from the Gil Blas) and the **Hotel Los Infantes** (which is on the edge of the old town). In Santillana del Mar the major attraction is atmosphere. It could fairly be called the most picturesque village in Spain and has retained its harmonious old-world feeling to an uncommon degree. The highly pure Romanesque architecture—from the Collegiate Church to the houses along Calle de las Lindas—will delight and amaze you. Just walk around and soak it in, not being too shy to glance discreetly into the ground-floor patios of the old houses, which occasionally shelter stables or shops. When you leave, you will know at least what it looked like to live in the Middle Ages.

Santillana is not on the ocean, but there is a large beach at **Suances** only 11 kilometers away, and it is only 30 kilometers farther to **Oyambe beach** at **Comillas**.

Another attraction of this area is its rich archaeological heritage. When we were there, a group of archaeologists were spending ten days based in Santillana to do nothing but visit regional caves. You can get a map (at the hotel) which shows where they are. It is true that the most famous one—the **Altamira Cave** with its 14,000-year-old paintings of bison and other animals—is practically closed. Its huge number of visitors were damaging the ancient paintings with the large quantities of carbon dioxide they exhaled in the caves every day. Currently, 20 people per day are allowed to visit (though the possibility of increasing the number is being considered), and most of those have either a professional interest or have written months in advance for the privilege. If you write at least six months in advance to the Director del Museo de Altamira, 39330 Santillana del Mar (Cantabria), you might be able to get on the list. If you do not have permission, check with the *conservador* at the museum in case there have been last-minute cancellations. But do not be too disappointed if not, for there are many more caves—just explore the possibilities.

One example is **Las Cuevas del Monte del Castillo** at Puente Viesgo. Head southeast from Santillana to Torrelavega, then east to Vargas, where you take the Burgos road to Puente Viesgo. Signs for the caves on the hill above the town can be seen. Discovered in 1903, the caves have drawings some 20,000 to 25,000 years old. There are actually three caves you can visit: the tour (in Spanish only) of the main one takes about 45 minutes; for all three plan on about four hours. They are closed during siesta time.

DESTINATION IV   HONDARRIBIA

When you have finished sampling the unforgettable atmosphere of Santillana, head east toward **Santander**, a mostly modern provincial capital whose old city was destroyed in 1941 by a tornado and the resulting fires. The road turns south to skirt the bay and continues inland through cultivated farmland to Colindres, where you regain sight of the sea. Shortly afterward, you reach **Laredo**, a popular seaside resort with a beautiful, large beach on Santona Bay (with a much larger resort development in the town of **Santona** out on the peninsula). The road again moves away from the coast for a bit, through green rolling hills. You become aware of how close the Cantabrian range comes to the coast during this stretch.

As you continue east, you soon enter the **Basque Region** (*Vizcaya*), where you notice many of the town names indicated in both Basque and Spanish. Unlike the other languages in Spain, Basque is not a "Romance" or "Neo-Latin" language. Indeed, no one is sure where it comes from. Here you pick up the freeway towards **San Sebastián**, bypassing (thankfully) the industrial city of **Bilbao**. If you are interested and time permits, take the exit that goes north to **Guernica y Luno**, the town bombed by Germans during the Civil War (1937) and immortalized by Picasso in his painting *Guernica*. The town has been rebuilt since the bombing, but still serves as a symbol of the brutality of the Civil War, which killed over a million Spaniards when Germany and Russia used it as a testing ground in preparation for World War II.

After you clear San Sebastian (following the signs for Irun and Francia), watch for the exit for **Hondarribia** (called Fuenterrabía in Spanish) and the airport (*aeropuerto*). The road continues 7 kilometers farther before passing under the massive stone gate into Hondarribia.

We recommend several hotels in Hondarribia. Look in the *Hotel Descriptions* section for details of each. However, if you can secure a room, our first choice for accommodation is at one of Spain's finest paradors, **El Emperador**. Not only is this hotel ideally situated on the main plaza, but since its renovation, the interior decor rivals any of the finest hotels in Spain. There is also a spectacular terrace that captures a sweeping view of the harbor. The Parador El Emperador is a 10th-century castle that was considerably remodeled in the 16th century by the Holy Roman Emperor, Charles V. It has served as host (while a palace) to numerous monarchs in its long history. Reflecting the fact that Hondarribia was often coveted by the French because of its strategic position, the castle was constructed with stone walls, many meters thick. When you look out your window through these walls, you really get a feel for what it was like to live in a medieval castle. Note: There is no restaurant at the parador (breakfast is the only meal served), but catty-corner across the square in front of the hotel is a charming, inexpensive place to eat, the **Restaurant/Bar Antxina**.

The small, intimate plaza in front of the parador is unforgettable. Though you almost do not notice it, you are only a stone's throw from the ocean. Walk to the north end of the plaza which overlooks a very blue and very pretty little port filled with colorful sailboats. On other sides of the square are brilliantly painted mansions with iron or wood balconies draped with colorful flowers,

Parador El Emperador, Hondarribia

accentuating the stern façade of the parador. The most interesting and charming stroll from your hotel is down the Calle Mayor. The narrow, cobblestoned streets, often too small for anything but pedestrians, impart a feel for life in long-ago times. There is a country-town atmosphere to the many splendid mansions with their escutcheons in this most picturesque quarter. There are also numerous other small plazas with similarly enchanting buildings.

Your next destination is the birthplace of one of Spain's most famous monarchs, Ferdinand of Aragón. He was a model for Machiavelli in his classic study of governing in the days of monarchy. He was also the husband of Isabella and the two were known as the "Catholic Monarchs" (Los Reyes Católicos) because of their strong support of the Church during the time of the Protestant Reformation.

Head south from Hondarribia into the lush green valley of the River Bidasoa toward Pamplona. Along here the river forms the Spanish-French border until you cross the bridge at Enderlaza, where the river returns to Spain and you officially enter the region of **Navarre**. The beautiful, winding stretch of road takes you through the **Spanish Pyrenees** and numerous quaint little mountain villages with stone-trimmed red-roofed houses sitting in this heavily forested region. **Sumbilia**, **Santesteban**, and **Almandoz** are all charming towns situated in the midst of magnificent natural scenery. After Oronoz-Mugaire you wind your way up to the **Puerto de Velate Pass**, through some impressively rugged mountains, then down the **Valley of the Rio Ulzama** into **Pamplona**. Pamplona was the capital of the ancient kingdom of Navarre from the 10th to the 16th centuries, and now best known for the "running of the bulls" festival of San Fermín (July 6–20), made famous by Ernest Hemingway's depiction in *The Sun Also Rises,* published in Britain as *Fiesta*.

If you would rather make Pamplona an excursion from your hotel, you can follow the signs which lead you around the city and toward the south where you bear left on N240. Besides the views from the **Puerto de Loiti Pass**, watch for a lookout about 36 kilometers over the **Lumbier Defile**, a gorge cut by the Irati river through the **Sierra de Leyre**. The vast fertile valley can be seen spreading to the horizon in all directions. Bear right to Sanguesa and, just before reaching the town, you see to your right the ruins of **Rocaforte**, a mountain where the people of Sanguesa fled in the face of the Moorish invasion. They later came back and settled in the area where the town is now. Also on your right is a giant paper mill that is the origin of the smell that you cannot fail to have noticed by now, and which certainly discourages a long stay.

You next cross the Aragón river, enter Sanguesa and follow the signs past a 13th-century church toward **Sos del Rey Católico,** a few kilometers farther on through fields of sunflowers on rolling hills. Just before arriving, you cross the line between Navarre and Aragón. Since Sos is perched atop a hill in the middle of the large flat plain, you will see it long before you arrive. It seems as though it might blend into the brown mountain if it were not for the square tower that juts up above the town. As you get closer, you see that it spills down the hillside under the **Sada Palace** where Ferdinand the Catholic was born in 1452. The **Parador Fernando de Aragón** provides you with a fitting introduction to the town's medieval atmosphere.

Plan some time to walk around the picturesque little village, which is a national monument and has undergone much restoration. You can also tour the Sada Palace and see the very bedroom (or so it is claimed) where Ferdinand was born. There are splendid views of the fertile countryside from the castle and church at the top of the hill.

You might also want to make a short side trip to **Javier Castle** (return to Sanguesa and bear right). It is an 18th-century castle built on the site of the birthplace of Saint Francis Xavier (1506), one of the early members of the Jesuit order and a very effective missionary to Japan in the service of the Portuguese. If you happen to be there on a Saturday night in the summer, you can see a sound and light show.

Another worthwhile trip is to the town of **Olite** (head west from Sanguesa). Passing through beautiful agricultural land with greens and golds predominating, you also see a number of small, fortified villages clinging to the hillsides. Olite itself is known as the "Gothic city," and you see why as you approach it from the east. In the center of town is the 15th-century fortress of Charles III that now houses the **Parador Principe de Viana.**

Return to N240 via Sanguesa and bear left for about 19 kilometers. Watch for the signs indicating Campanas and turn left. At Campanas go south and turn right to Puente la Reina. You pass the **Ermita de Eunate Hermitage**, a Romanesque chapel where pilgrims on the Way of Saint James were ministered to and sheltered. It was in **Puente la Reina** that two major French pilgrim roads joined before continuing on to Santiago de Compostela. As you leave town notice on your right the ancient medieval stone bridge over the Arga river, worn smooth by millions of pilgrims' feet.

Continue west on N111, which was the Way of Saint James, to **Estella** where, in the Middle Ages, pilgrims stopped to venerate a statue of the Virgin reportedly found in 1085 by shepherds guided by falling stars. The Kings of Navarre chose this as their place of residence in the Middle Ages. Be sure to see the **Plaza San Martín** with, among many beautiful historic edifices, the 12th-century palace of the Kings of Navarre, one of the oldest non-religious buildings in Spain.

As you continue southwest toward the wine center of Logroño, you pass the 13th-century monastery (on your left) at Irache and, as you approach **Torres del Rio**, you have a splendid view of the late 12th-century church towering above the town. This area is known as La Rioja Alta (Upper Rioja) and, as you will no doubt deduce from the quantity of vineyards, is the major wine-growing region in Spain. Navigate your way carefully through **Logroño**, whereafter the vineyards begin to be mixed with wheat and potato fields.

Soon after Logroño is the rampart-encircled **Santo Domingo de la Calzada** whose most impressive 12th-century cathedral has a live rooster and hen in residence in commemoration of a miracle supposed to have occurred when a young pilgrim's innocence was proved by the crowing of an already roasted cock. (They are replaced each year on May 12th.) On signs leading into town you see the brief poem summing up the legend, which says, *Santo Domingo de la Calzada/ cantó la gallina/ después de asada.* Although the legend says a cock, the poem says a hen was involved. Maybe it just rhymed better. In any case there is one of each in the cathedral. Its 18th-century belfry is famed as the prettiest in La Rioja.

It makes a good breaking point for your journey to overnight at the very atmospheric **Parador de Santo Domingo**, housed in a former pilgrims' hospice, right across the plaza from the cathedral. The saint was a local hermit who took in pilgrims on their way to Santiago de Compostela.

DESTINATION VII   MADRID

From Santo Domingo continue on the N120 through undulating wheat and potato fields (still following the Way of Saint James) to **Burgos**.

Burgos is a large, not particularly charming city, but of historical interest. The capital of Old Castile from 951 to 1492, when it lost its position to Valladolid, Burgos has strong associations with the victorious Reconquest. Spain's epic hero, El Cid Campeador (champion), was born Rodrigo Díaz in nearby Vivar in 1026. His exploits in regaining Spain from the Moslems were immortalized in the first Spanish epic poem in 1180 and subsequent literary works. He and his wife Ximena are interred in the transept crossing of the cathedral.

The **cathedral** is without doubt the leading attraction of Burgos. Surpassed in size only by the cathedrals of Seville and Toledo, the flamboyant Gothic structure was begun in 1221 by Ferdinand III (the Saint) and completed in the 16th century. The artworks in the many chapels inside constitute a veritable museum. The two-story cloister contains much stone sculpture of the Spanish Gothic school. Do not fail to walk around the outside to see the marvelous decoration of the various portals.

On the south side of the cathedral, if you walk toward the river, you pass through the highly ornate city gate called the Santa María arch. After crossing the river, you continue down Calle Miranda to the Casa de Miranda, an archaeological museum. North of the cathedral you can ascend the hill that harbors castle ruins and affords excellent city views. Enjoy the pretty pedestrian street along the riverfront, with its shops and lively bars and cafés.

When it is time to leave Burgos, head south on the N2 to **Madrid**. We recommend several hotels in Madrid in various price categories. Look in the back of the guide in the *Hotel Descriptions* section to see what most appeals to you. For details of what to see and do in and around Madrid, refer to our itinerary *Madrid and More*, pages 145–156.

Note: If you are weary of cathedrals, skip Burgos altogether and stop instead at one of our favorite petite towns in Spain, **Pedraza de la Sierra**. If this is your choice, approximately 120 kilometers after leaving Burgos, watch for the N110 where you turn right toward Segovia. After about 24 kilometers, turn right again in Matabuena, following signs for Pedraza. This medieval hilltop town is truly a gem, right out of a fairy tale. There is a wealth of marvelous restaurants. If you want to spend the night, we recommend two hotels, **La Posada de Don Mariano** and **El Hotel de la Villa**, both with rates far below what you pay for comparable comfort in Madrid. For details of these hotels, see the *Hotel Descriptions* section in the back of the book.

The Costa Brava and Beyond

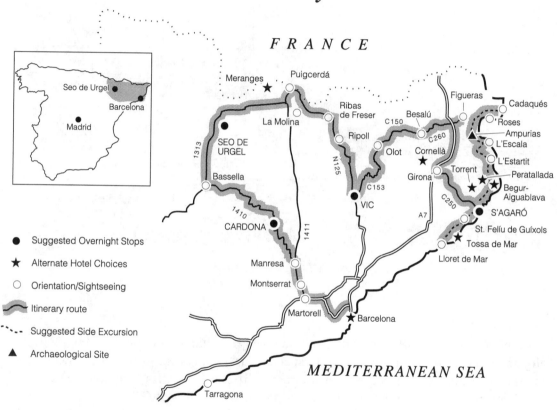

FRANCE

Meranges
Puigcerdá
Ribas de Freser
Besalú
Figueras
Cadaqués
Seo de Urgel
Barcelona
La Molina
C150
Roses
Madrid
Ripoll
C260
Ampurias
L'Escala
SEO DE URGEL
Olot
Cornellà
L'Estartit
1313
Torrent
Peratallada
N125
Girona
Bassella
Begur-
Aiguablava
C153
A7
VIC
C250
1410
St. Felíu de Guíxols
CARDONA
S'AGARÓ
1411
Tossa de Mar
Manresa
Lloret de Mar
Montserrat

- ● Suggested Overnight Stops
- ★ Alternate Hotel Choices
- ○ Orientation/Sightseeing
- ～ Itinerary route
- ‑‑‑ Suggested Side Excursion
- ▲ Archaeological Site

Martorell
Barcelona

MEDITERRANEAN SEA

Tarragona

The Costa Brava and Beyond

Tossa de Mar, Costa Brava

This itinerary is essentially a tour of Catalonia, and it includes a sampling of the multiple delights to be savored in this region: spectacular mountains, lovely old towns and castles, and beautiful sea coasts that alternate cliffs and beaches. Catalonia has been settled continuously since the Greeks landed in the 6th century B.C. In the 15th century Catalonia combined with Aragón to form a vast kingdom extending to Naples, Italy, and it became, somewhat reluctantly, part of the new kingdom created by the marriage of Ferdinand, King of Aragón, to Isabella, Queen of Castile.

The Costa Brava and Beyond

Catalonia has fiercely defended its autonomy during its entire history. As a Republican stronghold in the Civil War of 1936–1939, the region experienced a great deal of the bloodshed. When the Nationalists (under Francisco Franco) won, regional autonomy was suppressed. Only after the adoption of the new constitution of 1978 were the various regions allowed to regain a measure of autonomy, and Catalonia was the first to do so.

In addition to Spanish, the regional language of Catalan is widely used. As in Galicia and the Basque country, you often see things spelled in the regional dialect and since 1978, most official signs have been replaced with bilingual ones. Cuisine in Catalonia vies with that of the Basque region for the title of best in the country. It includes many seafood and meat dishes with a variety of sauces, reminiscent—and imitative—of French culinary style. In Catalonia the mixture of sandy beaches, rugged coastlines, gorgeous mountain scenery, and fine food offers something for everyone.

ORIGINATING CITY   BARCELONA

Barcelona is an impressive and prosperous city with much to see and do. But the rest of Catalonia also has much to offer, so when you have completed a tour of Barcelona, head into the interior to see another side of this lovely region. Note: For suggestions on sightseeing in Barcelona, see our chapter titled *Barcelona Highlights,* pages 163–168.

DESTINATION I   CARDONA

Leave Barcelona by going south on the A2 freeway to exit 25 just outside of town. Turn right on NII to **Martorell**, an ancient town where the Llobregat river is spanned by the Puente (bridge) del Diablo, said to have been built by the Carthaginian general Hannibal in 218 B.C. He erected the triumphal arch in honor of his father Hamilcar Barca. Continue on NII to Abrera and bear right on C1411 to reach **Montserrat**, whose ragged, stark-gray silhouette makes you see instantly why it is called "serrated mountain." After entering the village of **Monistrol**, follow the signs to the monastery on top of the hill—about 7 kilometers, along a zigzagging road offering ever-more-magnificent views. You can opt for the cable car (funicular) from a clearly marked point just before Monistrol, if you would rather avoid the mountain driving and the sometimes severe parking problem up top. Taking the cable car certainly makes the trip more enjoyable for the driver.

The golden-brown **monastery** at the crown of Montserrat contrasts strikingly with the jutting gray peaks of the mountain. The setting is ultra-dramatic, and it is claimed that on a clear day you can see the Balearic Islands in the Mediterranean. The monastery church is home to the famed Moreneta, or Black Madonna. The figure, reportedly made by Saint Luke and brought to Barcelona by Saint Peter, was hidden in the Santa Cueva (holy cave) at the time of the Moorish invasions, then found by shepherds in the 9th century. This is the patron saint of Catalonia, and is venerated by thousands of pilgrims annually. Numerous marked paths and cable cars take you to various viewpoints as well as the monastery along the 22-kilometer massif.

After you have visited this marvelous mountain, one of the most famous in the world for its unusual appearance and the inspiration for Montsalvat in Wagner's *Parsifal,* return to Monistrol and turn left to **Manresa**. Visit the elaborate 14th-century collegiate **Church of Santa María de la Seo** on a rocky cliff above the town. Follow the signs for Solsona and, as you leave town, do not fail to look back to catch a spectacular view of Montserrat in the distance. Follow the Rio Cardoner through red, pine-covered ridges, punctuated with little farming towns, to **Cardona**, beautifully situated and crowned by an outstanding fortress/castle, which just happens to be our hotel suggestion, the **Parador Duques de Cardona**. This magnificent parador retains much of its 10th- and 11th-century construction, and the purely Romanesque Collegiate Church of Saint Vincent is in the center.

Cardona's earliest significance was as a source of salt for the Romans. The conical mountain of salt to the south of town has been mined for centuries. The town itself is very quiet unless you happen to be there on Sunday, market day, when things are considerably busier. If you time your visit for the first half of September, you can experience the annual festival with a "running of the bulls," similar to that of Pamplona.

A lovely side trip is to the ancient brown-and-red village of **Solsona**, about 15 minutes away, which is entered through a stone gate in the old town wall. It has a salt and craft museum, and a quaint old quarter for wandering. The parador in Cardona is wonderful, but Solsona is a more interesting town.

Parador Duques de Cardona, Cardona

DESTINATION II   SEO DE URGEL

Head northwest out of Cardona following a lovely stretch of road through rugged hillsides, dotted with ruins of castles and monasteries, through Solsona (worth a stop if you did not make the side trip above).

Continue to Basella, then turn north, following the Segre river for the 50-kilometer drive to Seo de Urgel. At this point, the Pyrenees begin to make their brooding presence known in the distance ahead. Cross the Segre to reach the beautiful aquamarine Oliana reservoir. From the banks of the reservoir you get splendid views of the lake surrounded by its gray-green sheer cliffs, which occasionally seem almost man-made—like giant stone edifices. At the other end of the reservoir is **Coll de Nargo**, then **Organya**, both tiny villages stacked on the hillside like layer cakes. Beyond Organya, the cliffs become steeper and closer as you traverse the deep Organya gorge. The gray cliffs rise to 610 meters here and make an impressive backdrop before you come out into the fertile valley where **Seo de Urgel** (named for its Episcopal see, founded in 820) is located. The town's modern parador, the **Parador de Seo de Urgel**, is constructed on the 14th-century site of a church and convent. The generally contemporary decor is enhanced in the public rooms by the stone arches that remain from the original cloister. You will enjoy strolling through the old quarter around the parador.

A suggested excursion includes travel from Spain to **Andorra**, across into France, and then back again to Spain, all in the course of a day. Just 9 kilometers north of Seo you reach the border of the tiny principality of Andorra, which is under the joint administration of the Bishop of Urgel and the French government. Recognized throughout history for the fierce independence of its residents, Andorra is now known mostly as a duty-free zone, and thus a shopper's paradise. You see an infinite number of stores selling imported goods lining the streets of the capital, **Andorra La Vella**. Besides shopping, Andorra offers mountain scenery *sans pareil*. You ascend through pine forests crowned by the barren, blue-gray, snow-dotted peaks of the Pyrenees. It is truly a breathtaking drive. You see numerous ski areas as you cross the Envalira Pass and descend the mountainside to the French border. From here it is a short drive through the French Pyrenees to the quaint little town of **Bourg Madame**. Just outside of town you cross back into Spain at **Puigcerdá**, a small fortified border town. From here head west through the pretty valley of the Segre river back to Seo.

DESTINATION III   VIC

When you are ready to move on, more beautiful mountain vistas await. Leaving Seo, head east to Puigcerdá tracing the Segre river. Follow the signs for Puerto de Toses and Barcelona and head south on N152 along a mountainside with terrific views of the deep valley below where you soon spot the ski resort of **La Molina**.

The road winds through green mountains as you approach **Ribas de Freser**, a charming little village of pastel-colored buildings. In a short while, if you keep an eye out to your right, you see a waterfall bursting from the hillside. It is not far to **Ripoll**, a pretty town with pitched red-tile roofs topping tall, narrow buildings on the Ter river, and the home of a 9th-century **Benedictine monastery** founded by Visigothic Count Wilfred "the Hairy." Wilfred was responsible for freeing Catalonia from the domination of Charlemagne. The Ripoll Library was once one of the largest in the Christian world.

As you approach the ancient town of **Vic**, watch for a castle on the hill to the right. Your hotel is about 15 kilometers northeast of town, off the C153 to Roda de Ter. Watch for signs in Vic directing you to it. The **Parador de Vic** is a new parador built in the regional *masia catalana* style that is supposed to resemble an old Catalonian manor house (although to us it just looks like a large hotel). The nicest aspect of the parador is its setting on a high shelf offering a panoramic view of dramatic red-and-white stone cliffs surrounding the blue reservoir.

Although on the whole Vic appears to be a rather uninteresting town, at some point during your stay here go into the town of Vic and visit the pretty Plaza Mayor, surrounded by the 15th-century town hall and a 16th-century palace. A short distance down the Calle de Riera is the neoclassical cathedral.

DESTINATION IV   S'AGARÓ

After leaving the Parador de Vic, return to the C153 and turn right to begin the next stretch of your journey. A short drive brings you to the turnoff to the exquisitely preserved, 16th-century town of Rupit, which you reach past a huge gray mesa, itself a dramatic sight. **Rupit** is an utterly charming, typical northern-Spanish town. Park outside the gate and stroll through the age-old cobblestoned streets and plazas with their stone houses and iron balconies hung with colorful flowers. It is a perfect place for pictures and an old-world atmosphere pervades. There is a restaurant on your left just before you enter town where you can stop for coffee.

The drive from Vic to the medieval town of Olot is particularly lovely. The variety of scenery is incredible—vast forests crowned by rugged gray cliffs and mesas give way to equally beautiful, vast fertile plains with the blue Pyrenees as a backdrop. The spectacular scenery and poor road surface dictate a leisurely pace.

Besalú

Just beyond Olot, where the road improves considerably, you drive through **Castellfollit de la Roca**, which on your approach appears ordinary. Be sure, however, to stop and look back at it from the other side, where you realize that it is built on a giant rock at the very edge of a deep ravine.

Your next stop, **Besalú**, requires similar treatment. Go through town, cross the bridge, then turn around and come back for a spellbinding view of this perfectly preserved medieval town. Stop here for a while because the lovely little Plaza de la Libertad is wonderfully typical of ancient Spanish towns. It is an atmospheric and picturesque place to sit for a while and watch the activity in the colorful square.

The Costa Brava and Beyond

Leaving Besalú follow signs to **Figueras**, the birthplace of surrealistic painter Salvador Dalí (1904–1989). If surrealism interests you, we positively recommend a visit to the bizarre **Teatro Museo Dalí** where numerous (often humorous) paintings and sculptures by the famous artist are displayed.

You will be glad to find there is a freeway connecting Figueras to Gerona and a good highway from there to **S'Agaró** (take the Gerona South exit to San Feliu de Guixols and then the coast road a couple of kilometers north). The **Hostal de La Gavina** (seagull), where we suggest you spend the night, is a premier hotel, just north of the little town. Settle in for a few days of luxurious relaxation overlooking the beautiful Costa Brava.

S'Agaró is a small beach town sandwiched between two larger, more lively resorts—**San Feliu** and **Platja d'Aro**. Both are worth a visit for their chic shops, huge white sand beaches, and animated cafés and restaurants. Also, while staying at the luxurious Hostal de la Gavina, be sure to meander along the path below the hotel that traces the edge of the ocean. This is a marvelous walk that allows you not only to enjoy beautiful vistas of the sea, but also to gaze in wonder at the magnificent private homes lining the waterfront.

If you are in the mood for an excursion return to Figueras on the freeway and head northeast toward **Llansa**. You pass through rather barren country at first and, before you reach Llansa, you see the **Castello de Quermanco** on your right. Watch carefully, because it almost blends into the landscape on the hillside. From Llansa turn south down the **Costa Brava** (Wild Coast)—a lot less brava than it used to be with the appearance every few miles of another little resort settlement filled with white cottages with red-tile roofs and all the support and entertainment services that go with them. But the sea and the rugged coastline are as beautiful as ever. The water is a clear, deep blue and dotted with sail- and fishing boats. Continue south through El Puerto de la Selva, then wind the scenic way to **Cadaques**, a whitewashed and picturesque fishing-town-cum-artist-colony that surrounds the harbor. Take time to stroll along the waterfront and enjoy the play of the light on the colorful fishing boats.

Retrace your steps 5 kilometers and take a left toward Roses, located on a bay of the same name. Once a typical fishing village, **Roses** is fast becoming a holiday resort (as are most "villages" along this coast). Continue to the walled, old market town of **Castello de Ampurias**, turn south across the fruit-tree-dotted Ampurdán plain, turn left near Viladamat and follow the signs leading to the archaeological excavation at **Ampurias**. Scipio landed here in the Second Punic War in 219 B C. The town was founded in the 6th century B.C. as a Greek trading station. Tour the Neapolis, with many ancient walls and original floors. A museum displays the interesting artifacts that have been uncovered. A short freeway journey returns you to S'Agaró and the Hostal de la Gavina.

Other nearby spots to visit are reached by heading up the coast to **Platja d'Aro**, **Palamos**, and **Calella**, a pretty resort town with an impressive botanical garden on a cliff overlooking the sea at Cap Roig, just to the south of town. The beautifully planned garden has a shady walk through flowers and trees and spectacular views over the sea.

If you go south through San Feliu and continue along the coast toward Tossa de Mar and Lloret de Mar, you have a breathtaking and dramatic drive along a winding corniche road carved into the mountainside above the deep-blue sea. The rugged cliffs demonstrate clearly why this is called the wild coast. **Tossa de Mar** is a pretty little beach town with a harbor, and your first sight of it—crowned by a castle and surrounded by 12th-century walls and impressive round towers—is magnificent. **Lloret de Mar** (whose natural beauty is somewhat tempered by high-rise apartments and hotels) has a long golden beach, which makes it exceedingly popular, especially in the summer months (when its population more than triples).

Andalusian Adventures

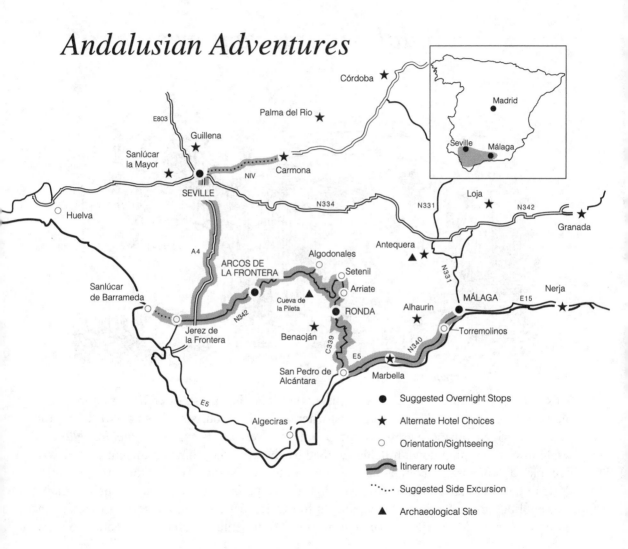

Córdoba

Palma del Rio

Madrid

Guillena

Seville   Málaga

Sanlúcar
la Mayor

E803

Carmona

NIV

SEVILLE

Huelva

N334

Loja

N331

N342

Granada

A4

ARCOS DE
LA FRONTERA

Algodonales

Antequera

Setenil

Arriate

Sanlúcar
de Barrameda

N342

Cueva de
la Pileta

RONDA

Alhaurin

MÁLAGA

Nerja

E15

Jerez de
la Frontera

Benaoján

C339

Torremolinos

N340

N331

San Pedro de
Alcántara

E5

Marbella

E5

Algeciras

●   **Suggested Overnight Stops**

★   **Alternate Hotel Choices**

○   **Orientation/Sightseeing**

    Itinerary route

·········   **Suggested Side Excursion**

▲   **Archaeological Site**

Andalusian Adventures

Antequera

This itinerary features western Andalusia, the area that most foreigners picture when they think of Spain, and surely the most-often visited by tourists. This part of the region is characterized by the warmth of its people as well as its climate. *Pueblos blancos,* white towns, stepping down hillsides topped by the brooding ruins of ancient castles will become a common, though never commonplace, sight. While this is primarily agricultural and cattle-raising country, this itinerary also includes one of Spain's major metropolitan areas, Seville—the country's fourth-largest city and the scene of Don Juan, Bizet's *Carmen*, Mozart's *Figaro,* and glorious 16th-century adventures to and from the exotic New World. It also includes the most tourist-intensive area in the country—the Costa del Sol from Málaga to San Pedro de Alcántara.

This is the part of Spain that extends to within about 15 kilometers of the northern tip of Africa and was the first area conquered by the Moors in 711. Except for the relatively small group of Moslems in Granada, Seville was also the last area reconquered by the Christians in the 13th century, and it is the area that retains the strongest traces of Moorish culture—not necessarily just architecture—to the present day.

The culinary specialties of the area include gazpacho and fried seafood dishes. Due to the warm climate, sangría is also delightfully ubiquitous. And, of course, this is the home of sherry, whose name comes from the English pronunciation of the wine-producing center of Jerez (formerly spelled Xerez, with the *x* pronounced *sh*).

ORIGINATING CITY MÁLAGA

Málaga had seen occupation by the Romans, Visigoths, and Moors, before being recaptured by the Catholic monarchs in 1487. Today, Málaga lies prey to a new onslaught, as tourists flock from Northern Europe to soak up the sun—an invasion that has somewhat dimmed its old-world charm. However, this seaside town still has much to offer. It is famous for its Málaga dessert and aperitif wines (sweet Pedro Ximenes, and Dulce and Lágrimas muscatel). Early works of Picasso can be found in the **Museo de Bellas Artes** on the Calle San Agustín. Explore the cobbled side streets off the main plaza where you can relax at outdoor cafés, and check out the bustling shopping street, Marquñs de Larios. From the 14th-century ramparts on the nearby **Gibralfaro** (lighthouse hill) are gorgeous gardens with magnificent views of the town and harbor, and just down from there is the 11th-century Alcazaba (Moorish fortress). Also situated on Mount Gibralfaro, high above the sprawling port of Málaga, is the **Parador de Gibralfaro**, a lovely hotel with a sweeping view of the coast.

Ahead is a short drive into some of the most attractive natural landscape in Andalusia. Leave Málaga on N340 along the coast (following the signs for Cadiz, among various other destinations) past touristy **Torremolinos** (which Michener's characters from *The Drifters* would no longer recognize) and Fuengirola before reaching **Marbella**. We suggest you spend some time exploring this chic playground (only about 30 minutes lie between you and your hotel)—this is the most aristocratic of the **Costa del Sol** resorts, with its hidden villas, lavish hotels, long, pebbly beach, and the inevitable remains of a Moorish castle. If you like shopping, you will enjoy the many elegant international shops in the city, where strolling along the main street and side streets is a pleasure. Numerous restaurants of all types and categories are available here, including La Fonda, with a Michelin star, on the Plaza de Santo Cristo. From Marbella, return to the N340 and continue west for a few kilometers west to **Puerto Banus**, where the marina harbors enough yachts to rival Monaco or the French Riviera. Unless your yacht is moored there, you will have to park in the lot just outside the harbor area proper and walk in. Inside are numerous chic shops, bars, and restaurants. This is the center of Spain's jet-set scene.

From Puerto Banus, return to the N340 for just a few kilometers and turn north on C339 towards **Ronda**. For sheer dramatic setting, Ronda takes the prize. Ronda is perched on the edge of the Serranía de Ronda, slashed by 153-meter gorges and cut in two (the old *Ciudad* through which you enter from the south, and the new *Mercadillo*) by the Tajo ravine carved by the Guadalevín river (which explains why every other sentence describing the site must necessarily include the word "view"). We suggest two hotels in Ronda. We fell in love with the **Parador de Ronda** which opened in 1994. This is one of the most dramatic paradors in Spain and also has the advantage of a large parking garage (an extra charge is made for parking, but is well worth it). From the parador there are incredible views of the gorge and sweeping landscape. Just across the plaza is the much

Ronda, Puente Nuevo

smaller **Hotel Don Miguel**. It does not have the pizzazz of the parador, but is less expensive and also has a superb setting overlooking the gorge.

After you have enjoyed a sangría along with the views from the hotel terrace, stroll to the **bullring** with its wrought-iron balconies. One of Spain's oldest (1785), it inspired several works by Goya. Francisco Romero, the father of modern bullfighting (he introduced the cape and numerous so-called classical rules), was born here in 1698. His descendants continued what is still known as the Ronda school of bullfighting. Farther on you discover the spectacular **Puente Nuevo** (the 18th-century bridge that connects the two parts of town and which you crossed on your way in) with its incredible view of the ravine. When you cross it, you are in the Ciudad section with its winding streets and old stone palaces. Visit the Plaza de la Ciudad and its church, **Santa María la Mayor**, whose tower (a former minaret) affords still more picture-perfect views. Some dramatic walking excursions (30 minutes each) can be taken on footpaths leading off the Plaza del Campanillo down to ruined Moorish mills; or look for the footpath to the upper mills that offer spectacular views of a waterfall and the Puente Nuevo. To the left of the Puente Nuevo (near the Puente Romano, or Roman Bridge) is the **Casa del Rey Moro** (note the Moorish azulejo plaque in the façade), a lavishly furnished old mansion with terraced gardens and a flight of 365 stairs cut into the living rock and leading to the river and the Moorish baths. The ancient ambiance is hard to beat and invites you to take your time strolling around the lovely streets and plazas. In the newer Mercadillo section of town, Carrera de Espinel is a picturesque, pedestrian-only shopping street. You find it running east from near the bullring.

DESTINATION II   ARCOS DE LA FRONTERA

Though Ronda encourages you to linger, take comfort in the fact that you are headed to another impressive site. Since today's drive is a short one, take time for a leisurely breakfast on the hotel terrace before heading northeast out of town, following the signs to **Arriate** and **Setenil**. The latter is a classic little white town with one very interesting aspect—at the bottom of the town, in the ravine, the houses are actually built into the cliff itself. All along this route you enjoy numerous spectacular views of the mountainous countryside. Leave Setenil in a westerly direction and follow MA486, then MA449, which seem to be taking you back to Ronda. However, on reaching C339, take a right and you'll be back on the road to Arcos de la Frontera.

Back on C339, after about 6 kilometers, you see a road (MA501) to the left indicating the way to the **Cueva de la Pileta**. Upon arrival in this desolate place, park your car and climb the steep path to the small entrance to the cave, almost hidden amongst the rocks. You need to join a group of other tourists and follow a guide to visit the caves. (Before leaving Ronda, best check with the tourist office or at your hotel to verify what hours the caves are open.) If there are only a small number of tourists when you visit, you may be allowed to see some of the ancient black-and-red animal drawings found here. The paintings are said to predate those in the famous Altamira Caves and apparently indicate that the caves were inhabited 25,000 years ago. The ceramic remains from the caves are claimed to be the oldest known pottery specimens in Europe.

Santa María, Arcos de la Frontera

Wind your way back to C339 and continue west. You are on a road called the **Ruta de los Pueblos Blancos,** or white-town route, and you soon see why as you pass several very picturesque little towns with their whitewashed buildings and red-tile roofs. On the right you'll see **Montecorto** and have a splendid view of the mountains in front of you. A bit farther, the town of **Zahara,** with a ruined castle and Arab bridge, rises to your left. Built on a ridge, it was a stronghold against the kingdom of Granada during the Moorish occupation. If you have time, you might want to stop and savor the atmosphere, but if you must rush, save your time for today's destination—the spell-binding town of **Arcos de la Frontera**.

(You notice on this itinerary several towns with the "de la Frontera" tag on their names. This means "on the border" and alludes to their status during the Reconquest of Spain from the Moors.) As you approach Arcos, you have several marvelous opportunities to capture its incredible setting on film.

Arcos de la Frontera clings impossibly to an outcropping of rock with the Guadalete river at its foot. Navigate carefully up its maze of narrow, one-way alleys or you may (as we did once) find yourself backing down those steep, twisty streets in the face of a big truck with traffic being expertly (sort of) directed by amused locals. Since you are approaching from the north, the route up the hill to the Plaza de España at the heart of the old town on top is fairly easy. Gracing one side of the plaza is a lovely white (of course) mansion, somewhat austere from the outside, but pretty within. It is the **Parador Casa del Corregidor** which is one of our suggestions for where to stay in Arcos. The parador was built in 1966, but manages to reproduce quite handsomely a Renaissance building. On the other side of the parador is nothing but a crowd-stopping view to the plains below, the full impact of which ought to be absorbed with a sherry at sunset from the terrace—a similarly spectacular view is available from the west side of the plaza in front of the hotel. In addition to the parador, we also highly recommend two others hotels in Arcos—the **El Convento** (a delightful, family-run hotel tucked onto a small street behind the parador) and **Cortijo Faín**, a stunning, 17th-century farm nestled in the countryside 3 kilometers southeast of Arcos on the route to Algar.

Although the view here is the main attraction, you will also want to see the **Santa María de la Asunción** church on the plaza and wander through the ancient, romantic, winding streets of the old town, where you get a real feeling that you have stepped into life as it was in the Middle Ages.

DESTINATION III   SEVILLE

The next destination is the centerpiece of romantic Spain and, appropriately, has retained its beauty and ambiance even in this modern age. We hope you have managed to leave enough time to enjoy its unsurpassable attractions. Leave Arcos heading west, still on the white-town route, and you pass rolling hillsides resplendent with sunflowers (if it is summer), numerous typical Andalusian *cortijo,* or ranches, and more dazzling white villages. Then the terrain becomes flatter and the roadside towns less impressive as you approach the famous town of **Jerez de la Frontera**.

The major reason for stopping in Jerez is to visit the bodegas where sherry is made. The traffic in and out of Jerez is exasperating, and we found the town to be dirty so only make this side trip if you are interested in wines. Most of the bodegas are open for visitors only from 9 am to 1 pm, so plan your time accordingly. Unfortunately, due to the ever-increasing number of interested visitors, some bodegas have instituted a reservation policy. To be on the safe side, call ahead as soon as you know when you plan to be in Jerez (ask for assistance from your hotel desk staff). English seamen in the 18th century found sherry wine an agreeable alternative to French wine and it still occupies a place of honor in English bars. The varieties commonly produced here are: *fino* (extra dry, light in color and body), *amontillado* (dry, darker in color and fuller-bodied), *oloroso* (medium, full bodied, and golden), and *dulce* (sweet dessert wine).

The Jerez region is also renowned for quality horse-breeding. The famous Lippizaner horses, still used at the Spanish Riding School of Vienna, originally came from this area. For information on equestrian-related events, check with the local tourist office.

When you are ready to call it a day and discover what **Seville** has in store for you, make your way to the A4 toll road, which takes you there in no time. From the outskirts, follow the signs indicating *centro ciudad*, while keeping your eye on the skyline's most outstanding landmark—the towering golden spire of the Giralda, attached to the magnificent cathedral.

All of the hotels we recommend are within a short walking distance of the **Plaza Virgen de los Reyes**, the large plaza just behind the cathedral. If you prefer a deluxe hotel, the **Hotel Alfonso XIII** is outstanding. For a less expensive place to stay without sacrificing location or old-world ambiance, the **Hotel Doña María** is a real winner. One of our favorites, the reasonably priced **Taberna del Alabardero**, is not only one of the best buys in Spain, but also has charming rooms and a fabulous restaurant.

In order to fully appreciate the many marvels of Seville, turn to page 157 where the itinerary *Seville Highlights* begins.

Hotel Alfonso XIII, Seville

Madrid and More

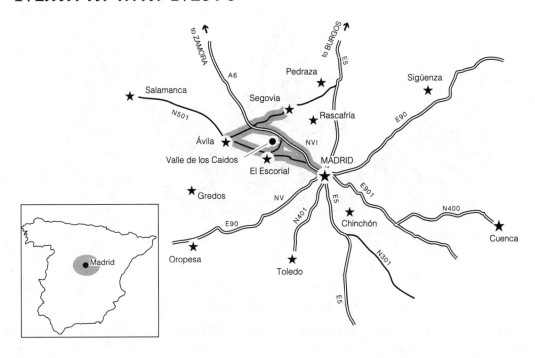

★ Destinations with Hotel Choices

● Orientation/Sightseeing

Itinerary route

Madrid and More

Parque del Buen Retiro, Madrid

We rediscover Madrid with increasing pleasure each time we visit. Our delight is mingled with increasing astonishment at the "new" face of the city that has emerged since Franco's death in 1975. Madrid (the highest capital in Europe) is a big, vigorous city—comparable in size to other western European capitals—but yet a comfortable one for the first-time visitor. Madrid's attractions will not overwhelm you if you have only a few days to devote to the city, but offer more than enough diversity and stimulation for a longer stay. If you are experiencing Madrid for the first time, a popular method of familiarization is to take one of the numerous city tours available in English (ask at the front desk of your hotel). You will get an idea of the city layout, and can return at your convenience to spend more time in places that pique your interest, or you may prefer to strike out on your own from the start, armed with a detailed sightseeing guide, a good city map (available at any bookstore or newsstand), and your sense of adventure.

A car is more trouble than it is worth in Madrid, which shares the traffic problems common to all large cities. If your visit here is at the outset of your trip, we suggest that you not get your car until you are ready to leave and, if Madrid is your last stop, that you turn your car in the day you get here. Otherwise, leave your car in a protected parking lot for the duration of your stay.

The major things to do and see are often within walking distance of downtown hotels, or readily accessible by "metro," the easily understood and extensive subway system that transports you swiftly and inexpensively to every important intersection in the city. Cabs are also reasonable for trips around town. But walk when you can, because downtown Madrid is made for wandering—with wide, bustling boulevards lined with gracious, old-world buildings and lively outdoor cafés, and narrow old streets winding through colorful neighborhoods and picturesque plazas. Below we mention a few of our favorite sights.

Probably the greatest attraction in the city is the world-class **Prado Museum**, housed in a splendid 18th-century building. Its facilities are constantly being expanded and upgraded, and it boasts one of the finest permanent art collections in Europe, as well as popular and well-presented special exhibitions. Most of the private collections of the Spanish monarchs are here. As with the Louvre in Paris or the Uffizi in Florence, you could spend days here and still not do justice to its treasures. Depending on your knowledge of and interest in the arts, we suggest you either take a tour of the museum's highlights (private if possible), or purchase a guidebook, study the directory, and set out in search of your particular favorites. The best of Goya, Velázquez, El Greco, and Murillo are here and should be seen, if nothing else.

Just a few minutes' walk from the Prado is another rare prize, the **Thyssen Bornemisza Museum**. Here you find a stunning collection of over 800 paintings that span the range of great masters from the 13th century to the present day. This art is the collection of Baron Hans Heinrich Thyssen Bornemisza and before finding its new home in Madrid, was housed in the Villa Favorita Museum near Lugano.

The **Parque del Buen Retiro** across the street is an enormous Central Park-like haven where *madrileños* stroll, bike, boat, and relax at all hours. The park also hosts outdoor concerts and theater (check the local paper or ask at your hotel desk for information).

A short distance south of the Retiro Park, near the Atocha train station on Calle Fuenterrabía, is the fascinating **Royal Tapestry Factory** (Real Fábrica de Tapices) where tapestries are being made as they have been since the 18th century. There are also some original tapestry drawings by Goya.

The neo-classic **Royal Palace**, at the west end of downtown, was conceived by Phillip V, but first occupied by Charles III. Napoleon proclaimed it the equal of Versailles, and it is definitely worth a visit. The extensive grounds and rooms, each a veritable art museum, provide a glimpse of how the Bourbons lived during their heyday in Spain. The beautiful **Plaza de Oriente** (so named because it lies on the east side of the palace) is downtown's largest and is adorned with over 40 statues of Spanish and Visigothic royalty, with an equestrian statue of Phillip IV at its center.

For archaeology buffs, the **Museo Arqueológico** emphasizes Iberian and classical material and includes the famous Dama de Elche.

If you are traveling with children, don't miss a visit to the huge **Casa de Campo** where there is a nice zoo (with one of the first pandas born in captivity), an amusement park, and a lake. The area used to be the royal hunting grounds.

Just southeast of the Royal Palace is the heart of the old city and one of the most monumental squares in the country, the 17th-century **Plaza Mayor**. An excellent place to people-watch from an outdoor café, the old plaza is completely enclosed by tall historic buildings and has a statue of Phillip III in the middle. If you depart from the plaza through the Arco de los Cuchilleros (on the south side), you will discover many typical bars and restaurants, tucked on streets which take you back in time.

Plaza Mayor, Madrid

There is a colorful flea market, called **El Rastro**, a few blocks south of the Plaza Mayor on Ribera de Curtidores street. Though it operates every day, Sunday is the liveliest time to go. Absolutely everything is sold here, both in permanent shops and temporary booths, and *madrileños* and tourists alike shop here in droves. You may even find some genuine antiques at bargain prices, but "buyer beware" is the rule here. Haggling over prices (*regateando*) is appropriate at El Rastro, unlike most other places in Spain.

About halfway between the Royal Palace and the Prado Museum is the huge plaza called **Puerta del Sol**. This is the center of activity in downtown Madrid and, in a sense, the center of Spain because all of the main highways (those designated with an "N") radiate from here. Inlaid into the sidewalk on one side of the plaza you find a plaque marking *Kilometro 0*. Some of the city's best shopping is to be found in the immediate vicinity, including a bustling pedestrian street lined with boutiques.

Shopping for antiques can be fun in Madrid. The largest concentration of antique shops is in the area southeast of the Puerta del Sol, especially on Calle del Prado between the Plaza de Santa Ana and the Plaza de las Cortes.

Madrid's night scene has something for everyone—from elegant dining and highbrow cultural events to colorful hole-in-the-wall tapa bars and pulsating, new-wave discotheques. Progressive and relatively liberal administrations following Franco's death have opened the door to new freedoms (or license, depending on your point of view) not experienced here as little as 20 years ago. The lifting of Franco's severe censorship has

paved the way not only for pornography, fast food, rock music, and divorce, but also for political argument, public gatherings, and displays of affection without fear of retribution; and you will most likely witness all of the above. Spain's recently condoned freedom of expression is nowhere as colorful and varied as in her capital city. Today, those same silent streets that were monitored by civil guards under Franco are not rolled up until dawn in many areas throughout Madrid. One of the liveliest (and safest) late-night spots in the city is located about halfway between the Cibeles fountain and the Columbus monument on the **Paseo de Recoletos**. Here indoor and outdoor cafés hum with the nation's favorite pastime: conversation. Your best sources for information about what is going on in Madrid, day or night, are the local newspapers, one of the numerous activity guides available at street kiosks and often found in hotel rooms, or, better yet, if you do not read Spanish, the concierge at your hotel can make arrangements for you, too—from dinner to bullfights to flamenco shows.

Madrid and More

SIDE TRIPS: **El Escorial**, **Ávila**, **Segovia**, and **Pedraza** may be visited in several ways. There are organized bus tours leaving from the Plaza de Oriente early every morning which include visits to El Escorial, Ávila, and Segovia (but not Pedraza) in one day. Your hotel can make the arrangements for you: the price is reasonable and the guides speak English. This method, however, is necessarily a rather quick tour of these wonderful towns and gives you very little flexibility. But, if all you want (or have time for) is a quick look, this is probably your best bet.

A better way to go, in our opinion, is to drive yourself. This allows you to allocate your time as you please. These towns are all close to Madrid and close to each other. If you leave very early in the morning and plan just a short time in each, you could see El Escorial, Ávila, and Segovia then drive on to Pedraza, where you could have dinner. But, if you decide you want to relax and not rush your sightseeing, just see part of the towns mentioned or else stay overnight en route (you will find hotel recommendations for all four towns in the *Hotel Descriptions* section).

Head northwest on A6 from Madrid, turning left about 30 kilometers out of town on C600 to reach the **Monastery of Saint Lawrence the Royal of El Escorial** (Monasterio de San Lorenzo el Real de El Escorial), better known as just **El Escorial** and one of Spain's most impressive edifices. Built by King Phillip II in the late 16th century, the building was designed to house a church, a monastery, a mausoleum, and the palace for the royal family. One of Phillip's main motivations was a promise he had made to dedicate a church to Saint Lawrence on the occasion of an important Spanish victory over France which occurred on the feast day of that saint. A second motive was that his father, Charles V, emperor of the largest empire the world had ever known, had expressed the wish that a proper tomb be erected for him. So when Phillip II moved the capital from Toledo to Madrid in 1559 in order to put the capital in the center of the country, he began construction of El Escorial on the site of the slag heap (*escorial*) of some abandoned iron mines. The construction took place from 1563 to 1584 and resulted in a huge complex that measures 206 x 161 meters and has approximately 1,200 doors and 2,600 windows. Perhaps no other building more faithfully reflects the personality of its owner than this.

Phillip II was a deeply religious man, obsessively so in the opinion of many. (It is perhaps understandable, since he spent most of his life in mourning. Seventeen of his close relatives died during his lifetime, including all of his sons but one, and his four wives.) He thus lavished great sums of money on the decoration of the religious parts of the building, while the palace itself was a simple, even austere affair from which Phillip ruled half the world. Subsequent monarchs added some decorative touches to the apartments or installed additional ones, as in the case of the Bourbon apartments. The Pantheon of the Kings, directly below the high altar of the church, contains the remains of almost all the Spanish monarchs from Charles V on (with the kings on the left, queens on the right). The lavishly decorated library contains some 40,000 volumes, and there and elsewhere in the building you discover examples of the works of all the great painters of the 16th century. El Escorial elicits varied reactions from visitors, some seeing it as a morose pile of rock with 2,600 too-small windows, others as a totally unique royal monument built by a unique monarch. There is certainly no denying its interest as a symbol of some important aspects of 16th-century Spain.

Head back toward A6 via C600 and watch for a turnoff to the left leading to the **Valle de los Caidos** (Valley of the Fallen). This memorial to Spain's Civil War dead is dominated by a 120-meter-high by 46-meter-wide cross (which has an elevator on the north side) and is the final resting place of Generalísimo Francisco Franco, who ruled Spain from 1939–1975.

Return to the A6 freeway and continue northwest to Villacastin, where you exit to reach **Ávila**, traversing pretty countryside of rolling hills. Approached from any direction, Ávila is a dramatic sight, but the most stunning view is when you arrive from the west. Enclosed by stone walls, it stands today as it must have appeared to potential aggressors in the Middle Ages. The 11th-century fortifications (the oldest and best preserved in

Spain) are over 2 kilometers long, 3 meters thick, and average 10 meters in height. They have 9 gates and 88 towers. A stroll along the sentry path atop the walls gives you a close-up view of the many storks' nests perched in the towers and rooftops of the city.

Ávila Wall

Within the medieval city, the fortress-like **cathedral** is a particularly fine one: mostly early Gothic in form, it contains some beautiful stained glass and ironwork. The **Convento de Santa Teresa**, a few blocks southwest of the cathedral, is built on the birthplace of the famous 16th-century mystic writer, who is generally credited with defeating the Reformation in Spain by carrying out reforms of her own. Inside there are relics related to the saint and some fine altars. In the immediate vicinity are some lovely and picturesque 15th-century houses. You will enjoy strolling around this ancient town with its tiny plazas and cobbled streets.

Just outside the walls on the northeast corner is **St. Vincent's Church**, founded in 1307. Noteworthy are the Tomb of the Patron Saints (12th century), a crypt with the stone where Saint Vincent and his sisters were martyred (in the 4th century), and the west entrance with its rich Romanesque sculpture.

Also outside the walls, via the Puerta del Alcázar gate and across the Plaza de Santa María, is **Saint Peter's Church**, with its impressive rose window. To the left is the Calle del Duque de Alba which leads (400 meters) to the **Convento de San José**, the first convent founded by **Santa Teresa**—now home to a museum of mementos about her life.

To reach **Segovia**, return the way you came to the A6 freeway and continue past it on N110. Segovia was an important city even before the Romans came in 80 B.C. It was occupied by the Moors between the 8th and 11th centuries, and was reconquered by the Christians in 1085.

The highlight of Segovia is the 14th-century **Alcázar** castle. Dramatically situated like a ship on the high sea, it is a sight not soon forgotten. This is the castle used in the film *Camelot*, from whose ramparts Lancelot launches into the song *C'est moi* before crossing the English Channel to join King Arthur's knights of the round table. Probably the most-photographed edifice in Spain, it is surprisingly barren inside—the tour is most memorable for its views. In 1474, Castilian King Henry IV's sister, Isabella, was here proclaimed Queen of Castile (which at that time included most of the western half of Spain and Andalusia). Isabella's marriage to Ferdinand, heir of Aragón, laid the groundwork for the creation of the modern nation.

Segovia claims one of the finest **Roman aqueducts** in existence today, and it still functions to bring water from the Riofrío river to the city. Thought to have been built in the 1st or 2nd century A.D., it is constructed, without mortar, of granite from the nearby mountains. It is almost a kilometer long and over 27 meters above the ground at its highest point as it crosses the Plaza de Azoguejo.

Madrid and More

A tour around the outside of the city walls to the north affords some excellent perspectives on the setting. Bear left from the aqueduct and you pass the old Moneda (Mint) and the Monasterio del Parral, on the left bank of the Eresma river. After crossing the bridge bear left, then right to the Church of the Vera Cruz, from where you can enjoy

Alcázar Castle, Segovia

a spectacular view of the city. A little farther north is the **Convento de Carmelitas Descalzos**, where the great mystic poet of the 15th century, Saint John of the Cross, is buried. To wind up your sightseeing with more city views, return to town via the Cuesta de los Hoyos.

In the old city are narrow, picturesque streets that deserve a half-day walking tour. The **Church of Saint Stephen** is a lovely Romanesque building from the 13th century. Farther down is the **cathedral**, said to be the last Gothic cathedral built in Spain. East another block is Saint Martin's (12th century), and a couple of blocks farther on is one of the most unique mansions in Segovia, the **Casa de los Picos**, a 15th-century home adorned with diamond-shaped stones. Northwest of there is the Plaza del Conde de Cheste with its numerous palaces. If you head south from here, you find yourself back where the aqueduct crosses the Plaza del Azoguejo.

Continue northeast on N110 for about 25 kilometers and turn left, following the signs for **Pedraza**, which is about 13 kilometers farther. Whereas El Escorial, Ávila, and Segovia are well-known tourist destinations, most people have never heard of Pedraza, a fact that makes it even more fun to visit. This walled, medieval hilltop village is truly a jewel. From the moment you enter through the lower gate, time stands still as you meander through the maze of little streets. There are no major sights to visit, although on the edge of town is a brooding castle where the sons of King François I of France were once held captive. The main attraction here is the town itself. The heart of Pedraza is its picturesque Plaza Mayor faced by houses that date back to the 16th century. The small side streets have many delightful boutiques, restaurants, and two lovely small hotels, **La Posada de Don Mariano** and **Hotel de La Villa** (both are described in the back of this guide in the *Hotel Descriptions* section).

Madrid and More

Seville Highlights

The Cathedral and Giralda, Seville

We should preface this section highlighting Seville with a frank admission of prejudice. It is one of our favorite cities, chock-full of fond memories of good times and good friends. Every time we return we fall under Seville's spell—and it won't surprise us a bit if you're enchanted, too. It is not that Seville is totally different from other Spanish cities, it is just that the town and its inhabitants are the quintessence of Spain. We strongly suggest several days in Seville. You need time to see its many sights, as well as time to wander along the orange-tree-lined streets and soak up the special feeling that the city imparts to its guests.

We recommend several places to stay in Seville, the **Hotel Alfonso XIII**, the **Hotel Doña María** , and the **Taberna del Alabardero**. All three are outstanding in their category (look in the *Hotel Descriptions* section for pertinent details) and in the heart of the city within walking distance of sightseeing.

After settling in your hotel, you must first visit the **cathedral**, one of the largest Gothic churches in the world, ranking in size with Saint Peter's in Rome and Saint Paul's in London. It was constructed between 1402 and 1506 on the site of a mosque. In the elaborate Royal Chapel at the east end is buried Alfonso X "The Wise," one of Spain's most brilliant medieval monarchs, who supervised the codification of existing Roman law in the 13th century. When his son Sancho rebelled, Seville remained loyal to Alfonso. Alfonso's gratified statement *No me ha dejado* (It has not deserted me) is the basis for the rebus symbol you are bound to notice painted and carved all over the city: a double knot (called a *madeja*) between the syllables "no" and "do," thus producing *No madeja do* which is pronounced approximately the same as *No me ha dejado*. Ferdinand III, later Saint Ferdinand, who freed Seville from Moorish domination, is buried in a silver shrine in front of the altar. On one side, in an ornate mausoleum, is one of the tombs of Christopher Columbus (the other is in Santo Domingo in the Caribbean—both cities claim to have his real remains).

Just outside the east entrance to the cathedral is the best known of Seville's architectural sights, the **Giralda**. Originally it was the mosque's minaret and was retained when the church was built. Be sure to enter and ascend the ramp up the 70-meter spire (stairs were not used in order to allow horses access). The view of the city is outstanding, especially in the late afternoon. The name *Giralda* means weather vane and refers to the weather vane on the top, which was added in the 16th century.

On the opposite side of the cathedral from the Giralda is an impressive Renaissance building—originally built to be a customs house but later converted into the **Archives of the Indies**—into which were put most of the documents (comprised of some 86,000,000

Alcázar, Seville

pages spanning 400 years) pertaining to the discovery and conquest of America. Students of colonial Spanish American history still come across undocumented material when they make pilgrimages here for a rich feast of research.

On the north side of the cathedral (a pleasant spot to sit and watch Seville go by) there are cafés that are slightly more tranquil than those along Avenida de la Constitución. To the south of the cathedral is the **Alcázar**—not as impressive as the Alhambra in Granada, but a lovely and refreshingly cool spot to spend a hot afternoon. Most of it was restored by King Pedro "The Cruel" (14th century), but he used Moorish architects and thus retained much of its authenticity.

If you leave the Alcázar by way of the southeast corner of the *Patio de las Banderas* (Flag Court), you are in the old Jewish Quarter, the **Barrio de Santa Cruz**. Looking something like a set for an opera, this is a mixture of old, typical whitewashed houses and shops—all, it seems, with flowers tumbling from wrought-iron windows and balconies. The painter Murillo is buried in the Plaza de Santa Cruz and the house where he died is in the nearby Plaza de Alfaro. Southeast of these two plazas, hugging the Alcázar walls, are the lovely **Murillo Gardens** (*Jardines de Murillo*), where painters are often engrossed in capturing the setting on canvas.

North from the cathedral you can stroll a few long blocks down the Avenida de la Constitución to the **Plaza de San Francisco** behind the city hall (*Ayuntamiento*), a center of outdoor events during Holy Week. Running parallel to Sierpes and out of the Plaza Nueva is Calle Tetuán, another major shopping street.

At the north end of Sierpes, turn left on Calle Alfonso XII, after which a few blocks' walk brings you to the **Museo de Bellas Artes** (Fine Arts Museum), housing one of the most important collections in Spain. There are well-presented paintings of El Greco, Zurbarán, Velázquez, and Murillo, among others.

On Calle San Fernando, flanking the handsome Hotel Alfonso XIII, is a golden 18th-century building, once a tobacco factory, where Bizet's beautiful and fiery Carmen worked. This is now the **University of Seville**. Feel free, if it is open, to go in and stroll its wide hallways through the collection of interior patios. Upstairs (to the right of the main entrance) you can find the university bar, where students and faculty convene for a between-class cognac, beer, coffee, or sandwich. A visit here gives you an insight into Spanish academic life.

Behind the university is the entrance to the **Parque de María Luisa** (laid out by a former princess of Spain), a popular local retreat from the summer heat. Here you'll discover the **Plaza de España**, a large semi-circle complete with boat rides and tiled niches representing each of the provinces of Spain, where Spanish families like to have their pictures taken in front of their "home-town" plaque. This plaza was constructed for the International Exposition in Seville in 1929, as were several other buildings in the park and as was the Hotel Alfonso XIII. In the Plaza de América, farther down, is the **Museo Arqueológico** with a very regional collection of Roman antiquities and an arts-

and-crafts museum. If you fancy being covered with doves, there is a spot where a lady sells you some seeds which, when held out in your hand, attract dozens of the white birds to perch greedily on your arms, shoulders, and head—this makes a fun picture to take home. There are also, of course, numerous spots to sit and people-watch.

You must not miss the **Casa Pilatos**, a stunning palace built in 1540 for the Marqués of Tarifa. The name derives from Pontius Pilate's home in Jerusalem (which supposedly the Marqués visited and admired). The palace is a delight—filled with brilliantly colored tiles, sunny courtyards filled with flowers, lacy balustrades, and Roman statues. A bit far off the beaten path (but within walking distance), the Casa Pilatos is usually not brimming with tourists.

The major festivals in Seville are Holy Week and the Feria (Fair) de Sevilla (about the second week after Easter). Although both are absolutely spectacular events, do not dream of securing a hotel reservation unless you plan a year in advance. And be aware that things can get pretty wild during the ten days of the Feria.

If time allows, you can take several good side trips from Seville:

CARMONA: Head northeast out of town on NIV through fertile hills to the ancient town of Carmona (38 kilometers), which still retains some of its ramparts and much of its old-world ambiance. The Puerta de Sevilla, a curious architectural blend of Roman and Moorish, opens onto the old town, where whitewashed alleyways and stone gateways lead to private patios of what were once noble mansions. The plaza is lined with 17th- and 18th-century houses. In the patio of the town hall (Calle San Salvador) there is a large Roman mosaic. Stroll down the nearby Calle Santa María de Gracia to the Puerta de Córdoba (built into the Roman wall in the 17th century diametrically opposite the Puerta de Sevilla) for a lovely view over a golden plain of wheat fields. The **Casa de Carmona** is an excellent place to stay.

The Church at Jerez de la Frontera

ITALICA: Just 10 kilometers out of Seville on N630, a little past the town of Santiponce, is the Roman town of Italica, founded in 205 B.C. by Scipio Africanus and birthplace of emperors Trajan and Hadrian. Still being excavated and restored, its baths, mosaics, and amphitheater are interesting and well worth the short drive (especially if you will not get the chance to visit the incredibly impressive Roman ruins at Mérida). Open-air dramatic performances are occasionally given in the amphitheater here (check with the tourist office on Avenida de la Constitución in Seville for a schedule if you are interested).

JEREZ DE LA FRONTERA: If you have an interest in going sherry-tasting Jerez, the sherry capital of the world, it is easily visited from Seville, being just a quick 67 kilometers south on the freeway (see the description in the *Andalusian Adventures* itinerary).

Barcelona Highlights

Barcelona

Barcelona is Spain's second-largest city, but its distinct history and regional culture make it anything but a small-scale Madrid. Its personality, architecture, customs, proximity to France, and long-term importance as a Mediterranean seaport make it a sophisticated and cosmopolitan city. The whole region of Catalonia, but especially its capital city of Barcelona, has long resisted absorption by Castile-dominated central authority. Catalans pride themselves on their industriousness and prosperity, both immediately evident to the visitor. Barcelona is a fascinating, bustling, charming city that will enchant you. There is a lot to see and do, so try to budget sufficient time to explore fully the delights the city has to offer.

As in most large, unfamiliar cities, a good way to start your visit is by taking advantage of an organized bus tour, which orients you and gives you a more enlightened idea of how and where to concentrate your time. There is a variety of tours available in English—ask the hotel concierge to arrange one for you.

Street signs (and maps) are often in the Catalan language. In Barcelona, you see *carrer* instead of *calle* for street, *passeig* instead of *paseo* for passage, *avinguda* instead of *avenida* for avenue, and *placa* instead of *plaza* for town square. The nerve center of the city is the large Plaza de Catalonia on the border between the old city and the new. It is singularly impressive, with many fine monuments and sculptures. Beneath it is the hub of the subway system and the shopping arcades along the underground Avenida de las Luces (Lights).

All of the downtown sights are within walking distance of the plaza, including the festive **Ramblas**—a cosmopolitan, stone-paved promenade running generally south from the plaza to the waterfront. Ramblas comes from the Arabic for river bed, which is what this once was. Now it is a chic and shady street, lined with shops and hotels and frequented by anyone and everyone visiting Barcelona. At the plaza end are kiosks selling newspapers and books in many languages; then a bird market takes over and the street is adorned with cages full of colorful birds. Next are lovely flower stalls, then a series of tree-shaded cafés, perfect for people-watching. On the right side of the street (as you walk toward the waterfront), just before you reach the flower stalls you find a busy public market where it is fun to stroll, enjoying the amazing variety of produce and fresh fish that Barcelonans have to choose from.

At the waterfront end of Ramblas is a monument to Christopher Columbus and a re-creation of his famous ship, the *Santa María*. King Ferdinand and Queen Isabella were holding court here when Columbus returned from his first voyage and announced the incredible news of his discovery of a route to the Orient (he still thought this is what he had found). Visit the *Santa María* and try to imagine what it would be like to set out into unknown waters on a two-month voyage as Columbus did in this tiny ship in 1492. You can also take boat rides around the harbor from here.

A few blocks east of the Ramblas is the colorful Gothic Quarter (Barrio Gótico), a virtual maze of old buildings, streets, and alleyways. A marvelous 15th-century cathedral dominates the area, which also contains the city hall (*ayuntamiento*), with its lovely sculptures and paintings and beautifully decorated chambers and halls. There is a rich selection of atmospheric *tapa* bars and chic shops, including some interesting antique stores, in this lively area.

Still farther east is the famed Calle Montcada, lined with handsome old mansions. Two of these contain the **Picasso Museum** with an impressive display of virtually every period of the famous painter's work. Although born in Málaga, Picasso spent much of his life (especially during his formative years) in Barcelona. His most famous paintings are not housed here, but the museum does contain many examples of his early work.

Even more intriguing are the works of another famous Barcelona artist, Antonio Gaudí (1852–1926), the avant-garde architect. His **Holy Family (Sagrada Familia) Church** is the city's most famous landmark, its perforated spires visible from various points around the city. You certainly want to take a closer look at this marvelous unfinished building with its intricately carved façades and molten-rock textures (it is best reached by cab). Even more fanciful is the **Guell Park** overlooking the city (Eusebio Guell was a wealthy patron of Gaudí)—also unfinished, but delightful in its conception and whimsical atmosphere. (Many of Gaudí's imaginative creations resemble life-size gingerbread houses.) Numerous examples of his work can be found in the city: the **Casa Batlló**, **Casa Mila**, and the **Pedrera** are on the Paseo de Gracia, west of the Plaza de Catalunya, and the **Palacio Guell** is just off the Ramblas. They all attest to the apparent rejection of the straight line as a design element in the highly individualistic style of this innovative artist. Because they cannot be moved from Barcelona, they are more an integral part of the city's personality than the paintings of Picasso or Miró which can be seen in art museums all over the world.

Another not-to-be-missed area is the **Parque de Montjuich**, occupying the hill of the same name south of the Plaza de Catalunya. Originally the site of a 17th-century defensive fort (which now contains a military museum), a number of interesting public buildings were erected here for the 1929 exposition. (This is a branch of the same exposition for which a number of buildings in the **Parque de María Luisa** were constructed in Seville. The exposition was divided between the two cities.) The **Museum of Catalan Art** is in the **Palacio Nacional** and it contains fine Gothic and Romanesque sections, featuring wonderful examples of religious art that have been rescued from abandoned churches all over the region. These are magnificently displayed, often as complete church interiors.

Holy Family Church, Barcelona

Also in Montjuich is the **Pueblo Español** (Spanish town) which is an entire little village, constructed for the 1929 exposition, utilizing the varied architectural styles of Spain. Some of the structures are re-creations of actual buildings, and some simply imitate regional styles. The entrance, for example, is a reconstruction of the towers of the city wall of Ávila. It is an impressive achievement and is now essentially a shopping area featuring *artesanía* (arts and crafts) from the different regions. If you have been to other areas of Spain, you will be struck by the unique juxtaposition of the various architectural styles.

Montjuich is also the setting of one of the most wonderful of all the sights in Barcelona—the beautiful **dancing fountains** (*fuentes*). For a truly unforgettable experience, ask at your hotel for the days of the week and the time at night they are augmented with lights and music. Music from classical to contemporary accompanies the multi-colored, ever-changing spouts in a symphony of sensory experience. If you go an hour early and are prepared to wile away the time watching the Barcelonans stroll around the park, you should be able to secure a seat in front of the palace.

Also in the park is the **Fundación Joan Miró**, with several hundred examples of this native son's bold and colorful paintings, along with works by other contemporary artists— definitely worth a visit if you are a modern art devotee.

Children particularly enjoy the new amusement park on the Montjuich hill, and an older one, reached by funicular railway, on the hill called Tibidabo. Both spots have fine city views. In the **Parque de la Ciudadela** there is a good zoo.

There is ample night life in Barcelona. The best approach is to ask your hotel concierge, since shows change constantly. One permanent offering, however, is the **Scala**, an international, Las Vegas-style review which is very professionally presented and is enjoyable even if you do not have an understanding of the Spanish language. There is a dinner show—the food is only passable—and a later show at midnight without dinner. You need to ask your hotel concierge to make reservations for the Scala, since it is highly popular both with locals and tourists.

Hotel Descriptions

This spectacular parador crowns the tiny fortified town of Alarcón on the rocky central meseta south of Madrid. Perched on a promontory, this dramatic 8th-century Arab fortress resembles an island surrounded by the deep, natural gorges created by the looping Júcar river below. The imposing castle-hotel is superbly preserved and retains a considerable portion of its original construction, including crenellated towers, ramparts, and the vigilant castle keep, featuring a guestroom on each floor. The main lounge off the entry patio is awe-inspiring: its towering stone- and wood-beamed ceiling arches over gigantic tapestries, suits of armor, and a corner fireplace—you can all but hear the rattling of swords borne by the Knights of the Order of Saint James who readied themselves here to combat the Moors during the Reconquest. There are few guestrooms, and each is unique, though they all feature traditional Castilian wood furnishings, high ceilings, breathtaking views beyond thick walls, and a mini-bar. Room 103 has windows so high that steps are carved to reach them. Room 105 is also special with a vaulted ceiling and balcony. Take a turn around the ramparts—it will make you realize why the Moors chose it as a stronghold and wonder how the Christians ever wrested it from them.

PARADOR "MARQUÉS DE VILLENA"
Manager: Joaquin Gutierrez López
Avenida Amigos de Los Castillos, s/n
16213 Alarcón (Cuenca), Spain
Tel: (969) 33.03.15, Fax: (969) 33.03.03
13 rooms, Double: Pts 19,000*
*IVA not included, breakfast Pts 1,300
Open all year, Credit cards: all major
Restaurant open daily
170 km W of Valencia, 85 km S of Cuenca
Michelin Map 444
Region: Castilla-La Mancha

The Parador de la Mancha is located in the flat countryside just outside Albacete, a city well known for its Archaeological Museum. The hotel (of fairly recent construction) is not a historic monument, but it has the appealing ambiance of a Spanish hacienda. The whitewashed building, accented by wrought-iron lamps and a terra cotta roof, is built around a large central courtyard, wrapped on four sides by a window-enclosed, wide hallway with a red-tiled floor. In this cheery corridor colorful plates and old prints accent the walls and green plants, nurtured by the sunny exposure, abound. A few antiques, such as handsome carved chests and saddles, lend a nice old-world touch. Behind the hotel, set in a grassy lawn, is a large swimming pool which offers a restful respite on a hot summer day. There are also two tennis courts for sports enthusiasts. The guestrooms and bathrooms are especially spacious. Although when we visited the paint on the doors was a bit chipped, the furnishings were very pleasant and in keeping with the mood of the building—headboards of black wrought-iron trimmed with brass, red-tiled floors, rustic wooden furniture, and windows enclosed by heavy shutters. There is a guest lounge with brown leather sofas, game tables, and a large fireplace. The dining room, appointed with simple wooden tables and chairs, serves La Mancha specialties.

PARADOR DE LA MANCHA
Manager: Carmelo Martinez Grande
02000 Albacete (Albacete), Spain
Tel: (967) 24.53.21, Fax: (967) 24.32.71
70 rooms, Double: Pts 15,000*
*IVA not included, breakfast Pts 1,300
Open all year, Credit cards: all major
Restaurant open daily, pool
180 km SE of Valencia, 4 km SE of Albacete
Michelin Map 444, Region: Castilla-La Mancha

On the top of a hill, dominating the town of Alcañiz and the beautifully fertile Maestrazgo valley, the Parador de la Concordia is installed in a majestic 18th-century Aragonese palace, once a 12th-century castle. Its double rooms have extensive views framed by thick castle walls and wooden windows (some windows set so high that steps have been built in to reach them), lovely rustic wood furnishings, pale-blue bedspreads and burnished red-tile floors highlighted by colorfully patterned rugs. All of the rooms have air conditioning, television, and mini-bar. Due to the spaciousness of the beamed hallways, sitting areas, beautiful, high-ceilinged dining room, and handsome lounge, the palace has deceptively few rooms to accommodate guests. Room 1 (a large corner bedroom with sweeping views in two directions) is especially outstanding. Your visit here will be a trip back through time. A 12th-century tower which was constructed when the Knights of the Order of Calatrava were based here is found on the grounds, and a small cloister and the remains of walls dating from the 12th through the 15th centuries share the hotel's dramatic hilltop setting. Medieval Alcañiz and its parador offer a lovely and tranquil stop for the traveler.

PARADOR DE LA CONCORDIA
Manager: Miguel Cruz Sanchez
Castillo de Calatravos, s/n
44600 Alcañiz (Teruel), Spain
Tel: (978) 83.04.00, Fax: (978) 83.03.66
12 rooms, Double: Pts 17,500*
*IVA not included, breakfast Pts 1,300
Open Feb to mid-Dec, Credit cards: all major
Restaurant open daily
105 km SE of Zaragoza. Road N-232
Michelin Map 443, Region: Aragon

In the verdant Andalusian hills, ten minutes from Mijas and less than an hour from the bustle of Málaga and the beaches of the Costa del Sol, a 300-year-old farmhouse has been restored by Arun Narang, an American, and his British wife, Jean. The rambling, red-roofed building is surrounded by orchards, a grass-edged swimming pool, and grazing horses. Arun is the chef and creates an interesting, international menu (including many Indian specialties and barbecue). Except in winter, meals are served on a shady terrace near the pool. Throughout there is a mood of easy-going informality—a "get to know the other guests," bed-and-breakfast atmosphere prevails. Enclosed within whitewashed walls are several garden patios and a sitting-room lined with books and enhanced with a cozy fireplace. The billiard room (where the former owner once housed lions) has been converted into a honeymoon suite complete with four-poster bed. The rather small guestrooms are decorated simply with dark-wood furniture, fresh white bedspreads, and floral fabrics (brought by Jean's mother from England) for the curtains. One of my favorites, the Panther room, has twin four-poster beds. With its pool, horse riding, tennis and mini-golf, for a budget getaway (but not too far), the finca provides a relaxed, family-oriented, friendly atmosphere. Note: Finca La Mota is not in the town of Alhaurín, but about 4 kilometers south on the road marked to Mijas.

FINCA LA MOTA
Owners: Jean & Arun Narang
Carretera de Mijas
29120 Alhaurín El Grande (Málaga), Spain
Tel: (95) 24.90.901, Fax: (95) 25.94.120
E-mail: lamota@maptel.es
15 rooms, Double: Pts 7,000 (shared bathroom)–9,000*
*IVA & breakfast included
Open all year, Credit cards: all major
Restaurant closed from Nov to Mar, pool
30 km NW of Málaga
Michelin Map 446, Region: Andalucia

For a rustic hideaway, tucked off the beaten path in the beautiful mountains of Asturias, La Tahona is an exceptional find. Besnes (La Tahona's official address) is so tiny that it rarely appears on any map—the closest town is Alles. The location is what makes this inn so remarkable: that in a beautiful, remote area you could possibly find such a Shangri-La. Please do not misunderstand: La Tahona is not a fancy hotel in any way, nor does it pretend to be, but it shines in its simplicity. From the C6312 (which runs between Cangas and Panes), you take a small road north toward Alles. In less than a kilometer, you take an even less significant lane on the left to Besnes and La Tahona. Then, in just a few minutes, you come to an appealing, two-story stone building with a red-tiled roof deep in the woods beside a small stream. The rustic charm continues when you step inside where there is a reception desk to the left and a fireplace nook to the left. Beyond is a charming dining room, surrounded with windows on three sides, looking out to the forest and a babbling brook. The tables, set with checkered cloths, lend to the country ambiance. A staircase lined with antique farm implements leads down to a guest lounge. There are thirteen rooms in this building which in days of yore was a bakery. Just down the lane is an old mill where six more guestrooms are located. All the bedrooms are appropriately decorated in a simple, rustic motif.

LA TAHONA
Manager: Lorenzo Nilsson
33578 Alles-Besnes (Asturias), Spain
Tel & fax: (985) 41 57 49, E-mail: latahona@ctv
www.karenbrown.com/spaininns/latahona.html
13 rooms, Double: Pts 8,800*
*IVA not included, breakfast Pts 750
Open all year, Credit cards: all major
Restaurant open daily
12 km W of Panes, 45 km E of Cangas
Michelin Map 442, Region: Cantabria

Surprisingly, this parador is not a bona fide restoration of the 16th-century original, but was in fact built in 1979, and principally the entry and attached church are all that remain of the former 1596 convent. However, the newness is hard to detect and you will marvel at the attention to detail. Everything from the bricks to the windows to the rough stones used for the floor were custom made. Elegant antiques abound in the public rooms. Cozy, quiet sitting areas, often with fireplaces, are located on each floor and 16 lovely patios are spaced invitingly around the premises. The bedrooms are impressive, with ancient-looking windows and quaint wooden beds surrounded by pretty ceramic-tiled walls instead of headboards. The other furnishings are harmonious in style and color, contrasting delightfully with the whitewashed walls. The bar is similarly enchanting: built in the style of an old wine cellar, it holds giant clay vats which extend from the lower sitting area through the floor above. Surrounding the vats are rough wooden tables which complete the ancient bodega atmosphere.

PARADOR DE ALMAGRO
Manager: José M. López Santos
Ronda de San Francisco
13270 Almagro (Ciudad Real), Spain
Tel: (926) 86.01.00, Fax: (926) 86.01.50
55 rooms, Double: Pts 17,500*
*IVA not included, breakfast Pts 1,300
Open all year, Credit cards: all major
Restaurant open daily, pool
218 km S of Madrid, 22 km SE of Ciudad Real
Michelin Map 444
Region: Castilla-La Mancha

This 1980's addition to the parador chain is of modern, whitewashed construction, built on a high point in town and overlooking the green sea of the Antequera plain. Just an hour from Málaga and two from Granada, it offers a restful, rural alternative to city sounds and pace, in a town with no less than thirty-eight churches and three remarkable prehistoric dolmens. The dining room and vast lounge are on split levels, complemented by a blonde-wood cathedral ceiling, Oriental carpets, and contemporary furniture. Wall-to-wall windows afford expansive countryside views from both. An immaculate green-and-white hallway leads past a tiny, sunlit interior patio to the guestrooms, all identical, with good-size white-tile baths, brick-red terra cotta floors with beige-weave rugs, pastel-print bedspreads, and wood and leather furnishings. All the rooms have lovely views, though if you request *una habitación en la segunda planta con vista de la vega* you'll get the best orientation. If you make a rest stop here, don't fail to visit nearby El Torcal, an incredible natural display of rock formations.

PARADOR DE ANTEQUERA
Manager: Eugenio Sos Roy
Paseo García de Olmo
29200 Antequera (Málaga), Spain
Tel: (952) 84.09.01, Fax: (952) 84.13.12
55 rooms, Double: Pts 13,500*
*IVA not included, breakfast Pts 1,200
Open all year, Credit cards: all major
Restaurant open daily, pool
58 km N of Málaga
Michelin Map 446, Region: Andalucia

If you wish, while driving through Andalusia, that you could spend the night in one of the beautiful estates you see snuggled in the countryside, then the Cortijo Faín will fulfill your dream. I can think of no other place to stay in Spain that exceeds the rustic authenticity of this marvelous old cortijo. From the moment you enter through the gate into the walled courtyard, you step back into a world long past—there is not a hint of modern commercialism. The discreet reception desk is in the old stables where harnesses hang from the walls and saddles stand ready for the day's ride. Across the cobbled courtyard with its old well stands a large, picturesque, tiled-roofed manor, whose thick, whitewashed walls are draped with bougainvillea. Inside is a spacious entry hall with steps winding up to a galleried upper level where most of the bedrooms are located. Antiques abound throughout. All but two of the rooms are suites. Of these, number 5 is especially enticing with a large terrace where you can look out over a grove of olive trees with huge trunks gnarled with age to the swimming pool. An air of faded elegance pervades the old cortijo–expect the family dogs to be present at dinner, do not expect decorator perfection or a staff that speaks English.

CORTIJO FAÍN
Owner: Jose Luis Jimenez
Carretera de Algar, Km 3
11630 Arcos de la Frontera (Cádiz), Spain
Tel & fax: (956) 23.13.96
11 rooms, Double: Pts 10,000*
*IVA not included, breakfast Pts 1,000
Open all year, Credit cards: all major
Set dinner Pts 3,000 per person, pool
80 km SE of Seville, 3 km SE of Arcos, road to Algar
Michelin Map 446, Region: Andalusia

The popular government parador in Arcos de La Frontera is frequently filled, but do not despair. Just behind the parador is an intimate, family-run inn that offers personalized service and wonderful prices. As you might guess from the name, this small hotel was originally a convent, dating back to the 17th century. In 1998 six new rooms were added, and the existing rooms renovated. Each guestroom has individual charm and has telephone, TV, air conditioning, and modern bath. Some are named for famous people, such as poets or journalists. Adorning the walls of these rooms are photos and press releases spotlighting the person for whom the room is named. Most of the rooms enjoy a view, and some have balconies. There is no public lounge—instead guests relax on an interior patio. The hotel's restaurant is located just down the street in a beautiful 16th-century mansion. Like the hotel, the restaurant (which specializes in authentic local cooking) oozes charm and hospitality. El Convento was opened in 1987 after extensive renovations by the Roldán family. They obviously have excellent taste because their hotel, although simple, offers a wealth of charm. The family also owns a second hotel in Arcos, Los Olivos, composed of several houses facing onto a small courtyard. Although not as centrally located, Los Olivos is a nicely decorated hotel that is recommended if a room at El Convento is not available.

HOTEL "EL CONVENTO"
Manager: María Moreno
Maldonado, 2
11630 Arcos de la Frontera (Cádiz), Spain
Tel & fax: (956) 70.23.33
www.karenbrown.com/spaininns/hotelelconvento.html
11 rooms, Double: Pts 10,000*
*IVA not included, breakfast Pts 800
Open all year, Credit cards: all major
Restaurant open daily
105 km SE of Seville
Michelin Map 446, Region: Andalusia

ARCOS DE LA FRONTERA   PARADOR CASA DEL CORREGIDOR   Map: 5c

This wonderfully situated inn was built in 1966 on the site of an old mansion on the Plaza de España in the center of the hilltop white town of Arcos. With the attention to authenticity characteristic of the parador architects, this parador was restored and reopened in 1985 and appears as a mansion several centuries old. The lobby and lounges are accented with antiques and enlivened with ceramic-tile pictures. The hallways are elegant with either open-beamed or lovely vaulted ceilings. Off the dining room is an enclosed garden patio that features an old tiled, stone well—a delightful spot for refreshment. The patio faces stiff competition from the terrace off the pretty little bar, which offers an endlessly dramatic view over the vast plains far below. The spacious bedrooms are extremely attractive, appointed with dark, carved-wood beds and deep-dred drapes and bedspreads which contrast beautifully with the stark white walls. Some rooms overlook the town's picturesque main square, or, for a small surcharge, you can request a room with its own terrace overlooking the valley.

PARADOR CASA DEL CORREGIDOR
Manager: Máximo Pérez
Plaza de España, 5
11630 Arcos de la Frontera (Cádiz), Spain
Tel: (956) 70.05.00, Fax: (956) 70.11.16
24 rooms, Double: Pts 17,500*
*IVA not included, breakfast Pts 1,300
Open all year, Credit cards: all major
Restaurant open daily
105 km SE of Seville
Michelin Map 446, Region: Andalucia

The Áran Valley, located in the high Pyrenees, is such a favorite target for skiers and sports enthusiasts that many of its once-picturesque villages are now buried behind giant condominium complexes. Happily, the tiny hamlet of Artíes, with stone houses lining its narrow winding streets, still retains much of its old-world charm. Driving into town, you cannot miss the parador—it faces directly onto the main road. The hotel has a cheerful, friendly look with honey-colored stone walls and a steeply pitched gray-tile roof, accented by two rows of whimsical gables. The original parador, which had only a few rooms, was built into the *Casa de Portolá*, the house of Don Gaspar de Portolá (a famous Spanish captain of the Dragoons who in the 18th century explored California, founded the Mission of San Diego, and went on to become the first Governor of San Francisco). In recent years, the parador has been greatly expanded. However a small chapel and the medieval core of the original mansion are still incorporated into one wing of the hotel. The decor is predominantly modern with dark-gray slate floors, contemporary chairs and sofas, and some abstract paintings. Relieving the newness of the decor are concessions to the inn's heritage such as an antique grandfather clock, heavy, wrought-iron chandeliers, and a beamed ceiling in the spacious dining room.

PARADOR DON GASPAR DE PORTOLÁ
Manager: Manuel Español
25599 Artíes (Lleida), Spain
Tel: (973) 64.08.01, Fax: (973) 64.10.01
57 rooms, Double: Pts 17,500*
*IVA not included, breakfast Pts 1,300
Open all year, Credit cards: all major
Restaurant open daily
170 km N of Lleida, 338 km NW of Barcelona
Michelin Map 443, Region: Catalonia

From the 14th until the 18th centuries, one of the most influential families in the ancient walled town of Ávila lived next to the cathedral in the mansion which is today the Gran Hotel Palacio Valderrábanos. Their escutcheons (family crests) can still be seen above the magnificent stone entryway, which today leads into a large marble-floored reception area accented with genuine suits of armor. Antiques are generously distributed throughout the grand, high-ceilinged public rooms. The bedrooms are comfortably furnished with occasional antiques, hand-woven rugs, and original art. Of the three suites, number 229 is most impressive: on two levels, it has vaulted ceilings and a view across the rooftops to the cathedral. Some front doubles also look onto the cathedral square, but they are noisier than the interior rooms. Breakfast is served in the cozy English-pub-style bar. The restaurant is quite good, although somewhat lacking in ambiance. The hotel is a fine choice in the ancient walled town of Ávila, both for its location and creative maintenance of its historic situation.

GRAN HOTEL PALACIO VALDERRÁBANOS
Manager: Tomas Beltran
Plaza de la Catedral, 9
05005 Ávila, Spain
Tel: (920) 21.10.23, Fax: (920) 25.16.91
73 rooms, Double: Pts 15,000*
*IVA not included, breakfast Pts 1,000
Open all year, Credit cards: all major
Restaurant open daily
113 km NW of Madrid
Michelin Maps 444
Region: Castilla y León

If you enjoy cozy, family-run hotels brimming with warmth and charm, the Hostería de Bracamonte will surely win your heart. This beige, stone mansion with wrought-iron balconies is typical of the many 16th-century homes that line the narrow streets in the spectacular walled city of Ávila. As soon as you step into the large reception room you also step back in time. You see to your left under an arched doorway a picture-perfect dining room with rustic charm—just a cluster of small wooden tables, dressed with fresh flowers and soft lighting, set against exposed stone walls. Also off the reception lounge is a sunny enclosed courtyard with greenery lacing the walls, an old well, stone oven, and wooden farm implements. The hotel also has an appealing bar plus a second beautiful dining room. A maze of immaculately kept narrow hallways lined with tapestries, antique chests, old clocks, and baskets of flowers lead to the guestrooms. Some bedrooms have genuine antiques, but all the furniture, even if new, blends with the old style. Each bedroom has its own tiled bathroom, usually with a small bathtub. There are several suites with two bedrooms, but unless you are traveling with a family, the regular doubles are certainly satisfactory. One of my favorites, room 108, has a double four-poster bed. If you prefer twin beds, room 114, decorated in tones of beiges and whites, is very pretty.

HOSTERÍA DE BRACAMONTE
Owner: Family Costa
Bracamonte 6
05001 Ávila, Spain
Tel: (920) 25.12.80 & (920) 25.38.38, No fax
20 rooms, Double: Pts 8,250–10,300*
*IVA not included, breakfast Pts 500
Open all year, Credit cards: MC, VS
Restaurant closed Tuesdays
113 km NW of Madrid
Michelin Map 444, Region: Castilla y León

The Parador de Ávila is tucked within the walls of Ávila, the first fortified Romanesque city in Europe. Partially installed within the 15th-century noble home of Piedras Albas, both the renovated palace and its new addition are in keeping with the original architectural style. The massive granite, limestone, and wrought-iron staircase off the lobby testifies to the success of this intention. The gracefully columned interior patio's focus is on its stone bull—a traditional symbol of nobility in the ancient Iberian past. In the bar are Arabic tiles salvaged from the original patio of the palace. After being closed for complete renovation, the parador reopened in 1996. We have not had the opportunity to see the hotel since its facelift, but if it follows the pattern of other paradors that have been rejuvenated, it should be more outstanding than ever. With Spain's top-notch decorators redoing the interior, you can expect the decor to be lovely. Note: While staying at the parador, be sure to stroll in the evening along the city ramparts.

PARADOR DE ÁVILA
Manager: Sr. Juan de la Torre
Calle Marqués Canales de Chozas, 2
05001 Ávila, Spain
Tel: (920) 21.13.40, Fax: (920) 22.61.66
61 rooms, Double: Pts 15,000*
*IVA not included, breakfast Pts 1,300
Open all year, Credit cards: all major
Restaurant open daily
113 km NW of Madrid
Michelin Map 444, Region: Castilla y León

The Colón is a stately hotel with some elegant touches, built in 1951 right in the middle of the enchanting Gothic Quarter (*Barrio Gótico*) of Barcelona. The lobby is entered up a broad, cream-carpeted stairway which passes through an impressive, square stone arch. The decor here, as throughout the hotel's public rooms, is perfectly lovely and makes you want to linger to watch the passersby in front of the massive cathedral across the street. On certain days local folklore buffs gather here for a session of the regional dance, the *sardanya* (ask at the hotel desk for the current schedule). Some 34 of its rooms overlook the city's famous cathedral—a few have terraces. When making reservations request a room with a terrace, preferably a quieter location on one of the upper floors, and, if the budget allows, a suite or double room with a sitting area, for more money, but also more space. All of the rooms have wonderful high ceilings and are accented with old-world touches which lend an intimate feeling to this fairly big hotel. The Colón is a good, not-too-expensive hotel which enjoys an incomparable location.

HOTEL COLÓN
Avenida de la Catedral, 7
08002 Barcelona, Spain
Tel: (93) 30.11.404, Fax: (93) 31.72.915
147 rooms, Double: Pts 23,700*
*IVA not included, breakfast Pts 1,700
Open all year, Credit cards: all major
Restaurant open daily
Across from cathedral in Gothic Quarter
Michelin Map 443, Region: Catalonia

Built in 1899 as an elegant mansion, Duques de Bergara still maintains the ambiance of a private home. From the outside, the hotel has an art-deco feel, created by a design of windows and balconies. In the center of the building there are four strips of balconies, each strip having six windows which are divided by stone columns, and to each side are single, iron-railed balconies. To enter, ornate front doors swing open to reveal an extraordinary floor with a harlequin design of black-, white-, and rose-colored marble. Enhancing the drama, a white marble staircase leads to the upper floors. Tucked under the stairs is a modern reception desk. Another architectural feature that adds to the richness of the interior is a charming stained-glass skylight. The bedrooms do not continue the old-world ambiance—they look like modern-day guestrooms seen in good hotels all over the world, with built-in headboards, good reading lights, TVs, mini-bars, and desks. Like the bedrooms, the bathrooms are almost identical, with handsome gray-and-white-grained marble walls and sinks. The Duques de Bergara has a large dining room with modern chairs. For warm days, there is a small balcony where breakfast can be enjoyed outside. The Duques de Bergara is a good choice for a well-located hotel that is not too expensive.

DUQUES DE BERGARA
Manager: Josep Balmanya
Bergara, 11
08002 Barcelona , Spain
Tel: (93) 426.26.00, Fax: (93) 426 04 00
150 rooms, Double: Pts 22,900*
*IVA not included, breakfast Pts 1,500
Open all year, Credit cards: all major
Restaurant open daily
In heart of Barcelona near Plaza Cataluña
Michelin Map 443, Region: Catalonia

Although not in the old quarter of Barcelona, the Gallery Hotel is close to very good shopping and within walking distance to most points of interest. A brochure available at the front desk outlines five tours you can take on foot from the hotel and what to see along the way. From the exterior, the Gallery Hotel does not have much to distinguish it from many other modern hotels—it has an unadorned stone façade with identical rows of windows facing the tree-lined street. However, once you are through the front door, there is an exceptionally cheerful, inviting ambiance. Large windows face onto the street, so the room is filled with sunlight during the day. A hand-loomed carpet adds accent to the creamy marble floor—a pretty color that is repeated on the walls. Dark-brown leather sofas, oil paintings, and potted plants give an ambiance that is neither modern nor antique, but just one of timeless good taste. Just beyond the reception area, a few steps lead up to the Café de Gallery, a pleasant dining room with one wall of glass which opens onto one of the hotel's nicest features—a courtyard where dark-green wrought-iron chairs and tables are romantically enclosed by a high wall draped in ivy. The guestrooms are similar in decor, with dark wooden headboards, built-in writing desks, and exceptionally nice bathrooms completely tiled in marble.

GALLERY HOTEL
Manager: Armando Rojas Aleix
Rosellón 245, 08008 Barcelona, Spain
Tel: (93) 415 99 11, Fax: (93) 415 91 84
115 rooms, Double: Pts 27,000*
*IVA not included, breakfast Pts 2,000
Open all year, Credit cards: all major
Restaurant open daily, gym
Off Paseo de Gracia, near Avenida Diagonal
Michelin Map 443, Region: Catalonia

The Hotel Mesón Castilla is a simple two-star hotel, but for those who prefer to watch their pesetas, it is not only moderately priced, but also well located and offers an old-world ambiance. It is on a small side street, just off the Plaza Cataluña and steps from Barcelona's popular Las Ramblas street. The mood is set when you enter into the reception lounge which is paneled (walls and ceiling) with a dark wood. Torch-like wall lamps give the room an almost mock-medieval look. A larger guest lounge and breakfast room are located one level up where the mood of days gone by continues. Here you find colorful antique wooden chairs with gilt trim, large wall murals, and stained-glass windows. A lighter note appears in arched windows which open off the breakfast room to a small inner garden courtyard. The bedrooms display the same style: each is individual in decor, but with similar furnishings of ornate painted headboards and coordinating chairs and chests. Some of these pieces of richly painted furniture are exceptionally handsome antiques, while others seem to be reproductions. Although this is a "budget" hotel, the bathrooms are newly remodeled and the rooms all have air conditioning, TVs, and direct-dial telephones. Just 50 meters from the hotel is the new museum of contemporary art (MACBA). Another bonus–there's a parking garage next door.

HOTEL MESÓN CASTILLA
Manager: Maria Quinto
Valldoncella Street, 5
08001 Barcelona, Spain
Tel: (93) 318 21 82, Fax: (93) 412 40 20
www.karenbrown.com/spaininns/hotelmesoncastilla.html
56 rooms, Double: Pts 12,000–17,000*
*IVA not included, breakfast Pts 850
Open all year, Credit cards: all major
No restaurant, breakfast only
In heart of city next to Plaza Cataluña
Michelin Map 443, Region: Catalonia

The Montecarlo, originally a private palace, has one of the prettiest hotel façades in Barcelona. Facing directly onto one of Barcelona's most colorful streets, La Rambla (affectionately known as "Las Ramblas"), the hotel looks like an ornate wedding cake with tiers of fancy frosting. The four-room-wide, cream-colored building rises six stories high—each floor a fantasy of ornate balconies and baroque stucco designs. The opulence of the exterior is not reflected in the decor of the reception area, or beyond in the lounge, bar, and breakfast room. Here you find a very contemporary look with white marble floors, leather couches, glass-topped coffee tables, and white wooden columns. Oil paintings accenting white walls add a more traditional touch. One floor up, the mood changes dramatically in the sumptuous lounge where the original architectural features have been meticulously restored, including a handsome, wood-paneled ceiling, crystal chandeliers, ornate fireplace, fancy wall sconces, gilt mirrors, and ornate windows. The traditionally furnished, air-conditioned bedrooms are all similar in decor and have good reading lamps, writing desks, mini-bars, TVs, and safe deposit boxes. There is no restaurant but the hotel has an extensive menu from which guests can order room service. The Montecarlo offers exceptional value for a friendly hotel with quality at a moderate price. Note: The hotel has a parking garage at pts 2,000 per day.

HOTEL MONTECARLO
Manager: Carlos Sanchez-Azor
La Rambla, 124
08002 Barcelona, Spain
Tel: (93) 41.20.404, Fax: (93) 31.87.323
76 rooms, Double: Pts 16,400-19,500*
*IVA not included, breakfast Pts 1,400
Open all year, Credit cards: all major
No restaurant, breakfast only
In heart of Barcelona on "Las Ramblas"
Michelin Map 443, Region: Catalonia

"Palace" denotes luxury, and this lovely old lady (formerly known as the Ritz) lives up to her name. The 1919 hotel has recently undergone extensive remodeling and the old rooms have only gained in ambiance. The walls are painted in soft colors and climb to ceilings that are at least 4 meters high. The bedrooms are immense by modern hotel standards, and furnished handsomely in old-world style—what the Spanish call *al gran estilo*. Salvador Dali's favorite room, and ours, is number 110, with a sunken Roman bath and its bed tucked into an alcove. The renovation of the Palace Hotel's public rooms is masterful, and the resulting lobby, central hall, lounges, and excellent restaurants are elegant without being intimidating. Gleaming marble floors, shiny, solid brass fixtures, stunning crystal chandeliers, gilded mirrors, bathtubs you sink into, subdued piano music, finest quality linens, turn-down service at night—all add up to a nostalgic, old-fashioned luxury and refined grace. The service is nothing short of perfection, and the English-speaking concierges go out of their way to anticipate your needs—a real asset in this city with so much to offer. You will feel pampered at the Palace and that is a feeling hard to come by in large city hotels these days.

PALACE HOTEL
Manager: Miguel Eugene
Gran Via de les Corts Catalanes, 668
08010 Barcelona, Spain
Tel: (93) 31.85.200, Fax:(93) 31.80.148
E-mail: ritz@ritzbcn.com
123 rooms, Double: Pts 35,000–43,000*
*IVA not included, breakfast Pts 2,450
Open all year, Credit cards: all major
Restaurant open daily
In the center of Barcelona
Michelin Map 443, Region: Catalonia

This fortress parador on the sea is undoubtedly one of the most remarkable in Spain. Isolated on a tiny, craggy peninsula just southwest of the little fishing village of Bayona, it is encircled by the ramparts of the former fortress of Monte Real, which protect it on three sides from the wild, crashing sea. The bedrooms, with wooden floors and ceilings, are large and charmingly furnished. Request well in advance a room with a view to the sea to fully appreciate the beauty of this popular spot. Room 102—with its circular corner balcony, private sitting room, and four-poster canopy beds—is spectacular and worth the splurge. Lovely antiques are as at home here and throughout the hotel as the comfortable, traditional wood and leather Spanish furniture. With its massive stone stairway and original stone, domed ceiling, the lobby is stunning and an interior patio with its fountain is delightful. An elegant dining room is found off the lobby and a more informal tavern, *La Pinta*, is located on the grounds overlooking the sea. Several days could easily be enjoyed in this romantic, luxurious hotel with its dramatic backdrop of the clear Atlantic Ocean. Note: As we go to press, the Parador de Gondomar is closed for renovations, but is planning to reopen in mid-April, 1997.

PARADOR CONDE DE GONDOMAR
Manager: Rafael Vázquez
36300 Bayona (Pontevedra), Spain
Tel: (986) 35.50.00, Fax: (986) 35.50.76
128 rooms, Double: Pts 20,000*
*IVA not included, breakfast Pts 1,400
Open all year, Credit cards: all major
Restaurant open daily, pool
114 km SW of Santiago de Compostela
21 km SW of Vigo
Michelin Map 441, Region: Galicia

The Hotel Aigua Blava (located on Spain's most dramatic stretch of coast, the beautiful Costa Brava) has a prime position on a promontory overlooking an incredibly blue inlet dotted with boats and rocky beaches. The Capella family converted their home into a small hotel in 1940 after it was returned to them following the disastrous Civil War. The original owner, the much-loved Xiquet Sabater who warmly welcomed all the guests, died in 1995, but his nephew, Juan (who worked with Xiquet for 46 years), has taken over the management and continues to run the hotel in the same friendly manner as his uncle. Now a fairly large hotel, the Aigua Blava retains the atmosphere of several homes jumbled together around flowered terraces and *rinconcitos* (little corners). Decorated by family members, each room is unique—from simple to elaborate—and many have sea views and terraces (for a surcharge). Set under a slanted ceiling, the Chez Xiquet room (containing family memorabilia) looks out to a large terrace and a fantastic view. For any room, however, reservations should be made well in advance during high season, as many guests return here year after year for their week or two in the sun. For a relaxing sojourn in an enchanting seaside spot with a family atmosphere, you can't go wrong at the Aigua Blava.

HOTEL AIGUA BLAVA
Manager: Juan Gispert
Playa de Fornells
17255 Begur-Aiguablava (Gerona), Spain
Tel: (972) 62.20.58, Fax: (972) 62.21.12
E-mail: habsa@ccalgir.es
90 rooms, Double: Pts 13,700–18,600*
*IVA not included, breakfast Pts 1,600
Open: late Feb to early Nov, Credit cards: all major
Restaurant open daily, pool
116 km NE of Barcelona
Michelin Map 443, Region: Catalonia (Costa Brava)

On the high, isolated, tree-covered point of Esmuts, overlooking the open sea on one side and a turquoise bay on the other, sits the Parador "Costa Brava"—a modern, secluded hideaway for the visitor seeking every comfort on the Wild Coast. Unlike most paradors, this one does not strive for an antique ambiance. The attractive public rooms are airy and open, accented in bright spring colors, and the bedrooms are spacious and bright with red-tiled floors and terraces with lovely views of either the ocean or the bay. There are six extra-large special rooms (*habitaciones especiales*), with large round bathtubs, separate, sunken showers, and exercise areas featuring exercycles and weights. For our money, these are special enough to merit the surprisingly few additional pesetas. There is in addition, a public exercise/game room downstairs with saunas. Guests here are two minutes by a footpath from the beach on the bay or can save the effort and choose to lounge around the lovely fresh-water pool overlooking the ocean. For a short or long stay, this contemporary parador above the idyllic white town of Aiguablava is an excellent choice.

PARADOR "COSTA BRAVA"
Manager: Jaime Sebestian Sánchez
Playa de Aiguablava
17255 Begur-Aiguablava (Gerona), Spain
Tel: (972) 62.21.62 Fax (972) 62.21.66
87 rooms, Double: Pts 19,500*
*IVA not included, breakfast Pts 1,300
Open all year, Credit cards: all major
Restaurant open daily, pool
116 km NE of Barcelona
Michelin Map 443, Region: Catalonia (Costa Brava)

Deep in the countryside of almond and olive groves, yet only a 15-minute drive from Ronda, Molino del Santo makes the perfect hub from which to venture out each day to explore the many wonders of Andalusia. Quite truthfully, you might forget all thoughts of sightseeing because the Molino del Santo is such a gem you won't want to leave. Originally an old grain and olive mill, the property was bought in 1987 by Pauline Elkin and Andy Chapell (formerly schoolteachers in England) who converted the mill into an outstanding small inn. The charming old water mill now houses the reception area, lounge, bar, and dining room. Sparkling white-walled guestrooms in cozy cottages, most with their own terrace, have been added over the years. Everything is faultless. The guestrooms are simply but tastefully decorated. Each has tiled floors, comfortable beds with good reading lights, attractive, wooden carved chairs, and handsome fabrics with a hand-loomed look at the windows. Every detail is well thought out by owners who obviously care. The solar-heated pool and the immaculately kept gardens display the same touch of perfection. In the morning, guests linger over breakfast on the flower-bedecked terrace listening to the gurgling mill stream as it meanders below. If you enjoy casual informality, for both price and ambiance, Molino del Santo is absolute perfection.

MOLINO DEL SANTO
Owners: Pauline Elkin & Andy Chapell
Bda. Estacion s/n
29370 Benaoján (Málaga), Spain
Tel: (95) 21.67.151, Fax: (95) 21.67.327
www.karenbrown.com/spaininns/molinodelsanto.html
14 rooms, Double: Pts 10,000–11,650
*IVA not included, breakfast Pts 950
Open Feb to Dec, Credit cards: all major
Restaurant open daily, pool
12 km SW of Ronda
Michelin Map 446, Region: Andalusia

This 12th-century palace on the edge of a sleepy village was practically devastated by the French in 1808, but was rescued and restored by the government as a historical monument. The royal family of Ferdinand and Isabella stayed at this delightful hotel on their pilgrimage to Santiago. Of the original castle, there remains only the Torreón, which can be visited on Friday afternoons. The tower bar, located in the cellar and remarkably reconstructed from the original foundation, is reached down a narrow stone stairway whose thick stone walls are draped with colorful tapestries, and whose vaulted, painted, 11-meter-high wooden ceiling has massive beams which support a huge, antique iron chandelier. Another highlight is the fabulous Mudéjar ceiling in the Salón Artesonado, brought here from the town of San Román del Valle in León and lovingly reassembled. The spacious bedrooms flank long, whitewashed hallways lined with antique benches and have a rustic, almost "western" ambiance, with tile floors and leather furnishings. They have lovely views of the town and countryside, and those on the upper floor have terraces.

PARADOR REY FERNANDO II DE LEÓN
Manager: Maria Concepcion Lechuga
49600 Benavente (Zamora), Spain
Tel: (988) 63.03.00, Fax: (988) 63.03.03
30 rooms, Double: Pts 16,500*
*IVA not included, breakfast Pts 1,300
Open all year, Credit cards: all major
Restaurant open daily
71 km S of León, 60 km N of Zamora
Michelin Maps 441 & 442, Region: Castilla y León

The setting of the Parador Monte Perdido is nothing less than sensational. From Bielsa, the road weaves down a beautiful, narrow valley, following the River Cinca for 14 kilometers, until the way is blocked by granite walls of some of the highest mountains in the Pyrenees. The hotel is perched on the side of the hill, looking across the rushing stream and idyllic meadow to a glacial backdrop of mountains laced with waterfalls. The gray stone building (of relatively new construction) blends well with the rugged landscape. The interior also blends in perfectly—the ambiance is that of a rustic mountain lodge. Throughout the hotel good taste prevails in every detail. The polished pine floors are accented by hand-woven carpets, the light fixtures are of heavy, black wrought-iron, the ceilings are supported by thick beams, the antique wood-paneled walls are accented by handsome oil paintings and framed prints. Green plants flourish in their window settings and comfortable brown leather sofas and chairs form cozy areas for friends to gather before the massive fireplace. The guestrooms have wood-paneled headboards, wrought-iron reading lamps, and sturdy wooden desks and chairs. Ask for the third floor—room 205 promises an unforgettable view!

PARADOR MONTE PERDIDO
Manager: Sra. Alicia Pierrette Bardin
Valle de Pineta
22350 Bielsa (Huesca), Spain
Tel: (974) 50.10.11, Fax: (974) 50.11.88
24 rooms, Double: Pts 16,500*
*IVA not included, breakfast Pts 1,300
Closed mid-Jan to mid-Mar
Credit cards: all major
Restaurant open daily
14 km NW of Bielsa, 184 km N of Lleida
Michelin Map 443, Region: Aragon

For those who want to overnight in Cáceres, the Parador de Cáceres is the choice place to stay. It is difficult to weave your way through the not-too-attractive new section of the city, but be patient and follow the parador signs. The quaint, walled old quarter of Cáceres (named as a national monument) is almost hidden within the new city. However, once through one of the medieval gates, you are suddenly immersed into a well-preserved city which in its heyday was home to many wealthy Spaniards who made their fortunes in the "New World." The 14th-century Parador de Cáceres, just off the Plaza de San Mateo, was built by Don Diego García de Ulloa. Like most of the mansions in town, it has a façade of cut stone with ornamental wrought-iron balconies stretching over the narrow street. Once through the massive doors and up a few steps, you enter an open courtyard and then the lobby. One of the nicest features of the hotel is its several interior gardens and courtyards. My favorite courtyard has whitewashed walls laced with bougainvillea and wicker chairs where you can enjoy the quiet. The guestrooms are large and attractive with tiled floors, white walls, and wooden furniture.

PARADOR DE CÁCERES
Manager: Enrique Comino Aguilar
Calle Ancha, 6
10003 Cáceres, Spain
Tel: (927) 21.17.59, Fax: (927) 21.17.29
31 rooms, Double: Pts 17,500*
*IVA not included, breakfast Pts 1,300
Open all year, Credit cards: all major
Restaurant open daily
265 km N of Seville, 217 km SW of Salamanca
Michelin Map 444, Region: Extremadura

One of the most dramatic paradors in the country, the Duques de Cardona has dominated the fortified town of Cardona for centuries from its 460-meter-high hilltop setting. This site was chosen as a home by the Duke in the 10th century and, although much of the construction is recent, the period flavor and authentic nature of the original building have been maintained. Behind the hotel are a unique 2nd-century tower and 11th-century church along with a beautiful Roman patio from which you can get a "bird's eye" view of the unusual salt hills, the pueblo, and the Pyrenees. All the bedrooms have been totally renovated during 1996. The restaurant is spectacularly situated in a forever-long, dramatic, vaulted-ceilinged room. The ochre-toned walls create a warm glow in the evening, making dinner a special occasion. Although out of the way, this parador offers a memorable night's stay in a carefully renovated historic setting with all the modern comforts of home.

PARADOR DUQUES DE CARDONA
Manager: Francisco Contreras
Castillo s/n
08261 Cardona (Barcelona), Spain
Tel: (93) 86.91.275, Fax: (93) 86.91.636
54 rooms, Double: Pts 17,500*
*IVA not included, breakfast Pts 1,300
Open all year
Credit cards: all major
Restaurant open daily
99 km NE of Barcelona
Michelin Map 443, Region: Catalonia

The exquisite Casa de Carmona, a noble 15th-century palace located in the picturesque town of Carmona, had fallen into sad disrepair when purchased by Sra. Medina. It took five years plus many pesetas, patience, and love to restore this masterpiece to its original grandeur. No expense was spared to bring every modern amenity, yet retain the authentic character of days gone by. From the moment you step through the massive wooden door into an inner courtyard, the magic begins. Wander through the maze of secluded "secret" patios—your heart will be captivated. Potted fruit trees, marble colonnades, fragrant flowers, the singing of birds, and the gentle gurgling of fountains are entrancing. A romantic walled patio with an exquisite formal garden features a picture-perfect swimming pool fed by five fountains. Doña Marta Medina personally oversaw the interior design and each room is outstanding. On the ground floor is a series of secluded lounges, each with elegant, English-style fabrics and superb antiques. Each guestroom has its own personality, yet maintains a similar look of refined elegance. One of my favorites, room 23, has a romantic view of the rooftops of old Carmona studded by many church steeples. As an added bonus, the Casa de Carmona has the personal touch of a manager who truly cares—Doña Marta Medina's personable son, Felipe.

CASA DE CARMONA
Manager: Felipe Guardiola Medina
Plaza de Lasso 1
41410 Carmona in Andalusia (Seville), Spain
Tel: (95) 41.43.300, Fax: (95) 41.43.752
www.karenbrown.com/spaininns/casadecarmona.html
30 rooms, Double: Pts 18,000–34,000*
*IVA not included, breakfast Pts 2,000
Open all year, Credit cards: all major
Restaurant open daily, pool
25 km E of Seville
Michelin Map 446, Region: Andalusia

The Parador de Carmona is ideally located in a small, ancient village, imbued with medieval ambiance, but still only 30 minutes from downtown Seville. Of the three castles built in the walled town of Carmona, one was converted into this parador in 1976. Formerly decorated by the same Moorish architects responsible for the famous Alcázar in Seville, the restoration has preserved the original Moslem flavor while adding rather more modern appointments. You will be charmed from the beginning by the entry through the castle gate into the courtyard surrounded by the restored castle walls. Entry into the building itself transports you into the Moorish past by the fantastic patio with its tiled floor, impressive fountain, and slender, graceful arches and columns. You will be delighted by the intricately patterned, colorful ceramic-tile decor throughout the hotel. The large guestrooms, decorated in traditional Spanish style, maintain the reliable parador high standards. For just a few pesetas more, request one of the 12 rooms with a terrace—and feast your eyes on the wonderful view from the hilltop vantage point over the vast plains below. The same panorama can be enjoyed from the terrace outside the pleasant bar.

PARADOR DE CARMONA
Manager: José María Ronda
41410 Carmona in Andalusia (Sevilla), Spain
Tel: (95) 41.41.010 Fax: (95) 41.41.712
63 rooms, Double: Pts 18,500*
*IVA not included, breakfast Pts 1,300
Open all year Credit cards: all major
Restaurant open daily, pool
44 km E of Seville
Michelin Map 446, Region: Andalusia

Part of the magic of Spain is its surprises. Who could expect to find a restaurant, recommended by Michelin with two red forks, located far off the tourist path in the beautiful, unspoiled countryside of Cantabria? As you drive through this unpopulated area, you will think you are certainly on the wrong road. But, sure enough, in the tiny hamlet of Carmona on a small knoll overlooking a cluster of charming pinkish-stone farmhouses, you find the Venta de Carmona. This nobleman's home, built in 1719 by Don Francisco Díaz, is lovely in its simplicity—a cut-stone, two-story house flanked by twin square towers. The hotel faces an idyllic view of rolling, lush green pastures stretching to wooded hills. The reception area has arched doorways that have been glassed in, allowing the sunlight to brighten the room. Beyond the entry with the reception desk a hallway leads to what makes this hotel so well known—the restaurant. Here you find a very simple dining room with wooden tables and chairs. There is nothing modern to jar the senses. Here country-style meals are served, with regional dishes always featured on the menu. Stairs lead up to the eight guestrooms. These are very basic in decor—just two strips of wood to form the headboards, wooden and leather chairs, and simple bedspreads. Although without an air of sophistication, everything is spotlessly clean and the bathrooms are modern.

VENTA DE CARMONA
Manager: Teresa Martínez Gutiérrez
39014 Carmona (Cantabria), Spain
Tel: (942) 72.80.57, Fax: (942) 32.30.58
9 rooms, Double: Pts 7,000–8,000*
*IVA not included, breakfast Pts 500
Closed Jan to mid-Mar, Credit cards: VS
Restaurant open daily
69 km SW of Santander, 162 km E of Oviedo
Michelin Map 442, Region: Cantabria

The Parador "El Adelantado" is definitely off the beaten path—do not plan to stay here just as a convenient overnight stop, but rather as a sightseeing experience in itself. The address reads Cazorla, but it is actually 25 kilometers away in the Cazorla Sierra nature reserve. Upon reaching Cazorla, follow the signs to the park—the road climbs up from the valley and into the hills. Once beyond the barricade and into the park, it is about 15 kilometers farther to "El Adelantado." The road is well signposted, but be sure to go in daylight or you might get lost. The setting on a small plateau with a sweeping vista of pine-covered mountains is beautiful. On the grassy terrace in front of the hotel there is a large swimming pool that captures the same lovely view. The newly built hotel has a traditional look (which is supposed to resemble an Andalusian farmhouse) with a white stucco façade and red-tiled roof. Inside, the ambiance is appropriately simple. The lounge has leather sofas, an enormous fireplace to warm the room on chilly days, and a spectacular antique oil painting of a hunting scene that almost covers one wall. The dining room has high-backed upholstered chairs, wrought-iron chandeliers, and French doors leading to a terrace. The bedrooms are spacious and nicely decorated with simple wood and leather furniture. Ask for a room with a view (number 1—an enormous room with a balcony—is the very best).

PARADOR "EL ADELANTADO"
Manager: Carmela Doña Diaz
23470 Cazorla (Jaén), Spain
Tel: (953) 72.10.75, Fax: (953) 72.13.03
33 rooms, Double: Pts 15,000*
*IVA not included, breakfast Pts 1,200
Closed mid-Dec 15 to mid-Feb
Credit cards: all major
Restaurant open daily, pool
46 km E of Ubeda
Michelin Maps 444 & 446
Region: Andalusia

Imaginatively and extensively renovated, this relatively recent addition to the parador chain is a member of the select group that merits four stars. It is located just off the main plaza in the charming, historic town of Chinchón (justifiably famous for its anise liqueur). The plaza, with its many overhanging wood balconies, is very picturesque. The parador is installed in a 17th-century Augustinian monastery, and fountains, hanging and terraced gardens, reflecting pools, and worn stone patios soothe the secular guest here with the same tranquillity once treasured by its previous religious residents. The pale-brick-paved central cloister features a glass-enclosed colonnade, lined with antiques and hung with tapestries. The guestrooms are simple and lovely, floored in red tile, with whitewashed walls and colorful wooden beds topped with cream-colored spreads. The rooms in *la parte vieja* overlooking the garden are particularly attractive, and room 8, with a private sitting room and balcony, is superior for not too many more pesetas. The cheerful dining room is accented with colorful *azulejos* (tiles) and offers an interesting variety of dishes. Try to fit in a visit to the historic restaurant Mesón Cuevas de Vino at the top of town, well known locally for its traditional grills and sangría. Note: The central plaza in Chinchón magically transforms into a bullring in summer.

PARADOR DE CHINCHÓN
Manager: José Menguiano Corbacho
Avenida Generalísimo, 1
28370 Chinchón, Spain
Tel: (91) 89.40.836, Fax: (91) 89.40.908
38 rooms, Double: Pts 17,500*
*IVA not included, breakfast Pts 1,300
Open all year, Credit cards: all major
Restaurant open daily, pool
53 km SE of Madrid
Michelin Map 444, Region: Madrid

Spain has so many lovely old cities that some gems almost go unnoticed. Such is the case with Ciudad Rodrigo, a most convenient overnight stop if you are on your way to Portugal. This walled town perched on a gentle hill is charming and delightfully lacking the hustle and bustle of tourists. Happily, the Parador de Ciudad Rodrigo offers excellent accommodations. The hotel is tucked beside the old stone walls, just a few blocks from the Plaza Mayor. The long, low, ivy-covered stone building is dramatized by a tall stone crenelated tower that rises just behind. Although the building is very old, it has been completely remodeled and some of the original old-world ambiance has been lost with the refinement of new construction. The decor, however, is much more tasteful than that found in many of the paradors and the overall look is warm and cheerful. The bedrooms are attractive. Room 26 (overlooking the back garden) is especially appealing, with hand-carved headboards, rustic wood furniture, and colorful striped, hand-loomed draperies and spreads. The lounge has leather sofas and chairs that stand out nicely against the parquet floor. The dining room is handsome with beamed ceiling and leather and wood chairs. One of the nicest features of this parador is its exquisite terraced rear garden, embraced on two sides by the city walls.

PARADOR DE CIUDAD RODRIGO
Manager: Angel Aliste López
Plaza del Castillo, 1
37500 Ciudad Rodrigo (Salamanca), Spain
Tel: (923) 46.01.50, Fax: (923) 46.04.04
27 rooms, Double: Pts 15,000*
*IVA not included, breakfast Pts 1,200
Open all year, Credit cards: all major
Restaurant open daily
294 km W of Madrid, 89 km SW of Salamanca
Michelin Map 441, Region: Castilla y León

The Hotel Albucasis is a welcome oasis of tranquillity in the bustling tourist center of Córdoba, just a short walk to the colorful mosque and other points of cultural interest. Although centrally located in the Old Jewish Quarter (*Barrio de la Judería*) with its maze of narrow, twisting streets, whitewashed houses, pots of colorful flowers, and romantic wrought-iron balconies, the hotel is quiet. Reflecting the Arabic and Roman style, the Albucasis faces onto its own small courtyard with fresh white walls laced with greenery and potted plants. From the courtyard you enter into the reception area that also serves as a bar and breakfast lounge. Light streams in through a wall of French windows, making the room especially cheerful. The decor is simple and uncluttered with white walls, terra cotta floors, and round tables with wooden chairs. There are nine double and six single rooms—all similar in decor with wooden headboards and matching desk and chair. Although not large, the rooms are of ample size so that you do not feel cramped, and the tiled bathroom are spacious. Best of all, this small hotel is spotless and the high standard of management is apparent throughout. There are many larger, more deluxe hotels in Córdoba, but we think this small, simple hotel offers some of the best quality in town. Note: The Albucasis is difficult to find. The best bet is to park your car, and with a detailed map, first find the hotel on foot (then a parking garage is available for Pts 1,900).

HOTEL ALBUCASIS
Owner: Alfonso Salas Camacho
Buen Pastor, 11
14003 Córdoba, Spain
Tel & fax: (957) 47.86.25
15 rooms, Double: Pts 9,500–9,950*
*IVA included, breakfast Pts 850
Closed Jan to Apr, Credit cards: MC, VS
No restaurant, breakfast only
143 km NE of Seville
Michelin Maps 444 & 446, Region: Andalusia

The grounds of this parador include acres of grassy hillside, a huge blue swimming pool overlooking the city, and tree-shaded areas ideal for cool walks on hot days—very inviting for travelers who simply want to relax and spend time in the sun. Being of the modern persuasion, this parador does not have the usual antique ambiance—that is certainly not to say that it is not attractive, however. The public rooms seem to cover almost as many acres as the lawn and command spectacular views of the valley and the city. Appointments are equally modern, with occasional tapestries and old-style chandeliers to remind you of the past. The spacious bedrooms are similarly furnished in contemporary Spanish style, and for a ten percent surcharge you can procure a room with the same gorgeous view you see from the lobby and dining room—over the lawn and trees to the city below. The vista is especially attractive at night. All this natural (and man-made) air-conditioned luxury is still only 15 minutes by car or taxi from the Mezquita and the fascinating and colorful old Jewish Quarter.

PARADOR DE LA ARRUZAFA
Manager: Manuel Vietes Rodriguez
Carretera de El Brillante
Avenida de la Arruzafa, s/n
14012 Córdoba, Spain
Tel: (957) 27.59.00, Fax: (957) 57.28.04.09
*94 rooms, Double: Pts 15,000 **
**IVA not included, breakfast Pts 1,300*
Open all year, Credit cards: all major
Restaurant open daily, pool
143 km NE of Seville
Michelin Maps 444 & 446, Region: Andalusia

Can Fabrica is a charming 17th-century stone farmhouse, only a little over an hour's drive from Barcelona yet blissfully set in the Catalan countryside. In every direction all you see are rolling fields dotted with woodlands and the Pyrenees rising in the distance. This is a simple place to stay—definitely not for those seeking sophisticated luxury, but if you are traveling on a budget, the ambiance, the amenities, the cooking, and the warmth of welcome far exceed what you would expect for such a modest price. (There is even a large swimming pool tucked on the terrace above the inn.) There are six moderate-sized bedrooms, each with a private bath, sweetly decorated by Marta, your enchanting hostess who speaks good English. All of the rooms are tastefully decorated with pieces of furniture either handed down as family heirlooms or found at antique shops and restored by Marta herself. One of my favorites is a corner room with pastel-blue walls, beamed ceiling, an antique queen-sized bed, and an old-fashioned washstand. The dining room, where simple, very good, home-cooked meals are served, exudes a rustic charm. Marta's husband, Ramón, is also very involved in the operation of Can Fabrica and gladly helps guests plan excursions to explore this lovely niche of Spain. Note: The hotel is tucked out in the countryside—ask for a brochure with directions.

CAN FABRICA
Owner: Marta Casanovas-Bohigas
Sta. Llogaia del Terri
17844 Cornellà del Terri (Girona), Spain
Tel & fax: (972) 59.46.29
6 rooms, Double: Pts 7,600*
*IVA & breakfast included
Open from Easter–Christmas
Credit cards: MC, VS
Restaurant open daily (hotel guests only), pool
112 km NE of Barcelona,14 km N of Girona
Michelin Map 443, Region: Catalonia

Have you ever wished you had friends in Spain who owned a romantic hideaway where you could spend your holiday? Wish no more. Staying at Finca Listonero, you will feel like a pampered guest in a private home—and indeed you are. Finca Listonero is the home of Graeme Gibson (originally from Australia) and David Rice (originally from Ireland), who for many years owned an extremely popular restaurant on the Costa del Sol, followed by an equally successful restaurant in Sydney. Now back in Spain they have found their dream—a 300-year-old farmhouse tucked up in the hills, not far from the quaint Moorish coastal town of Mojacar. Graeme is an interior designer, and David a talented chef—a perfect combination for their latest venture. The farmhouse, painted a deep rosy-pink, enhanced by bright-green shutters, laced with vines, and accented by a profusion of potted plants, is a happy sight to behold. Inside, the cheerful use of color continues: deep rose and green remain the predominant theme, but other colors are used boldly throughout. The eclectic decor reflects Graeme's and David's years of travel. Art Nouveau, European, and Oriental antiques; English fabrics; Spanish tiles; and hand-loomed carpets are cleverly combined to create a welcoming ambiance. Each bedroom has its own color scheme—the Blue Room, featuring pretty English floral fabric, is especially inviting. Finca Listonero makes a good place to relax after a few days in Granada (a two hour drive away). Note: Plan to dine here—David's meals are truly memorable.

FINCA LISTONERO
Owners: Graeme Gibson & David Rice
Cortijo Grande
04639 Turre (Almería), Spain
Tel & fax: (950) 47.90.94
5 rooms, Double: Pts 10,000–12,000*
*IVA not included, breakfast included
Closed all year, Credit cards: MC, VS
Restaurant closed Sundays
288 km E of Málaga
Michelin Map 446, Region: Andalusia

You cannot help falling in love with the Hotel del Oso, superbly located in the glorious mountain range called Picos de Europa. Although it is officially rated two stars, many deluxe hotels could take lessons from this gem. Rarely do you find such a combination of warmth of welcome, faultless housekeeping, superb cuisine, and beautiful displays of flowers. Undoubtedly this degree of excellence is the work of the Rivas family. Sr. Rivas designed the hotel which, although of new construction, maintains a traditional air, blending in with the other beige stone buildings in the region. His charming, friendly wife is the talented chef, and people come from afar to sample her fabulous food (specialties are regional dishes). However, the greatest asset is what few other hotels can offer—four wonderful, talented daughters (Ana, Irene, Teresa, and Cari) who assist in every aspect of the running of the hotel. Their sparkle and genuine hospitality would be difficult to duplicate. On the ground floor there is a wood-paneled reception room, a large dining room, and a cozy bar which opens up to a terrace where tables overlook a crystal-clear stream. The guestrooms are located on two upper floors (each level has its own sitting room). Each of the bedrooms has the same furniture—only the matching fabrics used on the spreads, the curtains, and the cushions vary. Ask for one of the rooms numbered 209 to 213—these have some of the best mountain views.

HOTEL DEL OSO
Manager: Ana Rivas Gonzalez
39539 Cosgaya-Potes (Cantabria), Spain
Tel: (942) 73.30.18, Fax: (942) 73.30.36
www.karenbrown.com/spaininns/hoteldeloso.html
36 rooms, Double: Pts 8,800–9,800*
*IVA not included, breakfast Pts 625
Closed Jan to mid-Feb, Credit cards: MC, VS
Restaurant open daily
129 km SW of Santander, 18 km SW of Potes
Michelin Map 442, Region: Cantabria

One of the latest stars to be added to the Spanish parador group is set in the spectacular 16th-century Convento de San Pablo. The hotel, crowning a rocky promontory, faces across the gorge to Cuenca, a breathtaking town hewn out of the rocks. When staying at the Convento de San Pablo, you can leave your car parked at the parador and take the long footbridge that spans the gorge between two giant outcrops of rock. The interior has been restored with skill to preserve the authentic soul of the old convent. The cloister still remains as the garden in the core of the hotel. The colonnaded walkway (which wraps around the cloister on four sides) now serves as a lounge area for guests, and is furnished with brown wicker furniture accented with cushions in tones of rust and green. The bar, entered through an ornately decorated portal, has dark-green wicker chairs with cushions in green and terra cotta, repeating the color in the potted palms and tiled floor. The vaulted ceiling is elaborately frescoed. In one of the wings there is a beautifully restored, tiny chapel. The dining room is dramatic, with a row of tiered chandeliers highlighting the intricately paneled ceiling. The guestrooms are decorated with reproduction painted headboards and floral-patterned draperies which are color-coordinated with bedspreads and chair coverings.

PARADOR CONVENTO DE SAN PABLO
Manager: José Navio Serrano
Paseo Hoz del Huécar, s/n
16001 Cuenca, Spain
Tel: (969) 23.23.20, Fax: (969) 23.25.34
63 rooms, Double: Pts 17,500 *
*IVA not included, breakfast Pts 1,300
Open all year, Credit cards: all major
Restaurant open daily, pool
164 km SE of Madrid, 209 km NW of Valencia
Michelin Maps 444 & 445, Region: Castilla-La Mancha

The Posada de San José, located in the heart of the walled city of Cuenca, is truly a gem. The inn is tucked onto a tiny cobbled lane behind the church on the Plaza Mayor in this fascinating old city. The entrance is easy to miss—just an antique doorway with a niche alcove above it featuring a charming statue of San José holding the infant Christ. Although not decorator-perfect, the uncontrived ambiance is one of a family-owned hotel that is striving (successfully) on a limited budget to stay true to the authentic, old-world charm of this 16th-century home with its thick stuccoed walls, beamed ceilings, and fabulous old tiled floors. The owners are always on the premises to assure that guests are well taken care of. Jennifer Morter (raised in Canada) speaks perfect English and is especially adept at lending a helping hand when language seems to be a barrier. There is no restaurant, but an ever-so-cozy bar offers light suppers and snacks. The hotel terraces down the hillside, providing most of the guestrooms with stunning views across the Huecar river gorge to the Convento de San Pablo, which is romantically illuminated at night. All of the rooms are pleasant: my favorites are room 33, an incredibly lovely corner room with two balconies, and room 24 with a small alcove with French windows opening to a glorious view. For value and charm, the Posada de San José is a real winner.

POSADA DE SAN JOSÉ
Owners: Jennifer Morter & Antonio Cortinas
Julian Romero 4
16001 Cuenca, Spain
Tel: (969) 21.13.00, Fax: (969) 23.03.65
E-mail: psanjose@arrakis.es
www.karenbrown.com/spaininns/posadadesanjose.html
29 rooms, Double: Pts 8,900*
*IVA not included, breakfast Pts 525
Open all year, Credit cards: all major
Bar serving light meals closed Mondays
164 km SE of Madrid, 209 km NW of Valencia
Michelin Maps 444 & 445, Region: Castilla-La Mancha

The stately Hotel Victoria Palace, with its English-country-manor flavor, is located a stone's throw from one of the most popular tourist attractions in Spain, yet offers a quiet and luxurious refuge from El Escorial's day trippers and the fast-lane pace of Madrid. To see the whole monastery-cum-palace properly, you will need two visits, and this hotel will make that a pleasant prospect. A welcoming garden café in front (seemingly created for the turn-of-the-century tea-drinking crowd) entices you into the marble-floored lobby and up a graceful, brass-railed double stairway to a spacious lounge with cozy brocade chairs, rich wood paneling, and corner fireplace. Upstairs, past wide landings dappled with sunlight streaming through stained glass, are tastefully appointed bedrooms with lofty ceilings, polished wood floors, and large windows overlooking the gardens. The service, though a bit formal, is correct and knowledgeable. By contrast, the warmly intimate, pub-style bar is charming and friendly. This impressive hotel, with its unique spired roof, will enhance a trip to Phillip II's palace.

HOTEL VICTORIA PALACE
Owner/Manager: J. Miguel Rico
Juan de Toledo, 4
28200 San Lorenzo de El (Madrid), Spain
Tel: (91) 89.01.511, Fax: (91) 89.01.248
87 rooms, Double: Pts 16,200*
*IVA not included, breakfast Pts 1,050
Open all year, Credit cards: all major
Restaurant open daily, pool
55 km NW of Madrid
Michelin Map 444, Region: Madrid

This parador has a distinctly different flavor from most of the other paradors in Spain. Instead of presenting an old-world look, there is an unpretentious, rather masculine, nautical ambiance—a most appropriate theme for its waterfront position. The square, three-story building (painted white with stone trim around the windows) is not very old, but definitely has a traditional feel. The setting (particularly if you are interested in ships) is very interesting: the hotel sits on a high embankment overlooking Ferrol's long row of naval yards, and beyond to the commercial docks. A wide terrace in front of the hotel has benches, rose gardens, a gigantic anchor, and several antique canons—poised guarding the harbor. To the right of the lobby (which has a handsome floor with a harlequin pattern of alternating large dark-gray and beige marble tiles) is a large lounge which looks a bit like a men's club with dark-red leather chairs and sofas, potted palms, fresh flowers, nautical prints on the walls, and a marvelous antique oil painting of two ships in the midst of battle. A sunny dining room with bentwood chairs set around small tables and two entire walls of windows overlooks the harbor. The guestrooms are spacious and traditional in decor. Number 25, a corner room, is especially large and has a great view of the harbor.

PARADOR DE FERROL
Manager: Amando Baños
Plaza Eduardo Pondal
15401 Ferrol (La Coruña), Spain
Tel & fax: (981) 35.67.20
39 rooms, Double: Pts 15,000*
*IVA not included, breakfast Pts 1,200
Open all year, Credit cards: all major
Restaurant open daily
104 km NE of Santiago de Compostela
Michelin Map 441, Region: Galicia

Granada's Parador San Francisco is the most popular parador in Spain—snaring a room is well nigh impossible in the high season unless reservations are made months in advance. An excellent alternate choice is the Hotel Alhambra Palace, a deluxe, well-located hotel with splendid views. From here you can gaze out from your room over the Alhambra, the cathedral, and the historic city through Moorish arched windows. The Hotel Alhambra Palace is on the road that weaves up through the wooded parklike grounds to the gate where you buy your tickets to visit the Alhambra. From the hotel it is a pleasant walk to this entrance. Opened in 1910, the Hotel Alhambra Palace has long been a mainstay of the Alhambra hotels. Andrés Segovia, the famous Spanish guitarist, played his first concert here, and it remains a favorite hotel choice in Granada for most visiting dignitaries. The sumptuous decor of the public rooms is enchantingly, almost overwhelmingly, Moorish—from the intricately carved ceilings, unusual decorative touches, to the symmetrically placed arched doorways and colorful tiled walls. The bedrooms are large and comfortable (the Andrés Segovia suite is magnificent). The hotel is air conditioned—a blessing in Granada's hot summer months. Savor one of the best views in Spain from the expansive bar area or the outdoor terrace.

HOTEL ALHAMBRA PALACE
Manager: Francisco Hernandez
Peña Partida, 2
18009 Granada, Spain
Tel: (958) 22.14.68, Fax: (958) 22.64.04
145 rooms, Double: Pts 21,200*
*IVA not included, breakfast Pts 1,350
Open all year, Credit cards: all major
Restaurant open daily
127 km NE of Málaga
Michelin Map 446, Region: Andalusia

Although officially holding just a one-star rating, the Hotel America is in our estimation far superior in many ways to some so-called "superior" class hotels. Its most outstanding feature is its location. No matter what you pay, you cannot be any closer to the portion of the Alhambra reserved for paying sightseers—the Hotel America is on the citadel grounds, just steps away from the entrance. But the America has more than location. The hotel is a pretty, cream-colored stucco, three-story building with red-tiled roof, enhanced by lacy vines and black wrought-iron light fixtures. To the left of the reception area is a sitting area with a cozy clutter of old-fashioned furniture. When days are balmy, guests' favorite place to congregate is the inner courtyard—an inviting small oasis enhanced by blue-and-white-tile tables and an overhead leafy trellis. My favorite room of all is the hotel's romantic little dining room, a real gem with beautiful antique paneling and walls decorated by oil paintings, handsome mirrors, and colorful plates. There are only eight tables, surrounded by pretty, country-style chairs with rush seats. The meals are reasonably priced and excellent. Remember that this is a simple hotel, so if you are fussy and like everything just perfect, this is not the place for you, but the Hotel America makes an excellent choice for a cozy, family-run hotel with an unbeatable location.

HOTEL AMERICA
Manager: Maribel Alconchel
53, Real de La Alhambra
18009 Granada, Spain
Tel: (958) 22.74.71, Fax: (958) 22.74.70
13 rooms, Double: Pts 15,200*
*IVA & breakfast included
Open Mar to Nov 9, Credit cards: all major
Restaurant open daily
127 km NE of Málaga
Michelin Map 446, Region: Andalusia

This is Spain's most famous and popular parador, and as a result reservations must be secured at least six to eight months in advance. Installed in a 15th-century convent, restoration has been carried out so as to retain much of the original structure, including the chapel where Queen Isabella was first buried before being moved to the cathedral downtown. Outside, lovely Alhambra-style gardens and walks blend well with the neighboring marvel. Inside, the decor is a mixture of Moorish and Christian. The former shows up in wonderful ceilings, carved doors, ceramic tile, and the graceful arches in the beautiful interior patio. The public rooms are rich in antique religious art objects— paintings, sculpture, and colorful tapestries. The guestrooms are comfortably unostentatious, with period accents and views varying from excellent to ordinary. The dining room is in a style apart—its walls are lined with handsome contemporary abstract paintings. An outstanding feature of the parador is its secluded location within the Alhambra—an oasis of calm in the usually bustling tourist area.

PARADOR SAN FRANCISCO
Manager: Juan Antonio Gianello Louro
Real de La Alhambra s/n
18009 Granada, Spain
Tel: (958) 22.14.40, Fax: (958) 22.22.64
38 rooms, Double: Pts 33,000*
*IVA not included, breakfast Pts 1,600
Open all year, Credit cards: all major
Restaurant open daily
127 km NE of Málaga
Michelin Map 446, Region: Andalusia

The Parador de Gredos, built in 1926 as a hunting lodge for King Alfonso XIII, was the very first in what has grown to be a large network of government-sponsored hotels. Surrounded by pine forests, mountains, large rock formations, green meadows, and rushing streams, the hotel is a favorite weekend getaway for residents of Madrid. The parador's charm is not immediately apparent: at first glance, it appears as a large, rather sterile, gray stone building with a French gray-tile mansard roof. Once you are inside, the charm of the hotel emerges. The decor is most appealing: nothing is cute or contrived—just a simple, hunting-lodge ambiance. The floors are wood-planked, the ceilings timbered, the furniture mostly leather. The white walls are decorated with hunting scenes, prints of wild animals found in the area, and hunting trophies. Wrought-iron chandeliers hang from beamed ceilings and fresh green plants are strategically placed throughout the immaculately kept rooms. The emphasis is not on antiques, but there are many hand-carved chests, authentic high-backed benches, fine writing desks, clocks, and rustic-style tables. The guestrooms continue the simple hunting-lodge look with wooden furniture, hand-woven-look drapes and spreads, and pretty scatter rugs on hardwood floors. There is a large play yard with gym sets and slides for young guests on a terrace behind the hotel.

PARADOR DE GREDOS
Manager: Fernando Alonso Almeida
05635 Sierra de Gredos (Ávila), Spain
Tel: (920) 34.80.48, Fax: (920) 34.82.05
77 rooms, Double: Pts 13,500*
*IVA not included, breakfast Pts 1,300
Open all year, Credit cards: all major
Restaurant open daily
170 km W of Madrid, 60 km SW of Ávila
Michelin Map 444
Region: Castilla y León

Shadowed by the famous monastery's towers, this inn was a Hieronymite hospital and pharmacy in the 16th century, but since the days of Ferdinand and Isabella has sheltered those who came to worship. Until 1960 visitors exchanged a daily donation of a mere 50 pesetas for accommodation. Still today, for value received and atmosphere, follow the footsteps of the faithful to this inn, as there is nothing comparable in Guadalupe, or anywhere else. Sharing and managing the edifice is an active Franciscan religious order, whose guides regularly conduct an insider's tour of their monastery, museum, and cathedral—a crazy and wonderful mixture of Mudéjar and Gothic architecture. The hotel rooms overlook the original stone-arched and paved hospital patio. Their decor varies wildly—some incredible, but all adequate and all with baths. To stay here is to live and breathe the history of Spain. Request a room on the gallery: number 120 is especially nice—given to visiting religious notables; the second-floor corner suite (number 108) is baroquely elegant and many third-floor rooms boast original Mudéjar ceilings. Delicious fare and homemade wine are served under a high wooden ceiling in a richly paneled dining room.

HOSPEDERÍA EL REAL MONASTERIO
Plaza S.M. Juan Carlos I
10140 Guadalupe (Cáceres), Spain
Tel: (927) 36.70.00, Fax: (927) 36.71.77
47 rooms, Double: Pts 7,750*
*IVA not included, breakfast Pts 825
Closed mid-Jan to mid-Feb, Credit cards: MC, VS
Restaurant open daily
225 km SW of Madrid, 129 km NE of Mérida
Michelin Map 444, Region: Extremadura

Built in the 14th century as a hospital to shelter and minister to pilgrims who came to venerate the famous Black Virgin of Guadalupe, this parador now provides admirably for the needs of the modern-day visitor. It is located directly across the street from the Franciscan monastery in a village from which the Catholic monarchs granted permission for Columbus's ships to depart for the New World. Whitewashed, with red roof tiles, the Zurbarán invites you to enjoy its cool, Moorish gardens sheltering a sparkling turquoise pool, and to dine on its outdoor terrace overlooking a tiled, Mudéjar fountain. Thanks to the local craftsmen, colorful tile is found throughout the hotel: the interior patio is especially lovely. When remodeled, the parador added 20 new rooms, all with garden-view terraces, which maintain the period ambiance faithfully. However, the old rooms with low, stone doorways are still the favorites—some have canopied beds, fireplaces, and balconies (ask for *una habitación antigua con terraza*). But, no matter the room, this is a special inn in a tranquil and picturesque locale.

PARADOR DE GUADALUPE
Manager: José Manuel Piña
Marqués de la Romana, 12
10140 Guadalupe (Cáceres), Spain
Tel: (927) 36.70.75, Fax: (927) 36.70.76
40 rooms, Double: Pts 13,500 *
*IVA not included, breakfast 1,300
Open all year, Credit cards: all major
Restaurant open daily, pool
225 km SW of Madrid, 129 km NE of Mérida
Michelin Map 444, Region: Extremadura

Just after you enter into the walled medieval town of Hondarribia by way of the Santa María gate, a small "Hotel Obispo" sign indicates that you turn right and go around the corner. Here you find wrought-iron gates leading into a completely enclosed courtyard, embraced on one side by the 14th-century ramparts of the town. The lush green lawn studded with colorful beds of well tended flowers is set off to perfection by the austerity of the cut-stone façade. A wide stone staircase leads up from the courtyard to the reception lounge where you might be greeted by the owner, Bihor Alza, who takes a very personal interest in the running of his intimate hotel. Throughout the hotel there are a few antiques plus some reproductions which are enhanced by lovely traditional fabrics. Each of the guestrooms has its own personality, with a color scheme set by the painted walls (in pink, blue, green, or yellow). My favorite, 202, is a most attractive room with walls painted a soft yellow, black wrought-iron headboard, a blue-and-off-white bedspread, and two small French-style carved wooden chairs with cushions in blue and cream striped fabric. There is a 14-person cozy dining room with exposed stone walls which is open in the summer, but one of my favorite rooms is the cheerful breakfast room, walled on one side with windows opening onto the lovely garden.

HOTEL OBISPO
Owner: Bittor Alza
Obispo Square, 1
20280 Hondarribia (Guipúzcoa), Spain
Tel: (943) 34 64.54.00, Fax: (943) 34 64.23.86
17 rooms, Double: Pts 12,000–16,500*
*IVA not included, breakfast Pts 1,000
Open all year, Credit cards: all major
Restaurant open daily
18 km E of Sebastián
Michelin Map 442, Region: Pays Basque

As you enter through the Santa María gate of Hondarribia and head toward the main square (Plaza de Armas), the Hotel Pampinot is located on the right side of the Calle Mayor in the shadow of the beautiful parish church of Santa Maria de Asunción. From the outside, the austere stone façade looks similar to the other 16th- and 17th-century gray stone mansions that line the narrow street—just a small hotel sign indicates you have found the proper house. Inside, a surprise awaits: the stern exterior does not hint at the opulence within. The reception is a spacious area with a massive stone floor and exposed stone walls which set off to perfection two large altar pieces, intricately and colorfully painted, which dominate facing walls. Beyond the entrance lobby is one of my favorite rooms, a delightful little bar tucked into what was once the fireplace. A huge antique chest set below the mantle serves as the "bar" and the entire space above the mantle is filled with a collection of brightly painted antique plates. A wide staircase with iron railings topped by a polished brass banister leads up to the guestrooms. There are only eight—four on each level—each individually decorated. One of my favorites, room 103, has whimsical clouds and birds painted on the ceiling. Pampinot is filled with history: in its days of glory it even housed María Theresa while on her journey to marry Louis XIV of France.

HOTEL PAMPINOT
Owner: Olga Alvarez
Manager: Fernando Navas
Calle Mayor 5
20280 Hondarribia (Guipúzcoa), Spain
Tel: (943) 64.06.00, Fax: (943) 64.51.28
8 rooms, Double: Pts 16,0 00*
*IVA not included, breakfast Pts 1,200
Open all year, Credit cards: all major
No restaurant, breakfast only
18 km E of Sebastián
Michelin Map 442, Region: Pays Basque

Parador El Emperador is located on the border of the Basque country, in the picturesque medieval walled town of Hondarribia (also called Fuenterrabía). Installed in a 12th-century castle, overlooking a beautiful square lined by brightly colored houses, the imposing stone castle has been occupied by Ferdinand and Isabella and also their grandson Charles V. The building's incredible 3-meter-thick walls have withstood countless assaults over the centuries. An outstanding feature of the Emperador is its stone-paved lobby, featuring lances, cannon, suits of armor, tapestries, and a remarkable, soaring 15-meter ceiling, overlooked through stone arches by a cozy lounge with a beamed ceiling. The interior glass-enclosed, flower-filled courtyard has comfortable wicker chairs where guests can relax. (One side of the courtyard retains the original stone wall.) Beyond the inner courtyard is a grand outdoor terrace with a sweeping view of the blue bay dotted with colorful boats. Not only are the setting and structure of this parador outstanding, but the interior (filled with astounding antiques) is stunning— rivaling the finest hotels in Spain. There is absolutely nothing to fault in this incredible parador. But be sure to book far in advance since it is very popular.

PARADOR EL EMPERADOR
Manager: Pilar de Miguel Hernando
Plaza de Armas, 14
20280 Hondarribia (Guipúzcoa), Spain
Tel: (943) 64.55.00, Fax: (943) 64.21.53
36 rooms, Double: Pts 20,000*
*IVA not included, breakfast Pts 1,300
Open all year, Credit cards: all major
No restaurant, breakfast only
18 km E of Sebastián
Michelin Map 442, Region: Pays Basque

Pikes (pronounced *Peekays*) has its own special personality. Not your "run-of-the-mill" hotel at all, this intimate inn is a favorite hideaway of the world's rich and famous and it is not at all surprising they flock here. Pikes offers 24 guestrooms, each decorated with a dramatic flair worthy of a stage setting. They are discreetly housed in a cluster of honey-beige-toned cottages that offer privacy. However, most of the guests I saw did not seem to be seeking seclusion, but were sunning by the swimming pool, playing tennis, taking advantage of the exercise room, or laughing with friends at the bar. An air of unpretentious informality prevails, conducive to guests becoming friends. Pathways crisscross through the beautifully tended gardens which include walls of cascading bougainvillea, roses, hibiscus, geraniums, daisies, carnations, and fragrant lavender. The heart of the property is a 300-year-old finca (farmhouse) where the stunning dining room and bar offer authentic rustic charm. The thick stone walls, arched doorways, low, beamed ceilings, and old olive press create a romantic atmosphere for tables set with pretty linens, fresh flowers, and softly glowing candles. And, best of all, the food is outstanding. If you can tear yourself away from this oasis tucked into the low hills outside of San Antoni, there are beaches, golf, and sights to see nearby.

HOTEL PIKES
Owner: Anthony J. Pike
Calle Sa Vurera
07820 San Antoni de Portmany, Ibiza
Balearic Islands, Spain
Tel: (971) 34.22.22, Fax: (971) 34.23.12
24 rooms, Double: Pts 20,800 *
*IVA not included, breakfast Pts 1,200
Open all year, Credit cards: all major
Restaurant open daily, pool
1.5 km E of San Antoni de Portmany
Michelin Map 443, Region: Balearic Islands

Words cannot prepare you for the magical setting of the Hotel Hacienda. As you approach, the road gradually climbs through a gentle forest of pines to a sparkling white building. When you check in, the Hacienda seems lovely, but not so different from other luxury hotels: it is only when you open the door into your bedroom that the absolute splendor of the Hacienda unfolds. The hotel is built into the hillside and what appears at first to be a one-story structure actually cascades down the hill with six floors of guestrooms—each with a view "to die for." Views just don't get any better. Spread before you are giant cliffs of granite that plunge into the sea, forming idyllic, small coves where the blue sea dances in the sunlight. All of the bedrooms have either a terrace or a balcony. The superior rooms and suites have large Jacuzzi tubs in front of picture windows. If your heart is not set on relaxing in your bath while soaking in the view, the standard rooms offer the same amenities, but, instead of a Jacuzzi, have a larger balcony. The public areas combine the feel of Ibiza with a touch of Andalusia, reflected in two inner courtyards, one with palm trees, the other with a covered pool. There are two more swimming pools, one romantically perched on the cliff overlooking the sea.

HOTEL HACIENDA
Owner: Sr Lipszyc
Xamena, 07815 San Miguel
Ibiza, Balearic Islands, Spain
(Mailing address: Apartado 423, 07800, Ibiza)
Tel: (971) 33.45.00, Fax: (971) 33.45.14
www.karenbrown.com/spaininns/hotelhacienda.html
63 rooms, Double: Pts 33,700–45,500*
*IVA not included, breakfast Pts 2,300
Open mid-Apr to Nov, Credit cards: all major
Restaurant open daily, pools
6 km N of San Miguel
Michelin Map 443, Region: Balearic Islands

For many years Ellen Trauffer came from Switzerland to Ibiza on holiday. In 1987 she purchased a whitewashed, centuries-old finca (farmhouse)—one of only a few that still exist on the island—and opened it as a hotel. You enter into a large living room exuding a fresh and pretty rustic charm. In the corner is a fireplace with a cozy grouping of white slip-covered chairs, and a blue-and-white-striped sofa. The blue-and-white color scheme continues in the cheerful dining room which has a flagstone floor and windows on three sides. The chef (who is co-owner of the property) prepares excellent meals using fresh produce from the island. All of the individually decorated bedrooms are attractive. Number 14 (with a four-poster canopy bed and a view of the garden) is a special favorite. Ibiza has many moderately priced hotels, but most from the same cookie cutter—modern white high-rises. In comparison, La Colina is truly a gem. Although not on the sea, it has a large swimming pool and makes a good base from which to venture out each day to explore Ibiza's many enchanting small beaches and coves. It is not by chance that this remarkably inexpensive hotel offers such quality since Ellen is no novice: she also has a hotel in Switzerland. Guests come back year after year.

LA COLINA
Owner: Ellen Trauffer
Carretera Ibiza a Santa Eulalia
07840 Santa Eulalia del Río
Balearic Islands, Spain
Tel & fax: (971) 33.27.67
www.karenbrown.com/spaininns/santaeulaliadelrio.html
16 rooms, Double: Pts 10,800–13,600*
*IVA & breakfast included
Open all year, Credit cards: MC, VS
Restaurant open daily, pool
5 km SW of Santa Eulalia on PM 810 to Ibiza
Michelin Map 443, Region: Balearic Islands

This engaging Parador Castillo de Santa Catalina crowns the ridge of Cerro (hill) de Santa Catalina, the patron saint of Jaén, and flanks the 13th-century Arabic fortress after which it is named and whose architecture it imitates. It is immediately apparent that much imaginative effort went into the construction of this "copycat" castle-hotel. The public rooms feature cavernous fireplaces, recessed windows, and tapestry-hung stone-brick walls which soar to carved-wood or granite ceilings. The drawing room is especially dramatic with 20-meter-tall crossed arches. The high-ceilinged guestrooms are spacious and bright, with rough-hewn brick floors trimmed in green tile, leather and wood furniture, cheery spreads and throw-rugs, and shiny green-and-white-tiled baths. Each has a roomy terrace commanding panoramic vistas over the city, the fertile Guadalquivir river valley, and an endless expanse of undulating hills studded with the olive groves for which this region is renowned. Tranquil will define your stay here, which should be combined with a visit to the Arab baths and the *barrio de Magdalena* in Jaén, which spreads out in the valley below the hotel.

PARADOR CASTILLO DE SANTA
CATALINA
Manager: Antonio Romero Huete
23001 Jaén, Spain
Tel: (953) 23.00.00, Fax: (953) 23.09.30
45 rooms, Double: Pts 17,500*
*IVA not included, breakfast Pts 1,300
Open all year, Credit cards: all major
Restaurant open daily, pool
90 km N of Granada
Michelin Map 446, Region: Andalusia

In the 15th century, the Counts of Oropesa built a fortress surrounded by gardens on the hillside above the fertile, tobacco-growing Tiétar Valley. Their noble home is now the Carlos V, beautifully preserved, with odd-shaped towers, ramparts, and a drawbridge completing the late-medieval picture. As you might guess from the name, Carlos V once briefly resided here, and the dramatic large fireplace in the lounge was added at his request since he found the castle chilly in winter. The wooded grounds surrounding the parador are beautifully tended and just beckon you to stroll around. Tucked into the gardens are a pretty swimming pool, a tennis court, and a children's play yard. The cool, stone-paved inner courtyard has ivy-covered walls and a placid central pool, overlooked by a terraced second-floor lounge with fireplace and lovely antiques. There are 16 guestrooms in the original building and an additional 37 in a modern annex. The parador has been redecorated by one of the best decorators in Spain and has as emerged as one of the "smartest" in the chain. The manager is "keen on cleanliness" and it certainly shows. The spacious high ceilings, rich wood floors, and antique furnishings of the castle chambers lend an atmosphere impossible to duplicate. The addition of a swimming pool and tennis facilities have only enhanced this charming hilltop hideaway.

PARADOR CARLOS V
Manager: Susana de la Rubia Gómez-Morán
Carretera de Plasencia
10450 Jarandilla de la Vera (Cáceres), Spain
Tel: (927) 56.01.17, Fax: (927) 56.00.88
53 rooms, Double: Pts 17,500*
*IVA not included, breakfast Pts 1,300
Open all year, Credit cards: all major
Restaurant open daily, pool
213 km SW of Madrid
Michelin Map 444, Region: Extremadura

Whereas many of the beach towns on Spain's popular Costa Blanca are dominated by towering hotels and condominium projects, somehow Javea has managed to keep a low profile. There is a small, pretty curve of sandy beach, rimmed by shops and restaurants. Embracing one end of the crescent of sand is a tiny peninsula that is home to the Parador Costa Blanca. The front of the modern hotel—a white stucco, five-story building—looks like a typical beach hotel but on the inside, the true merits of the hotel emerge. The spacious reception area opens onto the lounge with a wall of windows looking out to the terrace and garden. The decor is simple but pleasing, with Spanish hand-loomed rugs accenting cream-colored marble floors, comfortable brown-leather sofas, large paintings on the walls, and a profusion of green plants. Next to the hotel there is a terrace framed by colorful flowers in ceramic pots and beyond that is an expanse of meticulously tended lawn (dotted by large palm trees and rose beds) which stretches out to the sea. The garden is definitely the highlight of this hotel. There are even a few Roman ruins in the garden, attesting to the fact that the Romans, too, thought this a prime location. The bedrooms are spacious, furnished with contemporary, built-in furniture, and all but five have a balcony and view of the sea.

PARADOR COSTA BLANCA
Manager: Victor Teodisio Tirado
Playa del Arenal, 2
03730 Javea (Alicante), Spain
Tel: (96) 57.90.200, Fax: (96) 57.90.308
65 rooms, Double: Pts 19,500*
*IVA not included, breakfast Pts 1,300
Open all year, Credit cards: all major
Restaurant open daily, pool
110 km SE of Valencia
Michelin Map 445, Region: Valencia (Costa Blanca)

The San Marcos is elegantly installed in what was originally an elaborate stone monastery commissioned by Ferdinand (the Catholic king) at the beginning of the 16th century. Before its conversion to a hotel in 1965, it was used as a military prison and stable which saw lots of activity during the Civil War. Its immense façade is deceptive, as there are only 35 rooms in the historic part of the edifice (referred to as the *zona noble*). The rest of the space is occupied by an exquisite stone patio peopled with statues of saints, an archaeological museum, a chapel, spacious lounges and hallways lavishly furnished with antiques, and a modern restaurant offering a delectable menu (the scallops, or *vieiras*, are superb). The old rooms are discovered off a maze of creaky, worn hallways and are large and comfortable, with high ceilings, old-world ambiance and antique furnishings. The suites overlooking the entrance are a treat: enormous and secured behind walls now centuries old. The rooms in the new addition will not disappoint; they are quiet, maintain a traditional Spanish flavor, and overlook a lovely interior garden. The San Marcos is steeped in history and has a gracious staff.

HOSTAL SAN MARCOS
Manager: Manuel Miguelez
Plaza San Marcos, 7
24001 León, Spain
Tel: (987) 23.73.00, Fax: (987) 23.34.58
35 rooms, Double: Pts 22,500*
*IVA not included, breakfast Pts 1400
Open all year, Credit cards: all major
Restaurant open daily
194 km W of Burgos; 88 km S of Oviedo
Michelin Maps 441 & 442, Region: Castilla y León

This select hotel is an experience unto itself, spectacularly situated on over 1,000 acres of scenic countryside. No detail has been overlooked to offer every convenience in a distinctive atmosphere combining characteristic Andalusian style with contemporary elegance. Graceful Moorish arches, carved-wood ceilings, tiled patios, grilled terraces, marble fountains, and blossoming gardens surround the pampered guest in this intimate hideaway. A sampling of the services that come with the pricey accommodation here is: fitness equipment and programs, saunas, Jacuzzi, tennis, fishing (nearby), horseback riding, climbing, indoor and magnificent outdoor pools, concerts, and a staff that outnumbers the clientele. Each spacious guestroom is unique, richly and imaginatively decorated in soft colors, with a large bathroom (featuring both bath and shower), and either a balcony or garden patio from which you can enjoy the tranquil landscape. The orientation of rooms 1 to 6 (suites) and 7 and 10 (doubles) provides them with particularly ample upstairs terraces. In addition, you have your choice of two dining spots, one of which, La Finca, has gained justifiable regional renown. Note: La Bobadilla is not in Loja, but located north of Salinas (between Granada and Antequera) on C334.

HOTEL LA BOBADILLA
Manager: Klaudius Heckh
18300 Loja (Granada), Spain
Tel: (958) 32.18.61, Fax: (958) 32.18.10
E-mail: comercial@la-bobadilla.com
60 rooms, Double: Pts 38,500–48,500*
*IVA not included, breakfast included
Open all year, Credit cards: all major
Restaurant open daily, pools
72 km W of Granada, 71 km NE of Málaga
A-92 at Km. 175, 72 Kms. far from Granada
Michelin Map 446
Region: Andalucia

The good-value-for-money Hotel Arosa is in a large building in the heart of Madrid. The only part of the hotel at street level is the small lobby (serviced by a doorman)—the actual hotel is on the upper levels. Two elevators go to the different floors. The quaint one on the right—a tiny, five-sided affair—is unique, obviously having been constructed to fit the precise space available. Found on the third floor (Spanish second) is a pleasant reception, lobby, and restaurant area whose decorative style could be called intense: pseudo-French with antique accents. But it is spacious, attractive, and comfortable, and a veritable oasis in the heart of the noisy town. The bedrooms, each different in shape and size, are individually decorated. Some have a modern feel while others (such as 509, a pretty corner room with sprigged floral design on the walls) have a more traditional ambiance. An especially nice feature is that you can request a non-smoking room. The air-conditioning is not the best so you often have to have your window open which lets in a cacophony of traffic noise. Although you might see some "women of the night" a few blocks away, the location is very good: a few minutes by foot to the chic Puerta del Sol (a shopper's paradise) and the Plaza Mayor with its charming cafés. The Arosa remains one of Madrid's best buys.

HOTEL AROSA
Owner: Fernando de Leon
Calle Salud, 21
28013 Madrid, Spain
Tel: (91) 53.21.600, Fax: (91) 53.13.127
E-mail: arosa@hotelarosa.com
www.karenbrown.com/spaininns/hotelarosa.html
139 rooms, Double: Pts 17,000–21,000*
*IVA included, breakfast Pts 1,350
Open all year, Credit cards: all major
Restaurant open daily
Michelin Map 444, Region: Madrid

The Hotel Villa Real, facing a tiny plaza just off the beautiful tree-lined Paseo de la Castellana, is a rare jewel—a tranquil oasis of refined elegance. The location, in the heart of Madrid's famous triangle (formed by the Thyssen Bornemisza Museum, the Prado Museum, and the Reina Sofia Museum) is absolute perfection. Although a deluxe hotel, there is nothing intimidating nor stuffy about the Hotel Villa Real. Every one of the well-trained staff (from the receptionist to the maid who turns down your bed at night) is gracious and seems to take personal pride in making you feel welcome. From the moment you enter, there is a home-like ambiance—subdued lighting, rich wood paneling, fine mirrors, marble floors, and antique French chairs on fine Oriental carpets. Refreshingly lacking is the commercial hurly-burly usually associated with city hotels. The guestrooms are really special. Even the "standard" rooms are mini-suites: the beds are on one level and three steps lead down to a cozy sitting area with comfortable sofa, upholstered chairs, writing desk, and, of course, television. Most of the rooms even have a small balcony where you can step outside to enjoy the magic of Madrid. One of our favorites (room 315) overlooks the tiny Plaza de las Cortes. The Hotel Villa Real's goal "to ensure that whoever visits us will find a family atmosphere in which they can feel truly at home" is without a doubt fulfilled.

Hotel Villa Real
Manager: Félix García Hernán
Plaza de Las Cortes, 10
28014 Madrid, Spain
Tel: (91) 42.03.767, Fax: (91) 42.02.547
115 rooms, Double: Pts 34,000*
*IVA not included, breakfast Pts 2,000
Open all year, Credit cards: all major
Restaurant open daily
Michelin Map 444, Region: Madrid

Frequently referred to as one of the world's top ten hotels, The Ritz, across the street from the Prado Museum, is all one could ask for in a world-class hotel. The opulent old-world decor has been restored and creates a *Belle Époque* ambiance. The restoration is based on considerable research to ensure that the decor re-creates exactly its 1910 glory. A statue of Diana that had graced the upper hall bar was retrieved, restored, and replaced where it had stood for the first 40 years of the hotel's existence. The expanse of lobby and grand hall behind it are magnificent. The restaurant, which features regional specialties, is hung with dramatic tapestries that were refurbished by the original makers, the Royal Tapestry Factory. There is a delightful outdoor garden, an oasis of greenery, where guests relax on old-fashioned white wicker chairs. The bedrooms are spectacular in their decor and the same glorious hand-woven carpet that adorns the rest of the hotel has been custom-woven to fit each one. Everything, from the striking gold bathroom fixtures to the tasteful and handsome furnishings, will make you feel pampered. There is also a fitness center with sauna and massage. The Ritz successfully combines the luxury of the contemporary world with turn-of-the-century elegance. It is able to provide the comfort and facilities all guests could desire, whether they are royalty, diplomats, movie stars, or tourists who desire the finest accommodations.

THE RITZ
Manager: Alfonso Jordán
Plaza de la Lealtad, 5
28014 Madrid, Spain
Tel: (91) 52.12.857, Fax: (91) 53.28.776
158 rooms, Double: Pts 58,300–70,400*
*IVA not included, breakfast Pts 2,500–3,500
Open all year, Credit cards: all major
Restaurant open daily
Michelin Map 444, Region: Madrid

The Parador de Málaga de Golf is not actually in Málaga, but well located just a short drive west of town. It is easy to find, with a "Parador" sign marking the exit from the N340, which is also the airport exit. A pretty tree- and flower-lined lane leads to the hotel which, although of new construction, happily mimics the delightful Andalusian style, with white-stuccoed exterior, wrought-iron accents, and the typical red-tiled roof. You enter into a one-story-wing where the reception area, dining room, lounges, and game rooms are located. The guestrooms are found in two wings stretching out from these public areas, forming a U. In the center is a large lawn accented by flowerbeds, palm trees, and a swimming pool. The open end of the U faces the sea where a long, sandy beach beckons to be explored. All of the spacious guestrooms are attractively decorated with rattan furniture which is enhanced by very attractive, color-coordinated fabrics on the chairs, bedspreads, and drapes. As an added bonus, all the bedrooms have either a balcony or patio facing the gardens and pool. As the name might suggest, the emphasis of this parador is on golf and many guests come to play the course that surrounds the hotel. In winter (from November to the end of February) guests may use the golf course free of charge.

PARADOR DE MÁLAGA DE GOLF
Manager: Juan Garcia Alonso
Autovía-Málaga-Algeciras
29080 Málaga, Spain
Tel: (95) 23.81.255, Fax: (95) 23.82.141
60 rooms, Double: Pts 17,500*
*IVA not included, breakfast Pts 1,300
Open all year, Credit cards: all major
Restaurant open daily, pool
8 km W of Málaga, Airport-Coin exit off N340
Michelin Map 446, Region: Andalusia

Situated on Mount Gibralfaro, high above the sprawling port of Málaga, this premier parador commands a stunning view. Installed in an old stone mansion with wrought-iron grilles and arcaded wrap-around galleries, the hotel is surrounded by hillside greenery and located within easy walking distance of a ruined Moorish fortress that once guarded this proud town. This popular parador was closed for a lengthy renovation but reopened in the summer of 1995. Now, once again, if you want to stay along the Costa del Sol, this marvelous parador is truly choice for excellence of accommodation, ambiance, and, above all, the incredible setting. What had been a simple, 12-room hotel has grown in size and quality. In addition to the new bedrooms that have been added to meet the demand for accommodations, a small rooftop swimming pool with a view has also been built. The dramatic panorama is also available from the restaurant, making it an extremely appealing dining spot during warm weather (as evidenced by the number of locals who make the trip up the steep hill to dine). This newly enhanced parador is very popular, so be sure to book well in advance during the high season.

PARADOR DE MÁLAGA GIBRALFARO
Manager: Juan Garcia Alonso
Camino del Castillo de Gibralfaro
29016 Málaga, Spain
Tel: (95) 22.21.902, Fax: (95) 22.21.904
*38 rooms, Double: Pts 19,000 ** *
*IVA not included, breakfast Pts 1,300
Open all year, Credit cards: all major
Restaurant open daily, pool
On Mount Gibralfaro, E side of Málaga
Michelin Map 446, Region: Andalusia

Hotel Mar i Vent is without doubt one of the best values in Mallorca. For less than you pay for a room in most hotels, you also have breakfast and dinner included in the rate. This superbly run, small hotel has been in the Vives family for three generations. Originally it was owned by the grandfather of Francesc Vives, who is now manager. As was customary, his grandfather had to own a house before he could marry his sweetheart, so he went to America and saved enough money for a simple stone house in the small village of Banyalbufar, high in the hills above the sea. There were no cars or roads in those days, but travelers sometimes happened by who needed a place to spend the night. With a kind heart, grandfather Vives took them in and his wife fed them. The village priest suggested that they open their home as a wayside inn and today the same genuine hospitality exists. Francesc's pretty wife, Juana María, helps at the reception; his father, Tony, makes all guests feel special; his mother, Francisca, prepares the home-cooked meals; and aunt Juanita helps, too! Although this hotel is inexpensive, a high quality of service and accommodation exists. Each room is nicely decorated and has a terrace or balcony with a view over the terraced fields to the sea. The hotel is built into the hillside and on the lowest level is a large pool cantilevered over the cliffs with a panoramic view.

HOTEL MAR I VENT
Owners: Family Vives
Calle Major 49, 07191 Banyalbufar, Mallorca
Balearic Islands, Spain
Tel: (971) 61.80.00, Fax: (971) 61.82.01
23 rooms, Double: Pts 12,000*
*IVA & breakfast included
Open Feb to Dec, Credit cards: MC, VS
Restaurant closed Sunday night, pool
28 km NW of Palma
Michelin Map 443, Region: Balearic Islands

Finca es Palmer has been in Francisca Juan's family since the time of her great-grandparents. With farming less profitable, the house (located only 5 kilometers from the finest beach on Mallorca) was falling into ruins but it was rescued by Francisca, your charming young English-speaking hostess, and her husband, Pedro. With a labor of love and total devotion to their heritage, they have transformed the simple stone farmhouse, built in the typical Mallorcan style around a courtyard, into a very special small hotel. Dinner is served by candlelight in a garden-like dining room (covered by a glass roof in winter) using glasses and ceramic plates handmade in Mallorca. Almost all the food served comes from the garden where everything is grown as in days of yore, without the use of preservatives. In the picture-perfect kitchen, shelves are filled with row upon row of colorful jars of homemade marmalades, vegetables, and fruits. There are ten guestrooms, all decorated with artistic flair and rustic simplicity, using fabric woven in Mallorca, handpainted Mallorcan tiles, and family antiques. All have satellite television, mini-bar, shampoo, perfume, and even bathrobes. One of my favorites is a spacious corner room in the windmill. Since our original visit, a swimming pool has been constructed near the palm tree terrace.

FINCA ES PALMER
Owner: Francisca Juan
Carretera Campos-Colonia Sant Jordi, km 6.4
07638 Colonia de Sant Jordi, Mallorca
Balearic Islands, Spain
Tel: (971) 18.12.65, Fax: (971) 18 10 63
10 rooms, Double: Pts 19,100*
*IVA & breakfast included
Closed Dec, Credit cards: all major
Restaurant open daily (for guests only), pool
6.4 km S of Campos on road to Colonia de Sant Jordi
Michelin Map 443, Region: Balearic Islands

La Residencia, perched high in the hills with views to the sea yet just steps from the quaint village of Deia, is a faultless hideaway. This gem of a hotel, nestled in 34 acres, is imaginatively created from two 17th-century farmhouses built of the golden-tan stone of the region. In keeping with its past, the decor is elegantly simple with white walls accented by beautiful antiques and bouquets of fresh flowers. Even the reception is exceptional. Check-in is handled quietly and without fuss at an antique desk. Nearby are intimate lounges and bars where guests can sit quietly with friends as if in a private home. However, most guests "live" outdoors—the hotel has its own private club by the sea, serviced by a shuttle bus. For those who don't want to leave the property, the manicured gardens offer an exquisite retreat, with secluded shady nooks where guests can relax with only the fragrance of flowers and the song of birds for company. The hotel is built on a hillside with two swimming pools tucked onto terraces. Adjacent to the lower pool is a bar where guests can order lunch or have dinner if they want to dine casually. For those who want to dine elegantly, in the room where the olives were pressed, there is a gourmet restaurant, El Olivo, which holds a Michelin star for excellence. The bedrooms are all fabulously furnished. The suites are stunning, but even the standard doubles (such as number 9, overlooking the garden) are outstanding.

LA RESIDENCIA
07179 Deia, Mallorca
Balearic Islands, Spain
Tel: (971) 63.90.11, Fax: (971) 63.93.70
www.karenbrown.com/spaininns/laresidencia.html
65 rooms, Double: Pts 36,100–47,400*
*IVA not included, breakfast included
Open all year, Credit cards: all major
Restaurant open daily, pools
27 km N of Palma de Mallorca
Michelin Map 443, Region: Balearic Islands

Vistamar is perfection—a stunning country manor offering genuine warmth of hospitality and an ambiance of understated elegance without a hint of ostentation. You approach through an orchard of 900-year-old olive trees to massive, double wooden doors that open into the central courtyard where the old well still stands. When the wealthy landowner came to the mountains in the summer to escape the heat of Palma, he stayed with his family on the upper floor while the ground level of the home was the farmer's quarters. The farmer's living space has been converted into several intimate lounges, each tastefully decorated with chairs and sofas slip-covered with handsome Mallorcan fabrics. On the walls are original paintings (predominantly modern art) which nicely complement the handsome antiques. You dine in a glass-enclosed sunroom that looks out to a terrace embraced by a semi-circle of enormous palm trees. Beyond are towering pines through which you get a glimpse of the sea. Some of the guestrooms are in the main house, others in the old stables. Room 8 (formerly the homeowner's dining room) is fabulous, with beautiful, antique spool beds and an enormous balcony. But don't worry which room you get: each is superbly decorated. As an added bonus, there is a magnificent swimming pool on a terrace with a view to the sea.

VISTAMAR DE VALLDEMOSA
Owner: Pedro Coll Pastor
Cra Valldemosa-Andraitx, km 2.5
07170 Valldemosa, Mallorca
Balearic Islands, Spain
Tel: (971) 61.23.00, Fax: (971) 61.25.83
E-mail: info@vistamarhotel.es
18 rooms, Double: Pts 26,000–31,000*
*IVA not included, breakfast Pts 1,800
Open Feb to Nov, Credit cards: AX, VS
Restaurant closed lunch Mondays, pool
2.5 km W of Valldemosa on road to Andraitx
Michelin Map 443, Region: Balearic Islands

If your heart is set on a posh resort along the Costa del Sol, you can do no better than the Marbella Club Hotel. At one time this property was even more exclusive—it was the residence of Prince Alfonso von Hohenlohe who in 1954 began to take in paying guests. Of course, not just any guests—only such celebrities as Cristina Onassis, David Niven, Ava Gardner, the Duke of Windsor, and Grace Kelly were on the invitation list. The rich and famous still frequent the resort which blends nicely the formality of a staff in tuxedos with the relaxed atmosphere of a beach resort. Whereas most hotels along the Costa del Sol are high-rises, the Marbella Club is blessed with a large piece of land allowing for low-rise clusters of bougainvillea-draped, whitewashed, Andalusian-style buildings and cottages which house the suites and guestrooms. There is a swimming pool tucked in the garden and another facing the long stretch of excellent beach. Except for a new, deluxe complex of ultra-luxurious suites next to the beach club, the rooms do not have a sea view, but all have either a terrace or balcony looking out to the gardens. All the rooms are extremely spacious and include a large sitting area. The decorator-perfect decor is the same in all the doubles, with beautiful fabrics that vary only by color scheme.

MARBELLA CLUB HOTEL
Manager: Javier Rosenberg
Boulevard Prince Alfonso von Hohenlohe, s/n
29600 Marbella (Málaga), Spain
Tel: (95) 28.22.211, Fax: (95) 28.29.884
129 rooms, Double: Pts 51,500–61,500*
*IVA not included, breakfast Pts 2,600
Open all year, Credit cards: all major
Restaurant open daily, pool
3 km S of Marbella on the coastal road
Michelin Map 443, Region: Andalusia

Tucked high in a mountain valley, Meranges is one of the few remaining unspoiled Catalan villages in the Pyrenees. Clinging to the hillside are only a cluster of charming old gray-stone buildings weighted down with heavy slate roofs. As a child, Martha Sole Forn spent her summers in this remote valley with her grandparents—in the same farmhouse where her grandfather was born. She and her husband, Antonio, love this idyllic hamlet, and have bought a 200-year-old farmhouse that offers a few rooms and a charming small restaurant. The bedrooms are all simple, but extremely appealing and in absolute keeping with the nature of the building. Happily, nothing is contrived or too cute. The walls are painted a fresh white, the floors are of pine, the ceilings have natural beams. The only decoration on the walls are beautiful black-and-white photographs of the region, all taken by a local priest (now well up in his years) whose hobby was capturing on film the animals, people, and landscape he knows so well. Along with the lovely mountain setting, it is the restaurant (featuring Catalan country-style cooking) that draws guests. What in days-gone-by was the sheep stable, has been transformed into a cozy restaurant where stone walls, and a low, beamed ceiling, set a romantic stage.

HOTEL CAN BORRELL
Owners: Antonio Forn Alonso
C/ Retorn, 3
17539 Meranges (Gerona), Spain
Tel: (972) 88.00.33, Fax:(972) 88.01.44
www.karenbrown.com/spaininns/hotelcanborrell.html
8 rooms, Double: Pts 11,000–12,000*
*IVA not included, breakfast Pts 650
Open all year (Jan to Mar weekends only)
Credit cards: all major
Restaurant closed Monday nights & Tuesdays
185 km NW of Barcelona, 50 km NE of Seo de Urgel
Michelin Map 443, Region: Catalonia

The Vía de la Plata (named after a Roman road) is installed in a historic church-cum-convent-cum-hospital-cum-jail dating back to the 17th century. There is, in addition, strong archaeological evidence pointing to the conclusion that this was originally the site of the Concordia Temple of Augustus during the Roman occupation of Mérida. There are ancient artifacts scattered throughout the large, whitewashed hotel—all discovered nearby. The architecture is a crazy mix: for example, in the gorgeous, Andalusian interior patio you will discover elegant Mudéjar-style pillars with Roman and Visigothic stones, and the stunning front sitting room was the convent chapel. The Vía de la Plata was recently renovated to include an overall face-lift, additional rooms, and underground parking. The whitewashed rooms with dark Spanish furniture are very pleasant, and many have domed ceilings and colorful rugs brightening the red-tile floors. The doubles in back have balconies and overlook the delightful Moorish gardens. All in all this is a charming, unusual parador.

PARADOR VÍA DE LA PLATA
Manager: Victor Teodosio Tirado
Plaza de la Constitución, 3
06800 Mérida (Badajoz), Spain
Tel: (924) 31.38.00, Fax: (924) 31.92.08
82 rooms, Double: Pts 16,500*
*IVA not included, breakfast Pts 1,300
Open all year, Credit cards: all major
Restaurant open daily
195 km N of Seville
Michelin Map 444, Region: Extremadura

Perched at the edge of a 30-meter cliff overlooking the blue Mediterranean, the Parador de Nerja is a modern hotel. As you first see it from the road, the hotel seems unexceptional, but the interior (though it looks a little tired) is a definite improvement. Featuring just a few antique touches in the halls and public rooms, it offers an attractive alternative to the posh and expensive Costa del Sol resorts, and is a good choice for those who want to include in their trip a few days at the beach. The extremely spacious public areas are Spanish-contemporary in decor, and make extensive use of glass to capitalize on the marvelous view. The Andalusian-style central patio is quite pretty, with plants, flowers, and a typical little fountain—the result is a colorful and relaxed atmosphere. The hotel's best feature is the park-like terrace on the edge of the cliff at the back of the property where guests lounge around the large pool. At the corner of the terrace, just a few pesetas buys an elevator ride down to a beautiful, expansive beach with ample bars and restaurants, and boat rental facilities. After a day in the sun, you can return to an air-conditioned, spacious room commanding the same view as the public rooms.

PARADOR DE NERJA
Manager: Antonio Embiz Fabregas
Avenida. Rodríguez Acosta, s/n
29780 Nerja (Málaga), Spain
Tel: (952) 52.00.50, Fax: (952) 52.19.97
73 rooms, Double: Pts 19,000*
*IVA not included, breakfast Pts 1,300
Open all year, Credit cards: all major
Restaurant open daily, pool
52 km E of Málaga
Michelin Map 446, Region: Andalucia (Costa del Sol)

Nuévalos is hidden among the steep mountains of the *Sistema Ibérico*, a beautiful natural park of waterfalls, lakes, gorges, and stone grottos. In the center of this magical setting sits the Hotel Monasterio de Piedra, originally a monastery established by Cistercian monks in 1194 and active until 1835, when it was abandoned and tragically ransacked. General Prim came into possession of this spectacular piece of property and his descendants own it to this day. Curiously, because of the monastery's uninhabited period, neighboring villages can claim parts of it, too, as evidenced by some fabulous works of art (such as choir stalls, altars, furniture—even wine vats) that grace their otherwise relatively humble holy places. The site is large and rich in history, having fine architectural examples from the Gothic through the baroque periods. Wander at will, exploring every exciting corner, then enter the hotel from the beautiful cloisters. The antique-lined, arched-ceilinged marble hallways must be 6 meters wide and 10 meters high, through which it seems the slightest sound echoes endlessly, and the incredible windows that appear to be covered with parchment are actually made of alabaster. The wood-floored bedrooms are, not surprisingly, the original monks' cells, and therefore simply but nicely furnished, and overlook a natural park, an interior patio, or the cloister. Your stay here is guaranteed to be unforgettable.

HOTEL MONASTERIO DE PIEDRA
Manager: José Maria Montaner
50210 Nuévalos (Zaragoza), Spain
Tel: (976) 84.90.11, Fax: (976) 84.90.54
61 rooms, Double: Pts 9,000–10,500*
*IVA not included, breakfast Pts 550
Open all year, Credit cards: all major
Restaurant open daily, pool
118 km SW of Zaragoza
Michelin Map 444, Region: Aragon

Olite was the medieval capital of the Kingdom of Navarre, and Charles III made this castle fortress his summer residence in the early 15th century. Part of the extensive original dwelling has been incorporated into a charming parador (named after the young prince who spent his childhood here) which offers the modern-day resident unique lodging in this ancient walled town. Situated next to a tiny, elaborate church on a tranquil, tree-lined plaza, the inn has an impressive, almost intimidating, stone façade but, once inside, you will be delighted with the warm red-tile floors, stained glass, antiques, suits of armor, and intimate bar and dining room. Only 16 of its bedrooms are in the historic building, and they are wonderful, with canopied beds and wood floors; some are still sheltered by crude exterior walls dating back hundreds of years, and two (rooms 106 and 107) with massive stone fireplaces. The "new" rooms are also lovely (and larger), decorated in subtle earth colors, with traditional Spanish wood furniture and floors. If you prefer to stay in the old section, be sure you request *la parte vieja* when making your reservation.

PARADOR PRINCIPE DE VIANA
Manager: Antonio Bertolin Blasco
Plaza de los Teobaldos, 2
31390 Olite (Navarra), Spain
Tel: (948) 74.00.00, Fax: (948) 74.02.01
43 rooms, Double: Pts 16,500*
*IVA not included, breakfast Pts 1,300
Open all year, Credit cards: all major
Restaurant open daily
140 km NW of Zaragoza, 123 S of San Sebastian
Michelin Map 443, Region: Navarra

In the 14th century King Henry granted the medieval town of Oropesa, with its ancient castle, to Don García Alvarez de Toledo, who gradually restored the castle and added to it, as did his descendants. Converted to a parador in 1930, the hotel has handsome bedrooms with thick beige rugs on red-and-blue-tiled floors, beige bedspreads, rich wood furniture, ceramic and iron fixtures, and cavernous, dazzling-white bathrooms. All but a few overlook the fertile Sierra de Gredos Valley: the others look over the interior patio (originally a bullring), a 15th-century Jesuit church, and the remains of the ancient castle. This parador is home to an international cooking school and the cuisine exceeds usual parador standards, as does the dining room itself, laid out on two levels, with skylights, painted-wood ceiling, and large picture windows. In the lounge areas, cozy leather furniture and exquisite antiques cluster around big stone fireplaces. In the basement is a tiny cell where Saint Peter of Alcántara chose to stay when he visited here—it is intriguing, but he might have chosen differently could he have seen the accommodations available now.

PARADOR DE OROPESA Manager: Secundino
Fuertes Alvarez
Plaza del Palacio, 1
45560 Oropesa (Toledo), Spain
Tel: (925) 43.00.00, Fax: (925) 43.07.77
48 rooms, Double: Pts 15,000*
*IVA not included, breakfast Pts 1,300
Open all year, Credit cards: all major
Restaurant open daily, pool
155 km SW of Madrid, 122 km SW of Ávila
Michelin Map 444, Region: Castilla-La Mancha

The Hotel de la Reconquista, located just a block away from Oviedo's beautiful central park, is a real classic. From the first glance you will know this is not an ordinary hotel. The exterior is stunning—a superb 18th-century masterpiece (justifiably designated a national monument). The front of the two-story building is made of pretty ochre-colored stone. Wrought-iron balconies adorn the formal line of windows and a magnificent crest is mounted above the entrance. Inside the splendor continues: the entrance hall opens to an enormous arcaded courtyard (with a patterned red carpet and blue velvet chairs and sofas) roofed in glass to create a lounge that is protected from the sun and rain. This is where guests gather for a cup of tea or an aperitif before dinner, surrounded by an old-fashioned, understated elegance of a bygone era. Beyond the first courtyard, there is a second garden courtyard, and beyond, even a third. Throughout, the decor reflects a formal grandeur with gorgeous large mirrors, beautiful antique chests, fine oil paintings, grandfather clocks, fresh flowers, and green plants. The walls and hallways to the guestrooms are covered in a rich red fabric. The bedrooms are tastefully decorated in a traditional style, many with antique accents.

HOTEL DE LA RECONQUISTA
Manager: Ramón Felip
Gil de Jaz, 16
33004 Oviedo (Asturias), Spain
Tel: (98) 52.41.100, Fax: (98) 52.41.166
www.karenbrown.com/spaininns/hoteldelareconquista.html
142 rooms, Double: Pts 29,500*
*IVA not included, breakfast Pts 1,900
Open all year, Credit cards: all major
Restaurant open daily
445 km NW of Madrid, 121 km N of León
Michelin Map 441, Region: Asturias

This hospitable hideaway midway between Seville and Córdoba was a Franciscan monastery from the 16th to the 19th centuries, sheltering and educating monks on their way to missions in the New World, including the recently canonized Fray Junípero Serra, famous evangelizer of California. In 1828, when church property was being confiscated by the state all over Spain, the monastery passed into private hands—and subsequent ruin. It was eventually inherited by the Moreno family who, with care and attention to original historical detail, restored it over a three-year period, opening the tiny hotel to the public in 1987. (The family also raises fighting bulls, and the manager will happily arrange a visit to their ranch, if you're interested.) Tucked behind whitewashed walls in the heart of the typical Andalusian town of Palma del Río, you'll discover a superlative restaurant and cozy bar with artesonado ceilings, gardens, and orchards, and a beautiful cloistered patio supporting a gallery around which the guestrooms are situated. The twin-bedded, air-conditioned rooms are simple and comfortable, decorated in earth tones with dark-wood furniture and trim. They have modern, colorfully tiled baths and small sitting areas. Rooms 5 to 8 are particularly spacious and original. The Hospedería offers unique, economical accommodation not far off the beaten track.

HOSPEDERÍA DE SAN FRANCISCO
Manager: Iñagui Martinez
Avenida Pío XII, s/n
14700 Palma del Río (Córdoba), Spain
Tel & fax: (957) 71.01.83
22 rooms, Double: Pts 11,400*
*IVA not included, breakfast Pts 750
Open all year, Credit cards: VS, MC
Restaurant closed Sundays
82 km NE of Seville
Michelin Map 446, Region: Andalusia

In the picture-perfect hilltop village of Pedraza de la Sierra (only a short drive north of Madrid), Martin Arcones owns one of the most charming restaurants in town, the El Soportal on the Plaza Mayor. In addition, he runs an excellent restaurant in his Hotel de la Villa, located on an attractive side street lined with pretty boutiques. As you walk into the 17th-century, honey-tone stone building, the spacious lounge (painted a deep peach) with its modern chairs and sofas has a clean, contemporary look which is softened by a few antiques. Beyond the reception area and lounge, there is a large dining room opening onto an attractive inner patio. The guestrooms are located on the upper two floors. Each one has its own personality, but a stylish, traditional ambiance prevails with the use of coordinating fine fabrics, beautiful wallpapers, and some antiques. Suite 113, with a large bedroom and separate sitting room, is not only an excellent value (it costs only a little more than the superior doubles), but is also exceptionally pretty. It is decorated with tasteful wallpaper in tones of cream and beige and has exquisite, four-poster twin beds with white canopies. Another favorite is 216, a romantic room on the top floor, tucked under the sloping beamed ceiling. Its color scheme is extremely attractive—the walls and fabrics are color-coordinated in soft tones of green and cream.

EL HOTEL DE LA VILLA
Owner: Martin Arcones
Calzada, 5
40172 Pedraza de la Sierra (Segovia), Spain
Tel: (921) 50.86.51, Fax: (921) 50.86.53
26 rooms, Double: Pts 14,000*
*IVA not included, breakfast Pts 800
Open all year, Credit cards: all major
Restaurant open daily
126 km N of Madrid, 37 km NE of Segovia
Michelin Map 444, Region: Castilla y León

La Posada de Don Mariano is absolute perfection. To have such a jewel of a small hotel to complement one of Spain's most beautiful villages is almost too good to be true. The two-story, ochre-colored stone house is enriched by black wrought-iron lamps and balconies brimming with colorful pots of flowers. The reception area is small and simple. Probably one of the family members will be at the front desk to greet you since this is a family-owned and -run hotel. Steps lead to an upper level where there is a courtyard filled with flowers. About half of the bedrooms have balconies that overlook this pretty garden, while the others have views of the village and surrounding hills. Each of the bedrooms is individual in decor, but decorator-perfect in every way—the drapes match the fabric on the bedspreads and chairs and even coordinate with the shower curtains. Every detail shows the attention of owners who truly care. Some of the guestrooms are small, but all have an appealing simplicity with country-style antiques and English-style fabrics. You cannot go wrong with any of the bedrooms. One favorite is number 110 which has twin iron beds draped in a pretty peach-and-cream-colored fabric. Another winner is room 101 which has a canopy bed and is decorated in tones of white—even including white petunias on the balcony. This is not a luxury hotel, but very special. You will love it.

LA POSADA DE DON MARIANO
Manager: Mariano Pascual
Calle Mayor 14
40172 Pedraza de la Sierra (Segovia), Spain
Tel & fax: (921) 50.98.86
18 rooms, Double: Pts 11,400–19,600*
*IVA not included, breakfast Pts 950
Open all year, Credit cards: all major
Restaurant open daily
126 km N of Madrid, 37 km NE of Segovia
Michelin Map 444, Region: Castilla y León

Peratallada, a tiny village tucked in the countryside east of Barcelona, is designated as a historical monument. At one time completely surrounded by a moat, the village today still preserves its romantic medieval character. Boutiques, art galleries, and restaurants have been opened in the stone buildings that line the narrow cobbled lanes. One of these restaurants, the well-known Castell de Peratallada, is built within the walls of the old castle. It has several stunning dining rooms where tables set with fine linens and illuminated by candlelight look especially beautiful in the massive rooms with their vaulted stone ceilings. Most guests come just for the dining, but there are six bedrooms for those who wish to spend the night. These all have a somewhat dark, medieval ambiance with antique furnishings used throughout. Four of the rooms are in the house where the owner lived while restoring the property and there are two suites located in the same building as the restaurants. The suites are exceptionally large rooms with priceless antiques—staying here is a bit like living in a museum. Incorporated into the hotel is an inner garden courtyard, exclusively for the use of overnight guests. Part of the tower wall enclosing this garden dates back to the 9th century. Note: The prices listed below are for most of the year. In high season, which is the first two weeks in August, the prices go much higher.

CASTELL DE PERATALLADA
Manager: Josep Güell
Plaça del Castell, 1
17113 Peratallada (Girona), Spain
Tel: (972) 63.40.21, Fax: (972) 63.40.11
6 rooms, Double: Pts 25,000–30,000*
*IVA & breakfast included
Open all year, Credit cards: all major
Restaurant open daily in summer
130 km NE of Barcelona
Michelin Map 443, Region: Catalonia

Tucked in the shadows of the snowcapped Guadarrama mountain range, surrounded by pine forest, and within hailing distance of the ski area of Navacerrada, is the serene retreat of Santa María de El Paular. Less than one hour from Madrid, and located just outside the attractive village of Rascafría, the hotel is ensconced in the former living quarters of a monastery dating from the 14th century (and abandoned in the 19th)—in fact, the attached monastery is still active. It has been carefully restored and remodeled, and the most has been made of its marvelous original stone patios, columns, and stairways. Don't miss the small, barren chapel just left of the arch leading to the entry patio (complete with fountain, and outdoor tables in warm weather). In it you'll discover a striking figure of the black virgin Nuestra Señora de Montserrat. Inside the hotel, you'll appreciate the handsome public rooms with beamed ceilings supporting iron chandeliers, wood and red-tile floors, and capacious and cozy Castilian-style furnishings. The guestrooms—all offering tranquil vistas—are roomy, simple, and handsome, with provincial wood furniture, hardwood floors, and woven, earth-tone bedspreads and drapes. To top it all off, the dining room provides above-average cuisine, and the management arranges horseback excursions.

HOTEL SANTA MARÍA DE EL PAULAR
Manager:Manuel Irvela
28741 Rascafría (Madrid), Spain
Tel: (91) 86.91.011, Fax: (91) 86.91.006
58 rooms, Double: Pts 15,000–18,500*
*IVA not included, breakfast Pts 1,800
Open all year, Credit cards: all major
Restaurant open daily, pool
78 km NW of Madrid
Michelin Map 444, Region: Madrid

Facing the same plaza as the Parador de Ronda (where it is sometimes difficult to find a room), the Hotel Don Miguel has an equally outstanding setting overlooking the New Bridge and the dramatic gorge that slices the town of Ronda. This hotel is incorporated into what was once the home of the jailer who was in charge of the prison that was housed in the New Bridge. There is an entrance to the hotel's popular restaurant from the Plaza de España, but you need to go around the corner to discover the door that leads to the hotel's small reception area. Although the restaurant and the hotel have separate entrances, you can go directly to the restaurant without leaving the hotel. For a reasonably priced place to stay, the guestrooms are very pleasant. They are all similar in decor with wooden headboards, wooden desks and chairs, tiled floors, and attractive, off-white matching bedspreads and drapes. When making reservations, be sure to request a room overlooking the gorge. The location of this simple hotel is fabulous and the setting gives it another bonus—a restaurant with incredible views. If the day is warm, dine outside on the terrace and watch the old stone bridge change colors in the glow of the sunset. The food is excellent and the setting unsurpassed. One level below the restaurant is a pretty guest breakfast room where you can eat either inside or, if the weather is warm, outside on the terrace. Note: Plans are under way to add more rooms and a pool.

HOTEL DON MIGUEL
Owner: Miguel Coronel
Plaza de España, 3
29400 Ronda (Málaga), Spain
Tel: (95) 28.77.722, Fax: (95) 28.78.377
19 rooms, Double: from Pts 9,500*
*IVA not included, breakfast Pts 450
Closed mid-Dec mid-Jan, Credit cards: all major
Restaurant open daily
120 km NW of Málaga, 102 km NE of Algeciras
Michelin Map 446, Region: Andalusia

In 1994 a new pearl was added to Spain's parador chain, its new construction following the architectural style of Ronda's old town hall and market that previously occupied the site. Even if the romantic town of Ronda were not worth a detour in its own right, this dramatic hotel would warrant one. The hotel is built onto the cliff above the "Tajo," the gorge that splits Ronda, and from either inside or on the terrace by the swimming pool, you have views of the soaring arched bridge that miraculously crosses the impressive, 120-meter cleft formed by the Guadalevin river. You enter the honey-colored stone building into a sky-lit atrium where the reception desk is located. Beyond is a large seating area with comfortable sofas and chairs in tones of blue and yellow. The walls are a beige-colored brick and the floors white marble. The most attractive color scheme of blues, beiges, and yellows is continued throughout the hotel. There is no effort made to create an artificial antique ambiance. Rather, the furnishings are traditional in style with beautiful fabrics of excellent quality used on the sofas, chairs, and drapes in the public rooms and guestrooms. Each of the attractive bedrooms has a balcony. All the views are lovely, but for a truly memorable experience, ask for one of the corner rooms (such as 219) with two balconies that capture the sweeping view.

PARADOR DE RONDA
Manager: Jose Maria Ronda Arauzo
Plaza España s/n
29400 Ronda (Málaga), Spain
Tel: (95) 28.77.500, Fax: (95) 28.78.188
78 rooms, Double: Pts 15,000*
*IVA not included, breakfast Pts 1,300
Open all year, Credit cards: all major
Restaurant open daily, pool
120 km NW of Málaga, 102 km NE of Algeciras
Michelin Map 446, Region: Andalusia

In 1932 this luxurious "hostal" opened in the tiny fishing village of S'Agaró with just six rooms. The Gavina (seagull) and the resort town have come a long way since then, but the inn has remained in the Ensesa family, which is personally responsible for the extraordinary collection of antiques found throughout the premises. Everything you see—rugs, tapestries, tile, furnishings—is genuine; not a single reproduction blemishes the scene. Nor does a single room reproduce another: each is unique, and all are wonderful, spacious, and bright. Careful attention has been given to the tiniest detail in every corner of every room (a man is employed full-time to do nothing but polish the wood). This is a hotel of a style and quality of a bygone era, as we are certain such previous guests as Frank Sinatra, Sylvester Stallone, and Orson Welles would agree. The hotel is surrounded by lovely gardens and has a divine pool overlooking the ocean which features fine pool-side dining in one of its three restaurants. You are a mere five-minute walk from the beach that draws a jet-set crowd in the summer. The Hostal de La Gavina is very popular. Do not fail to reserve well in advance during the high season.

HOSTAL DE LA GAVINA
Manager: Anna Requena
17248 S'Agaró (Gerona), Spain
Tel: (972) 32.11.00, Fax: (972) 32.15.73
72 rooms, Double: Pts 35,000–48,500*
*IVA not included, breakfast 2,300
Open Apr to Oct, Credit cards: all major
Restaurants open daily, pool
103 km NE of Barcelona
Michelin Map 443, Region: Catalonia (Costa Brava)

If you are looking for a reasonably priced, superbly located hotel in Salamanca, you can do no better than the Hotel Don Juan, just steps from the Plaza Mayor. This is a simple, two-star hotel, but you are truly not compromising. In my estimation, the Don Juan is better than many of Salamanca's "luxury" hotels which cost almost twice as much, but are not as meticulously maintained. The four-story, cut-stone building, accented by black wrought-iron balconies, has two doors. The one on the left goes into the café/bar while the door on the right opens onto an intimate lobby with a pretty, green-marble floor and carved reception desk where you will be warmly welcomed. The two rooms have an interconnecting door that is convenient since breakfast is served in the bar. There is no lounge, but with the many wonders of Salamanca just steps away, I cannot imagine wasting time in a formal sitting area. From the lobby, both an elevator and a staircase lead to the rooms on the upper floors. All the rooms are identical in decor, with a pretty, soft, rose color scheme used throughout in the carpets, bedspreads, and draperies. There are light-wood, built-in headboards with good reading lights, pretty prints above the comfortable beds, satellite TV, and modern marble bathrooms. My favorite bedrooms are those on the top floor: ask for 402 or 404—both have exceptional views.

HOTEL DON JUAN
Manager: David Berrocal
Quintana, 6
37001 Salamanca, Spain
Tel: (923) 26.14.23, Fax: (923) 26.24.75
www.karenbrown.com/spaininns/hoteldonjuan.html
16 rooms, Double: Pts 9,000*
*IVA not included, beakfast Pts 550
Open all year, Credit cards: MC, VS
Bar with snacks, breakfast only
Half a block from Plaza Mayor
Michelin Maps 441 & 444, Region: Castilla y León

The Hotel Rector, located at the edge of the ancient walls of Salamanca, is one of Spain's finest small hotels with a special enhancement—gracious owners who oversee every detail. Although built in the 1940s, it definitely looks several centuries old. The handsome, three-story, beige-stone building (with beautiful sculpted designs over the windows and doors, and black wrought-iron balconies) blends in perfectly with the typical old houses of Salamanca. It is just a short stroll from the hotel to Salamanca's breathtaking cathedrals or an easy, seven-minute walk to the incredible Plaza Mayor. Whereas so many hotels seem to over-strive for the dark Spanish look, the Hotel Rector is refreshingly different. The decor throughout is one of tasteful, traditional ambiance. The colors are mostly pastel, with accents of deep rose. A whimsical touch, just as you enter, are two large arched windows with a colorful "Tiffany" glass effect. The reception area opens on one side to an intimate sitting area and on the other to a small bar with cane-backed chairs. Nothing is on a grand scale—instead, there is a refined, understated elegance. The guestrooms are lovely, with the finest quality, traditional-style furnishings and color-coordinating fabrics on the bedspreads and draperies. They all have large marble bathrooms. Breakfast is served in a pretty little dining room.

HOTEL RECTOR
Manager: Eduardo Ferrán Riba
Rector Esperabé, 10
37008 Salamanca, Spain
Tel: (923) 21.84.82, Fax: (923) 21.40.08
www.karenbrown.com/spaininns/hotelrector.html
14 rooms, Double: Pts 17,000–21,000*
*IVA not included, breakfast Pts 1,000
Open all year, Credit cards: all major
No restaurant, breakfast only
205 km NW of Madrid
Michelin Maps 441 & 444, Region: Castilla y León

If you love to be on the sea, yet off the beaten path, the Hotel San José (on the Costa de Almería) is sure to be your cup of tea. San José, a small village located about a 30-kilometer drive from the highway through an arid landscape, has miraculously escaped developers' bulldozers. It is a small, forgotten village with some whitewashed houses, a boat harbor, a smattering of shops, a few restaurants, and discreet clusters of holiday houses. Near the center of town on the slope of a small hill, the Hotel San José (a pretty white building with light-blue trim) offers a simple, yet delightful charm. The reception lounge has a fireplace, wicker sofas with white cushions, and a wall of windows overlooking the sea. The restaurant is extremely attractive, with dark-green chairs, fresh flowers on the tables, and a lovely view. Beyond the dining room is the hotel guest lounge, a cozy hideaway with chairs and sofas slip-covered in deep blue, green plants in large terra cotta pots, colorful ceramic plates on white walls, and antique accent pieces. In back of the hotel is a sunny terrace and a stone staircase leading down to a sandy beach. The bedrooms are all similar in decor (request one with a view of the ocean). Note: While staying in San José, be sure to explore the nearby secluded beaches backed by giant sand dunes.

HOTEL SAN JOSÉ
Manager: Eduardo Zarate
Calle Correo, s/n
04118 San José (Almería), Spain
Tel: (950) 38.01.16, Fax: (950) 38.00.02
8 rooms, Double: Pts 22,100*
*IVA not included, breakfast or dinner included
Open mid-Mar to Nov, Credit cards: MC, VS
Restaurant open daily, beach
240 km E of Málaga, 40 km SE of Almería
Michelin Map 466, Region: Andalusia (Costa Almería)

The Reyes Católicos, one of the most magnificent inns in Spain, is without a doubt one of the pearls of the parador chain. In the 15th century the building housed a pilgrims' hospice, which nurtured the sick and sheltered the humble who journeyed from all parts of Europe to visit the tomb of Saint James. The "hostal" has four interior patios (Matthew, Mark, Luke, and John) overlooked by enclosed third-floor gallery-lounge areas lined with antiques. The fabulous central court (where a music festival is held every August) has a 15-meter ceiling and beautiful stained-glass windows. Each room, hallway, ceiling, and floor is something special. In addition to its rich history, the Reyes Católicos offers truly sumptuous accommodation for the modern pilgrim. No two rooms are exactly alike, and the attention to detail is unsurpassed, resulting in harmonious old-world decor. The green-marble bathrooms are immense, featuring separate bath and shower and heated towel racks. In a city that must be visited, this is a hotel than cannot be missed, even if you merely take a tour (it is the second most popular tourist attraction in Santiago after the cathedral).

HOSTAL DE LOS REYES CATÓLICOS
Manager: Juan Carlos Morales
Plaza del Obradoiro, 1
15705 Santiago de Compostela
(La Coruña), Spain
Tel: (981) 58.22.00, Fax: (981) 56.30.94
136 rooms, Double: Pts 27,300*
*IVA not included, breakfast Pts 1,800
Open all year, Credit cards: all major
Restaurant open daily
Michelin Map 441, Region: Galicia

The Gil Blas, an imposing, 15th-century stone manor with wrought-iron balconies, is named after the infamous character in Le Sage's 18th-century novel. The parador sits on the cobblestoned main square in the heart of the enchanting medieval village of Santillana del Mar, the perfect base from which to explore the nearby archaeological wonders. There are 28 rooms in the main house, plus 28 more in an annex across the road. The entryway into the original house opens into a spacious, cobblestoned inner patio with massive stone walls and superb antiques. There is also a pretty interior garden where supper is served in warm weather. The hallways and charming sitting areas are planked with dark wood that gleams with the patina of age. The beautiful bedrooms are whitewashed and wood-beamed, and furnished with period pieces. If you want to splurge, 222 is a lovely large room with an enormous private terrace. Number 107, a corner room, is also especially attractive. Throughout, the decor is exceptional. Whereas paradors used to have the reputation of rather bland furnishings, the Gil Blas certainly breaks the mold. The interior abounds with splendid antiques which are tastefully combined with sofas and chairs covered with elegant fabrics. Parador Gil Blas is truly a jewel, further enhanced by being located in the quaint town of Santillana del Mar.

PARADOR GIL BLAS
Manager: Cesar Alvarez
Plaza Ramón Pelayo, 8
39330 Santillana del Mar (Cantabria), Spain
Tel: (942) 81.80.00, Fax: (942) 81.83.91
56 rooms, Double: Pts 17,500*
*IVA not included, breakfast Pts 1,300
Open all year, Credit cards: all major
Restaurant open daily
30 km W of Santander, 395 km N of Madrid
Michelin Map 442, Region: Cantabria

Flanked by pretty gardens, the handsome stone façade of the Hotel Los Infantes blends beautifully with the medieval village of Santillana. It is not located in the center of town, but on the main road just outside the pedestrian area. The 18th-century façade of this typical mountain manor was moved stone by stone from the nearby town of Orena and faithfully reconstructed here. Over the doorway are two carved escutcheons—one bearing King Phillip V's coat of arms; the other that of Calderón, the original landlord. The reception area and the first-floor salon are filled with antiques and are charming, with wood floors and beamed ceilings. The breakfast room on the main floor, with its central fireplace, and the good dining room downstairs are not original, but are cozy and decorated with an old-world theme. There are twenty-eight bedrooms in the main house, and twenty more in the annex. The bedrooms, with a few exceptions, are smallish and rather plain, though consistently spotless and equipped with modern bathrooms and tiny terraces overlooking the gardens. The three front-facing doubles with sitting rooms, wooden balconies, and antique touches cost a little more, but are the best rooms in the house. Los Infantes offers reasonable accommodation with historic flavor.

HOTEL LOS INFANTES
Manager: Sra. Marisa Mesones Gomez
Avenida Le Dorat, 1
39330 Santillana del Mar (Cantabria), Spain
Tel: (942) 81.81.00, Fax: (942) 84.01.03
30 rooms, Double: Pts 8,800–17,000*
*IVA not included, breakfast Pts 650
Open Easter to Nov, Credit cards: all major
Restaurant open daily
30 km W of Santander, 395 km N of Madrid
Michelin Map 442, Region: Cantabria

In the 12th century, Saint Dominico built a shelter and hospital on the site of an old palace belonging to the Kings of Navarre. His goal was humanitarian: a wayside hospice for pilgrims who passed through here on their arduous journey to Santiago. Today it houses a recently remodeled parador offering unique accommodation in the quaint old town in the heart of the Rioja wine country. The town of Haro, home to numerous fine bodegas, is only 16 kilometers away. The entrance of the hotel is through a small lobby into a vast lounge, buttressed by massive stone pillars and arches, with a wood-beamed ceiling and stained-glass skylight. The dining room is unusual, too, with dark, rough-hewn wood pillars throughout and the tables interspersed between them. The bedrooms are plain by parador standards, though they live up to them in size and comfort, with traditional Spanish wooden furniture and floors. Those in the old part are similar in decor to those in the new. Ask for one of the front-facing doubles which have small terraces overlooking the quiet plaza, across to the cathedral and a church.

PARADOR DE SANTO DOMINGO
Manager: Alfonso Sanchez M. Capilla
Plaza del Santo, 3
26250 Santo Domingo de la Calzada
(La Rioja), Spain
Tel: (941) 34.03.00, Fax: (941) 34.03.25
61 rooms, Double: Pts 17,500*
*IVA not included, breakfast Pts 1,300
Open all year, Credit cards: all major
Restaurant open daily
58 km SE of Burgos, 310 km N of Madrid
Michelin Map 442, Region: La Rioja

Segovia, with its remarkable Roman aqueduct and outstanding Alcázar, is most frequently visited as a day trip from Madrid. But if you have the luxury of time, you can enjoy Segovia more fully by spending the night there. When deciding on a place to stay, the 19th-century Infanta Isabel can't be beaten for location—the attractive, four-story building with wrought-iron balconies and red-tiled roof faces directly onto the Plaza Mayor. Although the address is Plaza Mayor, the entrance is on a small side street around the corner at Isabel la Católica 1. You enter into a simple reception area with pastel-yellow walls, marble floors, a large crystal chandelier, and pretty prints on the walls. A half-flight of stairs leads up to a small lounge that has a small, rather dated, sitting area enhanced by a large, ornate, antique mirror. More steps lead up to the bar whose walls are covered in a green-and-yellow-patterned design. The guestrooms are surprisingly nice and prettily decorated. Be sure to ask for a room with French doors that open onto a balcony overlooking the square and the majestic cathedral—these are truly special. Although not a hotel that exudes antique charm, the Hotel Infanta Isabel is definitely a winner for location.

HOTEL INFANTA ISABEL
Owner: Enrique Cañada Cardo
Plaza Mayor
40001 Segovia, Spain
Tel: (921) 46.13.00, Fax: (921) 46.22.17
29 rooms, Double: Pts 12,100–14,000*
*IVA not included, breakfast Pts 950
Open all year, Credit cards: all major
No restaurant, breakfast only
89 km NW of Madrid, 67 km NE of Ávila
Michelin Map 444, Region: Castilla y León

The Linajes is (not easily) found down one of the tiny stone streets that crisscross Segovia's quaint old quarter, the barrio of San Esteban, which sits on a hill above the modern city. The warm-stone and aged-wood façade of the hotel, known as "The House of the Lineages," is beautifully preserved from the 11th-century palace of the noble Falconi family, whose escutcheon can still be seen over the arched entryway. Inside, with the exception of the pleasantly modern bar/cafeteria downstairs, the hotel conserves an old-Castile flavor, with dark wood, beamed ceilings, and burnished-tile floors. An alcove off the lobby, decorated with antiques, looks into a glass enclosed garden patio on one side and over the open terrace in back, sharing its panoramic views over the city's monumental skyline. There are lovely views from every bedroom, too. In 1996 upgrades were made including new beds in all the rooms, new televisions, new curtains, and new quilts. We have not yet had a chance to inspect the hotel since these improvements were made and look forward to visiting soon.

HOTEL LOS LINAJES
Manager: Miguel Borreguero Rubio
Dr. Velasco, 9
40003 Segovia, Spain
Tel: (921) 46.04.75, Fax: (921) 46.04.79
www.karenbrown.com/spaininns/hotelloslinajes.html
55 rooms, Double: Pts 11,300*
*IVA not included, breakfast Pts 775
Open all year, Credit cards: all major
Restaurant open daily
89 km NW of Madrid, 67 km NE of Ávila
Michelin Map 444, Region: Castilla y León

Segovia's parador is one of the few ultra-modern offerings within the government-run chain, but, in accordance with its consistently high standards, it is a cut above any other contemporary competitor in service and style. Situated on a hill outside Segovia, the parador commands spectacular panoramas of the golden, fortified city. The hotel's architecture is every bit as dramatic as its setting: huge brick and concrete slabs jut up and out at intriguing angles, topped by tiled roofs and surrounded by greenery. The angled brick-and-concrete motif is carried inside, where black-marble floors glisten beneath skylights in the enormous lobby. Picture windows frame Segovia beyond a garden terrace with a pretty pool. The decor throughout is tasteful, Spanish-contemporary; the feeling open, airy, and bright. The bedrooms are spacious and decorated in earth tones, with pale wood furniture. Each has a balcony that shares the incomparable city view. The combination of the modern and the historical has an unforgettable impact on the guest here, that being the hallmark of Spain's paradors.

PARADOR DE SEGOVIA
Manager: Juan Carlos Morales
Carretera N601
40003 Segovia, Spain
Tel: (921) 44.37.37, Fax: (921) 43.73.62
113 rooms, Double: Pts 18,500*
*IVA not included, breakfast Pts 1,300
Open all year, Credit cards: all major
Restaurant open daily, pool
89 km NW of Madrid, 67 km NE of Ávila
Michelin Map 444, Region: Castilla y León

Constructed on the 14th-century site of the ancient church and convent of Santo Domingo, and next door to the Romanesque cathedral of La Seu d'Urgell (the oldest in Catalonia), this is nonetheless a parador whose byword is modern. But, as with all hotels in this government chain, the accommodations are something special. Of the original building, the stunning old cloister (filled with plants and ivy cascading from hanging pots) has been preserved and converted into the hotel lounge. Graceful stone arches form the foundation of a square central room, several stories high, bedecked with hanging plants. Since our original visit, the hotel has been refurbished and the rooms now are decorated in a Catalan style with mahogany furnishings. The demi-suite 121 costs more, but offers enormous space for the price. The dining room, with its glass ceiling, is sunny, bright, and attractive, as is the indoor pool—a rarity in Spain. Situated in a fertile valley, Seo de Urgel is surrounded by the sierras of Arcabell and Cadi.

PARADOR DE SEO DE URGEL
Manager: Juan Yepes Estebati
Santo Domingo
25700 Seo de Urgel (Lerida), Spain
Tel: (973) 35.20.00, Fax: (973) 35.23.09
79 rooms, Double: Pts 15,000*
*IVA not included, breakfast Pts 1,300
Open all year, Credit cards: all major
Restaurant open daily, pool
200 km NW of Barcelona
Michelin Map 443, Region: Catalonia

When the need for a fine hotel in Seville—one of the most popular tourist destinations in Spain—became apparent, architect Espinau y Muñoz rose beautifully to the task, creating the Alfonso XIII in an Andalusian style unique to Seville. The talents of local artisans were called upon for hand-crafting the rich interior. Dedicated to its namesake, the Alfonso XIII is reminiscent of an opulent Moorish palace surrounded by gardens, with fabulous artesonado ceilings, marble pillars, graceful Mudéjar arches, and colorful, hand-painted ceramic tiles throughout. The interior patio with its tinkling central fountain is elegant and peaceful, offering the perfect setting for relaxing with a cool drink at the end of a hot day. All of the public rooms are stunning: wide marble staircases lead to expansive landings on each floor, decorated with fine antiques under elaborately carved ceilings. Although some are more spacious than others, the high-ceilinged bedrooms are richly decorated in soft colors and handsome, classic wood furnishings. Many have Spanish "Oriental" rugs, specially made to fit. Some second-floor rooms have terraces over the patio. The Hotel Alfonso XIII is not only the choice of visiting dignitaries, but also the choice of Seville's élite when they entertain. For a deluxe hotel, ideally located for sightseeing, the Hotel Alfonso XIII is tops.

HOTEL ALFONSO XIII
Manager: Hector Salanova
San Fernando, 2
41004 Seville, Spain
Tel: (95) 42.22.850, Fax: (95) 42.16.033
149 rooms, Double: Pts 48,000*
*IVA not included, breakfast Pts 2,500
Open all year, Credit cards: all major
Restaurant open daily, pool
Michelin Map 446, Region: Andalusia

The Taberna del Alabardero (just a five-minute walk from Seville's cathedral) is a real find—almost too good to share. Here you can stay at a remarkably low room rate without sacrificing an ounce of quality, comfort, or ambiance. The charm begins with the exterior, a deep-salmon-pink, three-story building accented with white trim and black wrought-iron grille work. This was the home of Seville's beloved romantic poet, J. Antonio Cavestany. After meticulous renovation, taking great care to leave the original character intact, the home was reopened with the principal purpose of a gourmet restaurant where students from its hotel school could perfect their skills. Under the direction of one of Spain's finest chefs, Juan Marcos, the restaurant earned a coveted Michelin star in 1995. As you enter, you see a café with a bakery on the ground floor. The next level up is the restaurant—a series of intimate dining rooms. The top floor features a large skylight, below which a wrought-iron enclosed gallery opens onto the floors below. Around this gallery are seven guestrooms, named after the provinces in Andalusia. Each is impeccably decorated. Perhaps my favorite is the "Malaga" room, with Pompeii-yellow sponge-painted walls, beds with floral-patterned spreads in soft shades of yellows, rusts, and greens with matching fabric serving as headboards. From the sleeping area, steps lead down to a sitting area in front of a fireplace.

TABERNA DEL ALABARDERO
Manager & Chef: Juan Marcos
Zaragoza, 20
41001 Seville, Spain
Tel: (95) 45.60.637, Fax: (95) 45.63.666
www.karenbrown.com/spaininns/tabernadelalabardero.html
7 rooms, Double: Pts 18,600*
*IVA not included, breakfast included
Closed Aug, Credit cards: all major
Restaurant open daily
Michelin Map 446, Region: Andalusia

Just 18 kilometers from Seville in distance, yet a world away in atmosphere, lies the beautifully renovated Hotel Cortijo Aguila Real. When the charming Isabel Martinez and her husband bought the property it had fallen into serious disrepair but they saw the great potential of this handsome white farmhouse that had been the showplace of the whole region. In fact, the wealthy landowner who built the cortijo owned all the surrounding countryside—even including the town of Guillena. The Hotel Cortijo Aguila Real crowns the rise of a small hill, and, typical of the Andalusian style, you enter through a gate in the whitewashed walls into a large courtyard. Facing onto the courtyard is the family chapel which now serves as the reception area. Another door from the courtyard leads into an intimate library with prettily upholstered chairs facing the fireplace, a spacious living room, and a handsome dining room (although when the weather is warm, meals are usually served outside). The suites also open onto the central courtyard. The other guestrooms face onto a patio next to the gardens. Each of the bedrooms has a special flower motif which is repeated on the key chain, the fabric in the curtains, and in hand-painted designs on the headboards and dressers. There are many small gardens tucked around the property and also a large swimming pool, and even a private bullring. Another plus, the food is excellent and beautifully presented.

HOTEL CORTIJO AGUILA REAL
Owner: Francisco Venegas
41210 Guillena (Seville) Spain
Tel: (95) 57.85.006, Fax: (95) 57.84.330
www.karenbrown.com/spaininns/hotelcortijoaguilareal.html
11 rooms, Double: Pts 15,000–18,000*
*IVA not included, breakfast Pts 1,500
Open all year, Credit cards: all major
Restaurant open daily, pool
18 km N of Seville, 4 km E of Guillena
Michelin Map 446, Region: Andalusia

Just on the outskirts of Seville, only about 20 minutes by car, you can dwell in utter luxury. The Hacienda Benazuza caters to the rich and famous who want to be discreetly left alone, yet have their every need anticipated and fulfilled. This dazzling white hacienda, dating from the 10th century, belonged to Moorish royalty then, when the Moors were forced from Spain, it came into the hands of the Counts of Benazuza. In the mid-1900s the hacienda became the property of Pablo Romero, who was famous as one of the most outstanding breeders of fine fighting bulls. Today you can fall under the spell of these days long past as you walk the hushed halls, through various small courtyards, and pass fountains and formal gardens planned by the Moors so long ago. Although the niceties of today such as a beautiful swimming pool in the garden, satellite television, and luxurious modern bathrooms have been added, the ambiance remains faithful to the past with superb antiques used throughout. Each of the guestrooms is different. However, whether you are in a suite or a double room, you will find the decor faultless, with beautiful fabrics, quality carpets, antique furniture, and handsome pictures on the walls. The dining room, facing onto the courtyard, is beautiful and serves excellent meals, many of the recipes rooted in Andalusian tradition.

HACIENDA BENAZUZA
Manager: Javier Micueiz
Calle Virgen de Las Nieves s/n
41800 Sanlúcar la Mayor (Seville), Spain
Tel: (95) 57.03.344, Fax: (95) 57.03.410
44 rooms, Double: Pts 44,000*
*IVA not included, breakfast Pts 1,500
Closed mid-Jul to Sep, Credit cards: all major
Restaurant open daily, pool
27 km W of Seville, 72 km E of Huelva
Michelin Map 446, Region: Andalusia

Make a special effort to include the Parador Castillo de Sigüenza in your itinerary—you won't be sorry. The dramatic stone castle is perched romantically on a hillside overlooking an unspoiled cluster of old stone houses with red-tiled roofs. Happily, there are no modern buildings to interrupt the mood of the 12th century when the castle was a Moorish stronghold. The reconstruction was an overwhelming venture—take a look at the *before* and *after* photographs on the wall (just off the reception area)—you cannot help being impressed with what has been accomplished. Only the shell of the old castle remained, but the original walls have been repaired and the interior has been reconstructed with great care to preserve the original ambiance. Of course there are all the concessions to modern comforts for the traveler, but the decor (although perhaps too glamorous) is great fun. The lounge is dramatic: an enormous room with deep-red walls, blue sofas and chairs, red-tile floor, beamed ceiling, nine massive chandeliers, and a large fireplace. The hotel, following the original plan, is built around a central patio where the old well still remains. The spacious guestrooms are uncluttered and not too over-decorated: the walls stark white, the floors red tile, the furniture tasteful rustic reproductions, and the matching draperies and spreads of fine quality.

PARADOR CASTILLO DE SIGÜENZA
Manager: José Menguiano Corbacho
Plaza de Castillo, s/n
19250 Sigüenza (Guadalajara), Spain
Tel: (949) 39.01.00, Fax: (949) 39.13.64
81 rooms, Double: Pts 15,000*
*IVA not included, breakfast Pts 1,300
Open all year, Credit cards: all major
Restaurant open daily
133 km NE of Madrid, 191 km SW of Zaragoza
Michelin Map 444, Region: Guadalajara

Next to the ramparts in the ancient fortified town of Sos del Rey Católico, birthplace of the Catholic King Ferdinand, sits a contemporary parador which bears his name. Despite its recent construction, the hotel has a delightful, old-world ambiance and blends harmoniously with the centuries-old buildings around it. The setting is enchanting— surrounded by fertile countryside, resplendent with corn, wheat, and hay. The serenity is interrupted only by the chirping of swallows and the clanking of cowbells. The hotel's location is convenient for exploring the narrow maze of streets lined with low, sunken doorways and stone escutcheons, and for venturing up to the Sada palace where Spain's most renowned king, and Machiavelli's model prince, was born. In the lobby is a statue of the *reyito* (little king) alongside his mother, Juana Enriquez. Upstairs, the view can be enjoyed over coffee or cocktails on an outdoor terrace. Next to the terrace the dining room is attractive with leather chairs, wood-beamed ceiling, and elaborate iron chandeliers. The bedrooms have brick-red tile floors, cheerful, multi-colored striped woven spreads and drapes, pretty brass and glass lamps, and simple iron and brass bedsteads. Room 324 is especially pleasant with a large balcony.

PARADOR FERNANDO DE ARAGÓN
Manager: Miguel Rizos
50680 Sos del Rey Católico (Zaragoza), Spain
Tel: (948) 88.80.11, Fax: (948) 88.81.00
65 rooms, Double: Pts 15,000*
*IVA not included, breakfast Pts 1,300
Closed Dec & Jan, Credit cards: all major
Restaurant open daily
60 km SE of Pamplona, 423 km NE of Madrid
Michelin Map 443, Region: Aragon

The Hotel "La Rectoral" is a deluxe, small hotel tucked into the remote countryside of Asturias. When you arrive in the tiny village of Taramundi, you will wonder if you could possibly be in the right town. However, follow the signs up a small lane and you will arrive at an 18th-century stone house, similar to those you have seen dotting the lovely green countryside in the vicinity. But there is a big difference—this home (originally a rectory for the nearby church) has been totally renovated and now takes in overnight guests. The restoration has meticulously preserved the authentic, rustic mood. The bakery (with the old oven still in the corner) is now a small dining room with a skylight in the roof to lighten the darkened beams and thick stone walls. The dining room is especially attractive, with planked wooden floors, stone walls, and heavy beams blackened with age. Doors lead off the dining room to a wooden balcony where tables are set for dining in the warm summer months. The guestrooms are located in a new wing built in the same style as the original house and are decorated in a sophisticated, modern style with built-in headboards and all the latest amenities. Ask for a room on the ground level with a terrace—these offer a stunning view across the valley to the patchwork of beautiful green fields. For the sports enthusiasts, there is a well-equipped gymnasium, a sauna, and a large swimming pool.

HOTEL "LA RECTORAL"
Manager: Jesús Mier
33775 Taramundi (Asturias), Spain
Tel: (98) 56.46.767, Fax: (98) 56.46.777
18 rooms, Double: Pts 12,000*
*IVA not included, breakfast Pts 975
Open all year, Credit cards: all major
Restaurant open daily, pool
167 km NE of Santiago de Compostela
55 km E of Villaba
Michelin Map 441, Region: Asturias

The Parador de Teruel, located a little over a kilometer from the city, is a recently remodeled parador, incomparably graced with Mudéjar architecture. Surrounded by appealing grounds sheltering an attractive pool, the hotel has the appearance of a large private home, built in Mudéjar style, with a warm yellow façade and gently sloping tiled roofs. The unusual, somewhat formal octagonal lobby, dotted with antiques, features marble pillars and a high, sculpted ceiling. A massive stone archway frames marble stairs leading up to the bedrooms. The sunny, glass-enclosed terrace off the dining room and bar has the feel of an atrium, with pretty pastel-colored, flowered upholstery and wicker furniture, making it an altogether inviting spot for cocktails or supper. The bedrooms are parador large, with wood floors and woven earth-tone spreads on dark-wood beds. Although this is not a stellar example within the government chain, the hotel is nonetheless pleasant and commodious throughout, and it is unquestionably the best choice of accommodation when visiting the architecturally and archaeologically rich province and city of Teruel.

PARADOR DE TERUEL
Manager: Antonio Escobosa Blazquez
Carretera N 234, Carretera Sagundo-Burgos
44003 Teruel (Teruel), Spain
Tel: (974) 60.18.00, Fax: (974) 60.86.12
60 rooms, Double: Pts 13,500*
*IVA not included, breakfast Pts 1,300
Open all year, Credit cards: all major
Restaurant open daily
149 km NW of Valencia
Michelin Maps 443 & 444, Region: Aragón

The Gran Hotel is located on a tiny peninsula that is connected to the mainland by a narrow bridge. Surrounded by pine trees and with a view of the inlet of Pontevedra, this large, turn-of-the-century hotel whose white façade is accented by yellow awnings appears as a grand old mansion. One of the finest white-sand beaches in Spain (La Lanzada) is a five-minute drive away, and the hotel has its own health and fitness club, which includes Olympic-sized saltwater pool, Jacuzzi, steam bath, sauna, and gymnasium. There are also tennis courts, and a nine-hole golf course overlooking the sea. For those who like to try their hand at the game table, there is also a casino just steps from the hotel. Famous among Europeans for decades for its thermal baths, this somewhat dated, spa-style hotel is a reminder of the grand hotels of days gone by. The sparkling-white lobby offers the first taste of the formal public rooms. The vast, grand dining room is dramatic, with a huge stained-glass skylight and gleaming marble floors. One of the most attractive rooms is the sun terrace, looking out to the pool and the inlet (dotted with platforms for the cultivation of mussels). This bright and cheerful sun terrace has a ceiling draped in yellow and white, a motif carried out in the upholstery on the white wicker furniture beside glass-topped tables. The totally renovated modern bedrooms are spacious, catering to the comfort of the many long-term guests who return each year.

GRAN HOTEL LA TOJA
Manager: José Felix Alvarez
36991 Isla de la Toja (Pontevedra), Spain
Tel: (986) 73.00.25, Fax: (986) 73.12.01
197 rooms, Double: Pts 28,600–32,600*
*IVA not included, breakfast Pts 1,750
Open all year, Credit cards: all major
Restaurant open daily, pool
62 km N of Vigo, 70 km SW of Santiago
Michelin Map 441, Region: Galicia

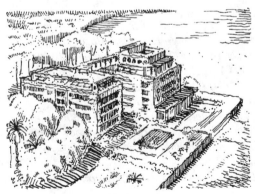

The Hostal del Cardenal, a former archbishop's summer home, is an absolute jewel. As an added bonus, it has a convenient location—on the northern edge of Toledo, with an entrance next to the Puerta de Bisagra (the city's main gate). Your introduction to the small hotel is through a dramatic 11th-century wall and into an enchanting garden with a reflecting pool reminiscent of that found at the Alhambra. Climb the stairs on the right to reach the tiny foyer of the hostal. The stunning stairway, the patio with its lovely fountain, and the cozy sitting rooms embellished with antiques all reflect the hotel's 18th-century heritage. The period furnishings in the inviting guestrooms seem to blend into a tasteful whole. Although smallish, the rooms provide modern comfort with an unbeatable ambiance of past centuries. The indoor dining rooms (which are used only in the winter) are fabulous with their heavy wood beams and fireplaces. In warmer months, meals are served in the garden in the shadow of the medieval walls. The kitchen is outstanding and serves Castilian specialties such as suckling pig. The Hostal del Cardenal has a natural grace and authentic old-world charm frequently lacking in more deluxe hotels. With its gardens, excellent management, and lovely ambiance, this is definitely the finest place to stay in Toledo (and the price is low for value received).

HOSTAL DEL CARDENAL
Manager: Luis Gonzalez Gozalbo
Paseo Recaredo 24
45004 Toledo, Spain
Tel: (925) 22.49.00, Fax: (925) 22.29.91
www.karenbrown.com/spaininns/hosteldelcardenal.html
27 rooms, Double: Pts 9,115–12,150*
*IVA not included, breakfast Pts 875 (continental)
Open all year, Credit cards: all major
Restaurant open daily
70 km SW of Madrid
Michelin Map 444, Region: Castilla-La Mancha

The Parador Conde de Orgaz has a choice setting on the hillside across the Tagus river from Toledo, one of the most beautiful ancient towns in Spain. If ever you're willing to pay extra for a view and a terrace, this is the place to do so. The bar and the restaurant also have terraces with a view, so what you are paying for is privacy—your own balcony and view. We think it is worth every penny to see the city change from golden brown to pink in the setting sun. In any case, you will be happy with the rooms—large, comfortable, and tastefully decorated with gaily colored wooden headboards and red-tile floors with pretty rugs. The open-beamed ceilings are especially attractive. Indeed, the newly built, regional-style building is handsome throughout. The impressive, two-story lobby with its giant wood beams is magnificent when viewed from the gallery above which leads to your room. Liberal use of colorful ceramic tiles and local copper pieces adds a delightful touch. There is also a pool surrounded by a pretty lawn. As lovely as the parador is, however, it has one drawback: you have to drive into town.

PARADOR CONDE DE ORGAZ
Manager: Fernando Molina Aranda
Cerro del Emperador s/n
45000 Toledo, Spain
Tel: (925) 22.18.50, Fax: (925) 22.51.66
76 rooms, Double: Pts 18,500*
*IVA not included, breakfast 1,300
Open all year, Credit cards: all major
Restaurant open daily, pool
2 km S of Toledo on circuit road
70 km SW of Madrid
Michelin Map 444, Region: Castilla-La Mancha

Unlike some of the paradors that are historic monuments, this one in Tordesillas should not be considered a destination in its own right. However, it certainly makes an excellent choice for a stop en route. The hotel is an especially appealing choice during the hot summer months because in the rear garden, facing a lovely pine forest, is an exceptionally large, attractive swimming pool. The Parador de Tordesillas is newly built, but in an old-world style and with many accents of antiques such as hand-carved chests, grandfather clocks, and old mirrors. The exterior is painted a pure white, the windows outlined in tan bricks, and the roof made with a heavy terra cotta tile. The hotel faces directly on the main highway into town, but a green lawn dotted with tall pine trees gives an appealing country air. To the right of the reception area is a large, attractive lounge with an enormous tapestry, fine oil paintings, and a large open fireplace flanked by leather chairs and sofas. The dining room is outstanding: a bright and cheerful room with a wall of windows looking out to a lovely pine forest. The guestrooms are attractive, with traditional wood furniture, wrought-iron reading lamps, and gleaming parquet floors accented with colorful area rugs. One of the nicest aspects of the hotel is that it is immaculately kept throughout.

PARADOR DE TORDESILLAS
Manager: Alfonso Sánchez-M. Capilla
47100 Tordesillas (Valladolid), Spain
Tel: (983) 77.00.51, Fax: (983) 77.10.13
71 rooms, Double: Pts 15,000*
*IVA not included, breakfast Pts 1,300
Open all year, Credit cards: all major
Restaurant open daily, pool
182 km NE of Madrid, 142 km SE of León
Michelin Map 441, Region: Castilla y León

Mas means an old farmhouse, implying perhaps a simple place to stay. Such is definitely not the case at the Mas de Torrent, a hotel of absolute luxury and stunning charm, idyllically set in the countryside near the beaches of the Costa Brava. The enchantment of the 18th-century, honey-toned stone farmhouse remains, while further enhanced by an outstanding interior design. The walls and vaulted stone ceiling are painted a delicate, muted salmon—an ever-so-appealing color scheme that is repeated in the fabrics and fresh bouquets of flowers. There are several cozy sitting areas, each tastefully decorated with antiques from the region. What was once the kitchen is now the bar, and you can still see the massive chimney for the fireplace and the original deep stone well. A new wing, which blends in beautifully with the original structure, has been added and houses the gourmet restaurant. Ten of the bedrooms are located in the original farmhouse— splurge and request one of these. Each is individually decorated with antiques, each is a dream. My favorite (room 1) has a gorgeous antique bed, exquisite armoire, and large terrace overlooking the pool and garden. There are also 20 guestrooms in a newly constructed garden wing. Although not antique in decor, these are beautifully appointed and have the luxury of individual, private terraces.

MAS DE TORRENT
Manager: Gregori Berengui
17123 Torrent (Gerona), Spain
Tel: (972) 30.32.92, Fax: (972) 30.32.93
30 rooms, Double: Pts 30,000*
*IVA not included, breakfast Pts 2,000
Open all year, Credit cards: all major
Restaurant open daily, pool
133 km NE of Barcelona, 36 km E of Gerona
Michelin Map 443, Region:Catalonia

As you drive into Tortosa, you will see the Parador "Castillo de La Zuda" crowning a hill at the northern end of town. The location is significant, for this historic parador is nestled into the ruins of an ancient Arab fortress that guarded the city in former times. As you wind your way up the hill, the road enters through the ancient walls which still stretch in partial ruins along the hilltop. Although the architectural style is that of a castle, most of the hotel is actually of new construction with a somewhat traditional hotel look. The dining room is very attractive and strives for an old-world feel with wrought-iron light fixtures and a beamed ceiling. The cuisine features specialties of the Catalan region. Each of the guestrooms is furnished exactly alike with wood and leather headboards, home-spun-looking drapes and matching spreads, and dark-wood chairs and desks. Every room has a balcony and the views from this lofty hilltop setting are lovely in every direction, whether it be to the fertile Ebro river valley or the mountain massif. One of the nicest aspects of this parador is a romantic swimming pool tucked into a terrace framed by the ancient walls of the castle. There is also a children's play yard for those traveling with little ones. The bustling town of Tortosa is not terribly picturesque but the hotel, surrounded by acres of land, creates its own atmosphere.

PARADOR "CASTILLO DE LA ZUDA"
Manager: Manuel Esteban
43500 Tortosa (Tarragona), Spain
Tel: (977) 44.44.50, Fax: (977) 44.44.58
82 rooms, Double: Pts 15,000*
*IVA not included, breakfast Pts 1,300
Open all year, Credit cards: all major
Restaurant open daily, pool
188 km SW of Barcelona
Michelin Maps 443 & 445, Region: Catalonia

Restaurants, boutiques, and souvenir shops now line the maze of narrow streets that spider-web back from Tossa de Mar's beach, but once you get past the high-rise hotels and condominiums, the heart of the town still retains the feel of its fishing village heritage. Most tourists opt for one of the modern hotels with swimming pool and up-to-date amenities. However, if you don't mind sacrificing luxury for location, the Hotel Diana offers a lot of charm. The setting is prime: the hotel fronts right onto the main beach promenade. A bar, with small tables set outside to watch the action, stretches across the front of the building. Arched windows, dark-green trim, and a white exterior lend a small villa-like atmosphere to the hotel. Within, the hotel has the character of a private home. Marble floors, antique furnishings, grandfather clock, painted tile decoration, inner courtyards, fountains, statues, and stained-glass designs all add a romantic, if somewhat worn, appeal. The simply decorated bedrooms have TV and telephone. Ask for one of the best rooms, such as 306, 307, 206, and 207—the headboards are antique, the bathroom modern, and, best yet, there is a good-sized balcony with a lovely view of the beach and the old fortress on the hill. If you don't expect too much from this two-star hotel, the Hotel Diana is an excellent value.

HOTEL DIANA
Manager: Fernando Osorio Gotarra
Plaza de España, 6
17320 Tossa de Mar (Gerona), Spain
Tel: (972) 34.18.86, Fax: (972) 34.18.86
www.karenbrown.com/spaininns/hoteldiana.html
21 rooms, Double: Pts 10,400*
*IVA included, breakfast Pts 1,000
Open Easter to Nov, Credit cards: all major
No restaurant, breakfast only
79 km NE of Barcelona, 39 km S of Gerona
Michelin Map 443, Region: Catalonia (Costa Brava)

Henri Elink Schuurman and his Spanish wife, Marta, bought a beautiful 19th-century farm with two granite houses, an olive press, a winery, and a house chapel 14 kilometers outside Trujillo (on the road to the captivating town of Guadalupe). With patience and love he has tucked guestrooms into the various buildings—taking great care not to disturb the ambiance of the farm (finca) that makes a stay here so special. Of course you must be the kind of person who would chuckle to find a lamb looking through your window in the morning or ducks waddling by your door. Henri (who before retirement was a Dutch diplomat) and his family live in Madrid, but are frequently at the finca where Henri oversees the ongoing project of renovation and Marta, an artist and decorator, has created a beautiful ambiance of rustic simplicity. My favorite guestroom (the "red room") is on the ground floor of the main house and has two charming antique iron beds, pretty red-print, country-French-style material on the spreads and curtains, a predominantly red Oriental carpet, and a window overlooking a tranquil garden where dinner is often served. Steps lead from the garden to a swimming pool surrounded by a lawn stretching out to groves of olive, cherry, and almond trees.

FINCA SANTA MARTA
Owners: Marta & Henri Elink Schuurman
Pago San Clemente, Por la carretera de Guadalupe
10200 Trujillo (Cáceres), Spain
(or: Juan Ramón Jiménez, 12-8.º A, 28036 Madrid)
Reservations (91) 35.02.217, Tel & fax: (927) 31.92.03
E-mail: henri@facilnet.es
www.karenbrown.com/spaininns/fincasantamarta.html
12 rooms, Double: Pts 9,000*
*IVA not included, breakfast included
Open all year, Credit cards: MC, VS
Restaurant open daily upon request, pool
14 km SE of Trujillo on C 524, sign on right
Michelin Map 444, Region: Extremadura

Installed in the 16th-century convent of Santa Clara, the Parador de Trujillo, opened in 1984, blends harmoniously with the Renaissance and medieval architecture in Trujillo. Enter through the outdoor stone patio, and be sure to notice the *torno* (revolving shelf) to the right of the doorway. The original residents were cloistered nuns, and it was by way of this device that they sold their homemade sweets to the town's citizens. Inside, 18 of the hotel's bedrooms were originally the nuns' cells, and retain their low, stone doorways (be careful not to bump your head). These rooms surround a sunlit gallery (whose walls are laced with climbing vines) overlooking a cloistered garden patio with an old stone well at its center. An attached annex houses new bedrooms surrounding another, whitewashed courtyard. Although there is a special flavor to the original bedrooms, the new addition has views of the valley and maintains a traditional Spanish ambiance with pale-wood furnishings, brick-tiled floors, leather sling chairs, and iron fixtures. This parador is a charming spot from which explore the beautiful town of Trujillo and to launch explorations of Extremadura, whose native sons launched their own explorations to the New World.

PARADOR DE TRUJILLO
Manager: José Rizos
Plaza de Santa Clara
10200 Trujillo (Cáceres), Spain
Tel: (927) 32.13.50, Fax: (927) 32.13.66
46 rooms, Double: Pts: 15,000*
*IVA not included, breakfast Pts 1,300
Open all year, Credit cards: all major
Restaurant open daily
252 km SW of Madrid, 88 km NE of Mérida
Michelin Map 444, Region: Extremadura

This parador is installed in a 16th-century palace on Ubeda's monumentally magnificent Renaissance main square. It features no less than three interior patios, one lined by slender stone arches and dotted with outdoor tables, another overhung with its original wooden terraces, and the third converted to a lovely garden. All but the five newest guestrooms are found at the glass-enclosed gallery level, up a massive stone stairway flanked by suits of armor. The hotel has undergone two renovations, resulting in a variety of rooms off the antique-lined hallways, all of them lovely, with gleaming white baths, colorfully tiled floors, and wood artesonado ceilings. Our personal favorites are those overlooking the golden Plaza Vázquez de Molina and El Salvador chapel, largely furnished with antiques (room 112 is especially romantic, with a small corner balcony peeking out at the cathedral). The more recent additions are decorated in a modern style and are more spacious (one has a sitting room for an additional 3,000 pesetas). Detailed attention to faithful historic preservation is obvious throughout the parador's public rooms, with the exception of the recently constructed but pleasant restaurant, whose menu offers an unusually creative variety of dishes. Don't miss a visit to the Taberna, a lounge/bar in the stone basement, whose decor includes huge, ceramic storage vats.

PARADOR "CONDESTABLE DAVALOS"
Manager: José Muños
Plaza de Vázquez Molina, s/n
23400 Ubeda (Jaén), Spain
Tel: (953) 75.03.45, Fax: (953) 75.12.59
31 rooms, Double: Pts 16,500*
*IVA not included, breakfast Pts 1,300
Open all year, Credit cards: all major
Restaurant open daily
120 km NE of Granada
Michelin Map 444, Region: Andalucia

Four kilometers west of the sleepy town of Verín, its brooding stone towers visible from afar, stands the medieval castle fortress of Monterrey (the most important monument in the province of Orense), facing the parador of the same name. Reached by driving through green vineyards, the hotel is constructed in the style of a regional manor, having a somewhat severe exterior of cut-stone blocks with a crenelated tower at one end. The Parador Monterrey is perched atop a vine-covered hill and surrounded by lovely views in all directions from its high vantage point. The lobby features warm wood decorated with suits of armor and other antique pieces. Fifteen of the twenty-three bedrooms enjoy the countryside vista, eight overlooking the dramatic castle (ask for 102, 104, 106, or 107). The large rooms are pleasantly decorated in beige and brown, with wood floors and comfortable, contemporary Spanish furniture. The tranquil setting of this parador, along with its pretty pool in the middle of a lovely green lawn and the delightfully cozy reading room with its unusual fireplace, makes it an ideal spot for overnighting, especially if you can squeeze in a visit to the castle and its 13th-century church.

PARADOR MONTERREY
Manager: Tomas Cardo
32600 Verín (Orense), Spain
Tel: (988) 41.00.75, Fax: (988) 41.20.17
23 rooms, Double: Pts 12,500–13,500*
*IVA not included, breakfast Pts 1,200
Open Feb to mid-Dec, Credit cards: all major
Restaurant open daily, pool
209 km NW of Zamora, 182 km SE of Santiago
Michelin Map 441, Region: Galicia

Situated in the pine-green mountains outside the medieval town of Vic (also spelled Vich on some maps), this parador overlooks the reddish, gorge like rock formations and the blue Sau reservoir which is fed by the waters of the Ter river. Its setting is singular in beauty and tranquillity. The hotel is within easy walking distance of an ancient monastery that can be reached only by foot and within easy driving distance of several of the most picturesque villages in the region (Rupit being the most notable example). The building itself has somewhat of an institutional look with a severe façade of pale-gray granite with arched windows, iron balconies, and red-tile roof. The two-story patio/lobby has heavy polished-wood columns, a large modern mural on one wall, and a vast stained-glass ceiling that casts blue and gold light on a shining white-marble floor. One of the nicest rooms is the sitting room with antiques and a cozy fireplace. The wood-paneled bar has a terrace with views over the lake below. Most of the bedrooms have terraces with splendid views over the lovely swimming pool and lawn and on to the hill-ringed lake beyond. The bedrooms are large and pleasant, decorated with wooden furniture and lovely brass and iron lamps. Note: The well-signposted parador is located about 15 kilometers northeast of Vic, off the C153 to Roda de Ter.

PARADOR DE VIC
Manager: Anna María Puigdollers
08500 Vic (Barcelona), Spain
Tel: (93) 81.22.323, Fax: (93) 81.22.368
36 rooms, Double: Pts 15,000*
*IVA not included, breakfast 1,300
Open all year, Credit cards: all major
Restaurant open daily, pool
80 km N of Barcelona
Michelin Map 443, Region: Catalonia

Although the tiniest of Spain's paradors, the "Condes de Villaba" is a real gem. As you drive into town, you cannot miss this small hotel which is incorporated into a very old stone tower—the only remaining fortification standing in Villaba, which otherwise has lost its medieval ambiance. The ground level holds an excellent restaurant—a romantic room with two enormous iron chandeliers, antlers on whitewashed walls, massive stone floor, and just ten tables. Steps lead up to the reception area encompassing the entire second level. Colorful medieval paintings on the walls and a soaring ceiling give this room a proper castle atmosphere. Each of the next three floors of the octagonal tower has two guestrooms. There is a small elevator, but if you want some exercise, it is fun to wind your way up the stairs to the various levels, peeking out as you climb through tiny slit windows in the thick stone walls. All of the bedrooms are spacious but the even-numbered rooms (2, 4, and 6) are enormous. The decor is extremely attractive, with plain wooden headboards, wrought-iron reading lamps, simple wooden writing desks, beamed ceilings, and pretty area rugs setting off the gleam of hardwood floors. The stone walls are so deep that you must actually walk into them to look out through the original tall, narrow windows.

PARADOR "CONDES DE VILLABA"
Manager: José Ceferino Vázquez
Valeriano Valdesuso, s/n
27800 Villaba (Lugo) Spain
Tel: (982) 51.00.11, Fax: (982) 51.00.90
6 rooms, Double: Pts 17,500*
*IVA not included, breakfast Pts 1,300
Closed Dec 20 to Feb 9, Credit cards: all major
Restaurant open daily
65 km SE of Ferrol, 140 km NE of Santiago
Michelin Map 441, Region: Galicia

The setting of El Montíboli is nothing short of superb—completely dominating its own rocky peninsula which juts into the sea. The entrance is through a well-kept garden, enhanced by long reflecting pools rimmed by a series of terra cotta jugs which have been converted into merry little fountains. Although of new construction, the exterior reflects Moorish influence, with a stark white exterior and arches incorporated throughout the design. The interior is much more contemporary in feel—sort of a "Miami Beach" look with light streaming in through purple, turquoise, and white translucent windows. In the center of the lobby is a gold-leaf table with an artificial silk flower arrangement. To the right is a sitting area with modern brass and leather chairs. Because the hotel is terraced down the hill, the lounge, bar, conference rooms, and dining room are built at various levels, cleverly designed to take full advantage of the fabulous views. Most of the guestrooms too capture a vista of the sea. In addition to tennis courts, there are two pools, one a gem of a small oval pool crowning a promontory overlooking the sea, and the other next to the beach and tennis courts. Best yet, whereas most hotels would be happy just to have a bit of sand, the El Montíboli has not one, but *two* excellent beaches, one on each side of the private peninsula. Amazingly, the hotel is not super-expensive—for all the amenities it offers, it is a good value.

El MONTÍBOLI HOTEL
Manager: José Castillo Aliaga
03570 Villajoyosa (Alicante), Spain
Tel: (96) 58.90.250, Fax: (96) 58.93.857
53 rooms, Double: Pts 22,300*
*IVA not included, breakfast included
Open all year, Credit cards: all major
Restaurant open daily, pools
3 km S of Villajoyosa, 145 km S of Valencia
Michelin Map 445, Region: Valencia (Costa Blanca)

The Hotel la Casona de Amandi (dating back to 1850) is a typical home of this area—an appealing, two-story white house with a wide expanse of small-paned windows wrapping around the second level and a steeply pitched red-tile roof. It faces directly onto a small street, but there are extensive manicured grounds surrounding it on three sides. Some of the gardens are formal, with a French flair, others have a more casual English look. Inside, the ambiance is very homey, much more like an intimate bed and breakfast than a hotel. The owners live on the property and take pride in seeing that guests are well cared for. The furnishings throughout are antiques, nothing pretentious or decorator-perfect, just fine family pieces displayed as in a real home. The spacious living room is lovely with comfortable sofas (slip-covered in pretty floral fabric) flanking a large fireplace. Antiques abound, but the one that is particularly gorgeous is an enormous 17th-century wooden chest under one of the windows. Breakfast is served in an intimate, old-fashioned little parlor. The guestrooms, like the rest of the house, are decorated in antiques—all are different, but have the same old-world look. Number 1, a twin-bedded room, is especially attractive, with beautiful antique headboards, pretty matching floral draperies and bedspreads, and windows looking out on two sides.

HOTEL LA CASONA DE AMANDI
Owner: Rodrigo Fernández Suarez
33300 Amandi-Villaviciosa (Asturias), Spain
Tel: (98) 58.90.130, Fax: (98) 58.90.129
9 rooms, Double: Pts 11,300*
*IVA not included, breakfast Pts 850
Open all year, Credit cards: all major
No restaurant, breakfast only
32 km W of Gijón, 39 km NE of Oviedo
1,300 meters S of Villaviciosa
Michelin Map 441, Region: Asturias

Cortés was the conquistador of the Aztec empire in Mexico in 1521. He was born in Medellín, east of Mérida, but was taken on as a protégé by the Duke of Feria, whose ancestors built this wonderful fortified castle in the 15th century. Cortés actually lived here for a short time before embarking for Cuba as an ordinary colonist. The castle has been faithfully restored and put to use as a highly attractive hotel. Virtually surrounded by towers, the exterior is somewhat intimidating, but the tiny plaza in front of it is charming and, once inside, you will love the lounges and public areas with antiques in every available space. There is a glorious chapel with an incredible golden cupola. The central patio, with its graceful stone columns, is equally enchanting. The bedrooms vary somewhat, since they were often installed in the original castle rooms, but they are all attractively decorated with regional furniture and the traditional parador good taste. In 1991 the parador was completely renovated: several new guestrooms were added including three with a terrace and several with a special romantic decor. Sala Dorada (room 314) has a stunning ceiling and room 303 has a Jacuzzi. This parador affords a marvelous opportunity to lodge in an authentic castle without sacrificing a single modern comfort.

PARADOR DE ZAFRA
Manager: Antonio Atalaya Diaz
Plaza Corazón de María, 7
06300 Zafra (Badajoz), Spain
Tel: (924) 55.45.40, Fax: (924) 55.10.18
45 rooms, Double: Pts 15,000*
*IVA not included, breakfast Pts 1,300
Open all year, Credit cards: all major
Restaurant open daily, pool
135 km N of Seville
Michelin Maps 444 & 446, Region: Extremadura

The Parador "Condes de Alba y Aliste" is a stately stone mansion built in the 15th century by the counts whose names it bears. The exterior is somewhat austere, reflecting the style of the times, but inside, you will be charmed. The elaborate use of antiques with regional furniture makes a terrific impression. The central patio, surrounded by glassed-in, stone-arcaded galleries, is wonderful. Masterful antique tapestries and chivalric banners abound on the walls, and many of the interior doorways have intricately carved façades. Sitting areas are arranged around the galleries and afford a lovely view through rich wood shutters of the interior patio with its old stone well. The hotel closed for extensive renovation in 1995 and reopened in the spring of 1996. Twenty-four new bedrooms were added and the hotel refurbished. This delightful parador has always been one of our favorites, and after its face-lift, is even nicer. Its prime setting in the heart of Zamora has, of course, not changed. It faces onto a small stone-paved square, a convenient hub for exploring the narrow, picturesque streets of the old quarter.

PARADOR "CONDES DE ALBA Y ALISTE"
Manager: Sra. Pilar Pelegrin Gracia
Plaza de Viriato, 5
49001 Zamora, Spain
Tel: (980) 51.44.97, Fax: (980) 53.00.63
51 rooms, Double: Pts 17,500*
*IVA not included, breakfast Pts 1,300
Open all year, Credit cards: all major
Restaurant open daily, pool
206 km N of Salamanca, 257 km NW of Madrid
Michelin Maps 441 & 442
Region: Castilla y León

Maps

Regions of Spain

Santiago de Compostela

Galicia

Asturias

Cantabria

Navarra

La Rioja

FRANCE

Catalonia

Barcelona

Castilla y León

Aragon

PORTUGAL

Madrid

Madrid

Castilla-La Mancha

Valencia

Extremadura

MEDITERRANEAN SEA

Andalusia

Murcia

ATLANTIC OCEAN

Málaga

Key Map to Hotels

Map 1: Northwest Spain

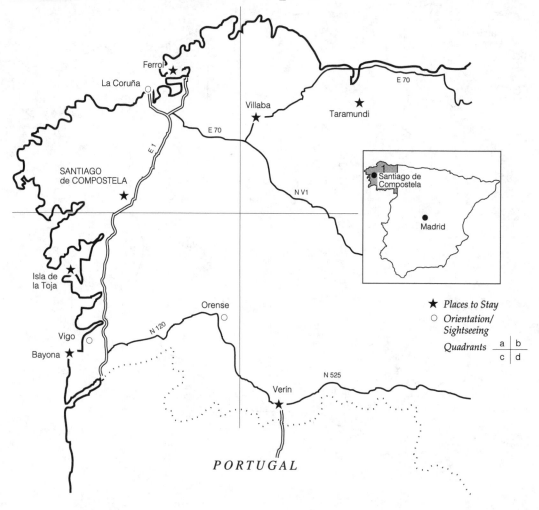

Ferrol

La Coruña

Villaba

Taramundi

E 70

E 70

E 1

SANTIAGO
de COMPOSTELA

N V1

Isla de
la Toja

Orense

N 120

Vigo

Bayona

N 525

Verín

PORTUGAL

Santiago de
Compostela

Madrid

★ *Places to Stay*

○ *Orientation/*
Sightseeing

Quadrants

a	b
c	d

Map 2: North Central Spain

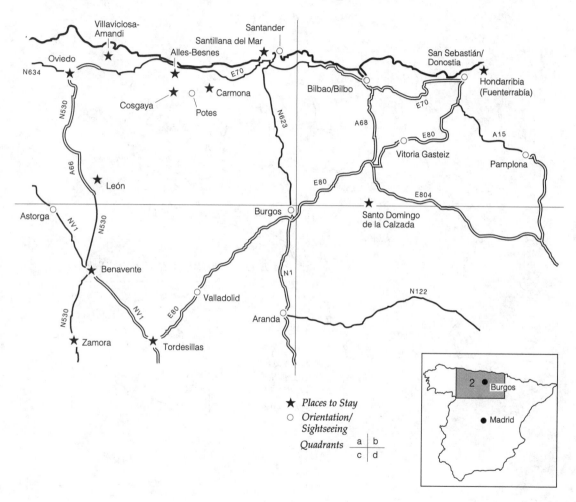

Villaviciosa-Amandi
★

Santander

Santillana del Mar
★

San Sebastián/
Donostia
★

Oviedo
★

Alles-Besnes
★

N634

N530

E70

Hondarribia
(Fuenterrabía)
★

Cosgaya
★

Carmona
★

Potes
○

Bilbao/Bilbo
○

E70

E80

A68

A66

N623

Vitoria Gasteiz
○

A15

Pamplona
○

León
★

E80

E804

Astorga
○

NV1

N530

Burgos
○

Santo Domingo
de la Calzada
★

Benavente
★

N1

N122

N530

NV1

E80

Valladolid
○

Aranda
○

Zamora
★

Tordesillas
★

★ *Places to Stay*
○ *Orientation/*
  Sightseeing
Quadrants

a	b
c	d

2 ● Burgos

● Madrid

Map 3: Northeast Spain

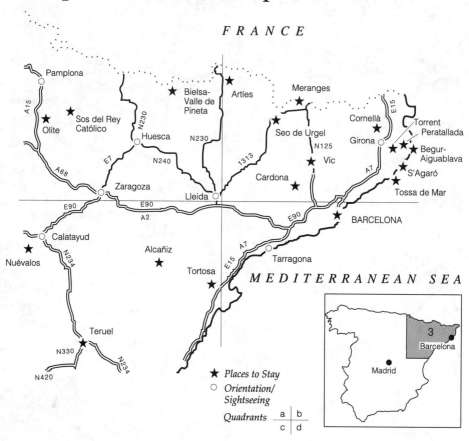

FRANCE

Pamplona

Bielsa-
Valle de
Pineta

Artíes

Meranges

Cornellà

Torrent
Peratallada

Sos del Rey
Católico

Olite

Huesca

Seo de Urgel

Girona

Begur-
Aiguablava

N125

S'Agaró

Zaragoza

Lleida

Vic

Cardona

Tossa de Mar

BARCELONA

Calatayud

Alcañiz

Nuévalos

Tortosa

Tarragona

MEDITERRANEAN SEA

Teruel

★ Places to Stay
○ Orientation/
   Sightseeing
Quadrants

a	b
c	d

Barcelona

Madrid

Map 4: Southeast Spain

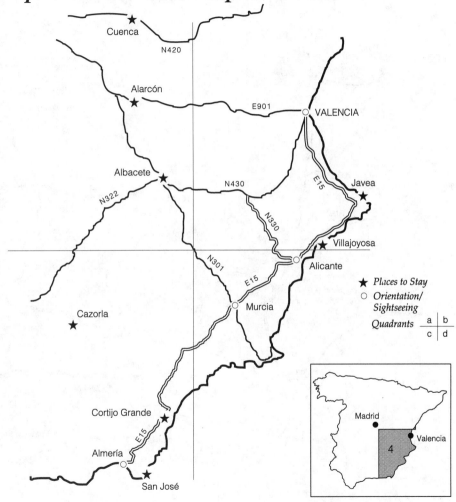

Cuenca

N420

Alarcón

E901

VALENCIA

Albacete

N430

E15

Javea

N322

N330

Villajoyosa

N301

Alicante

Cazorla

E15

Murcia

★ Places to Stay
○ Orientation/
   Sightseeing
Quadrants | a | b |
          | c | d |

Cortijo Grande

E15

Almería

San José

Madrid

Valencia

4

Map 5: Southwest Spain

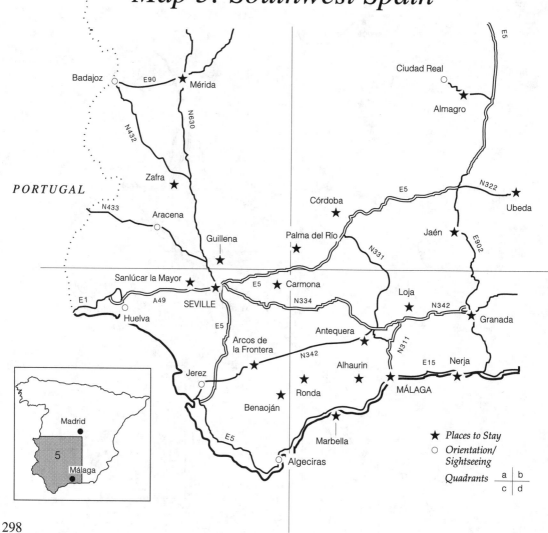

PORTUGAL

Badajoz ○   E90   ★ Mérida   Ciudad Real ○

N432   N630   ★ Almagro

Zafra ★   Córdoba ★   E5   N322   ★ Ubeda

N433

Aracena ○   Palma del Río ★   Jaén ★   E902

Guillena ★   N331

Sanlúcar la Mayor ★   E5 ★ Carmona   Loja ★   N342   Granada ★

E1   A49   SEVILLE   N334   ★ Nerja

Huelva ○   E5   Antequera ★   N311   E15

Arcos de la Frontera ★   N342   Alhaurin ★   MÁLAGA ★

Jerez ○   Ronda ★   ★

Benaoján ★

Marbella ★

E5   Algeciras ○

Madrid ●   ★ Places to Stay
○ Orientation/
   Sightseeing

5   Quadrants | a | b |
             |---|---|
             | c | d |

Málaga ●

298

Map 6: Central Spain

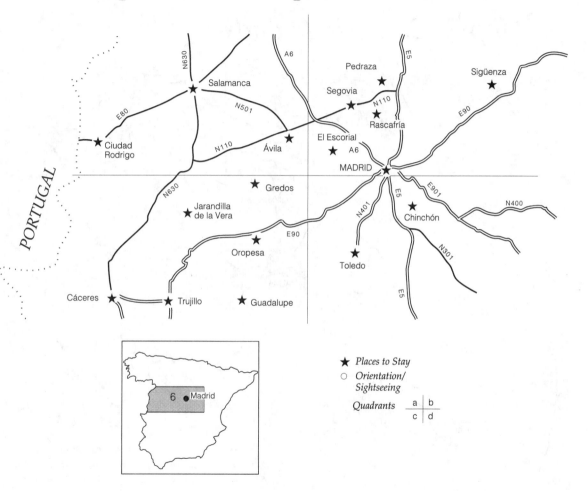

★ Places to Stay
○ Orientation/
   Sightseeing

Quadrants

a	b
c	d

Map 7: Balearic Islands

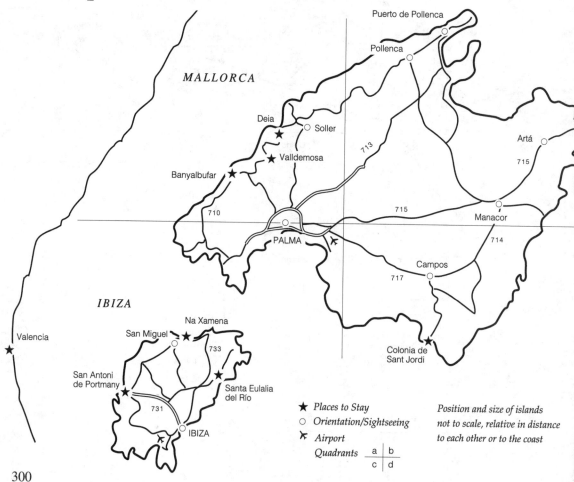

★ Places to Stay
○ Orientation/Sightseeing
✕ Airport
Quadrants

a	b
c	d

*Position and size of islands
not to scale, relative in distance
to each other or to the coast*

300

Reservation Request Letter in Spanish and English

HOTEL NAME AND ADDRESS—CLEARLY PRINTED OR TYPED

Muy señores nuestros:
Dear Sirs:
Rogamos reserven para _____   *noches (s)*
We are writing to request (number)   nights (s) at your hotel
a partir del día _____ *de* _____   *hasta el día* _____ *de* _____
Arriving (day)   (month)   departing   (day)   (month)
_____   *habitacion(es) sencilla(s)*
          number of single rooms
_____   *habitacion(es) doble(s)*
          number of double room(s)
con cama extra _____   *con vista al mar* _____   *con terraza*____
with an extra bed   sea view   with a terrace
con vista al patio ____   *con vista a la plaza* ____ *en la parte antigua* ____
facing the patio   facing the plaza   in the old part
Somos _____ *Persons.*
We are (number of) persons in our party.
Les rogamos nos informen sobre la disponibilidad de habitacion(es), el precio de la(s) misma(s), y el depósito requerido. En espera de su respuesta les saludamos, atentamente,
Please advise availability, rate, and deposit needed. Awaiting your reply, we remain, sincerely,

YOUR NAME AND ADDRESS CLEARLY PRINTED OR TYPED.

Index

A

About Hotels, 35
About Spain, 3
About This Guide, 2
Aguilar de la Frontera, 57
Aiguablava-Begur
    Hotel Aigua Blava, 191
    Parador "Costa Brava", 192
Al-Andalus Expreso, 23
Alarcón
    Parador "Marqués de Villena", 170
Alba de Tormes, 103
Albacete
    Parador de la Mancha, 171
Albarracín, 82
Alcabre, 72
Alcala La Real, 57
    Fort of La Mota, 57
Alcañiz, 88
    Parador de la Concordia, 88, 172
Alcaudete, 57
Alcazaba, 137
Alcázar de San Juan, 52
Alfonso IX, 105
Alfonso X "the Wise", 105, 158
Alfonso XI, 99
Alhambra, 36, 58
Alhambra Palace Hotel, Granada, 57
Alhaurín El Grande, 62
    Finca La Mota, 173
Alles-Besnes
    La Tahona, 174
Almagro, 52
    Corral de Comedias, 52

Almagro (cont.)
    Parador de Almagro, 52, 175
Almandoz, 120
Almodóvar del Rio, 56
Almuñécar, 61
Alpujarras Mountains, 60
Altamira Caves, Santillana del Mar, 117
Amandi
    Hotel La Casona de Amandi, 288
America (Hotel), Granada, 57, 214
Ampurias, 134
Andalusia, 54
Andalusian Adventures–Itinerary, 135
Andalusian Express, 23
Andorra, 130
Andorra La Vella, 130
Andújar, 54
Antequera
    Parador de Antequera, 176
Aracena, 94
    Gruta de las Maravillas, 94
Arcos de la Frontera, 25, 141
    Hotels
        Cortijo Faín, 142, 177
        Hotel El Convento, 142, 178
        Parador Casa del Corregidor, 142, 179
    Santa María de la Asunción, 142
Arenas de Cabrales, 113
Arevalo, 66
Arosa (Hotel), Madrid, 230
Artíes
    Parador Don Gaspar, 180
Arzua, 76
Avila, 25, 103, 151, 152
    Carmelite Convent, 103

Avila (cont.)
  Cathedral, 153
  Church of Saint John, 104
  Convento de San José, 154
  Convento de Santa Teresa, 153
  Hotels
      Gran Hotel Palacio Valderrábanos, 181
      Hostería de Bracamonte, 182
      Parador de Ávila, 183
  St. Peter's Church, 154
  St. Vincent's Church, 153

B

Baena, 57
Baeza, 54
Balearic Islands
  Ibiza, San Antoni de Portmany
      Hotel Pikes, 222
  Ibiza, San Miguel, Na Xamena
      Hotel Hacienda, 223
  Ibiza, Santa Eulalia del Rio
      La Colina, 224
  Mallorca, Banyalbufar
      Hotel Mar i Vent, 235
  Mallorca, Colonia de Sant Jordi
      Finca es Palmer, 236
  Mallorca, Deia
      LaResidencia, 237
  Mallorca, Valldemosa
      Vistamar de Valldemosa, 238
Banks, 3
Barcelona, 26, 79, 90, 163
  Casa Batlló, 165
  Casa Mila, 165
  Dancing Fountains, 167
  Fundación Joan Miró, 167
  Gothic Quarter, 165
  Guell Park, 165

Barcelona (cont.)
  Holy Family (Sagrada Familia) Church, 165
  Hotels
      Duques de Bergara, 185
      Gallery Hotel, 186
      Hotel Colón, 184
      Hotel Mesón Castilla, 187
      Hotel Montecarlo, 188
      Palace Hotel, 189
  Museum of Catalan Art, 166
  Palacio Guell, 165
  Palacio Nacional, 166
  Parque de la Ciudadela, 167
  Parque de Montjuich, 166
  Pedrera, 165
  Picasso Museum, 165
  Ramblas, 164
  Santa María, 164
  Scala, 167
Barcelona Highlights–Itinerary, 163
Basque Region, 118
Battle of Salado, 99
Bayona, 70
  Parador Conde de Gondomar, 70, 190
Begur-Aiguablava
  Hotel Aigua Blava, 191
  Parador "Costa Brava", 192
Belchite, 88
Benaoján, 62
  Molino del Santo, 193
Benavente
  Parador Rey Fernando II de León, 194
Berlitz Phrase Book, 7
Besalú, 132
Besnes-Alles
  La Tahona, 174
Bielsa-Valle de Pineta
  Parador Monte Perdido, 195

Bilbao, 118
Bishop of Urgel, 130
Bishop Teodomiro, 73
Black Madonna (Moreneta), 128
Boabdil, 57, 60
Burgos, 123
   Cathedral, 123

C

Cabra, 57
   Castillo de los Condes, 57
   San Juan Bautista Church, 57
Cáceres, 97
   Old Cáceres, 97
   Parador de Cáceres, 196
Cadaques, 133
Calatayud, 87
   Kalat-Ayub, 87
Calella, 134
Calzada de Calatrava, 53
   Castle of Calatrava la Nueva, 53
Cambados, 73
Campo de Calatrava, 52
Campo de Criptana, 51
Can Borrell (Hotel), Meranges, 240
Can Fabrica, Cornellà del Terri, 206
Cangas de Onís, 113, 115
Canido, 72
Cape Verde Islands, 66
Car Rental, 4
Cardenal, Hostal del, Toledo, 275
Cardinal Lorenzana, 50
Cardona, 128
   Church of St. Vincent, 128
   Parador Duques de Cardona, 128, 197
Cariñena, 87
Carmona in Andalusia, 26, 161
   Casa de Carmona, 161, 198

Carmona in Andalusia (cont.)
   Parador de Carmona, 199
Carmona in Cantabria
   Venta de Carmona, 200
Casa de Carmona, Carmona in Andalusia, 161, 198
Castell de Peratallada, Peratallada, 250
Castellfollit de la Roca, 132
Castello de Ampurias, 134
Castello de Quermanco, 133
Castillo de las Guardas, 93
Catholic Monarchs, 120
Cazorla
   Parador "El Adelantado", 201
Cerro de Mulhacen, 60
Cervantes, 51
Charles III, 121
Charles V, 55, 59, 103, 118
Chinchón, 26
   Parador de Chinchón, 202
Christopher Columbus, 100
Ciudad Encantada, 82
Ciudad Rodrigo
   Parador de Ciudad Rodrigo, 203
Civil War, 18, 118
Climate, 3
Clothing, 4
Coll de Nargo, 129
Columbus, 106
Columbus, 17, 158, 164
Comillas, 115, 116
Córdoba, 55
   Hotels
      Hotel Albucasis, 56, 204
      Parador de la Arruzafa, 205
   Jewish Quarter, 55
   Mosque, 55
   Street of Flowers, 55

Cornellà del Terri
  Can Fabrica, 206
Cortijo Aguila Real (Hotel), Guillena-Seville, 268
Cortijo Faín, Arcos de la Frontera, 142, 177
Cortijo Grande
  Finca Listonero, 207
Cosgaya-Potes
  Hotel del Oso, 113, 208
Costa Brava, 133
Costa del Sol, 138
Count of Oropesa, 103
Counts of Alba and Aliste, 109
Covadonga, 114
  Basilica of Our Lady of the Battles, 114
  Santa Cueva, 114
Cradle of the Conquistadors–Itinerary, 91
Credit Cards, 44
Criptana Hermitage, 51
Cubillas de Rueda, 111
Cuenca, 26, 80
  Casas Colgadas, 80
  Cathedral, 80
  Hanging Houses, 78, 80
  Hotels
        Parador Convento de San Pablo, 81, 209
        Posada de San José, 81, 210
    Meson Casas Colgadas, 80
    Museum of Abstract Art, 80
Cueva de La Pileta, 140
Cueva del Navazo, 83

D

Dalí, Salvador, 133
Daroca, 87
Del Oso (Hotel), Cosgaya-Potes, 208
Despeñaperros Gorge, 54
Diana (Hotel), Tossa de Mar, 280
Díaz, Rodrigo, 123

Don Francisco de Toledo, 102
Don Juan (Hotel), Salamanca, 255
Don Miguel (Hotel), Ronda, 252
Don Quixote, 51
Driver's License, 4
Driving, 4
Dukes of Alba, 103
Dulcinea, 52
Duques de Bergara, Barcelona, 185

E

Economy, 7
El Cid, 67, 123
El Convento, Arcos de la Frontera, 142, 178
El Escorial, 151
  Hotel Victoria Palace, 211
El Greco, 49, 80, 147, 160
El Hotel de la Villa, Pedraza de la Sierra, 124
El Hotel de La Villa, Pedraza de la Sierra, 156, 248
El Montíboli Hotel, Villajoyosa, 287
El Toboso, Dulcinea's home, 52
Electric Current, 4
English, 7
Entre Dos Lagos, 115
Ermita de Eunate Hermitage, 122
Estella, 122
  Plaza San Martín, 122
European Union, 7

F

Favorite Places, 25
Ferdinand, 17, 154, 164
Ferdinand and Isabella, 57, 59, 73, 120
Ferdinand III, 158
Ferdinand the Catholic, 121
Feria (Fair) de Sevilla, 161
Fernan Nuñez, 57

Ferrol
  Parador de Ferrol, 212
Festivals and Folklore, 7
Figueras, 133
  Teatro Museo Dalí, 133
Finca es Palmer, Mallorca, 236
Finca La Mota, Alhaurín El Grande, 173
Finca Listonero, Cortijo Grande, 207
Finca Santa Marta, Trujillo, 99, 281
Flamenco Dancing, 55
Food and Drink, 8
Francisco de Icaza, 58
Francisco Romero, 139
Franco, General Francisco, 18
Fray Luis de León, 106
Freeways, 6
Fuendetodos, 87
Fuenterrabía, 118
Fuentes de Jiloca, 87

G

Gallery Hotel, Barcelona, 186
Gasoline, 5
Gaudí, Antonio, 90, 165
Gavina, Hostal de la, S'Agaró, 254
Generalísimo Franco, 76, 152
Geography, 14
Government, 14
Goya, 87, 139, 147
Gran Hotel La Toja, Isla de la Toja, 72, 274
Gran Hotel Palacio Valderrábanos, Ávila, 181
Granada, 27, 36, 57
  Albaicín quarter, 60
  Alcaicería, 59
  Alcázar, 59
  Alhambra, 58
  Cathedral, 59
  Church of St. Nicholas, 60

Granada (cont.)
  Generalife Gardens, 58
  Hotels
    Alhambra Palace Hotel, 57, 213
    Hotel America, 57, 214
    Parador San Francisco, 57, 215
  Palace of Charles V, 59
  Sacromonte (Gypsy Cave Dwellings), 60
Gredos
  Parador de Gredos, 216
Guadalupe, 27, 99
  Hotels
    Hospedería El Real Monasterio, 100, 217
    Parador de Guadalupe, 100, 218
  Virgin of Guadalupe Monastery, 99
Guernica y Luno, 118
Guillena-Seville
  Hotel Cortijo Aguila Real, 268

H

Hacienda (Hotel), Ibiza, 223
Hacienda Benazuza, Sanlúcar la Mayor, 269
Hanging Houses, Cuenca, 80
Hartzenbusch, 84
Hemingway, Ernest, 120
Híjar, 88
History, 15
  Early Period, 15
  Modern Period, 17
  Moorish Period, 16
  Reconquest Period, 16
  Roman Period, 15
  Visigoth Period, 15
Holy Roman Empire, 59
Holy Week, 161
Hondarribia, 28, 118
  Hotels
    Hotel Obispo, 219

Hondarribia (cont.)
    Hotel Pampinot, 220
    Parador El Emperador, 118, 221
    Restaurant/Bar Antxina, 119
Horreos, 114
Hospedería de San Francisco, Palma del Río, 247
Hospedería El Real Monasterio, Guadalupe, 100, 217
Hostal de La Gavina, S'Agaró, 133, 254
Hostal de Los Reyes Católicos, Santiago, 73, 258
Hostal del Cardenal, Toledo, 50, 275
Hostal San Marcos, León, 110, 228
Hostería de Bracamonte, Ávila, 182
Hotel Aigua Blava, Begur-Aiguablava, 191
Hotel Albucasis, Córdoba, 56, 204
Hotel Alfonso XIII, Seville, 144, 158
Hotel Altamira, Santillana del Mar, 116
Hotel America, Granada, 57, 214
Hotel Arosa, Madrid, 230
Hotel Can Borrell, Meranges, 240
Hotel Colón, Barcelona, 184
Hotel Cortijo Aguila Real, Guillena-Seville, 268
Hotel de la Reconquista, Oviedo, 246
Hotel de La Reconquista, Oviedo, 246
Hotel del Oso, Cosgaya-Potes, 113, 208
Hotel Descriptions, 35
Hotel Diana, Tossa de Mar, 280
Hotel Don Juan, Salamanca, 105, 255
Hotel Don Miguel, Ronda, 139, 252
Hotel Doña María, Seville, 144
Hotel Infanta Isabel, Segovia, 262
Hotel La Bobadilla, Loja, 229
Hotel La Casona de Amandi, Villaviciosa, 288
Hotel La Rectoral, Taramundi, 272
Hotel Los Infantes, Santillana del Mar, 116, 260
Hotel Los Linajes, Segovia, 263
Hotel Monasterio de Piedra, Nuévalos, 243
Hotel Montecarlo, Barcelona, 188
Hotel Obispo, Hondarribia, 219

Hotel Pampinot, Hondarribia, 220
Hotel Pikes, San Antoni de Portmany, Ibiza, 222
Hotel Rates and Information, 41
Hotel Rector, Salamanca, 104, 256
Hotel Reservations, 42
  Fax, 42
  Letter, 43
Hotel San José, San José, 257
Hotel Santa María de El Paular, Rascafría, 251
Hotel Victoria Palace, El Escorial, 211
Hotel Villa Real, Madrid, 231

I

Ibiza, San Antoni de Portmany
  Hotel Pikes, 222
Ibiza, San Miguel, Na Xamena
  Hotel Hacienda, 223
Ibiza, Santa Eulalia del Rio
  La Colina, 224
Illescas, 49
Infanta Isabel (Hotel), Segovia, 262
Introduction, 1
Isabella, 17, 66, 154, 164
Isla de la Toja
  Gran Hotel La Toja, 72, 274
  Lanzada, 72
Italica, 162
Itineraries
  Barcelona Highlights, 163
  Cradle of the Conquistadors, 91
  Madrid and More, 145
  Moorish Memories, 47
  Old Castile and the Cantabrian Coast, 107
  Overview of Itineraries, 45
  Seville Highlights, 157
  The Costa Brava and Beyond, 125
  Treasures off the Beaten Track, 77
Itineraries–General Information, 24

J

Jaén
  Parador Castillo de Santa Catalina, 225
Jaraba, 86
Jarandilla de la Vera, 103
  Parador Carlos V, 103, 226
Javea
  Parador Costa Blanca, 227
Javier Castle, 121
Jerez de la Frontera, 143, 162
Juan Carlos, 19
Juan Diego, 84
Juana the Mad, 59, 66

K

King Phillip II, 151
Kingdom of Asturias, 16
Kings of Navarre, 122
Knights of St. James, 97

L

La Alberca, 103
La Casona de Amandi (Hotel), Villaviciosa, 288
La Colina, Ibiza, 224
La Coruña, 76
La Guardia, 71
La Mancha, 51
La Molina, 130
La Posada de Don Mariano, Pedraza de la Sierra, 124, 156, 249
La Rectoral (Hotel), Taramundi, 272
La Residencia, Mallorca, 237
La Rioja, 123
La Tahona, Alles-Besnes, 174
La Toba, 82
La Toja, Gran Hotel, Isla de la Toja, 274
Lago Enol, 115

Lago Ercina, 115
Lanjarón, 61
Las Cuevas del Monte del Castillo, Puente Viesgo, 117
León, 28, 74, 110
  Cathedral Santa María de la Regla, 111
  Convento de San Marcos, 110
  Hostal San Marcos, 110, 228
Letter-Reservation Request, 301
Linajes, Hotel Los, Segovia, 263
Llansa, 133
Lloret de Mar, 134
Logroño, 122
Loja
  Hotel La Bobadilla, 229
Los Reyes Católicos, 17, 120
Lucena, 57
Lumbier Defile Gorge, 120

M

Madrid, 29, 49, 65, 79, 124, 146
  Buen Retiro Park, 65
  Casa de Campo, 148
  Casa de Miranda, 124
  El Rastro, 149
  Hotels
    Hotel Arosa, 230
    Hotel Villa Real, 231
    The Ritz, 232
  Museo Arqueológico, 148
  Parque del Buen Retiro, 148
  Paseo de Recoletos, 150
  Plaza de Oriente, 148
  Plaza Mayor, 149
  Prado Museum, 147
  Puerta del Sol, 149
  Royal Palace, 148
  Royal Tapestry Factory, 148
  Thyssen Bornemisza Museum, 148

Madrid and More–Itinerary, 145
Madrigal de Las Altas, 66
   Convent of St. Francis, 66
   Our Lady of the Lugareta Nunnery, 66
Málaga, 62, 137
   Castillo de Gibralfaro, 62
   Gibralfaro, 137
   Hotels
      Parador de Málaga de Golf, 62, 233
      Parador de Málaga Gibralfaro, 62, 137, 234
   Museo de Bellas Artes, 137
Mallorca, Colonia de Sant Jordi
   Finca es Palmer, 236
Mallorca, Deia
   La Residencia, 237
Mallorca, Valldemosa
   Vistamar de Valldemosa, 238
Manresa, 128
   Church of Santa María de la Seo, 128
Maps
   Hotel Locations, 35
   Itinerary Maps–How to Use, 24
   Key Map, 293
   Map 1, Northwest Spain, 294
   Map 2, North Central Spain, 295
   Map 3, Northeast Spain, 296
   Map 4, Southeast Spain, 297
   Map 5, Southwest Spain, 298
   Map 6, Central Spain, 299
   Map 7, Balearic Islands, 300
   Michelin Maps, 36
   Regions of Spain, 292
Marauder de la Reina, 115
Marbella, 62, 138
   Marbella Club Hotel, 239
Marketing Ahead, 23, 40
Martorell, 127
Mas de Torrent, Torrent, 278

Medina Azahara, 56
Mellid, 76
Meranges
   Hotel Can Borrell, 240
Mérida, 29, 93, 94
   Alcazaba, 96
   Casa Romana del Anfiteatro, 96
   Museo Nacional de Arte Romano, 95
   Parador Vía de la Plata, 94, 241
   Plaza de España, 96
   Roman Arena, 95
   Roman Theater, 95
Meson Casas Colgadas, 80
Michelin Green Guide, 24
Michelin Maps, 24
Mijas, 62
Miño Valley, 70
Miró, 167
Molina de Aragón, 85
Molino del Santo, Benaoján, 193
Mombuey, 68
Monasterio de Piedra (Hotel), Nuévalos, 243
Monasterio de Piedra Park, 86
Monasterio de Piedra, Nuévalos, 85
Monasterio de San Lorenzo el Real de El Escorial, 151
Monistrol, 128
Monreal del Campo, 85
Montana de Covadonga Nature Reserve, 115
Montecorto, 141
Montemayor, 57
Montes Universales, 82
Montíboli Hotel, Villajoyosa, 287
Montilla, 57
Montón, 87
Montoro, 54
Montserrat, 127
   Santa Cueva, 128
Monturque, 57

Moorish Memories–Itinerary, 47
Moreneta (Black Madonna), 128
Mudéjar, 83
Murillo, 147, 160

N

Navarre, 120
Nerja, 61
   Parador de Nerja, 242
Nerja Caves, 61
Noya, 76
Nuévalos, 86
   Hotel Monasterio de Piedra, 243
   Monasterio de Piedra, 85

O

Obispo (Hotel), Hondarribia, 219
Off-Season Travel
   Seasonal Discounts, 39
   Senior Discounts, 39
Oficina de Turismo, 22
Ojén, 62
Old Castile and the Cantabrian Coast–Itinerary, 107
Olite, 121
   Parador Principe de Viana, 121, 244
Orena, 116
Orense, 69
Organya Gorge, 129
Orgiva, 61
Oropesa
   Parador de Oropesa, 102, 245
Oviedo
   Hotel de la Reconquista, 246
Oya, 71
Oyambe Beach, 116

P

Padrón, 73

Palace Hotel, Barcelona, 189
Palamos, 134
Paleolithic Caves, 83
Palma del Río
   Hospedería de San Francisco, 247
Pampinot (Hotel), Hondarribia, 220
Pamplona, 120
   Running of the Bulls, 120
Parador "Castillo de La Zuda", Tortosa, 279
Parador "Condes de Alba y Aliste", Zamora, 66, 290
Parador "Condes de Villaba", Villaba, 286
Parador "Condestable Davalos", Ubeda, 283
Parador "Costa Brava", Begur-Aiguablava, 192
Parador "El Adelantado", Cazorla, 201
Parador Carlos V, Jarandilla de la Vera, 103, 226
Parador Casa del Corregidor, Arcos de la Frontera, 179
Parador Casa del Corregidor, Arcos de La Frontera, 142
Parador Castillo de Santa Catalina, Jaén, 225
Parador Castillo de Sigüenza, Sigüenza, 270
Parador Conde de Gondomar, Bayona, 70, 190
Parador Conde de Orgaz, Toledo, 276
Parador Convento de San Pablo, Cuenca, 81, 209
Parador Costa Blanca, Javea, 227
Parador de Almagro, Almagro, 52, 175
Parador de Antequera, Antequera, 176
Parador de Ávila, Ávila, 183
Parador de Cáceres, Cáceres, 196
Parador de Carmona, Carmona in Andalusia, 199
Parador de Chinchón, Chinchón, 202
Parador de Ciudad Rodrigo, Ciudad Rodrigo, 203
Parador de Ferrol, Ferrol, 212
Parador de Gibralfaro, Málaga, 62, 137
Parador de Gredos, Gredos, 216
Parador de Guadalupe, Guadalupe, 100, 218
Parador de la Arruzafa, Córdoba, 205
Parador de la Concordia, Alcañiz, 88, 172
Parador de la Mancha, Albacete, 171
Parador de Málaga de Golf, Málaga, 62, 233

Parador de Málaga Gibralfaro, Málaga, 234
Parador de Nerja, Nerja, 242
Parador de Oropesa, Oropesa, 102, 245
Parador de Ronda, Ronda, 138, 253
Parador de Santo Domingo, Santo Domingo, 123, 261
Parador de Segovia, Segovia, 264
Parador de Seo de Urgel, Seo de Urgel, 130, 265
Parador de Teruel, Teruel, 83, 273
Parador de Tordesillas, Tordesillas, 277
Parador de Trujillo, Trujillo, 98, 282
Parador de Vic, Vic, 131, 285
Parador de Zafra, Zafra, 94, 289
Parador Don Gaspar, Artíes, 180
Parador Duques de Cardona, Cardona, 128, 197
Parador El Emperador, Hondarribia, 118, 221
Parador Fernando de Aragón, Sos del Rey Católico, 121, 271
Parador Gil Blas, Santillana del Mar, 116, 259
Parador Marqués de Villena, Alarcón, 170
Parador Monte Perdido, Bielsa-Valle de Pineta, 195
Parador Monterrey, Verín, 68, 284
Parador Principe de Viana, Olite, 121, 244
Parador Reservations
   Marketing Ahead, 40
   Paradores de Turismo, 40
Parador Rey Fernando II de León, Benavente, 194
Parador San Francisco, Granada, 36, 57, 215
Parador Vía de la Plata, Mérida, 94, 241
Paradores de Turismo, 39
Paradors, 36
Pedraza de la Sierra, 29, 124, 151, 156
   El Hotel de La Villa, 156, 248
   La Posada de Don Mariano, 124, 156, 249
Peratallada
   Castell de Peratallada, 250
Phillip the Fair, 59, 66
Phrase Books
   Berlitz, 7
Picasso, 62, 118, 137

Pico de Veleta, 60
Picos de Europa, 30, 111
Pikes (Hotel), Ibiza, 222
Pinturas Rupestres, 83
Pizarro, 98
Platja d'Aro, 133, 134
Plaza de España, Mérida, 96
Plazas, 19
Pontevedra, 72
Portillo de la Canda, 69
Posada de San José, Cuenca, 81, 210
Potes-Cosgaya
   Hotel del Oso, 208
Pozuel del Campo, 85
Puebla de Sanabria., 68
Pueblos Blancos (White Towns), 61
Puente del Arzobispo, 102
Puente la Reina, 122
Puente Viesgo
   Las Cuevas del Monte del Castillo, 117
Puerto Banus, 138
Puerto de El Cubillo Pass, 82
Puerto de Loiti Pass, 120
Puerto de Paniza Pass, 87
Puerto de Velate Pass, 120
Puerto del Suspiro del Moro, 60
Puigcerdá, 130
Pyrenees, 120, 129, 130

R

Rascafría
   Hotel Santa María de El Paular, 251
Rates, Hotel, 41, 44
Reconquest of Spain, 114
Rector (Hotel), Salamanca, 256
Regions and Provinces, 20
RENFE, 22
Reservation Request Letter, 301

Reservations, Hotel, 42
Responsibility, 44
Ría de Vigo, 71
Riaño, 112
Ribadelago, 68
Ribas de Freser, 131
Rincon de La Victoria, 62
Ripoll, 131
    Benedictine Monastery, 131
    Ripoll Library, 131
Roads, 5
    Road Numbers, 5
Rocaforte, 120
Ronda, 30, 62, 138
    Bullring, 139
    Casa del Rey Moro, 140
    Hotels
        Hotel Don Miguel, 139, 252
        Parador de Ronda, 138, 253
    Puente Nuevo, 139
    Puente Romano, 140
    Santa María la Mayor, 139
    School of Bullfighting, 139
    Tajo Ravine, 138
Roses, 134
Running of the Bulls, Pamplona, 7, 120
Rupit, 131
Ruta de los Pueblos Blancos, 141
Ruta del Vino, 57

S

S'Agaró, 133
    Hostal de La Gavina, 133, 254
Sada Palace, Sos del Rey Católico, 121
Saint Peter's Church, Teruel, 84
Salamanca, 31, 104
    Casa de las Conchas, 105
    Hotels

Salamanca (cont.)
        Hotel Don Juan, 105, 255
        Hotel Rector, 104, 256
    New Cathedral, 105
    Old Cathedral, 105
    Patio de las Escuelas, 105
    Plaza Mayor, 105
    Puente Romano, 106
    St. Martin's Church, 105
    University, 105
Salobrèña, 61
Samil, 72
San Feliu, 133
San José
    Hotel San José, 257
San Martin de Castaneda, 68
San Sebastián, 118
San Vicente de La Barquera, 115
Sanlúcar la Mayor
    Hacienda Benazuza, 269
Sant Yago, 73
Santa María de El Paular (Hotel), Rascafría, 251
Santa María del Prado, 102
Santa Teresa of Ávila, 103, 154
Santander, 117
Santesteban, 120
Santiago de Compostela, 31, 73, 123
    Cathedral, 74
    Hostal de Los Reyes Católicos, 73, 258
    Plaza de España, 74
Santillana del Mar, 32, 116
    Altamira Caves, 117
    Hotels
        Hotel Altamira, 116
        Hotel Los Infantes, 116, 260
        Parador Gil Blas, 116, 259
Santo Domingo, 122
    Parador de Santo Domingo, 123, 261

Santona, 118
Seat Belts, 6
Segovia, 151, 154
  Alcázar Castle, 154
  Casa de los Picos, 156
  Cathedral, 155
  Church of St. Stephen, 155
  Convento de Carmelitas Descalzos, 155
  Hotels
      Hotel Infanta Isabel, 262
      Hotel Los Linajes, 263
      Parador de Segovia, 264
  Roman Aqueduct, 154
Seo de Urgel, 130
  Parador de Seo de Urgel, 130, 265
Serranía de Ronda, 138
Setenil, 140
Seville, 93, 143, 157
  Alcázar, 159
  Archives of the Indies, 158
  Barrio de Santa Cruz, 159
  Casa Pilatos, 161
  Cathedral, 158
  Giralda, 143, 158
  Hotels
      Hotel Alfonso XIII, 144, 158, 266
      Hotel Doña María, 144, 158
      Taberna del Alabardero, 144, 158, 267
  Murillo Gardens, 160
  Museo Arqueológico, 160
  Museo de Bellas Artes, 160
  Parque de María Luisa, 166
  Parque de María Luisa, 160
  Plaza de España, 160
  Plaza de San Francisco, 160
  Plaza Virgen de los Reyes, 144
  Pueblo Español, 166
  University of Seville, 160

Seville Highlights–Itinerary, 157
Seville-Guillena
  Hotel Cortijo Aguila Real, 268
Seville-Sanlúcar la Mayor
  Hacienda Benazuza, 269
Sierra de Aracena, 93
Sierra de Covalierda, 115
Sierra de la Culebra National Reserve, 68
Sierra de Leyre, 120
Sierra Nevada, 60
Siesta, 20
Sigüenza, 33
  Parador Castillo de Sigüenza, 270
Sir Francis Drake, 71
Solsona, 129
Sos del Rey Católico, 33, 121
  Parador Fernando de Aragón, 121, 271
  Sada Palace, 121
Spanish National Railways, 22
St. Ferdinand, 158
St. Francis Xavier, 121
St. James the Apostle, 16, 73
Suances, 116
Sumbilia, 120

T

Taberna del Alabardero, Seville, 144, 158, 267
Talavera de la Reina, 102
Taramundi
  Hotel "La Rectoral", 272
Tarrancón, 79
Telephone
  Calling Home from Spain, 20
Teruel, 83
  Cathedral, 84
  Chapel of the "Lovers of Teruel", 84
  Parador de Teruel, 83, 273
  Plaza del Torico, 84

Index   313

Teruel (cont.)
  Saint Peter's church, 84
The Catholic Monarchs, 17
The Costa Brava and Beyond–Itinerary, 125
The Prado, 20
The Ritz, Madrid, 232
Tipping, 21
Toja–Isla de
  Gran Hotel La Toja, 274
Toledo, 34, 49
  El Greco House and Museum, 51
  El Tránsito and Santa María la Blanca Synagogues, 51
  Hotels
      Hostal del Cardenal, 50, 275
      Parador Conde de Orgaz, 276
  Santa Cruz Museum, 51
  Santo Tomé, 51
Toll Roads, 5
Tordesillas, 66
  Parador de Tordesillas, 277
  Santa Clara Convent, 66
Toro, 66
Torre del Mar, 62
Torremolinos, 138
Torrent
  Mas de Torrent, 278
Torres del Rio, 122
Tortosa
  Parador "Castillo de La Zuda", 279
Tossa de Mar, 126, 134
  Hotel Diana, 280
Tourist Offices of Spain
  Chicago, USA, 21
Tourist Offices of Spain, 21
  London, England, 21
  Los Angeles, USA, 21
  Madrid, Spain, 21
  Miami, USA, 21

Tourist Offices of Spain (cont.)
  New York, USA, 21
  Toronto, Canada, 21
Traffic, 6
Train Reservations
  Iberrail, 23
  Marketing Ahead, 23
  Rail Europe, 23
Trains, 22
  "Estrella", 23
  "Talgo", 22
  "Train-Hotel", 23
  Andalusian Express, 23
Treasures off the Beaten Track–Itinerary, 77
Trujillo, 34, 98
  Church of Santa María la Mayor, 98
  Convent of Santa Clara, 98
  Hotels
      Finca Santa Marta, 281
      Parador de Trujillo, 98, 282
  Palace of Hernando Pizarro, 98

U

Ubeda, 54
  Parador "Condestable Davalos", 283
  Plaza Vázquez de Molina, 54
Una, 82
Unquera, 115

V

Valdecabras, 82
Valdepeñas, 53
Valle de los Caidos, 152
Valle de Pineta-Bielsa
  Parador Monte Perdido, 195
Valley of the Fallen, 152
Valley of the Rio Ulzama, 120
Velázquez, 147, 160

Velilla, 87
Venta de Carmona, Carmona in Cantabria, 200
Venta del Quijote, 52
Verín, 68
  Parador Monterrey, 68, 284
Vic, 131
  Parador de Vic, 131, 285
  Plaza Mayor, 131
Victoria Palace (Hotel), El Escorial, 211
View of Toledo (Greco's Painting), 49
Vigo, 71
Villaba
  Parador "Condes de Villaba", 286
Villajoyosa
  El Montíboli Hotel, 287
Villaviciosa
  Hotel La Casona de Amandi, 288
Virgin of Covadonga, 114
Virgin of Guadalupe, 100
Vistamar de Valldemosa, Mallorca, 238
Vivar, 123
Voltage, 4

W

Way of St. James, 16, 74, 76, 111, 122
Windmills, 51
Wine Road, 57

Y

Yuste, 103

Z

Zafra, 94
  Parador de Zafra, 289
Zahara, 141
Zamora, 66, 109
  Cathedral, 109
  Parador "Condes de Alba y Aliste", 66

Zamora (cont.)
  Parador "Condes de Alba Y Aliste", 290
  Parador de Zamora, 109
Zurbarán, 160

Become a Karen Brown Preferred Reader

Name _____

Street _____

Town _____

State _____ Zip _____ Country _____

Tel _____ Fax _____

e-mail _____

We'd love to welcome you as a Karen Brown Preferred Reader. Send us your name and address and you will be entered in our monthly drawing to receive a free set of Karen Brown guides. As a preferred reader, you will be the first to know when new editions of Karen Brown guides go to press, and receive special promotions and updated information on hotels & B&Bs.

Please send to: Karen Brown's Guides, Post Office Box 70, San Mateo, California 94401, USA
tel: (650) 342-9117, fax: (650) 342-9153, e-mail: karen@karenbrown.com, website: www: karenbrown.com

SHARE YOUR DISCOVERIES WITH US

Outstanding properties often come from readers' discoveries. We would love to hear from you.

Please list below any hotel or bed & breakfast you discover. Tell us what you liked about the property and, if possible, please include a brochure or photographs so we can share your enthusiasm. We keep a database of all of reader recommendations for future consideration. Note: we regret we cannot return photos.

Owner _____ Hotel or B&B _____ Street _____

Town _____ Zip _____ State or Region _____ Country _____

Comments:

Your name _____ Street _____ Town _____ State _____

Zip _____ Country _____ Tel _____ e-mail _____ date _____

Would you be willing to share your discovery with other Karen Brown readers?

Do we have your permission to electronically publish your review(s) on our website? Yes _____ No _____

If yes, would you like commentary anonymous, Yes ___No ___, or may we use your name? Yes___ No___

Please send report to: Karen Brown's Guides, Post Office Box 70, San Mateo, California 94401, USA
tel: (650) 342-9117, fax: (650) 342-9153, e-mail: karen@karenbrown.com, website: www.karenbrown.com

SHARE YOUR THOUGHTS ON PLACES YOU STAY

We greatly appreciate firsthand evaluations of places in our guides. Your critiques are invaluable to us. To stay current on the properties in our guides, we keep a database of readers' comments. To keep our readers up to date, we also sometimes share feedback with them via our website.

Please list your comments on properties that you have visited. We welcome accolades, as well as criticisms.

Name of hotel or b&b _____ Town _____ Country _____

Comments:

Name of hotel or b&b _____ Town _____ Country _____

Comments:

Your name _____ Street _____ Town _____ State _____

Zip _____ Country _____ Tel _____ e-mail _____ date _____

Do we have your permission to electronically publish your comments on our website? Yes ____ No ____

If yes, would you like commentary anonymous, Yes ___No ___, or may we use your name? Yes___ No___

Please send report to: Karen Brown's Guides, Post Office Box 70, San Mateo, California 94401, USA
tel: (650) 342-9117, fax: (650) 342-9153, e-mail: karen@karenbrown.com, website: www.karenbrown.com

VISIT OUR WEBSITE

karen@karenbrown.com

- View color photos of a selection of hotels and B&Bs
- Link directly to places featured in Karen Brown's guides
- Learn about our latest discoveries—before they go to press
- Access up to the minute news on Karen Brown properties
- Share readers' comments on hotels and B&Bs
- Order Karen Brown's guides—at special prices

KB Travel Service

Independently Owned and Operated by

Town & Country Travel

Quality * Personal Service * Great Values

- Staff advised by Karen Brown to help plan your holiday
- Reservations for hotels, inns, and B&Bs in Karen Brown's Guides
- Countryside mini-itineraries based on Karen Brown's Guides
- Special offerings on airfares to major cities in Europe
- Special prices on car rentals—ask about free upgrades

For assistance and information concerning service and fees, contact:

KB Travel Service / Town & Country Travel
16 East Third Avenue
San Mateo, California, 94401, USA
tel: 800-782-2128, fax: 650-342-2519, e-mail: kbtravel@aol.com

auto ⊛ europe®

Karen Brown's

Preferred Car Rental Service Provider

for

Worldwide Car Rental Services
Chauffeur & Transfer Services
Prestige & Sports Cars
Motor Home Rentals

Seal Cove Inn

Located in the San Francisco Bay Area

Karen Brown Herbert (best known as author of the Karen Brown's guides) and her husband, Rick, have put 22 years of experience into reality and opened their own superb hideaway, Seal Cove Inn. Spectacularly set amongst wild flowers and bordered by towering cypress trees, Seal Cove Inn looks out to the distant ocean over acres of county park: an oasis where you can enjoy secluded beaches, explore tidepools, watch frolicking seals, and follow the tree-lined path that traces the windswept ocean bluffs. Country antiques, original watercolors, flower-laden cradles, rich fabrics, and the gentle ticking of grandfather clocks create the perfect ambiance for a foggy day in front of the crackling log fire. Each bedroom is its own haven with a cozy sitting area before a wood-burning fireplace and doors opening onto a private balcony or patio with views to the park and ocean. Moss Beach is a 35-minute drive south of San Francisco, 6 miles north of the picturesque town of Half Moon Bay, and a few minutes from Princeton harbor with its colorful fishing boats and restaurants. Seal Cove Inn makes a perfect base for whale-watching, salmon-fishing excursions, day trips to San Francisco, exploring the coast, or, best of all, just a romantic interlude by the sea, time to relax and be pampered. Karen and Rick look forward to the pleasure of welcoming you to their coastal hideaway.

Seal Cove Inn • 221 Cypress Avenue • Moss Beach • California • 94038 • USA
tel: (650) 728-4114, fax: (650) 728-4116, e-mail: sealcove@coastside.net, website: sealcoveinn.com

KAREN BROWN wrote her first travel guide in 1976. Her personalized travel series has grown to thirteen titles which Karen and her small staff work diligently to keep updated. Karen, her husband, Rick, and their children, Alexandra and Richard, live in Moss Beach, a small town on the coast south of San Francisco. They settled here in 1991 when they opened Seal Cove Inn. Karen is frequently traveling, but when she is home, in her role as innkeeper, enjoys welcoming Karen Brown readers.

CLARE BROWN began her career in the field of travel in 1969 when she opened her own travel agency. Her specialty was countryside itineraries in Europe for her clients. The focus of her job remains unchanged, but now her expertise is available to a larger audience—the readers of her daughter Karen's guides. Clare lives in Hillsborough, California, with her husband, Bill, who shares her love of travel.

JUNE BROWN'S love of travel was inspired by the *National Geographic* magazines that she read as a girl in her dentist's office—so far she has visited over 40 countries. June hails from Sheffield, England and lived in Zambia and Canada before moving to northern California where she lives in San Mateo with her husband, Tony, their daughter Clare, two German Shepherds, and a Siamese cat.

BARBARA TAPP, the talented artist who produces all of the hotel sketches and delightful illustrations in this guide, was raised in Australia where she studied in Sydney at the School of Interior Design. Although Barbara continues with freelance projects, she devotes much of her time to illustrating the Karen Brown guides. Barbara lives in Kensington, California, with her husband, Richard, their two sons, Jonothan and Alexander, and daughter, Georgia.

JANN POLLARD, the artist responsible for the beautiful painting on the cover of this guide, has studied art since childhood, and is well-known for her outstanding impressionistic-style watercolors which she has exhibited in numerous juried shows, winning many awards. Jann travels frequently to Europe (using Karen Brown's guides) where she loves to paint historical buildings. Jann lives in Burlingame, California, with her husband, Gene.

Travel Your Dreams • Order your Karen Brown Guides Today

Please ask in your local bookstore for Karen Brown's Guides. If the books you want are unavailable, you may order directly from the publisher. Books will be shipped immediately.

_____ *Austria: Charming Inns & Itineraries* $18.95

_____ *California: Charming Inns & Itineraries* $18.95

_____ *England: Charming Bed & Breakfasts* $17.95

_____ *England, Wales & Scotland: Charming Hotels & Itineraries* $18.95

_____ *France: Charming Bed & Breakfasts* $17.95

_____ *France: Charming Inns & Itineraries* $18.95

_____ *Germany: Charming Inns & Itineraries* $18.95

_____ *Ireland: Charming Inns & Itineraries* $18.95

_____ *Italy: Charming Bed & Breakfasts* $17.95

_____ *Italy: Charming Inns & Itineraries* $18.95

_____ *Portugal: Charming Inns & Itineraries* $18.95

_____ *Spain: Charming Inns & Itineraries* $18.95

_____ *Switzerland: Charming Inns & Itineraries* $18.95

Name _____ Street _____

Town _____ State _____ Zip _____ Tel _____ email _____

Credit Card (MasterCard or Visa) _____ Expires _____

For orders in the USA, add $4 for the first book and $1 for each additional book for shipment. California residents add 8.25% sales tax. Overseas orders add $10 per book for airmail shipment. Indicate number of copies of each title; fax or mail form with check or credit card information to:

KAREN BROWN'S GUIDES
Post Office Box 70 • San Mateo • California • 94401 • USA
tel: (650) 342-9117, fax: (650) 342-9153, e-mail: karen@karenbrown.com
For additional information about Karen Brown's Guides, visit our website at www.karenbrown.com

Stacey: Marcus. Brian?

The Things They
Carried.
Tim O'Brien

475 5230
5239

Bill Zabielski

THE COMMON GROUND BOOK

THE COMMON GROUND BOOK
A Circle of Friends

O

Remar Sutton and
Mary Abbott Waite

**BRITISH AMERICAN
PUBLISHING**

Published by British American Publishing
19 British American Boulevard
Latham, New York 12110
Typesetting by C.F. Graphics, Albany, NY
Typeface: Garamond

Manufactured in the United States of America

96 95 94 93 92 5 4 3 2 1

Library of Congress Cataloging-in-Publication Data

Sutton, Remar.
  The common ground book / by Remar Sutton and Mary Abbott
Waite.
      p.   cm.
  Includes index.
  ISBN 0-945167-46-6
  1. Conduct of life.   I. Waite, Mary Abbott.   II. Title.
BJ1581.2.S85   1992
081—dc20   92–15693
                                                    CIP

To our friends
who shared their stories for this book

Contents

1. Standing on Common Ground   1
2. A First Memory   6
3. Things That Shine   19
4. Early Memories   23
5. Holding Hands   32
6. A Special Moment with a Parent   34
7. Hanging Together: A Portrait   50
8. An Early Friendship   54
9. Mutual Respect: A Portrait   63
10. A Pet   66
11. It Takes My Breath Away   71
12. Your First Intimation of Mortality   76
13. Life without Father: A Portrait   89
14. An Awkward Moment with a Parent   91
15. A Vivid Dream   98
16. A Treasured Possession   103
17. Somebody You Could Talk To: A Portrait   110
18. Someone Other Than a Parent Who Had a Major Influence on You   113
19. The Ex-Mother-in-Law: A Portrait   135
20. The Time You First Felt Like an Adult with Your Parents   138
21. Busking: A Portrait   150
22. A Summer Job   153
23. If I Say Money, What Comes to Mind?   161
24. Standing Tall on the Coca-Cola Crates: A Portrait   164
25. Finding Work   166
26. Failing   176
27. Art with and without Merit   179

28. Village Life: A Portrait 182
29. Simple Things That Bring Pleasure 184
30. Your Moment of Glory in Sports 192
31. What Makes You Give Up? 201
32. Overcoming Adversity: A Portrait 206
33. What Gives You Courage to Go On? 208
34. Serendipity 214
35. City Fathers: A Portrait 220
36. Your Lowest Moment 222
37. Unexpected Threats 230
38. Unexpected Treats 233
39. An Unexpected Special Moment 236
40. Letting Veronica Go: A Portrait 249
41. A Moment of Loneliness 251
42. Once on a Rainy Afternoon 262
43. Holding Hands: A Portrait 268
44. A Special Relationship 270
45. Friends and Family at Their Funniest 272
46. Vile Things 283
47. An Unexpected Moment Provoking Compassion 285
48. Airplanes: A Portrait 294
49. A Moment of Real Fear 296
50. Something Sweet 311
51. Discovering Courage: A Portrait 314
52. A Discovery about Myself That Surprised Me 317
53. Birds Flying South 335
54. An Unusual Friendship 338
55. Burying a Friend: Martin Hoose, a Portrait 341
56. Burying a Friend 343
57. Your Greatest Fear 350
58. No Grieving for Peyton, Please: A Portrait 353
59. A Fear for Your Children 355
60. What Makes You Feel Young? A Portrait 359
61. What Makes You Feel Young? 360
62. Regrets 364
63. A Legacy to Pass On 367

64. Something You Want to Do   377
65. Things Are Going to Be Better: A Portrait   380
66. Something Worth Waiting For   383
How We Met   390
Springboards for Discussion with Your Own Friends   420
Acknowledgments   423
Index   425

1. Standing on Common Ground

If you enjoy and are nourished by a really good conversation—where the barriers are down and the trust is high—you're going to have a very good time in this book. *The Common Ground Book* is first a book of fascinating stories about all facets of life. The storytellers include famous writers and royalty, cooks and island fisherman—all friends of ours.

Common Ground also is a book about communication and self-discovery, initially for the people who share their stories with you, but much more important, for you.

The book springs from a group of fifty questions. What's your first memory, for instance? Or who, other than your parents, had the greatest impact on your life? We asked our friends for honest, unrehearsed answers. Their responses will make you laugh, move you, and make you think about your own life, family, and friends.

We think *Common Ground* reveals a lot about life as it is lived in our times, too. In a fragmented world where genuineness and honest feelings too often are masked by the roles we all play, the intimacy and trust offered here will surprise you at times. These extraordinary people reveal themselves in unexpected ways as they face the human issues we all face every day.

How the Book Works

Though it certainly doesn't have to be read this way, *Common Ground* works front to back. Read in order, it offers a chronological look at life from first memories to reflections on last thoughts. Selected answers to each of our questions are shaped into chapters, some short and whimsical, others longer and more substantive.

There are also several other interesting ways to approach *Common Ground*. You can simply pick out a question that catches your fancy. Or you can read all an individual's answers at once if you want to get to know that person quickly. The index will guide you. Or, read the book according to the topic discussed. Duck stories, for instance, are listed quite logically under *duck*. Under R for *rooster*, we even have a story of a countess and her cockerel if you're really into feathers. Design your own imaginative journey using the extensive index.

If you'd like to meet the storytellers before you begin reading, flip to "How We Met" in the back of the book. There, you meet our friends as they recount how *we* met. One couple met Mary Abbott while they were working together at a breakfast for the homeless. "She hasn't got the grits right yet," they report. I met George Plimpton because of a professional football game I staged in Paris. "Soon," he says, "Bubba and I were sharing hot-air balloon rides over Florida with a man named Thunder Chicken." George retired from the balloon circuit shortly thereafter.

Looking at the Past
The backward glances in *Common Ground* are about the role memory and the past play in shaping who we are.

"Being bitten by my sister" is Silvia Munro's "First Memory," opening the next chapter. Her mother's unusual reaction is the dream response of every child who has been badgered by an older sibling. Norman Lear has never forgotten his spiel as a barker working on Coney Island one summer: "Hey, hey, you want to be in pictures? Six for a nickel, five cents!" A nice "Summer Job" for a future director.

And while we're at it, how do we all end up doing what we do for a living, anyway? In "Finding Work," Princess Pamela Strobel recalls leaving South Carolina by herself, after the deaths of her mother and grandmother, to go "north" (125 miles to Winston-Salem) to find work as a cook. She was thirteen. "I

remember piling up wooden Coke cases to reach the sink,"
Princess says. Washing dishes was where she started, but pretty
soon "the salad lady was making cole slaw my way." It's still made
that way in Princess Pamela's restaurant.

The Present
Current experience plays a big role in *Common Ground*, too. In
"An Unusual Friendship" Kurt Vonnegut, an atheist, talks about
the fundamentalist preacher who is roofing his house.

Actress Doris Roberts *didn't* talk with the person in her
"Unexpected Special Moment." She received instead a hilarious
message on her answering machine from Lord Laurence Olivier.
Underwater cinematographer Paul Mockler was on his last dive
on the wreck of the *Titanic* when he encountered an
unexpectedly moving sight.

And how does a person teach courage? In "Burying a Friend,"
a father shows his son mortal courage when they visit a friend—
still vibrant and giving—who's dying of AIDS. Marla Hanson, as
she talks about the vicious attack that ended her modeling career,
reveals other roots of courage.

What's Ahead?
Anticipation drives many of *Common Ground*'s telling moments.
How important is success in business to you? Asked about his
"Greatest Fear," an automobile dealer friend said, "I'd rather be
dead than fail"; a powerful statement in the context of his life.

Do you worry much about what others think? For composer
Phoebe Legere, "Something Worth Waiting For" is "that moment
when you suddenly realize you don't give a damn about anyone
else's opinion, that the work is good enough."

Did you ever love a pet? In "First Intimations of Mortality,"
actress Stephanie Beacham says that's how we begin to understand
death: "Human beings when they die are whisked out of
everybody's vision," Stephanie says. "And then there's this
uncomfortable three hours, possibly in a pair of squeaky shoes."

But with a pet, you "dig the hole and make a wooden cross and put the flowers and cry."

Portraits

Scattered throughout the book are seventeen slightly longer stories that look at a topic from the perspective of individual storytellers. "Hanging Together" looks at what we all want in lifetime friendships and honest relationships through the experiences of three ostensibly carefree college students, a Jamaican cook tells you a lot about perseverance in "Things Are Going to Be Better," and one friend even tells you why you shouldn't have pets in "Mutual Respect."

Finding Common Ground in Diversity

What holds this book together? On an obvious level many tales are about the same subjects. This book has three duck stories, a lot of people's scariest moments happened in small airplanes, and nobody wants to die anytime soon. But on a more profound level, very diverse stories—many told casually—resonate with each other. A memory of raising ducks in rural Minnesota tells us as much about compassion as does a hospital volunteer's nurturing crack-addicted babies at a public hospital in New York City. The death of a wild squirrel in Florida rings as true in the sense of loss it conveys as the death of a special nanny in Scotland.

The biggest patch of common ground, not surprisingly, was the impact of family on our storytellers. Sonya Friedman's childhood was "chaotic and filled with loneliness. My family had very limited expectations for my life," Sonya says. But meeting her future mother-in-law completely changed her life. By the time a young doctor was twenty-three, he had lived in more houses than he had years, but his grandmother became the "one big taproot" that anchored his life. Lyn Lear worshiped her brother so much she once at his request happily offered her back as a human dartboard.

As the natural order of life drives *Common Ground*, we hope you'll appreciate the extraordinary cross-section of the people here as much as you enjoy their observations. A couple of our friends can't read, and others have written some of the best-read books in the world. Some are richer than you can count, and quite a few make those penurious church mice seem rich; one's family rules a country, and one has spent his life on an island no bigger than a modest country farm. The storytellers in this book define diversity, and that's the best way to get a compelling picture of life in our times.

Finding Your Own Common Ground with Friends and Family

We found out very quickly during these interviews that *everyone* has something interesting and valuable to say, *if* someone will just listen. This, of course, is the most important lesson in this book.

It's as true for your friends as it is for ours. The next time you're with the right group of people and are yearning for a more substantial passage of time, why not use our questions to delve a little into the topics and thoughts explored here? In the back of the book, you'll find a complete set of questions and some cues to help make them work.

We said in the beginning that *Common Ground* was a book of self-discovery. As we talked with friends and began to shape the book, Mary Abbott and I found that these stories and observations made us see our own experiences in a new light. We also were encouraged by this group's courage, humor, and sheer vitality. In shaky times, it's reassuring to see that there is firm ground to stand on. We hope you will feel the same way.

2. A First Memory

Silvia Munro

First memory? I remember being bitten by my elder sister. And my mother biting her back. I was two.

George Plimpton

I remember vague things about Paris—a sense of the wallpaper in the apartment, the Punch-and-Judy shows in the little marionette stages in the parks—how violent they were: *whap! whap! whap!* I remember the ocean liner, the *Bremen*, coming back—the taste of bouillon. Oddly, one of the earliest memories I have of New York is of a large, cylindrical washing machine that sat in a bathtub. It was sinister looking, and when it operated, it did so with a rumble and shook slightly, as if something was within. I wouldn't go near the bathroom when clothes were being washed in there.

Zar Rochelle

Just a flash of somebody ugly standing over my crib. I guess I was under one.

Then I remember, when I was a toddler, seeing a cord dangling in the kitchen and wanting to know what was at the end of it. So I pulled it. At the other end there was a pot of perking coffee, which came down on my head. I remember pulling the cord. And I remember Mother ripping my shirt off. But I don't remember the coffee falling on me or being in a cast for three weeks with my arm straight out. I didn't pull any more cords. Amazingly, there were no scars.

Helen Barbour

At three months, I went with my parents to West Africa. My first memories are just flashes: the monkeys in the garden—with babies on their backs; lush semijungle, hot brown grass; the ocean near our house; pineapple growing up the driveway; avocados; and frog spawn on the top of the pool.

Jock Munro

Before I was walking, I was napping in my pram one afternoon in front of the house, Ardullie Lodge, in Scotland. I woke up and was restless. Though the pram was an old-fashioned black pram with big wheels, I managed to tip it up and went for a wander. I crawled up the Spring Walk, which was a walk my mother had made with a little pocket covered in lots of wild grasses and flowers and trees. When Nanny came out to the pram, there was no baby. Though I wasn't walking yet, they couldn't find me anywhere. Finally they found me several hundred meters away from the pram, crawling quite happily through the long grasses.

John Marston

My earliest childhood memory is probably crouching over a rose bed in San Jose, reaching down and picking up a dirt clod and sticking it in my mouth. I remember the salty, earthy flavor of the dirt, the crunching in my teeth.

Dorothy Cross

The first memory I have is being able to stand up and just see over the top of a table on a farm in Michigan.

Norman Lear

Three first memories, all flashes: A group of adults on a lawn with a hedge about four feet high. I remember my father leaping over the hedge—it seemed impossible, but he did it. I was three or four and I was thrilled.

Another flash is of sledding down a hill—"belly whopping," we used to call it—on a Flexible Flyer. My father's father was at the bottom of that hill with his arms outstretched as I came to him. I was about six, and it's the only memory I have of him.

And then perhaps the same year, that same grandfather died, hit by a car. It was a terrible surprise. My mother idolized him more than anybody in the world; my father adored him. I remember Father coming up the stairs where he saw Mother crying, and they embraced. Maybe she told him while they were embracing; I couldn't hear. I just remember them holding each other, turning 360 degrees in each other's arms and weeping.

Foxy Callwood

I liked to walk on the beach with my mother. But when she's going home, I want her to lift me up, and this afternoon she decides not to. So she goes and leaves me in the road. Whenever she is far away, I get up and walk and wait and cry. But then my grandmother had some honey hives in a box, and a bee come out and hit me in the head, so I take off and Lord-Jesus-Christ-honey-bee, I'm going home! I take off running and I overrun the gate. From then on, all my mama had to say to me was, "I gonna send for the honeybee for you."

Win Rockefeller

My first clear recollection is at my grandparents' farm during a northern Indiana winter: getting up in the morning, pulling my socks on and puttering onto the linoleum to the unheated bathroom. And then I'd pull a chair from the dining room into the kitchen, pop the wood stove open, and stick my feet in to get them warm. I couldn't have been over five.

Peggy Hackman

I remember standing with my grandmother in the back of our restaurant while she baked. She was always baking. She used to make very thin phyllo pastry by hand, working with a broom handle on a marble table. The pastry would twirl around the broom handle, getting thinner and thinner.

I also learned what Greek I know in that kitchen so that I could talk to my grandmother, who spoke no English.

Most of our lives circled around the restaurant—Lindell's in Lake Linden, Michigan, a small town on the Upper Peninsula. It was in the family for about forty years.

Richard Duke

I have a very vivid memory of chocolate cookies with chocolate frosting made by a housekeeper whom I remember only vaguely. These cookies were fairly large, but more important, were chocolate on top of chocolate.

Princess Pamela Strobel

Because Beauty, my mother, was working as an A-number-one pastry cook in Massachusetts, I was raised by my grandmother on Park Avenue in downtown Spartanburg, South Carolina—I was never a country girl. And my first memory is how strict Grandmama was—with *everybody*. In that house, you learned how to mind. Everybody minded, too: her children, my uncles, my mother.

Grandmama was a pillar of the biggest church in Spartanburg, the Majority Baptist Church. You know those cornerstones? Her name's right there. That church and cleaning were her life—and ours. I got in trouble once for washing a handkerchief after sundown on Saturday. That was the Lord's time, you know.

I remember Grandmama stayed home and cooked all the time, *especially* if pound day was coming. That's when Reverend Coleman would come around, and you gave him a pound of everything: canned fruit and cakes and pies.

One reason I've got so many names was Grandmama's cooking. We had a pretty home with manicured hedges, and food was always on the table for anybody. But ladies would come over to eat and would be my play mamas. You know about play mamas. That was a delight, and Grandmama would let them name me!

Grandmama was staunch! You didn't think about it, you just had to mind.

Jerry Preston

I remember singing with my mother in dusty Brownsville, Texas. We were driving somewhere when I started singing with her, and it absolutely blew her away that I was singing harmony. Mama belonged to a Pentecostal church, and pretty soon I became a minicelebrity on the church circuit. Mama would stand me on the altar bench to sing. "Jesus Knows" was real popular: "Before the sunshine comes the rain; after the harvest comes the grain." We sang at funerals a lot too; "I Won't Have to Cross Jordan Alone" and "Pearly White City" were standards.

Mama would carry her accordion with her wherever she went. Once we were on the train going to visit my father when a guy came up and wanted me to sign a recording contract. Of course we couldn't do that, since singing was *For The Lord Only*.

And then Mama got involved with a very, very fundamental Pentecostal group. Everything was sinful: comics, even dominoes, something my dad played on Saturday nights at the domino hall. I remember once we'd been singing on the street corner and the preacher had been preaching when Mama decided we had to march into the domino hall and save those domino players! All my life I've thought that must have been horrifying for my dad: your wife conducting a Salvation Army-type preaching service in a pool hall in front of your friends.

At the same time, everybody did seem to like the singing. I think Daddy did too.

Mildred Sutton

I remember coming to Georgia with Daddy from South Carolina in a horse and buggy. We spent the night in Hepzibah with one cousin on the way to Midville to spend the night with cousin Myrtis. That night in Hepzibah they sat out on the porch while they wanted me to go to bed. But I was afraid to go to back to that strange room by myself, and Daddy wouldn't make me. He let me lie down in the swing and go to sleep.

It took us two days to go about eighty miles. Why Daddy brought me I don't know, but I was about three. That was quite a trip, just the two of us.

Marynell Waite

When I was sick with the chicken pox and measles at the same time, I remember Brother and Sister, who were eighteen and sixteen years older than I, taking me to ride in my new red wagon—a special treat. I was sitting on a bed pillow, which was not usually allowed, and my eyes were covered with my brother's cap. As we toured through the backyard and around the church, I was delighted to be the center of attention. And I loved to ride and go places even at age three, but I felt so sick I surprised all of us by saying, "Take me back in."

Lyn Lear

When I was two, my mother wasn't well, and we visited my grandmother in Palm Springs for a couple of months. I very clearly remember locking myself in the bathroom, climbing on top of the sink, getting into all the makeup, and having a great time with lipsticks and powder. I remember Grandmother outside banging on the window, frantically trying to get me to open the door. I was wanting attention from my mom, but she wasn't able to give me much those days.

Phoebe Legere

I have two first memories: looking up into my mother's face, at her shoulder and her ear and her beautiful blonde hair and thinking she was so beautiful I wanted to get older so that I would be old enough to draw her. I must have been one or two. My second memory would be around the same time. I would take my nap each day in the library. As soon as I was put into bed, I'd get out and peek at all the little tiny beautiful things. I can remember fine, tiny, bound books and tiny carved ivory.

Sonya Friedman

My first memories are chaotic, filled with loneliness. My father never wanted to have anything to do with me, although I was his only child. He left when I was three. My mother simply had difficulties surviving. I can't give you a specific memory, but I was very aware of a lack of cohesion and approval, aware of very limited expectations for me by the authority figures in my life.

Doris Roberts

I remember living with my grandmother and grandfather and my aunt and uncles in an apartment in the Bronx. I remember being awakened at five in the morning by the smell of fish being fried. My grandfather loved fish, smelts, I think. It was the worst smell, and I hate fish as a result.

Nancy Perkins

Itching with chicken pox when I was three. Mother kept putting baking soda all over me to take the swelling and itching down. I looked like a white ghost.

Don Brunson

When I was about three, in Midfield, Alabama, we lived across from a park that had a small creek with a little bridge. I was kneeling on the bridge watching the little bitty minnows in the water. When one of them started swimming up underneath the bridge, I leaned over farther to keep it in sight and fell off the bridge and hit my head on a rock. It wasn't a long fall, but it scared me since I cut my head open and a lot of blood gushed out. I remember running home, being comforted by my mother, and taken to the doctor to have stitches.

Marla Hanson

I was at a park with my grandparents—I hardly knew them my whole life—and there was a swinging rope bridge across a gully. My grandparents and parents were trying to push me onto the bridge, and I was screaming and crying.

Barbara Bailey

I remember being very angry and kicking a hole in my bedroom wall. I must have been under four. I don't know what I was in a tizzy about.

Virginia Kabl

I remember hitting my brother over the head with one of those pins they used to exercise with, pins like those in a bowling alley. He was playing with something I wanted to play with.

John Englander

I remember going out to the garage when I was about three and releasing the emergency brake on a car. It rolled over my leg. It was just amazing that it didn't break my leg.

Judy Rose

During the war we lived in the country in England, where my parents had a hotel. Though I don't remember any bombing, I remember carrying my parents' double bed into the kitchen and the pale green bedspread. I also used to scream hysterically at the air raid sirens.

Ben Rose

What I remember most vividly is the whole ground just rumbling and rumbling—this was during the war in England. And I remember the U.S. forces moving through. All the kids would stand around and ask the Americans, "Give me some gum, chum." Or chocolate.

John Emmerling

On V-E Day, when the whole family went downtown to the big Detroit parade celebrating the end of the war, I had the measles and had to stay home. I sat at the window watching them all go off and felt very much deprived. But when they came back, my grandfather picked up one of his shotguns and took me out into the tiny backyard. There in the alley was a cement trash can. As firecrackers went off in the neighborhood, he fired off the shotgun into the side of the cement trash can. What an incredible boom! My grandfather did it as a special celebration just for me.

Robert Abrams

When I turned five, my Aunt Jeannette fixed me a German chocolate cake, and my dad got store-bought drinks for a special treat. After we'd had dinner and ice cream, I started pushing Aunt Jeannette and other folks to leave the birthday party. I wanted to have more than one of those soft drinks for myself.

Stephanie Beacham

My first memory is *weeping*, weeping behind the red velvet curtain in our living room as I was not allowed to go fishing because boys went fishing. My father and my brother were going fishing, and I was probably simply too young. It wasn't anything boys did at all; that was just the excuse I was given. I was three and about to be totally troublesome on a fishing trip.

Alastair Barbour

I grew up on the end of Loch Tunnel, near Pitlochry, Scotland. I remember learning to ice skate with a chair. I remember picnics in the summer with lots of cousins and aunts and uncles around. My grandmother, a matriarchal figure, drove us around in an old yellow van. Later I remember learning to ride bicycles by riding among the cowsheds.

Mary Randolph

Having a tea party with my dog Poochie when I was three. He was sitting in a chair and I was sitting in a chair at this small table.

Medora Plimpton

Feeding the hummingbirds at the Bird Lady's with my parents and my friend Wendy in Barbados is a vivid memory. The birds would come sit in your hand. I was five.

Michael Bornn

My first memory goes back to our little baseball field here in the Virgin Islands—getting clocked in the head with a baseball bat.

My brother and I were playing baseball. I was catcher and I was behind the plate and I got clocked. I still have the scar. The "field," you understand, was this courtyard, about ten by twenty feet.

Edith Bornn
My first memory may be playing baseball with my father and my sister. I was going to say up here in the garden, but that was my own children. My father playing baseball with my own children in the garden is also a fond memory.

Torre Andrews
Peashooters. My friend's father took us up to a little hill behind the military housing we lived in and taught us how to make them. Take a piece of paper and wrap it around a pencil; then pick up pebbles and shoot them through the thing. What I remember was that I swallowed most of the pebbles. I was less than two.

Edward Colquhoun
I remember playing in the backyard in Texas. I had a horned toad that lived under the water faucet. I'd climb up an oak tree on a fat rope that had big knots in it. And I remember climbing on the horizontal pieces of the back fence and leaning over to talk to the garbage men coming down the alley or to the next-door neighbors.

At night, I could hear the wallpaper, which was evidently loose, blow in and out in the Texas wind. I was about three.

Later I looked up the house, and, of course, the backyard had shrunk!

Alvis Waite
I have a fleeting impression of how far the church seemed from the parsonage at Midland, Georgia, where we lived when I was two. I discovered how close they actually were when I returned twenty years later to serve that same church.

I also remember the new car that Dad got while we lived at Midland—a Model T with isinglass curtains that rolled up and buckled. That was the car involved in a famous family adventure.

Dad was driving from Midland to Upatoi, another church on the circuit, and I was with him. As we pulled slowly up a hill on a narrow red clay road, two men leaped out of the woods and onto the car. Since Dad had both the curtains and the luggage rack up, they couldn't get a good hold. He brought his elbow down on their hands, they fell off and he kept going. He was going too slowly to hurt them. With no telephones to pass the word, he had no idea who they were until he got the paper later in the week—two convicts had escaped, jumped a freight, and left the train near where we encountered them.

Jim Hallett

When I was about four years old, I wanted to go to work for a gas station, and so about five or six o'clock in the morning I got up. Still wearing my Dr. Dentons, I snuck out of the house and walked uptown to a Texaco gas station where I liked to hang out as a four-year-old. Going up in the dark in my Dr. Dentons. And when I got there, the gas station, Burgess's Texaco, was just opening. Jim Burgess called Mom to tell her that I was up there in my Dr. Dentons. It was great! I loved it.

Vince Spezzano

My father loved to go to see the Rochester Red Wings play baseball. The first time I remember going to a game, as we walked into the stadium, a ball came up over the fence and rolled almost to our feet. Dad handed it to me and said, "Marty Marion hit that ball." I treasured it.

Some time later, maybe a year or two, it occurred to me: how did he know it was Marty Marion who hit that ball? He couldn't see anything—we were outside the fence.

Buck Johnson

I got a tricycle when I was about four. I had it in the yard of our house in Twin City, trying to back up. And for some reason it wouldn't back up, so I yelled, "The son-of-a-bitch won't back!" My folks got on to me about that.

Bill Peck, Supper Club

I remember falling down off a porch on a tricycle. I was probably about three or four years old and was after a cookie from the rolling store. My mother bought me one every morning. As the youngest at the time in a family of six, I was the only one who got a cookie. My brothers and sisters who are in their seventies and sixties now, still won't let me forget it.

Deni McIntyre

On a really snowy morning in Wisconsin, I was waiting on the front porch for a neighborhood car pool to pick me up for nursery school. The wrought-iron porch railing was covered with ice, which, for some reason, I decided to lick. I got stuck.

There was nothing I could do. I screamed, but enough of my mouth was engaged with the railing that I must not have been making much sound. It was so cold and I stood there bent over with my tongue on this railing until the car pool came.

Then my mother came out and poured a cup of some warmish water over my tongue. I had pulled so much that my tongue was bleeding, but Bobo and Billy, my little friends, said, "Well, just get in the car and go to school and if your blood fills up your boots we'll bring you home." That's the first thing I remember anybody saying to me.

Dana Warrington

The school bus driver passed our house on the way home from kindergarten, and I started to get nervous. But the driver finally circled around and left me off. Since no one was home, I fell asleep on the porch.

Carolyn Abrams

I was watching my mother take my older sister through her reading lessons. My sister was having a hard time grasping the next word. "Recipe," I said. My mother looked at me in amazement. I was only four.

Timothy Sultan

Though they lap over one another chronologically, the memories from my childhood in Laos, where my father worked for the Agency for International Development, are very vivid. I think back to them often and still go through my father's slides when I go home.

One of the earliest is going to a fair at night in Vientiane. I remember only that the fair was located near the river, the Mekong. It was raining steadily as we walked by shooting booths, where you could win gold-painted wooden carvings of slender Buddha figures. Some time in the evening, we rode the Ferris wheel that overlooked the soaked and mostly deserted fairgrounds.

Another early memory, I might have been four, was running to find Santa Claus. It was the afternoon of a tropical day, and for some reason I was late reaching where he was supposed to be. When I got there, I found only one adult who told me that Santa Claus was about to leave and told me where—behind a house on Dead End Street, my street. Perhaps I could still catch a glimpse of him. I ran back, feverishly upset, and as I got to the field, Santa Claus was just taking off, hovering over the grass and waving from his helicopter. And so I learned that reindeer just aren't native to Laos.

Dave DeGrandpre

My first memory? Christmas Eve, hidden in an upstairs hallway, I'm peeking over the stairs watching my parents bringing the presents from the closets. They had already told me Santa didn't exist, but that had only made me more excited. That meant I could sneak down at 4:30 and check out all the presents without worrying about him! I'd get a bit of sleep and go down to check out all the stuff—not just mine, but everyone's! I was seven.

3. Things That Shine

Henry Kemp, Supper Club
Going eighty-five in an Oldsmobile.

Zar Rochelle
The top of my head.

Nan Thomas
The water on Little Apple Bay. On certain days the light is such that the ocean's like floating diamonds.

Marla Hanson
As I watched from the balcony of the house overhanging the cliff in Little Apple Bay one evening, the rays of the setting sun burst from behind the island of Jost Van Dyke in the distance and across the water, lighting up the bay and a fisherman for one final second.

Paul Mockler *different kind of shine*
I like to see qualities in people that shine. Like loyalty; a sense of honor. I sense loyalty in my real friends, and I appreciate that in other people.

Jerry Preston *aging*
My mother's first cousin was very plain when she was younger. But now that she's seventy-seven, she has this warm glow about her. This lady has gotten truly beautiful in her old age.

Sonya Friedman
My skin when it has no makeup on it.

Dan Buettner
> I think well-defined goals shine.

Alvis Waite
> Preaching, when the sermon is going well.

Edith Bornn
> The thing that gives me the greatest pleasure is when my children all band together to help each other to accomplish something. Maybe only one will actually do the job or get the credit, but they have to all work together. That shines for me.
>
> I remember one horse show where my sons Mike and Dave were entered in competition, and in the warmup prior to it, David's horse fell over a jump and David's shoulder was broken. At that point, their brother Steve said, "I'll take his place." Within moments Steve took his position, and with tears in their eyes, Mike and Steve went out to compete as a team in place of David and Mike. They had a stunning win against the other team. That shone.

Torre Andrews
> My grandmother's datebooks from 1923 when she was at the University of Chicago and met my grandfather, Frank Andrews. The appointments vary at first: "John in the afternoon." "Bob's party." "ATO formal." Then there's the first reference to my grandfather: "Swimming with Frank." Pretty soon, every page has something about Frank.

Mildred Sutton
> When somebody comes up and tells you they love you, that you mean something to them, that makes you warm all over because we all want to be loved and appreciated.

Shannon Kelly
> This sounds absolutely corny, but Mary Lou's smile when I first saw it on TV. I remember it clearly, watching her as she performed for that perfect ten during the Olympics. I had never met her, and

I certainly wasn't the only person in America taken by that victory smile. But I did say to myself right then, *that's* the girl I'm going to marry. And I did.

Murial Sichveland, Wednesday Bridge Club

My husband of fifty-three years keeps a little account book in his office. And he adds to my account on all kinds of occasions. He'll give me a nice little note and tell me, "I've added to your account."

He's gone through a lot of those little books over the years, adding to my account. And it's really grown, since I don't spend much. I did subtract a little bit to take him for lunch the other day.

Peggy Kemp, Wednesday Bridge Club

Shining shoes, gosh!

Joy Melton Prickett

Waxed Chevies. My hunter green, two-door, '69 Impala Sport Coupe. Every time I came home from college for the weekend my daddy and I waxed it. First the rubbing compound, then the wax, the chrome shiner, the whitewalls. That's a shiny car.

John Marston

The right corner fender of my '76 Celica. The one I sawed the roof off of.

Last January I decided to get the little racy, red convertible I'd always wanted. I couldn't afford one of those fancy new Miatas, and I couldn't bring myself to sell the '76 Celica, the car I learned to drive in.

So I went down to Wannamaker Rents and rented a Saws-All for about $15. A Saws-All can saw through metal plates. It has a diamond blade. I called up my friend Bob Thompson who knows a lot about auto design and so knew what was inside the car, what's behind that panel, what's behind that seat.

We laughed and drew guidelines in dust on the car and sawed the roof off. It took about fifteen minutes.

Now I'm building a soft top for it. And I took it in to get it painted yesterday. It's going to be Mercedes Benz signal red. The whole car shines.

Amy Holloway

Standing in a spotlight. A moment that shines is when I conducted *No, No, Nanette.* I walked out for the first performance and the spotlight came on *me.* I picked up the baton and saw my shadow. It gives me chills now to think about how it felt: *You're doing this!* I was the first woman to conduct a musical performance at the Clarence Brown Theatre.

Bunny Johnson

The searchlights during the war. Papa was an airplane watcher in south Georgia; he even had this little hat to wear. He'd count every plane that came over and check to see if it was an enemy plane. They made camouflage nets in the gym at the high school.

But right behind Mama and Papa's flower shop was a great big searchlight. All night, if you were at Mama's, you could wake up, and that light would be shining out there, the brightest thing I've ever seen in my life.

Buck Johnson

When they first turned on the electric light in my house, it was almost a ceremony. I was thirteen years old; it was 1945. We had a single bulb hanging from the ceiling, and we had a string. At night we'd pull that string to turn on the light, and the whole room lit up. Compared to lights now, that light was dim, but it seemed extra bright at the time.

I remember we usually turned on the lights at full dark, and we could hardly wait till then. That's one of the reasons we loved Roosevelt so much: the Rural Electric Administration.

4. Early Memories

Carol Hallett

As soon as World War II was over, we moved to Carmel, where my sister and I attended a one-room school. We're actually stepsisters. My mother had died when I was born and my sister's father had died four months before she was born. Our parents met as widower and widow, each with a baby. They were married just a month before I was two and just after my sister turned two. So we grew up happily ever after—really a very close family. When we were small, people would ask us if we were twins, and we would say, "No, but we're going to be."

In Carmel my father built the house we lived in. While he was building it, we "pioneered." We had an outhouse, and until my father had the bathroom built, we showered by turning the spigot on this great, big, 12,000-gallon tank and getting under the water as it spurted out of a huge pipe.

Myrtis Brown

I have lived in Greene County off and on my whole life. I was born there, on the Little plantation where my father and mother, Henry and Claudy Hurt, were sharecroppers. When I was a baby, Miss Ida and Watt Little, the owners of the plantation, wouldn't let my mother and dad take me in the fields, so they kept me in a box in the kitchen. And when I was big enough to get around, I played in the kitchen and around the yard. I always wanted to chase the chickens. And I grew up there with the families I loved. We took care of each other and we're still close.

When I got big enough to go to the fields with Mother and Dad, though, I thought it was fun to be there. I was always chasing around and getting in my mother's way. She couldn't get anything done, and when she'd go home to fix dinner, I'd be right behind her. Finally, she got Ann Eliza Jackson, a young girl from another black family, to stay with me so she could get some work done. When my sister Cora Beth came along, Ann Eliza took care of both of us.

By the time my baby brother Charles came along, we'd moved off the place to Atlanta.

Ollie Ferguson

Most of my first memories are at Camperdown, my grandparents' home in Nassau, where I was brought up. Basically it is the old family home with a little cottage off to one side. They had an extensive orchard, probably fifteen acres, with sapodilla trees, mango trees, orange trees, tangerines, guavas, grapefruit. We even had an akee tree that I planted as a child. The akee is a very bizarre fruit that's only edible when its hard shell cracks open, and if you don't prepare it properly, it can be poisonous. Yet people eat it all the time. I never ate the fruit, but I remember going down to the orchard with my grandmother with my little red wheelbarrow, and she said, "OK, you are going to plant this tree. This is going to be your tree." I dumped horse manure on it and nurtured it, and it is still in the orchard to this day.

Camperdown also was the original site of what turned out to be our family's ranch. It started out with just my grandparents' two horses, one called Love and the other called Yamacraw. The stables are down there, too. It was a collage of different scents and odors, a big playground full of adventure.

Nassau in my childhood was a paradise. We had beautiful beaches, ideal weather, lots of friends, lots of things to do, not a care in the world, and all the time in the world to do all of those things. Summers for me ranged from spending the day on the beach body surfing to going out in the boat spear fishing or water skiing. In great packs of ten or twelve, we'd ride our trail bikes aimlessly on the street, on the beach, on trails. I remember the absolute abandon, not reckless or irresponsible, but absolute abandon, the freedom to do whatever you wanted. In my childhood I felt invincible and immortal. It was just incredible.

George Plimpton

My grandparents had this wonderful place in Ormond Beach, Florida, a compound somewhat like the Kennedy compound in Hyannis Port and just as lively when the families turned up. We went down there on school vacation at Easter time on the train. I think the train left New York at noon. I remember walking through the cars to the dining car and the big, squat glasses with the ice tinkling in them. At night, if you had the lower berth in the Pullman you could lift up the shades and see the towns going by, and then the dark fields and maybe a light way off in the distance.

Then in the early morning you'd wake up, and a little later the train'd get to Jacksonville, where the electric engine would be changed for a steam engine. You'd get out and walk along the station platform to see this, and once it happened there was always the excitement that maybe the train would leave without you.

Campion Platt

I was four or five, and we were all naked there on the beach at Toom Island on Cape Cod. I have good memories of that; it felt really natural and nice.

Jim Swann

When I was a kid, my dad, who'd become semiretired at an early age, went fishing almost every day in Tampa Bay back before it was polluted and when there were still fish there. And I'd go with him every time I possibly could. He had an old, beat-up 1950 green Chevrolet where he kept all his fishing tackle and bait. It smelled like hell.

And every afternoon after we went fishing, he'd stop at a bar and leave me in the hot sun baking with those smelly fish, while he went in and socialized. Since kids didn't go in bars, I'd sit out there and suffer along with those poor dead mackerel.

Kathryn Hames, Supper Club

My daddy had a Model T Ford that we thought was the most wonderful car in the world. When it rained, remember, you had to put up those side curtains. And every summer they'd save up money to take my sister and me down to Tybee Island for a vacation. We used to live for that treat. I remember it took two days and two nights to get there from Marietta—about 300 miles. We'd camp out in tents along the way.

I remember that the first time any of us ever saw the ocean, my daddy just kept driving down onto the beach. And we got stuck when the tide came in—something we hadn't thought about.

David Prowse

I used to wait outside the house when my father was coming home from work. I'd see him in the distance on his bike, and I'd race up the road to meet him. Father would give me a lift on the crossbar of his bike. I was three. And then when I was five, Father developed a duodenal ulcer, and they said, "You have to have it seen to." The operation was a great success, and I had lots of letters from him in the hospital saying, "Look after your mom. Make certain Bobby is OK." And then on the tenth day after the surgery, the whole thing burst and he was dead within a day. Just like that. I still have the letters.

Paul Mockler

I remember going duck hunting with my father when I was five. He had a twelve-gauge shotgun and I a popgun with a cork. I remember killing several ducks with that cork gun.

Chris Keefe

Going to a little Irish pub with my dad. He'd get me a bag of chips and a Coke, and I'd sit in a booth or play the piano and stuff. I was about six.

Mary Lou Retton

Going to get a haircut with Mom at the beauty parlor, and I was really scared! I had gone with her a lot, and finally it was my turn to sit in the chair. I was so scared because I didn't know what would happen, was afraid the scissors would hurt me. But Mom held my hand, and it was OK. I was probably three.

Dan Buettner

When I was four, my grandmother, Irene Palermo, gave me my first bicycle. She had the custom of giving the children in the family their first bicycles. Mine was a small, red push bike with training wheels. I rode it in a square pattern around the front yard. I had that bike for two years, then I got a Stingray, which was far cooler because it had the banana seat and big U-shaped handlebars.

Buck Johnson

One of my funniest early memories: Mama had back trouble, and one winter night—we all slept in the same room where it was warm—Mama said to Daddy, "Grady, you have got to rub my back." Well, we didn't have electric lights, so Daddy got up in the dark and got a bottle of liniment and rubbed Mama down. And she said, "Oh, that's the best stuff." Then she went to sleep in about thirty minutes, saying, "That is the best liniment I've ever seen." When we got up next morning, we saw Daddy had rubbed her down with O-Cedar furniture polish. I was about six or seven then.

Rodney Cook

On our farm, I had a cozy room on the top floor with dormer windows and a slanted ceiling. My bed was stuck into the dormer, and I remember lying in bed looking out the window as my mother sang to me.

One evening when my parents were out, I locked myself, for no apparent reason, in the bathroom that led off that dormer room. When I refused to come out, the sitter threatened to call my parents away from the party they were attending, and she did. I came out of the bathroom and looked out the dormer to see my father arriving in his T-bird, one of those with the porthole in the back. The driveway was so far away from the house that he had cut over the grass and through a hedge to drive right up to the house.

I knew trouble was really coming. So I ran back into the bathroom, locked the door and again refused to open it. In a moment, I saw the end of a saw blade slip through the door over the hinge. They sawed off the door to get me. And that's all I remember. I don't remember being punished, though I must have been. What I do remember is that I did it for no reason at all.

Mildred Sutton

The first time I ever remember hearing a radio was about 1918 in Swainsboro, when Daddy carried us up to a filling station at the corner of Main Street where they had a radio with earphones. We stood in line and put the earphones on. The miracle was you heard something through those earphones. Daddy wanted us to know about things, so he took us up there.

Barbara Bailey

I remember the planes dropping bombs over London during the First World War. My grandfather, a very nervous man, would take us to the coal cellar, and we'd sit on little, hard, wooden chairs. The smell of coal dust and mildew brings that very pungent memory to me immediately.

Timothy Sultan

As a child in Laos, I was mostly oblivious to the war that was taking place in the mountains, but I have two direct memories. One is a vague image of a Pathet Lao soldier in a wooden cage in the market at Vientiane. The other is more vivid. It happened when the Lao National Army, which was losing its war, came to our house looking for young Lao men to draft. They had been going from house to house. Our gardener, Peng, came to my mother for help. She hid him in the bathtub when the soldiers came to our door. Later, in order to sneak him past the guards at the entrance to our community, she put a wig on his head and dressed him in her clothes. I'm sure he felt embarrassed thus clothed, but my mother successfully drove him to his village. There his wife and children hid him beneath some bamboo sticks and leaves for three weeks until the danger had passed.

Hamilton Fish

We lived in Ireland. My father was in the foreign service after World War II, and my mother at that time apparently was an indifferent cook. She didn't know the relative value of weights and measures: once she ordered enough potatoes to feed all the Irish in America. That's what we ate much of the time we were in Ireland. I was about two.

Helen Barbour

In Sierra Leone, we had a night watchman called Palomino who patrolled the house to guard against the snakes and beasties and burglars that might get in. My mother was overprotective, so I was not allowed to talk to him, but I used sometimes to sneak off to his mud hut and just look in. It was a tiny hut, perhaps ten circular feet, with a smooth mud floor pounded down by his feet. He had a bench and a little wooden bowl for eating out of and a wooden spoon he'd made from sandalwood. I couldn't believe he lived there and with so few possessions.

Stephanie Beacham

I remember a lake was a terribly important place in my upbringing, the center of all society as far as we young bicyclers were concerned. We used to meet there from the age of seven. I can remember one whole spring, the Easter holiday of the oak tree, when this hugh oak tree fell in a storm, and before the council cleared it up, we children made encampments. The boys wanted to make army barracks and the girls, of course, wanted to make houses. All these leaves and sort of entrances. I remember this whole society of girls wanting homes and boys wanting army barracks.

Jock Munro

Some of my earliest memories of playing are of special secret places outdoors. There was a holly hedge so old that the bottom of it had hollow places underneath the branches that a child could get right under. We also had similar hideaways under the yew bushes.

Then we had a marvelous rowan tree that I used to climb up. It had lots of little side branches so I could go right up to the top. If someone wanted to cut my hair—I wanted to have a fringe like the Beatles—I'd climb up this tree, so they couldn't get me. But they always seemed to nab me later.

Silvia Munro

We had secret places, too, particularly the clock tower that had some little rooms at the top. Actually, we weren't allowed up there because the clock was easily upset and there was danger of getting hit by the works. And the noise was really loud if you got caught in the tower when it chimed. But we used to sneak up anyway. When the man who used to look after the clock saw footprints, he would run around and check our feet and find the sole that matched and say, "It was you!" He almost always got it right.

Henry Kemp, Supper Club

I had to look after a cow, and I'm talking about a four-legged cow. She was my responsibility to milk, and she *got* milked—sometimes at five or six in the afternoon, sometimes at midnight. It was kind of hard for me to work in some of my social life with milking a cow.

Rose Wing, Supper Club

When I first came to Marietta to teach school, all the singles in town used to eat down at Miss Abbott's Tearoom, near the town square. Another teacher and I would walk down Lawrence Street from our rooming house, around the square, to the restaurant. If you didn't have a date when you went in, you hoped you would when you left.

Nowadays you can walk around the square or eat out and not see a person you know. But not then. I remember that the way we walked home took us by the Methodist parsonage and the preacher would be sitting out on his porch. This was when I was just starting to date Steve. And when my friend and I would walk by, the preacher would look at his watch and say, "You'd better hurry; he'll be there in about five minutes."

He knew exactly what went on in the neighborhood. Everyone did.

5. Holding Hands

Jim Swann

I love little children's hands. They're beautiful. I hold hands with my children at night when they're in bed, and we make up stories. We have a great game. It would be fun for grownups to do if they could let their hair down. The kids give me two animals and I make up a story. Of course they try to think of the most outrageous combination, like a cat and a roach; animals that will stump me.

Stephanie Beacham

Sitting on my father's shoulders when I was a small child.

Jane Burke

In fifth-grade gym class, I got the worst partner for folk dancing—Eugene, who had sweaty, warty fingers. I had to hold hands with him.

Dan Buettner

Skating in a game called Snowball at the Rosedale Roller Skating Rink. We were all about fourteen. In Snowball, one couple starts skating in a circle while all the other men and women line up on either side of the rink. When someone blows a whistle, the first couple breaks off, each going to the lines to pick another partner. As the whistle blows again and again, the number of people skating increases.

You stood there hoping the girl you had an eye on would pick you or that you'd have a chance to pick her first. Then you'd hold hands and skate round the rink—at thirteen or fourteen, the highest gratification.

James Royce

The first time I held hands with my fiancée, Lisa. I haven't held hands with too many people, haven't been close to that many people. Lisa and I were skating at the ice rink in Central Park. I grabbed her hand because I couldn't stand up by myself.

Nan Thomas

I remember that when I was finally allowed to go to the movies and held the hand of the man I eventually married, I didn't know how to stop sweating.

John Marston

I do it every day. I hold hands with a surf board.

Mary Lou Retton

I love it! Shannon and I hold hands more than we put our arms around each other because of our height difference. He's six feet two inches and I'm four feet nine inches.

Ollie Ferguson

I always held hands with my grandparents. As a matter of fact, I took a trip with them when I was twenty-eight or twenty-nine, and I would be driving in the car, just holding hands with my grandmother. There was nothing spoken between us, nothing said to instigate it, we would just hold hands. Any time I see any of my family, male or female, we always hug and kiss as a greeting. I have been very, very lucky to have a family like that.

Kurt Vonnegut

The most intimate thing you can do.

6. A Special Moment with a Parent

Norman Lear

I'd just gotten my license and had a date to see my favorite play—*Lilliom*—at the Westport Playhouse, a three-hour drive from home. Tyrone Power and Annabell were playing. It was the biggest night of my life! The play, those stars, and my father had promised to be home in time for me to take his Hudson rather than my old jalopy Model A Ford.

He was due back at 5:00, but he wasn't there; 5:15 came, 5:40, he still hadn't come. So I jumped in my jalopy, tears pouring down my face, and picked up my girlfriend. Two hours later, I'm on the Merritt Parkway nearly to Westport when I hear this honk, honk, honk. My father had arrived minutes after we'd left and chased me two hours to exchange cars.

My father disappointed you day in and day out, and then he did these incredible things.

Kathy Bater Brackett

When I was very small, my mother took my sisters and me on vacation to Catalina. We were having a great time when I remember my mother sitting me down and saying, "Do you like it here?"

"Of course." My sisters and I were in heaven.

And we stayed. My mother bought a hotel, the Seacomber. And I remember as a little child, about six, standing out in front of this hotel and saying, "I really want to live here, but Mom, you don't know anything about hotels." She said, "You don't have to worry about that; let me worry about that."

34

The hotel was like Fawlty Towers. The pipes were always honking and rattling. The place was falling apart and didn't do well. But Mother didn't share her troubles; with her, everything was always fine.

Foxy Callwood

My father beat my leg with a saw once, and it got worse and worse. I was around five. It was bad all the way from my toe to knee. See? The hairs is still not there, and only now skin has started to come back.

All the doctors did was make it worse. But Grandmama took care of that foot. She got a physic-nut bush, the black physic-nut, and she would do it like this—rub it up in the water and warm the water and sop it on my leg all the time. She took care of it.

It took a while for me to walk again, and then I goes up the hill and I walks a little. Did'ya know I only rode in an automobile once since they're here? There's only six. But years later, I rode to take my father from the house to the dock to take *him* to the hospital. Any place I want to go, I get in my dinghy or my boat or walk.

But that day I rode. My father died in the hospital in St. Thomas.

Sonya Friedman

I hate to tell you this, but there wasn't a special moment. Because I cried so much, I used to think that God should have given me windshield wipers on my eyes instead of eyelashes.

Hamilton Fish

A problem with special moments is that they don't often seem special until later when you look back on them, when you have the tools of an older person to assess them. My father was an unassuming man without any overt sense of self-importance. My grandfather was a wildly egotistical and self-important individual whose primary communication with us was in the first person singular and whose usual MO was to squash people who competed with him for the limelight. And so I think I will always be grateful to my father for having essentially deflected this raging personality from his children. We were able to grow up without being unduly steered by my grandfather and, more important, without ever feeling too angry toward him because he ignored us.

I think the same was not true of my father; I think he took it on the chin and paid a steep price. But he certainly protected us, and realizing that was certainly a special moment for me.

Dan Buettner

As a kid, I had a great terror of sticking my head underneath water. I have fragments of memory from age three or four of my mother sticking my head underneath the bathtub faucet to wash my hair. And then I have a much clearer memory of my father once washing my hair by gently lowering my head to the water in the tub and splashing water lightly up on my hair rather than putting me under the faucet.

Carolyn Abrams

My dad, who was seventy-seven when he died in 1965, was both a father and mother to us after he and my mother were divorced. To take care of us, he cooked, cleaned, ironed, sewed—did whatever it took. He worked up until he couldn't. When he retired from cleaning streets with a pushcart for the City of Hattiesburg, he did yard work. He recovered from one stroke and went back to his yard work again because he had to "take care of my chaps." He did his best. He was a good friend. And he believed in me.

He was quite a storyteller, and sometimes I was the only one who would sit down and listen. He took me to visit some relatives in Hattiesburg where I remember walking with him through this long field while he told stories.

And I remember writing letters for him. He only got to the second reader in school, the second grade, but he taught me the first word I learned to spell: compressibility. "Do it like this," he said; "Com, c-o-m; press, p-r-e-s-s; i; bil, b-i-l; i; ty, t-y. Compressibility." I had no idea what it meant at the time.

The way he presented himself impressed me. When he had to go downtown on business, he'd always dress up. He always wore a hat. And he'd change his mode of speaking: he'd get real proper.

When he had a second stroke, he went to bed and couldn't get up. Over my dad's protest, I called Dr. Graves, but there was nothing he could do. Dad told me he needed to talk to me and told me he was going. I said, "No, you're not dying." Then he said, "Yes, it's time to go." I was holding his hand when he died. I was sixteen.

Mildred Sutton

I remember when I went to school at Milledgeville, you couldn't go off campus beyond town and you couldn't go dancing. And I remember my daddy came to school one Friday to pick me up to take me home. Instead he carried me to Macon, hours out of the way, to my boyfriend's fraternity dance. That was very, very special, shocking in that day and time, 1928. No one but my daddy would have done that.

Jerry Preston

My daddy worked in the oil fields in Texas, so I didn't see him a lot and we moved all the time—wherever the work was. Mama would just pile everything in the car and sometimes a trailer and we went. We moved so much we couldn't have a piano—and I really wanted to play the piano.

Then Daddy got promoted. I will never forget: *movers* came to move us. We didn't have to load a thing. That was a very special moment, because I was sure we'd get a piano. And we did.

David Prowse

I always remember my father helping me put together the money to buy a book, *Youth at the Zoo*. Even at five I was doing odd jobs earning various bits of money. The book had the most fantastic, beautiful pencil drawings of all these animals. I worked weeks to earn the money and remember bringing the book home and showing Father. I've still got the book.

Bunny Johnson

I remember just a flash of my daddy singing in the choir at the First Baptist Church and being so proud of him. He had a good voice. Then I have a very vivid memory of Mother and Daddy coming back from driving some cars down from Detroit for a local car dealer and bringing me a doll. It was just a little doll, but that was the first time I remember anyone bringing me something.

But most of my early memories are not real happy. They're of going home to Mama's and Papa's because Mother and Daddy were fighting.

Kate Learson

My father, who had been poor, worked very hard to reach the top of his profession. To do so, he traveled so much I used to think that dads only came home for weekends. One time when he came home, all sorts of things needing fixing around the house. Unlike my sisters, I chose to help when he asked. So he taught me how to hammer and nail, how to splice electrical wires, how to fix the toilet, how to bend the float if the water level was too low. I felt so close to him. I felt so helpful; I was learning and I love learning. I look back and think that in a way I formed a relationship with my father that went on from cleaning up the linen closet and painting the bathroom and hammering and nailing to scraping the bottom of the boat he bought the richer he got. I was always like his little handyman and enjoyed it.

Henry Kemp, Supper Club

My father was a general practitioner, and I used to like to ride with him when he was making house calls. So I learned to drive an automobile early. I was the only sixth-grader at the Waterman Street school who drove to school. I don't know if it was legal or not, but nobody cared and there were no driver's licenses then. The car was a Model T. And Atlanta Street was the only paved street then in Marietta.

Mary Randolph

We had huge family reunions in Arkansas, and at family reunions, all the children used to sit at one table, the small table. Moving to the big table was a rite of passage. It also meant you had to help with the dishes.

Tommy Sammons

My father operated a sawmill in Waynesboro, Georgia, when I was about six. And Mama let me take his lunch in a bucket to his job. He worked a long ways away for a six-year-old—a mile and a half across town. I loved doing that!

The pail was a syrup bucket. I'd take corn bread, peas, vegetables, maybe some meat. I'd take it in and hang around while he took lunch, then head straight home.

Win Rockefeller

When I was a teenager, my stepbrother Bruce and I went on a float trip down the Buffalo with Dad. For a couple of days, Dad had been carrying an umbrella around on the boat, and Bruce and I were having quite a chuckle about it—an umbrella on the river! Then it began suddenly to pour down rain like a cow on a flat rock. The boat leaked, our gear was drenched, we were waterlogged. Bruce and I had obviously not considered rain gear in the middle of July in Arkansas. We had to get off the river, and Dad had the last laugh.

Kim Litton

Up in Montana or Wyoming, when I was five, the whole family was out in a boat fishing. We had a guide and everything. And I wanted badly to catch a fish. My dad said, "Kim, come hold my rod."

He put it in my hand. All of a sudden something jerked and I just pulled like crazy. I had a fish!

I didn't figure out for years that my father had probably already hooked the fish.

Peggy Sammons

I'd be so excited when I knew that Daddy was going to come in from the mail route and we were going to go fishing. Mother, Daddy, and I would go out to the Ohoopee River, where we'd fish from the bank. We never caught any fish, so Mother always took bacon and eggs for us to cook by the river. We'd fish for several hours—not catching anything, of course—then build a fire.

I went fishing with Daddy the last day I saw him alive. We'd been at our cabin on Lake Allatoona, and I went from there to a meeting in Atlanta. He died that night.

Michael Bornn

When I was a kid, I used to go hand line fishing with my dad off the great docks at the West Indies Company—where the cruise ships tie up, and where pirates used to anchor. We'd bike over there along the waterfront, all along the harbor. My first fish I ever caught was right off that dock. I remember it vividly: a lizard fish. You don't eat them, but they made great first fish to catch. I was sitting on the pier with my little red hand line, and that spotted fish looked like two hundred pounds to me. I think it was six inches long.

Last year I went hand line fishing with my father again right there, and it brought back good, good memories.

Edith Bornn

There were moments when my sister and I left St. Thomas and went to college stateside. I don't think our parents would have ever let us leave the island if they had thought we would be gone more than two months without seeing them. Then the war came. Quite suddenly we couldn't travel because of the troop convoys and supply ships. And they couldn't even make phone calls from St. Thomas. So my parents would travel to Puerto Rico in order to speak to us on the telephone. Those were very special calls. We didn't see them for two years.

Zar Rochelle

Most moments with my mother were special. God, was she a character! Often unconventional; sometimes zany; but always interesting, fun, and ahead of her time. She once got bored and dyed her hair fire truck red, and once for Christmas she dyed it green. Everyone loved her. It wasn't unusual for me to come home and find some of my friends there. They hadn't come to see me. They had come to see my parents.

Carol Hallett

My dad just loved deer hunting. And my dog Monty, a Gordon setter, always went hunting with us. I can remember trudging around the mountains with my dad, carrying this gun and never having an opportunity to shoot at a deer.

The summer after I graduated from high school, Daddy and I were hunting, climbing up and down hills, when I saw this great big buck. I was in front of my father; my dog was with me. And I started shooting. Well, I wasn't even aiming I was so excited. The deer just stood there and stared at me. I mean it's terrible, I could never shoot a deer now, but at the time it was important.

Suddenly I had only one shot left, and I thought, *I've got to aim*. I aimed and I got the deer. My father came running; he was panting and out of breath and the dog was barking. For my father—I will never as long as I'm alive forget it—it was the most thrilling moment of his life, to see me actually go out hunting with him and be the one to get the deer. An unusual experience for a daughter.

Alvis Waite

When I was a senior in high school and president of the student council, Ralph Hood, the principal of Glynn Academy, called me into his office and said, "Alvis, I'm not sure that you know that your great-grandfather was once principal of Glynn Academy"— actually I was surprised that he knew, since we'd lived in Brunswick only two years—"and we'd like for your father to read the scripture at graduation. If your grandfather can attend, we'd also like to have three generations of Waites on the platform."

It was a special moment to stand on the stage with Grandad Waite as Dad read the scripture from the Waite family Bible, which had been given to my great-grandfather, James Thomas Hamilton Waite, by the school when he left the position of principal.

A generation later, that special moment of connectedness was recalled when I gave the invocation and read the scripture from the same Bible at the baccalaureate service for my daughter Mary Abbott's graduation from Glynn Academy. Dad was in the audience, and she was an honor graduate. Part of what is so special is that so many generations of our family should have a connection with one public high school since three of the four fathers were ministers and moved fairly frequently.

Doris Roberts

My mother was a woman who worked; that's what she knew to do. I don't think she had a great sense of herself, but she was a very giving, funny woman. And she, too, helped send me into this world of the theater.

She worked for and finally owned the oldest public stenography service in New York City, a great, duplex office in the *Times* building. They typed all the scripts and books of the plays for the Broadway scene. So into that office came some of the greats of the theater.

As a young child I would spend extra hours with her there, working. At nine or eleven years old, I would collate. Later I learned to type and helped with that.

When Mother would get free tickets for a theater matinee, she'd allow me to stay away from school to go to the theater that afternoon. So I got to see most everything that was on Broadway.

That also contributed to this great appetite I have for acting.

Campion Platt

The overwhelming thing I remember about my mother is that during all those formative years when everyone else was being

restricted by their parents, I was given the wide expanse of life.
Mother wanted me to explore. She cut me loose to find my own
way. She had this wonderful attitude: Do it yourself! Talk to me
about it, I'll help you think it through, but do it!

Deni McIntyre

Even when I was really small, my parents seemed to treat me just
as they would treat each other or one of their friends.

Occasionally, for instance, my mother would help me play
hooky from school. I would either stay home in the morning or
call her with some problem midway through the day. She always
told me I could do that. So when I got ticked off at the nuns, I
could call her and say, "Come get me out of here; they're driving
me nuts."

And she would come and we would go out to lunch. Then
we'd go to a movie or the art museum. We would spend the day
just like a couple of girls out on the town. And when we talked
it was always equal, sort of give-and-take.

Phoebe Legere

Both of my parents were painters. They loved flowers and loved
to be outdoors, and I have a wonderful memory of picking
blueberries with my dad.

While my father painted in his studio, he would listen to jazz.
I would be playing nearby, so I could smell the turpentine and
hear Charlie Parker and Ella Fitzgerald. I think that experience
somehow instilled in me the deep passion I have for black music.

Mary Lou Retton

When my parents decided to let me move to Texas by myself at
fourteen to train with Bela Karolyi, they sat me down and talked
to me completely honestly and supported me 100 percent. It was
a touching moment because they were going to let me try to
achieve what had been my dream since I was seven: to go to the
Olympics. I had watched Nadia Comaneci in the 1976 Olympics
in Montreal. I was already taking dance and acrobatics at the time,

and I looked at Mom and said, "I'm going to win the Olympics." Mom patted me on the head and said, "Sure, honey." During the talk about moving to Texas, I remembered that moment.

I think my parents knew our relationship would change with that move, and they accepted that.

Cliff Robertson

I was absolutely stunned one summer by my grandmother. I was going through what I call my Richard Halliburton phase; I'd always been adventuresome. I wanted nothing more than to get on a train and just go somewhere that summer. And I didn't want to go with anyone. My grandmother had a sister who lived down in Dallas, so I said, "Maybe I'll go down to see your sister," expecting her to say, "Well, that's just ridiculous."

But she said, "All right. The only thing that I would suggest is that you use your own good judgment." I was so thrown by her accepting this and then saying use your judgment. I was fifteen.

Edward Colquhoun

My father was a very strict disciplinarian. And when I was just starting to drive I smashed up the front part of the car, a fairly new station wagon. I'd waved to a friend and hit a tree. I headed home absolutely mortified—I was never going to drive again, etc., etc. Uncharacteristically, my father didn't say anything negative. He had the car fixed and insisted that I take the car out again. That was special.

John Jaxhiemer

I guess for me a special moment would be last year, after I got caught cheating on a final exam. My parents were both very understanding, and they pretty much just helped me get through that and were right behind me. That kind of surprised me.

Stuart Perkins

I never really had one; I was brought up by governesses until I went away to boarding school at age six. When I was home it was apparent that my mother and father never really agreed about anything, and I'd be scooted away to my room.

But my grandfather, Harry Hutcheson Cooke, was an absolutely nifty guy. I really loved him. He was a retired VP of manufacturing for the Link Belt Company and had made a blooming fortune selling short in '29.

When he died at eighty-seven, he'd seen a doctor only twice in his life—once when he slammed his finger in the trunk of an old Packard and when he had a stroke at age eighty-seven. Since this stroke totally paralyzed him and left him near death, the family had set up shifts to keep watch.

My uncle, his son-in-law, whom he absolutely despised, was sitting his turn when I went over to relieve him. As I walked into the room, my grandfather was trying to say something. His lips were quivering, and my uncle was trying to lead him on and being a little silly about the whole thing. What he should have said was, "Don't worry about it."

Suddenly the clot must have moved, and my grandfather sat straight up in bed, looked my uncle right in the eye, and said, "I'm hungry, you goddamn fool!" And fell back dead.

I could tell immediately. I howled. I had to go out of the room. When a nurse asked what was the trouble, I laughed and said, "I think my grandfather just died." I never had the slightest sorrow about that man's death. In his eighty-seven years everything he did was fantastic. He taught me to sail. He taught me to drink a martini when I was seventeen at the Germantown Cricket Club. He was a great man.

Stephanie Beacham

My mother is unconditional love. I saw this most when my husband and I were splitting up and, though she was in tears for me, she said, "Darling, never expect me to say anything bad about John; he's the father of your children, my grandchildren." No matter how much resentment and anger there was, she said there is only love. I realized that the cleanness with which my ex-husband and I have become friends is because there was no taking sides, just love.

My father's strength was hands-on caring, as so many special moments during childhood reveal. For instance, he taught me to ride a two-wheel bicycle. I remember saying, "Daddy, don't let go of the seat." But he did and kept running along beside me. "Daddy, you let go, you let go! Oh, I can ride." He taught me love of horses. He ran around the field holding the reins as I took my first six-inch jump on our fat pony, Custard. And he taught me love of plants.

John Emmerling

I have two separate moments.

When I was very young, after my brother Kurt and I put on our pajamas and got ready for bed, my father would call us down into the living room. We'd sit on either side of Dad as he read children's books to us. One book we really loved was *The Last of the Mohicans.* Dad is a somewhat reserved man, but he has a great dramatic reading voice and acted out the characters. For a father who seemed distant, that was a close and loving time. We felt secure. His reading to us every night is a warm and special memory.

My mother was loving and caring. One summer morning, I came down to breakfast that Mom had set out as she always did. It was not her birthday or a holiday or a special occasion, but for some reason I just felt that I wanted to get her something. I was probably eight years old. So I went outside and crossed James Cozzens Highway—a four-lane divided road we were not supposed to cross—to get to the flower store. There, for fifty cents, I found a little ceramic bird that had an opening in its back and a little flowering plant poking out. I bought that and brought it back before lunch and said to my mother, "I want to give you this." That was very uncharacteristic of me, and if she were alive today, she would remember it like yesterday.

Lyn Lear

My dad was sick a lot after he came back from World War II. I remember him screaming in the middle of the night because of the nightmares. The whole house would shake.

We would sit and listen to him talk in his sleep about those terrible war events: his best friend getting blown up in front of him; fights. It was very dramatic. We would sit around and Mom would write all the dreams down. I realized then my father was damaged; I realized what the war had done to him. It was an insight into why my father was the way he was. It changed my relationship with him.

Dave DeGrandpre

My special feelings have happened lately. About two years ago over the holidays my dad and I were wrapping presents, and all of a sudden we were having a really open talk about plans and what was going on with each other. I was also becoming very in touch with my own feelings at the time. But this was the first time I really said, "Dad, I love you," with full force. It meant a lot to me. It meant a lot to him, too. I don't think many fathers are in touch with their emotions in general.

Damian Miller

This past spring when my mom dragged me down—well it felt like I was getting dragged down—to France, where she owns a cottage. The idea was to clean it out, to completely redo it and just make it look good. I expected two weeks of a lot of heavy work and stuff, two weeks with my mom, and I thought it might get a bit boring. But it turned out to be a really good experience. For the first time we talked about all those things I was just old enough to understand—for instance, experiences she shared with my father. I was very surprised; it was a beautiful place and a beautiful time.

Chris Keefe

When I won the New England Three-Meter Intercollegiate Diving Championship. My father is very loving, but he was never much for words, so we'd never communicated much. He was always the authority figure, and I was always sneaking around behind his back trying not to get into trouble. And this day he wasn't that talkative at all. He'd had his leg amputated weeks earlier, and healthwise he just wasn't doing well.

Anyway, I looked over the scorekeeper's shoulder, and I had won! So I looked up at my dad and gave him the number one sign. Dad jumped up in his seat and punched the air, "Yeah!" That was the most dramatic emotion I have ever seen in my father. I think it was the first time I saw emotion on my father's face.

Dorothy Cross

One afternoon in the fall I'd come home from school and my father came in from picking apples. My mother, who taught school, was not home yet. My father and I were sitting in the kitchen and he was talking to me a little bit about life and what I might be able to do. He said, "You may be growing up on a farm now, but you will go to school and you'll go away and come back and surprise them all." I was probably twelve, and he was showing me what great faith he had in my ability. I've never forgotten.

Medora Plimpton: A Special Moment with a Parent

During a ten-day trip to Africa, I remember sitting in a bar with my dad, having a beer, and talking about things we'd never talked about before. It was the first time we talked on an equal level about personal experience and relationships. It was fun, and I didn't feel intimidated like a child often does. Since then, I've had a different outlook on him.

George Plimpton: A Special Moment with a Child

My daughter Medora and I were in Africa on safari. I was one of the tour guides. The last night in the bush, I made everybody get up and talk about what they remembered about the trip. I nearly didn't call on Medora, because she was by far the youngest there, fifteen or sixteen, but I said, "All right, Medora"—she was the last one.

She stood up from her chair with great confidence. She said, "You know, I've never realized what fun it is to be with adults. I had a great fear when I came on this trip that I was going to be bored." She got the strongest applause of the night. All of us, especially her father, realized that she had made a transition in her life, crossed a barrier, indeed, that she was on the way to becoming an adult herself. It was wonderful.

7. *Hanging Together: A Portrait*

Aubrey and Erik Peterson, Scott Smith

Aubrey: We've known each other since we were zero, but I think our sense of being inseparable friends began when we started biking together in East Hampton.

Scott: Yeah, all our bikes had names. Mine was the Yellow Hornet, and my garage was the Hornet's Nest. We'd go in there and be grease monkeys, taking our bikes apart into as many pieces as we could, getting covered in grease. We thought we were so smart about it even though the bikes kept falling apart.

Erik: We went everywhere on those bikes. We'd go to the Broken Down Bridge on Dunemere near the Maidstone golf club a lot because the big bass were there. We were nine. And then we'd cruise through the duck pond sanctuary on David's Lane in East Hampton, even though you weren't supposed to.

Scott: But we'd see a lady walking her dog there, and you weren't supposed to walk dogs, either; so it was OK for us to break the rules a little. We used to talk a lot about what was right. We'd camp right outside my parents' window and stay up all night.

Erik: We always pushed each other to the limit, like in the S Club. To be a member, you had to have an S in your name. As a member, you had to do anything a club member challenged you to do. I remember the challenges started at the duck pond. There was ice by the waterfall, and we were talking about crossing it; that's how it started. It doesn't get that cold in East

50

Hampton, so the ice wasn't very thick. The first person would cross, then the next, then the ice would get pretty bad. Once we had an Ice Breakers Club. We'd jump on the ice and use sticks to break it so the ducks could swim in the winter. We took a real interest in that pond and those ducks, pruning trails. Once someone had thrown a bench in the pond, so Scott and I went in that cold, black water to get it. Eels were slithering all around the base and our feet, and when we pulled the bench out, they were wrapped around it, too. It's funny, but doing those things was really important to our friendship, though we didn't think about it then.

Aubrey: We could also talk about our parents when we were worried. I remember the first time I saw my parents argue. My dad came home late, and they had an argument. My mom ran to her room and slammed the door. When she came out, I said, "Mom, are you guys going to get a divorce?" "Yeah, maybe we will," she said. The fight was still going on, and I thought she was getting her anger off at me. It scared me, but I didn't really think they would get a divorce. I was nine.

Scott: The fight I remember between my parents happened when my sister got permission from my dad to go out after my mom had said no. Mom and Dad got in a huge fight, and Mom went into the guest room. I remember the cat ran after her, and they lay there on the bed, the cat and my mom.

Then one night I was watching "The A-team." My parents said they needed to talk to me, and I was pissed because I was watching the show. So I waited until a commercial to go into their bedroom. I remember the whole scene. Dad was on the right side of the bed, and Mom on the left, and I was pacing back and forth griping, "Hurry up! I'm missing the show," not knowing what was up at all. That very day, I'd talked to my best friend in the fourth grade about divorce, said it was the worse thing that could happen.

Then Dad said, "Well, your mother and I have decided to divorce." Just the word made me snap, made my heart stop, and I broke into a sweat. I was holding this green apple I'd taken three or four bites out of, and I cocked my arm and chucked it as hard as I could, smack in the center between them, splattering it all over the blue headrest. I ran into my brother's room and started crying. Then I started looking through a magazine and saw an ad for Atari. I slid the Atari ad under the door—this was like October—and for Christmas I got an Atari. That was our last Christmas together.

Erik: The first time I totally knew my parents were going to get a divorce was when Mom got back from India when I was in the tenth grade. Maybe China. Aubrey and I were right there, and Mom was sitting there sunbathing. Dad came in; it was the first time they'd seen each other for two months. Their hug was so unaffectionate, like a quick pat on the back. I knew then.

Aubrey: So, Erik and I expected it. But Oliver, our little brother, freaked out. "You can't do this to me! Fuck you!" He ran out of the room crying; so Erik followed him and said, "Hey, it's like we're going to spend plenty of time with both of them, it's going to be awesome," and he totally calmed down.

Scott: So our parents being split up got Erik and Aubrey and me closer together. Even in the tenth grade we would wake up at my mom's house and just talk, and it would be awesome. By the time we all went off to different prep schools, we were hugging each other good-bye, and by that time we had an unspoken understanding that we'd be hanging out together for the rest of our lives. We all say now we'll sail around the world together with our wives, raise our kids together, and their kids, too.

Aubrey: I can remember that being close was different with Erik because he was my brother. Even now I hug Erik less than I hug the others. It's assumed, you know. But I can't even think about life without my brother. If either of these two were to die, I'd just freak. I always think about that. I think that's one reason I hug people good night now. I don't say "I love you" all the time, but I think it's nice to affirm it every once in a while.

Erik: At prep school, we stayed in touch; we'd send each other tapes. "I still love that girl and this girl," you know. But we really wanted to go to the same school. Then my girlfriend told me how awesome Montana was. We all applied, we all got in, an awesome feature.

And we started getting closer to our parents then, too. I think we got really honest with our parents when we quit smoking pot.

Aubrey: That's exactly what I was going to say. Because when we quit, we could be honest about the fact we did then but we don't now. And that helped us talk about drinking. That was taboo for a while, but I started talking with Mom about it right then, and with Dad in the last two years.

Scott: You know what's awesome? I've learned that if you're going to get through a relationship, you can't hide a thing, you've got to openly confront things. I can do that now, even with my dad. I used to talk with him and he'd say, "Scott, you know you can talk with me about anything." I'd say, "Yeah, Dad, sure, I understand." Then I'd feel so lonely because I didn't think I could talk about *anything* important. Communication is everything.

Erik: Yeah, like you and Aubrey communicate! You want to hear a story? Aubrey and Scott are like "Divorce Court." The first year at school here in Montana, they roomed together. And they would start freaking out, and punch each other, and Aubrey would say, "OK, that's my stereo. You can't ever listen to it again!" And Scott would say, "Fine, Aubrey, you can't watch my TV!" And Aubrey would say, "And don't you touch my VCR or I'll deck you!" Then they'd go to breakfast and all would be fine.

Aubrey: So, a little argument was how we communicated. We still loved each other.

Scott: Yeah. Even our parents find our friendship special. My parents think I get along with people well enough to be a teacher.

Aubrey: Christ, Scott, what are you going to teach? Recess?

8. An Early Friendship

Lyn Lear

My brother, four years older than I. I would do anything to play with him. When I was eight, he was in his terrorist period, and I was his guinea pig for scientific experiments. I learned how to withstand "antigravity": he twirled me around by my feet. Or I'd have to hang upside down from the backyard tree and try to drink soup—a way to learn to eat during weightlessness. Once he locked me in the closet for two hours to see if I could withstand isolation. Another time he invited all the neighborhood kids over and charged them a nickel to watch him throw pin darts at my bare back. I just thought I was in heaven.

Mary Lou Retton

My brother Jerry. I was very much a tomboy, and Jerry and I hung out all the time. He didn't like it, but I always tagged along. I was the only girl allowed in my brother and his friends' fort. But for the privilege they made me sweep the floors all the time.

Bunny Johnson

Old Brother Durden was our preacher. He was one of those preachers that hollered big. Well, my friend David Bird and I were in church, talking too much. We were about four. Mother kept saying, "You've got to be quiet, you've got to be quiet, or the preacher's going to get after you."

All of a sudden Brother Durden hit the pulpit and yelled "*And David!...*" When he did, David Bird fell on the floor. The preacher was of course talking about that other David. But we didn't talk anymore, and I don't remember David Bird going to church with us anymore, either.

Ben Rose

My best friend was Terence. We used to go swimming or wading in the brook collecting sticklebacks, then come home and swear we hadn't been in the water. We had wet socks and shoes and usually had our underwear on backwards and our shirts wrong side out, but we'd swear we hadn't had our clothes off. We never could figure out how our parents knew. We'd also sneak across the brook and into an apple orchard and get the worst stomach-aches from eating big, hard, green apples.

Eric Edmondson

We moved when I was five right next door to Johnny Findley, who was a year younger. Our favorite pastime was digging this large hole in the backyard. Why, no one really seems to remember. But we started out with a foxhole and ended up with a hole big enough to contain a Volkswagen beetle easily.

We'd just go back there and dig. We piled the dirt up around it. My father never complained about a big hole in the yard; he thought it was great: it kept us out of trouble. Digging is pretty safe stuff—you can't fall anywhere, you don't get cut, we didn't dig deep enough to get buried.

But after we got through digging and got all the dirt piled up, we could sit back and not be seen. It was sort of like a subterranean tree house. Sometimes we'd have other of our friends over, and we couldn't understand why they didn't think this hole was the greatest thing in the world.

Nancy Edmondson

Paula, her little sister Dotty Ann, and I were the Three Musketeers. They lived next door, and we did everything together. They were crazy about playing horses, which I didn't particularly care for. I'd be the master, and they would be the horses and run around with pieces of string hanging out of their mouths, whinnying. Paula blames her broken arm on me for my making her jump over a bush. Well, it was a horse show, and I directed her to take that jump. She tripped. We last played horses about twenty-five years ago, but I still see Paula weekly because she bought her parents' house and still lives next to my parents.

Michael Bornn

Hilary Thompson, this girl I grew up with riding horses. She's my first girlfriend. I got married to her in the tackroom when *Love Story* was the big thing, and we had a big ceremony. We were eight.

Silvia Munro

What was funny was that my classmates at the village school expected me to be wealthy because I lived at Ledreborg, but I had hand-me-down clothes. I was number four. Number seven had them, too. My school bag was the same school bag my elder sister had; my first bicycle was hers, too. People didn't expect that. They thought I would have a brand-new bicycle, a brand-new school bag. Once we got to be friends, the children told me they had expected me to wear a crown to school.

Jane Burke

I had a crush on Ricky Bell in the second grade. I kissed him in line one day—a very innocent kiss on the cheek—and got in trouble. He told me one day that if I'd let him borrow my eraser, he'd marry me. Another day, he told me if I lost five pounds, he'd marry me. He lied both times.

Mary Randolph

I remember my childhood sweetheart, Jimmy Williams. He lived three houses down. I couldn't speak very plainly—of course, I get accused of that now—and Jimmy translated everything I said to teachers in kindergarten and first grade, those wonderful, formative years when you really want to be heard. I was heard, but I was never understood. Jimmy was always very special. I haven't seen him in probably thirty years, but I think he still lives in the same house.

Mildred Sutton

Margaret and Lillian were my dearest friends in Swainsboro, from the second grade on. We were roommates in college. I'll always remember them because they made me feel so welcome when we moved to Swainsboro. I was a newcomer and they were natives and they took me right in and gave me a special security.

Lenny Berman

Henry was the first friend I had after my mother died when I was ten. The day she died, I went to school that morning and was released to walk home when my dad called to say my mother had died. When I got home, I was met outside the apartment by relatives who put me in a car and took me to another city. I never returned to where I had lived ever again. In this new city, Henry was the son of an aunt's friend. We've known each other ever since; he's the longest-running friend I have.

Chris Keefe   *grandfather friend*

My Grandfather, Nicholas Spagnola, who took me everywhere. Grandfather was much more important to me than my friends. I was with him his last night, too. I was maybe fourteen, and we'd been to dinner in town. He took me home and then had a heart attack in his own driveway. They found him slumped over the wheel, the horn blowing. Pop was my guy.

Hamilton Fish   *Nannies*

My mother brought her English-Canadian ways to our childhood. One feature of this was the annual succession of young women from England brought over as our companions and caretakers. They became our closest friends. Their arrival was always a period of skepticism and caution, and their departure always a period of emotional sadness.

Emily Cook   *Parting of ways*

Maria Maracich was my best friend for years, from the time I first went to Sun Valley when I was nine. Her father ran the Sun Valley skating rink where I practiced for competitive skating. I was never good at it, but I followed the routine, up skating at 5:30 and so on. Maria practiced a lot with me.

During the summer and long holidays, we did everything together. I'd arrive in Sun Valley, so excited since I hadn't seen her in months. I would get out of the car and race up three stories of stairs into our apartment to call Maria. Absolutely breathless, I'd shout into the phone, "I'm here!"

And we always got in trouble. We'd get caught smoking cigarettes or joints. Or we got caught breaking into somebody's house because we didn't like them. It was always something. We shared a lot.

She also had two of the neatest parents I ever met in my life. Their house was my refuge when times were hard at home, though they never had a clue they served that role for me since no one outside knew about my mother's alcoholism or how difficult that made life. But they were always there.

As years went by, Maria and I grew up differently. I became a barefoot hippie in a school in Virginia. She was a downhill ski champion who skied in two Olympics. Though we changed, I appreciated her strong personality and character. She was very loyal, feisty, not afraid of things. She still means a lot to me.

Dave DeGrandpre Sports group - part of sister
Erik Gamans, who lived right up the road from me. Erik was a year older than me and taught me how to play basketball, baseball, soccer, the works. We were baseball nuts. We memorized the name of every player on every team, we knew how and generally where every player would hit, and we developed these baseball games like we thought the players would play. We would throw each other line drives, pop flies, ground balls—whatever the hitter was likely to do. The games would go on forever!

We're still friends, although he's a lot more interested in my sister now than he is in me.

James Royce

Shannon Kelly, and did it start out precariously! Shannon has been my best friend since we were in little league football. He was a rail, a skinny thing, the Eddie Haskell type. He was always there when you needed him, very courteous and kind, very together. But beneath that exterior he was ready to get in trouble any minute. I was a good kid and didn't understand him at all. One night Shannon enticed me to come over to box. We started duking it out—I was smaller than he was—and he leveled me. That's the first and last time he's ever done that.

Dorothy Cross

I had a little girlfriend who lived about a mile and a half cross-lots from me. I was an only child, and there were no children around me on any side, and she used to walk from her farm to mine to come over to play. But she moved to the other side of town. I missed her. Then one morning I was out in the yard, and she came walking in. She'd walked four miles to come over to play.

A. J. Hiers

When I lived in Cocoa, I remember this kid across the street that was adopted. He was an Eskimo, almost black. He was my buddy. When we moved, I lost the connection. I was probably his only friend; because he looked so different, nobody cared for him.

Joy Melton Prickett

As a native of Mableton, Georgia, I found Melanie Wilsden, my best friend in junior high, fascinating because she and her family were from England. Just by the way she spoke, Melanie gave me something. Everybody around here called me *Jaw-ee,* but when she said my name in her English accent there was no diphthong. She said *Joy.* It was so pretty. I thought, gosh, maybe that's really how my name is supposed to sound.

Marla Hanson

I grew up in a really violent household. Whenever things got bad, I would run to my friend Julie Sinn's house and hide. When I first decided to run away, Julie and her mother would hide me in their garage so my parents couldn't find me. That's a pretty good friend. I haven't seen her since sixth grade.

Amy Holloway

When I was ten, I was sick in bed for a year with rheumatic fever. Rather than miss the fifth grade or have a homebound teacher, the telephone company ran a special line from the elementary school to my house and I had a little intercom system. I could hear what was going on in the classroom and I could talk to them by pressing a switch. I did my assignments and sent them in.

I saw Mrs. Queener, my teacher, just twice. Once she brought the whole class to my house and they brought me a big box of things you can do in bed—crossword puzzles, cards, games. The little girls that lived on my street came by often and the Girl Scouts came. I'm sure my mom was behind all this, seeing that I didn't miss out. I hated the illness, having to be carried to the bathroom even, but being in contact, being able to hear the laughter and the activity in class was wonderful.

Zar Rochelle

My best friend Charlie Strickland and I played together every day. Always.

One summer day Charlie and I were playing in my bedroom upstairs, and through the open window we heard my sister drive into the garage from grocery shopping. Our house was on a hill so that you walked up steps to the front door and down steps from the garage to the back door. Just as my sister came through the garage door and started down the steps, I said, "Charlie, scare her to death. Jump out."

And he did. I couldn't believe it. Suddenly, all I saw was Charlie's heels. It worked. It scared her to death. She threw groceries all over the backyard. Charlie didn't get hurt. He landed in an ivy bank. But from then on I've never on an impulse told somebody to do something.

Margaret Mason

My best friend from the first through the fourth grades and I were so comfortable together. I could bring her home after school and give her an apple and a book, and we'd both sit and read together. We didn't have to talk. She was very hard to leave when we moved to Minnesota.

Mary Costigan, Supper Club

When we were in high school, my friend Helen lived in the country. I'd go out from town and we'd ride horses—big, old workhorses. And her mother was a wonderful cook. Once we had a very rainy season, I remember, and Helen's brother picked a lot of wild mushrooms and her mother fried them for us. She'd dip them in batter and fry a big platterful. They were the most delicious things—I can still taste them.

After high school I lost touch with Helen until fifty years later. We started corresponding again and took a delightful trip together to Boston and Canada. We visit each other often now.

Alvis Waite

I had a buddy in Brooklet whose dad was the engineer on the short-line railroad that ran from Egypt, Georgia, to Claxton. The train made one trip a day to serve a lumbermill.

While we lived in Brooklet, the S & S, another short-line railroad, went out of business. They pulled up the rails but abandoned half the spikes. My friend said, "I'll get a spike puller. We'll use your wagon and we'll pull spikes and make us some money by selling them to my daddy's railroad."

We worked hard and loaded my wagon with a hundred spikes. We hauled it down to the railroad and went in and told the manager we'd come to sell him some spikes, that we'd worked hard and wanted a penny apiece.

He said, "Boys, I don't need any spikes." Our faces fell; of course, we hadn't asked if they wanted spikes. "But I'll give you a dollar for your load of spikes; then don't you go pull another one."

Rodney Cook

My first cousin Allison was my best friend for the first decade of my life. We had a great time playing on the creek behind our house. Vines hung from the trees, and we could swing over the creek on them. While we had rough woods around our house, he had manicured gardens around his. Some huge planters surrounded his courtyard—probably five feet tall and five feet in diameter. Even though they had dirt in them, we'd climb into them and pretend they were space ships. We'd hide there, too, and watch our parents or the staff come and go with no idea that we were there.

David Prowse

No, none a'tall. I've never had a best mate other than my wife Norma. I've been thinking about it quite a bit lately, because somebody said, "Why don't you go have a night out?" and I couldn't think of anybody I could call.

9. Mutual Respect: A Portrait

Jerry Preston

I have always loved wild creatures and nature, even when I was a baby. Even when Mama used to take me to Holy Rollers church, I'd crawl on the floor, fascinated by the bugs drawn by the single bare light bulb hanging from the ceiling.

It's really amazing I didn't die because I was always fascinated by anything that moved. I'd catch scorpions and rattlesnakes and put them in jars and bring them home, and I wouldn't understand why Mama was upset.

I used to love big hognose snakes. If they saw they couldn't escape, they'd play possum—roll over and play dead—and I'd be thrilled, pick them up, and take them home. Mama would get up early the next morning, though, and let them loose.

One of my first pets was my gopher. I'd carry this little guy in my shirt pocket, and he had these huge teeth and cheek pouches full of seed. I also had a prairie dog owl, a little owl that inhabits the same burrows as the prairie dog. The owl was nifty because you'd set him in the middle of the room, and as you walked around, his head looked like it was on a swivel.

I also had a dog, Bugeyes, that went everywhere with me. Then there was my crow, Pete. Daddy would give Pete beer, and Pete would have trouble walking. He'd imitate a dog's bark and say, "Help, help!" even though I hadn't split his tongue. Crows make good mimics even if their tongues aren't split.

Years later, one of my favorite pets was a curly-tailed lizard smuggled in from Bubba's house in the Bahamas. We were to fly back in a private plane, and the pilot had forbidden me to bring it in because of customs regulations, but I had spent three days catching that thing. So I put him in the refrigerator for about thirty minutes just before we were to leave, until the lizard was completely torpid. At the very last second, I took him from the refrigerator, put him in a sock, and stuffed him down my pants.

Well, everything went OK for a few minutes, and I forgot the lizard was there. But as we got to the airport, my body heat finally woke it up—abruptly. I was riding in Bubba's little blue dune buggy with George Plimpton and three others when suddenly I nearly jumped out of the buggy. "What's wrong?" Plimpton said. George had seen me fiddling with the lizard at the refrigerator earlier. "Nothing, George," I said, settling the lizard.

Then at the hanger the pilot's wife said, "Jerry, I just know you've got that lizard somewhere."

"Well, let's just say I'm not usually this sexy."

The lizard stayed right there the whole flight, too. At home, I installed him in a specially heated outdoor rock garden where he lived for several years. Archie would come to me any time I did my special whistle. A pileated woodpecker and a blue jay come to me now.

Then there are the raccoons. I buy whole trays of stale bread for a dollar to feed them. Very often after a meal, I clean out the frying pan and pots with the bread. That way the raccoons get something nice to eat; it also helps to clean the pots and pans and saves the sink.

Usually the raccoons are in a big oak tree behind my house, where they wait for me. When it gets about dark, here they come looking in the back door. There are paw prints all over the door.

I've been feeding this one particular family of raccoons for fifteen years. It started out with their great-great-grandmother. And then each mother would bring her babies up, and they would bring their babies up. So they've become old friends.

One thing I've learned about animals is that at all levels of life their experiences parallel human experiences and feeling. They make character judgments. I learned a long time ago, for instance, that if one animal sees another animal—even another species—being comfortable with you, then you're OK.

For a long time I had a pet squirrel, Susie. She would exhibit the ultimate expression of friendship and trust in the animal world: when I would give her something to eat, Susie would turn her back on me and eat without facing me.

Susie was also violently jealous of my relationship with other animals, particularly her niece, Ragged Ears. Susie absolutely *hated* her and would chase her around the tree if I was in the yard at all. One summer day, I was sitting on the back stoop feeding Susie peanuts, having a pleasant visit, but every time Ragged Ears came near, Susie had a fit. So Ragged Ears went up on the roof, and pretty soon I noticed her looking down at me. In my bare feet, I stood up on the rail and started to hand her a peanut. At the sight of that, Susie jumped up on that rail and clamped on to my big toe, saying plain as day in anybody's language, "Don't give her any." She didn't hurt my toe—she just got my attention.

I watched Susie age. It took her longer and longer to climb up the big oak, and eventually she couldn't even chase Ragged Ears away. One day she just wasn't there for a peanut. I miss her friendship.

You know, there's a big difference in having an animal for a friend and having an animal for a pet, a big difference. It's all based on mutual respect. And some attention. And a little food. They're like anybody else.

10. A Pet

Helen Barbour

I've never been much of a pet lover, but we were fond of Charlie the Crawfish in the Bahamas. Charlie, a Bahamian lobster, lived in a fishtank at our house for a while, before we put him back in the sea. I'd like to think he's eluded the fishermen, but I'm afraid we felt, as he was sinking to the depths the night we released him, that he was probably doomed.

Eric Jensen

I was very proud of my mallards. We lived in the woods of rural Iowa, and because I was six years younger than my five brothers and sisters, I spent a lot of time raising animals. I raised mallards from birth. I'd take them out to the end of our long driveway, give them a start by running at them to scare them a little, and watch them circle the perimeter of our property, about ten acres. They'd fly around and around, and I'd call them back with my duck call.

We had some geese that essentially acted as foster parents to the ducks. The geese seemed to get worried about the ducks when they flew away, so they'd call them back with that *honk!* It was so much fun to watch! The wild ducks would land occasionally during migratory season and waddle over looking very confused. You know, like "OK, we're here now. What are we supposed to do?" Then they'd fly off again.

Once during hunting season, I was flying my ducks when some hunters started shooting. I was really worried, so I ran over yelling, "Hey! Stop it! Those are *my ducks!*" They stopped shooting, but one duck got a shotgun pellet through the bill. I

66

fixed it by folding the fragments back into the proper position and it healed.

We had so many mallard eggs that sometimes we'd have them for breakfast. I loved my ducks, but I didn't mind eating their eggs occasionally, either.

Silvia Munro

In the wing where we lived, which my parents had beautifully converted from part of the stables when we needed more room, my sisters and I had sixteen cats and a cockerel. The cockerel finally had to be put outside because my sisters didn't dare go outside to get their bicycles—the cockerel would nip at their heels. He was my pet. He went to live in the hen run where he grew into a beautiful bird until the fox got him.

Princess Pamela Strobel

Beauty, my mama, was working at a fancy place in Massachusetts, and one day a mail truck stopped at our house and dropped me off a miniature house with a steeple on it. Inside was a dog like you'd never seen: a purebred wire-haired terrier. The ears and tail had been clipped, like you do with purebreds, and that little thing came to Spartanburg, and nobody on my block had seen a dog like it. Bobbie Lee was his name.

When I left home to go away and work at thirteen, I didn't take him, but he kept visiting my family all over the neighborhood, and pretty soon there were grandbabies. Years later when I went back to see my uncle Hun, I got to see Bobbie Lee's great-grandchildren. They didn't exactly look like my dog, but I knew them on the spot.

Marla Hanson

My little brother's bulldog, Sweetie. He wanted to name it R2–D2, but we decided that was a terrible name for a girl. Sweetie was a dog that didn't know she was a dog. We'd take her to my cousin's, and she'd run around with the pigs and horses and try to sit at the dinner table with us. We found her poisoned one day; a neighbor had done it.

Emily Cook

At boarding school, I got in trouble for keeping a groundhog named Ichi Anomahu in my bathtub. Knowing I took care of a lot of injured animals, people in town would find road-injured animals and bring them to me. That's how I acquired Ichi, who had a head wound.

I was not about to keep him in the science lab since someone had recently poisoned a lot of the animals there with arsenic. So Ichi lived in my bathtub. Unfortunately, the head of my dorm and I didn't get along very well, and she reported me. I went through fourteen hours of "supreme judicial court"—fourteen hours!—before they threw the case out. I think they told me "no more animals and do ten hours of community yard work." It was a joke. Everyone was laughing when I went into the dining hall at dinner.

Timothy Sultan

In addition to the usual assortment of cats and dogs, our neighbors in Laos had a monkey that would periodically climb over the fence and take the freshly washed clothes off our wash line in the yard. This would cause our Chinese maid, Sing, to charge out of the house waving a broom, sending the monkey scurrying away. Their Asian brown bear, which had a light V-design on its chest, would also break loose and come barreling through our yard.

Our family also had a number of odd animals, including an Asian fruit fox that would sleep during the day, hanging upside down beneath mattresses and wherever else it could dig in its claws.

Chris Keefe

One day just as my dog Gypsy was running around the corner of the house, a friend came racing around the corner from the opposite direction and accidentally kicked Gypsy really hard. Gypsy collapsed. I saw it happen and knew she was dead, and for the first time had this heat rush shoot through my body. Gypsy was just stunned, but the moment stands out clear in my head. It's the first time I thought I was seeing death.

John Emery

My grandparents' dog Sherry got me in a lot of trouble when I was five. I grabbed hold of her tail, and we took off from the house, went down the railroad tracks, then around the lake and through Rollins College in Winter Park, Florida. I remember the people at school seemed to like the sight, but the police finally picked us up. Our first run-in with the law.

George Plimpton

I found my cat, Blue, on the street, a wonderful, strange cat. Blue used to sit on my shoulder and watch me shave.

Peggy Sammons

Remember the cat that wouldn't drink water? Instead Nippy would stick a paw down in a vase where flowers had been and lick it. Perhaps the water was sweeter there. My parents had a hothouse and floral business, so there was no shortage of vases.

Jane Burke

Buford T. Pussy was a walking-tall tomcat. He came to live with us when he bit the hand that fed him—we had to keep him two weeks to check for rabies. By then he was our cat. He was tough on crime. He even foiled the clandestine attempt of Granny, who thought he was a poor excuse for a pet, to stuff him in a pillow-case and take him to the country. All the evidence we found of the dirty deed was a shredded pillowcase in the garage. Granny took the Fifth, and Buford never ratted.

Eric Edmondson

When I was very young we had a little bulldog, Thumper. Thumper didn't stay with us too long because he had this tendency to chew holes in everything. He chewed a hole in my pup tent, a hole in my swimming pool, a hole in the kitchen wall behind the dryer. When he started chewing on my mother's shoes, Thumper went to the farm. We have relatives in Fairburn and we shipped Thumper out. Our next dog, Cookie, was very laid-back, very bright, never chewed holes, and lived to be nineteen.

Dan Buettner *gerbil*

Since my mother was terrified of dogs and my dad hated cats, we had a gerbil. When we'd had the gerbil a couple of days, my brother Tony and I—we were about six and eight—took the gerbil to the playground where we sent it down the slide. Then we began playing catch with the poor creature. As Tony caught it after the third throw, the gerbil snapped his jaws down on Tony's finger. I tried to get it off by tugging lightly, but Tony screamed and the gerbil held fast. We ran home the two blocks, blood streaming down Tony's hand, the gerbil still clamped on. My dad eventually had to use pliers to break the gerbil's jaw. That was the first and last pet.

11. It Takes My Breath Away

Norman Lear

Biting into a ripe peach.

John Jaxhiemer

Seeing a lawyer in a trial. I think it's pretty amazing the way they are always prepared for anything that comes their way.

Zar Rochelle

A Frank Lloyd Wright house. Just the perfection of it. The incredible balance and design and flow.

John Emmerling

It is 6:00 A.M., a July morning on Cape Cod. I go over to the little airport. There is a low, 500-foot ceiling, and it's gray and a little bit rainy. There are hundreds of sea gulls sitting on the warm runway. I do my complete preflight, start the engine, and taxi out. First I have to taxi up and down the length of the runway to wake up the sea gulls so that I don't run into them on my actual takeoff.

The gulls fly off. I'm on an instrument flight plan and radio for my takeoff clearance. I give it full throttle—I'm gaining speed down the runway, I come back on the yoke, I lift off, and retract the landing gear. Ten or twelve seconds and I'm into the overcast, rain streaking on the windscreen. It's gray and it's dark and I'm going up—1,000 feet, 1,200 feet, 1,500 feet. It's starting to get lighter as I climb toward the top. Suddenly I burst out into this absolutely blue-sky dawn. The altitude I have been assigned by

Cape Approach puts me right in the tops of the clouds. The sun is rising behind me, and I'm clipping along in and out of the tops of these clouds.

Ahead about 300 yards there's a larger cloud rising 200 feet. It's all white and puffy because the rising sun is catching it. I'm coming at it at 200 miles per hour; now suddenly I see a dot on the cloud. It's the shadow of my airplane. It gets bigger and bigger and bigger as I approach the cloud. Bam! I go right through it, then burst out the other side of the cloud. I look ahead—there's another big cloud 400 yards away. I wait and wait for it. Here comes my shadow. It's incredible to see this tiny shadow of an airplane grow bigger. I see the wings, the fuselage growing—bigger and bigger. Then I smash into it! Wow! It's the most exciting thing I've ever done.

Win Rockefeller

Too many cigarettes, to start with.

Nan Thomas

The smell of Mount Gay rum.

Egbert Donovan

Cleaning these shells—*that* takes your breath away! They smell a lot. So when I bring them in, I sit them in some clorox water for a while. That cools it out. I give the conch meat to people.

Timothy Sulton

Mowing ski trails with a hand scythe. Not long ago I spent a summer doing that in Vermont.

Dan Buettner

Cycling over Slippery Rock in Utah. Slippery Rock suggests a lunar landscape because it has absolutely no topsoil. Cycling up and down over the twenty square miles of big hills and big crevices feels like skiing huge moguls except that in the back of your mind you know if you wipe out, your femurs will be reduced to bone meal.

Damian Miller

Jumping in a mountain stream.

Jane Burke

When I have to sing a solo and I see it coming up—it's two pages away—I can still breathe OK, but my pulse starts getting quicker. A page away, I'm singing on the left and I can see my solo coming up on the bottom of the right-hand page, the less breath I get. I have such horrible stage fright. That absolutely, literally takes my breath away.

Kate Learson

I paint, and sometimes it takes my breath away to see what a painter can do. To see, for instance, how Rembrandt managed light in a painting—how he used tonalities of white paint, an object on a flat surface, to make light that seems to shine through a window or give atmosphere to a room or capture the luminous quality of real pearls around a lady's neck. I can't get over it.

Mimi Taufer

Some works of art take my breath away. I feel like I try to absorb them through my eyes, to take them in, consume them, as much as I can. I feel like I'm pulling them off the page, the canvas. I recently read a children's book called *Diego* about the life of Diego Rivera in which the illustrations are little paintings. They're so beautiful. That was my last experience of having my breath taken away in that respect.

Emily Cook

I'll be curled up in bed watching a movie, totally concentrating on it, and I'll turn over, not really thinking about Rodney, and see him. And it will register, here I am in this home. I have a home. I have a husband. I have my daughter English. We all love each other. There's a feeling of just peace and the rightness of things at that time.

Sonya Friedman

It can take my breath away to walk into a situation and have someone say they're delighted to meet me.

Edith Bornn

Sometimes when I see people helping others at risk to themselves, doing something special for the community, or doing something you wouldn't expect of an individual, I feel overwhelmed. For example, a few days ago, I saw someone stop in traffic to help an older person. On St. Thomas, we have very heavy traffic, narrow streets, and everybody yelling and screaming, but this driver saw a person in need of help. Right there on Synagogue Hill, a very steep street, with a lot of steps to the sidewalk, he stopped his car and got out and held up a line of traffic. It made such a big difference to an older man who was afraid of crossing the street and getting to the steps on the other side. Things like that take my breath away.

Mildred Sutton

Sometimes seeing a great deal of waste takes your breath away. You think how terrible it is, how it could be used so much better when you see things squandered.

Jim Swann

The world is such a crazy place I can't imagine having your breath taken away by anything. There's nothing that shocks or surprises me enough to do that—I'm just not that type person.

Kurt Vonnegut

The beauty of some women actually does because I simply gasp sometimes—just on a bus or on the street or anywhere. A respiratory experience. Some women are absolutely stunning. And of course a lot of women, I think, feel the same way: the beauty of a lot of women takes the breath of other women away, too, as much as it takes mine away.

Gerry Cooney

Life takes my breath away. There's a great book out about going through life with blinders on. That was me all my life. I remember one day getting into a glass hotel elevator. I looked downstairs where they had a goldfish pond. And I thought about it. Those goldfish would stay there forever. They're never going to go anyplace. They're going to live in that goldfish pond. And that's how life was for me for many years. To me life is about letting go and being there—really getting out, stepping out. That's exciting.

12. Your First Intimation of Mortality

A. J. Hiers

It was the lowest day of my life. We were at my mother's funeral, and my sister was five years old and she didn't realize that mother was in a casket. She looked at my cousin, who was older than we were, and said, "Why do those people have my mother in a suitcase?"

Stephanie Beacham

Losing Smudge, one of our dogs, on the Great North Road in London. When I was very young, I went to the convent school. I used to come home every day on the 84 bus. I'd get off at the bus stop where Mummy would meet me with Smudge. One day when I got off the bus, Smudgie was lying there by the bus stop, and I said, "Smudgie, Smudgie, Smudgie," and she didn't move. I thought, Oh, she's sleeping.

Then I went closer to her and I noticed there were flies on her eyes and then I saw my mother on the other side of the high road, waving. She said, "Stephie, stay right there! Don't touch Smudge! Don't touch Smudge!" And, of course, the dog had been run over, and my mother had phoned for help and not been able to get back to stop me from seeing poor Smudgie dead.

It sounds callous to say, but I think that's almost the purpose of pets for children: the nurturing, the caring, the loving—and the realizing of the life cycle and the mourning. The other thing is that you can be responsible. I always have pets around for my children because I was able to see Smudge *personally* into the

76

earth. There was no mortician. There was nobody taking Smudge away. I was able to dig the hole and to make the wooden cross and to place the flowers and to cry. And all of it was able to happen in front of my eyes.

Human beings when they die are whisked out of everybody's vision. And then there's this uncomfortable three hours, possibly in a pair of squeaky shoes. It doesn't register to a child in the same way as it does if you are responsible to see that *that* is what life and *that* is what death is.

Cliff Robertson

I don't remember my mother; she died when I was two and a half. So I think my first experience of death was when my little dog Bingo was poisoned. He used to follow me on my magazine route in La Jolla, California. He might wander off, but he knew my route, and ten minutes later he'd be back. One day I was riding along and he'd gone off fifteen minutes or so, when I saw a group of people down at the corner looking down at something. I rode over to see what they were looking at and it was him. Some horrible person had poisoned him.

It's hard to describe what I felt then. Emotion has a lot of colors. Because I was so young, mine was embarrassment. I don't know why. I was heartbroken but I was embarrassed because of all those people, perhaps because they were intruding on a very personal experience.

John Emmerling

When we were very young, my brother and I had a parakeet named Petey that we loved a lot. We'd let him out of his cage often to fly around the house because he never flew away. We had an old RCA Victor radio, a floor model with a top that lifted up so you could reach in and adjust the dials. One day, we were playing the radio, and Petey came over and landed right on the edge. I bumped the top accidentally, and bang! Petey was gone. There was just a little blood. I tried to breathe life into him, to bring him back to life.

It was the first time that something we loved died and, unfortunately, died because of something that I did. So a lot of guilt was involved. Like most children, I really believed that if I did the right thing I could bring him back. As my childhood went on, I lost a lot of older family members. When I saw them in their coffins, I would think if I could just figure out the right thing to do, I could make them come back.

After the third or fourth funeral, I gave up.

Nan Thomas

When we were children, we had kittens and dogs around the house all the time, and we had a special place, a cemetery, for them. We had funerals and the whole neighborhood would come—the neighborhood kids, the cook, the chauffeur, my father. I don't think my mother had the guts. We'd plant flowers and make grave markers of twigs. The kitten I remember was Mittens who fell out of the window more than nine times and one time didn't make it.

Mildred Sutton

Daddy's younger brother, Uncle Oliver, was killed by lightning. He was shaving with a hand razor on the back porch in North Augusta; they used to have shelves on the porches where you'd sit a bowl of water. He was killed instantly. I remember us going up there, and that's the first family death I can remember.

Margaret Mason

I think I was about five. I was sitting on a piano bench with my mother when she was playing the piano, and we were singing a song. The words must have had something that gave me the idea that all of us die. I couldn't believe it. I remember questioning my mother: "Me too? Everybody? I have to die?" And she said, "Yes." Very matter-of-fact. I remember being just appalled at the idea and angry.

I still feel it's such an inconvenience. I like that recent line: "Dying is something you do while making other plans."

George Plimpton

I think I got it all straight lying in bed one night. My earliest years I lived in a maid's room of the family apartment, a very narrow room that looked out on a back courtyard. Earlier that night, my parents had told me that one of my great-aunts had died. I thought about it: she had died; my parents were going to die; my brother was going to die; the family dog was going to die; *I* was going to die. It was immensely depressing and I remember bursting into tears. I had a small stuffed animal I took to bed—a squirrel with bead eyes—and I sobbed to it that I was afraid.

Not long after my grandfather kind of reaffirmed it. He was a scientist. We were talking out in front of his house in Florida when he suddenly reached for a stick and broke it in half. "This is life—snap! Life ends like this!" I think he'd just been told he was very ill.

Zar Rochelle

I don't know how old I was, but I'd gone to bed. I don't know why I was thinking about such things, but it suddenly dawned on me that my mother would die someday. Perhaps a pet had died, or a neighbor. So I jumped up, went downstairs to find Mother sewing at the breakfast table and cried, "You're going to die someday!" which was no news to her.

She explained that, yes, everyone dies eventually. That it's all temporary had never occurred to me before.

Campion Platt

When my father died, I was five. My parents had already divorced, and Father had been living in South Carolina. Mother woke me about one in the morning, crying. I don't really think I felt much sorrow at that moment. But from mother's reaction, I knew something was ending, life would change radically or that person just wouldn't be there any more.

I had very little time with my father, but I have very good memories of him.

◉ *Kate Learson*

A child in my grammar school died, and I remember that either the nuns or my grandmother said, "Well, God always calls the good ones early." I remember thinking about that deeply. I thought it very odd because shouldn't the good ones stay around and try to make things good around here? It was a very conflicting thing for me to figure out: First of all, am I good? I know I want to be good, I know I should be good, but then will I die early? To this day when I hear about children dying, as I do at the hospital where I volunteer, often I remember that notion that the good go to God early.

David Prowse

I can't remember at five seeing my father dead, can't even remember his funeral. But I remember Grandmother when I was thirteen. She had terrible diabetes, and she actually died in one of our bedrooms. My mother came up to me and asked, "Do you want to see Gran?" I always remember going and seeing her, deathly white, laid out.

Helen Barbour

In my Africa days, when I was about five, I remember going to the health clinic and seeing the little children running around in rags and bare feet and with horrible sores on their bodies. And my mother taking my hand and whisking me out of the way and saying, "Come on, don't look." And just thinking...

I think I felt sad for them. There I was with shoes on my feet and clothes on my body, and there they were with horrible sores and no money to pay for the medicines to get them better. I always remember that.

Phoebe Legere

I always knew. I first contemplated suicide at age seven, so I must have known what death was: an escape to freedom. I always knew about death because they talked about it in church. I first had to confront my own death when a friend of mine tried to kill me, tried to poison me, and I felt myself going into the black. I didn't want to go. I was fourteen.

Jock Munro

I realized about life and death with a sudden shock. My father kept sheep on the farm and we had pet sheep, orphan lambs. We'd put them in warm, coal-fired ovens, not very hot, to bring them back to life. My first two lambs were Oswald and Albert. But it didn't really bother me when they disappeared after awhile. Gertrude and Esmerelda followed. Then I had a black-faced lamb called Lariat that I really loved. Lariat would jump in the car with me and would follow me everywhere I went as a boy. When I bicycled around, it followed me. As a full-grown sheep, feeding in the field, Lariat got its horns stuck and broke its neck. That's the first time life and death struck home. My father buried him; I was about six or seven.

Alastair Barbour

We learned to shoot when we were very young and learned quite quickly how easy it is to take life. You learn that life is finite, so I don't think there was anything dramatic when somebody I knew died.

Marynell Waite

The summer I was seven, my mother was very ill. She was unable to eat, but the doctor thought that a little squab might help.

We had some pigeons that Mother had been raising. I had helped her with the birds, and I was very fond of them, as was Mother. When my father asked Mary, who came every day to cook and help out while Mother was sick, to fix some of the squab, she said, "Well, sir, I don't think Miz Sampley's gonna like that."

And he said, "Yes, but the doctor thinks it might help, so we'd better try."

So Mary butchered and prepared a few squab and took them up to Mother, who cried, "Oh, you've killed my babies; I can't eat them."

I think that's the first time I realized that we killed to eat. I made the connection between the little birds I liked and the food. And I just cried and cried.

Mary took me up in her arms. She was a wonderful, kind woman, large and stout. She fasted from Saturday to Sunday noon, the better, she said, "to sing to the glory of God." As I wept, Mary comforted me and said, "With every life there's a death, and I'll sing you a song about it." And she sang an Easter hymn.

Lyn Lear

I think I knew at an early age, especially when my animals died. I had tremendous crying jags. I was very aware of mortality, but I think that was the basis for my faith. I just knew there had to be something more than this life.

Norman Lear

When Toots Shor closed. I couldn't believe that an institution like Toots Shor could ever close. When institutions fail, it's somehow more telling than an individual's death.

John Marston

The most intense experience was the summer I spent preparing cadavers for the anatomy class at San Diego State.

Barbara Bailey

Though I was a doctor, I don't think I was conscious of mortality during my professional life. But then I had a very bad heart attack, a congenital deformity of the aortic valve of my heart.

Edith Bornn

I thought I had cancer about three years ago. I took it rather calmly. I very firmly believe that you fight like hell if it's something you can do something about; if it's beyond your control, you've got to accept it and do the best you can from there. I cleared the decks here and went up to New York expecting to spend three to four months with radiation, but when they took a biopsy of my breast, it was benign. So in the time I had cleared, what did I have? A knee operation. I had been needing it for about seven years.

The Librarians

Mary Randolph: When you're brought up in the South, you know death from childhood because you have family reunions and funerals, which I think is healthy. It's just a natural thing. You get together for births and for holidays and for weddings and for funerals.

Virginia Kahl: When I was young, I knew several cousins or almost cousins from twelve to twenty who died. It still never connected with me. But when my uncle died, that hit me. Then I suddenly realized the family was going to go down and dwindle.

Dorothy Cross: Well, on a farm you have animals that die and kittens that get stepped on by horses. But I don't think I really made serious connections about mortality until the time I was facing cancer surgery, and then it became very personal. I realized that I was very mortal indeed.

Surviving changed my priorities. I used to be much more precise about making sure that my house was in order, and now it's a total mess, because if it's a nice day, I go out and walk in the leaves. I also retired even though I had just received a very substantial promotion. I decided it was my life I was spending rather than money I was saving up—for what?

Sonya Friedman

The most powerful time was in Israel twenty years ago. My family life as a child was so disjointed I was never able to know anything about my family history. I knew nothing about my mother's side except that they were probably from the Polish-Russian border from a town that no longer exists; the Nazis destroyed it. Even my grandfather and uncle weren't sure how to spell it, but they thought it was Urubashov.

But in Israel there is a memorial to all the lost towns. I went there with my husband and children to see if we could find that name. A guide pointed to a tombstone on a wall. I touched it, and collapsed as a wail escaped from me. I realized that if my grandparents had not left that town, I would not be alive and my two children would not be alive.

John Emery

When my stepmother died eight years ago. I took my son Anthony over there the day before she died. As we drove up, I explained that she had this tube up her nose to help her breathe and that she was very, very sick and might be dying. Anthony was only four. Well, he bounced up on that bed, and Mother's face lit up because she loved him in particular. Anthony blurted, "Hi, are you going to die?" I wanted a hole to open in the floor for me, but she smiled weakly and said, "No honey, I'm not going to die this minute."

I realized much later that the rest of my family had left the room so that I could be alone with Mother to say good-bye. But, you know, I couldn't. And she knew that I couldn't. She died the next day.

Vince and Marge Spezzano

Vince: The death that has had the most impact was our daughter's, six years ago.

Marge: Then you know it can happen to you.

Vince: It was totally unexpected. We knew something bad had happened when we tried to get Christine and could get only her answer phone.

Marge: Her friends had called us because it was unlike Christine to not be at work and not call in. She had missed two days of work.

Vince: We knew something was wrong. She'd gone to the mountains with her boyfriend. I called a friend, Tom Johnson, then the publisher of the *Los Angeles Times*. I said, "I wish they could start looking around that mountain area."

So he called the sheriff of Los Angeles County and said that
he was going to send the paper's helicopter over the area
to search.

Marge: That's when they found the car, parked with a flat tire.

Vince: Christine and her friend could have walked away. But the
following day they found them down at the bottom of the
mountainside.

It was hard to get through that. You're stunned for a
long, long time.

Doris Roberts

I first saw mortality when I saw my mother's hands get old,
probably about 1968. The skin got very translucent and crinkly
and lined. It looked like all the juice had gone out of it. She was
wonderful. At eighty she was going to senior citizens' homes and
playing the piano and entertaining them.

And I'll tell you the second time. My husband Bill had
leukemia for seven years. For seven years we lived in denial all
the time. We never for one moment gave in to it or believed that
it would bring him down. Then the last weeks before he did die,
I stayed in the hospital with him, in the same room with him,
so I was there all the time and never left. I was glad I was, because
I learned something that a lot of people avoid or try to avoid.
You know, if someone is terminally ill, you tend to allocate the
care of that person to the nurses and the doctor and you either
sit in a chair or wherever in a room with them. But you isolate
yourself to one side. It's the worst thing in the world you can do
because what you need to do is get into that bed with that person
and put your arms around them and be there for them. They need
it more than you do. You're so terrified that they're going to leave
that you can think only about yourself. What you should be
thinking about is that person.

So I did that. And I told Bill constantly what his love meant
to me in my life and how he had changed my life and what he
had done for me. Then I would get advance notices about his
book, *Had I a Hundred Mouths*, and I would have them blown

up and put all over the room. And I got the advance of the *New York Times* review in which Vance Bourjaily said some of Bill's short stories were the greatest of the century.

So he heard all of that, you see. I made sure that he knew all that, and I made sure that he felt a warm body holding him because most of us in life—I mean—sex is great but you know what we want more than anything else is to be held and told it's OK.

James Royce

I enjoyed life so much I used to be scared to death of dying. I'd cry myself to sleep wondering what would happen after you died. I was even scared to get older. Every day you got older, you got closer to *it*. I don't worry about that as much any more. I think when it's your time, you go on. Lately I've become much more comfortable with the fact there's something up there, you know.

Win Rockefeller

I guess my early knowledge of death came from being around animals. But that didn't really affect my own personal sense of mortality. Getting into my midthirties did that. I went ahead and had my midlife crisis at thirty-five. I figured if the basic premise is three score and ten, and thirty-five's half of that, that's cool.

Lenny Berman

One instance that comes to mind has a funny twist. A while before our wedding, I began to have headaches and then some chest discomfort on the opposite side from where the heart is. As the day for the wedding drew nearer, the pain grew more intense. Now the anxiety of it all may have had something to do with these symptoms, but I was sure I had a problem that was going to be fatal. Here I had waited so long to get married, had the right person, had the date, people were going to show up and I was going to die before it happened.

Edward Colquhoun

The day Mimi and I got married, an hour and a half after the ceremony I was hit by a taxi and lay in the street with a broken leg and a dislocated shoulder. I then spent a week in the hospital. I think in a way it was very lucky; it was a good time to have that lesson hit home.

Jonathan Peter

I had been invited to a party up in the mountains of Cyprus to provide some local interest and younger people for a group of tour operators. At the party we sat around the fire and drank gallons of wine and had a lot of fun. Late at night, when we were leaving, there was a small car going down the mountains, but there were six of us and we couldn't all get in. So two of us ended up on the roof.

On the winding mountain road the driver mistook a street light across a gorge for the direction the road went—which was very lucky for us, in fact, because instead of turning the corner too fast, she went straight off the cliff, airborne. I saw the headlights shining on the pebbles, the shadows of the pebbles on the edge of the road going out into the infinite darkness, and my thought was, this is going to be a hassle. Something's wrong. And when I woke up my first words were, "You couldn't get a ride like that in Disney Land."

Now I was drunk, of course; everybody was. And the others somehow thought they'd run over me. But between sailing out and coming to I had lost consciousness and had tumbled down the mountain. My blue jeans were torn. I had lacerations and bruises all over me. My glasses had been smashed. I'd been tumbling down the mountain unconscious, I guess, and could easily have broken my neck and been dead. But what I remember—and that's not a good word—was a sensation of floating in an atmosphere that was sort of greeny-gray in tone when in fact it was every color of the rainbow. The sensation was one of total relief, complete and total relief. It was like, *aaah, that's done, great.* It was a really wonderful sensation. And it left me not worrying about death any more.

This was a situation where God looks after drunks, fools, and children. None of us was hurt.

Gerry Cooney

I never really put it together for myself about dying. To be honest with you, just of late I've started understanding as I see the kids growing up. Because I've become the other side; I'm the kid up on the top now.

Jim Swann

I haven't realized that I won't live forever yet. I keep hoping they'll figure out some way to be immortal.

13. Life Without Father: A Portrait

James Royce

My natural father wanted to start a new family. He bailed out on us when I was three and when he was the age I am now. As a kid growing up in that situation, I obviously wondered what was up, why I didn't have a dad and everyone else did. I've seen him a total of two weeks in twenty years.

A little later, Mother remarried. I have mostly fond memories of Ralph because he was more like my real father. He started me off in baseball and football, but baseball was his thing. We were always off playing pitch and catch in the front yard, and he was always my coach. Ralph was very much a disciplinarian—more than anyone I've known in my whole life, now that I think about it. But I think that's important, don't you?

Then a couple of years into this marriage, my brother John came down with Burkitt's lymphoma, a virulent form of cancer. My mom had brought three kids to this marriage in the first place, then a few years later one gets cancer, and here's $300,000 worth of bills. It put a lot of pressure on the relationship. They split up.

That was a very awkward time for me. I was about thirteen—a very impressionable time—and seeing my mom bringing home another man was very odd. I was so protective of her. I've always been close to her, and when you combine that with not under-standing why Ralph wasn't there, I'd get pretty angry.

Two years later, I went to visit my natural father in Dallas. I needed him to give me some direction, I think, some help in finding out what I should do with my life. My friends always talked to their fathers about that. But that weekend he didn't know how to handle or talk to me, and I didn't know what to do, either. It was a miserable visit, and I went home crying.

Then in 1988 my father decided to come back in my life again. At first, I think, most of it had to do with settling matters in my grandfather's will. Whatever the reason—maybe he's feeling mortal or something—he's suddenly being much more pleasant toward my sister Julie, my brother John, and me. I think we're beginning to accept each other's faults and maybe I am forgiving him for not being there.

My mother did everything she could for my life. But I missed the finished picture, the good balance I think a father brings to his children.

My dad and I are planning a couple of trips together. But it's not really a father-and-son relationship, and it's OK if it doesn't work out. I wanted that father figure when I was growing up. I don't really feel the need to have a father at this point. Now I think I can keep everything in perspective a little better. But it would be nice to have him as a friend. We're trying to start out that way first.

14. An Awkward Moment with a Parent

Marla Hanson

Perhaps when my mother would kiss me when I was younger. I remember she had really hard lips and didn't kiss us very often because there were just too many kids—I had fifteen brothers and sisters.

Phoebe Legere

I felt that maybe Daddy wanted a son. So, I tried to be very physical and tried to build up my upper-body strength. I made myself quite fearless.

But it was very awkward at about age fourteen when it became quite obvious that I was not a guy. From that time on it's taken many years for my parents to adjust to the way in which I somehow always have had one foot in each sex. All mothers, when you turn thirteen or fourteen, try to make you act like a lady, and I resisted. Then you get put into the category of bad girl, on the wrong side of the toast. It became very awkward.

Judy Rose

Mother's little talks made my heart sink. She'd say, "Judy, it's time to have a little talk about being nice to your sister" or my laziness or my attitude—the usual teenage stuff. She was a tiny little woman, but she always made me feel even smaller.

Timothy Sultan

When I was younger, eight or nine, watching romantic scenes on television with my mother in the room was awkward. There was nothing licentious about the films—black-and-whites from the forties—but during the prolonged kissing scenes, I'd conveniently go to the kitchen.

Mary Costigan, Supper Club

I got caught once with my hand in the cookie jar—not by my parents but by a neighbor boy's mother. The boy was probably two or three years older than I was, and he said, "I know where the cookies are at my house. Come on, I'll show you." He took me in the kitchen. "What you do is climb up on this cabinet and you reach right up there and get the cookies." So he got me up there reaching in, then slipped out when his mother came in and caught me. She was probably amused, but I'll never forget how absolutely humiliated and terrified I was.

Rose Wing, Supper Club

I remember when I had to stay in at school, I knew I'd be taken care of at home, for sure. So I would rush home every step of the way and run to the woodhouse, get a pile of wood, take it in, and fill up the woodbox. That was the one chore I hated, and I never did it if I could get out of it.

Now I realize my parents were smart enough to know what was up, but they never called me on it.

Steve Wing, Supper Club

We had a big Jersey cow when I was a freshman in high school, and that cow had a calf. It was my job to look after them. And one day, when the calf was only a month old, the durned calf got out while I was at school. When Daddy couldn't catch the calf, he called me up at the high school and said, "Come on home and get the calf in." That put me in an awkward spot. I didn't know what to do, but I went to Mr. Hill, the principal, and said, "Sir, I've got to go home and put the calf up." He said, "You have to stay a month in detention hall if you do." And I said, "OK, that'll be fine." And I went and did that chore.

But the next morning in chapel the principal said, "Do you know I had one boy yesterday during study hall tell me he had to go home and put up the calf?" Everybody knew who it was and laughed. I was so embarrassed I didn't want to go back to school. But I made sure that calf never got out again.

Buck Johnson

Daddy drank. And I was going to steal his bottle. Daddy was a lot older than me, of course, and he was overweight, so at age six I figured I was getting big enough to do what I wanted to do because I could outrun him.

And so I grabbed his bottle, and he said he was going to whip me. But I ran. He caught me in just a few minutes. I found out quick I could not outrun him.

Jerry Preston

It was *really* awkward when I asked mother where babies came from. I was nine or ten. My total sex education from her was this: "God plants a seed under a mother's heart, and it grows." I think I believed that for a few years.

Jonathan Peter

In my early teens when my parents were discussing separating, I walked in on the conversations I'd been overhearing for some time. I tried to talk them out of it. I think adults have things they have to work out and children often complicate it very much.

Dave DeGrandpre

When I was growing up I didn't like my dad very much. My parents were divorced, and I grew up with my mother who really colored my views of him. He knew that I didn't like him and didn't want to spend time with him.

Dad had a summer house in New Hampshire about an hour's drive from where I grew up. It's a lake house in the town where he grew up. He wanted me to love it, but I didn't want to go there and remember telling him that I didn't want to see him. We went anyway, and, boy, was it awkward. I was about ten.

Now, I love to go to the pond house. The water is so pure it's amazing. I always skinny-dip and it feels so good, like silk.

My dad and my uncle Jed made a totem pole there one year. They cut down the tree and everything, and it took a long time. There are three different carvings: one has wings, one has a real long nose, one has freckles on it. When I was growing up, I had tons of freckles, and they put the freckles on there for me.

Joy Melton Prickett

One morning I was late for an early-morning college class. You know how it is on an empty back road—you pick up some speed. So I was zipping along, about fifty miles per hour in a thirty-miles-per-hour zone, when I topped a hill, looked up in the mirror, and to my great shock saw a blue light flashing. The first time ever. Horrible.

By the time the policeman got to my window, I'd started to cry. What was I going to tell my parents? How would I pay the ticket?

As the policeman took my license, who do I see coming down the road but my dad, coming home from his shift at the fire department. As soon as I saw the white pickup, I really started crying. Dad *waved* as he drove by.

Dad turned the truck around, came back, walked up and said, "Sug, what's going on?"

"Uhuu-u-u, uhu-u-u," I was sobbing so hard I couldn't speak.

Dad walked over to the policeman and came back and handed me the ticket. It had WARNING written across it.

All day at school I worried about what Dad would say when I got home. All he said was, "You know, hon, the next time you're speeding I want you to think about me driving by. This time you were simply pulled for a citation. But I could have found you off the road in a crashed car. I'm glad it was just a citation. You think about that and be careful."

Chris Keefe

When I had to tell my parents I was addicted to crack. I had to call them from the treatment center. All my life I had been an overachiever. Whatever I wanted to do, I excelled in. And then I had to tell them I had failed and failed badly. It was the hardest thing I've ever had to admit.

Nan Thomas

The morning of the day I was married, my father came up to me and said, "You know, Nan, we've never had a little talk." And he looked very nervous as he went on, "I've just been wondering if you know what getting married is all about and what's expected of you." And I was so embarrassed for my father that I looked at him and said, "Oh, Dad, sure!"

I didn't know a damn thing.

Peggy Hackman

When I married the first time, I didn't tell my parents right away that my husband was black. At first they were upset, but after our son was born, they were very accepting.

Mary Lou Retton

My mom and dad had the idea that after my gymnastics training days were over, I'd come back to Fairmont, West Virginia, to live. My mom really had her hopes up that I'd come home, so it was really awkward when I didn't. But by the Olympics, my life had changed so much that I just couldn't live that lifestyle any more. Now, I think they accept it completely.

Medora Plimpton

When I had the accident in my fifty-dollar car. I was sixteen. I didn't have a license yet, but I could look at that car in the driveway and have something to look forward to. I just wasn't supposed to drive it.

One night, I was hanging out with my friends before my parents got home, and I'd had a couple of glasses of wine, and I decided to drive down to the beach. Along the way, something happened—it wasn't at all the drunk driving part; I think an axle broke or something—but the car went out of control and I hit a good friend's new jeep. My head went right through the windshield, and I almost hurt the whole other carload of people.

I lied to my parents about that, said it was all because of the axle and that I'd been stupid to take the car. Then a week later they heard at the yacht club that I was drunk driving. My father could have said I was a stupid ass and that wouldn't have bothered me. But he said, "I'm very disappointed in you," which was the worst thing he could ever say.

George Plimpton

My father appeared for a trustees' meeting at Exeter. He came down to the baseball diamond where we were practicing. I was very proud of my junior varsity baseball uniform. I was out in center field. He took one look at my hair, which was growing over my ears from under the baseball cap, and he ordered me off the field and down into town to get a haircut. Right then and there! Very embarrassing! He was a stickler for such things. I doubt if he'd done it if a game had been going on against Andover, the great rival, but the thought would have crossed his mind. I told my son about this the other day. He has been growing his hair long, and perhaps he means to test me . . .

Taylor Plimpton

With my dad, the spray paint incident in the city. One of my friends sprayed paint on the outside of my house. An obscenity. Really big. And I thought they were going to be really small. The words were in white paint on a black building, facing FDR Drive. I felt really awkward when Dad came home, and everybody was talking about it. I knew it was dumb, and I knew I wasn't thinking. My dad was really disappointed. He rarely gets disappointed, but that was one of the times.

My awkward moment with Mom occurred with Bubba and Mom when we were on Grand Bahama for spring break. I was fourteen and had met a beautiful eighteen-year-old girl. Of course, I couldn't tell her my real age, so I said I was eighteen.

Well, Mom and Bubba didn't like that. "Taylor, relationships have to be honest," they said, nearly in unison. "She's going to like you anyway," Bubba said. So, I thought about it and said, "You're right. I'll be honest with her."

The next day, Mom asked me if I'd told her the truth, and I said yes. What I didn't tell Mom is that I decided to tell her I was sixteen.

At least I was closer to the truth.

15. A Vivid Dream

John Emmerling

As a child in Detroit, I dreamed several times that I ran downstairs and outside and around the corner of the house to find the whole side of the house missing. Instead, a green dragon, twenty feet high, flames shooting out of its mouth, was living in the side of the house. The dream was very frightening, but it would calm me for some reason.

Michael Bornn

I dreamed as a child of being in a room with the walls coming in. I never knew what the hell it was all about, and as I got older, I haven't had it.

Silvia Munro

I often dreamt that I was in my bedroom asleep and would wake up to find an old lady, a witch, sitting between my sister and me. When she got up, all the door handles would disappear off the doors. After that I'd wake up, but I'd remember you couldn't get out of the room because there were no door handles.

Taylor Plimpton

I had one dream when I was younger about two people having a war in my apartment in the city, in the hallways, which are cold, gray and barely lit. They would take me and use me as a hostage. They couldn't kill me, but if one was about to kill the other, he'd grab me and put me in front because I couldn't be killed. And I remember coming downstairs and going in my closet and being grabbed and dragged out into the hallway through a secret passageway. I had that dream continuously for a couple of years.

Shannon Kelly

In my dream I was being chased by the police, and I would run underneath the freeway near the Astrodome. A big warehouse under there was filled with nothing but clocks with human faces. I'd run into the warehouse, and one clock would give me advice on how to get away from the police. I don't think the police ever caught me. I had this dream for about five years starting when I was four.

Kim Litton

For years, I dreamed that I was in the schoolyard on this huge jungle gym. All the kids were trying to get to the top but someone had greased it and we were falling. I had this dream until I was in my twenties.

David Prowse

As a kid, my dreams were always about money, always. I'd put my hand out in the dream as somebody was going to give me some, and the money would drop straight through my hand. I'd try to scrape it up from the floor and I could never get ahold of it.

That dream sort of predicted my life, actually. Money just kept going straight through.

Campion Platt

Right before my father died, when I was five, I dreamed my mother and father and I were walking along this wharf, and my parents were ahead of me. I was looking at the boats, when the planks underfoot just disappeared, and I fell into the water. I woke up just as I fell, but the sensation was still there. The water rushed up past my feet to my knees and my hips and then my chest and then over my head, and I was in blackness. It was the most intense physical feeling. I can still feel it twenty-five years later.

I enjoy my dreams. I usually set my alarm for much earlier than I need to so I can wake up and remember my dreams.

Jim Swann

When I was a kid, after my dad died, I had a dream of a large man hitting me with a sack of something that hurt. It was a vision as much as a dream because it only occurred when my face got down in the crack between the bed and the mattress. If I was asleep, I'd have a dream, and if I was awake, I could see it just as vividly. All I had to do was put my face in that spot. That's a weird deal, isn't it? I still can do that. Not as well and only upon occasion. But sometimes I can put my face in that same spot and have that thought come to me. I hate it.

Phoebe Legere

In Italy I had a dream. I was holding a little baby boy about eleven with beautiful blond hair and blue eyes and very delicate features. I thought, "Oh, look at that nice little boy!" Then someone said, "Yes, his name is Phoebe Legere, and he does everything you do. He plays piano and he sings and he paints and he's very smart!" I was completely confused until I realized he was my son.

Ollie Ferguson

I had a dream that haunted me for the better part of my youth. I was sitting on the front porch of a house. A horse with a spiked harness ran up on the porch and chased me off the porch and down the street at full gallop. I was running for every bit of life in me, running at full blaze down this road that never ended, and the horse was at a full gallop, so close that every step I took I felt was my last. All of a sudden my mother ran up and spanked the horse on the nose and saved me.

John Marston

Here's a weird one, morbid actually. I dreamed that a stampede of bulls broke out of a poorly constructed aluminum corral and ran into a crowd of football fans down by the beach and started thrashing everybody. I was running to help some of these poor victims when I saw this phalanx of beef coming at me. I ran back—and woke up.

John Emery

I had serial dreams when I was young, usually about sex. They started when I was fourteen and continued until I got married and started doing the things I was dreaming about.

Johnathan Peter

I'm walking in a column of white light—there's a cross and intersection. As I approach the intersection of white light, it's always very uplifting, very exciting, almost orgasmic. There's no fear. I've had the dream several times—not yesterday or last month—but I always remember it.

Win Rockefeller

I was in college at Oxford at the time, and I woke up one morning having dreamt about meeting Prince Charles and Princess Anne. In the dream, the event seemed small and the atmosphere fairly casual, and I remember saying, "Do you mind if I call you by your name?" or something to that effect. And within about two or three days, I'd received an invitation to an event they were holding at the White House welcoming Prince Charles and Princess Anne to the United States. That's fairly vivid.

Jim Hallett

I like to swim underwater. Since I'm good at holding my breath for long periods of time, I like to swim laps on the bottom. I have one recurrent dream of swimming underwater while breathing away quite comfortably.

Edward Colquhoun

For some reason I felt very depressed as a teenager, but I had these wonderful flying dreams. And that cheered me up. I would be flying in my own person and watching the clouds go by.

Kate Learson

After one of my favorite dreams—I have lots—I woke up exhilarated, hopeful, like I never felt before. In the dream a funny little snail was going over this whole expanse of sand, leaving a trail. When I woke up, I felt the promise of my life, the predictability of my life, was indicated by that snail. It was on the earth; it was leaving a trail. I got the sense that, OK, I've left a mark, too. It gave me the most solid feeling.

Lenny Berman

I am in an airplane and the airplane starts to take off. It never crashes but it never gets more than a few feet above the ground. It flies through the trees or whatever is there, and in spite of any efforts to get that plane into the air and in a safe place, it just never rises.

George Plimpton

A lot of ships sink in my dreams. Usually within the sight of shore, for some reason or the other, which is beyond reaching.

16. A Treasured Possession

Jock Munro

My bagpipes. They were my great-great-great uncle's and are now over a hundred years old. There are different types of pipes—Irish, French, German—but these are typically known as great highland war pipes.

I like to go out in front of the house where there's a little rise in the ground and the acoustics are great and just play there by myself. It's a sort of a form of meditation. After you've been playing for half an hour, you feel relaxed.

Starting at age eight, I learned to play from an old pipe major called Pipe Major Stott, or Stottie, as we used to know him. He had a gammy leg, a bad leg, and he used to come up from the local village where I went to school. His claim to fame was that he had fought in the Boer War. So he was pretty ancient by the time he taught me. If he was pleased with the lesson—we always had an individual lesson—he'd dig into his old tweed jacket pocket and bring out a rum-and-butter toffee for you and say, ''That was fine today.'' If he wasn't pleased, and you hadn't been doing your exercises, you didn't get one of those at the end. He was quite strict. He had a small stick or pencil he'd tap your fingers with if you were playing the wrong notes. But he was a great old fellow.

Torre Andrews

Having my grandmother's desk is nice. It sat in the corner of her bedroom under a window, and she used to sit there to write all her letters. She kept every letter ever written to her. If I open the drawers and stick my head in, it still smells like her stuff—talcum powder.

A. J. Hiers

We didn't have a lot of material possessions, but one thing meant a lot to me. When I was about ten, my mother bought me a transistor radio that probably cost five dollars. The thing doesn't work, but I have it today. I don't even know what brand it is, but I know that she didn't have any money, and she bought it for me, and her hands have touched it, and to me it's precious.

Win Rockefeller

For my twenty-first birthday Dad gave me something that I use every now and then. Every time I get a chance to use it, it's another special moment. Dad wrote me a book, two or three privately printed copies. It was just a little bit of his life history until he married Mom. I've had people ask me if I would have it published, but though I'll share it with my friends, it's still a private book.

Amy Holloway

My father's paintings. I have a number, but my favorite is a study he did of me washing my hair. When I moved into my first apartment, I asked him for that painting for my birthday. He framed it for me and I hung it over the fireplace.

Jane Burke

A patchwork quilt Granny made just for me from pieces of cloth she'd saved from just about every dress or outfit she'd made me through the years.

James Royce

A picture taken at my sister's wedding in Acapulco last July. It contains my brothers, my sister, my mom, and my natural father.

The Librarians

Mary Randolph: If the house were burning, I would take my dog Boozer. It's a name, not a condition. People have a tendency to get weighted down by possessions. I think if you have your health and your mind, which is sometimes questionable with us, that's what matters.

Virginia Kahl: I'd go out of the house with a diet book.

Dorothy Cross: An arsonist burned our house down with a lifetime of treasured possessions, and that was hard because I have practically no family and they were my material heritage, the connection to my past. But after a while you realize that's not where it is; it's in your thoughts and memories. I still find it somewhat difficult to go back and drive past the farm and see there's no house there.

Richard Duke

If the house were in danger, I'd grab this panel from a cedar blanket box made by the Haida, an Indian tribe that inhabited islands off the northwest coast of British Columbia.

Such storage containers were one of the more utilitarian things they created. They cut a single big sheet of cedar, grooved it, steamed it, and folded it into a rectangle, then fashioned the bottom and top. It was called a bentwood box. My panel, about twenty by thirty inches, is the short side of the box. You can see on the right hand side where it was bent. You can also see some holes where there were traces of cedar root which bound it together or provided handles.

Finally it was decorated. The design on this panel is probably a bear. The two big ovals on the bottom are the hip joints. And the two big ones on the top are eyes; the two things above that, ears. Their style was cubistic, in a sense, a couple of centuries before Picasso. You have a representation of an animal through much stylized forms of the basic important parts of the creature—face, legs, arms, hips—in a flat perspective that could not exist in nature. It points to a contradiction in my thinking in that I've never felt so comfortable with cubism, for instance, yet I'm attracted to this, which is in a sense based on a similar principle. It says something to me.

Why I became particularly fond of it, I don't know. I'm not one who, I think, oversentimentalizes the native American. This tribe, the Haidas, for example, practically wiped out some of the tribes that lived in what is now Washington state by persistent slave raiding. And occasionally when they built a new building, they killed a slave and put the body under a particular corner of the house, which was considered lucky. So my interest is not grounded in some degree of oversentimentality about the noble savage. The Haida were pretty nasty people at times. But somehow I'm attracted to the art they created.

Paul Mockler

A tiny piece of the *Titanic*. I took this sample myself, broke it off the captain's cabin, and put it in our Mir-submersible's collection basket 13,000 feet below the surface. We brought it back to the scientists for evaluation.

George Plimpton

I have an enormous tennis trophy I won with Vijay Armitraj, an Indian Davis Cup champion, in a pro-celebrity tournament in Las Vegas. We each have one. Vijay had his shipped home by sea rather than by air. Too expensive. Absolutely gigantic trophy, largest I've ever seen. The two of them were on a table at courtside when we went out to play, and I thought they were for the professional championship scheduled for later in the day. I'll describe it: a large round base, surmounted by four pillars within which is the statue of a poet reading a scroll. The pillars support a bowl, and then, on top of the bowl is a replica of a tennis player hitting a forehand (he is wearing long trousers à la Donald Budge). The whole thing is about four feet tall—wonderfully tasteless, but then since my tennis trophies have always been little ashtrays for being a finalist at the yacht club Labor Day tournament, I treasure it enormously. It's the biggest thing in the house short of the piano.

Gerry Cooney

I love my saxophone. I play it because I always loved to hear a sax. I also love my bike. That to me symbolizes life, that changed me because all my life I would be doing one thing but I'd be thinking about getting to the next place. Riding my bike symbolizes that I can slow down and just enjoy the moment.

Dave DeGrandpre

My baseball cards. When I was a kid, baseball was my world. I had this huge collection, and I'd organize it every day. I had every team set up, every player in alphabetical order by position, team, and league. And then I'd find a new way to organize them. Whenever anybody was traded, I put them in their new place.

Then I started buying valuable cards. In fact, I have some pretty good cards. My favorite right now is a Sandy Koufax rookie card from 1955. It's beautiful! Sandy Koufax was a great pitcher for the Brooklyn Dodgers, a left-handed pitcher; and I'm left-handed.

Jonathan Peter

A book called *On the Loose*. It was a Sierra Club book and I still have a copy given to me twenty years ago. The book expressed this search, this feeling for "out there" with nature and how we communicate with it and how we commune with it and learn about ourselves. It's a very simple book, but I treasure it.

Kathy Bater Brackett

I don't think I have any treasured possessions. I was thinking just the other day that when I was younger it was very important to have a really good piece of jewelry. The size of the rocks in the ring I was wearing was important; the label on the dress I was wearing was important; the make of the shoes. Now, it's a release—those things aren't important to me anymore.

Deni McIntyre

When we're traveling, I think about this leather chair in our living room that's the place I always want to be if I'm sick or jet-lagged or really tired. I think about just being at home in that overstuffed chair with my legs up over the arm—it's the most comfortable place in the world.

Wednesday Bridge Club

Peggy Kemp: I treasure my house that my mother left me. She loved that little house better than anything in the world. Ed Stevens built it for her with just what she wanted, and she lived in it from 1940 until about 1975. She lived alone after my father died, and she absolutely thought that was the nicest little house. I know how she felt. I've enjoyed it too.

Mildred Sutton: That's why I treasure so many things here. They aren't worth anything to anybody else, but I associate so many with my husband Remar. Like that little wooden bowl out there on the table. That was Remar's mother's bread bowl that she made her biscuits in all those many years. And it's worn thin. She was a wonderful person and I treasure that a lot. It wouldn't mean a thing to anybody else, but it was hers.

Mary Costigan: I treasure that lamp I have in the living room with the Tiffany glass shade because it was my mother's years and years ago. I remember when she got it—my brother, who ran away to St. Louis to become a telegrapher, gave it to her with some of the first money he earned.

They put it in the parsonage, and it was so much more elegant than anything else that we had in the home. I just loved it.

After my parents broke up housekeeping, the lamp disappeared until I rescued it—all dismantled—from my sister's basement and restored it.

Kurt Vonnegut

Well, I just delivered it to my daughter. We own it jointly. It's a painting my father bought when he went to school in Europe before the First World War. By a guy who was a friend of Henry James—Frank Duveneck—and it is a knockout painting. Just the head of a boy. All American painters who were any good used to go to Europe. The painting is swell. But anyway, that's the big family heirloom and I have four heirs. They're just going to have to figure out what the hell to do about it.

Sonya Friedman

A charm necklace I put together. It has five symbols: first is a New York subway token so I never forget where I came from. The second is my initial, so that I don't forget who I am. The third is the hand of God—I'm not very big on organized religion, but I am spiritual. The fourth is a die I got in Las Vegas. I once realized that the harder you work, the luckier you get. And the fifth charm is two words: Trust Me. It's important to me to be bankable, and most people who say those words aren't.

17. Somebody You Could Talk to: A Portrait

Torre Andrews

Until I was twenty-three, I had lived in more houses than I had years. My dad was in medical school, his residency, and then the army, so we were always moving. We'd move to a place and be there as a family. Then my dad would be reassigned. He'd go to the new place ahead of us; my mom would stay behind, clean up, pack up, and move us. Then we'd be there for the next six months, but the last two months he'd be gone to the next place. It was a very tumultuous situation. We had no roots.

But every year we would go to my grandmother's house for Christmas or she would come to visit us. She was always coming from the same place, her apartment in Chicago, wherever we were. Whenever we went to visit her, we went to her home in Chicago. She was the one stable connection. If somebody's always cutting off the roots, you concentrate on growing one big tap root instead of a lot of superficial runners. My grandmother was the solid connection I always went back to. I always wanted to go to her house; my dad thought that was nuts. But no matter where we were, I visited her for two weeks every summer until I was twenty-four. That summer she died.

She was my dad's mother: Evelyn May Thompson Andrews. Crippling arthritis made her all but an invalid, and she lived by herself in an apartment tailored to her needs. For instance, she had a sink with no cabinets so she could roll her wheelchair right up. Nothing ever changed in that apartment. When I was five, I put a paper star on the door of my room that said, "This is Torre's room." When I went to clean out the apartment twenty years later, it was still there.

Every visit was the same, too. She'd let me do exactly what I wanted, whether I was eight or twenty. When I was five or six, I would get up in the morning and go mix myself up some pancake batter and make pancakes because she couldn't get out of bed easily. And she was very encouraging: "Oh, you're such a wonderful kid. You're so smart to do this. I can't wait to tell my friends that you came and made your own pancakes." Which, of course, made me make more pancakes. I learned to be an independent person because from age five, my parents would put me on a plane alone and send me off to Chicago, where I would spend my couple of weeks making pancakes.

I always liked to fix things; and as I got a little older, Grandmother would have a big list of things that needed to be fixed. She would keep things around and not get them fixed and not throw them away even if she didn't need them anymore because she knew that when I came, I would want to fix them. For instance, every year I'd rebuild her wheelchair—take all the wheels apart and grease them up. Once I put in a smoke detector; then when the smoke detector went off every time she cooked, I put a little switch in it so that if she was going to cook she could turn it off.

We liked to watch TV in the evenings. I'd help her into bed and then sit beside the bed in her wheelchair to watch. She might say, "Let's watch Johnny Carson; I see Gerry Cooney's going to be on tonight." She loved Cooney.

As the big highlight of every trip, we would go to Greenfield Mall. Getting there was quite a production. We always had to have a careful plan because somebody had to drive us, but never someone who was allowed to stay—it was our trip. My grandmother would be impatient waiting: "Fred is a great guy, but he's always late." So Fred would show up and we'd carry the wheelchair down and come back up and get her. She could just barely walk at all, but we'd get her in the car and off we'd go. When we got there, we'd eat and I would push her around to all the stores.

I'd say, "OK, Grandmother, I'm going to push you really, really fast. I'm going to crash you into things." And she'd pick her feet up and say, "Let's go." She would make siren noises as we were whipping down the mall. She'd be screaming and I'd be careening her around the turns and people'd be jumping out of the way. She always used to say people probably thought she was a crazy old lady. Then I would take her to a shop and drop her off; she'd look at clothes and I'd go to the toy store or ride up and down in the elevators for an hour and a half.

Her final illness was real sudden. She had a stroke and she was in the hospital. I talked to her once while she was in the hospital, and I think she could understand me but she couldn't talk. I heard her making these funny noises in the phone, which made me very uncomfortable, so I ended the conversation pretty abruptly. That was the last time I ever talked to her.

My grandmother was always someone you could talk to. She was always home. You could call her anytime, night or day, and she would be home and she would answer the phone. I remember one time I thought I was going to get a C on an important chemistry test, but I made an A. I was so excited and relieved that I wanted to call everybody and tell them. And she was the only person home because she was always home.

Just after she died and I cleaned out the apartment and came home to California, I used to call my grandmother's phone number just to listen to it ring. I would sit there in my apartment and I would listen to her phone ring. She was always somebody you could call and talk to. That phone rang for hours.

18. Someone Other Than a Parent Who Had a Major Influence on You

Stephanie Beacham

Mrs. Ohly who ran the Abbey Arts Center. She used to call me her little lioness. When I was twelve, she gave me Flaubert's *Madame Bovary*, which is not necessarily what you would give a twelve-year-old. I can remember having a headache. She said, "Oh, lie down in the library." And I lay down in her library, which was full of more wonderful books than I had ever seen. The Abbey Arts Center was smothered in Henry Moores and many other wonderful artists' works she'd accepted as an alternative to rent payments.

This was a woman who showed me, just by being, the alternative structure of life. The freedom to be whoever you are. Whatever your imagination tells you is where you can get to. My family life was so middle class and cozy. I was sweetly brought up as the third of four children. The values of my parents were such that money was never discussed. But Mrs. Ohly stood out as someone who was, I suppose, thought of as a little odd and a little eccentric.

There was my art teacher, Mrs. Zable, who if we'd made a wonderful lino cut, would say, "Ooh, would you do some on material for me?" So you'd do your lino cut print all over some material and a week later she'd turn up in this badly made skirt with your lino cut print all over it.

So it seemed to be the artists I met who had the freedom of choice that seemed to me the best way to live. They had the freest thinking. They would laugh at more strange and silly things. They would collect a pebble from the beach. They wouldn't have to have a tea set behind glass.

John Emmerling

My uncle Gordon McAlpine. A very successful salesman, he has great personality and enthusiasm, and he would say to me, "What are you going to do? Where are you going to go in life? Where are you going to college? You need to go to a good college." He would spin tales of selling that made great impressions upon me.

My family almost never went out to restaurants. One day, when I was nine or ten, my uncle took me out with him on a sales call and we stopped at a little roadside restaurant for lunch. When the check came—let's say it was four dollars—he left a dollar tip. This was in the late 1940s. I could not believe that somebody would leave one dollar. I was tempted to pick the dollar up and put it in my pocket. Then it struck me: what incredible style! Gordon continued to influence me, to ask my opinion, to want to hear what I thought about my future. He was the main person in my childhood who did that, and it meant a great deal to me.

Ollie Ferguson

When my grandfather, Etienne Dupuch, was knighted, he decided on a family motto that summed up the way he lived, what he gave our family: Being Bound to Swear to the Dogmas of No Master. What that means to our family is that you should always try to do what is right and do it to the best of your ability, that as long as you feel that what you are doing is right, you should never let anybody make you back down or waver from your path. In his public and private life, my grandfather embodied that ideal. In his newspaper business, he always stood by certain ideals and morals, for what he believed was right for the country, not necessarily for himself personally, no matter what it cost. And it did cost him, and it has cost the family who have followed his example; but it has always kept us going, too, and always reminded us why we were doing what we were doing.

I owe my grandfather so much. I don't know that I ever told him outright with so many words, but I tried to show him how much he meant to me by leading a life that would make him proud, by trying to be a good person and the best at whatever I do. I think that's all the thanks he ever would have wanted.

Deni McIntyre

Our family moved a lot because my father, a turnaround specialist for Kimberly Clark, was always being sent to help another troubled plant. So the family didn't stay one place long enough for one person to have a big effect.

But do historical figures count? There is almost no time in my life that I can't remember being under the influence of one literary or historical figure, sometimes real, sometimes fictional. It sounds a little suspect to claim that you're really influenced, say, by Joan of Arc: "Man, old Joan and I, we used to sit around on the hills and listen to the voices while tending the sheep, and she'd say, 'You know, Den,' . . ."

But I'd get on jags where I read everything I could find about one historical figure or another. Joan of Arc and Elizabeth I were important. I was going to be Robin Hood, or, for a while in high school, T. E. Lawrence. Male or female didn't matter. These people became part of my life.

My father used to have the passion of the week. One time he discovered Beethoven, and for a while we were reading Beethoven biographies, listening to Beethoven records, and I was buying music staff paper and writing down notes, although I didn't have the least idea what I was doing. I was going to be a composer and with any luck go deaf. The next week it would be sailing. Or chess.

Bunny Johnson

Miss Almareta, my friend Rita's mother. I have more happy memories at her house than I do at my own. That's where I listened to the "Inner Sanctum," a radio program that started every Saturday night with a squeaking door, and where I went to play with Shirley Temple dolls. I meant to ask Rita if she still had those dolls. And that's where we roasted marshmallows outside.

Buck Johnson

Other than family, Rosey Tweeks probably meant the most. Rosey was black. She worked with Mama. She would say things like, "If you don't behave, I'm going to gnaw the white off a ya." And she was the one who told me I had to stay away from haints. She said if a haint ever slapped you, you'd walk with your head sideways the rest of your life. So any time after dark, I was scared to get away from Mama or Daddy, somebody bigger, because I was scared I'd get caught by a haint.

We lived in the country on a dirt road where not many cars ever came through. And there was a window on the kitchen and another window on the pantry. When Mama and Rosey would hear a car, they'd run to the side window to see the car coming. And then as the car passed in front of the house, they would run to the other window to see the car go by. They'd try to figure out who it was. If a car they didn't recognize came through, it would tear them up all day long: "Who do you think that was?" "Well, I don't know; I never seen that car in my life." "What are they doing through here?"

Edward Colquhoun

Eddie Jackson, our mailman in Jacksonville, was a black man who had dropped out of medical school to care for his family. In addition to working for the Post Office, he was the Boy Scout leader for the entire northeastern Florida region, which was a paid position for the white Boy Scouts but a volunteer position for the black Scouts. I used to walk with him and talk. I don't remember any specific conversations or any words to the wise—I just know that he presented himself as a person to me. In that way I learned that a lot of what I was hearing about racial issues was not right, that much was racist. This was in the early fifties.

Campion Platt

Dan Sacks, a family friend who taught at Harvard. Although he was dying of cancer and must have been in a lot of pain near the end of his life, Dan never talked about that and I didn't know it then. I remember him because he used to come over on crutches and tell my sister and me Paul Bunyan stories in "longhand." I remember it all! He told us about this immense mythical character, and we'd sit around for hours and listen. Dan and I had a really close bond. He died when I was very young. I felt a great sense of loss for the person, but I didn't really understand the physical ramifications of death then.

Mary Lou Retton

My coach, Bela Karolyi. Bela saw me at a competition in Reno and said he wanted me to come to Houston. Bela *was* gymnastics, the best coach in the world, and at first I was intimidated just to meet him. I'd heard these horror stories about how mean he was, how strict.

Bela just came up to me and said, "Mary Lou, I want you to come to me. I will make you Olympic champion." I was looking around to see if there was another Mary Lou somewhere. I trained with him for three years.

Eric and Nancy Edmondson

Our friend George who died of AIDS in March 1989. George had a lot of class, a lot of style. He had a great sense of humor and a great love of music. We used to sit around and sing together sometimes.

George had a wide range of friends—wealthy friends who were real socialites and buddies like us. He lived just a hundred yards away. We did everything together: Saturdays seemed to be spent, for instance, at the Home Depot. We were always eating together or just dropping in to visit with each other.

He told us when he discovered he was HIV positive. In the summer of 1988 it became full-blown AIDS. We were with him constantly the last year and a half. Eric took George to the hospital the last time he went in. George wasn't going to ask for help—he had that kind of mental strength—until Eric met him by chance at the end of the drive and said, "Hey, where are you going?"

That was just before New Year's, because we spent part of New Year's Eve with him in his room. George was always very upbeat and he kept that spirit. The last month, when dementia set in, was the saddest—he just barely recognized people though not much else. But he was a great friend—to so many people. A big crowd came to his funeral at All Saints Episcopal. It was Easter Sunday—perfect for George.

Jim Hallett

Jim Burgess, who owned the Texaco station in Carmel, was important early in my life. I liked gas stations, and I liked to work. I liked to ride in the tow truck to tow in the wrecks or to fix the batteries or change the tires of stranded cars. They used to take me down to all the old wrecks. I did this every day when I was four or five.

And I drove them crazy. They used to send me on errands. I'd go up the street, two blocks away, to pick up all the parts at the parts store. Then as a reward I'd go to Bluett's, the creamery there, and pick up ice cream cones—softies—for everybody and carry them back to the station. I did that probably a couple of times a day. That's how I got overweight.

Will McIntyre

Foremost for me is Opie Pace, who was the chief of police for over thirty years in Spring Hope, North Carolina. He is a great-big guy who lived very near us out in the country. He'd been a professional baseball player—a pitcher in the Boston organization. And I dreamed of a big-league career.

After my father died when I was nine years old, various uncles and other men in the community filled in as my father. Opie did things like take me to baseball games and spend time showing me how to do things. We'd go hunting together. I don't think we ever killed anything, we'd just walk around out there. He taught me how to drive tractors better, which of course I needed.

And he let me hang out around the police station. When I was playing Little League baseball, he'd take me to town at noon on Saturday when he went to work. My mom would come to watch the game, but I'd stay in town after the game and go home with Opie at midnight. Sometimes I'd sleep in the jail until he got off work.

Shannon Kelly

My first-grade teacher. Mrs. McKeller was special because you could just tell she cared about us kids; she was never in a bad mood. And *that* certainly says something. I remember when she would come up and put her hand to the back of your head and pat you on the back whenever you asked a question.

Jonathan Peter

In my freshman year of architecture, I took a great books course taught by Miss Flood, a teaching fellow who, for the first time in my school experience, talked to us seriously about ideas—the great books: Plato's *The Republic*, Socrates, Aristotle. And she was a teacher whose ideas about these books had changed from the year before or six months before. She'd say, "I used to think this meant . . . but I think it's now. . ." I was amazed that this could be.

Alvis Waite

Miss Lola Wyatt, my sixth-grade teacher in Brooklet, broadened my vision beyond the sixth grade; she helped me set my sights high. There were no accelerated classes then, but she pushed me out of the rut of the everyday.

She encouraged me to go way ahead on homework. She'd make special assignments and I'd go over to her house on Saturday for additional work and tutoring. She was not only a good teacher, she was a good friend.

Timothy Sultan

Bill McBride, a former English teacher of mine, who encouraged my writing in his class even though I rarely turned anything in. He later moved to the Midwest to work for an educational publishing firm and has become very active in the gay community there. He was the first admittedly gay person I knew. It is rare for his letters not to contain the news of another of his friends' deaths; and yet he is one of the funniest, most tenacious and spirited persons one could know. He has that rare ability of always looking forward. Rather than drawing him down into a hole, the past enriches his present.

Doris Roberts

Sandy Meisner was my teacher at Neighborhood Playhouse. A couple of years ago I was very moved to find him and call him and tell him how much he had influenced my life, that he really began the whole process for me. I remember we had a terrible time toward the end because he asked you to do something three different ways: as it was written, as an English drawing-room comedy and as an Italian melodrama. And because I was too inhibited to do it as an Italian melodrama, I questioned his authority and he just let me have it. I remember biting the inside of my mouth just to stop from crying, but he gave me the tools with which to begin work and he gave me a belief in myself and he challenged me and I met that challenge. I had to call him and tell him that, because we don't do that in life. We just kind of keep going and we pick up all the good stuff and forget where we began and who gave us that chance.

Carol Hallett

My grandmother really had a big impact on me. She was a real pioneer, and she raised me until my parents were married. My father had built her log house as well as his, and she lived next door to us. We did wonderful things together like baking potatoes every day in the fireplace in the coals and making biscuits and things like that in addition to going to rummage sales, which today people would call flea markets. She used to braid rugs and, oh, a lot of interesting things. To me it is so sad when kids don't have an opportunity to grow up near grandparents because the stories she told me about her childhood, doing things by horse and by carriage and covered wagon and all of those wonderful things of the West, were important. She died in 1952 at age ninety-six.

Kate Learson

My grandfather, Dennis Murray, my mother's father. He was a telephone lineman. He was the kindest, most wonderful man, a combination of Santa Claus and God, I thought.

Since my parents couldn't afford to send us to summer camp, they sent us to my grandparents for part of the summer, which was so heavenly. They lived in this rundown place on the water south of Boston called Nantasket. Those summers were the most glorious times of my life.

My grandfather was extremely artistic. We would walk the rocky beach, picking out the most round or most oval flat rocks. We'd bring them home and paint them all white to make little canvases. Then we would take very little brushes and paint on them, often an altar with the crucifix and candles. Then we would make little easels out of Good Humor sticks.

Other times we would get up early in the morning and go clamming as the sun came up. My grandmother was just as loving and kind, though a little bit more reserved. There was no question that they thought I was wonderful. They loved me and I totally trusted them and I felt I could say anything, do anything, and that would be just great and fine.

Dan Buettner

I can trace what I'm doing today as an adventurer and writer to Joel Kacheal and a conversation in the school cafeteria when we were in the seventh grade. Over lunch he told me that in ten evenings out selling subscriptions you could earn a trip to Disney World. It took 220 points. That seemed like fiction to me. I'd never even stepped on an airplane, though I'd dreamed of doing it. So we went out one night. Knocking on that first door was a little nerve-racking, but I earned twenty-two points selling subscriptions that night. That was the start. Later he got me involved in serious bicycling. So one conversation led to all these fantastic trips and later to my addiction to travel.

The serious cycling began when we were in high school. We both worked at a Sambo's, he cooking, I washing dishes. At our wages of $2 an hour, he scraped together enough money to buy an $800 custom-made bicycle that was top-of-the-line everything, and he passed the enthusiasm along to me. We used to bicycle at night because we both had night jobs and on our days off our body clocks kept us up. We'd start at midnight on these sixty-to-seventy-mile rides through the city.

There was no traffic. Sometimes we'd go down these streets covered with mist that had an almost storybook quality. We'd ride down the Mississippi, up on the Indian mounds overlooking the river, down to Minnehaha Falls. We'd go into the working-class neighborhoods by the Schmidt Brewery, which were very foreign to our suburban existence. When the sun came up about eight in the morning, we'd bike home to sleep.

When we were twenty, he died suddenly. I had seen him two weeks before and we'd planned to go to a party together. When I heard he was dead, the news just sounded absurd. That was the first time in a long time that I actually cried. His ashes were spread in the Lake of the Isles because he liked to bicycle there.

George Plimpton

The brightest in the class—both at St. Bernard's in New York and later at Phillips Exeter Academy, which we both attended—was a kid named Toby Wherry. Very sophisticated, the class literary figure. He was one of those people who never seem to have a childhood. He was an adult at ten. I remember once at Exeter, a group of us were sitting around at a play rehearsal, waiting for our parts to come up, and Toby set us a sort of literary exercise. It was to describe in a paragraph a character going into the woods, getting lost, and what he was like when he came out. He got five or so of us writing these little themes, and then he read them out—something to do while we waited. He was too polite to say out loud which was the best, but I remember him whispering in my ear. He said, "You are the writer." I wish I could remember what I wrote—I don't recall being especially proud of it—but hearing that from him meant infinitely more than it would have coming from one of my teachers. I've often wondered if it didn't provide the spark for me to do what I've been doing for a lifetime. I was eleven at the time.

Mimi Taufer

In high school Cary Rick and I had a little silkscreen business. Cary was a very creative person who was involved in theater as well as art and later became a dancer. He introduced many, many things to me.

I helped with the theater—sets and costumes. And we painted a lot together as well as designed things and silkscreened them in my basement. We sold our work, usually at art fairs. Cary and I could always share. He was my best friend.

Marge Spezzano

My calligraphy teacher. I began in 1984 because I knew it was something I would like to do. One reason is that it is something constructive that you can leave behind—a legacy of sorts. But I didn't really think I could do it; my handwriting is barely legible. Now I spend a lot of time on it and a lot of trouble. Practically all the gifts I give now—baby gifts, wedding gifts—I do.

Virginia Kahl

At Milwaukee Downer College, I had an English professor who also taught writing. She was very encouraging, a great influence. All the assignments! You knew you had to write and you began to enjoy writing.

Miss Hadley's been gone a long time, but I still remember all the quotations that I learned in her class. There's one I quote a lot in the fall:

Margaret, are you grieving
Over Goldengrove unleaving?
Leaves, like the things of man, you
With your fresh thoughts care for, can you?
Ah! as the heart grows older
It will come to such sights colder
By and by, nor spare a sigh
Though worlds of wanwood leafmeal lie;
And yet you *will* weep and know why.
Now no matter, child, the name:
Sorrow's springs are the same.
Nor mouth had, no nor mind, expressed
What heart heard of, ghost guessed:
It is the blight man was born for
It is Margaret you mourn for.

(Gerard Manley Hopkins, "No. 55, Spring and Fall")

Peggy Sammons

Both my sisters. I had three mamas. My sisters Mildred and Edna (Bill and Tootsie to the family) were teenagers when I was born. Bill insisted that I learn to write thank-you notes, that I learn manners. She'd jump all over me if I didn't do right and talk right.

And the highlight of my week was riding in the car every Friday afternoon with Tootsie out to Summertown and on to Stevens Crossing to get Bill from school. I would stand up on the seat beside Tootsie and we would sing. I was scared of the hilly dirt roads. And I remember her saying one time, "If you think this is bad, wait till we start down."

Mildred Sutton

Aunt Jessie, who was my great aunt on both sides—my mother and daddy were first cousins. Going to Aunt Jessie's house in Aiken, South Carolina, was like going to a grandmother's house.

One of my grandmothers had died before I was born and my other grandmother taught school and traveled in the summer, so I had no grandmother's house to visit. But Aunt Jessie's house was always there, and her granddaughter Elizabeth, whom she raised, was my very favorite cousin. I could go over to Aunt Jessie's anytime I liked and stay as long as I liked. If Mother and Daddy said it was time to come home, and Aunt Jessie said no, then I got to stay. I enjoyed being humored and spoiled by Aunt Jessie, who treated me just like a grandparent would have done. When I got to Aunt Jessie's, I felt like I'd reached heaven.

Silvia Munro

My grandmother, my mother's mother. She was a very good, kind person. A very great lady and a very humble lady. In a house full of servants she still insisted that when you came back from school you picked up your school bag and took it to your bedroom. You didn't wait for the servants to take it. If you did, you were in trouble.

She was a very special person, not because she was the Grand Duchess, but because of the way she lived. For instance, when her family went on holiday to their hunting huts in the mountains, she'd teach them to cook and things like that, which people in her position normally wouldn't bother about. But she always taught us that no one's better than anyone else.

Jane Burke

My Granny, Beulah Grace Hale. Granny had great flair, a generosity of spirit, and an ability to laugh and have a good time no matter what she was doing.

Though she grew up in east Tennessee without much money, Granny had style. She was a very tall, beautiful woman with dark hair. She made her clothes in the latest fashion and she made all mine. We'd go out shopping, not to buy but to look. I'd find a dress I liked on the rack, and she could go home and make it from memory.

Granny did everything with energy and flair. She'd burst into the house if you were expecting company ready to help you clean and cook—just for the fun of it. She'd make going to Shoney's for strawberry pie an occasion. Part of my love of performing must have come from Granny's expansive approach to daily life.

She loved glamour, and to her the theater was glamour with a capital G. Even if she didn't care for the play, she came to every show I was in—including one where I played a foulmouthed character who provoked audible gasps from Granny in the third row. After she died, we found a box full of newspaper clippings; all my reviews were there.

Granny was my biggest fan. She applauded for me and laughed with me when I needed that, and she taught me to laugh at myself when I needed that. I loved Granny's name, Grace, because that's what she was for me, true grace, a gift.

Princess Pamela Strobel

My uncle Hun. His name was Isaacs, but I called him Hun, because he looked like a hunter to me, just like Yul Brynner. Hun dressed so well! Everything he wore had to be Longines and blue serge and Stetson hats and Zeniths.

Since I was born around old folks and spent most of my time around the house helping Grandmama, Hun would come by and "give me a day," he'd say. That was my day to do anything I wanted to in the world, and I enjoyed that more than anything. Hun even took me to his friend's house.

When he was old, Hun called me up in New York and said "Lord, everything is wrong with me! You'd better come see me while you can." Well, somehow I got on a plane and rushed down there. I sat on that glider on the front porch—where I used to sit and tell him how much I loved him. We talked and talked and then I noticed he wasn't limping. He said, "Well, that's one way to get you here!"

Even on that trip, Hun would let me do anything I wanted as long as I showed respect to his wife, Aunt Anna. All he wanted us to do was respect people, ever.

I talked with Hun the day he died. He said, "Princess, you were always special in my heart because I always knew you can make it because you're strong." I think about that a lot even now.

Jock Munro

My wonderful old nanny had an enormous impact. Her name was Barbara Bowen, but she was always Nanny. She stayed with us for twenty-five years; she died when I was nineteen. In my early years, she looked after me more than my mother. She fed me, changed me, changed my clothes, and spoiled me to death. That's why I'm such an impossible person now. I'd say, "Oh, Nanny, I don't like to have my potatoes and meat and vegetables on one plate. Can I have it on different plates?" And she'd do it for me. Which is ridiculous. My mother put a stop to it.

My mother rescued Nanny from her kindness another time when she noticed that Nanny was looking more and more tired and asked, "What's wrong with you?"

"It's wee Johnny. He's not sleeping at night."

"What do you mean," my mother said, "he's not sleeping at night?"

"Well, he keeps getting his foot stuck in the bars of the cot."

So Mummy said, "Let me sleep with Johnny for a while and see if I can cure him." So she did. My foot got stuck once and she tucked the foot back in. Then it happened again. After two or three times, my mother just let me scream. I quickly discovered that the trick that brought Nanny running, "Oooh, poor little child," didn't work with my mother.

Nanny was the kindest person I ever knew. At Christmas, for instance, she'd take the trouble to get up early and put red cloth on the barbed wire of the gate that goes up to the railway line. Then she'd take us children for a walk on Christmas afternoon and say, "Oh, Father Christmas must have torn his trousers." With warm parents and this wonderfully kind Nanny, my childhood was a happy time.

Marynell Waite

Mrs. J. Q. Smith, who worked with the young people in the church in Quitman, was a woman with a vivid sense of humor. Any number of funny things would happen to her. She was the first person I ever saw who had furs hanging over her, tails and feet dangling. But she was also a very generous woman.

Her family took ours on a trip to Florida once. We started out early in the morning, and as daylight arrived, I suddenly noticed that she had her dress on wrong side out. I started to giggle. Mother pinched me. I giggled some more. Then Mrs. Smith caught me looking, glanced at her dress, and died laughing at herself. For years after we got a Christmas card from "Wrong-Side-out Smith."

Mrs. Smith had a tremendous influence on all the high school young people and particularly me. She had a prom party just for me, where I was the guest of honor. Other children had prom parties, but I'd never had anything like that happen.

Patrick Goddard

My grandmother, Ada Saunders, whom I always knew as Nana. Because of my parents' problems she really raised me and was the dominant force in my life, the biggest influence on the way I live now.

Nana first taught me about perseverance. Since we'd moved around, I was behind in school, way behind. So each afternoon she would spend what seemed like forever going over my homework with me. She was relentless, too, and I hated it at the time. But she finally convinced me that I was equal to the other kids, that I wasn't a dummy if I'd just work. Looking back, it was a question of self-esteem.

Nana also taught me about money and responsibility. She had me selling magazines in the first grade. And then I became a great fruit salesman. We had thirty-four different kinds of fruit trees in the backyard, so something was always ready to harvest. She'd bundle me up with a paper bag full of fruit and avocados, and off I'd go through the neighborhood. Nana wanted to teach me the ethic of work. What a tremendous edge that must have given me!

That lady started me surfing too. She took sheets and sewed them together, then taught me how to run along the beach against the wind until the sheets were full and then somehow quickly tie a knot. Since I could never figure how to tie the knots right, she'd tie it and hand it off to me. Then we'd go out into the surf, and when a big wave came along, we'd plop down in front of it and ride that air bag in. Nana was always showing me things like that.

She'd let us carry on like kids, too. Once at Christmas we were sitting in a store parking lot and occasionally shooting pinto beans with my beanshooter at passing cars. We weren't exactly shooting rockets, so Nana ignored it. And then one car came to a screeching halt and the woman driver started screaming at us. Apparently a direct hit! I was petrified! And do you know what Nana did? She just said, "We all want to wish you a Merry Christmas." She defused the situation with this great aplomb, and she protected us. She also confiscated the beanshooters and ammo.

Nana died at ninety-two, a very young-thinking person. It was interesting, because my grandfather had died forty years earlier. Nana had lived without him for all those years. And one day my mother was commenting on a friend of hers who was considering a remarriage; I could tell Mother really disapproved of the idea.

Well, Nana looked at her and said, "You know, it's a terrible lot to live without a companion, without someone to share your life with. I hope that woman marries him and is happy."

I'd never realized my grandmother had been lonely until then. I might not have even realized how many needs she had until then, either. But I've never forgotten how special she was and how much I've loved her.

Sonya Friedman

Meeting my future mother-in-law allowed me to believe you need only one person in your life to change the entire direction of your life. Her name was Dr. Leah Hecht-Friedman. Even when I was a very young girl, I desperately wanted her close to me. Leah said yes: to my education, and to my dreams of doing something special with my life and career. She lived long enough to see me start my job at CNN, but she died that week.

Lenny Berman

Personally rather than professionally, my counselor Margaret has been very important. I luckily found her when I was going through a bad ending to a long-term relationship. Things in my life were at bottom. Before that point when times were tough, I'd say to friends who asked, "Don't worry, I'll get through." This time I wasn't sure.

But with her help I was able to end the bad relationship and begin to develop new ones. By helping me have self-confidence and confidence in relationships, she really did change my outlook about myself as a person. I'd go so far as to say without her, I wouldn't be sitting here happily married to Julie at this point.

Julie Rogers

After I left teaching school to work for the D.C. City Council, I worked for about six years for the grand old lady of the council, Mrs. Shackleton. She was in her seventies then, at the end of her political career. I had innate political skills, but watching this woman operate with incredible sets of liberal values and great political skills taught me a lot.

She's very sharp, a hawk; she counts votes. She showed me that if you really want to do good and legislate well, you have to be tough and trade things; you have to be more of a realist and a pragmatist. Her example taught me that you can have ethics and values and work your will in the writing of laws in your jurisdiction if you are also sharp and smart and able to work with your colleagues and line up the votes. The lessons have served me well.

She still lives here, now retired, and we often have dinner together.

Vince Spezzano

That would have to be Al Neuharth. In the sixties, Al took over what became *Florida Today*. And one of the first things he did was send me down here. My assignment was to bring him a list of the 500 most influential people in Brevard County without identifying myself or talking to people at the other papers. I spent a week and came up with a pretty good list. That's when I got to know most of the bartenders, waiters and waitresses in the area; a lot of them are still friends.

Al impressed me because he trusted me with many professional and personal matters and would bounce ideas off me. My career owes a lot to him.

Dave DeGrandpre

I'd have to say three people: Aubrey and Erik Peterson and Scott Smith because they've allowed me to be as open as I want to be. I have such a special friendship with these guys. They can accept anybody for anything. I met them in the freshman dorm here at the University of Montana. They were somewhat of an oddity—crunchy; they had long hair; they would clown around and be at a level we couldn't understand.

But in time we understood each other. They've given me a level of freedom. Anything I think, anything I feel, I can tell these guys without reservation. I've felt very close to a couple of girls, but I've never had this kind of relationship before.

Peggy Houlihan

My sixth-grade teacher, a nun, was a great influence. She challenged her students to go far beyond their own expectations—academically and otherwise. This teacher taught all of us to try the unknown and to stretch ourselves into new areas. She encouraged me to write a play for our grade school. I chose to write on the life of Joan of Arc. I enjoyed it so much that I ended up as producer, director, casting director and star of the play. It was a success, and although I never pursued the theater again, it was a wonderful experience.

Margaret Mason

I have two. One was my third-grade teacher who brought me home on her noon hour and showed me a robin's nest. I was to read a poem in class: "We have a secret, just we three, the robin and I and the sweet cherry tree. The bird told the tree and the tree told me. . ." It goes on. So she wanted me to see a robin's nest. We had lunch together, too—tomato soup and a grilled-cheese sandwich, I think. You can imagine what a thrill that was for a third-grader to be singled out by the teacher. We talked about poetry and about words, about the importance of each word in the poem. And we talked a little bit about expression in reading and so on.

The other person was also a teacher, and he directly influenced my career choice. He was a journalism teacher at Central High in Red Wing, Minnesota. He really felt that I should go into journalism. He cleared the way for me to edit the high school paper. Though I'd edited the grade school and junior high papers, I hadn't taken it seriously. But he took me so seriously that I think I started taking myself seriously as a writer and editor. A couple of us would go to school early to work on the paper and he'd come in, too. He had a way of showing each of us that the individual way we looked at the world was important. He made us see that it was important to figure out our perspective of the world and then try to put it on paper.

Amy Holloway

Mr. Fields, who was a theater director at the University of Tennessee. My mother forced me to audition for the University's summer theater company at Hunter Hills, up in the Smokies. I got in and Mr. Fields was the director.

Hunter Hills was a huge, beautiful, open-air theater with hemlock trees all along the back of the stage. Because it was so huge, in rehearsals in Knoxville they kept telling us, "You've got to remember to 'dress the stage'—spread out. Even if you're supposed to be next to someone, keep that distance."

Well, I was the quietest, shyest person there. And I did exactly as rehearsed when we took *Li'l Abner* up to Hunter Hills. My legs were so thin and white—I was the only girl in pants—I felt a little self-conscious about running across all that expanse of green.

At any rate we're rehearsing, I'm at the back of the stage spreading out as told to do, and Mr. Fields suddenly calls out,

"Amy, if it's the last thing I do, I'm going to get you out of the hemlock trees." All the other kids were theater majors and were crowding up front. So he was wonderful. He had confidence in me and did more to instill confidence in me than anyone.

He gave me roles I'd not auditioned for because he felt I could do them. He made me believe I could be good. He got me out of the hemlocks.

Rodney Cook

My paternal grandmother Bess Mims Cook was an extraordinary lady. I called her Mimi. She was a great cook and knew just the things to cook that I liked.

She also knew that I played out on the creek between our house and hers, building cities all over the banks with mud and bricks. And she knew I could smell the food cooking from down there and would come running through the woods, across the vines and up to see her. She also had this wonderful balcony, high up looking over the steep hillside. It was the scene of some great conversation and sharing.

I eventually went on to build cities out of paper where I could play with them all the time. When it rained, my cities on the creek would be flooded. And she let me put these paper cities in her basement where I'd go to play in the winter and on wet days. That was the beginning of my designing. I have, interestingly enough, built a lot of the buildings I did as a child.

Emily Cook

Oh, that's easy. Rodney. I remember the first time we met in 1978. I was working in New York at New York, New York, Disco and was part of that scene. My grandmother in Atlanta, who I thought was a lovely lady, wanted me to make my debut. I didn't really want anything to do with it but agreed to please her.

For this particular ball, I had attended none of the rehearsals but came just for the night. I didn't know what I was doing, but I did have this outrageous dress—fifty percent Scarlett O'Hara, fifty percent New York, New York, with diamond bracelets and eight-foot-long bits of chiffon trailing off into nowhere. In those days, the more insecure I was, the more I paraded. So I arrived this evening with no idea what to do.

I noticed that when all the debs would go down, there was polite applause. When I came down in this strange costume, there was not much applause, just murmurs. I curtsied to the wrong person, shook hands with the wrong person. It was awful. So, I was prancing!

Rodney and a dear friend of ours heard the murmurs, turned to see what was going on and saw me. Our friend reports Rodney saw me for the first time, and our friend said, "Uh-oh, this is it."

We met that evening for sixty seconds when he came up and introduced himself by saying, "I'm living in the pool house of your grandmother's old house."

I remember looking up. He was tall, handsome, dashing, had very blue eyes. It is truly funny that I don't remember who my date was that evening or anything else about the rest of the evening, except meeting him.

We didn't get together right away. It was almost as if God said, "OK, you guys meet now, but you're such children and have so many problems to work out, you're going to be separated for a while." We dated other people through the years. We went through periods when we didn't keep in touch. But whenever we met, the sparks would fly.

Rodney also says that whenever I came to town to visit my grandmother, he'd get this mysterious call from Kate, my grandmother's longtime housekeeper: "Roddy, she's here." Click. That's all.

But starting from that first time and growing through the years, Rodney has been the most important influence, the most important person to me.

19. The Ex-Mother-in-Law: A Portrait

Nancy Daugenberg Sutton Perkins

I was about fourteen when I met Bubba's mother. Bubba and I were in the same grade in high school; George, his brother, was a year ahead of us.

And then I fell in love with George. We eloped in June of 1959 after I graduated from high school and George finished his first premed year at Emory University. George was still living at home, and our plan was to keep the marriage a secret for a few years. Good luck. Just a couple of weeks later, Mrs. Sutton was playing bridge on the porch with friends when an insurance man knocked on the door: "I'd like to talk to your married son George about life insurance." *That* stopped the game for a minute, but Mrs. Sutton went on to win as usual.

I remember two things after Mr. and Mrs. Sutton got the news: how afraid I was to see them, and how they quickly accepted me though they didn't really think marriage at our age and stage in life made sense.

From the beginning, Bill—what I call Mildred—taught me a lot. My mother had taught me to be a lady, but Bill taught me how to be a gracious Southern lady, and more important, the value of family. I had never lived around any of my family and loved being part of an extended one. Though Bill never said it in words, everything she did showed me the importance of sticking together, of depending on each other. For a while, I couldn't have been happier. Mr. Sutton bought us a house close to Emory University;

in 1961 and 1964 my daughters Dawn and Sue were born; George, my husband, was finishing medical school early.

But in 1966, I began to drink. By 1970, when George was in the service, I was drinking a lot, and by 1971, I was in the hospital. In 1972, George asked for a divorce. Since I couldn't see any future in life right then, I gave him custody of Dawn and Sue. That seemed better for them until I could get straightened out. Two days after the divorce, George remarried. I was no longer a Sutton.

It took two years for me to get straight, and then in 1974, I came down with Guillain-Barré disease. By the time I recovered from the paralysis, George's new wife had pretty much convinced George that I should never see the kids again. She convinced the kids not to want to see me, either. I felt like I'd hurt them enough and didn't want to push them. Until the summer of 1989, seventeen years after my divorce from George, I didn't see or talk with them.

But during all those years, Bill Sutton never forgot me and never let my children forget me either. She wrote me constantly. I still have every letter. She told me what the children were doing. She told me what the family was doing. She told me how strong a person I was when I needed to hear that. In 1979, Mrs. Sutton even invited me to town to stay with her and Mr. Sutton for our high school twentieth reunion. No one will ever know what it meant to me to drive up to her house again and feel at home.

Bill Sutton did all this without her son George's knowledge or permission, since he had forbidden contact with me. And as the kids grew up, Bill would risk being told off by them whenever she talked about me. She told them about me anyway.

Then in 1989, I was in Florida with my husband Stuart Perkins when I picked up the phone and heard George Sutton's voice for the first time in seventeen years. George had remarried again, and his new wife wanted Dawn and Sue to know their mother.

My husband and I came to Atlanta to meet my children in September of 1989. I was a complete and total wreck. "Nancy," my husband said, "you can do it! And what's the worse that can happen? They can look at you and say, 'You are an absolutely unmitigated bitch and we don't ever want to see you again!' If they do that, we'll be exactly where we were yesterday, and we were happy yesterday.'' He was right of course. I had learned how to live without.

Or I thought I had. When I saw my children, even though we couldn't really talk seriously then, so much of my life came together. Even from the first, I knew them well. Dawn and Sue were surprised at that, and even more surprised when they found out Bill was the reason.

During these last few years, Dawn and Sue and I are a lot closer. We're friends more than anything. We're at Bill's constantly, on that porch where she learned I was her daughter-in-law, or in front of that big fireplace. And during many of those visits we talk about the importance of family, and the great influence Mrs. Sutton has been in making this family whole again, giving us the courage to live through the awkward moments. Christmas is especially important at that house, because we're all together— and Bill can sit and hold her great-grandson, my daughter Dawn's child.

Mildred Sutton has been one of the most important persons in my life. She has stuck with me through life's roughest moments. She taught me and my daughters *that's what families do.*

20. The Time You First Felt Like an Adult with Your Parents

Virginia Kahl

When I was a child, I thought that if you were an adult you always knew the end of stories. My mother always knew the end. I would hear her talking to friends, and she'd say, ''Yes, there's someone who has tuberculosis in their family. And there were six sons and daughters, and they all died of tuberculosis. And then the mother died.'' And that was the end of the story. It seems all the stories she dredged up were always complete, and I thought, I never know the end of a story. Somebody's doing something, then he goes off; my friends go off to school, I never know the end. That's when I'll become an adult, when I know the whole story.

Norman Lear

I was treated like an adult very early by my parents, when I was allowed to hear their most vociferous arguments in those small places we lived in. Mother and Father were pretty much at each other's throats a good deal of the time, and the arguments were in full view.

I used this once in a picture called *Divorce American Style.* The couple were fighting in the kitchen, and the kid was in the upstairs bedroom listening through a transom, sitting in bed with a clipboard. When the camera peeked over his shoulder to look at what he was writing, the kid was judging the argument downstairs, giving them points. He was scoring the argument as I used to do.

But there was no upstairs, downstairs at that point in my life. I would sit at the kitchen table and score the argument as a way of protection. Mother usually won.

Kathy Bater Brackett

Mother always treated me like an adult—with respect. We could pretty much talk about anything. The only problem that I had in relating to her was that she was such an optimist. Sometimes it is difficult to weigh a problem when you're not looking at both sides. Even if she thought about the down side, she would not express it. She really, really believed in positive thinking, positive speech, positive actions.

Will McIntyre

My dad was always sick. As the foreman of a granite rock quarry, he ran what they called the "hole." He was dying of lung cancer, ulcers and other ailments from the time I was about four. He died when I was nine. So I think from the time I could talk, my parents were preparing me for adulthood because pretty soon I'd have to be a small adult.

Dorothy Cross

As a farm girl with no brothers, I got a lot of farm work. I took on the responsibility of milking a cow at age eight. A little later, I felt very adult because my father let me drive the team when he was spraying his orchard.

Campion Platt

My mother has had a difficult life, and she's tried to be independent and do the best she could with it. But when I was eleven, she went into the hospital. When she came out, there was a definite change. By the way she was acting, I knew I would have to play more of a father role than a son role. We had a different relationship from then on.

Deni McIntyre

From an early age, we were not only allowed to have our own opinions but expected to. The times my parents would really get upset with us were those when we would swallow something wholesale from our classes and not think for ourselves. But thinking things through on our own was great. We were even allowed to argue with our parents.

Barbara Bailey

I remember my mother treating me like a kid when I wasn't, and that felt better than feeling like an adult! I was twelve and had fallen down, taking all the skin off my knees. Mother sat me on her lap and comforted me. I was much too old to be sitting on Mother's lap, but it left me with a very loving impression. That happened in southeast London while my father was off at war.

John Emmerling

While I was thirteen, we had an old 1939 green Ford sedan, and I wanted very much to learn how to drive it. Though I was a year away from a learner's permit and three years from a license, my mother took me out to some gravel back roads and gave me a driving lesson. She showed me how use the clutch to shift and use the brake, and I drove up and down shifting into first, second, third, and reverse. It was the first sense that I had that I was about to be free and that I had been given this permission to be free by my mother because I very much saw a car as my ticket to freedom.

Wednesday Bridge Club

Peggy Kemp: When they finally let me wear lipstick and dress up like I was grown-up. I was fifteen.

Murial Sichveland: Before I went to college, my dad took me to Butte, the nearest large town, to pick out my wardrobe for school. I felt so grown-up as I picked out clothes all by myself. I'll always remember a beautiful green three-piece suit with a fox collar. And I had to pick out a long dress and the tunics that were popular in 1936. I felt just great when I came home with that wardrobe.

Mary Costigan: When I was thirteen, I was allowed to make my mother a dress. I thought, oh, here they've entrusted me with all this pretty material. I felt so big and grown-up to be able to do it. And the dress turned out so well. I can almost see my mother swish around in the full crepe skirt now.

Peggy Sammons

I thought I was really grown when on Saturday morning I begged and begged and was finally allowed to drive to go get the clothes from the washwoman. We'd take the clothes once a week. Of course, I wasn't old enough to have a driver's license; I got that later when I was fourteen.

Tommy Sammons

When Mama let me drive the car in 1940—back and forth, in and out of the garage. I'd learned how to shift gears, and I asked her. The car was a '37 Chevrolet that my dad had painted black— with a paint brush.

Edith Bornn

When I was fourteen years old, my father took me to Puerto Rico with him on a business trip. Everywhere Father took me on this trip, I was greeted as Mrs. Bornn, and he had to correct them. It didn't happen once or twice, it happened repeatedly over the space of a week. I said, well I must be mature. I've never forgotten it.

Bunny Johnson

Mother taught school and had three jobs in the afternoon, then went to school on Saturdays. So I had to take responsibility for Pat, my younger sister, from the time I was fifteen. But no matter how much responsibility I assumed and how grown I was being, I never felt like I did a good-enough job.

Nan Thomas

When I was given a clothing allowance. I was fifteen and I got twenty-five dollars a month, a fair allowance for 1947. But I always wanted more than that would buy, so I'd go to my grandmother and get the difference. I could get anything I wanted from her.

Marynell Waite

In Quitman we lived in the center of town, but the new high school was well out on the other side of town—a very long walk. I had just turned fifteen and had my learner's license. Just around the block from the parsonage was the one fine hotel in town at which all the single teachers boarded. And four of the women needed a way to school.

I'm not sure how it was arranged, but I was allowed to drive my sister's car to school if I took the teachers. So every day I pulled up at the hotel entrance to pick up the four teachers and drove them to the schoolhouse where I had a regular parking space just like faculty! Then I reverted to being a student all day long. In the afternoon I took them home again to the hotel. I was proud of the responsibility, particularly driving the whole block and a half to and from the hotel unaccompanied.

Buck Johnson

In high school I went to Macon to make a speech with the FFA, Future Farmers of America, and I got a standing ovation. My daddy came up to me looking proud. He didn't know how to express it, but when he said, "That was pretty good," I felt like an adult. I was sixteen.

Gerry Cooney

I was sixteen years old, and my father and I were going to the Golden Gloves. He was directing me around to do this and to do that and do this, and I looked at him and said, "Hey, who am I doing this for? For me or for you?" And my father looked at me and walked away.

Hamilton Fish

When I was seventeen, I was at a point in my relationship with my mother where I was older but still her child. My mother would give permission and set limits, and I think I was basically comfortable with that. And then she was killed in a car accident.

My father was suddenly without this source of family stability, bereft of the person who set our family norms—at the very time his career was blossoming. After trying for several years, he had won election to Congress; that whole world was beckoning. And suddenly he was blasted in the face by this accident. He was only forty-three. Though Dad must have been frustrated having to feel his way on both the home front and the professional front, he supported his children and allowed us to feel our own way, too. From then on, he essentially said, "I'll back you."

Anne Brunson

When I was a camp counselor, a copperhead snake appeared. All the girls started screaming, and I realized that I wasn't one of the screaming girls, that they were coming to me—the grownup! I killed the snake.

Carol Hallett

One of the things that really made my sister and me seem very grown-up was that my parents wanted us to learn how to drink before we went to college. So every night the summer before we went to college when my father came home, we would sit down and have a drink together. They tried all sorts of different drinks on us, from scotch and soda to martinis. They wanted us to really know what we were getting into. This was unusual, but I can remember drinking too much only one time at school.

Shannon Kelly

I was recruited by all the Big Ten schools, the Big Eight, the Southeast conference, the PAC 10. My parents said, "Shannon, we'll help you, but it's got to be your choice." Well, I didn't want to hear that, really; I wanted them to take that from me. But they wouldn't do it. And then I realized that being an adult was a lot more than just being older: you had to make lifetime decisions.

Alvis Waite

I was active in the Methodist Student Movement, and in the summer of 1939, after my freshman year in college, Dad let me take the family's only car and drive from Brunswick to Athens for a student conference, about 500 miles round trip. He even let me go by Waycross to pick up another student. He turned me loose with the car! That trust made me feel adult.

James Royce

Mom and I always had a dual relationship. Since she was mom and dad, we had twice the fights, of course. But she has always been a pillar to me. My "growing up" has happened over the last fifteen years, and I'm twenty-six.

I know she was very impressed I went to school on a 100 percent academic scholarship. But at the same time, I'd come home from school and at times she would be very *un*impressed with my attitude; she'd say I was immature and not handling myself like an adult. Most of the time she was right. No self-respecting kid says that, though. There's a certain growing up you have to do inside emotionally. That takes longer than body growth.

Lenny Berman

I had a rocky time in college and graduate school, something my dad didn't understand and that affected our relationship badly. I left to go to graduate school in Colorado on nonspeaking terms with him. Five years later, I'd finished school and was working professionally. It seemed ridiculous then to have such a nonrelationship with my dad. So I sat down and wrote him a letter, basically saying what had happened to me and asking to reconnect and communicate. Soon after I had an opportunity to go home to visit. As we talked, my dad recognized I was working in a professional relationship and that I was in charge of my life. That complex of events was probably the first time I felt like an adult with him.

John Emery

When someone said *sir* to me in my early twenties. I was married then, but I always looked so young. It made me feel uneasy.

Egbert Donovan

Most people when they reach twenty, twenty-one, feel like they've reached the stage where they've got to stand on their own. When I made twenty-one years, I had my house coming up. What you see around me, my family owns. They gave each child a spot to put up their own house. This is the spot they gave me, and I put my house here.

So at twenty I felt I ought to have my own home, and I built one section. In the island here, the people live together. Any time you're going to build anything, everybody come together and they help you. Some is carpenter, some plumber, some electrician— you have a little food and drink and everybody helps. My parents help too. I've always been close to my parents. Parents and children is very close here.

Ollie Ferguson

I was talking about getting married, and my mother said, "Great! Wonderful! But when you get married, you're going to have your own home and take care of your wife on your own." It had never crossed my mind that I'd have to move out. Her saying that made me sit down and think, wow, you're an adult now.

Kathryn Hames, Supper Club

Perhaps when I married and left home for the first time. I'd never been farther than Florida or Alabama, and the army had promoted Luther to lieutenant colonel and sent him to Cambridge, Massachusetts. That was something to leave the little southern town of Marietta and go to Boston and Cambridge—in the dead of winter, too. It was another world.

Eric Edmondson

The first Christmas we were married, Nancy and I gave our first big party. My mother and father had been throwing great parties for a zillion years.

But we arranged this one. We had all sorts of great stuff to eat and the right drinks and everyone was having a good time. I was standing over to one side enjoying this, when my dad walked over to me, stuck out his hand, and said, "You give a pretty good party here." And I thought, well, hell, I guess I've made it—I can give a party that my father can come to and enjoy.

Nancy Edmondson

This past fall. First, Guinevere, one of our cats, died after a long, distressing illness. Then, suddenly, absolutely unexpectedly, my brother-in-law Donnie died of a heart attack in November. I felt like God had abandoned me. All I'd ever prayed for was the safety of my family.

I was telling my mother that I'd always been a basically happy person but I didn't feel that way anymore, didn't think I'd ever feel that way again.

And she said, "Well, you're an adult now."

Edward Colquhoun

My mother's brother contracted Lou Gehrig's disease when I was forty. Everybody was in a quandary about what to do. I did some research, made some calls, and got things started. I was able to find a special National Institutes of Health study program through which he had an operation that helped some. While there was no long-term cure, I was able to help.

After that, I think my parents looked at me and my work from a different perspective. Being able to contribute is an adult role.

John Marston

My plans last summer to come to Alaska and be a boat gypsy, a professional hobo, weren't as exciting to my parents as to me. I had, after all, filled the traditional mold they expected as a rising executive at Disney and then at a graphic arts firm. But when I started sending them checks, I think Dad finally stepped back and said, "He's going to be all right no matter what he does. He's out there having a good time and making some money."

Amy Holloway

In a way your parents' house is that safe haven where you can be a kid again. You don't have to be adult with your parents. Just this Valentine's Day, my sister Erin and I, aged thirty-five and forty-two, were decorating sweatshirts with puff paint in her old bedroom. Suddenly the dachshund jumped on a sweatshirt, getting puff paint all over him. Erin grabbed the dog, we ran into the bath laughing.

My mother came in and said, just like a mother, "What are you doing?"

"Washing the dog." Giggle. Giggle.

"Well, you sound just like you did when you were into trouble when you were little."

Stephanie Beacham

A genuine, genuine adult? Not until I had said, "You must come to Hollywood," and Mummy said, "Darling, we can't because of Lucy." The dog.

I said, "Lucy can be looked after."

"Well, Darling, Daddy's hip."

"No problem, I will get the limousine to take you from Dunstan to Heathrow. If you need two first-class seats each, you can have them. You will come."

So they let me arrange it and came to visit me in my lovely house. And they said, "Stephie, we don't know how you've done all this." Then, I felt adult with them because I knew that I was the nurturer.

Feeling adult with your parents is not as simple as personal adulthood. Adulthood for a child, perhaps, does not happen until the parents allow the child to look after them.

Jerry Preston

My brother and I *never* used foul language around our parents. But when I was home just a few months ago, I said damn in front of my dad for the first time. I guess at fifty-six I'm feeling somewhat like an adult.

Judy Rose

Feeling like an adult didn't happen suddenly. It began in my early twenties when Mother used to come out every two years to visit me in my house rather than me going to the family home. That had a different feel. Then as your parents get older, a complete role reversal gradually takes place. Then in the last stage, your parents die and you move to the top of the tree. It's a terrible feeling when there's nobody to go and ask anymore; instead you're the one everyone turns to. I realized that when my mother died ten years ago.

Marge Spezzano

I think I remember more than anything else that moment when I realized that my daughter thought about me like I thought about my mother—on an adult level—and that was very special.

I remember in the last years of her life, when she was in a nursing home, my mother saying to me, "It's like becoming the child. Now you're the mother." And she made it a positive statement, not sad.

Kate Learson

A few years ago my father was very ill in the hospital and needed several serious operations. My father had the old-fashioned notion that doctors are gods and wouldn't ask them to explain and justify the proposed treatments. So I queried the doctors constantly, making them explain this and then that. They hated me. But I remember looking at my father at one point and he sort of put his head back on the pillow; I could see that he was exhausted.

He's a brilliant man and a tough man, but he was sick, in pain, worried—and I saw just a brief flicker of "I appreciate your doing this for me." At the time I was in my midforties, he, midseventies.

Princess Pamela Strobel
Never. Never!

21. Busking: A Portrait
Jock and Silvia Munro

Jock: I went busking around Europe with my bagpipes the summer I was seventeen.

I did it the first time when I was sixteen—just by chance. When a group of us on holiday in the south of France went into the village just for fun, I brought my pipes along and started playing them in the street. Then someone put the bagpipes box out in front of me. Lots of people started looking on. I played for probably ten minutes, having great fun, then packed up and went on to dinner with my friends. The next morning, I opened the box to get my pipes and saw how many francs there were. "That," I said, "is a lot of money for ten minutes playing on the bagpipes. There's something in this."

So the next summer, I went to Paris to play. Being an ignorant seventeen-year-old Scotsman, I had a bit of a shaky start when I played on the tomb of the Unknown Warrior and that wasn't too popular. So after the police moved me off, I played in the Champs Élysées, Montmartre, St. Michel, St.-Germain—very successfully. I never played more than about twenty minutes in one place because though the pipes' loudness attracts people from a long distance away, it also drives people working in nearby offices or shops crazy after about half an hour.

After Paris, I played in St. Tropez, Rouen, Munich, Cologne, then back to Paris, where Silvia joined me.

Silvia: I took the hat around.

Jock: My taking went up by at least fifty percent when Silvia passed the hat.

Silvia: The first time I did it was at Notre Dame. Jock said to me, "I start playing, you wait five minutes, and then you walk around with the hat and you shake it with a little bit of money." I said, "Jock, I'm sorry, I can't do it. I'm *not* doing this." And he said, "Yes, you are." "I can't. I *can't*."

"You are." And he started playing and kept looking at me with these black eyes, saying, now walk—making it so obvious that finally I did. It wasn't bad at all. Then we discovered people gave quite a lot of money when I passed the hat—a hundred-franc note sometimes.

My family thought it was a big joke; though they were a little worried about whom I might meet on the street. When I once saw an old school friend, I ran away and hid.

Jock: And we had some funny experiences. Like the time I was playing on the Champs Élysées. I'd played there for two weeks a month earlier without problem. And the first evening back, I had played a while and stopped, when a man who'd been watching came up and reached into his inside jacket pocket. I thought, that's great, because now and again you get someone who'll give paper money rather than coins. A hundred francs, I thought.

It was his police identification card. "No more playing around here," he told me. Thinking I'd just been unlucky, I came back the next night and played. Sure enough within five minutes: "You're under arrest, come with me."

Just as I was packing up my box to go, this loud voice with an American accent booms in my ear, "Are you a Munro?"

"Yes." I assumed that he recognized the tartan of my kilt.

Then he said, "Are you John Munro?"

"Yes."

"Are you the son of Capt. Patrick Munro of Foulis?"

Meanwhile, the little French detective was sitting beside me tapping his foot on the pavement, not understanding a

word of English. And the American said, "Well, gee, that's
great. I just come down from Foulis Castle in Scotland and
we're doing a tour of Europe and your father told me you
were going to be in Paris playing. And we think this is just
great we found you here. That's fantastic. Now I'd like you
to meet my wife, Mary Ann, and my son here, George, and
my other little daughter, Janie."

I'm shaking hands with all of them, "It's great to meet
you."

"Vite, vite," the policeman was impatiently gesturing
that we should go.

I said, "It's terribly nice to meet you, but I've just been
arrested. Excuse me, I've got to go."

Whereupon this guy's jaw dropped open. He did say,
"Can I help you? Can I do anything?"

And I said, "No, don't worry."

I didn't retire, but I did move on. I had another amusing
encounter in Rotterdam when I was playing and suddenly
felt this hard poke in the back. Quite hard. I stopped and
looked round. A little old woman was prodding me with
her walking stick saying, "The Lord God said men should
wear trousers and women should wear a skirt. And you're
a man and you're wearing a skirt and you're sinning."

She was a Dutch Reformed Church fanatic—absolutely
off her rocker. I wasn't in any danger since she was pretty
ancient.

"I'm terribly sorry," I said, "but I don't seem to recall
that Jesus Christ wore trousers."

"Aawhhh, you're just making fun of the Lord.
Aawwh. . ." she went and started poking me again.

I still enjoy playing my pipes for whatever ears might
be listening, but I haven't put the box out recently. Still, you
never know—given the current economy.

22. A Summer Job

Don Brunson

I worked on the oil rigs in the Gulf of Mexico for a couple of summers during college and also over one Christmas holiday.

This oil rig in the Gulf of Mexico had a pretty hardened crew, including ex-criminals and others who were really rough, rough people. Under our Christmas tree on the rig was just one present for the whole crew. We had no idea what it was. So we all woke up that Christmas morning and opened up our present—a hula hoop. All that day, each of these tough men would take a turn doing the hula hoop there in the little dining room.

Norman Lear

When I was thirteen, we lived in New York for a year and a half or so. That summer, I had three jobs on Coney Island, two of them barking. I sat with a megaphone in one of those telephone-booth-like structures and angled my head six different ways: "Hey, hey, you want to be in pictures? Six for a nickel, five cents! The only place on the island!"

For two summers I got a job driving a Good Humor truck. I used to check out at seven in the morning, which meant I had to get up by five. In those years, Good Humor trucks used to park and cars used to drive by.

That first summer my father was ill, and I supported the family. I made over $100 a week; not bad for an eighteen-hour day.

Buck Johnson

We gathered pine burrs, pine cones, for seed and sold them for a dollar a bushel. I started when I was about fifteen.

You picked the cones in September when they were ripe by climbing the tree and knocking them off with a stick. Not long after picking, they would release their seeds. We used to float them in motor oil to see if they were ready to take to the drying kiln to finish opening up. If you got them too green, it was like picking fruit before it was ready.

I climbed those pine trees for several years. In fact, every September now I want to go climb a pine tree. The first year I was in the business, I made $18,000, and back in 1956, that was a lot. That was just before the pine cone warehouse burned, and we went out of the pine cone business.

Helen Barbour

In my late teens I used to go up with a friend who lived on a lovely estate in Aberdeenshire to earn some pocket money on the holidays as a beater for the hunts. The head beater organized the team of thirty or so men, women, and young boys and just added us. We'd go off on one side of the hill, the guns were on the other side, and as we walked up through the trees and heather, they'd shoot whatever grouse we managed to flush.

We'd earn pocket money, about a couple of pounds a day.

Alastair Barbour

I also worked as a beater at first, for ten shillings, fifty pence a day. Later I earned thirty shillings a day as a loader. Loaders stand in the butt with the shooter and load his gun for him. He'd have two guns, and you'd load one while he was using the other. You'd basically chaperon him around the hill.

Kathy Bater Brackett

When the steamer came into Catalina from the mainland, the docking always took twenty minutes or longer. As it was docking, there wasn't anything for the four hundred or so tourists to do except stand on deck waiting to get off. So as kids, we would all swim out and line up in the water the length of the ship. Then we'd scream, "Throw a coin." And they'd toss these coins in the water, and we'd dive down for them.

The water near the fantail was probably about thirty feet deep. It was the greatest job in the world because you could go whenever you wanted. You'd be on the beach and you'd think, Gee I'd really like to have a hamburger but I don't have any money. Hey, the steamer's coming in at noon, let's go!

You could make good money—literally as much as you could hold in your cheeks. And you could hold quite a bit. Not five dollars, but enough. A hamburger then was thirty-five cents; a *really* good one was fifty cents.

On average there'd be a dozen kids. We all had our spots. There was a real hierarchy. The younger kids were in the shallower water, and the older kids were out in the deeper water. The deeper water was by the fantail lounge where all the drunks were and they threw more money. We small kids were in the shallow end not because they were looking out for us but because there wasn't much money at the bow of the boat. As you progressed within the diving community you got a new, more lucrative spot. You just went to the new spot, and if you were strong enough to hold it, you stayed there. The steamer pier's gone now.

Jane Burke

I worked at a wedding shop dying shoes, making rice bags, and printing napkins—one at a time on a little hand press. Sometimes I got to sugar the grapes for the groom's cake. Intellectually stimulating.

I worked at Allmart as a cashier on a ninety-nine-key register—I could fly on that thing. At Christmastime the lines would meet in the middle of this huge store, but I was, I'll have you know, cashier of the month for three months running, including December. I got a little plastic rose to wear that said Cashier of the Month. It *was* a thrill.

Those were probably the two worst jobs except for the one at Sears. I opened a new Sears in Knoxville in the lingerie department. We were told we'd have permanent jobs, but, no, we were really just hired to open the store. For two weeks solid, I ironed slips. That's all I did. The store opened, they kept me on for two more weeks showing little elderly women how to try on brassieres—like they hadn't been doing it for sixty years. That was exciting, and then I was laid off.

James Royce

I worked all the time, but when I was sixteen, I started my own lawn-maintenance company and eventually had a pool of 178 lawns. At that point, I had four full-time employees working for me. Then I sold the business to a friend and for the next six months made a commission on all the lawns *he* cut.

Deni McIntyre

When I was twelve I decided that contact lenses would make all the difference in how I felt about myself. My parents said, "OK, get them, but you have to earn the money yourself." At the time contacts were more expensive than eyeglasses. My allowance was not going to be enough.

A Polish couple across the street, however, needed someone to care for their preschool son, Denes. They both worked as chemists, and their nanny had quit. So though I was only twelve, I got this kind of grown-up job staying with Denes for the summer.

I would go over every day at 7:30 to make breakfast. And every day it was the same thing—bacon fried to exactly the same degree and put on these little squares of bread with the crusts cut off. I was also fascinated by the exotic things in their refrigerator: marzipan and quinine and other stuff my family didn't have.

At the end of the summer I had saved around four hundred dollars and went and got contact lenses, which I then couldn't wear because my eyes could never get used to them. It was a big disappointment.

Richard Duke

I was an apprentice engineer one summer at a Union Carbide plant that made titanium. In one particular process they put limestone in the top of a several-story kiln, heated it, and removed what they wanted from the bottom. But what was coming out of the bottom had too much sulphur in it. My summer project was to find out where that sulphur came from.

Was it in the stuff put in the top? Did it somehow come out of the gas burned to heat the kiln? Was it some other factor?

I scampered around on top of boxcars to take samples of the stone waiting to be dumped into the kiln. I fashioned six-foot-long spoons to take it out of the bottom, the second story, and the third story of the kiln. Back in a makeshift lab I used my freshman-level chemistry to examine all these samples. I never figured out where the sulphur came from. They never figured it out either.

But I was an engineer. And I had a hard hat. A gray hard hat—that was significant. The whole place was color coded. The gray hat meant I was a salaried employee, not an hourly worker. On summer afternoons a number of employees might be sitting between cars having a nice long afternoon break when they should have been working. That was not something that a salaried person was supposed to see. So when a gray hat appeared, even if it was on a college sophomore who didn't know what he was doing, all sorts of people jumped up and pretended to work. The effect of my gray hat bobbing about was amusing.

Tommy Sammons

In addition to delivering newspapers—I'd deliver eighty copies of the *Atlanta Journal* before school—I worked as a desk clerk at the John C. Coleman Hotel, the only two-story hotel between Savannah and Macon. They had a rathskeller and served wonderful meals. A lot of the Yankees who came down for the great quail hunting would eat there.

There were immense quail preserves on the John C. Coleman estate, which was an original land grant and reached all the way into South Carolina. Nobody here owned any property; you rented your house from the Colemans. And they didn't want to sell. When Reid Watson's daddy sold his big pecan orchard, that was the first time people were buying.

Joy Melton Prickett

I rang up hamburgers at Six Flags over Georgia. When I picked up my till from the cashier's pool every morning—it was only a couple of hundred dollars—I felt the weight of the world on my shoulders until I got that money to the shop.

I used to play games—got pretty good at it, too. I'd try to guess what people in line would be eating by how they looked. For instance, a clean-cut yuppie type always had a cheeseburger and milk; rarely fries. I enjoyed watching people—funny things would happen, but to keep from hurting anybody's feelings my standard trick was to drop some change and duck under the cash register until I regained my composure.

To keep from losing their money on the rides, kids would put their dollar bills in their shoes. They'd come in—all too often from the log flumes—and fish this wet dollar bill out of a soggy tennis shoe to pay.

The cash register was big enough to have a pocket for every currency amount, including half dollars. Since we didn't use half dollars, I kept that pocket full of Sugar Babies or some other snack. I enjoyed that job. I was sixteen.

Robert Abrams

The summer before I went to college I worked at Price Brothers making up heavy-duty steel water pipe. I would put the rings on and then weld it. I had two sixteen-pound hammers and I beat them all day. I was only the third person able to do that job. I rode my bicycle about five miles to work and then after work I'd bike another five over to Carolyn's house to see about her—she was sick with anemia that summer—and then I'd bike the ten miles home. I was crazy.

Zar Rochelle

I worked at the Myrtle Desk Company two summers on a glue reel, veneering desks. The job was not a lot of fun, but I got to know a group of people who had different lives and values than mine. So that was interesting. Compared to my opportunities their lives seemed more limited. High Point was all they knew and all they seemed to want to know. It was their new watch and their new Chevy. They played ball on Saturday or maybe went bowling once a week and watched television. It was sort of sad. Religion came up once and, just for shock value, I told them I was an atheist. There were people who would not get near me because they thought they were in physical danger, that something horrible was going to happen to me.

Will McIntyre

My Uncle John, who ran the general store right across from our house, had a pretty-good-size tobacco farm. And I really wanted to work.

Finally, when I was about eight, my mom said, "OK, it's time you learned how to work in tobacco," and, using grape leaves off our backyard grapevine, she began to teach me how to hand tobacco leaves out of a tobacco truck to a looper, who ties them to the drying sticks. After a bit, I felt like I was fully trained and ready to go to work.

The first day, they put me at what they called the "house," the scaffold, with all the women. The men were out at the fields, see, where an eight-year-old boy doesn't have a place. Right away the women were making fun of me because I was handling tobacco leaves, which are huge, like they were grape leaves, which are small. You'd think you couldn't screw up handing a leaf to a looper, but it was a real mess. Anyhow, I got where I could do that pretty well, but I still wanted to go out to the field and drive the tractor.

I finally prevailed upon my uncle and the people who were actually running the farm to let me drive a tractor. I got to drive only in the field, only in a straight row. At the end of a row, one of the adults would come and turn the tractor into another row. So all I did was drive it up and down the field. You really can't mess that up. I'm still good at that. I'm an excellent straight driver.

And one day, toward the end of the day, the boss man was out there in the field. His name was John Henry Thigpen. Isn't that a wonderful name? He lived in the house right there at the field we were working in. And he had to go back into the barn. So he said, "William Bill, would you like to drive the tractor?"

"Oh, yes."

So I drove the tractor and John Henry stood on the back. It was extremely dangerous but, hey, we were in the country. We didn't care. We didn't know it was dangerous at the time because everybody did it.

Well, on the left as we came out of the tobacco field was John Henry's back porch. On the right was John Henry's garden, which had already begun to flower and produce. And right in between the two there was a crate of soft drink bottles.

Now I knew that you should not run over the soft drink bottles because you would cut the tires on the tractor. And I knew that you shouldn't run over the garden because people worked hard to plant that garden and the garden was flowering and you wouldn't want to mess it up. So I got over near the house.

As I got nearer to the house, I was looking to my right and I saw that I avoided the soft drink bottles and I avoided the garden, of course, but I started hearing this noise. It sounded like planks being pulled up. I looked over on the left to see a washing machine come flying through the air, one of those old handcrank washing machines. Water was spilling out of it and it was coming off the porch.

As I drove along the boards were going up and down like piano keys. All these things were flying up, the boards, the washing machine and everything. And John Henry was on the back. And John Henry had not said a word. Finally after I had enough sense to figure out that I'd hit the porch with the tractor, I pushed in the clutch and mashed the brake and stopped.

By this time, though, I'd already run through John Henry's entire porch. And John Henry was still on the back of the tractor. I cut the tractor off. A whole crowd had gathered. John Henry had still not said a word, and I was just frightened to death. Then as I turned around, he said this wonderful thing: "Well, I needed a new porch anyhow."

23. If I Say Money, What Comes to Mind?

Win Rockefeller

Money's like a hammer or a screwdriver or a fishing rod: it's a tool. The first time I heard that, I looked at the person and said, "That's crazy." But fundamentally it is just one more tool, one more implement, one more resource.

Dave DeGrandpre

Opportunity. I don't think I'm going to make a lot of money in life, though in a way I'd like to. If you have a lot of money you can have a lot of opportunities. But it seems more important for me to put a lot of time into more valuable pursuits.

Foxy Callwood

I think of fruit trees. I think, well I could get some more money to clear land and plant fruit trees or make pasture. I would get into that, not raise condominiums. I like to see the seedlings rise.

Gerry Cooney

I worked hard for what I did. Money's not happiness to me. Money is money. If I had my way, I'd have a little farmhouse someplace and be happy with family and people I love. Then I'd be really rich.

John Jaxbiemer

My job, because that's the only reason I do it.

Jonathan Peter

A big problem for me. I have never been able to get a grip on money. Never been able to make a lot of it. I have always been able to live, of course, but money's just a puzzlement. Money is a real struggle.

Rose Wing

How much things have changed. When I started teaching during the Depression, I made $900 the first year of teaching. Then they gave me a $5-a-month raise—$45 for the year, which was big money. It was also cash. At that time a lot of teachers in other districts were being paid in scrip. But I never had to put up with that.

Wednesday Bridge Club

Mildred Sutton: It reminds me of how much money it takes to go such a little distance—how much it costs to live today.

Murial Sichveland: I think the main concern older people have about finances is that you want to be able to live independently and not be dependent on anybody. One of my children keeps telling me, "Mother don't worry about a thing. I can take care of you, I can do anything you need, just don't even think about money." But I'd hate that, I wouldn't want him doling out his money to me under any circumstances.

Mildred Sutton: When we were growing up, we would have all thought if we had what we have to live on today that we would be rich. But it won't even start.

Murial Sichveland: There's been such tremendous change since the thirties. Young people can't imagine how different life is.

Mildred Sutton: When I first taught school, I taught eight months and I made $50 a month. That's a poor day's wage now.

Peggy Kemp: I think we have a fear now, looking back at what happened in the Depression when fortunes and people's money were suddenly just gone. That's what worries us now—that something like that could happen again when we've saved and struggled. What would we do now?

Mildred Sutton, Supper Club
The sincere wish that if I ever get to heaven, I hope I don't have to keep a checkbook.

24. Standing Tall on the Coca-Cola Crates: A Portrait

Princess Pamela Mary Elizabeth Martha Strobel

I was thirteen when Mama and Grandmama were dead, so I decided to go on my own up north—about 125 miles to Winston-Salem. That was certainly North to me. I rode a bus and had three pigtails, my mother's suitcase and diamond watch, and a big white bow in my hair, but I didn't even have a place to stay. So I asked a man on the bus where the colored section was, and he sent me to the worst part of Winston-Salem.

I saw a lady walk by when I got out of the cab. Her name was Maude, and the first thing she asked me was, "Did you run away?"

I said, "No, ma'am." And I kept asking her if she had a room to rent. Finally that lady said she had a mother-in-law in a wheelchair about a block away. "Maybe you can stay there, because she's holy and righteous," she said. And I did, and she was.

Early mornings, I'd go look for work right there by the R. J. Reynolds tobacco plant. You had a lot of little restaurants around there because of those thousands of people. Well, there was this little place on the corner, where a lady had already said I was too young. So, I decided to go see her at home when she was sick.

"You're too young, honey, what can you cook?" she said.

I wanted that job so bad! So I said, "Well, *who* is gonna cook the food for lunch?"

Pretty soon, she'd sent me to the restaurant to help the salad lady. When I got there, I saw this high sink was filled with dishes, and I couldn't even reach the sink! So I looked out back, and there were some Coca-Cola crates, and I kept piling them up until I could reach the sink.

I washed those dishes, and after that, I took the chops out of the icebox, and I made chops and I made steaks. You know how you take the steak and flatten it out and then fry them off and then make gravy? You talk about something good.

I even started making the slaw my own way that day, and pretty soon the salad lady made it that way. When I started there, I couldn't even lift the frying pan down without someone helping me!

That was the beginning of what I'm doing now. I learned a lot from Mrs. Smith, and I loved her. The only day I wouldn't go work there was Sunday, but I'd go anyway and sit with her in that little restaurant because that luncheonette was her life.

I think I learned how to cook the best food in the world between Mrs. Smith and my grandmama, and I'm trying to keep my place what our food is about. I try to keep the music that goes with our food, the jazz. I have to pay for the musicians out of the chicken money, and it's hard. And I sing hard. But I'm from staunch stock, and don't you forget it.

25. *Finding Work*

George Plimpton

I wrote for the school newspaper at Phillips Exeter Academy. When I was on probation for misdeeds or fluctuating marks, I had to use a pseudonym. V-A-G-U-E was my byline. That was one of my nicknames because I never seemed to be listening.

One fall day I went out for a walk alone and got lost in a deep wood, the kind that stretches up to the Canadian border and beyond, really quite spooky. I finally walked out hours later and made it back to my dormitory about eleven o'clock at night. I wrote a poem about the incident that I sent in to the undergraduate literary magazine, the *Exeter Monthly*. Gore Vidal was one of the senior editors, and he thought it was quite promising. But he was voted down by the rest of the board. They said it was juvenile and sensationalistic, I don't know what. A long prose poem, simply the babbling of a youngster who had gone through a traumatic experience in the woods. It was a start. I remember Gore telling me years later he'd recognized my "talent" even at that age.

John Emmerling

I earn my living as a professional idea man. I think of ideas, of advertising; I wrote a book about ideas. But at sixteen I thought that I would be an automotive engineer because most of my friends wanted to be automotive engineers. Then I decided I would like being an architect. I knew I was talented graphically but I had no sense of creating ideas. I enrolled in the architectural school at the University of Michigan. In my spare time I had discovered *The New Yorker* magazine and begun to read it religiously. I was absolutely enamored of the cartoonists—Charles

Addams in particular. So one night during my freshman year, after I finished my homework, I started to try to think up gag cartoons. I thought of four or five and sketched them out.

I thought they were pretty good, so I did a two-page questionnaire and naively sent it off with a SASE to the twenty top *New Yorker* cartoonists. I asked them such questions as How do you think of ideas? How much do you get paid? Do you think you will ever run out of ideas? I got about ten responses back and that encouraged me further. Out of the very first batch of cartoons that I sent off to *The New Yorker*, they held one for further consideration. I moved on to doing greeting card gag lines and selling them. After about six months, I said I can think of ideas and I can sell them. This eighteen-year-old kid who was thinking about ideas and selling them was such a different person from the sixteen-year-old kid who thought he was going to be an automotive engineer. Knowing I could sit down at a desk, think of something, represent it on paper, put it in an envelope and get a check back was a watershed moment in my life.

Stephanie Beacham

I suppose the ability of imagination is my God-given talent, which means that I could have been a writer, a successful advertising person, or a storyteller in ancient times. But I became an actress. Some of the instances that made me become an actress were not obvious. What I'm trying to say is so often we choose in opposition.

First, there's my deafness. That fact says, well, maybe you shouldn't be an actress, so that's the very reason one says subconsciously, I am going to do it. As a child I didn't realize I was deaf until one day when I was taken to this specialist who said to my mother, "She's unilaterally deaf but she's not stupid, she's not retarded." And I said to Mummy, "What is tarded?" She said, "*Re*tarded, darling. It means you're not stupid." I therefore had this fear that if I ever said I was deaf, people would think I was stupid and that has stayed with me forever. Since it's just one ear, it doesn't show but it has tremendous effect. That fear, of course, caused me to push myself further than I might as a child.

Then I remember at the age of four—so many things happen at four—because I was the smallest kid in school, I had to carry a huge bouquet the same size as myself up on stage, give it to this visiting reverend mother, and say, *"Au revoir, bon voyage."* (It was a French-speaking convent.) Now that speech is not very long, but for a child who has learned very little French, *au revoir, bon voyage* is the canon of Shakespeare. So I got up these enormous stairs with this enormous bouquet and looked at these rows and rows and rows of black-dressed nuns and couldn't remember what it was I was meant to say. That's probably why I'm an actress— compensation for early failure.

But my first acting? A school play. They were going to do *Electra*, Sophocles. I wasn't in the drama society, but they said, "Do you want to be in the school play?"

And I said, "Yeah, sure, why not," though I knew nothing about acting. At the time I was ballet mad.

"We want you to play Chrysothemis."

"Hang on," I said. "What's the name of the play?"

"Electra."

"Well, either I play Electra or I don't think I'll bother," I said. I played Electra.

And walking on stage that first time before an audience was total. Even then, I still planned to teach mime to deaf children. But I found mime, which I studied in Paris, a very dry subject. A chance acquaintance of one of the founding members then led me to the Liverpool Everyman, a very idealistic young theater company. I'd gone to the Royal Ballet often, and to the English pantomime with my parents, but I don't remember going to the theater ever. I saw a production and I smelt that theater and I thought, this is theater! It seemed the most wonderful thing ever.

I auditioned and got in as stage management. I was fired from stage management within twenty-four hours for being a distraction and was put onto wardrobe. I was locked away in the wardrobe and only let out to play the juvenile lead. Then I went to the Royal Academy of Dramatic Arts after that. So I fell into acting.

Torre Andrews

My dad had a house on stilts on a steep hillside in Laguna Beach, and he had tied a rope underneath the balcony on which we would swing. I was always wild, pushing limits, swinging way out. I finally fell, breaking my femur. I wound up in traction in the hospital for six weeks and then in a body cast. That's when I decided I wanted to be a doctor.

Although my dad was a doctor, that never meant anything to me. But in the hospital I saw what doctors did for the first time. Everybody knew my dad and I got a lot of attention. Plus I thought what doctors did was really interesting. As I lay in bed for six weeks, I learned the names of a bunch of bones from the Time-Life *Child's Book of Health* or some such. Though being tied to a bed for six weeks was very frustrating, it was an important experience, and it probably changed the course of my life.

Myrtis Brown

At last count I have nursed 460 babies. All I have wanted to do is love people and help people. And that's what I have done all my life. And I still love it and want to go where I'm needed. A person up on their feet can do for themselves, they don't need me in their door all the time. I have had lots of wonderful experiences. One earlier time comes to mind.

Things in the forties were real tight. I had been doing baby nursing. I had two boys, but my husband had left; he wasn't ready for a family. So my mother took care of my boys and I answered an ad out of the *Atlanta Constitution* and went to Chicago.

I didn't know where I was going. When the train got almost into Chicago, they commenced to calling, "We're entering into Dearborn Station, Chicago." I said, "Oh, Lord, here I am in a big place and don't know where I am." You know how a country girl is.

So I got there, and as I went up the steps into the station, the Lord pictured it out to me, and I walked up to this lady and said, "Would this be Mrs. Wolf?"

She said, "Yes. This is Myrtis? You're so pretty. You aren't what I was looking for."

I said, "Well, thank you."

So I stayed with the Wolfs for nine years. My main responsibility was to cook and care for the youngest child, Joanie, who I'd noticed limped badly. But they hadn't told me what was wrong and I didn't want to ask. So I worked it to go to the doctor with them, and I asked him. He said, "Polio."

I said, "I've had a little experience working with that in Greensboro."

He said, "What experience have you had?" I told him how I exercised a child's leg in warm water to keep the muscles from drawing up. And he said, "Well, thank God, we've got what we need then with you."

I took care of Joanie, I did the cooking, I would pay the bills, go to the market, and I said, "I am just as green as I want to be, but, Lord, teach me how to go about these things." And he did. I would go to the kosher market for the meat. I learned to cook their way and enjoyed it. After a while, I was able to bring Thomas and David up.

And Joanie's leg started straightening up, and she didn't have any more symptoms. That's also where I learned to play golf. On Thursdays to exercise her leg, we'd play golf and I'd caddy for the child. It was a happy thing for me to do with the Wolf family.

We went back home after nine years when my mother got sick. She had "sugar" so bad that she had to have one leg amputated. I took care of her and began baby nursing in Atlanta again to pay the bills.

Barbara Bailey

I was into the evangelical thing, you see? And I decided to be a missionary. I thought medical missionaries were much more useful than ordinary missionaries. An arrogant thought, really. But by the time I met my husband Robert I didn't want to be a missionary at all. I've been a doctor for forty years.

Will McIntyre

How did I come to photography? I actually started out as a writer. I wanted to be a sportswriter. No. The truth is I wanted to be a big-league baseball player. If you said chuck everything and be a big-league ballplayer today, I'd be in that line. I still like to think that if my eyes had not gone bad, I might be in the Hall of Fame by now. But if I couldn't hit a fastball, I decided I'd write about it.

And in high school, I had a good turn as a sportswriter on a little weekly paper. Then one day the guy who normally shot pictures couldn't make it to the ball game. So the editor of the paper came in and said, "You're going to have to shoot your own pictures tonight."

I said, "I've never shot pictures before. I don't know how to do this."

"Well, hell, you've got two hours. You can learn." And she threw me the camera and a book. I read and I shot pictures. I found I liked shooting pictures. So I started doing more and more of that and less and less writing. So by the time I went to college I had a bunch of photographs. Since I liked it, I kept on doing it.

Deni McIntyre

Will has a great theory that you end up doing something that not only appeals to you on the positive side but is an area where you can tolerate the downside.

For instance, you say, oh, teaching, now there would be a worthy profession. I once thought I would end up in academia. Wouldn't it be great, I thought, to inspire others to think or to appreciate literature or to create? And then the more I got to see of the downside of academia—the publish or perish, the committee meetings, the politics—the less appealing it was.

I came to photography from writing because we always thought that it would be really great to be a writer/photographer team until we discovered that the world isn't organized that way. Unfortunately the places that used the kind of writing that I wanted to do didn't seem to use photography, or if they did, used bad photography or used it badly. We found also that magazines rarely sent writers out with photographers.

Plus the rhythms were all wrong, we discovered. One of our first jobs as a writer/photographer team was to do a story on Philippe de Rothschilde during the grape harvest in Bordeaux.

We spent about a week on the Rothschilde estate during the harvest, interviewing and immersing ourselves in everything that was happening. And the problem was that just when I wanted to be a fly on the wall and record a scene in my mind the way it was, it wasn't that way anymore because Will would be in amongst it with his cameras, changing it. It's like you want to spectate at the pool and your companion keeps throwing little pebbles. You don't know how it would have been.

So our work together has evolved. Will and I do different kinds of photography, which makes our team more versatile. He doesn't have much patience with detail but can grab things on the fly. I like to go into situations that seem to have no visual potential and bring together things that seem meaningful and make a photograph.

I thoroughly enjoy what I'm doing, but I really always thought I'd be knocked off my horse on the way to Damascus. And in a way I'm still waiting.

Edward Colquhoun

One spring my high school biology teacher said, "Would you like a job in a hospital?" And I said, "Yes."

So I worked in the operating room for four summers at the county medical center. Since my best friend's father was the head of the psychiatric unit, I would go over and help out with electric shock therapy. I would sit in on consults with patients, or I would stay in the emergency room for hours. That was a real growing-up experience. Later I combined my liberal arts education—my major was English—with that practical experience when I went into science and medical writing. That is exactly where my career comes from: one of those lucky crossings.

John Emery

At Walt Disney World I danced in the bicentennial parade for over a year. I was a repairman, part of the electrical inventions section.

An iron, a telephone, a gramophone, and the handy repairman made up that section, and I usually danced next to the iron. I danced for a living, but it really was crazy: seventeen bosses out of sixty employees and the heat. We lost several each day to heat prostration or muddled management. I don't recommend dancing as an appliance or even as a repairman.

John Englander

I first came to the Underwater Explorer's Society, UNEXSO, in 1968 to take an instructor's diving course. My parents had given me the course as a high school graduation present. When I graduated from college in 1972, I moved down to the Bahamas to work for UNEXSO as a dive instructor. They also gave me some managerial things to do.

The company, however, was really struggling. By '73 or '74 they were ready to close the doors. Freeport was doing poorly after Bahamian independence and the U.S. was in a recession. Everybody that could give me advice said, "Leave."

But it seemed like an opportunity to me. The place had such a mystique and obvious potential. The diving here was good. The proximity to the U.S. was great. It was a special structure. I just couldn't walk away from it and let it crumble back into the earth. It seemed worth the wait to see if we couldn't learn from the mistakes and do it right.

So I just hung in there; I was tenacious. I didn't know any better. I could read financial statements and I could conceptualize and plan and write, but I did not have a wealth of business experience. It was very tough for a long time. We existed day to day for a while; we had to take in money to pay out. At one point our water was cut off because the hotel next door was closed and our water had come through them. We got down to three or four employees and no idea how to pay them. That was *really* difficult.

But I just had this calm, this confidence that somehow we were going to work this out. We didn't have money, but we did have a methodical plan. I had pages of yellow pad notes laying out how we were going to get from where we were to where we wanted to be. And I kept rewriting those scenarios and plans and staying calm no matter how great the crisis.

UNEXSO's success is a great satisfaction now. I taught scuba diving in college and ran a summer business teaching scuba on Martha's Vineyard. But this has been my only "real" job.

Virginia Kahl

Years ago I worked in Austria as an army librarian. It seemed as if you couldn't not write there because it was such a fairy tale country or a comic opera. So I thought, I guess I could try writing a book. And I did. I used school paints to do some illustrations and sent it off.

I had everything wrong. I sent it to one publisher and got it back the next day—it was too long, had too many colors, etc. But then I got a very nice letter back from a Scribner's editor saying, "If you could write a thirty-two-page book illustrated in no more than four colors, we'd be interested. Too bad you're not here where we could work on it."

Well, I had a year left in Austria, so I worked on it and came home with this book about a dog that pulled a milk wagon. I took it in to the editor and she laughed and said, "Sorry I don't have my glasses." That seemed to be a gimmick to avoid giving me an answer. But she asked me to lunch the next day and said she'd take it. That was *Away Went Wolfgang*, the first of sixteen books for Scribner's.

Mary Lou Retton

I have a lot of respect for my parents, because they sacrificed a lot to raise us five kids, and growing up in a big family is a lot of fun. But being the youngest really isn't a lot of fun sometimes because you have to fight for your independence, you have to fight to show them that hey, *I* can do it, too! Just because I'm the youngest, don't forget about me. I really feel that's where I get some of my competitive spirit.

But being athletic and competitive was in our blood, too. Our folks didn't teach us, it was natural. I was at a baseball diamond or on a basketball court or football field more than I was anywhere.

John Marston

I spent last summer in Alaska fishing on all kinds of boats. I was a boat gypsy. Going to Alaska was a catharsis. It was breaking out of what society expects from a young college grad with the looks and the savvy and the contacts. I was on the fast track at Disney, then I was the general manager of a graphics company, and I wasn't happy. My way wasn't working; I needed to try a different way. So I said to hell with it—I'm going to go and see how people do it up north. I can make it with $100 in my pocket and the shirt on my back. It was kind of a personal vendetta, too—against the system, against my family—you watch and I'll show you!

So a buddy and I took off for Alaska and ended up in Petersburg, a little town of 3,000 people, a totally different world.

My first job was pitching halibut out of boats. For twenty-four hours I pitched slimy fish, probably 100,000 pounds, out of a hole. You throw them into a net, and the net is lifted by a crane. You tie the 300-pounders with a rope and lift them singly.

Later I worked on salmon boats, black cog boats, gill netters. For the most part you work constantly, as long as there's an opening, you're working. It's a real grind. After a while, the work's boring. But there were times up there when I'd never felt more peaceful or happy. So I'm going back.

26. Failing

Kurt Vonnegut

Failing is part of the job. I've got a wastebasket and I disappoint myself again and again and again.

Taylor Plimpton

It seems to me that it's all right to fail other people's goals, because that's not what matters. It matters because that's what grades are, but if you fail yourself in any sort of way, it hurts a lot more, I think. So I'm much more scared of that than I am of failing a course.

George Plimpton

I was very poor at exams, almost invariably because I rarely studied for them, or at least sufficiently. My senior year at Harvard I took a geography course to fulfill a science requirement, Geography 103, the geography of South America—a small class of fifteen or so. It was reputed to be very easy—a gut course in the parlance of the day—largely because the final examination was invariably (so I had been told) based on a reading list of a dozen books. Because of this I rarely, if ever, went to class that spring—relying entirely on the assumption that I would be able to pass the final exam by reading the required books. So I read the books, quite carefully, and sure enough, the questions on the exam focused on them. I wrote at length and with a kind of smug satisfaction that I had pulled it off. But then to my horror the self-addressed card I'd inserted into my paper for my mark came back with an E on it, in fact an E−, which meant among other things that I didn't have the sufficient science requirements to graduate that spring. So I hurried up to see the professor—his name was Whittlesly, as I recall—to find out why I'd failed despite my formidable work on the exam. I said to him, "I thought I wrote a good exam."

He looked at me (I was standing opposite his desk) and asked this awful question: "Have I ever seen you before?"

I didn't really know how to answer him because, in essence—considering the few times I'd been to the class—it was a perfectly pertinent question!

"I hope you understand," he went on, "that I cannot give a passing grade to someone I've never seen before." He was quite agitated.

So that was it. I came back that summer and took a course in anthropology to get my science requirement. It wasn't what I expected to do that summer, but it was all right because I passed the anthropology course with a gentleman's C+ and fell in love.

Michael Bornn

Statistics. At Georgetown, it was one course that baffled the life out of me. I eventually passed it, but, boy, until that final exam I wasn't doing too well. For some reason, statistics just kicked my butt.

Zar Rochelle

I failed Family Living once in high school. My teacher got real frustrated with me because in class discussions I would suggest that children should be boiled in oil or put in boxes until they were twelve. No, I did not take Family Living all that seriously. So my tendency to be rather sarcastic earned me an F for one six-week period. Then I lightened up a little bit and passed.

Mildred Sutton

Languages aren't my strong suit. After everyone in my class had long since passed French in college, I was still struggling. If I didn't fail it, I came so close that I decided right then that I'd have to get a B.S. degree rather than an A.B. because I'd never pass the language requirement. That's the truth.

Gerry Cooney

The toughest failure I had was when I lost to Larry Holmes, I think, because I really did not like him as a man. A lot of racism was brought up in that, too. It turns out Don King was doing that. But when I went into the fight, I didn't care if I won or lost—so I thought. All I wanted to do was hit him, give him a nice whack. I wanted to kick his ass.

After that fight, it took me a good year and a half to get moving again. Holmes and I get along now.

Nan Thomas

I guess you could consider divorce failing.

Norman Lear

I'd like to have been a better husband. I'd like to have been a better father. I think I've been adequate to those tasks, but I could have been better.

John Marston

I try to take the attitude that there's no such thing as failing. The scientific view point, for instance, is that there are no good versus bad test results. Everything is just a result. Actions have consequences. To say that I'm failing in something is a very negative way of looking at things. I would rather think of it as one other way not to build a light, one other way not to treat someone. Until I find the right way, I'm always searching—never failing.

Jock Munro

I've written at the top of my diary, "If you treat catastrophes as mere incidents and certainly never treat an incident as a catastrophe, you can get through life."

Sonya Friedman

Everyone fails at certain things, but it doesn't mean you're a failure. I think that's a lesson in maturity which takes most of us a long time to learn. If you don't fail, you don't live.

27. Art with and without Merit

Marla Hanson

I don't know if there is art without merit. I think if somebody takes the energy and time to put down his or her perceptions of the world, there is merit in it even if the presentation is shallow.

John Marston

Art with merit is like business ethics—there is no such thing. Art is anything you can get away with. Everybody wants to promote his or her own morality or idea through art.

Art to me is not so much an end in itself as a process. The merit is in the act of creating it.

George Plimpton

Art with merit is almost impossible to define, but I would guess it is something that moves you though you may not quite know why. For example, a great photographer can take a picture of a street you know well and yet tell you something you never knew about that street.

Phoebe Legere

Merit is to me an adherence to certain principles of intelligence. Art with merit would show a conscience, reflect high ideals and high moral principles.

I don't like to think too much about art without merit. I'm exposed to a lot of it every time I go to the store or to the drugstore. I hear a lot of it being played on the radio. I watch television as little as possible, maybe once or twice a year so I won't be exposed to art without merit.

Art without merit is created basically to sell a product, to make people feel bad about themselves so they will have to go out and buy products to fix themselves. For instance, fashion magazines are really art without merit because they are designed to make women feel ugly and unsexy.

Now, fashion is art, and photography is art, but fashion advertising is an art designed to make you feel incomplete so you will go out and spend money on clothes.

Art without merit is art without compassion.

Richard Duke

There's a woman I read of just lately who built a balloon filled with something like 10,000 liters of air that was to represent the amount that would be breathed by a person during the time required to read *Anna Karenina*, or some such. She displayed this in a gallery as her homage to Tolstoy. I'm not making this up!

It says something to her and to someone else, perhaps. To me it's without merit. Once the balloon is explained to you, of course, you could be led to think, well, yeah, that's a lot of air and that took a lot of time and this says something about such a large work, and so forth. But accessible? You have to go through a whole chain, be prompted at the start, given the explanation, go on through, and then come out with something. It's certainly far from something that one responds to on an emotional level. I've said that I don't particularly like cubism, for instance, but I react to something like Picasso's *Guernica* immediately. You need not know the history of the Spanish Civil War or the details of Franco to have a reaction to it rather quickly. That's different.

John Emmerling

I would say that art with merit is art that gives pleasure. If, say, a bus driver on holiday visits San Francisco and stops on Grant Avenue to buy a painting on black velvet of a child with big eyes that some hack in a back room knocked off in thirty-five minutes, then because that painting gives him pleasure, that is art with merit. However, for a fine arts elitist that same painting would almost certainly be art without merit.

David Prowse

I admire people's ability to see and then to be able to transpose what they see onto the canvas.

Kate Learson

Any art that is done with the intention to do something wonderful has merit. The artist could be a two-year-old child or a Rembrandt. We may not always understand what we see or hear, but the integrity of intention should come through. So many people who say they are artists are just technicians who are trying to capture the PR wave of something avant-garde; the work may be different, but the intention sometimes looks so shallow. So many people now, not only in painting and sculpture but in music and probably literature, seem to be producing cheap knockoffs and are into just promoting themselves.

28. *Village Life: A Portrait*
Paul Mockler

Until I moved to the village of Smith's Point, I had either been on the road for two-and-a-half years for the Canadian Broadcasting Corporation or in Toronto, and I was tired of travel and the big city. So I moved to Grand Bahama Island, left for a four-month expedition, and came back to find every single thing stolen. Even the mattress on the bed.

Disgusted, I went for a drive in my jeep and ended up right here in Smith's Point at the White Wave Club. Smith's Point has only ninety people and maybe sixteen structures, an easy place to meet people. So I grabbed a spear from the back of the jeep and went on a really successful spearfishing trip with some of the guys here in the village.

We came back, and as I was sitting at the bar, for the first time I really noticed this derelict, broken-down shack, about ten by fourteen feet. My closet in Toronto was bigger than that. But it was fifty sandy feet from the ocean and surrounded by other modest houses and shacks. Utterly simple. So I turned to Mama Flo, the matriarch of Smith's Point. I didn't know Mama well then but had met her at the White Wave Club because she owns it. She's a killer pool player even at eighty. So I asked her who owned the shack. Turns out she did.

"Mama Flo, I could make me a home there," I said without thinking.

"No, honey, it's a wreck."

"But I could fix it up."

Well, we walked over there, and it was indeed a wreck. The roof and floor were caved in; the shack was held up by two-and-a-half cement blocks and was all twisted out of shape. But it looked like an interesting project to me, so I rented it from Mama and became the only white man in Smith's Point. My first night there, I slept on the bare wooden floor and hooked up a hose and an extension cord at Mama Flo's to have water and electricity.

I have now seen a couple of generations of kids grow up in Smith's Point. For years they hung around my little porch just to watch me. They really had no idea how a white man lived, and I became their entertainment, a living movie. What does a white man do when he comes home? I'd have a date, and the kids would sit in my doorstep and just look at us. I'd melt lead for my diving weights in a pot on the porch, and they'd be amazed. Everything I did they thought was extraordinary, including eating cucumber sandwiches.

And do you know what? In twelve years, I've never locked a door and never had anything stolen. I've also made some of the best friends of my life, and I don't think any of them ever had shoes on.

29. Simple Things That Bring Pleasure

Nan Thomas

Simple things that bring pleasure? Believe it or not, the rats running around the kitchen. I don't know why. I'm not one to jump on chairs and scream and yell and tear my hair out over mice and things like that. But these things are as cute as can be, even though they're a nuisance. They're simple and I've learned to live with them. None are pets, but I don't jump when I see them. You can't keep them out on an island. And the lizards, too. But I'm terrified of snakes, which there are very few of around here. Thank God the lizards have feet because otherwise I wouldn't be here.

Hamilton Fish

I'm pleased by unexpected things because I'm not working to squeeze enjoyment from them. They just suddenly rear up.

Jock Munro

Once or twice a week, a good cigar in the evening. Rising at five on a weekend morning to go riding—just when the sun is rising and there's a bit of mist around. Curling up in a chair when the *Economist* arrives and reading it cover to cover—it really covers what's going on all over the planet.

Torre Andrews

Fixing things.

Kate Learson

I love holding the little babies I care for at the hospital and trying to make eye contact with a child who is withdrawing from methadone, cocaine, or whatever. When you do make eye contact and if, in fact, you ever get a smile out of little faces that are constantly frowning, what a moment that is. It's like two souls meeting each other for one little moment, and God knows when these kids are ever going to have that again.

These are boarder babies, babies the hospital has kept because they were born addicted or ill with AIDS, syphilis, TB, hepatitis B and have parents who are also addicted or ill and unable to care for them. The life ahead of them is dismal.

Dave DeGrandpre

Hugs. Aubrey and Erik have really brought that out in me, shown me it's OK.

John Marston

Dogs. I'm kind of a dog slut—any dog will bring me pleasure. I enjoy dogs that are just passing on the street.

Jerry Preston

Just being with any of my animals. For instance, I love my chickens. They're booted Bantams, rather fancy. Whenever I get rattled about anything, I go outside, pick one up, and talk to it. I don't tell them about my affinity for fried chicken, though.

I also like sitting under that giant oak in the backyard. It's huge, so big the city of Melbourne gave us a Grand Old Tree award. When I die, I want to be cremated and have my ashes spread around that tree so I can be absorbed by it, become part of it.

Zar Rochelle

Watching my goldfish swim.

Michael Bornn

When we were kids, our family would go right out here in this yard on Friday or Saturday afternoons and create a destination. My mother has worked with the UN and always been internationally oriented. So every weekend we'd travel to a different place—Mexico one week, Italy another. We'd have Italian food, for instance, Italian decorations, Italian maps, and so on.

Travel—mental and physical—was very much part of our growing up, and other than Australia and South America, I've traveled everywhere. They're in the future.

Joy Melton Prickett

Decorating the family Christmas tree. We hardly ever bought a tree. We'd find a nice tree on land Daddy was leasing to hunt, shape it up during the fall, then cut it down together. We even had a regular old pine tree once. It was beautiful. We'd make ornaments as a family project. Mom's and Dad's looked good, and then there are the ones my sister and I made. My mom still hangs all of them on the tree.

Peggy Sammons

I grin thinking about riding with Mother. Everyone said she had no sense of direction, but she loved to go to ride. So we'd just tear off down the road and not know where in heaven's name we were going. We'd get off on some road where she thought something used to happen or somebody used to live. We might end up in a sand hole. But we'd have the best time—and laugh and laugh.

Mildred Sutton

A call from the family.

Gerry Cooney

Hanging around with kids is the simplest pleasure because the kids are so innocent. There's no ulterior motive and it's just really basic love. And I like to work out, I like to boat, and I like to communicate with people. I like to go into different cultures and listen to them and see what makes them breathe. All that simple stuff that just kind of fills you up, you know.

Richard Duke

A good beer. A good book. Would you call a book a simple thing? That may not be fair.

To the author it's not a simple thing. After reading so many, I may treat them too lightly. But a book sprang to mind—perhaps it's simple in the sense that we have easy access to books. It is not hard for us to get a book, to find it and read it, to buy it or go to the library for it.

That may be overprecise—the effect of my mathematical background.

Jonathan Peter

I used to have a rule of four things that you wanted to have: good weather, good friends, good food and music, and something worthwhile to be doing. I've been down to where it's only good weather. But if you can get three of those, then you can stay with it until you feel the balance fall in place.

Timothy Sultan

The fall. My friend Chris says it only makes him think of death and decay, but it reminds me of long motorcycle rides in the fall on the innumerable dirt roads in rural Ohio—blue sky over yellowed and browned grasses, trees so red you'd think someone poured paint over them. Stopping to look at the cows and sitting on railroad trestles watching the water below; trying to make evening bats chase tossed rocks and sticks.

John Jaxhiemer

Girls.

Taylor Plimpton

Laughing.

Eric Jensen

My fishtank. That tank has gone through many developments! I developed a reef tank that was basically self-sustaining—its own little ecosystem. It even produced its own food. But I decided to change that because the water had to be perfectly balanced for the ecosystem to function, and that took a lot of time and money. I had to buy purified water from school, special sea salt, and various trace elements. So it wasn't really self-sustaining at all, was it? I sold it all in one whack, and now I have things like trigger fish and eels—a lot easier to care for.

Helen Barbour

Snorkeling for crawfish. Deep-sea fishing. Zooming out on the boat for miles with no one around us and having a wonderful time in the ocean, just the two of us.

Kurt Vonnegut

This man just dived into my pool here and that moment when you're under and you haven't come up again yet gives me enormous pleasure.

I can't drink martinis anymore, but I can remember that *cachong* of the first martini. That was awfully nice. And I've tried to do it again with martinis and it just doesn't work, I don't get that *cachong*, but I remember it.

Digging in the ground, just planting things, gives great satisfaction. I've taken the burlap off the rootball, dug the hole, put the thing in, mixed in the fertilizer, the peat moss and everything, the ground's all level, and I turn on the hose. And that is just terrific satisfaction. Because, by God, there it is and it's really going to be all right and nobody did it but me. These are sort of nitwit answers, but . . .

Margaret Mason

A walk in the woods.

Edith Bornn

Gardening brings me the greatest amount of pleasure. It seems to run in the family. The van Bederhoudt side of the family had a generation of fabulous gardeners. My grandmother's entire life was gardening. She hardly went out. She spent hours on her roses. At an early age she gave me some rose trees to take care of and develop. At age thirteen, I fell off the parapet when I was watering my gardens and nearly broke my back. I had been quite a sprinter, and I thought I'd never be able to run again. And then my grandmother's brother had a garden, again mostly of roses, down where we have Riiser's Alley on the waterfront. It was such a fantastic, fabulous garden that people would come to St. Thomas just to see it.

And my grandmother's sister, who got married later in life and went to live on St. Croix, did nothing else but garden. I have loved gardening, but I don't spend anything of the time these other members of the family did before me.

Now my son Michael has the gardening bug, to my great delight.

Egbert Donovan

My pleasure is working on my museum, the North Shore Shell Museum.

My family has been here a long time, eighty or ninety years. When I was a young kid coming up, I used to make these little log sailboats like I have in the museum, and I know many of the people here had shells, fish traps, bottle floats, and these other things around home. But I found our culture was down; people find that they can make money faster and they change their course and stop doing a lot of these old things. People realize that you don't have to work hard like this.

But I kept studying about it. I keep thinking and keep studying and I start putting it together. Before I did the museum, there was nothing here. Then I built this open building, just like people used to do. Put up pieces of wood, then the galvanized tin for a little shade. I started going out and gathering shells and then I had the inside full with the shells. And people bring me things, too. Sometime I sit and make these bowls. People used to make the baskets, the hats, and that is something I plan to do.

That's how people used to do. They'd get pieces of wood or anything like that. And they put the shells on just like that. They didn't know anything about fancy things. Everything was just put together, patch it up. You see how it is. My greatest pleasure is working on this museum, so people can see what their culture is. A lot of our people, young people, ought to know what people used to do for a living.

Alvis and Marynell Waite
Being with each other.

Don Brunson
Going to the woods with my family—camping and hunting. Once on the opening weekend of duck season, the five of us went to a hunting lodge in Arkansas.

And the good ole boys were there, too—these guys from North Carolina who come down every year to play poker all night and drink hard and cuss and tell jokes. And this year, guess what? This family of five people shows up at the same place—wife, little girl, two little boys.

These men were magnificent in the way they handled themselves around us. We ate supper with them that Friday night, we shared some fun together, and then we departed to one of the bunkrooms and let them have their fun.

The next morning the five of us got up and got all dressed and went out to one of the blinds. Of course, you are wishing for a wonderful day full of ducks. But the ducks were not flying that day. It was still fun. It always is.

Will McIntyre
Being in our own home and preparing our own food, sitting down and having a nice bottle of wine—things that don't happen often because our work keeps us on the road. It's the rare things that give the most pleasure.

That reminds me of something Dr. Hugh Matthews, a friend in the mountains, once said. He'd grown up in the Depression and was talking about building the beautiful house he lived in. "To us now," he said, "a purchase is just a purchase. But I remember the time when a purchase was a triumph." Being at home doing nothing is a triumph for us.

Wednesday Bridge Club

Peggy Kemp: I think of my friends and how I love to be with them. To see what they're doing.

Mary Costigan: Yes, my friends are like my family now because I came here from St. Louis in 1945 and have the same friends that I had when I came. They're the equivalent of a family now.

Mildred Sutton: You've been with them longer than you've been with your family. That's true for most of us.

Murial Sichveland: I think friends take on more importance as you get older, because you're real busy raising your family when you're younger and you haven't as much time to spend with friends.

Mildred Sutton: One of the most important things they do, I think, is love you in spite of. . .

Mary Costigan: They understand. . .

Murial Sichveland: They overlook. . . .

Mildred Sutton: That's it—because they have some of the same problems you do, they overlook them.

Peggy Kemp: And you share the same interests. Friends keep you going.

30. *Your Moment of Glory in Sports*

Norman Lear

My greatest moment of sports came at my fiftieth high school reunion. In high school I tried out for junior varsity even though I wasn't athletic because my father loved football and always wanted me to play. I wasn't good though I tried hard. My idea of playing well was to make sure I was at the bottom of the scrimmage, and I was. I would have even welcomed getting hurt because that would have made me somewhat of a hero with my father, I thought.

Then after a couple of weeks of practice, Fred Stone, the coach, took off my helmet and handed it to me and said, "Get out of uniform. You can't play."

Fifty years later at our reunion, a terrific halfback from back then came to me and said, "I've been wanting to ask you all these years, why did you quit football?"

I said, "Because I couldn't play."

And he said, "What the hell are you talking about? Nobody could stop our all-city fullback Bill Maloney in scrimmage, and there you were for a couple of weeks stopping him four out of five times. We couldn't get over your quitting."

Then I told him my memory, and he said, "Bullshit! That never happened!"

So my greatest sports memory is hearing a story at my fiftieth high school anniversary that I knew wasn't true.

Shannon Kelly

In front of 80,000 fans at Memorial Stadium in Austin. We are down with twenty seconds left in the game against North Texas State, and I throw the winning touchdown pass as time runs out. Absolutely exhilarating!

Lyn Lear

In high school I wanted so much to be a cheerleader. I worked for months trying to get my routine down and I got out there and I did it! I knew it was a great job! I knew I had it!

Then I found out I hadn't studied enough for the Constitution test, flunked it, and wasn't eligible for cheerleading anyway.

Will McIntyre

I played football on the Southern Nash High School Firebirds in the first year of the team's existence. Though we had few experienced players, our school's new consolidated size meant that we played larger schools with established football programs. If we scored a touchdown in a game but still got beat 66–6, we considered that something of a moral victory.

My worst moment in sports came on a pass play in one of these games. I was offensive center, and the quarterback dropped back into a shotgun formation while I thought he was still right behind me.

I snapped the ball. I heard the crowd roar and saw pandemonium on the field. I had hiked an interception. When we watched the game film, the coach delighted in showing the play four or five times in slow motion: You see all these people lining up and then you see the ball shoot straight up behind the center's butt and sail right up to the level of the camera up in the stands and straight back down into the hands of the outside linebacker from the other team. Embarrassing.

Two weeks later we were, amazingly, winning a game. With just minutes left, we had a one-point lead. But Wakelon was threatening to score. I played middle linebacker on defense. They lined up to pass. They got the ball off—I intercepted on the one-yard line. That saved the game—our only win of the year.

That was my moment in sports. The crowd yelled and screamed, and I got kissed by more cheerleaders that night than I can remember. It made up for hiking that interception.

Michael Bornn

I wasn't even present for my greatest moment. I played on the football team in high school and participated in horseback riding. One weekend, I had to be in New York for a horse show and missed the football game. I came back home on Monday morning to find that our team had gotten their butts kicked, and the feature of the newspaper story was not the loss but that Michael Bornn wasn't there and that cost the team the game. Though everybody used to give me grief about having such a big ego about it, that made me feel pretty good—to be the featured player and not even be present.

Robert Abrams

Awards day my senior year in high school. I wasn't born with natural ability; I had to work for every skill I had. When they read off that I had fifteen football scholarships and three track, I knew I had earned every bit of it. And I knew that I had the grades to take advantage of the opportunity. Even though I did well and tried out with Kansas City—a cracked kneecap put an end to that—and the Packers, that awards day in high school was my glory in the sun.

Cliff Robertson

Recently I got my diamond in soaring. That means I flew a glider up over 26,000 feet by riding the winds. That was a great day. I took off out of Mindon, Nevada—a beautiful, flat valley. You get towed up by plane to a prearranged altitude, then you release yourself, and you're on your own. It's the next thing to being a bird. I fly airplanes, too, and I've raced in the Reno air races. That's fun and fast; you've got thousands of people watching you run the pylons, and that's terribly exciting. But soaring is almost poetic. You're working with nature, not against.

Dan Buettner

The biggest moment is finishing my very first trek from Alaska to the tip of South America. I had dipped my rear bicycle wheels in Prudhoe Bay, Alaska, and bicycled southward for 15,536 miles through North, Central, and South America toward Tierra del Fuego. We'd gone through cold and tropics and back to cold. We'd been pushing our bikes for the last three days through snow. As I mounted the very last hill, I could see the town of Ushuaia fanning out to the sea and the whitecapped waters of the Beagle Channel. I glided down the very last hill and my three teammates and I, one by one, dipped our front wheels in the water and finished that trek. Glorious moment.

Gerry Cooney

I was twenty-three and fighting Ken Norton in Madison Square Garden. My first million-dollar payday. We came out in the first round, and I was feeling him out. I thought, let me take a shot and see how he takes it. So about ten seconds into the round, I threw a good body shot with my right hand and connected. Then I turned over a left hook that caught him on the chin and knocked him out in fifty-four seconds of the first round. It wasn't a bad place to be that night.

David Prowse

Winning the British Weightlifting Championship in 1962. I won again in '63 and '64, but it never had the appeal it did the first time. I remember sitting in the dressing room when it was all over, thinking, *I'm the strongest man in Great Britain*. I was there stripping off, getting ready to have a shower, when all of a sudden the team manager comes in the dressing room. "Well, are you going to sit on your bloody laurels, mate? You've got more work to do!" So, my euphoria didn't last very long. I was twenty-seven.

Peggy Houlihan

Winning a national championship award in 1970 with my horse, Old Josh. We won the Bengt Lundquist Award in dressage. It was so exciting then—and even six years later when Ballycor, the horse that finished second to us in that event, went on to win a gold medal in the Montreal Olympics.

Doris Peck, Supper Club

I loved to ride horses as a kid. On this particular afternoon when we went over to the farm to ride, for some reason they didn't want me to ride this horse, but I got on anyway.

No sooner was I up than the horse took off for the barn and his stall. He was going to run right under the door and knock my head off, but at the last moment I grabbed the door frame, let the horse run out from under me and dropped down. What a stunt! But I never got on that horse again.

Stuart Perkins

Polo is the greatest game in the world. I played my first match when I was fifty-seven. I was tearing down the field at the Boca Raton Polo Club playing number one. The number-two guy behind me was notorious for wild play that hurt other players. Riding in front of him, I tried to watch my neck as much as anything else. As he let one fly, I ducked and suddenly there's the ball right in front of me with the goal straight ahead. So I took this nifty swing at the ball and missed it completely. But the pony's front hoof hit the ball right through the goal. Everybody thought I'd scored a goal. I didn't protest too much.

Nan Thomas

Making the FIS squad—Federation of International Skiing—a professional competitive ski team. If you're a professional skier—I was a ski instructor—you can't race in the Olympics, you race FIS. I made the Eastern FIS squad then had to drop out when I got pregnant with my first child.

Sonya Friedman

I learned to snow ski when I was nearly fifty. I did it because I was afraid of getting up on everything from a chair lift to a hill, and skiing was learning to control being out of control.

I won the trip in a church auction and wanted to share it with my friends. So I took them all with me, and we had the best time. I ski in Aspen every year now.

Zar Rochelle

I always knew I would be good at snow skiing. I told my friends, "I'm going to be able to do it." And they all laughed at me. "Wait till you get them on your feet. Then see how it works."

So we went to ski one weekend in the North Carolina mountains—my first time. I was about thirty-two.

We got there. I put the skis on. My friends, who were experienced skiers, insisted that I go to the beginner's slope. I got bored halfway down.

"I want to go up in the chair lift," I insisted.

So up we went. I beat them both down the hill, did a spinning stop, and was standing there waiting for them when they arrived. They were shocked. They refused to believe I had never been on skis before.

I don't know why I was so good. But I just knew I could do it and, sure enough, I could. I had a great afternoon, and I've never skied since. I've done that.

Peggy Kemp, Supper Club

Learning to play bridge when I was twelve. That was the best thing that ever happened to me; it's given me a lifetime of enjoyment.

Foxy Callwood

Though I've been fishing all my life, I caught my first blue marlin about two months ago! Three hundred pounds. I was on a friend's boat from St. John. It felt powerful, powerful. We released it.

Medora Plimpton

In a sailing race on a day when the wind was really blowing and we capsized four or five times in freezing water, just finishing was a moment of glory.

Deni McIntyre

Will and I, for a while, played on a coed soccer team. I played halfback and had two goals, but though it isn't really glory, I was prouder of another moment.

Even though it was a coed league, the women were tolerated rather than encouraged. In this particular game, one guy kept calling out that he was open when I was standing right on him. I stayed right with him, but he kept yelling, "I'm open, I'm open!" When he said it right into my face, which is kind of like denying my existence, I finally came back at him, "The hell you are!" And the next time that somebody passed the ball to him I just gave it the last bit of oomph, stepped in front of him and stole the ball and took off just as fast as I could and left him gaping. Estrogen makes its mark! Having somebody act as if you're insignificant—what a great incentive.

Jock Munro

I always played in the second fifteen in rugby. I enjoy sports but can't get into them too seriously. So only one moment—sweet if not great—comes to mind. During one match at school, an opposing player raised his knee real hard at my groin. Somehow he missed, connected with my elbow or something—to this day I'm not sure just what—and fell writhing to the ground. Watching him writhe about, knowing he'd got what he deserved—that's my greatest moment in sports.

Mary Randolph

Getting my black belt in karate at fifty felt really good. At the same time we were training for the Conchathon, a minitriathlon. I had karate two nights a week and swimming three times a week. You really felt on top of it. But getting in the pool to swim that first minitriathlon was the crowning glory because I used to be scared to death of the water. As I swam I thought, *you're doing it.* It was really something.

Kim Litton

Competing in that first Conchathon in Grand Bahama in 1988 meant so much. Finishing there pushed me on to other things.

As I was running in the first one, I realized that I was nearly last. And I thought, oh, God, if I'm the last person, I'm going to be embarrassed. But I also realized that I could finish! That's when it hit me that finishing was what mattered. I went on from there to do other triathlons. I knew I could complete something, that I could do lots of things if I put my mind to it. I finished that first race next to last, but I really won.

Damian Miller

My moment came in a national cross-country event, 3,000 meters, when I was thirteen years old. There were 500 of us running. As we lined up, the line seemed to stretch for a quarter of a mile. I knew I was one of the favorites, but with all those people I didn't think I stood a chance.

After the first loop, I was in third place. And I was almost content to be there. I thought, this isn't bad. Then something happened.

We were going up the biggest hill of the race and the iron front started dropping back. For the first time, I realized this was it—I had a chance to win a big event! One guy stuck with me as we came down to 200 yards from the finish. Then I broke away and won it by five seconds. That's the biggest highlight.

Joy Melton Prickett

Well, it had to be when I got third place in the Sardis Frog Wallow Waddle. As in Sardis, Georgia, a large metropolis. I used to call on the bank there to sell checks. I had just started to jog when the bank manager mentioned the bank was sponsoring this road race and said, "Why don't you come and run in our race."

I was nervous about this because I'd only run a mile and a half. This was a great distance—five K. But they assured me it was flat ground and no one had been training hard.

So I went to this road race. There were only about twenty-five or thirty participants. Sardis hasn't got but about a hundred folks when it's full. I started off at my slow pace, got halfway through, and decided it was time to walk a while. Except for one other woman, I was soon left behind. The most embarrassing thing was the police escort, trailing along behind us with blue lights flashing. So we decided to finish by picking up the pace just a little.

The guy in the police car is saying, "Come on, girls, you can do it." So it was a moment of glory to finish. It was an even greater moment when they announced that I had won third place in my age category. Fortunately, there were only four people in my age category and one of them was the other woman who walked in with me, one step behind. So I have a ribbon and I have a lot of fun with it.

31. *What Makes You Give Up?*

Margaret Mason

People who don't like life make me stop. People who are just putting in their time, just doing something to pass time, give me a thud inside, and I have to get away from them.

Kurt Vonnegut

Anger on the part of the person I'm dealing with. No matter what's going on, if somebody gets angry, I will walk away—no negotiation, no conversation.

Nan Thomas

A car! At least here on the island. Getting it fixed is impossible if you aren't a native. So Ben takes care of that.

Mildred Sutton

Sometimes when you get a bad surprise—like an unexpected big expense on the house—you say, "Can I do it, or will I just have to give up?"

But I tell you when you get this age, you realize that if you give up, that's it. You just can't. You've just got to keep on fighting one way or the other. Sometimes when I get tired of having to make decisions out here, I stop and think that if I'm going to live here and live alone, I'm going to have to do those things. If I can't do them, I can't live alone. So you just have to go ahead and do it.

Dave DeGrandpre

Ignorance. When someone just won't listen. Aubrey Peterson and I did a paper on the Aryan Nation, and we met with them, tried to throw out new ideas, and they kept referring to isolated passages in the Bible. Their faith's so sure it seems closed-minded. When people don't have an open mind, there's nothing you can do.

Julie Rogers

If I smell failure around the corner, I shut down and withdraw from the situation. I was raised with an expectation of success on all fronts; a lot of my self-esteem is wrapped up with needing to be successful. So faced with something I think can't be accomplished, I leave rather than easing myself in and giving it a try.

Lyn Lear

Giving up has such a negative reality. But I think one of the things we need to learn to do is to fail gracefully or just to see failure as a learning experience. If you want something really badly and you don't get it, I think there comes a time when you need to realize it is not meant to be.

Norman Lear

Giving up comes very hard to me. I think for most of my life giving up represented failure, and I couldn't stand to give up. Now I have a better understanding of my own limitations, and I find it perfectly permissible not to give up but to think of it as just not being able to accomplish something. There is no shame in that.

Lenny Berman

Periodically the government gets so ridiculous I can't stand it anymore and I close up temporarily. For example, until today, I hadn't opened the paper in a week. I'd walk the dogs as usual and pick up the papers at the end of the drive and leave them in their plastic on the counter. The situation is so depressing that to continue to participate in it by reading, hearing, and discussing it makes me so glum I feel almost physically sick. So I temporarily shut down until I feel the storm has passed or I can deal with it.

As Julie says, we're facing some hard questions about what people of conscience can do in this state of affairs in American political life. It's very hard not just to get cynical and leave. That's frightening because we're both very committed to issues and social justice in our work and personal lives; and if we're not prepared to participate through the process, then who is?

Jim Swann

I'll give up in a heartbeat if I think defeat is imminent, is going to happen no matter what. That came from my stepfather, Jack Eckerd. He was always superloyal to his employees and commitments, but he was always willing to admit his mistakes and go on. Don't try to live in a dream world and hide your mistakes, because if you do that, you'll end up spending a lot of time wasting your life, trying to fool yourself and other people.

Campion Platt

There are two levels on which to give up: emotionally and then physically. I try not to give up on either. For instance, I've been through some incredibly taxing days businesswise, personally, and intellectually, but all of it has taught me so much. And intellectually the bad times have even appealed to me: How do I deal with this? What have I learned from it? What did I do wrong?

Gerry Cooney

One day, about a year and a half after I lost to Holmes, I just sat in my house all alone. Man, I was going nowhere. I had no answers, had tons of people hanging around. And I sat there crying to myself, and I said, you know, it's just not working out. I don't know what's going on.

Someone explained to me once it's like going to a toy store to buy a great big toy to put together. You're all excited as you bring it home, and you open the box—and there are no instructions. So you don't know how to put it together. Well, no one told *me* how to be.

It got to a point where I had to say, OK, quit. Give it up. Try something else. That was when my life turned. I learned that you draw people to help you and people hook up together and connect. When it stops working, they can then take what they learned from that and they go and share somewhere else.

Egbert Donovan

The first year I worked on this shell museum, I had only twelve or thirteen people come, and I felt like quitting. But you have to have a strong faith. So I say, no, give it time and let it go on. The second year, things look better 'cause people get to know it.

Will McIntyre

It doesn't happen very often, but every now and then you produce a photograph that you really worked hard on and you think is really just right. But when you show it to the client, he either doesn't think it's right or doesn't understand it. Lack of response is even worse. Hostility, stubbornness, being contrary—anything is better than lack of response. That's the most off-putting thing that I can imagine.

John Emery

When I've completely lost control. Once, when I was married, I'd just lost my job and had just flunked a major exam and was on the way to pick up my wife when the car broke down. I didn't have a dime to fix it, either.

Medora Plimpton

When things get overwhelming, when I have too much work to do and it keeps piling up. If I look at everything as one whole thing, rather than pieces, then I tend to give up by losing interest.

Kathy Bater Brackett

Me. I think I'm very hard on myself. Most people are very hard on themselves. It's self-talk. Though I try to keep it out of my brain, the majority of the self-talk I have is negative: *You can't do this or you shouldn't be doing this or this is gonna go wrong or this was a bad idea*—that kind of self-talk. I fight it all the time.

On the other hand, I try to keep cheering for myself. For example, if I really need to lose some serious weight, I'll stick a picture of a very attractive woman on the fridge. I'm looking at where I'm going, not where I am now.

Myrtis Brown

Nothing. Not one thing will make me quit because I think God's got me out here to go, not to quit. Not to quit anything. And I'm in full voice.

32. Overcoming Adversity: A Portrait

David Prowse

You have to cope with adversity the best you can. If things go wrong, you just pick up and go on to something different. When I was a kid, I was one of the top schoolboy sprinters in the country, I was greased lightning. I had a whole career mapped out for myself: I was going to play rugby for England and be an England International sprinter. And then at thirteen the problems started with my knee. They kept me in a hospital bed—actually tied to the bed—for a year. I couldn't go to the toilet or anything like that. And then they put me in a leg iron similar to the brace I've got on now, but instead of going up to my knee it went up to my groin. I had that on for three years. My athletic career was ruined.

Then I thought, this bodybuilding thing, I'd like to take it up. I did bodybuilding for ten years and got to the Mr. Universe contest. "I'm very, very sorry," the judge had the cheek to say, "you're never going to get anywhere because of your feet." Well, I thought, how stupid! I can't do anything about my feet. I might as well do something else. That's when I took up weightlifting, where strength counts rather than looks, and I became a champion.

Then I was nearly defeated in my gym business just last year. First my hip gave way with inflammatory arthritis, and then my ankle went. I'd gone into the hospital for six weeks and came out on crutches to find my gym manager had been fiddling me rotten for years, really fiddling me badly. I owed £39,000 to the bank,

I also had other debts to the tune of another £35,000. I was at the lowest ebb financially of my career.

Well, I thought, I've got to get this business back on a proper footing again. I sacked everybody. From nine in the morning to ten at night, six days a week, I ran a gymnasium on five floors just me on my own, hobbling on crutches up and down those flights of stairs. I put an exercise bike by the door and spent hours there reaching the phone, reaching the door entry system, instructing classes from the gym bike.

It took me over a year, but I reduced the £39,000 overdraft down to £10,000. The firm I owed £20,000 to now owes me £20,000. It was bloody hard work, but I enjoyed every minute of it, and at the end, I'd achieved something, and *that* was well worth waiting for.

I don't worry about my leg getting better, either. If the deterioration means it's got to come off, it's got to come off. I was very anti about it coming off at one period, but then I saw the disabled Olympics on TV and saw one guy with a wooden leg run a hundred meters in 11.8 seconds. Well, I thought, if he can do that with a wooden leg, there can't be much wrong with having a wooden leg. So, if it comes off I'll probably be a lot more mobile than I am now. It doesn't worry me in the slightest.

I'm always trying to think on the positive side of things all the time. A lot of people if they'd gone through what I have would have applied for disability allowance, packed up work completely, retired, and packed it all in. I'm working harder now and doing more than I've ever done before.

33. What Gives You Courage to Go On?

John Emery

My grandmother used to say, "Life is a do-it-yourself proposition." Another friend said, "You just make life up as you go along." I've sort of melded the two. If you wake up, you've got another day, so just make up the day as you go along.

Nan Thomas

Well, I'm just a damn Yankee.

Jim Swann

I don't think it takes courage. I think you have to enjoy life. If you don't enjoy life, you might as well kill yourself, right? If you enjoy life, you go on.

Cliff Robertson

The past. I've tried to tell my kids: Look at every obstacle as an opportunity in disguise. Whatever comes to you—sometimes you get a green light, sometimes yellow, sometimes red—that's life. Get on with it.

Looking back over my life, I see a few obstacles here and there, including the three years I didn't work after exposing Hollywood corruption in the infamous Hollywoodgate scandal, as fuel for the future. What you learn from the past gives you the insight to go on.

Deni McIntyre

It's knowing that nobody expects me to. Expectations intimidate me. But if it's something that nobody thinks that I have a prayer of doing, then I'm free to really give it all I've got because there's nothing to lose.

Chris Keefe

A view of the future, an understanding there *is* a future. I think that was the most important lesson in my experience with crack. Once I realized that I could get over that need, I began to move forward again. It's like a record stuck at one part that you think you can't get off. But if you just tap the needle, it goes on to the next part.

Peggy Houlihan

I'm always waiting to see what's 'round the bend, always finding another adventure or challenge. I have a to-do list that's three miles long.

Virginia Kahl

I have eighteen cats to feed. What do you do? They never stop eating. I've willed them all to Mary. Really, I have.

Zar Rochelle

Recently, book deadlines. The galleys are out and you want the drawings when?

Damian Miller

I want to go on to make my mark in the world, to do something to be remembered for, something that I feel good about. Just to leave something behind.

Win Rockefeller

I suppose the courage to go on is nothing more than a personal commitment, really. A lot of times it's just the circumstances. The guy that wins the congressional medal of honor for killing a hundred or a hundred fifty of the enemy's troops and for defending his wounded comrades despite great personal risk will probably turn around and tell you, "Well, hell, it was either that or get killed, and I really didn't want to get killed."

Marla Hanson

When the whole trial process ended after my attack, I was faced with all these choices. I had this vast landscape in front of me, and I couldn't do anything. I couldn't model anymore, really. I had to start my whole life over again, and that was scary because it was all up to me. So I dealt with the situation by sleeping all the time. I didn't return phone calls; I locked myself in my room and slept sometimes for three or four days.

Then I couldn't sleep anymore, and I couldn't escape anymore, so I had to confront what I'd been through. It was the first time in my life I felt really, truthfully alone.

I didn't have the choice of going to my family, so I went to a really good therapist. He said, "Look at your choices," and I said, "I don't have any choices." He said, "You do. You can either fall apart or find someone to attach yourself to or you can just go on and continue." I find myself remembering that advice now, knowing that I've got to go on and continue.

Kathy Bater Brackett

The belief that I do have a choice. I know I don't *have* to go on. I have a choice.

Mildred Sutton

I think your faith does. You know that no matter how bad things seem to be at the time, God's still in his heaven and you'll make out somehow. It's my faith that keeps me going a lot of times when I can't see my way. Then the love of your family keeps you going, you have to keep on going for them.

Myrtis Brown

I say a lot of times we are trialed. God tries us to see how strong we are. Others look at me and say, "Why you always don't bitch out at people?" I say, "I ain't got time for that. God don't want me to do that. He's got me here for me to tell you young generation these things. You haven't been through things like I have."

You've got to pray over the things you want to do first, and God will get you on the right track. I always study over things first before I jump in the fire. And I talk the idea over with others before I jump out there by myself. Do that and you can keep going.

I never will forget one of my nieces was going to lose her house. I didn't have any collateral to go to the bank to get the money that she needed. I went there and talked to the lady and she said, "Oh, yes, Myrtis, I'll let you have it." She thought I needed it for myself, not my niece.

That Friday it was raining like everything, and I said, "Otis, get up and go to Atlanta and carry this money so she won't lose her house."

And every month—they ain't giving me anything to help— but every month the Lord fixes where I can meet that note at the bank. It doesn't come out of my little Social Security check. The Lord has let me go somewhere and make it. A hundred and ninety-five dollars, I've always got it to go and pay that note. See I went there and I talked to God first. If you do something in his name, he's going to let you take care. You just don't get out there by yourself.

Dan Buettner

I really have little sporting talent, average intelligence, few natural social graces. That has been a blessing because I think you derive your strengths from weaknesses. Since I've had so many weaknesses, I've been able to develop a keen sense of perseverance, which for me has paid off more in the long run than any natural ability.

Jane Burke

I've always had big dreams. That's probably what gives me courage. When I look at some of the things I've done, I still can't believe that I did them. For instance, I moved to Atlanta at one of my lowest points with a goal of getting into Symphony Chorus. Within a week, I had a job and I was in chorus. In acting and singing, I've gone after some roles that I never thought I'd have the courage to go after—like the lead in *Sister Mary Ignatius Explains It All for You*—and I've gotten them. When I look back at what I've done, I think, why can't I do that again or do more?

Doris Roberts

I saw a play in San Diego about a year and a half ago presented by a Russian company from Leningrad. It was much like *Nicholas Nickleby* in that you went to a matinee and then you went out and had dinner and then you came back. I saw forty-eight Russian faces and personalities on stage, and for the first time I knew who I am. I really am Russian. I have their personalities. That's in my genes. And there's something about the Russian spirit that when it gets absolutely terrible, when life is just awful, you dig deeper into the earth. It's like dancers you know. In order to leap you have to go down first before you leap up. That's what the Russian spirit does, I think—it goes down into the earth to give itself strength to pull back up and leap forward up into the air. And I think that's what I do.

Desy Campbell

Getting busy helps. This summer I found out I may have to have two back operations, and I know I'll have to have hip replacements done sometime. When I heard I might have these operations, whenever they may be, I panicked. So I work on my own house—I wallpaper and I strip paint. It's an old house, part of it goes back before the Civil War, so there's always something to do.

Medora Plimpton

On the second day of my first Outward Bound trip in 1989, I was climbing up the mountain and crying. Down the mountain, I could see a town far away. I wanted a pack of cigarettes so badly I started running toward the town—it must have been twenty miles away. I felt I couldn't take it anymore!

But I stayed and finished that course and have gone on another trip. The experience made me realize I can do things I didn't think I could. I learned endurance and self-reliance and acquired more self-understanding. Most of all, I've learned that you can get through what seems overwhelming by breaking it into pieces and tackling those pieces one at a time.

Margaret Mason

I've always been gutsy. It came from my mother, who was always upbeat. Her attitude was, we're here and whatever we're handed, our only choice is to go on, so we might as well be upbeat. She'd wake up in the morning and sing things like "Oh, what a beautiful morning."

And she taught me to breathe. She'd always say, "Breathe deep." That was almost a metaphor for living. From the time I was small, I learned that this is your life and it's wondrous. We'd go for walks in the woods and she'd say, "Put your shoulders back. Breathe deep."

34. Serendipity

Kathy Bater Brackett

I've lived on Grand Bahama Island eighteen years because I got drunk in California.

I hadn't seen my father in a long time, because he lived outside the country, when he called me up and said, "I'm in San Francisco for two days. Come up and visit."

I flew up from southern California. The first night was OK. The next morning at eight when we went to have breakfast in the hotel, the restaurant wasn't open but the bar was. So we thought we'd have a couple of Bloody Marys. We did not get out of that bar until after midnight. I hadn't seen him in years, so we just talked and talked and drank and talked.

At some point he said, "I've got this property in the Bahamas, and it's not doing too well. I want you to go have a look at it."

I never did go back to southern California. The next thing I know I'm on a plane at four in the morning—wearing a wool suit and carrying just the little overnight bag I brought to San Francisco. My dad said, "If you're going to do it you've got to do it now."

The plane stopped and I stepped out in Freeport. It was August. The heat and the humidity hit me. I didn't even know where the Bahamas was. I was so hungover.

My dad had condominiums, newly built. Independence had just come and everybody was leaving town and he couldn't sell them. In fact, he didn't want to sell. I turned them into long-term rental properties. And I stayed long-term myself.

Nan Thomas

My book *Toby the Sea Turtle*—it's funny how that came about. We were out fishing one day and stopped on Sandy Pit, a tiny island near Sandy Cay. As we were walking around Sandy Pit, we saw the tracks of a mother sea turtle who was going up to lay her eggs. We watched her dig the hole, lay the eggs, and cover it up.

We kept checking on them regularly, and one day we saw them hatched. The tiny turtles climbed up through the sand and ran to the beach. One turtle was running faster—far out in front of the group—that was Toby. They clustered into a tiny wedge and tumbled around and—bang!—they were gone.

I thought about this idea for several months. I'd told my children stories when they were small and drawn pictures to illustrate the story, but I'd never written a book. Toby was the first. It's now in its third printing and the second book has just come out—*Further Tales of Toby the Sea Turtle*. I'm so excited.

Now I do turtle surveys for the government, too, since sea turtles are an endangered species. So I feel very close to Toby and all his relatives out there.

Stephanie Beacham

My fear of dying fish brought me to Hollywood to do "The Colbys."

My children and I were vacationing at my parents' beach hut—the first holiday I'd had in three years—when my agent called to say Aaron Spelling had seen me perform and wanted me to do a screen test for this series. "I've sent you a few pages of script," he said.

I thought, oh, yeah, they've got some American actress signed up but are just trying to frighten her off—I didn't take it seriously. In fact, when the wind off the sea picked up the pages of script and sailed them away like a kite, I didn't care.

Then the phone rang. It was my next-door neighbor who had been watching my fish and plants at home. "I've done a terrible thing," she wailed; "I've locked your key inside your house." Well, the plants could cope, but I didn't want my fish to die. So I went up to London to save the fish and tested for "The Colbys" at the same time.

Bill and Doris Peck, Supper Club

We met Rose and Steve Wing because we lived in the same apartment house. In fact, we had to go through their living room to get to our apartment. We lived on the upper level and they on the lower level. Steve would joke we had to get clearance to go home.

Dana Warrington

Meeting my future wife in an elevator in Manhattan. We both worked for Eastern Airlines and were living in the same apartment building but might have missed knowing each other but for that lucky ride.

Emily Cook

Rodney is famous for drawing on napkins. And at a special luncheon one day he was seated beside John Saladino, the famous designer, who was to speak. When Saladino discovered that Rodney designed houses, he asked, "What kind?" Rodney immediately drew our house on a napkin.

Saladino looked at it and said, "Have you been published?"

"No."

"Would you like to be?"

"Certainly."

"Which publication would you like to start with?"

"Well, how about *Architectural Digest*?"

So that's how that came about. It was serendipity. But it doesn't stop there. After our house appeared in the magazine, we received a call from a woman who'd been trying to build a museum for years and, though she'd dealt with a number of architects, had never found just what she was looking for. She was about to go ahead with the best plan from a competition she'd held, even though she wasn't crazy about it, when she opened the magazine and saw our house. The Latin inscription, translated

"To the glory of God," at the top of our house caught her eye. She read the article, then called Rodney and said, "Please come see me." That was the start of a wonderful relationship.

Sonya Friedman

I had never thought about being on TV. I had a clinical practice with my Ph.D. and was on a book tour doing an interview on CNN at 2:00 A.M. The president of CNN saw it the next day and called me out of the blue to offer me a job.

John Englander

Life is timing. I think more than anything else we need to have a sense of opportunity and know when to seize an opportunity. Sometimes we seize too many at once and do them all badly. Sometimes in hindsight, we see one we should have taken and didn't.

I've been unusually fortunate that I've been at the right places at the right times, where there have been unique opportunities. Like saving UNEXSO. Or much later, being able to have the skills and instinct to say yes to the opportunity that became the Dolphin Experience.

The world is full of a million possibilities. We can do anything. But we can do only so many things well. The challenge is how do you make those decisions and turn down certain opportunities so that you are free to do others.

Sometimes, too, I think there are either far greater coincidences in the world than I can understand mathematically, or there are some metaphysical or "big picture" patterns at work that are truly beyond coincidence. Certainly I've seen that in the way the Dolphin Experience has grown: the growing world concern with whales and dolphins, the research we are doing and are going to do, the appearance of the right scientist to head the research at the right time, and the way the project started in the first place, having the right business acumen to make it work, the right water. So part of me says this has gone beyond coincidence, and that's a little spooky.

Don Brunson

I remember one positive aspect of getting the message of my brother's death aboard ship. A year later, when I was back in Georgia, I got a call from a shipmate, Mike Crowley, who was headed to Atlanta and wanted to see how I was doing. Anne and I said, "You ought to meet Anne's sister; she lives in Atlanta." He did and they ended up getting married and having four kids and living happily ever after!

Judy Rose

My ex-husband won a raffle prize of a free introductory scuba lesson in 1982. He doesn't like the ocean or beach so he said, "Here, you do this." That single instance introduced me to a new sport that brought me new friends, including my husband Ben, and those friends introduced me to the theater group and more new friends. That one point changed my whole life.

Ben Rose

Meeting Judy and having her bend my ear for two hours the first night. We were invited to the same dinner party and she dragged me into a corner and promptly told me her life's story. When she came over to apologize at another dinner party the next night, she did the same thing again. I went back to her house for a nightcap and never left.

Mimi Taufer

Jill, a friend from when I lived in Florence, had been traveling in Italy in 1972 with her husband and two children; and when she came back to the States, the first thing she said was, "I bought a castle in Italy."

They had met a man who invited them to explore an abandoned monastery he had discovered. When they peered over the wall of the monastery, they saw an abandoned village built within the walls of a medieval castle. It was so wonderful they thought they'd get together a group of people to purchase it, restore it, and have homes there.

That's how we came to Santa Giuliana in Umbria. It was a labor of love to do just the right amount of restoration—learning its history, finding out the way the windows should be, replacing stones that had fallen down. It gives you a special feeling to live in a place that has such a long history, and it's a very beautiful, tranquil place.

I spent eight years in Florence, so having a place in Italy and being able to return there and spend time with my Italian friends and my American friends and continuing my Italian experience is very important to me.

Umbria is a wonderful part of Italy; it's just south of Tuscany. By now I've spent twenty-five summers in Italy, and there's always something wonderful to discover.

Dan Buettner

In Ulan-Ude, just north of Mongolia, 6,600 miles from the nearest place to buy a new twenty-six-inch mountain bicycle wheel, my front wheel completely disintegrated. The aluminum layers split apart. There was absolutely no way to fix it. Soviet wheels were thirty inches in diameter and wouldn't fit my frame.

About thirty seconds after this disaster, however, I noticed a cyclist riding what appeared to be an abnormally good bicycle toward me. I flagged him down and through charades explained what had happened. He gestured for me to follow him.

As my other team members caught up, we followed Sasha, as he was named, to a garage near the center of town. In his workshop he built bicycles out of tubing he got from a nearby MiG fighter factory.

As he took a thirty-inch Soviet wheel down, I said, "No way you're going to get that thirty-inch wheel on my twenty-six-inch mountain bike."

He said, "Watch me."

He then cut all the spokes out of the Soviet wheel, chopped out a section of the rim and welded the smaller rim in place with a coat hanger, then drilled thirty-six new holes for spokes, and in the course of a day he built me a wheel stronger than the one I'd left the Twin Cities with. He refused to take any money for it, fed us dinner, and sent us on our way.

35. City Fathers: A Portrait

Jonathan Peter

My first disillusionment came when I was a Boy Scout, fourteen or fifteen—and I think this probably led in part to my funny, existential life. I was up for my board of review for Eagle Scout and went to the basement of the federal bank building to meet the board. I had all these merit badges, a good school record, and all these other achievements. For instance, I'd participated in the Freedom Walk, where we followed part of the Underground Railway to Michigan. So the city fathers looked over all my qualifications, all these things I'd done, then looked at me and said, "You're ready. You've got all the requirements, except for one question: Do you go to church?"

I said, no. I had often envied people who had Sunday school; in fact, I had insisted earlier that my parents let me go to Sunday school so I'd know what all the kids were talking about. But I wasn't going to church at the time, and these city fathers told me I had not demonstrated my duty to God, which is part of the Boy Scout oath. They said I would have to go to a church of my choosing for three months before they would award me the rank of Eagle Scout, which I had otherwise attained.

I was stunned. I'll never forget it. I was absolutely stunned. First of all, I thought going to a church had nothing to do with one's duty to God. To me that was a completely personal thing. I do feel we do have responsibility there, but going to a physical building and sitting through a liturgy of some kind was not this expression. I was stunned to think they would insist that it was. I was very disillusioned.

But I went along with it. I looked at everybody. It seemed to me that the people who were practicing the closest to what they preached were Quakers. But I have a problem with Jesus being the son of God and the immaculate conception. I think that many people have probably been divinely inspired: Jesus, for sure. I think others also. Maybe even Gandhi. But we have teachers throughout history, and the door of heaven is not closed on them if they happen to be born in Papua, New Guinea, and never know anything about Christianity. So I looked around and I thought the Quakers were very close but I had trouble with that. So I ended up joining the Unitarian Universalists and went to services. Three months later the board awarded me my Eagle. By that time I had collected enough extra merit badges that I was now a Bronze Palm, which is like a two-star general or something. Then I dropped out of the Boy Scouts.

I think Scouting was a good experience for me. It brought me in contact with other people from all walks, and I enjoyed the whole process, but I was disillusioned by the city fathers.

36. Your Lowest Moment

A. J. Hiers

An ambulance out front. My father had just passed away at our home. My stepmother and I didn't quite see eye to eye at that time—she was very young—so I took my brothers and sister, and we moved out. I knew a guy who was in the small-loan finance business, and he made me a $2,500 loan. I used that money to put down on a house. As a matter of fact, we were in the house for almost a week with no electricity because I didn't have the money to turn it on.

But then, again, we seemed to be happy. My brothers and sister and I always stay together. I talk to them every day.

Kim Litton

I can give you a day and a time. I flew down to the University Medical Branch in Galveston to see my brother Greg before he died. He'd been sick such a long time. When I got to his floor, I walked around the corner and his stuff was packed and sitting there. I knew something was terribly wrong. I walked through the door about 10:05 and my mom walked out and just put her hand up, shook her head, and said he was gone.

Losing him has been difficult to get over. I'm a critical-care nurse. I've walked through death with many people; I always thought that would make a difference. I thought it would be easier for me, but it hasn't been.

Bunny Johnson

There would be three. First, the day my grandson Justin was born. We'd been out to eat, and when we came back, he wasn't in the nursery. Buck left and came back with his face ashen white, and he said, "The baby's having problems. I've got to go get Doug. Justin's in ICU." He needed heart surgery right then.

And the day in August the doctor told us my granddaughter Melissa had spina bifida.

And when our daughter Holley was four months old, and they took her away to do exploratory brain surgery.

My lowest points all relate to sick babies. And they all turned into high points. It happened because we were blessed. They could have all been so much worse, and now each one is doing so well. They are really our greatest joys.

Don Brunson

In October 1970, I was on a naval LST in the middle of the Pacific; we were coming back from Vietnam with a lot of marines and equipment aboard. We were headed to Honolulu, then to San Diego to drop the marines off at their base. We were creeping along in the middle of nowhere—those LSTs go about eight to ten knots, and we were nursing a bunch of slow minesweepers back to the U.S.

I was in the wardroom having breakfast when the messenger of the watch came in with a message and gave it to the captain. He was sitting right across from me at the table. He read it to himself, then handed it to the executive officer who said, "Don, I need to see you in my stateroom." We walked upstairs, sat down, and he gave me the telegram. It was from the American Red Cross. It said my brother, Capt. Bob Brunson, a U.S. Air Force pilot, had been killed in action in Cambodia.

Being on the ship when the message came in about my brother was my lowest moment. I remember going down to the bowels of the ship through all these various doors and back up into compartments of the ship where no one seemed to have gone in about forty years. I sat there by myself and cried my eyes out. I made that trip several times. I spent about two or three hours there the first time; you have to get your composure back and get back into things.

I remember thinking so much about my parents at that time. I remember writing a message to them. It was sent over the radio back to them in Birmingham, but I felt so very, very far away from them. I sent them a second message on the second day. Of course, they wanted me to come to the funeral, but there was no way to get there, absolutely no way. When we eventually got into Hawaii, the first thing I did was call my parents.

Myrtis Brown

When my son Wallace was killed in an accident, that was very hard. It didn't hit me until it was all over, after I had gotten everything taken care of, and he was put away and everything. It hit very hard. You sit there and you stay where are you. That's the only thing ever hit me that hurt me so bad.

My mother's and father's deaths didn't bother me because they both suffered. But for a week after Wallace died, I just stayed away from everybody. And I had to pray mighty hard. A friend I'd worked for sent me a book in the mail. And that book gave me more consolation than anything. "God always plucks the best flower in the garden"—that's what was in that book.

And I got to thinking. Wallace was such an easygoing child; he liked to be by himself. He'd say, "Come see so and so—see how you like it." And I never would say I disliked anything he did because I figured he liked it. He was a very sweet kid.

There's a passage of scripture: "God wipes away all your tears"—I sat there and one day he wiped the tears up and I got up and went back to work and I felt better. When you bring them into the world, you don't know how they're going, you don't know what kind of death they are going to have, and so after that got to me, I was able to put it behind me. I was happy he didn't suffer, that he wasn't an invalid or a vegetable. I had a lot to be thankful for.

Margaret Mason

I was mugged by a gang of kids with knives and guns. It was horrible. Awful. Afterwards, I couldn't get my rage out. It was almost as if I hovered on the brink of madness. But I came back, and I knew at that moment that I had been to the very bottom and was able to come back. And, therefore, nothing could really get me again. I would survive.

Dave DeGrandpre
By the time I was sixteen, I was nearly crippled because some of my vertebrae were resting on my spinal cord. It started at age twelve, and it hurt like hell, getting worse and worse all the time. At the end I couldn't walk more than a hundred feet without crouching over in pain.

Then I went to see this fantastic doctor named Seymour Zimbler who said I needed a spinal fusion. I was in the hospital for two weeks, and in a body cast for the entire summer, but my back is fine now.

Timothy Sultan
One Friday or Saturday when I was in high school in Germany, I had drunk beer until I couldn't drive my motorcycle home, couldn't even stand, and lay wretchedly on the sidewalk. A kind German walked by, helped me sit up, got my home phone number, and called my mother, who had to come and pick me off the pavement, seat belt me down in the car to keep me from swaying too much, and drive me home. My classmates that year voted me most likely to be found under a bar.

John Marston
Definitely Christmas about four years ago. There was an incredible polarity in my life. I was a rising executive at Walt Disney Studios, working at the happiest place on earth with a future ahead of me, and I was miserable.

Why? I was a miserable drug addict. I snorted all the Christmas Club money and couldn't buy anybody any presents. I was feeling really sorry for myself and couldn't think of any good reason to go on living. I checked into a rehab. I got sober.

I don't have any regrets about the experience. I like to look forward rather than back. It was a character-building experience that helped me get where I needed to go.

Anne Brunson

I had bulimia. I found out I had it probably about ten years ago. I realized I had it because I was reading a magazine that described the condition and its symptoms. I thought that was so disgusting, then suddenly I realized that was me. I tried to straighten it out myself and couldn't, so I found help in a good psychiatrist.

I had probably been bulimic for a year or year and a half before I realized it. Don hadn't seen it because he traveled a lot, so it was easy to cover up. He was supportive when I told him. It took probably six months to a year to feel that I was over the worst.

John Emmerling

In 1979 I had been married for ten years; Samantha was five; Jonathan was three. I had started my advertising agency, we had moved into a new apartment, and my wife Mary was becoming a successful decorating editor. She had just signed a contract for her first book, and I was working in my business and building what I thought to be a successful, contemporary, cosmopolitan family life.

Two beautiful children, a beautiful apartment and two exciting careers, and my wife, with no previous discussion, said, "I want a divorce." She gave me no notice. I felt I had worked hard to try to make things come out, and to have the plug pulled—just because the other person just didn't want to go on—shattered me.

Of course, I didn't know Kate was around the bend.

John Englander

From a business or life's work perspective, the toughest time was when UNEXSO's future looked worst. We'd run out of money. The banks and creditors had more or less cut us off. The local economy was in a depression; the business was falling apart. I can remember one guy, who'd been coming to dive with us a long time, began diving with a competitor. That really hurt. And given the difficulties with the business, there were times when it was very difficult with the staff because I was mentally in one place and they were in another. They'd be having a party, for instance, and I wouldn't want to crash it and they didn't feel comfortable inviting me. That was real strange. I didn't know how to correct it at the time; I just had faith that if everything fell into place, things would come round and, in fact, they did.

Marla Hanson

My early life was so violent. I remember my stepfather would come home drunk waving his gun around. I remember my stepfather and mother with whips—they'd hit each other and then hit us; they'd drink and fight and rip each other's clothes off, be out in the yard screaming and fighting. Then the police would always come and take us away to foster homes. It was a terrible, terrible scene.

But my sister Bobbi was fearless. She wasn't afraid of my mother or stepfather, and she could keep them under control—keep them away from me.

One day she blew up at Mother. "I'm leaving!"

"That's fine! Don't ever come back!" Mother yelled. And then Bobbi stormed down the street. I stood there crying and Mother yelled, "Get out! Get out!"

Bobbi was hiding in this big drainpipe. I kept begging, "Please, don't go. Please, I can't live without you. Please let me come with you." So she crawled out of the drainpipe and said, "OK, you can come."

A few minutes later here came my brother Mark crying, sobbing, "Please, I want to come, too." So we went on this little adventure. First we lived in an abandoned house for a day with ninety-seven cents between us to survive. We bought a loaf of bread and some candy. Then we ran out of money and food and went to Sue Ellen's house, a girl we thought rich. Of course, she wasn't, but Sue Ellen lived on a farm, and she hid us in the horse barn, bringing us food every day until her mother caught us and called the police.

My brothers and I survived the violence, I think, because we simply didn't question it too much. Everybody lived like that, I assumed. You just accepted it and had good times, anyway.

My mother doesn't remember that violence. Once I felt the need and anger to bring it up, and all she did was cry and say, "I did *that?* I didn't do *that,* did I?" And then I started to look at her and understand where she was coming from and why she did the things she did. I started seeing her as a human being rather than this big, mean figure.

Dan Buettner

On the Sovietrek, I was three or four hundred miles into what was essentially 650 miles of roadless terrain in Siberia. I was trying to bike along this mud track where big tractors had passed, leaving something very much like mud skiing moguls. We'd cycle way down in one and up in another.

I hit a big one and my front wheel went flying up. I lost my balance, twisted my wheel and went flying over the handlebars. When I got up, I found that my wheel rim had bent to a forty-five degree angle.

My teammates were ahead, so I took the bike and hobbled a couple of miles through the brush to the rails of the Trans-Siberian Railway, where I used the metal rail to help bend the rim back in shape. I had to take off all the spokes, reshape the rim, then rebuild the wheel. The mosquitoes were biting; I was hungry and thirsty; my friends were lost. For twenty-seven days, we'd eaten only pig fat and buckwheat porridge, so I also had a severe case of diarrhea.

After about four hours I got the wheel true enough so it would spin in the bicycle frame. I got back on and started cycling on. After about a mile, I hit another mogul rut—up, down and over. Again my rim twisted. In eight hours, I'd gone two miles. I felt like quitting.

Mary Lou Retton

The USA vs. China, and I fell off the beam three times. I was humiliated, crushed. But I got back on, and it's funny, I won the gold on vault and floor.

37. *Unexpected Threats*

Cliff Robertson

I think possibly the most frightening threats are things that you discover within yourself that are potentially counterproductive, potentially damaging, potentially threatening.

Timothy Sultan

Once in Laos, my schoolmate, Bobby Wagner, and I were playing in his backyard before lunch, when he suddenly leaped up and pointed behind me yelling, "A snake!" I turned and looked but couldn't see anything but grass. Bobby kept shouting. After about half a minute, I finally saw a small cobra only a few feet away. I jumped up just as Bobby's father came chasing around the corner of the house with a shovel. With one swing he decapitated the snake. Soon after as we were eating lunch, however, the father brought the snake's head in and left it, still writhing, on a napkin in the middle of the table. I was shocked and revolted.

Stephanie Beacham

We hated living with nannies. If they were sloppy nannies, the kids loved them and I hated them because I never knew what was happening. If they were efficient nannies, all of us were frightened of them. So our triumvirate decided: no more nannies.

Edward Colquhoun

To have your health threatened; when that has happened you really know that health is number one. Everything flows from good health. There is no quality of life without health.

Win Rockefeller

Disease. My dad died of cancer when I was twenty-four. It was very quick. He felt positive he was going to beat it, but he could not.

Jim Hallett

This threat turned out to be an important milestone. In 1981 when I went for my yearly physical, I didn't have my regular doctor. I didn't like the new doctor's personality or attitude, but I had the physical, and when it was over, this doctor looked me in the eye and said, "You know, Jim, you are in terrible shape and you are never gonna make fifty." He made such an impression on me, I bought my first stationary cycle within the week. And Carol and I took a whole new approach to maintaining fitness and health.

The disquieting thought, however, is that if I'd had my regular doctor I would never have gotten the message. Even when he was telling me what I should hear, he was probably too close a friend to put the message in the blunt terms I needed, and I probably liked him too much to take his gentle admonitions seriously.

Deni McIntyre

Bad weather in a small plane. Usually it's on the way home at the end of a job. You don't have a lot of resistance. You've spend your energy doing the day's work. You just want transportation—"Take me home, James." You're not looking for a challenge. And then you look up at that little radar thing to see those massed blocks of bright color that mean get out of the way, major thunderheads. It's like, oh, God, now I have to gather the energy to be afraid. I dislike being afraid. All I wanted was a ride home, and instead I'm going to have an adventure. Oh, hell!

Jonathan Peter

They're always out there in the sea. They happen all the time. When rigging fails, for instance, that's an unexpected threat. In order to be a good sailor, you have to anticipate what might go wrong. A lot of people say, "Live in the here and now; if you don't worry, things won't happen to you." But the longer you're involved in boating, especially living aboard, the more you start to behave to the outer world like a worrywart. You have to keep thinking ahead. You try to keep unexpected threats from happening by trying to get spares, by going through your systems, by always anticipating. Still, that's not always the healthiest way to live because you don't live in the here and now.

Jane Burke

Once when I played the Mother Abbess in *The Sound of Music*, I had to make a publicity appearance on the local TV station's early-morning show. So I was flying down the interstate at 5:30 in the morning in full nun's regalia, late as usual. I had just tossed a cigarette out the window of my Celica, when I saw the blue lights flashing. Oh, Jesus, Mary, and Joseph.

So I pulled off, shaking. I'd never gotten a ticket. I was afraid I'd miss my call. I rolled down the window, braced myself, and turned to the officer, who took one look at my wimple and veil and said, "Oh, I'm sorry, Sister, you go right on." I guess he thought I was headed to St. Mary's Hospital, an exit away, on some emergency. He must have missed that cigarette.

38. Unexpected Treats

Doris Roberts

Meeting Fellini.

At a party once we were talking about how we never tell people the wonderful things about themselves while we can and how we ought to. Just then Fellini walked into the room. I thought I would die. I think he's one of the great geniuses of this century.

So I went up to him. I told him how I felt that his first film—which I know frame for frame—was like a writer's first book. Everything he's done since has been an extension of the same story. We talked forty-five minutes and he was wonderful.

At that point, someone said to Fellini, "Have you seen Miss Roberts's work? She's starring on Broadway."

Fellini just looked at me, then said, "You are an actress?" I nodded.

"You are the most unpretentious actress I have ever met," Fellini said. "Not once did you ever ask me for a job."

Win Rockefeller

Making new friends as opposed to new acquaintances.

Jonathan Peter

Having friends show up by sheer chance. Remarkably, even though I'm always moving around on my boat, that happens a lot.

Dave DeGrandpre

Going to boarding school. I knew only one or two people when I went there, and it was a little nerve-racking. But it was like a slumber party! I met people pretty easily, and we would hang out until all hours. I wasn't into school at all then, I was getting poor grades. I was chewing tobacco, and we all smoked pot and got drunk once in a while. It was awesome!

Edward Colquhoun

In about ten or twelve years, to have David's college funds all completed and to have some sort of a nest egg and be able to retire at sixty-five. I don't see it, but that would be an unexpected treat.

Robert Abrams

One happened this morning at the Breakfast Club for the homeless when all the guys sang "Happy Birthday" to me. People never realize how much I love those folks and how I look forward to being with them. And to hear them sing "Happy Birthday"—I can't take stuff like that very well—it was special. Unexpected and special.

Foxy Callwood

The first year I was in business, I decided to do what all businessmen does—take a vacation. So I was saying, "I'm going to New York." And a good friend from New Jersey I met here that liked me said, "Oh, when you coming in?" And when I arrived at Kennedy Airport, he was there to pick me up. And he had a house party for me with twenty-five guests and then toured me all around—New Jersey, Baltimore, Coney Island, Buffalo. Everywhere I went—"Welcome Foxy!" For the seven-and-a-half weeks that I was there—my first trip to America—I was not allowed to spend a dime!

Kathryn Hames, the Supper Club

A number of us in the supper club lived in Pine Forest when our families were young. After some friends bought the first television on the street, we'd all go down there at night in the summertime and take our folding chairs. Our friends would put the TV up in a window, and we'd all sit around in the yard and watch the wrestling match!

Kurt Vonnegut

I'm trying to remember, there was a dance company performing in some improbable space, probably the Metropolitan Museum of Art, in some open space there. I don't know exactly how this happened, it was totally unexpected, but they got me and they blindfolded me and they passed me from hand to hand, touching me. That was totally unexpected and quite nice.

Damian Miller

My grandmother in England knows how monstrous my appetite is. So when I arrive home late, maybe ten or eleven at night, and haven't eaten, she always makes a point, no matter how tired she is, of fixing something. That's always an unexpected treat.

Ben and Judy Rose

A whole week all by ourselves.

Jim Hallett

Our times in Hawaii were very special to us. Our favorite place is the big island of Hawaii on the Kona coast. Each year when we would go there, at sunset I made up a thermos of mai tais. We took them out to the edge of the rocks on the ocean, watched the sun go down and drank our mai tais. Once or twice, we even took Van Camp's pork and beans, some hot dogs, and a tiny barbecue to cook supper. Those times to us were *the* most important treat.

Don Brunson

When Anne brings home the Nutty Buddies.

Dan Buettner

On a bike trip—good pavement.

39. An Unexpected Special Moment

Doris Roberts

Laurence Olivier's wife Joan Plowright and I became good friends when we did the movie *The Diary of Anne Frank*. Sometime later, I got this wonderful call from Olivier on my answering machine. He said, "This is Larry Olivier of London"—like there are nine of them—"and this is for Doris Roberts and I'm coming to your country Thursday next and wish to take you to dinner on that following Sunday, if that's all right. Would you leave word on my son's telephone service which is 764...no, 762...76...oh, shit" and hung up.

I did indeed meet him for dinner on that Sunday and it was wonderful. I had a note someone had given me for him, and during the dinner I said, "Oh, I have a note for you," and went to my purse to get it.

He stopped me and said, "No, don't give it to me."

About twenty minutes later, I said, "Do you want to know who it's from?"

"No."

I said, "I hope I live long enough to not want a note or even know who it's from." We giggled and had a grand time.

On another occasion, Olivier's son was doing *Ubu Le Roi* at a little theater off Melrose. I'd been invited to come over after I finished my performance. So I went over to find a long line waiting to get in at midnight. Someone yelled my name out and I was ushered inside to find Olivier sitting there in the theater all by himself with a bucket of ice and champagne and two glasses chilling waiting for me. And we sat and drank champagne and watched the performance with the others. I said good-bye to him at three o'clock in the morning in the parking lot behind the theater, thinking I had just died and gone to heaven.

Silvia Munro
Every day at four o'clock we used to go up to the main house for tea with my grandmother. She had a lovely tea and was fun to talk to. And she was the first one to have a television; she had it hidden behind a screen in the living room. If there was something special, we'd be allowed to watch TV with her. We watched children's programs and perhaps once a week, a film.

Win Rockefeller
Camping out up the Sylamore Creek in Arkansas, I woke one morning to the sound of bagpipes. I shook my head to clear it; I still heard bagpipes. I lifted the tent fly to see the fog settled low over the valley. I just sat there a while, looking at the morning over the meadow with the fog hanging about twenty feet above it, listening to the gurgle of the stream behind and the sound of the pipes.

Alastair Barbour
Before Helen and I married, I was going to go down to London to train.

And my grandmother, Helen Victoria Barbour, thought it would be a terrible waste if Helen and I lived on opposite sides of London, renting two flats and spending all our time traveling between the two. So she suggested that we live together.

She brought the subject up, I think. She was a grand old lady in her eighties then but very forward thinking.

We took it for an official blessing, said "Thank you very much," and off we went.

Helen Barbour
A group of us were driving up to a place in northwest Scotland. There were three of us in the backseat, Alastair, me, someone else.

And we went past a house on the left side of the road which had turf on the roof with crocuses growing. It was March or April. And I turned to Alastair and said, "One day, when we have a house like that, we'll have crocuses and daffodils on the roof." Then I was immediately quiet because I realized what I'd said.

Alastair was very quiet for the next day or two. . .then he proposed.

Edward Colquhoun

Getting David from the children's hospital in Brazil was a *shared* peak experience—a moment that is still very vivid. Everything about that first hour when we first held David was joyous, and it seemed as if everyone was radiating love.

Almost everyone we came in contact with regarding the adoption was especially helpful, and even the travel agent who drove us to the airport when we were leaving the town where David was born told us, "Everyone who knows about this thinks it is a wonderful thing."

Anne Brunson

For me that goes back to being pregnant. Before it starts showing, before you've told anybody and just you and your husband know, it's like your own special secret.

Campion Platt

It's the most amazing thing: holding my son the day he was born. He's one and a half. I don't think I had a sense of myself and where I fit in chronologically and culturally until he was born. Jeremy has been an incredible addition to my life. Being with him has been a turning point in my own life. I have this incredible feeling that watching your child is the first time since late childhood we sense our lives dramatically changing, reshaping. I can see all the good and bad habits and jealousies and discriminations which shape us.

And to watch him explore! My son brings this fresh attitude to my own life. It's like if you take up a new sport, you want to know the history of it, you want to know how it's done, and want to practice it. A child experiences that every day.

Being a father has seemed the most natural thing to me. I knew from the moment my son was born how to hold him, how to change his diaper. For me it was completely innate, and even talking about this makes me want to be with him.

Rodney Cook

One night recently, Emily was asleep, and I'd been working all day. I was tired but I had a fire going downstairs and I brought English, who's two, down with me and curled up in front of the fireplace with her. She slept. We just stayed there for an hour or two. That was the best.

Margaret Mason

Mynot, North Dakota, had incredible blizzards—I'm talking second-story blizzards where we could jump from the second story onto the snow. We were in the middle of one of those blizzards one day, and my father, who traveled a lot, was gone. My mother, who was a tiny but very determined person, had all three of us children home with the mumps. We were all alone in the house, with snow piled up all around the windows.

Perhaps she was a little nervous in this situation, but she created this wonderful comfortable time. It was close to Christmas. And all three of us, our swollen heads tied up in handkerchiefs for the mumps, were gathered around her in the warm kitchen as she read Dickens. *A Christmas Carol*. It was wonderful.

From that experience I think I distilled the knowledge that even in the worst of situations you can create a warm place. You can create your own reality.

Gerry Cooney

I learned how to swim when I was eleven. And how I learned was I went to the town pool and said, "Well, this is it," and jumped off the diving board. And I swam.

Years later because I loved my brother so much, I got him to do the same thing. I said, "Don't worry about it. I'll be there for you; I'll be there for you." And he almost drowned me! It was great—he looked like Mark Spitz for about ten strokes.

Eric Jensen

I am big brother to a twelve-year-old boy who has been emotionally abused severely by his father. Consequently this kid isn't trusting of adult males and has been slow to accept me. But we've been going to air shows together, going boating, running errands, and working on my fishtank.

Not long ago, he returned from a two-week stay with his grandparents. He brought me a little key chain from there and a little wristband. He was so proud to give them to me, and it meant so much to me, too! I knew at that point that he had accepted me and would stay in the program, and that was a special moment for both of us.

Dan Buettner

My dad and I went on a four-day weekend camping trip up in northern Minnesota with a couple of friends. We'd canoed through half-a-dozen lakes, up two rivers, and four portages to get to a small island on Polly Lake. At the time I went to church every Sunday with my dad, though he never said much about it. This Sunday, he took me into the woods and up to the highest point on the island. He put his hand on my shoulder, and we had a little bit of silence to replace that hour of prayer. That moment of silence did more for me spiritually than ten years of church did.

Bunny Johnson

In 1950, I wrote and recorded an essay for the "I Speak For Democracy" contest sponsored by the National Jaycees. One day they called me to the office over the loudspeaker at Swainsboro High School; a telegram had come telling me I had won the state contest. I don't know how to tell you how it felt.

Number one, I was going somewhere, and I had never been anywhere. We went to Williamsburg and gave our speeches in the colonial assembly. I drove up with Horace and Totsy Evans, the state Jaycee president and his wife, and spent the night on the way in an inn—a new experience. Then they left all the young people together. I had never been where young people could gather in rooms and talk. The winners from Virginia and the rest of the thirteen original colonies were there.

I also won a television set as part of the state contest. There were no TVs in Swainsboro, and we thought we'd sell it. Well, you can't sell a television when there are no television stations anywhere around. So it cost Mother a lot of money for us to keep it since she had to buy a telephone pole and put the antenna on top the pole. Then we put green cellophane paper over the screen and watched mainly the snow. The first thing we got was the Democratic National Convention. Every now and then you'd see somebody, but very seldom. I laugh now to think that the first people in town to own a TV lived in an upstairs garage apartment.

Buck Johnson

It's special to think about our son Doug being vice president in charge of A&R for Epic Records and remember how we used to listen to music from Nashville. We had one of the first radios, a round wooden thing. On Saturday night, we'd have neighbors come in, and we'd all sit there looking at the radio and listening to the "Grand Ole Opry." Roy Acuff would play "Great Speckled Bird."

Nashville to us then was like Paris would be to me now. Music from Nashville was music coming from heaven. If Mama or Daddy or I had known that we would have a son head of a big record company in Nashville, we would have passed out.

When Kristy Lane sang a song my son wrote on the country music awards, I told my mama, "Doug's song has just been played before fifty million people." And she said, "God almighty! How'd you get 'em together in one place?" She really did.

A. J. Hiers

A special moment no one knew about? When I was made a partner in the business. No one knew about that until ten seconds later when I could call my wife.

Egbert Donovan

Making these drinks is special to me. After I put them together, people come and start thinking about them. I won the bartender contest twice—once with this Shack Special Daiquiri (it's got mango and soursop) and the next year with my Soursop Daiquiri. I use the local fruit to make them: mango, guava, soursop, sugar apple.

Virginia Kahl

About the time I was writing my second book, I attended a party in Madison, Wisconsin. Dr. Seuss was also a guest and he sort of drifted over to me, and we talked about an hour until the hostess came and separated us.

Kurt Vonnegut

When I lived on Cape Cod, I was remodeling a barn up there, where one of my kids lives now. And I built a staircase. I went to the library, and I got a book on how to build a staircase. You know, the risers aren't all the same height. And I built a staircase, and I went running up and down that thing. It was solid as a rock. And it was just utterly private.

Carolyn Abrams

For me the moment came when I got past the ninth grade. For some reason, I measured things by my mother. She quit school in the ninth grade. When I finished the ninth grade, it was like the lock had been taken off and I could make it through high school and on to college.

My next milestone was that I had to get to twenty-two years of marriage, because that's when my mother and father divorced. I know their situation was different: My mother, at nineteen, came home from work one afternoon to find that her grandmother and aunt had arranged for her to marry my father, Mr. Hall, that evening. Her mother had died, and she was responsible for her four brothers and sisters. He was a widower of fifty-one. Though he was kind, she felt her life was cut off. So even though their lives were different, celebrating our twenty-second anniversary was special to me.

Ollie Ferguson

Traveling with my grandparents was an absolutely wonderful experience. I particularly remember meeting the Pope with them when I was nine.

We first sat for what seemed an endless time in a huge room. The ceiling must have been thirty feet high and the room so incredibly large that I felt like a small, insignificant thing sitting there alone with my grandparents waiting to see the Pope.

Finally we were called in for our audience, and my grandparents began to talk with the Pope and present different articles for blessing. But the one very vivid memory I have of the meeting is that the Pope wore red velvet shoes with little curly toes on them. In one of the pictures taken of our audience with the Pope, there I am looking down at those red velvet shoes.

Alvis Waite

After we moved to Guyton, we lived just thirty miles away from Savannah, where Grandmother and Granddad Waite lived. We'd drive into Savannah to visit in our Model T. The road was dirt until the Chatham County line and then narrow pavement. At an average of fifteen miles an hour, the trip took about two hours.

When we went on to Tybee Beach, another eighteen miles, we'd usually spend the night with Granddad because it was too long a trip to go to the beach and back home in one day. I enjoyed spending the night as a six-year-old because I got to stay on the sleeping porch. Most old two-story houses then had a sleeping porch on the back of the second story.

The summer I was six we'd been to Savannah for the Fourth of July, and Granddad Waite said, "I want Alvis, Jr., to stay, and tonight I'll carry him to Daffin Park to see the fireworks"—I'd never seen fireworks—"and tomorrow I'll put him on the train home." I can hear my mother now, "All by himself?" That was a special time with Granddad and quite an experience—riding home thirty miles on the train by myself.

Nancy Edmondson

I used to travel a lot with Daddy during the summers when I was a child. As a treat one trip when I was nine, we spent the night on Jekyll Island, which had a kid's train ride close to the ocean.

There was a huge full moon that evening, and after we rode around once on the train, I wanted to ride again.

Daddy said, "You can ride one more time, but these things aren't made for adults. I'll let you ride by yourself, if you don't mind."

I said, "OK," and got in. I was about the only rider except for the conductor. As I was riding along in the back by myself, looking at the ocean, I started singing "My Wild Irish Rose" at the top of my lungs.

Will McIntyre

Deni and I were riding Arabian horses in the desert in Egypt, and we'd never really galloped on horses before. But the first morning out we took off, boom, lickety-split right across the desert. What a wonderful feeling of exhilaration, going full speed! We were up in two-point stances like jockeys, and I was in the lead. I was just wondering how Deni was, whether she liked it or not, when all of a sudden on my right I heard this galloping getting louder and louder and louder. I thought, "Who in the hell is that?" Then I turned, and there was Deni coming by me. I thought I was going full speed, but she was flying. If I'd been a jockey in the home stretch of a big horse race I would have been left at the final turn. As she came by me, she had this great look on her face. She was so cool. She just waved with one hand like, "Hey! How ya doin!" And I thought, "No problem, she likes it just fine."

Carol Hallett

Yes, I have piloted an F18 and an F16, but the single most difficult feat I've ever accomplished was passing the water survival course to prepare to fly the F18. It was an all-day event that took me three months of training.

I had to spend three hours in the water in a flight suit and boots doing a variety of different things. The course ends with the instructors putting you in a mockup helicopter and lowering you down eighteen feet underwater, blindfolded and upside down, and you have to get out. Then you have to do it again.

That is the single most difficult thing I've ever done in my life because I've never been a good swimmer. I grew up being afraid of deep water. So to me, flying the F18 the next day was just like flying another airplane. The aerobatics were exciting but no big deal; I had done aerobatics in a J3 Cub twenty years before. But passing the underwater survival course, that was a big deal.

Patrick Goddard

A trip to Machu Picchu, Peru, with my son Patrick when he graduated from high school. There's a peak there called Huayna Picchu. People climb it during the day, and I didn't even like that idea since I don't like heights—great cliffs, narrow paths and sheer drop-offs are all that come to mind. And this particular climb was hand-over-hand on slippery rocks. You could fall a million miles any second, as far as I was concerned.

Well, our guide asked us if we'd like to climb it during the full moon. I didn't like the idea at all. But since this was Patrick's trip and he was eighteen, I said, "Whatever you say." I think he was nervous, too, but Patrick said, "Let's just start up and if it gets bad, we'll turn back." That sounded sensible. But I was still afraid.

The climb was terrifying in a way. Drop-offs at night are sheer black, and at the top there was no defined area, just drop-offs. But my son was excited. An eternity later, we were sitting on the top crags. Patrick had squirreled away a small book of poetry by Pablo Neruda, *The Heights of Machu Picchu.* He read it out loud.

The moon was full; I was transported. I was very proud. I'll never forget how magnificent it felt to climb up there with my son.

Jane Burke

When the Atlanta Symphony Orchestra and Chorus toured Europe in 1988, we sang Beethoven's Ninth at the Schauspielhaus in what was then East Berlin. The day before the concert we toured East Berlin. Though it was Sunday afternoon, few people were on the streets and no one smiled. In a crowded beer garden everybody was quiet, no one was laughing. We were allowed to stop only in certain places. It was all very depressing.

When we arrived at the Schauspielhaus, a beautiful building, guards were posted at various spots around the hall to keep us from going where we weren't supposed to.

As the concert began, I looked around the hall from my vantage point on the top row of the chorus. That elevation put me level with the gallery that rings the hall. I could see people's faces as the orchestra played the first three movements before the chorus begins to sing in the fourth. They were absorbed.

Beethoven's music is very important to the German people. As we started to sing Schiller's "Ode to Joy," *"Freude, schoner Gotterfunken"*. . . , I glanced over and saw a woman seated about twenty-five feet away and she was sobbing. I caught her eye a moment later, and I had tears streaming down my face. It was very hard to finish the performance. I thought about her the day the wall came down.

Edith Bornn

In 1988 I was invited to go to Russia by the League of Women Voters to consult with the Russian Women's Committee working on a document that Gorbachev was then circulating with respect to representative government. I had been a member of the league's National Board and had worked in international relations with the league at the UN. So with the league president and a former congresswoman, I went to Russia and met with the Russian women as they worked to analyze the document—what it meant; what their rights and obligations should be under it; what should they require for citizens, including women.

The exchange of ideas had been planned as a panel discussion. First several women designated by the Russians spoke, and then the U.S. delegation was to respond. When my turn came as the last member of the panel, rather than give a speech as the others had done, I asked questions of the Russian women and they responded. We really began to exchange ideas.

This apparently wasn't the proper thing to do. But when it finished, the Russian women said to me, "That's the best thing you ever could have done for us. We wanted to give you information but we did not have the freedom to initiate the discussion. We were told, however, to answer any questions if you asked. And you certainly had all the questions as if in a cross-examination!" I responded, "Well, that's my nature, my business." That was a fabulous experience.

Ben Rose

The afternoon we found the Lucayan caves on Grand Bahama. Marine life is one of my great interests. I had a friend on the island, Father Underhill, who knew this, and in the early sixties he told me about some caverns in the middle of the island that he had found by chance.

As a missionary, he did the whole route back and forth between West End and East End and Sweeting's Cay. The roads were just rocky tracks when you got beyond Freeport, and travel was rough. He'd have radiator trouble from time to time, running out of water. One day, when he had broken down, friends from one of the settlements said, "Come, we know where there's water," and took him off through the woods and climbed down a tree root into a hole and emerged with fresh water.

Since I'd been collecting fish in a number of other caverns near the harbor, he told me about all the fish he'd seen in this one. I didn't follow up for a long time.

Then one Sunday when we'd had a cold front or a storm and it was miserable, rainy, and too windy to go out and dive, a group of us went hunting the cavern for something to do. We trudged through the woods for about three hours on foot. We'd just about given up hope, when we found the sea cave. The trees were growing right up to it. We actually walked between the trees, where the ground had been eaten out by the sea. But we saw no fish in the water in the cave.

We decided to go back to the car to get the snorkeling gear. As we started walking through the woods to go to the car, I suddenly froze. I'd pushed the trees apart to take the next step and suddenly realized there was this big hole in front of me. We could see tree roots going down the side, so we climbed down the roots on to the breakdown pile, where the rocks had fallen in, and straightaway we could see all the fish. These caves are part of the Lucayan National Park now.

John Englander

Ice diving in the Arctic was really like another world. Though I'd had some cold-water diving experience, I had done no ice diving. And there we were up in the Arctic, diving through a three-foot-diameter hole, through ice ten feet thick, and in water that was below freezing—minus 1.6 degrees Celsius. Eskimos and Inuits were peering over the edge. The water was crystal clear, true icy blue. It was like another planet.

Paul Mockler

Sitting in a dogsled crossing the Arctic, my sense of amazement as the landscape went by.

40. Letting Veronica Go: A Portrait

Carolyn Abrams

When I think of loneliness, I think of Veronica, our second daughter. Veronica died when she was two days old. The circumstances were so tragic.

When I woke up that morning in 1971, Robert was at my hospital bedside saying that she was in trouble, that they had called him at home. To that point my biggest worry had been that Veronica had been born on August 17 and Andrea's birthday was August 5 and would we have one birthday party or two. And then I wake up with Robert standing there.

His parents were out of town. We were by ourselves crying and praying and hoping everything was all right, that the doctors who were working on her were having success. Then the hospital maid came in and offered her condolences. That's how we found out that our baby had died. They brought Veronica into us after that.

In the next few days, Robert showed a strength I don't think I could have had. He had to arrange everything by himself. He had to plan the funeral. He had to buy the burial dress. They wouldn't let me go to the funeral. He had to do it all. Talking about it is still hard for him.

And through the years it has been so hard for me. Coming to closure with this loss and grief finally came for me in January 1990. I didn't share this, not even with Robert, for a while. But about three o'clock in the morning I woke up. Through the years

I had wondered if I had done something wrong that had caused Veronica's premature birth. Could I have prevented it? I felt I had resolved that, but I'd always wanted to go to the funeral and couldn't. That bothered me, and I couldn't let go.

Then sitting there in our den at three in the morning I got my Bible and opened the Methodist Hymnal to the order for the burial of the dead and offered the service. I thought about my child. I cried. I prayed. I did "ashes to ashes." I did the benediction.

There was a sense of peace. It was as if something had been lifted. I recorded it in my Bible and told no one. But I could begin to let go.

Now I am able to share more with the other children about Veronica. Since all six of my children were born in three months of the year, each child has seemed part of a pair. But there are four years between Andrea and Stacy, and it's always been like part of Andrea's pair was missing. Now the whole family has been able to ask questions; in letting go we've been able to make Veronica more a part of the family because we can talk about her.

41. A Moment of Loneliness

Dan Buettner

When we reached Nicaragua on our bike trek through the Americas, I flew back to Spain to be with my new son on the first days after his birth. While I was in Spain, my three teammates called from Panama to say that, in spite of their promise, they had decided not to wait for me. They were going on alone through the most dangerous part of the trek—walking through the Darien Gap, the jungle between Panama and Colombia.

A week and a half later I flew back to Nicaragua and began bicycling southward. Six weeks later, I caught up with the team. During that time, I felt lonely. I remember one night two days after returning, I was spending the night in a hotel in southern Nicaragua. For thirty-three cents a night, I got a cinder block room. There was a bed but it had only one filthy sheet. There was a huge puddle filling the middle of the room that came from a toilet flooding over down the hall. I can remember lying there thinking of my newborn son and wife. Instead of being home looking after them, as most people would think proper, I was in this squalid room, miles from my team, and absolutely alone.

Jim Swann

The first time I went to camp. I was probably nine years old. I was taken to the Greyhound bus station, put on a bus with fifty kids I didn't know, and taken all night long through the back roads of North Carolina and Georgia. I can remember vividly going to the bathroom at a bus stop with some drunk laid out underneath all the toilets. I'd never seen such. I'd never been on a Greyhound bus before. It was horrible. My response was, "I'm going home!

This is not for me; I made a mistake stuck here for five weeks. I don't like these people!''

My little daughter had basically the same reaction. She wrote me only one letter: "I don't like any of these people! I'm lonely! I'm homesick!" Then we didn't hear anything from her after about five days. You know how worried you get, so Johnnie called the camp. "Oh, she's fine, one of our greatest campers."

When she comes off the airplane at the end of the summer she's covered with yellow clay, hasn't taken a bath, hasn't washed her hair, and she brags about not brushing her teeth for two weeks.

So I go, "How did you like camp?"

She goes, "Oh, it was the most fun I ever had in my whole life. I didn't want to leave and I want to go back," and on and on. My daughter talked for two hours and didn't slow down and she's not that kind of kid.

That loneliness the first time you get sent away is a horrible experience. But you have to do it. You've got to go away one day.

Jock Munro

At the age of eight I was sent to a relatively strict boarding school on the east coast of Scotland just south of Aberdeen. I had had a wonderfully warm, cocooned upbringing as a child with a wonderful nanny and nice, kind, warm parents. My friends were the farm workers' children and local schoolmates. It was a very pleasant but a very innocent childhood. I'd never had to face any aggression or stand up for myself.

Suddenly I was plunged into a boarding school with 150 other little boys between the ages of eight and thirteen, where you slept in iron beds and wore shorts 360 days a year even though the school was right beside the sea. We used to have Vaseline put on our knees in the evening before we went to bed because our knees were chapped from the cold. So I was thrown into this Spartan life.

I was not prepared, not at all. I remember right to this day coming with a box—everyone went to school with a small wooden trunk in which you kept your books, the small toys allowed, and a bit of sweets—I remember the boys gathered around as I opened my box: "Oh, what are those?" "Can I borrow that?" "Can I have this?"

I said sure. I looked in the box after some twenty minutes and everything had gone. Even the toys that were lent never came back. And of course the sweets were eaten immediately. I was so naive. Though I learned to stand up for myself and had a lot of friends, it came as an enormous shock to begin with, and I felt deeply, deeply lonely, missing my mother and my nanny. I cried for weeks and weeks.

Desy Campbell

In ninth grade I attended school with my friends until Christmas, then my hips were operated on in January. That's when I lost contact with everybody. I was either in the hospital or at home in a body cast until June. I was fourteen—a big transition time for children.

When I went back for tenth grade at public school, everybody had grown up and I was still little. There were five of us that had been short like I was until ninth grade. But after the operation I didn't grow much more and everyone else shot up. I'd also missed out a lot in that half year.

For all those reasons, my friends didn't accept me the same way anymore. I soon went off to boarding school.

Doris Roberts

I felt very much alone as a child. I never knew my father, who left when I was an infant. Since my mother was forced to work to support us, I lived with my grandparents and their children. Later I went to an aunt. I just never quite belonged, always a boarder in somebody's home. It seemed to me the only reason I was allowed to stay there was the fact that money was left on the table every Friday night for my support.

My lonely childhood is probably one of the reasons I started acting. My fantasy life was the thing that got me through that period.

Lenny Berman

When my mother died of Hodgkin's when I was ten, my family essentially dissolved. Though I got some support from my aunts, I felt that from that point on I was by myself and raised myself. From the time I was in the sixth grade, I got myself out of bed in the morning, got myself ready for school, and came home to an empty house. My dad left for the factory at 5:00 A.M. and got home at 6:00 P.M. and was too tired to do much but take a nap.

Eric Edmondson

When my brother Evan died, I felt like the whole world had deserted me. I was very close to my brother. It hit the whole family very hard. I was a freshman in college, and he was three years younger. From the time Evan was diagnosed as having aplastic anemia until he died was only six weeks. I don't think I'd really considered the possibility of his not making it. The doctors were trying a variety of treatments, and while I'd had schoolmates killed in car accidents, people my age got well when they were sick.

The day he died my grandmother had called to say that perhaps I ought to come home for the weekend, since Evan was not doing well. I left after lab and came on home. All these people were there when I arrived and my grandmother told me.

That first night was especially bad. Mom wasn't home because she didn't think she could stand coming back to the house right away. My friend Roddy came over to spend the night, but he was in one room upstairs and I in another downstairs. Our whole family was in different spots for a while. We didn't know what to say to each other. Like most families, we'd never had to go through anything like that. It took a while.

Phoebe Legere

I think I've been lonely ever since I left my family. I think suffering and solitude and silence are the key to creativity. But it's terribly lonely. A woman without a husband and children is lonely.

David Prowse

I think I was most lonely when my mother died in 1966. A lovely lady: big, very jovial, blonde—oh, such a lovely attitude about life! I lived with Mother until I was twenty-eight, and then I went to London. I became the British Weightlifting Champion, I had a job working for this American weightlifting company, and I started doing film and television work. Playing the bodyguard in *A Clockwork Orange* was a big break.

As the money started coming in, Mother could never understand how I earned money. You know, why would anybody pay me to endorse a product or to act? Mother and I drifted apart then.

Barbara Bailey

I miss someone to touch. I miss just touching my husband's arm, brushing against him. When you are alone after fifty-six years of comfortable closeness, the feeling of physical isolation can be deeply lonely.

Mildred Sutton

The first night I spent in our house after Remar's, my husband's, death. That's a real loneliness, and I still feel it lots of times, eleven years later.

Lyn Lear

So many. . .I remember in New York right before I moved back here, a feeling that you'd almost rather be in a bad relationship than no relationship at all—even though you know in the back of your mind that isn't right. To be so lonely is the worst kind of pain. I've been in a couple of bad relationships, and the positive thing was really being able to get the strength to break away from them and deal with the loneliness afterward.

Norman Lear

This is a great presumption, but I think I have known a greater loneliness than Lyn's. She was not married, but she had a stronger relationship with things eternal. I was married, but having a ton of friends and a marriage and children and everything without having a real sense of one's place in the universe is probably a worse loneliness.

Stephanie Beacham

I think loneliness has a lot to do with lacking self-worth. I can think of an actual instance of huge loneliness just when my marriage split up, and I knew I had to be surrounded by roses. I wanted to make my life happy again. I bought on sale two of the cheapest rolls of wallpaper covered in huge roses. I didn't have any money at the time. I went home after the theater one night and cut out individual roses, got the wallpaper glue, and began to make a collage of roses from the two different rolls.

My babies were asleep in the room next door, but I felt a terrible feeling of loneliness, the most enormous loneliness. Then, my babies woke up and came in, and they said, "Mummy, can we help, can we help, can we help? Mummy, why are you crying?" And I can remember saying, "Oh, darling, I'm not crying, it's just that the wallpaper glue is making my eyes run."

Then of course what happened is the children and I had a wonderful party with sticky paper and glue, and gosh did the room look a mess the next day.

Sonya Friedman

I spent the first thirty years of my life feeling lonely inside even though I was married and had children. I didn't have the ability to really maintain attachments. I really believe it takes some of us a while to understand that physical closeness doesn't necessarily mean closeness. You can be in the same room with somebody, work with them all day, and still not feel close to them. Or you can be apart from people physically and feel very close to them.

Stuart Perkins

The worst was three days after I arrived in Boca Raton. I had gone through a dreadful divorce; I had nothing but debt up to my eyeballs. I'd come down on a friend's yacht to this beautiful town that was going to solve all my problems, and it hadn't solved a one. I was alone, depressed, had some medical problems. It was the worst time I ever had in my life. I was so angry, a year later I was writing my ex-wife's name on the balls when I played polo. But for the first time in my life I listened to other people. I listened to my therapist. I listened to friends. I kept going. Slowly but surely things got better.

Win Rockefeller

Which one? The worst times are when I'm in a room filled with people who know me but with no one I can call a real friend.

Mary Lou Retton

I have a lot of loneliness because I'm on the road so much by myself. At times I'm the loneliest when I'm around people who recognize me, but I don't know them. It's much harder to make real friends, now. Everybody wants to know you and so forth, but it's difficult to make good friends.

Mary Costigan, Supper Club

I flew out to visit my sister in Kansas City and nobody was there to meet me. I waited, but no one arrived. I didn't have her number and didn't know how to use the complicated pay phone. That was a lonely feeling. When I finally managed to call her, she said, "Where are you?"

"At the airport."

"Oh, I thought you were coming next month."

Timothy Sultan

My moment of loneliness is not negative. I remember swimming out on the lake in the late afternoon and lying on my back and with slow arm strokes pushing my way against the current of the lake. My ears underwater, staring at the sky, I could hear nothing but my breathing. My body felt large, like a planet, entirely alone and self-aware.

Dave DeGrandpre

I took last winter off from school, left a girl I was in love with, and drove around the West. I was on the road four weeks all by myself cruising different ski areas, and it was a pretty lonely time. But it felt good because I knew just being by myself would force me to do a lot of thinking. It did. I'm not afraid of being alone as much anymore.

Kate Learson

When I was in grade school, we lived in a small house and my three sisters and I shared two bedrooms and one bathroom. There was a lot of hostility and anger in the household. The anger was so great that I couldn't breathe, and I'd climb out of the bathroom window and sit on a little roof there just to get some air.

Another thing I would do was go out to a special place in the woods. Behind our house was a much bigger house on a lot of property. In the woods was an old Indian or settler's log cabin. Below it were huge boulders. I would climb down to one big, big boulder with a little overhang that I could sit under. It was my friend and I would talk to it. I did that for years. I never named it, but that boulder was like a human to me. It was my friend, a place where I could weep quietly and feel enormously sad for myself but feel ever so slightly protected.

Torre Andrews

When I was eleven, my dad married my stepmother and we moved into her house with her three kids. Since I was mostly on my own with three kids I didn't like very much, I starting spending a lot of time at my mom's house. I would ride the Greyhound bus down to San Diego every weekend and ride it back on Sunday night. We lived close enough to a major intersection that I could ask the bus driver just to pull over at the next stoplight. I would get off and walk a mile or so up the street in the dark, back to the house where I had to be. The whole trip back, from the time we left Mom's house, through the bus ride, and along the dark walk was all prelude to opening the door and walking in and hoping nobody would start yelling at me. That was a particularly lonely time.

Virginia Kahl

The loneliest moment was probably when I landed in Berlin in 1948 during the blockade. It was my first job as an army librarian in Europe, and I knew no one. Berlin was in ruins. For mile after mile there was nothing but ruins. It was a divided city, too. We could go into our sector and the English sector anytime, but if we went into the Russian area, we had to tell someone where we were going and when we'd be back so that someone could try to get us out if we did not return at a reasonable time.

That was a very lonely time until I began to know some of the people at work. Our library was called "Uncle Tom's Library" because it was located on Onkel Tom Strasse, so named because a black gentleman had once lived in the area. Soldiers and some British nationals used the library. It was an unsettled time. I remember that one Englishman had borrowed a book and then lent it to his German driver who traveled to the Russian sector. When the book became overdue, I mentioned it to the man, who said his driver had disappeared, as people did sometimes. The book was Thomas Wolfe's *You Can't Go Home Again*.

Rodney Cook

When I was young, the mayor of Atlanta in the early sixties had had a wall built in one part of town to keep blacks from moving into what was then a white neighborhood. Though the mayor realized quite quickly that it had been a stupid thing to do, my father had been about the only person who had come out publicly in opposition to it.

As a result, shortly after, when my parents went out of town, the Ku Klux Klan burned a cross on our lawn. Standing on the third floor with my sisters and Bertha, the black maid who raised us, and looking out at these bizarre people burning this cross on the yard was the strangest feeling I have ever had. I was probably seven or eight, and I remember being the only male there. I cared about these people and I felt I was supposed to protect us, but it was an extremely lonely feeling as I thought, What am I supposed to do? It made me angry to see Bertha's face and how frightened those strange people made her.

Of course, the police came. No one was hurt—they didn't even approach the house. But I remember how angry and lonely I felt.

John Emmerling

When I was twenty-five, I left my job in San Francisco and went to Europe by myself on a five-month trip I had lusted after. I had been away from San Francisco for two months when I woke up one morning in a borrowed apartment in Stockholm. I remember sitting in the living room and playing a Tony Bennett album with the song "I Left My Heart In San Francisco." I played it over and over, feeling a tremendous sense of homesickness and vulnerability that I don't think I had ever experienced before. I am someone who surrounds myself with people I enjoy, yet I had put myself into the lonely situation where I was in a strange place, strange apartment, strange city. I sat on the floor and cried.

Chris Keefe

Two moments of loneliness, both related to crack. I would get real lonely when I knew I couldn't get any more crack for the night and knew I had to go to work in a couple of hours. I'd lie down to get some sleep and couldn't, of course, even though I'd chug a ton of booze.

The second moment occurred when my brother dropped me off at the treatment center in Miami. Flying over from the island, it hadn't hit me yet, because I was still with someone who loved me. I was in a daze, anyway. Even when I checked in, it still wasn't bad because my brother was still there.

Then after checking me in, they took me on an elevator to the third floor. My brother had run out to get me some toothpaste and stuff, so I watched the people in the adult wing. Some of them looked completely normal, and some looked pretty weird. But I handled that.

The loneliness didn't hit until a woman came to the third floor with the things my brother had bought me. I wasn't allowed to go downstairs, and he wasn't allowed to come up. But Bill had written me a note. I don't think he'd ever done that before. And I know we hadn't talked about feelings that much openly. But he told me he loved me and he knew this was the best thing for me.

I have always idolized my brother, wanted him to look up to me. But right then, looking out the window and reading his note, I didn't think he ever would again. That was probably the most depressing, lonely instant in my life.

42. Once on a Rainy Afternoon

Amy Holloway

Rainy days are the best—gray and misty. I get a lot done on gray days. I don't mind my hair frizzing or the dampness.

You can look at me and tell I'm obviously not a sun person. The kids at Northside High where I taught used to tell me I was the whitest white woman they knew. I was not meant to tan. My whole family loves rainy days; we must have lived on the moors in some former life.

Taylor Plimpton and John Jaxhiemer

Going to the movies, going bowling because we're bored.

Nan Thomas

One rainy, winter afternoon at Sugarbush, my friend Albert came over. "Ah, this is just awful!" he said. "What are we going to do? The skiing's a wreck."

"I don't know," I said.

"Wait," he said, "I've got an idea. You know, I hear the kids are smoking pot."

"Albert! You're not going to do anything like that!"

"No—but—I heard that if you take banana peels and bake them, you get something not as bad but something you can still get a kick out of."

So he went downtown and bought two corncob pipes, and we baked banana peels and cut them all up and stuffed them in the pipes. It was the most god-awful taste, and nothing happened.

Peggy Kemp, Supper Club
Rainy afternoons make playing bridge even better. You never have to feel guilty because you ought to be doing something else.

Gerry Cooney
Once on a rainy afternoon, I sat by the fire and was read to by a special person. *The Velveteen Rabbit.* It's about what's real.

Carolyn Abrams
I'd wish for a chance to sit down and finish a book without anybody calling "Mama."

Dave DeGrandpre
Sometimes on a rainy afternoon as a child I would go out on the porch with my mom, and we would kind of bundle up, cuddle, and sit there. The rain would be coming down really hard, the thunder and lightning would be cracking, and I would get these chills because it was cold and eerie—a really nice sensation.

Dana Warrington
I remember being anchored off Bimini in the Bahamas when a major-league squall came up in the pitch black night: howling winds, seas crashing over our little sailboat, our hull scraping against the reef. Three terrifying hours in the rain I could have done without.

Barbara Bailey
One horrible, cold, wretched, miserable day in London in January 1965, I was flipping through a women's journal and saw an advertisement for a development on Grand Bahama Island; a picture of a beautiful beach, palm trees, blue skies, and all the rest. It rather intrigued me, so I filled in a coupon almost accidentally. We first visited the island the same year and retired here in 1969.

Princess Pamela Strobel

My grandmama didn't like me associating with a lot of people, particularly boys, and she had a way of telling me things I'd never forget.

One rainy day Grandmama told me if I even ate an apple given to me by a young man, I'd have a baby. She had a way of saying things like that: "Don't ever accept anything from a man. Not even an apple! See those apples on the table? If you want one, eat it at home, because something *bad* can happen to you." I was a real late bloomer and still don't eat many apples.

Cliff Robertson

When Dina and I split up, I went up to a friend's tiny cottage in the woods in upstate New York for two weeks. I stayed there with nothing but music and books, trying to separate some trees from the forest.

Dan Buettner

On a gray, rainy afternoon near Chita in the Soviet Union, I topped a hill and started down the other side. My brakes were so worn I couldn't control the acceleration; the rain was coming down so hard it bounced off my eyeballs, causing rapid blinking. The countryside that afternoon rolled by like the image of a flickering, early motion picture.

Joy Melton Prickett

Coming home on a cold, rainy afternoon to a pot of hot vegetable soup on the stove.

Doris Peck, Supper Club

When it rained, we'd go over to the creek on our farm and wade in the mud and play and just have the best time there ever was.

Timothy Sultan

On rainy afternoons in Laos, I would wait in the darkened house rather excitedly, for often the backyard would fill so quickly with water that later in the day we could take the bright red washtubs out and paddle around in the newly created pond. During longer rains the water would rise beneath the stilted Laotian houses; streets, cars, and rice fields were flooded.

When we lived in the Ivory Coast, the rain slamming down on the tin roof would cause a roar throughout our house.

Phoebe Legere

Once on a rainy afternoon in Maine, I went on a walk through the woods to a place that had about six hundred varieties of moss, deep green moss all wet on the shiny, shiny trunks of each tree; all those intricate root systems covered with moss. There's nothing like virgin woods for the druid mind.

Mary Randolph

When I was in junior college, any time it rained, we had an open invitation to go over to one of the professor's apartments and just sit and talk. When it was getting sort of dry, you prayed for rain. It was a time to get out, walk in the rain, get all wet, enjoy a hot cup of cocoa, just talk about all of the important and unimportant things in the world.

I lost that teacher, Joanne, for twenty-eight years. She was one of the three most important people in all my college life, and there were a lot of people in my life then. I found her two years ago and had dinner with her just two weeks ago, and it was an absolutely delightful find, a present.

Kurt Vonnegut

Once on a rainy afternoon after my first marriage broke up, I was living alone in New York City. I didn't know what to do, so I went out and bought a phonograph record and brought it home and it turned out that was a good idea. Must have been Rossini's Overtures, I guess. It was really the right thing to do.

Campion Platt

Being at a Van Morrison concert. He's very awkward in concert, and I think he's had a very hard life; but his voice and music are special, and he's my favorite artist.

George Plimpton

Mother took us to see the movie *Waterloo Bridge* on a rainy day in Huntington, Long Island. I was ten years old. My mother thought this film was about something else. In fact, it starred Vivian Leigh as a prostitute who falls in love with an army officer during the war. My brother and I didn't understand the film at all, and we were too young to have it explained to us. We wondered why Vivian Leigh was so worried about her background. I remember that afternoon very vividly. My first grown-up film. Mother must have loved it, because we sat through the whole thing.

Silvia Munro

When we were married, we spent two weeks in a cottage up in the mountains in Bavaria and it rained almost every single day. We played a lot of backgammon. It didn't matter.

Zar Rochelle

One rainy afternoon when I was young, I was so bored I counted all the books in the house. There were several thousand.

Doris Roberts

Fiftieth Street, top-floor apartment, Bill Goyen listening to me, just sitting and talking.

There's a sweet story that reminds me of. When Bill first moved into that apartment, I was working on some television show, and I said I'd come by at the end of the day to help him unpack books and stuff like that. So I came to the building where he had the top-floor apartment and I rang the bell. There was no answer. So I rang the bell again and again. No answer.

Since he didn't have a phone yet, I went across the street to the fire station. The guy on duty said, "Are you his wife, lady?"

I said, "No, no, I'm just a friend. He just moved in and the bell doesn't work and he doesn't have a phone in yet and I don't know how to reach him."

Do you know what they did? Brought the fire engine, New York's second largest, halfway out of the building, put on the lights and the siren, and asked me if I wanted to go up the ladder, which I would have done had I been wearing long trousers.

Everybody on that street opened their windows to see where the fire was except Bill Goyen. The man who lived in the building next to him on the top floor went over his roof and knocked on Bill's door and said, "Look out your window." And there I was. So then he let me in.

Patrick Goddard

There's great power and emotion in the elements. I'm looking forward to this weekend. We're supposed to have a rainstorm.

When I was five, I remember my mother coming home from a date. I was waiting by myself in the darkness, perched in a tree branch all bundled up in a peacoat. The wind was howling, but it didn't seem cold to me. I also remember my grandmother's house. In the winter, I'd open the windows when it was really cold, take all the covers off my bed, and lie there, pretending I was a cowboy out on the prairie at night with my horse. Then I'd grab the covers and bundle up. What safety, what security that seemed to give me! It was an emotional thing.

John Emmerling

On a rainy afternoon during Christmas in Venice, Kate and I are staying in a beautiful room looking out over the Adriatic. Through the misty rain, we can see the early evening walkers in San Marco Square and the lights coming on. The pink glass of those street lamps illuminates the view with this incredible color. We decide that we're not going to go out, we're going to make love. To me a rainy afternoon has always been the most sensual, lovely, marvelous time to make love.

43. *Holding Hands: A Portrait*

Carol and Jim Hallett

Carol: Actually, we don't hold hands.

Jim: No, we're not big hand holders. The thing that distinguishes us is that through thirty-four years of marriage, Carol and I have been friends. That's the basic tenet under which we live.

Carol: But we depend a lot on one another.

Jim: Even though we're independent, we're very dependent on each other.

Carol: We stay in constant communication, no matter where we are. For instance, I do a lot of traveling. But I always call Jim. We talk to each other twice a day, no matter where we are.

Jim: Anywhere in the world.

Carol: And from some of the most inconvenient places— Hungary, Turkey, South America, rural Mexico—because that's important.

Jim: We talk over things that are important to us. Shortly after we were married, for instance, we made an important decision: not to have children. That was one of the smartest decisions we ever made because it set us on two professional career tracks. It has allowed us to do a lot of things that people with children can't do. For instance, Carol probably wouldn't be where she is today if we'd had children. She never would have become this flying nut that she is today.

Carol: Or a state legislator. Remember I got my first job in politics because I could fly.

Jim: I would still have been teaching at the university; I'd have loved to finish my career there. But we've done so many exciting things together. I've changed professions six times. Carol has had challenging government positions. This constant change has been healthy for us mentally. I don't think we've ever made a wrong turn in the road which had significance for us.

Carol: Jim said something there that is really important: together. That's the uniqueness in our marriage that I don't see as much in other marriages. For instance, Jim had been teaching at Cal Poly for ten years and I had been running a joint office for two legislators when I was asked to run for the state assembly. Jim and I must have talked for a hundred hours going through the pros and cons trying to decide, because that was still at a time when, you know, husbands weren't real enthusiastic about their wives going on and doing something.

Jim: This was a whole new direction in our lives. We knew it would be, and we had to set our ground rules. The funniest part is that I agreed to go along for one two-year term . . .

Carol: To see if it worked.

Jim: Was I ever naive! I mean Carol has been political since before we married.

Carol: I'm the eternal optimist, too.

Jim: Well, she won and was very successful. One thing led to another. As Carol's political career advanced, I finally left my job teaching at Cal Poly and became the president of the Western Agricultural Chemicals Association.

In the beginning, as is very normal, I got the job and Carol came along and took what work she could find—secretarial position, whatever. Then things evolved and now it's just the other way around. And that's great. I've had a good career and Carol has too. We know where we are going—what's going to happen in five years, ten years. We have a goal. And it's all done together.

44. A Special Relationship

Cliff Robertson

It sounds funny to say a relationship with your kids, but both of those kids are my daily blood supply; they're transfusions, whether it's on the phone or a letter or being with them. We have a very open relationship. It sounds old-fashioned, but my older daughter insisted that her husband ask me for her hand in marriage. Victorian!

Foxy Callwood

I'll sing it:

"I really really got to give you that message,
The relationship that I practice, my marriage
Well, all you got to agree with me
I need nothing more than my Lord and my family."

Ever since I was a teenager I've been playing and singing. But after I fell out of a coconut tree and broke this finger joint out of place, I only play in C. Whatever I do, I play in these three chords.

George Plimpton

The love of my father for my mother, and she for him. It was lovely seeing them together. When my father was made an ambassador to the United Nations, he was sworn in in the General Assembly. He was sitting next to Adlai Stevenson. With Mother up in the balcony, I saw him give a little thumbs-up sign to her, very private, a prearranged signal. They shared everything.

Ollie Ferguson

With my grandparents I think it was almost love at first sight. It appeared to me to be unquestionable, unwavering love from day one until my grandfather died last year. Even when they argued, you could see the underlying love.

They both had their own space. The thing that I found incredible about their relationship was neither one of them said *You should do this* or *You should do that.* They both could do whatever they wanted, but whatever they did they wanted to be together. In other words, they weren't like two people who say *Well, since you like this and I like that, you can have your space here and I'll go there.* They had the same option, but their choice was always to be together. I found their enjoyment of that unwavering, total commitment to each other enviable and admirable and probably the single greatest thing that I remember from their relationship.

Phoebe Legere

My relationship with my grandmother. Her name was Bessie Hemenway. She loved me. She died one year ago, maybe a year and a half. Grandmother came to New York with my grandfather to watch me perform, but she was not critical of me. Once she said, "Oh, your grandfather and I just love those rock beats!"

45. Friends and Family at Their Funniest

Buck Johnson

Cousin Sally wanted an air conditioner, so she went into Metter to buy one, and they said, "Miss Sally, what size you want?"

She said, "I don't know."

They said, "Well how many BTUs do you want?"

She said, "I don't know a thing in the world about BTUs. All I know is I want an air conditioner with enough BTUs to cool a b-u-t-t as big as a t-u-b." She was really large.

Virginia Kahl

I worked with this nice woman who was Catholic, and one day she said, "Oh, it's Friday, and I can't eat any meat, so probably I'll have to have some eggs tonight. I'm so tired of them."

I said, "Well, gee, that's what you get for not being a Protestant. I can go home and have a nice dinner."

So I went home to find my mother beating up a storm. We were having scrambled eggs, she'd made custard, and she'd made egg cakes and angel food cake and yellow sponge cake. I asked what happened. We had this gentleman who was a friend of the family who had moved to a little area outside of Milwaukee and started a chicken farm, and he began to deliver eggs to all his friends. Actually my father had eaten in his restaurant for years, and so some of his restaurant customers would take eggs. He would come in on a train, and then he'd take a taxi around to his customers. When he had got to our house that day, he had fallen out of the cab with his eggs, and my mother had said, "Well, I'll take whatever eggs are broken." There were fifty-nine broken eggs. And we ate them. That's what you get for being a Protestant.

Mary Costigan, Wednesday Bridge Club

When I taught kindergarten in a church basement, the men's room was a couple of doors down from the kindergarten proper. I missed a little boy but knew that he was probably in the rest room. I waited a little while and he never came back. So I went down and spoke to him through the door, asked him if he was having problems or anything. I didn't get any answer. I kept talking to him, telling him to hurry up. No answer. Finally, I told him I was going to come and get him. To which the pastor's voice replied, "I'm in here."

Rose Wing, Supper Club

Many years ago, I was just teaching away one day. History. And this boy said, "Mrs. Wing, you're such a good history teacher." Well, with that, I just beamed. My day was made. Then he added, "You've lived through so much of it."

Torre Andrews

My grandmother loved to teach and was an excellent tutor. Of course, students came to her since she couldn't get out.

For some reason once, a student gave her a couple of joints. Probably she knew or suspected that he had them and didn't want him to smoke them and so said, "Why don't you give them to me? I'd like to try them." At any rate, he did.

She treasured those joints. She kept them under glass, so she could bring them out at bridge parties and shock her friends. It never occurred to her to smoke them, but they were so obscene to her friends she couldn't resist suggesting they could get stoned if they wished. I think it was neat that a student would trust this old lady enough to give them to her.

Nancy Edmondson

Aunt Maude was one of everybody's favorite relatives. She had lived in Washington while her fiancé went off to fight in World War I. When he was killed, she never married but stayed in Washington and lived at the Bellevue Hotel for almost fifty years.

When she could no longer care for herself, she came to live with my parents. But as far as she was concerned she was still living, perfectly happy, at the Bellevue. She dressed and went down for dinner every night—she wore gloves, took her pocketbook, and locked her door.

Once after dinner we were in the family room relaxing and talking, and Aunt Maude was sitting there gloved, holding her pocketbook, when she noticed some shoes on the floor. "Whose shoes are these?" she asked. When we tried to ignore the question, she said, "WHOSE SHOES ARE THESE?"

"Mine," said my niece Kelley.

"The lobby is not a good place to leave your shoes, young lady."

Bunny Johnson

We've some good friends who put words together more entertainingly than most of us. For instance, at Christmas they put "ointments" on the tree. Once when she went to visit the Mennonites up in Jefferson County, she stopped to ask the policeman where the "morphodites" lived.

When his ulcer was acting up, he reported that the doctor had told him "not to eat any more plumage." That gives new insight into the meaning of "roughage," doesn't it?

World-class achievements go into the "Gideon's Book of Records." And once after a "hockey expedition game," they took us out to eat "garnished hen."

They've had such an influence on their friends that sometimes we can't remember whether the color, for instance, is really "burgamy" or not.

Cliff Robertson

When my daughter Stephanie was five, I was taking her fishing, and en route to the boat, she announced with the wisdom of a five-year-old, "Daddy, I'm not gonna catch any fish."

I said, "Let's just wait, dear."

As the boat was going out of the harbor, she looked up and said, "Daddy, I'm not gonna catch any fish. I know."

I said, "Wait."

We got beyond the three-mile line of demarcation, and as her line was dropping into the water, she looked up again and said, "Daddy, I am not going to catch any fish."

"Stephanie, damn it all, in fishing as in life you must *always* be positive."

"All right," she said. "I'm positive I'm not going to catch any fish."

Edward Colquhoun

My mother and her best friend (a sixty-year friendship) took a car-repair course. If you saw my mother—she's a demure little lady—you'd never expect her to know anything mechanical.

And one day my mother was under the hood in the A&P parking lot and some fellow in a baseball cap and T-shirt came up and said, "Can I help you, little lady?" And she said, "No, I'm just adjusting the timing." Which, of course, he didn't know how to do. I'd like to have seen his face.

Anne Brunson

My daddy never went shopping, but while my mother was sick, he had to take me to buy a bathing suit. I was four or five, and he bought me an adult size-fourteen bathing suit, a size which I have never worn in my whole life.

When he got us home, Mother asked, "Why did you get her that bathing suit?"

He said, "That's the one she wanted."

Evidently he had said, "Pick out a bathing suit," and I had—a white two-piece. I can still remember it because you can't return a bathing suit, and every year I would try it on thinking that it might be the right size. It never was.

Silvia Munro

Jock sleep*talks*. When we were newly married, we lived in a two up, two downer—bedroom, bathroom upstairs, sitting room and kitchen downstairs—with a steep staircase with a door at either end between the kitchen and our bedroom. Our dog lived in the kitchen.

I woke up one night to hear Jock calling out, "Be quiet! Sit up!" and whistling at the dog, "Come in here, you silly dog. Come here." Downstairs the poor dog was howling and screaming, trying desperately to get through the shut doors and up the stairs. Jock was sound asleep.

Patrick Goddard

Mother sent my brother and me home from church one Sunday with instructions for Nana to spank us because we'd acted up. I was six. Well, she asked what I'd done, and I didn't know. But she dutifully sent me out to cut a switch, and that spanking hurt! I'd brought in an apricot switch with all those little blossoms on it.

When mother got home, Nana asked what I had done to deserve a spanking. Turns out I hadn't done anything. I just got the message mixed up and took that spanking for nothing.

Joy Melton Prickett

My grandmother Melton loves answering machines. She'll call me up and say, "I can't find anybody home. And I thought to myself I'll just call Joy 'cause even if you're not there I can talk to you anyway." She'll use all the time, then call back and leave another message. She tells me all kinds of things. It's great. One time she told me how she got the flu at Uncle Hambone's and "upchucked all over his house." Or she'll tell me about all the vegetables she's gotten out of the garden.

I'm always delighted when I come home to find one message light blinking or two, and I hit the rewind button and it takes forever. I know that Granny has called. They're verbal letters.

My other grandmother, whom I lost recently, was an interesting character, too. Even if she was wrong, she was right. For instance, Geraldo may pronounce his name *Heraldo,* but no, for Granny, it was *Geraldo:* "It says right there on the screen G-e-r-a-l-d-o." When I gave her a Kodak instant camera, she used it to take pictures of every neighborhood stray or every flower she had growing in the yard. I guess that was her world, so she had piles and piles of pictures of the flowers and dogs. The camera quit working once, and she said, "I don't know why it's not working. I spilt some milk inside but I wiped it out." When Kodak issued a recall on those cameras, that was the most exciting thing my grandmother had ever had happen and the most fun. You got to send it in and get money.

Jane Burke

I was singing in the Civic Opera production of *Lucia di Lammermoor* and Roberta Peters, whom I idolized, was playing Lucia, well past the age any self-respecting singer would do Lucia, but that didn't stop her. And Granny was sitting there in the front row supporting me as usual. Since she was a little hard of hearing, she spoke loudly. Well, the local tenor, George Bitzas, who sang the national anthem at the Tennessee football games, was playing a role in the opera. As he made his first entrance, a very dramatic one, I was onstage and I heard out of the front row, in my Granny's lovely voice, "Why, that's George, isn't it." Half the audience heard it too; you could hear the choked-back snickers. So that's a night at the opera with my granny.

Zar Rochelle

I have a favorite story each about my father and mother.

When my father was not too far from dying, and he knew it, he called his nurse in and sent her to the closet for a particular sports coat and shirt. She brought them out and he said, "That's what I want to be buried in."

Now the sports coat wasn't gaudy, but it was loud—red and yellow plaid. Pretty bright. And the nurse said, "Zalph, these are spring clothes. These are spring colors. And it's winter."

"Well, goddamnit," he said, "then prop me in the corner and wait till spring, but that's what I want to be buried in." And four days later, he was.

My father was the cofounder of GTI, Guilford Technical Institute, in North Carolina, which began as a trade school to help train new furniture makers because the old furniture makers in High Point were dying off. For a number of years he also served as chairman of the board of trustees.

After a few years of success, the president of GTI, supported by many of the board members, decided that the school should become a junior college—a move to which my father as board chairman was adamantly opposed. A great controversy erupted in the area. I remember one headline quoted my father: "The last thing North Carolina needs is another Mickey Mouse junior college."

About that time I had talked my mother into taking art classes at GTI. But because of the fight over the institute's destiny, the president of the school had it in for my mother and my father.

He made his first move when my mother parked her car on campus for class and a security guard came over and said, "You can't park there."

"Why not?" She'd parked in the usual spot.

"That's a no-parking zone."

"There are no signs that say No-Parking Zone."

"Well, I haven't gotten around to putting them up yet. But if you park there, I'll have to give you a ticket."

"Then, suppose you don't get around to giving me a ticket till you get around to putting the signs up," she said and went off to class.

When she came out, there was a ticket on her windshield. She took the ticket, tracked the security man down, tore it up and handed it to him. So she got a call the next day before class that the president wanted to see her. "Mrs. Rochelle, your car is just too big to park in normal parking spaces" (she drove a Lincoln). And he assigned her a place way at the far end of the campus where nobody parked.

So she drove in the next day past her assigned parking place and right up to the president's home, which was on the campus. She drove into his driveway, pulled out on his front lawn right in front of his house, parked her car, and went to class. I think that went on for about five days. The student body got behind her. Finally, they decided that, well, maybe she could park where everybody else parked.

Not too long after, the president was fired, and he took everything that wasn't nailed down—the carpet, light fixtures, bath fixtures. And in two years he died. See what you get for screwing around with my mother? You didn't mess around with Jacqueline Rochelle!

Amy Holloway

I had jury duty. I was number fifty-six out of sixty-four people on the panel from which the lawyers were trying to choose their twelve. And they were asking every single juror multiple questions. This lady next to me had been filing her nails the whole time; the Braves victory parade had ended up right outside the courthouse windows and all we could hear was that chant—it was driving me crazy.

Finally they get to me. Without looking up, the D.A. says, "Miss Holloway, they have your birth date down here as 1904? You don't look like you were born in 1904. Surely you're not?" Instantly everybody turns around to see the decrepit old lady. And "Oil of Olay!" pops out of my mouth. Really. I couldn't help it! They were all laughing anyway.

Well, in spite of working at the TV station, I got picked for the jury. Miss Fingernail File also got on the jury. We heard all the testimony in this drug case and then retired to the jury room to decide this man's fate.

We began expressing our opinions in turn—until we got to Miss Fingernail File, who was obviously chosen because she had no brain. She says, "I can't say anything against him. I don't believe in it."

When the time comes to vote, she says, "I have to vote?" Everyone else has voted guilty, but she says, "I can't say anything against him. Not guilty."

A young man across from me says to the foreman, "Does everybody understand what a hung jury is?" So the foreman explained that the decision had to be unanimous or the case would be retried. One of the jurors asked her, "Do you have a reason for saying he's not guilty? Maybe we're not seeing it the way you are. Just explain to us why you can't say anything."

Ignoring this intelligent question, Miss Fingernail File said, aghast, "You mean we're going to have to go through this again? Well, guilty." Not exactly *Twelve Angry Men*.

Alastair Barbour

Some years ago, we are told, one of my grandfathers had a full-scale portrait painted of him standing in his kilt on the hill at Bonskeid, a former family residence and quite a house. The portrait was hung above the landing at Bonskeid as soon as it was completed, but some of the ladies of the day adjudged the kilt too short. So they recalled the artist and had him paint an extra inch on the bottom of the kilt while the painting hung on the wall.

Rodney Cook

At the time of the Civil War, my great-great-grandfather Ezeriah Mims had a farm located between what's now the stadium and airport in Atlanta. A colleague of my sister, who works in historic preservation, said to her one day, "Are you related to this Ezeriah Mims who was paid reparations after the Civil War?"

"Well, yes," she said.

And he said, "That's interesting. You had to prove you were a Northern sympathizer to be paid."

So that sent waves of shock and astonishment through the family. Everyone reeled into a depression for weeks after we sent our five dollars off to the Library of Congress and got the record back. My great-grandmother's three daughters couldn't believe it. Another aunt said, "Don't worry about it. The war devastated everybody, and most folks tried to get payments because they were so poor after the war. There's nothing to it."

But there was something to it. Atlanta is not the so-called gracious belle it has pretenses of being. It's an old railroad town. And Ezeriah was a railroad man. Not only was he a Union sympathizer, he had sent his sons off to Union County in north Georgia so they wouldn't fight for the Confederacy, and he had directed Sherman's troops around the city, pointing out all the rail lines so they could cut them.

My great-aunts were mortified when they saw their grandfather's and their father's signatures on this document. They pretended they had known nothing about it. I thought my father, who's a Civil War buff, would be horrified too. But he thought it was kind of nice. He said it took guts for this guy, in the heart of the Deep South, to stand up for what he felt was right at that time. Obviously he had felt that the Constitution and the Bill of Rights and the founding fathers and the Union were the way to go, and he stood by what he believed.

Emily Cook

The family has always taken pride and pleasure in Captain English, an ancestor who was the courier at Appomattox at the end of the Civil War. After the war, not having much in the way of funds, he returned to Atlanta carrying part of the tree that the surrender was signed under, and he'd sell off pieces to raise funds. From that, he built himself up and eventually became mayor. If I've got the story straight, he also opened the first brothel in Atlanta after the war. We laugh about that.

Doris Roberts

Jimmy Coco was wonderful, my best friend. He was another one like my uncle, who would say, "Turn it around honey. Turn it around." He would always make you laugh.

He'd take you to Mr. Chows and order the most ridiculous amounts of food. And you'd say, "Oh, Jimmy, that's too much, too much." He'd say, "Darling, put it in your mouth; and if you don't like it, you can always spit it out."

I met him in 1968, and we fell upon each other. You know that kind of wonderful feeling that you don't have with everyone? We were just hysterically funny.

We did a lot of things together after Broadway. We did the movie *A New Leaf* and we did *The Diary of Anne Frank* and we did "St. Elsewhere" that we won our Emmys for. And we did two "Love Boats." My husband Bill died before I won the Emmy, but he knew I was up for one, and I remember him saying, "Oh, darling, I hope you win just to prove to the world that you do better work than 'Love Boat.'"

46. Vile Things

Mary Randolph
I thought you said *file*. Now that's really vile.

Edith Bornn
Vulgar language. I've said often that Edith Bornn can tell somebody just where to get off, but you never hear her using obscene or vulgar language. Many people have an idea you can't tell a person off without using vulgar language. I can assure you I can.

Zar Rochelle
Chewing gum. Pushy people. Dirty ashtrays.

Mimi Taufer
Ignorance and prejudice. Racial prejudice.

Timothy Sultan
Economics over environmentalism. The *Homo sapiens uber alles* mind-set.

Jonathan Peter
People lying. Especially people in positions of authority and responsibility.

Damian Miller
A nasty character. Someone with a lot of anger who goes out of the way to hurt people for no reason.

Dorothy Cross

I hadn't been in France long, about 1960, when I went with a group of soldiers to a French village that had been totally destroyed by fire. The Germans had locked the women and children in the church and set fire to it. One woman and one little boy escaped to tell what happened. The French have kept this just the way it was, all the burnt-out buildings. There's still an odor about it.

Phoebe Legere

I abhor the greed and self-centered materialism of today's singer prostitutes who dominate the airwaves with their vulgar propaganda and push down on anyone else who is trying to make it.

Kathy Bater Brackett

Potato bugs. It's one of those memories from childhood that isn't very pleasant. You're outside; it's a sunny day and you're pretending like you're a farmer and you're digging around and planting your vegetables and all of a sudden, you turn up this big, awful, vile bug. They're probably not that bad, but this is a seven-year-old's memory.

Nancy and Eric Edmondson

Cruelty to animals.

Dan Buettner

In Cuzco, Peru, a local fellow took me to a restaurant for its specialty—something called *cuya*. The dish turned out to be a deep-fried, skinned hamster. "Now, before you start to eat," said my friend, "be sure to check the paw. In cheap restaurants they'll give you a rat and the paw's the only way you can distinguish the two."

Vile Things

Edward Colquhoun: *Racism. Sexism.* Mary Lou Retton: *Smoking.* John Emery: *A lie.* Dave Degrandpre: *Hate and ignorance.* Gerry Cooney: *Abuse. Injustice. Not knowing.* Cliff Robertson: *Exploitation of any kind.* Win Rockefeller: *Snobbery. Self-righteousness.*

47. An Unexpected Moment Provoking Compassion

Paul Mockler

I hold the record for the longest dive to the *Titanic*. Because the ship carried a lot of shoes as cargo, it's not uncommon to see fancy shoes littered on the ocean floor around the ship. The women's shoes had a cotton upper portion, and most of that is generally eaten away. Men's shoes were all quite well preserved. I got used to filming a lot of fancy, nice shoes 13,000 feet under the ocean's surface.

But on this final dive, I came upon a pair of old, heavy work boots with thick, well-worn soles and heels. It was obvious someone had been wearing them. A coal stoker came to mind. They were lying side by side in the forward part of the stern section. I was four feet away from those boots when I thought about the last moments of that poor man's life.

Torre Andrews

When I was on the obstetrics rotation my first year out of med school, this young pregnant woman—her name was Ann—came into the hospital. She was healthy but nauseated and vomiting. Over three weeks she got worse. We did all the tests possible and could not find the cause. It was clear that she had an obstruction of the bile duct, the biliary system, but nothing, not even surgery, revealed the cause.

After exploratory surgery, Ann was transferred to the ICU. Two days later and two months early, the baby was suddenly delivered. Ann couldn't even warn her nurse because she was so weak and had a breathing tube in her throat. The ICU team called for help, so the OB guys and the pediatricians came running from four floors up, scooped up the baby, and ran up the stairs to the pediatric ICU. The baby did OK, but Ann was too sick to see her. Her husband took a polaroid photo and taped it up over Ann's bed.

Even after her baby was born, Ann continued to go downhill. One night she was doing so badly, her husband was called in. By the time he arrived, she was "coded," undergoing CPR. I heard the code called overhead and came down to help because I was afraid it might be her. The team worked on her for an hour. But she still died.

Another doctor and I walked out of ICU to talk to her husband. This was a county hospital—no flair. There were plastic bus station seats in an elevator lobby with a pay phone. No carpeting, no nothing—except some cigarette butts thrown on the floor by patients sneaking a smoke.

And there's this guy, all by himself in the elevator lobby, at two o'clock in the morning, down on his knees on the floor with his head in the seat. He was obviously praying. We waited until he finished. When he looked up, we said, "We did everything we could, and we couldn't help her." He stood up and walked away from us down the hall, stood there a while then came back. He just said, "Thanks."

It was devastating. I can't really describe what it was like to walk out there at two o'clock in the morning in this shitty hospital, the lousy little plastic seats, the dirty floor, and this guy on his knees, by himself, doing the only thing that he could do. He did all he could; we did all we could. Together we couldn't do enough.

Hamilton Fish

My day at Human Rights Watch is filled with reports about great tragedy, torture, and death. After awhile, you have to stop reacting emotionally to the single event or you lose your ability to function. So, my unexpected moments that evoke compassion are quite simple: the success of my child in a school play or an underdog who has overcome obstacles.

Richard Duke

For several summers during college, I was a bartender at Geneva-on-the-Lake, a modest beach resort on Lake Erie. And I remember how much the people who came to the resort enjoyed the idea of being somehow connected to the place—being able to call the bartender, say, by his first name. Or being called by their first name. I think we've all done that.

We've all gone out of our way to get away from home to some new, strange place, but then we like it if somehow we can feel we belong there. If the bartender doesn't have to ask what you drink but just puts it there, you get a buzz out of that.

I also remember being shown I don't know how many newspaper clippings about someone's child and his performance in Little League baseball or on the high school football team. This was not a resort for the wealthy. The guests were modest folk. They wanted to tell you something, and the thing they had to brag about was their children.

I've observed it ever since in myself and been more aware of when I'm showing the same reaction. I think we all have it. It would be interesting to ask why, what need does that fill for us? It's clear that most or all of us really treasure some feeling of belonging. We feel that we're connected somehow, and that's important to us.

David Prowse

In Australia, I went to an arthritis camp for children, and among the children was this six-year-old girl, Victoria, who was very seriously ill with arthritis. Her parents had flown her down from Darwin to this camp, but Victoria wouldn't even speak; she just sat huddled up in a little wheelchair. So, I got her out of her wheelchair and onto my lap, you see? I tried to involve her, asked her questions, but nothing, nothing. "She never speaks," her mother said.

Then I started to lead the other children in a sing-along. Some time ago I'd made an LP record of me singing children's songs, including "Old MacDonald Had a Farm." All the kids joined me in that song but Victoria. We were all making animal noises—you know them!—and when we got to the pig, I put the microphone up to Victoria, and she went "honk honk!" Marvelous! Lovely! She sat straight up! So, from then on, no matter what the animal was, every time I put the mike up to Victoria she would "honk, honk."

We finished the song, and next thing I know she's smiling. I say to her, "Oh, come on, Victoria, what's it like in Darwin?" And she starts telling me about her family. It was fantastic! It was lovely! If I didn't ever do anything else in my life, that was one of the great experiences.

Mary Lou Retton

Any moment with a person who is disabled moves me and impresses me because of that person's strength. I've been so fortunate and am proud of what I've done, but when I see the incredible strength and independence of people who are physically impaired, I don't think I've done anything.

Damian Miller

During the Tiananmen Square disaster, that man who walked out to the middle of the street when the tanks were rolling along. Remember? He had two suitcases, or a briefcase, in one hand, and he stood there. When the tank moved to one side, he moved in front of it. The tank moved again, and he also moved in front of it. That was a moving, courageous act.

Michael Bornn

I recently went on a Scouting trip to Philmont, New Mexico, with twenty youths. It was a pretty grueling trip, and this one guy, Vincente, had been charging along doing a great job for the whole week. On the last day, we had to climb the mountain at Philmont to the top—a straight-up climb. Since I'd done Everest, the climb, though tough, was a walk in the park for me. But these kids were going through a really rough experience. Only eight of the twenty were making the climb. Vincente got halfway up this hill that day and physically just died. I saw his engine just turn off; there was nothing physically left of him. But that kid said, the hell with this, I'm going to make it. I've come this far, I'm gonna go to the top of this hill. He made the rest of that hill on his guts. He practically crawled it. I didn't help him physically, but I coaxed him up. I drew on my Everest experience. I told him to dig down and he responded.

Amy Holloway

Our family's first house was near the quarry, near a poorer section of town. These people were so poor that one family of eight lived in a chicken coop just up the road from us. Almost all kids then wore a lot of hand-me-downs; we thought nothing of it. One of my mother's piano students who was older than us, for instance, would pass on something she'd outgrown; our mother, who made beautiful clothes, would pass on our outgrown things to other friends. And we had clothing drives at our elementary school all the time because these children from the quarry had no one to hand-me-down to or from.

I had a favorite skirt that my mom had made—a black border print with clowns all around it. As I grew, she kept letting out the hem until it had gone as far as it would go. Then she put it in a clothing drive.

Shortly after I saw my skirt on practically the only kid in school smaller and skinnier than I was. I came home saying, "Mom, Lois had my skirt on."

She said, "Now don't say anything about that skirt. Don't tell her it was yours. You enjoyed it. You're too tall. She'll enjoy it." She made me think about Lois's feelings, something I've not forgotten since.

Medora Plimpton

Our dog Gaia was acting up in the car as I drove her back from the vet. I glanced away from the road to get her to sit down and looked back to see this orange blur in front of the car. I slammed on the brakes but couldn't avoid hitting a mother cat carrying a kitten in her mouth. I jumped out, but they were dead. Since the mother cat was carrying one kitten, I knew there must be others. I found two others, about four weeks old, beside the road and took them home.

Gaia was pregnant with her puppies then and immediately adopted the kittens. They nursed with her puppies, and she raised them as dogs. They live on campus now and still act like dogs—chasing twigs and jumping about more like dogs than cats.

Timothy Sultan

Hearing of animals being mistreated by people. Such compassion is different than that which one has for people. People can at least reason or perhaps understand the cruelty inflicted upon them, can recognize the action as a human quality, but I don't think animals have this comprehension. There's a look in the eyes of injured animals that reflects no understanding of what happened to them.

John Marston

Hauling in several thousand fish at once—I've never seen so much life and death in a few minutes. Have you ever looked at a face in a photograph that seems to stare straight at you no matter where you are in the room? Well, a fish's eyes go straight out too. Imagine a couple of thousand fish on deck, all watching you. It was kind of sad, but I got used to it. That's scary—that I got used to all the carnage. But I think that's what we are—hunters, not just gatherers.

Phoebe Legere

Every moment of life provokes compassion. Every time I walk out onto the street every single person that I meet needs compassion.

Edward Colquhoun

You can hardly pick up the newspaper without reading about a child killed in a drug shootout, starving, homeless. As soon as you have a child, you start projecting and identifying with what happens to other children.

Norman Lear

During the war I was stationed in Italy. They'd be selling watermelons off wooden carts, and I'd buy all of them and hand out slices to the kids who were in such despair; little boys who approached you saying, "Joe, sleep with my sister."

Lyn Lear

Driving through the east part of town or through New York and seeing very young girls with tiny babies that probably won't get past that block. You feel such a tremendous sadness and a tremendous helplessness.

Ollie Ferguson

A young girl had a diving accident, and we had to retrieve her from the bottom in about fifty feet of water. At first, I was not afraid; the whole way through I was just doing what I'd been trained to do—searching for her, finding her, giving her life support, right up to turning her over to advanced medical care.

Yet as we were doing the search pattern on the bottom and I saw her lying on her back, face up and motionless on a coral bed about ten feet off the bottom, I remember saying to myself, *This person is not alive. This person is not alive.* I knew immediately that we were retrieving a dead body, not a living person. My response was not so much fear as shock, then brutal realization. The actual rescue procedure was more mechanical, making sure we did all the right things so that by the time we turned her over to advanced medical help she had a pulse even though rigor mortis had set in. She had been down for about two hours, so she was obviously dead.

It was not until after the rescue was complete, until after she had been turned over to medical care that the realization of what I had just been through hit me. I was standing in the shower when I got all these feelings. I went from being very calm to sobbing, just absolutely sobbing.

I've been part of six retrievals since then. They don't get any easier.

John Jaxhiemer

I saw a lady in New York City who had been hit by a car and she was lying dead on the street. One of her friends was there crying.

Taylor Plimpton

Finding that dead woman in the ocean in South America. When I stopped thinking about the actual excitement of finding someone dead, it hit me. Then I was as sad as I've ever been.

Kurt Vonnegut

When I lived in New York, I was walking up Second Ave. I used to walk every afternoon because I'm very stupid in the afternoon. And a woman came up to me and told me she'd just read my book, *Hocus Pocus*. That was nice. Then she asked me what I thought about the Gulf War and all that and said she'd spent time over there and had worked for ARAMCO. It turned out she was out of work and living in a shelter. And, dear, dear, dear, dear . . .

Dan Buettner

One evening I was in San Miguel, El Salvador, straddling my bike and paging through a guide book looking for a place to sleep and get something to eat. Across the street in a garbage dump this old woman dressed in dark brown clothes with a ragged scarf on her head was scrounging around in the garbage. I watched her for a moment. She found a black plastic garbage bag and turned the thing inside out where she found rotting garbage. I figured she would just throw the thing away and keep on scavenging; instead she lowered her mouth to the garbage and started eating it. About halfway through, she realized I was looking at her and she turned toward me with this face of utter shame and this greasy garbage all over her mouth and dropped it and walked on. It's a face I remember when I sit down to Thanksgiving dinner.

48. Airplanes: A Portrait
Buck Johnson

It wasn't fearful, but, boy, was it exciting. I don't know if I'd ever been to an airport—we lived in south Georgia on a dirt road miles in the country. Airplanes flying over gave a strange feeling, like they might be going to fall on us. As Mama said, "The Lord spoke: 'Lo, I am with you always.' He never said anything about 'high.' " So we were fascinated by airplanes coming over.

One Saturday afternoon, we heard an airplane circling. We all ran out on the porch, and this airplane came up and landed in a field right there! Well, Mama got so excited she couldn't talk; I got so excited I nearly peed on myself; and Daddy, he just couldn't stand it. We all cranked up cars and trucks, and two minutes after the plane landed there were fifteen or twenty cars around it. I mean, it was the greatest thing that ever happened around home.

What had happened was this old boy was stationed in Jacksonville, and his wife lived cross the field from Mama and Daddy, and he had stolen—well, taken—a plane he wasn't supposed to and flown home and landed in the field up there to spend Saturday night with his wife.

We found out what time he was going back, and we had dinner on the grounds at church that Sunday. I don't think we even had a service. Everybody gathered up. He was going to leave at three, so some of us got there at eight in the morning.

The plane went down in the cornfield and took off, and we were all just standing there cheering, and Gail Sanderson, a big old fat girl, was standing there—she thought the plane would be higher—and the tip of the wing just touched her head, and she fell on the ground and went to kicking and screaming, and Mama went out there and said, "They killed Gail! They killed Gail!" And I saw the plane coming, so I went and got behind a bunch of dog fennel—you know, bushes—thinking that would save me. And the plane hit a barbed wire fence, and said *flip!* and turned over backwards.

Well, we went up and grabbed them and got them out of the plane—we didn't know planes burned up and all that kind of stuff.

And Mama was a hollering and a screaming, "Oh, my God, they're dead! Save 'em, Lord, Save 'em!" Well, Mama always had ammonia. And anything that'd ever happen, she'd give 'em some ammonia. We went and drug the boys out, and you ain't never heard such hollering and carrying on in your life. Fanning 'em and wiping their faces off, and Mama giving them ammonia. "Smell some more! Come on, smell some more! You wanna live! You wanna live! Oh Lord, they'll never make it!"

We laid them out there in the pecan trees. They made it. That was in 1946. Afterwards, we stayed by the plane for a day or two until they came and got it.

49. A Moment of Real Fear

Gerry Cooney

When you can't see what's coming at you, that produces fear. We just don't know how to handle it, don't know how to deal with it.

Paul Mockler

Stuck in a tiny submarine 1,000 feet down off the coast of Labrador in 1974. We were surveying the wreck of the *William Carson*, and as we went around the stern of the wreck, a vortex current swept us out of control and thrust us under the wreck. And as if things weren't bad enough, the hatch started to leak slightly, sending sprays of ice-cold water into the sub, we were well off shore, the weather was building, and our mother ship kept drifting off location. We were stuck for over six hours. Fear builds in a situation like that, and let me tell you, by the end of six hours it can build a lot.

We finally worked our way gradually from under the wreck and through the debris field, blew our ballast, and shot to the surface.

Mary Randolph

When I first got to Vietnam, I was staying with one of the librarians in Saigon. There was a lot of incoming fire at night and flares all over the city. Even at two o'clock in the morning, it was so light you could read.

There was a double bed in the apartment and a very thin mattress. As the shelling continued, I thought, *I'm really scared to death. I've never been in a situation like this, I'm not reacting the way I thought I'd react.* And I pulled this mattress up over me, just as if it were going to protect me. I was hyper; I was scared.

One night in the middle of this I realized I was going to suffocate with this mattress over me.

So I thought, OK, you've got three options: You can wake up in the morning and pay your way home; you can wake up in the morning, stay here and go home in a basket crazier and loonier; or you can wake up in the morning and realize you have to stay here and do the job and not let this bother you anymore. And I chose the third option.

At that point I really became a fatalist. Nothing bothered me after that. Absolutely nothing. I realized I was going to live until I die, and that was it. But it was a very lonely night as I considered what I had subjected myself to and what the possible outcomes might be. I learned a lot in that year.

After that, I've had this tremendous desire every couple of years to go out and pit myself against something in which the odds are maybe a little bit hard for me. You do this so that you'll turn around and appreciate the little moments of life more. That was the benefit of spending a year in a war zone.

Bill Peck, Supper Club

After the war was over, I was put in the Army of Occupation in Austria. I was sent out from my camp in Czechoslovakia to go on duty way out in the Austrian forest guarding SS troopers who were cutting wood to supply the people with heat.

I'd been out there about two weeks when another fellow came on duty, sent out from my old camp. When I told him that, he said, "Who're you with?"

"Twenty-sixth Infantry Division," I said.

"Well, they're going home," he said, "leaving for France in the morning."

I've never felt as afraid as I did when I heard that. There I was in the wilderness with enough points to go home and no word from anybody. I didn't know what to do; the other guy couldn't tell me.

Finally I got my duffel bag, got out on the highway and started thumbing army trucks. I finally got back to my division, walked into the orderly room, and the first sergeant said, "Peck, where in the world have you been? We've looked everywhere for you. We leave for home tomorrow."

They'd lost me. I really thought I was stranded in that forest for the rest of my life. And I was nearly right. That's the most afraid I've been.

Dan Buettner

About 5,000 miles into Russia on our Sovietrek, the road stopped abruptly at a Siberian town called Kachael. There we four team members spent three days converting military lifeboats into a river raft and the next four days floating down the Shilka River in freezing conditions and with no way to steer the raft.

Near the end of the river, at about one in the morning, we were drifting around a hairpin turn in the river on our raft, at the mercy of the current. It was pouring rain. We were freezing. The greatest danger was that we might run into one of the occasional barges that steam up the river. As the current pulled us round the bend, we were suddenly illuminated by a blinding search light. We couldn't see anything, but knew we were in the path of a freighter. We paddled frantically. But the harder we paddled, the more we were pulled into the path of the boat. If we had fallen into the freezing water, we'd have been history. We kept paddling.

Then as we got close, we saw it wasn't a freighter, but a gunboat. Two KGB soldiers had rifles pointed at us. Suddenly another floodlight hit us, directed from a tower. We managed to steer the boat to the shore. The soldiers were yelling at us and waving their guns. "Soviet-American Bicycle Marathon" Alexander yelled back in Russian. "Soviet-American Bicycle Marathon." When they finally spotted our bicycles, they backed off and found us a cardboard box in which to shelter for the night.

George Plimpton

The year he was thinking of running for the presidency, I went on a rafting trip down the Colorado River with Bobby Kennedy, his family, and guests, a group of twenty or thirty, I'd say. One day a couple of us climbed some cliffs across the river from where all the rafts were drawn up and the others were having a picnic. After the climb, we should have had a raft come across for us, but instead we walked upriver about half a mile and decided to swim over to the other side.

The Colorado is glacial, extremely cold, I would guess fifty-nine or sixty degrees. Halfway across I realized I was in trouble. The other two with me midstream, being swept down the river, were having no trouble at all—one of them was an American who had climbed Mount Everest—but I was *really* in trouble. Panic began to set in. Ahead, about a quarter mile, were the Thunderbolt Falls, a cataract that really would have done me in forever.

The great legend, of course, is that at moments like this your life flashes before your eyes. Sure enough, the odd vision that came popping to mind was a blue box in a closet back home in New York. A pale blue box that held about six or seven old pornographic films that a friend and I had collected. They were all quite bad; we had renamed them with titles like *Doctor Yes* and *The Nun's Habit*.

Well, this blue box popped into my mind, and I thought, my God, if I get into the Thunderbolt Falls and succumb, my mother is going to look into this blue box and watch those home movies, assuming they will show her son mountain climbing or on a camping trip in the Adirondacks. And instead . . . she's going to be introduced to *Doctor YES!*

So, with renewed vigor my limbs began to function, and I practically walked on the water to the picnic.

Peggy Hackman

As a child I was afraid of fires, perhaps because we were home alone briefly at night when my father went to the restaurant, just a block away, to help my mother close up. So I always had my closet arranged—all the hangers one way, shoes laid out—so I could grab my clothes and run out. I was about nine.

Virginia Kahl

In 1980 an electrical storm knocked out the electricity for some hours one night in the home I shared with an eighty-six-year-old aunt. We went to bed, but I left the lights on so I'd know when the power came on. Suddenly the lights went on, and I smelled smoke. I went downstairs and saw the couch in flames. I called the fire department and was told to get out immediately. I woke Aunt Martha; we'd reached the top of the stairs when the lights went out again. I held on to her as we felt our way down the stairs to the door. We opened it and got out and had taken only two steps when the windows exploded and the flames poured out. I lost seven cats. That was probably the most frightening experience of my life.

Dorothy Cross

I'd gone back to Michigan and was staying alone in the farmhouse after my parents had died. I woke in the pitch black to loud cracking sounds throughout the house. For a minute I was really terrified. Then I thought, I can't really do anything about this. So I went back to sleep. I found out the next morning that it had been a tornado. And it had been six in the morning, when it should have been bright day, not the middle of the night. The trees all around were flat, but the house was still standing.

Medora Plimpton

Several weeks ago I was lying on the metal-frame daybed in the TV room, watching a show, and petting the cat Shadow who was lounging on my chest. I hadn't paid any attention to the thunderstorm outside when—out of nowhere—an intense electrical shock hit. The TV switched off and on, the cat sprang up, scratching my chest, the dog tore screaming and squealing around the room, and all my hair literally stood on end.

Campion Platt

On a visit to both sets of grandparents in Georgetown when I was about ten, I was walking back from swimming at one house to the other and carrying a small bag with my swimming suit in it, when about six black kids pushed me into an alley to beat me up. They took my watch. Then the leader looked in my bag and saw the wet bathing suit. I just focused on that guy. I told him, "Hey, this isn't the way to impress your friends here—to take a cheap watch and a wet bathing suit, to mug some kid who can't give you anything of value."

They let me go, with my watch and bathing suit. But, God, was I scared.

Edward Colquhoun

I was probably less afraid than I should have been when marching and participating in sit-ins with other students and civil-rights workers in Atlanta in 1961. There was such a sense of community that even though the Ku Klux Klan was counterdemonstrating as we picketed Rich's Department Store or sat in at lunch counters, we were not afraid. In retrospect—that is, in light of the murders in other parts of the South—we should have been. Also, looking back, that was a very special experience—one that had its beginnings in those walks with Eddie Jackson the mailman and Boy Scout leader.

Mimi Taufer

In our health class in grade school and high school, we were weighed in front of the class. I was very heavy as a child and adolescent and didn't tell anybody how much I weighed—ever.

Health class, as I recall, was on Tuesday, and on the first Tuesday of each month, we were weighed in alphabetical order. The teacher would weigh you and then shout out your weight to the person who was filling it in on a chart in some other part of the room.

So I was automatically absent each first Tuesday. I would have a fake stomachache. And then, because I couldn't admit this to any of my friends, I would have to subtly figure out what point in the alphabet they'd gotten to in the weighing—they didn't always reach T—to see whether I had to be absent the second Tuesday. Fear of exposure in front of my peers panicked me enough to fake a health problem.

Damian Miller

Fear? Recently it was with a girl. It just seemed like a long time since I'd had to go through the whole process of meeting a girl, taking her out, trying to be charming, trying to please her. And then just getting involved again. It was so weird. I'd never feared that in my life before; I'd always looked forward to it; but for the first time, I started thinking *uuhhhh*.

Desy Campbell

When I had my hips operated on in 1965—I was in the ninth grade—I thought I was going to die. I'd been born with multiple skeletal problems, and this operation was supposed to fix some of those.

I don't know why I thought I was going to die, but they took great care to take me to see our minister the night before I went to the hospital. The day I was supposed to go into the hospital we had a snow day, and Dad took us into Philadelphia to see *The Sound of Music*—we never went into Philadelphia to see a movie. And I had only a vague idea of what they were going to do. All these things must have contributed to my fear.

James Royce

Standing in front of a thousand people giving a speech on something I don't have a clue about.

Nan Thomas

Driving on Tortola. When I first moved here, the roads were terrifying—narrow as outstretched arms and steep. I'd been driving in Vermont through all kinds of blizzards and icy conditions, but those were nothing! Nothing!

Foxy Callwood

My father and I was walking, chasing the cows from one pasture to the other, when all of a sudden I saw these three men; each had two rocks in their hands. And they started pelting, and my father got one. I saw where he rolled over and I pulled aside the bushes like this—I was just a kid—and the garden shield me and they went right down in front. I went down through a cut and saw an old man coming up, so I told him they killed my father up there. I kept on coming down and was hiding in the pop bush because I don't know what to do now, where to go. Then I heard them coming, Oh, Lord Jesus Christ, Mother.

But they caught them and took them to Tortola where they had the court business. The guys went to jail. My father got OK.

Eric Jensen

Being with the whales with Bubba and Ollie Ferguson. Bubba and I were at his house in the Bahamas when a call came from the Explorer's Society: a yacht miles offshore had spotted a pod of whales. Ollie rushed over in Bubba's boat, and we raced out far from shore, and sure enough we found hundreds of short-fin pilot whales—all different ages, big bulls, females, and dozens of calves. Ollie turned the boat off, and we started drifting in their midst as they rested.

I decided to swim with them and slipped over the side of the boat. There I was about ten miles from shore in water five or six thousand feet deep surrounded by these great creatures. Light rays penetrated down thousands of feet, and below me whales were diving to feed, or moving in formation, or rising from the depths. Just below the surface three whales went under me and never took their big eyes off me. You could sense such a powerful intelligence there.

I didn't even have my fins on, and at some point, I started getting so excited I looked up and noticed that the boat was hundreds of yards away and that the whales had moved away too, and I was in that black, bottomless ocean alone. I tried swimming to catch up with the whales' lazy pace, but by now my mind was racing, imagining how deep the water was. You can think too much. I started to panic a little. The boat was far away; I didn't have on my flotation device. By God, I could *drown* out here easily. I realized quickly that this was *their* world, not mine. It was scary.

Steve Wing, Supper Club

A group of us were putting the supporting crosspieces in a bridge over a creek. And we were up under the bridge working when it started to rain. A regular deluge. We were pretty dry under the bridge, but the water started to rise. And, boy, it kept coming, higher and higher and higher. We were stuck between the water and the bridge. Finally we wriggled our way out through the crawl pieces before the water covered the bridge. It scared me so bad I can still show you right where that happened.

Kathryn Hames, Supper Club

When I was young, we used to ride the streetcar into Atlanta, about twenty miles away. The line crossed the Chattahoochee River on a trestle bridge. One day we arrived at the river crossing, and the streetcar stopped. The river had flooded and was up over the tracks. We had to get out and wade over the bridge—that was scary—and get on another car on the other side of the river. I'd never do it now.

Kathy Bater Brackett

A moment of absolutely horrible fear—being stuck on a pyramid in Mexico.

It wasn't hard going up, but once up there, I went completely out of control. The top was a small square. There was no rail and there were all these people. I couldn't watch them go near the edge. So I stood in the middle trying to get myself under control: *OK, talk yourself out of it; this is ridiculous. Look at all those people. They're having a good time; they're not panicking. Don't make a scene. Work it out.* I'd get myself to the point where I thought, *OK, I can go down now,* then get to the edge and go *o-o-oh.* I was there for a long time. I got down—on my stomach feet first. And I had a cab waiting the whole time.

Amy Holloway

While on tour in Paris, I had gotten brave about taking the Metro where I needed to go. I caught the train after dinner one night at 10:30 or 11:00 to go home. I wasn't worried: I knew where I lived—52 Rue de Carmélite.

So I got off the train at my stop and started down the street, only to realize that it was not the Rue de Carmélite. There was nobody out. No cars. Nothing. I was scared to death.

I ran back to the station and here came another train. There were six men scattered around the car as I got on. I must have looked like a ghost because when I began asking one man in poor French if he knew the Rue de Carmélite, all six gathered around.

The men began to say "Rue de Carmélite" to each other and gesture that it was two stops farther on. When we reached the station, the train stopped and waited. All six men got off with me, walked up the street to the corner and watched till I reached my door. Then they waved and headed back to the train. How amazing—guardian angels.

Dave DeGrandpre

Skydiving last November. I'd been on a three-day binge and took the six-hour course hung over. I wasn't feeling that well, but I got in the plane. When the guy opened the door, the wind and noise knocked me over. I had to crawl out and put my foot on that little pedal and lunge. The guy said, "Go!"

I was so incredibly terrified! It was the greatest fear I've ever felt. I knew that I would be OK, I trusted the equipment, and I trusted the instructor. But I was still damn scared.

Kim Litton

Being strangled by ski ropes. My brother Greg was driving a powerful new boat and pulling six or seven water-skiers. Several skiers behind me fell, but I couldn't see that or their ropes dragging through the wake toward the center of the boat. Suddenly the ropes hit my legs and wrapped round my chest and stomach and dragged me underwater. I was fighting but knew I was drowning. I couldn't scream underwater. Greg didn't know I was trapped. The ropes kept tightening. After what seemed forever, the boat stopped, and I popped to the surface, badly bruised but with nothing broken.

John Englander

A few years ago, when I was president of NAUI, I went diving off Santa Cruz, California, with some fellow members, dive shop owners. Most of my diving has been in warm water, not cold. We went at six before they opened their dive store. They're master divers and I'm a master diver, and as happens, unfortunately, we were a little blasé about the equipment.

They tossed me a "stab jacket," actually a backpack, and said, "This is the only one available. Does it fit?" It was a small or medium, but I tried it on and it seemed OK—a little snug perhaps, but what the heck.

And off we went. First we had to do a surf entry from a cliff—jump down a fifteen-foot drop—something I'd never done. That was a little scary. Then we go offshore, and the Pacific surge is very different from the Atlantic. It's just this rolling sea that comes in twenty or thirty feet and goes out continually. I wasn't used to that. Since I was fighting an unusual current as we swam around a little island with some sea lions, I ran out of air early. Though embarrassed to admit that I was low on air, I put air in my vest to increase my buoyancy in order to rise to the surface. Then I unexpectedly started getting out of breath. I didn't realize at the time that the vest, as it inflated, was restricting my breathing. I thought it was tightness from stress and panic. And the more I couldn't get my breath, the more that made me panic.

And getting out of the water was not easy—the rocks were slippery and steep. At first it was funny. Then I began to think we wouldn't get out. As I clung to the seaweed, each surge seemed like it was going to pull me back into the ocean. And each breath seemed harder. I was starting to lose it. Finally, I said, "I need help."

That was a big admission. Eventually, we were all able to get up the slippery rocks. But it took a while and was extremely difficult.

Bunny Johnson

When I was nine or ten, I had my own room. During the summer nights, I would wake up to hear through the open windows people hammering or building something when everyone was asleep. It scared me because what they were building couldn't be good if they did it when everybody was asleep.

So I'd go into my mother's bedroom and pull her big toe until she waked up. Then I'd ask, "Can I turn on the bathroom light?" She'd say, "Yes, and go on back to bed."

I'd turn on the light, get back in the bed, and pull the cover over my head because I knew the minute I'd turned on the bathroom light, those people who were building out there could see me. Nobody had ever told me that the hammering came from woodpeckers busy in a tree beside the house at night.

Peggy Houlihan

Playing in a hayloft when I was fifteen, I slipped between some hay bales and slid right into a nest of yellow jackets. They stung me in over a hundred places. I really thought I was going to die—and spent a month recuperating from the terrible experience. To this day, I am terrified of bees.

Phoebe Legere

I remember the first time that I was up in a tree, and I felt a branch give away beneath me. My heart left me. I would have been killed, but I somehow caught another branch. As I was resting on the branch afterwards, I noticed that the effect of the fear was almost exactly the same as the sexual feelings I was starting to have.

Timothy Sultan

One August night in my college town, my friend Joy and I decided to hike to Walker's Pond, where I'd never been. It was near midnight when we walked past the last houses. The pavement turned into crumbling mud. We crossed several fields with late-summer Queen Anne's lace, climbed a couple of fences, and finally got to the wood where the pond was located. We continued through the trees and low brambles until we reached the pond, which was so covered with algae that the air above the water was illumined with a green, waxish light.

We sat on the ground sloping down to the water and were mostly silent, enjoying listening to the sounds in the pond and surrounding trees. We felt comfortable out there in the night woods.

After perhaps ten minutes, I glanced up over our heads and noticed an odd silhouette. A straight line descended from a branch above—too straight to be a branch. It had to be man-made. We both peered more closely at the sharp symmetrical outlines of whatever was dangling at the end of the line. A sculpture perhaps? In the darkness, we couldn't really see. But we both suddenly felt an unspoken unease: this unnatural object had been hanging over our heads unseen, as if to watch us. Fear rapidly overwhelmed unease, and we both bolted, fleeing through the trees and brambles until we reached an open pasture. There we stood panting and laughing hesitantly before walking home.

Carol Hallett

I was flying the Bonanza back to San Luis Obispo from Sacramento, after the legislature recessed, to bring the cats home for the winter and to make a speech that evening. Since there was a storm coming in, I'd checked the weather all day long. All the predictions said it wouldn't arrive until about ten that night.

So I took off in the afternoon and flew down the valley because clouds were already coming. I could hear various tower conversations discouraging people from flying over the mountains.

It was almost dark. I had five cats in the plane. One, Freddy, always flew outside of his cage, sitting in the seat and watching. Suddenly I got into very, very rough weather. I found an airport, but I couldn't really see for the rain. I couldn't even see which way the wind was blowing because it was raining so hard. Meanwhile all the cats were yelling their heads off. The plane was bouncing all around. And I had to get Fred back into his cage and hold on to the plane. He was screaming and scratching my arms. I didn't lose confidence, but I was real tense.

I was on the radio trying to find out what runway to land on, but there was no tower. The airport was way out in the country. The conditions were such that I couldn't even really tell which runway was which. And frankly, I wasn't paying that much attention to my headings, I just wanted to get on the ground. Somehow I did.

Now here's what's so amazing. This shows the friendships and the trust among pilots. I got the plane down but I was still miles from my destination. And a couple who had a crop-dusting business at the airport said, "Well, just take our car." A Cadillac. So I piled the five cats in their cages into their car and took off for the hour-and-a-half drive from that airport to home, dumped the cats off, changed my clothes, and went on down to San Luis Obispo and gave my speech.

In a couple of days, when the storm passed, the couple flew my plane over and picked up their car.

Win Rockefeller

We were flying in Dad's King Air one time, and his pilot said, "Oh, these planes glide wonderfully," as he feathered both engines. I thought he was shutting them down. It's a very, very strange feeling to be sitting in a six-thousand-pound glider with lots of fuel on board.

Cliff Robertson

In a glider once I experienced the most sustained high concentration, on the cusp of true fear. The good thing about flying a glider is that with no engine you're busy, the master of your fate. If you were a passenger with nothing to do but sit there, that would be worse.

I was alone, flying cross-country in the High Sierras. I was going to go about sixty miles north; and I had pretty good altitude, I knew the territory, and I'm very conservative about flying. But the best-laid plans. . .

As I got up about sixty miles, suddenly there was a cloud bank. I had mountains about 13,000 feet high in front of me that I couldn't see. I thought, I'm getting out of here. I knew where I was exactly, and I started to head back to the airport. Then I saw this heavy fog bank in front of me and knew I wouldn't be able to get back. There'd be no lift at all in the very damp air, and I was going to be coming down; indeed, I was already coming down.

I figured I could go five minutes at that speed and then better bank away toward the valley so that I wouldn't hit the mountain and would hopefully be out of the fog.

It was a wild experience. It was exhilarating and stimulating but slightly scary. But I was so busy flying, concentrating on the glider's basic instruments as I came down and got right on top of the fog. Then I was in the thick fog, in the middle of a marshmallow. There was no frame of reference, no horizon. I had to concentrate on my instruments to make sure I didn't get into a death spiral, which happens many times, with power planes as well, when a pilot loses his orientation or second-guesses his instruments. So I realized I had to concentrate on the instruments. I started talking to myself. But I started talking to myself as an instructor: *watch this, watch that, watch this . . .*

I talked myself through the whole damn thing. That was great because I was forcing myself to concentrate. If I'd been quiet, I might have had too much room to let something interfere. Panic, say.

That's why I like flying gliders: it builds self-reliance. And you don't bruise or abuse the environment.

50. *Something Sweet*

Jerry Preston
My aunt Hazel Misenheimer's egg custard pie.

Edward Colquhoun
When I smell freshly cut grass. It takes me back in time.

Margaret Mason
Roses. I have several rose bushes I love. Roses become like friends, don't they? And they can be almost like barometers of your life if they aren't being tended.

John Emery
A thoughtful act.

Rodney Cook
Mama Jo, Emily's grandmother. How she treats Emily.

Myrtis Brown
My granddaughter was born premature. I explained to the doctor, "We don't have the money to keep her in the hospital, but if you let me take her home, I know I can see to it." About that time, I was taking some children up to Atlanta to see Dr. Heinz Roberts and asked his advice. He told me to bring her home, get a basket, put a lamp under it, line it and keep the infant warm. He told me the temperature to keep it. I brought the child home when she didn't weigh but three pounds. And Dr. Roberts sent me SMA milk in premature bottles down to Greensboro on the bus.

It was such a miracle. I know God did this, working through man for me. And my mother who was in a wheelchair took care of the baby while I started working at the hospital to help. At three months, the baby had gained five pounds and was released to go to New Jersey with her mother to rejoin her father, my son David.

Now the little lady is thirty-two years old. She's five foot three and weighs 146 pounds. I have taken care of my family my whole life. It's happiness to me.

John Marston

Apple-cinnamon hot cakes over red-hot coals in the middle of a forest. Tongass National Forest in southeast Alaska. Or wild-blueberry hot cakes. You can never appreciate that stuff until you are out in the middle of nowhere.

Timothy Sulton

My famed raspberry and strawberry crepes.

Edith Bornn

Every Sunday morning I sweep my hill in Charlotte Amalie—the sidewalk beside my house up to Government House. It's one of the things I enjoy doing. We descend from the Dutch, who are great sweepers, and our regulations have long required that merchants and landowners sweep their property right down to the street. Everyone starting with the boss on down did it. So on Sunday, I go to church very early so I can come back and sweep using a good old St. Thomas whisk broom.

Eric Edmondson

When I'm sitting here doing nothing and suddenly the cat jumps up and nuzzles me for no apparent reason.

Will McIntyre

I took a horse over a jump for the first time in my life recently. I was riding around the ring and I thought, *Gee, there's no reason in the world why you can't jump.* And so I said, "OK, let's see how we feel next time." The horse was doing real well and everything was going great. So I said, "OK, it's time." There was no hesitation at all in my brain. I knew we were going to do it and I just went right over it. No problem. And I had fairly good form. It was sweet.

51. Discovering Courage: A Portrait

Marla Hanson

I am surprised at my strength. When the men who slashed my face first came up, I thought they were going to rob me. I knew this was the end of my life because they had these knives. Somebody once said to me that fear is only intense excitement, and I remembered that when they grabbed me. I thought, it's true, I'm only feeling an intense excitement and anticipation. What's going to happen in the next minute? I completely accepted that I was going to die, and that I had to face it by myself, but I was completely serene.

Then they began to carve on my face. I didn't feel it, but all these different memories began coming back to me. That childhood memory on the swaying bridge, and my mother doing her hair. She had long, beautiful hair, and with one twist of her finger she would put it up in a bun and put a stick pin in it. And then I remembered my father singing to us in the car.

Then I had this horrible, horrible fear: someone once told me they believed that you die when you've learned all you can learn in your present form; then you come back in another form to learn more. And I suddenly thought, Oh God, I'm going to die in the next two minutes, and then I'm going to suddenly be an infant coming out of the womb, and I'll have to start all over again. It was the worst, most terrifying feeling. I thought, God, I just don't think I can go through another twenty-four years like I've been through. So suddenly, I went from being five feet away from my body to being in my body and saying, I've got to live. I had to take control.

That moment when they cut me ended up being the easy moment in it all, out of my control. I got up from the sidewalk as the two men that cut me ran away. My landlord—the guy who paid them—just stood there a minute, then tried to drag me into the parking lot. There was no one to help me, so I elbowed him in the gut. I had to make a decision right then: I was bleeding really badly. Did I try to go to a police station, which was a half block away or back in the bar I'd left a few minutes earlier? I went in the bar because I didn't think I'd have to explain anything there, and I started screaming, becoming hysterical. But everybody just looked at me like I was the Bride of Frankenstein. *Right then* I realized it was up to me to take care of myself or I would bleed to death.

So I started barking orders: "Somebody get me wet towels! You, please call 911! You, please call the police!" Then I sat down and closed my eyes and held the rags to my face.

I remember waking up from surgery in the hospital, trying to grasp what had happened to me. I was in a room with three other women, and the afternoon had been quiet. Then we turned on the television, and there was my face and people talking about me like I was dead. The other women got very excited, "Hey, you're somebody famous, ain't you? Who are you anyway, some soap star?" Within the hour the whole hospital was swarming with people and flowers and notes and reporters and police and prosecutors, and nobody was there helping me.

Then my mother came to see me in the hospital. She sat by my bed and tried to be a mother. As she sat there, I realized I didn't know anything about her. But she tried, and it was the first time I really loved her. From that moment, I saw her in a completely different light. But I've never really been around her since then.

Afterwards I went through a year and a half of trials, civil and criminal. Testifying in the second trial became so nasty because they tried to turn everything around and started blaming me and accusing me. Taking the stand was the most terrifying moment in my life in a way. I couldn't fall apart and cry; I had to listen to every question, and my concentration wasn't there. Those jurors were deciding my fate, too, and every time somebody asked a question, I had to remember to turn and look at the jury and try to be sincere even though I was terrified.

I don't know where my strength comes from. But it's like an internal mirror. In situations like mine, when you're really tested, you have to look inside yourself and say, *OK, what am I made of?* And you don't have any guide, any mentor, because you haven't seen anything like this. To survive you have to say *this is how I really feel and what I really am.*

52. A Discovery about Myself That Surprised Me

Hamilton Fish

How much I eventually enjoy doing those things I always put off. I don't have a good work ethic. I work hard on things that come easily and postpone those that don't. I always regret I didn't make more time for my postponed tasks because in the end they're the most satisfying, the harder tasks.

Mary Lou Retton — *gymnast*

I'd like to say my independence—I'm a very independent person and have been on my own since I was fourteen—but sometimes I don't know if I *am* that independent. All my life I have been coached and told what to do: you do this and eat this; point your toe here. I'm very good at taking direction. But now that I'm into life, it's hard to make my own decisions at times. I'm always asking everybody Do you think that's OK? Is this the best? What should I do?

That surprises me because of my independence. I'm trying to have more control over my decisions now, trying not to care what other people think. My husband Shannon has been good for me about that.

Alastair Barbour

My parents were keen for all their children to spend some time overseas before going to university or a job. So at the suggestion of my mother, I took a bus from Clapham Common in London with an intended destination of Connaught Circus, New Delhi, India.

After two-and-a-half months, however, we had to abandon the bus in Kabul in Afghanistan because the Indians and Pakistanis had just had a little war and the border was closed. The bus company offered two choices: to drive the passengers to Tashkent in Russia or to give us a ticket to Delhi and leave us on our own. For the first time in my life, I had to make a decision and nobody was there. I was in a totally foreign place, by myself at eighteen, and I had to do it.

Having made the decision, I realized how easy it is to get on in life. No great soul-searching needs to go on. I won't say life's been easy, but it's not been difficult to face up and make decisions since.

Dave DeGrandpre

Growing up, my parents always told me I was adopted. I was never interested in finding my biological parents because I always felt my parents were my parents; I never felt the need.

Then just this year I decided, yeah, maybe I do want to look into my roots a little bit. That kind of surprised me, because I love my parents. But the more I've thought about it, the more I've realized that maybe my roots are important, maybe I want that sense of grounding.

So I talked to my dad. He said if I wanted to go for it he would help all he could. I contacted an organization in New Hampshire my dad found. Then over Christmas I talked to Dad about it again. I think he was a little threatened then. This is something he and I haven't dealt with yet.

But I talked on the phone to a lady at the organization. She asked me to write a letter about what I was feeling, a letter I would want my biological mother to see. So, I did. It was really a good experience for me because it was the first time I'd really articulated this even to myself.

In the letter, I first said, OK, I don't want you to be threatened by this. I have no idea where you are in your mind, and maybe giving me away was a really, really painful experience, one she wanted to keep in the past. Then I said I wasn't angry, I had no ill feelings for her at all. And I thanked her. I could have been aborted. My biological mother and father obviously gave me up out of love, love for life and love for me. She wanted me to have more opportunity than she could give.

So I guess I just wanted to thank her. And kind of give her a hug, and look at her. I don't know . . .

Will McIntyre

When I was nine years old, I discovered that I could tackle my Uncle Whitey, who weighed 250 pounds. He seemed like the biggest person on the face of the earth. One Saturday he came down to our house to play football with me. Just Uncle Whitey and me. He'd run down the sidelines, and my job was to tackle him.

I hit him as hard as I could, though I had no hope ever of stopping him. But I did. I brought him down to the ground and he rolled. It was just like on television. It was great! I felt so good. That was my discovery that I could actually tackle adults.

Judy Rose

When my first husband and I split, I was left in fairly dire straits with a lot of responsibilities, an eight-year-old daughter, a house full of animals, and very few resources. But I managed somehow to survive and to start doing something and turn it into a little business—catering and bed and breakfast. Looking back after a few years, I realized you can do anything.

Sonya Friedman

My strength and my ability to deal with adversity without falling apart. When you're young, you have a tendency not only to dramatize but to catastrophize, making things even worse.

Chris Keefe

That I had so little control over crack. I've always been in control. But then in about 1986 that stuff overwhelmed me for a time. I was doing $300 worth a day working on an island in the Caribbean. I would start out first thing in the morning by running up to my supplier's house—a grandmother—and then running home to fire up as much as I could before going to work. I was always twenty minutes late. Then I'd shoot back and forth between work and the apartment all day, doing little hits here and there.

As soon as lunchtime came, I'd lock myself in my room, maybe eat, maybe not. After work, I was usually out of stuff, so I'd go back to grandma for more. That supply would usually last me from six until about one, when I'd get some more. Then about four or five, I'd pass out for an hour, and start the whole routine again.

Emily Cook

It took me a long time to realize that I was a strong person, that I was a good person. I didn't realize it until I got into a program of recovery. In 1982, my world totally fell apart. A friend found me huddled in a corner. He said I was keening, that he'd never heard a sound like that. And I was drinking.

I knew about the Betty Ford Center because when it first opened, they'd tried to get my mother through the program. It's a good facility. They break you down in order to build you back up. A lot of places break you down and more or less leave you there. But you really leave Betty Ford on a note of hope. By the time I got out of that program ten years ago, though I continued to struggle, I had learned more about life than I ever had. I was twenty-two then, and it was the beginning of recovery.

Lyn Lear

I'm sort of surprised my life has turned out so gloriously when I had such an insecure and difficult childhood. I'm surprised I was so strong and stable throughout it all. But a lot of that had to do with Norman.

Campion Platt

When I really began to grow and mature, I realized that you find out more about your faults from other people than from yourself. You also find out how much your actions impact another person. Until I realized that, I was a much more private person, not mixing emotionally with many people. Now, I try to look out into the world and be conscious of the interaction taking place there. Because I'm very reserved, people tell me at times I come off as cold or possibly a little arrogant. When I find an interesting person, I try really hard to overcome that impression, because I'm not arrogant or reserved. I think I'm just careful.

Medora Plimpton

The way I use to treat my brother Taylor surprises me. When he was about four years old, for instance, I used to put on boxing gloves and force him to put on gloves, too. Though I was twice his size, we'd punch each other and have a boxing match. He didn't want to fight at all, but I told him I was training him for the Olympics. I even broke his nose. I'd also make him do a hundred push-ups and once tried to drown him by pushing him underwater in the pool at the house. I don't know why, but I took out all my aggressions on him.

That behavior surprises me because I would never do that now. It's almost as if he weren't my brother anymore, but more like a friend. I think the first time we could talk to each other like normal people was on a trip to St. Thomas in 1989. Now we are totally best friends. We kid around together, and we help each other through family things that we don't really enjoy attending.

Torre Andrews

When I was about twelve, I had a terrible temper—I'd throw tantrums, smash things, kick holes in doors, beat on my sisters. One afternoon in the car, my sister and I had been jostling and bickering in the backseat and suddenly I was kneeling on her, punching her head. My stepfather pulled to the curb, reached over the seat, grabbed me off her and out of the car in one motion.

Then he turned to help my sister, who was bleeding where her lips had caught on her braces. As he helped her, my stepfather said, "I bet you really feel like a big man now."

Suddenly, for the first time, I thought, he's right. What does beating up my sisters prove? I haven't accomplished anything. I've only hurt them. That's when I decided I was never going to do it again, and I never did. That's when I began to understand that my actions had consequences.

Win Rockefeller

Probably the most surprising discovery was the possibility that when I do become angry, violence can come as a result of it. One night in college after someone had rolled my car, I had wandered down through town to look for it. And this guy who had been pushing and pushing me all year long mouthed off at me. It was the wrong thing to say at the wrong time, and I went monochromatic and came across the table for him.

I'd been angry before, but I had never gotten to the point where I realized that deep down inside there is the animal that exists, I suppose, in all of us. I haven't had a fight since then, but I haven't forgotten the potential is there to revert to one's very primitive instincts.

Taylor Plimpton

I am surprised that I can be very cruel without thinking about it, without meaning to be cruel.

John Jaxhiemer

I didn't realize I was self-conscious until about a year ago when I was sitting around at boarding school with a couple of friends, and we were just talking about what our fears were and things of that nature.

Jim Swann

How emotional I am. When the doctor handed me my first baby, I burst into tears. I had never cried in years. My father died when

I was seven years old. And the nanny woke me up and told me I was now the man of the family. When I started crying, Nanny told me, "You're the man of the family, you've got to quit crying and take care of all these women." And I had never cried for nearly thirty years until I had the first baby. Then it just came out. Now I have a blast. I can cry at movies; I can cry when I'm happy; I have a great time being emotional. Maybe because I didn't do it for so many years, I appreciate it now more than most other folks do.

David Prowse

My ability to get on with children. I can go anywhere, and I've got all the kids on my side. It all started in 1976 when I became the Green Cross Code Man in England, the spokesman for the British DOTransport's Child Pedestrian Road Safety Campaign, and when I also began to play Darth Vader in the *Star Wars* movies. Those two things basically altered the whole of my life. The children were being killed, you see, because they would step unthinking into the paths of cars. So, I became the Green Cross Code Man, all dressed in a Superman-like outfit, and with a sidekick droid who looked an awfully lot like R2–D2. My droid and I visited all the schools and taught the children to "stop, look, listen, and think."

Paul Mockler

All my life I thought sexuality was the most important part of a relationship. Maybe it's a function of old age—I'm forty-seven—but now I think I'm more interested in friendship in a relationship than anything else.

Doris Roberts

That people think that I'm a sexy woman. I guess that's one of the silly things.

More seriously, I am a generous spirit. Sometimes I learn that I give to an extent that is harmful to me, and that's a discovery that surprised me. I think you have to differentiate if it's some sort of a power play or not and that's another discovery that's surprising. What happens is you find yourself adopting people. That can be lovely, but if it's at your own expense then there's nothing left. My husband Bill Goyen used to say, "If you have a doubt about something, ask yourself is the bread that good or are you that hungry?" Isn't that wonderful? Once you get that clear, you know exactly what to do.

Dan Buettner

I was born with the social agility of a small soap dish. But I can remember deciding when I was a freshman in college that I was no longer going to be the male equivalent of a wallflower. So I started reading books and paying attention to other people who were good at being social, and I've turned into somebody who managed to make "Late Night with David Letterman" and be reasonably glib on national television.

Anne Brunson

I've been surprised about how I stand up for what I believe is right. I just never thought that I could do that. Recently I was teaching and some of my students cheated on some tests. It was hard calling their parents and telling them, and as a substitute teacher it would have been easier not to. But I did it.

Edward Colquhoun

I always thought I was homely, and I don't think so now. Not to think you're ugly is a definite change in attitude.

Why did I think so? OK, here's a deep secret. My eyes have kind of an oriental fold, and even people from Asia have asked if I have Asian ancestry. Of course, when I was a child during the forties, the Japanese really were the enemy, so some of those cruel little kids called me Tojo. It's nothing I've thought about in forty years, but it does say something about how our self-images are shaped.

Lenny Berman

I was surprised that I was able to do a minitriathlon. When I started training in January, I'd put on my heavy coat and mittens at nine o'clock at night and walk-jog through the neighborhood, hoping no one would see me huffing and puffing. By the time spring came along, I was in shape enough that I wasn't embarrassed to be out in the daylight.

But I still had an extremely low confidence level. Up to the morning of the race in Key West I was afraid. I thought I'd drown during the swim; I was so glad the water was shallow. I had that much fear. But I finished. That I was able to go from being worse than a couch potato to finishing a triathlon surprised me.

Kate Learson

I was raised with the idea that women should be totally feminine: you should never develop a muscle because down the road that muscle is going to sag. You should never be competitive about sports; even tennis was almost unacceptable.

But when my marriage was ending—I was in my late thirties—this notion that I should take an Outward Bound trip came into my head. So I called the head of the program, Hank Taft, whom I knew slightly because I swam at the same pool with his wife, and said, "Hank, I want to take an Outward Bound trip."

"Have you ever been camping?" he asked.

"I've never even been in a sleeping bag," I said.

He later told me he'd never heard anybody ask so desperately to go on a trip. I don't remember that. But Hank arranged for me to take a trip with a bunch of businessmen—just me and the men. The activities really pushed us. I couldn't get over how I enjoyed moving my body around—climbing, rappelling, bouldering. When I went to sleep out by myself in the open for the solo part, I was so fearful. It was bear country and I said, "Oh, God, they're going to eat me." But when the solo ended, I didn't want them to come and get me. The experience was a total revelation about how much I enjoyed doing physical things, how important the can-do attitude is.

Now I've trekked the Himalayas, climbed Kilimanjaro; I jog, play squash and tennis: I'm a regular jock—and all this started for me at age thirty-eight.

Margaret Mason

My physical endurance surprised me the most. A woman of my age wasn't even supposed to sweat. I'd been physical as a kid, but nothing structured. I did compete once in swimming but was terrible at baseball and soccer. So I was surprised to find an athlete lurking inside this fifty-year-old body. Even after completing two marathons, I still can't believe it.

Peggy Hackman

That I like running surprised me. When I was young, I hated it. But when my husband began training for the Marine Corps Marathon, I rode a bike along with him. I'd also drop him off for a run, take him water, stuff like that. And my friend Margaret Mason was running. I'd watch them running as I rode my bike and think how crazy they were.

But the months went on and the marathon drew near. After my husband went down for the start of the marathon, I thought, what the heck, I'll run around the school, which is about a mile, and I'll be with him in spirit for the start.

So that's what I did. I more or less jogged around the school. It was hard, but I was surprised at how good I felt. So I just kept adding. My husband helped me till I reached three miles; then I kept going on my own. It took two years to reach twenty-six miles and the Marine Corps Marathon.

Nan Thomas

Really, being able to look at people and life in a totally different way than I had been accustomed to. Unhurried, number one. I was born and brought up outside Boston; my family was active on the Boston social scene. I'd spent most of my adult life in resort management—my family helped develop Sugarbush Resort in Vermont. Life on Tortola is different—I sailed around visiting a number of islands before I settled here. I wanted a friendly place, like Vermont but warm. There's no social class here, so to speak; you talk to everybody. You take life and people as they are. I like that.

Jock Munro

Discovery? I think I'm rather surprised at our life in the last ten years. It never entered our heads that we'd work in Honduras, the Bahamas, and now here at Ledreborg. It all came about by chance.

In my last year at agricultural college—Silvia and I had just married—I was dining with friends in France. A banker sitting beside me said, "What are you doing when you leave college?"

"I'm not sure at the moment," I said, "but we would like to see a bit of the world." And for no particular reason I added, "I've always thought South America would be an interesting place to see."

A couple of minutes later the banker said, "Well, you know I'm actually involved in a project growing papayas in Honduras, and we might be looking for an assistant manager. Would you be interested?"

"Yes, I would," I said, "but to be perfectly honest, what's a papaya and where's Honduras?"

Amazingly I got the job. Though my studies had been European agriculture—wheat, barley, cows, sheep—I'd read up quite a bit on papayas before we got to Honduras and the frontier life.

Then we moved to the Bahamas to work on a farming venture there and wound up moving into big business matters—another surprise. And the third surprise came when Silvia, who'd gone to Denmark for Christmas earlier than I, called and said, "You're not going to believe this, but the family wants us to take over Ledreborg, if you're prepared to live here and run it."

So if anything's been a surprise in our lives, it's the different twists our lives and careers have taken.

Vince Spezzano

When Al Neuharth asked me to leave the news side and go into the business side of the paper, that startled me. And surprised me because I was a good reporter. I covered politics, I was well known, I was breaking stories left and right. I was calling the election night returns on the radio before they had computers. I had a system for predicting the returns, and I was right for ten straight years. So Al Neuharth's asking me to leave the news room was a surprise. Then he asked me to help start *USA Today*. That I could excel at publishing as well as reporting was a discovery.

Norman Lear – *TV Producer*

For me it would easily be the extreme pleasure I get from reading and examining what the great minds throughout history think about the spiritual and religious. I can't believe how much pleasure and excitement I derive from reading in these areas. I don't consider myself religious because religions are bridges to the spirit, and my bridges are uniquely irreligious. It has much more to do with our appetite for the original gift, more about our capacity to believe. I'm interested in what we make of that capacity.

I've got a two-volume encyclopedia of American religions, 2,600 of them. That fascinates me! The human mind can take a capacity and make so much of it. That utterly thrills me.

The Librarians

Mary Randolph: That I'm a librarian.

Virginia Kahl: I'm surprised that I actually sat down and wrote a book and finished it. I mean, I hardly ever finish anything. And now I've done it sixteen times.

Dorothy Cross: Well, my whole life was a surprise, but I was certainly surprised to find myself working in Europe as an army librarian, and I was very surprised to finish my professional career as the chief of the Pentagon library. To earn money, I used to pick strawberries on a farm in Michigan. I never dreamed that I would leave home, let alone work overseas or wind up in the kind of position that I had.

Edith Bornn

That I could do such a good job in oral argument. When I went to law school I didn't intend to become a practicing lawyer nor did my father want me to become a practicing lawyer. He just wanted me to have legal training. My class, the first postwar class at Columbia, was twice the size of the usual class, and its members were older. By our third year, I was one of four women in a class of 111. We started out as 188 with eight women. In our third year, we had moot course cases with oral argument and briefs. I got the highest marks—way above the others in oral argument by a large amount. I said, well, I have to rethink this. Maybe, in fact I ought to be a lawyer, maybe I truly ought to use this skill.

George Plimpton - *Writer*

That I can write. I thought I was going to be an editor. Putting other people's words right seemed much easier than putting my own words to paper. I had a vague notion about liking words and appreciating how they were put down and being struck by pieces that I thought had quality. I began to realize that I had a certain gift at it myself. Particularly a gift for humor, which is the hardest, I think, to write. Of course, I continue to be unsure.

Phoebe Legere

I'm surprised that I went into show business. Where I come from in Massachusetts there is a very great pressure not to call attention to yourself. The women are encouraged to be very above it all, not to distinguish themselves in any way. I remember my mother saying to me, "I can't believe that you're turning out to be a music fanatic." That was the worst insult she could possibly muster, but I'm sure she was trying to help me, keep me from stepping out too far from the crowd

My parents came to see my musical—*Hello, Mr. President*—which is about the first black woman president of the United States. It starred Laverne Baker, and I was playing about ten different parts, including the part of a black man. They liked it. Somehow it's starting to make sense and it's very nice for me. They were so embarrassed by it when I first started to become famous.

Ben Rose

I was surprised when I realized I could teach. The first time I taught about marine life, the class had a lot of UNEXSO staff members and I had no confidence in myself at all. But everyone seemed to like it and want more. As I realized I could do it, then I began to teach more and more.

Jerry Preston

I was surprised that I can compose music. Although I composed my first piece when I was in high school, I really didn't do anything serious till a few years ago. Sometimes I'll sit down and play something just out of the blue and it seems as if someone else is playing and I'm just listening. I really have no idea where it comes from, but sometimes it's very special. I've done a lot of musical portraits of friends.

Kathy Bater Brackett

That I was smart. When I was in school, I didn't do very well. And people seemed to reinforce that. You know: *You're not too bright, so we're going to put you in dumbbell English and dumbbell math.* I remember my school counselor sitting me down and asking me what I wanted to do. I said, "I'd like to work with criminally insane people, in a mental hospital." He said, "You can't go in as a psychologist, and you couldn't be a nurse, because 'you're not college material.' So you could probably get in as a nurses aide or a technician." I perfectly accepted what he said. I thought he was really directing me because I really didn't think I was capable.

Then I moved off Catalina Island and met a really great college student named Mark Hirsch. Mark said, "Kathy, you're really wasting your time." I was then working at the state mental hospital as a nurse's aide. I was in my twenties.

So Mark said, "You should go to school," and I said, "I can't go to college." I hadn't even finished high school; I'd dropped out after my counselor's advice. I thought, *I'm wasting my time here; go out and get a job.*

So my friend kept nagging at me and nagging at me. At first I thought he was pulling my leg. I couldn't go to college! That's where all the smart people go. But he kept at me, so finally I said OK.

At first I sat the exams for the state college. And of course I didn't pass. I said, "See, Mark! You're pushing me into something that's only going to cause me a lot of aggravation and unhappiness; I'm not capable of this."

"Oh no, no," he said. "You can go to a junior college for two years. You won't have to sit the entrance exams."

That's what I did. I enrolled in college in Huntington Beach, and it was a piece of cake. When I left college, I had a grade point average of 3.85, and I was not only in college, I was working full time and I was supporting myself and my daughter.

But I was scared to death at first. I can remember sitting in class sure the teacher was going to come up and say, *What are you doing here! You're not college material!* I felt like a thief or something.

Without Mark Hirsch, who knows what would have happened to me? I'd probably still be working at the state mental hospital. I've lost contact with him, unfortunately. It's really sad.

I never saw the counselor again. Mr. Lipscom. I would love to see him, to find out where he is and what's he's doing. I would love to make sure he is not counseling children.

Jane Burke

I started acting out of spite because I didn't like this girl who "knew" she already had the lead in the church play. And she had attached herself to *my* church and was singing in *my* choir—you know how kids think they own something. So I decided that I was going to get that part that she knew she had. And I did.

But what surprised me more was that I was good and that I enjoyed it as much as I did even though I was scared to death to get up and do it. The enjoyment surprised me. There was that adrenalin rush when you're nervous but you're having a ball at the same time. It led me to do more.

My junior year in high school I had accompanied for *Carnival*, so everyone assumed I was going to play for the musical my senior year, which was *Once upon a Mattress*. I played for all the auditions, then politely said, "I would like to audition." They were surprised. But I got a real good role, had a ball doing it, and didn't have to play the piano. I was hooked.

Deni McIntyre

This was not so much a discovery as knowledge forced upon me. I discovered that I could not sing. This was news to me because I used to go around the house singing at the top of my lungs. But at school we were supposed to sing in unison with some kind of melodic consistency. I wanted to be one of the leaders of the class, so I was simply taking my customary place when I sang just slightly louder than everybody else.

After about a week of practicing for some kind of parents' night, Sister Mary Lidwin decided there were about five of us who were undermining the quality of the performance. She came around and, one by one, asked us if we would please consider just mouthing the words, singing silently. She put it as diplomatically as she could—I think she said something about singing in our heads. I haven't sung full voice since.

I've had to perform on stage, even with microphones, and I still don't sing full voice. I'm not tone-deaf and can carry a tune, but my vocal quality really sucks. Sister Mary Lidwin was right.

Don Brunson

Looking back, I'm a little surprised at how quickly the transition occurred from being a young, carefree adolescent still supported largely by my parents to being a married, independent adult. I think it came very fast.

One of the things I remember is that our first two or three months of married life were like college all over. Anne and I had an apartment, we were around people our own age, we were having a good time. Anne had just graduated from college and I was in the naval supply school in Athens, Georgia. Then all of a sudden we were both headed to Japan; we had about four days together to find a place for her to stay, to buy a car, to get her situated. Then I'm on an airplane by myself headed right into Saigon. That whole transition happened real fast. From being a sort of carefree, fun-loving college type of a kid in Athens, Georgia, to the next day waking up in Saigon by myself in officers' quarters that had chain link fence angled out from each of the windows so that when people threw hand grenades up there, they'd roll away from the building and not kill as many of the people who were sleeping inside.

Stuart Perkins

I think I finally began to feel mature at fifty-six, when I learned to laugh at myself. My definition of maturity is a lack of fear about anything; being able to laugh at yourself is an important part of that ability to keep plugging ahead whatever happens.

I learned to laugh at myself because I ran into a real smart female counselor who taught me. I'd gone to see her because I'd just been divorced for the fourth time. After four divorces you begin to think that there's something wrong here.

I'd left Stonington after the last divorce with just two suitcases. Nothing else. I was understandably bitter and upset. And one day the counselor said to me, "I think I can help you get over this anger."

"I know you're a good accountant," she went on, "and you know exactly how much money this woman took you for."

"Yeah, she took all my family possessions and $67,321.26."

"You also have a reasonably good memory, and I'm sure you can remember how many times you went to bed with her."

I flinched, "Yeah, I probably could."

"All right," she said, "I want you to go home and figure out how many times you slept with her and how much money you lost; then divide one into the other and figure how out much it cost you per crack. Then I want you to look in the Yellow Pages under 'escort services' and call and find out what the going rate is so you can see how you did."

I did just that, and, boy, I made out like a bandit! Suddenly the true nature of the whole relationship came to me, and I burst out laughing. That was the first time I hilariously laughed at myself.

Kurt Vonnegut

It was always easy for me to read and write, and when I was a little kid this was commented on. But that was obvious to me and not worth commenting on, so I had a "so-what" feeling about it. I guess nothing has surprised me except that I seem to be in very good health at the age of sixty-eight, and I'm certainly not entitled to be. That's the big surprise.

Murial Sichveland, Wednesday Bridge Club

That I, an older person, can care as much as I do about everything that goes on in politics and can get so stirred up about it. That surprises me. Why don't I just forget about it?

Barbara Bailey

How I've managed to survive since my husband Robert died. We were best friends for fifty-six years and lived happily together. Then suddenly life became *me* instead of *we* and everything belongs to *you,* not to *us.* It's an enormous change to reconstruct your life so that you don't sink into depression, very difficult to make yourself do things alone. I made up my mind that I wouldn't succumb to despondency or inactivity.

Mildred Sutton

I think it surprises me how hard I have to still fight to keep going. I didn't know you were going to have to work this hard to keep going when you get older. Oh, yes, it's worth it. If you stopped, it would be the end. You have to keep on. But I didn't know that with every year you'd have to work a little bit harder at it.

53. Birds Flying South

Timothy Sultan

On our lake in Virginia, there is one lame goose that can no longer fly and has been spending the winters there. One evening as I was rowing, a large flock of geese circled the lake, all honking as if they were notifying any stragglers that this was the moment to get up and go. And this one crippled goose was on our dock with its wings flapping and its neck stretched up, honking excitedly. After several circles, the flock turned away and their cries became increasingly dimmer until all I could hear was the occasional honks of the remaining goose.

Gerry Cooney

Change. Since I've been out here on Long Island, I've really gotten into birds, watching them flying south. It's part of the cycle we all go through—the change, the process of moving on.

Will and Deni McIntyre

Going to Brazil. We'll be doing something that's got all our attention, when something breaks through—a little samba rhythm or the smell of limes—and we'll catch each other's eye and just kind of nod our heads and go, "Time to go to Brazil."

Princess Pamela Strobel

They're traveling home because it is rough up here in New York.

Phoebe Legere

When the summer is over in Bridgehampton and those birds start to fly south, it is like a little taste of death. It's a melancholy that is so wrenching. Summer is over and those birds are getting out.

Damian Miller

I think of the old house over by the beach on a gray, gloomy fall, almost winter, afternoon—absolutely gray. And silhouetted against the sky, in a vague V shape, maybe seven or eight geese just heading out.

Mildred Sutton

Every time I see wild birds flying south, it never ceases to amaze me that they can fly, that they are so graceful, and that they succeed against all the obstacles in their way. They are such tiny specks in the universe.

Edward Colquhoun

It's a beautiful thing in October and November to see the geese taking turns, breaking up the air currents for those behind. It's such a fascinating thing to watch the cooperation.

The Librarians

Dorothy Cross: On the farm in southwest Michigan it was terrific because toward the fall you could see geese going over frequently. More recently, we were camping in Pennsylvania in October on a nice, clear night, and I awakened to the sound of the geese going over. It was just gorgeous.

Mary Randolph: The honking has to be one of the warmest feelings in the world. It doesn't matter what type of congested area you're in, it just transforms you to another place, another time. It makes you realize that there's just something more than bricks and concrete and I-95s. Sort of keeps a certain balance. I think everyone identifies with birds and a sense of freedom.

Virginia Kahl: I worry about them.

Mary Randolph: I'll say I saw a beautiful deer this morning, and Virginia will say "Oh, my gosh! How terrible! It's going to get hit! Oh, it's never going to make it!" And I say, "Virginia! It's a beautiful sight, enjoy it," and she'll say, "Oh, it's terrible!"

Mary Lou Retton
Hunting. I went once in my life, and I'll never go again.

Shannon Kelly
Hunting season, winter time, and football!

Zar Rochelle
Watching the flocks of blackbirds or starlings gather on the ground and start turning leaves over is fun. It's like the ground is moving or vibrating.

Jean Dorrance
Sometimes there are birds that fly around my window, little yellow and green birds that look like parakeets or bananakeets and go "wee, wee, wee, wee . . ." Maybe that's good luck.

Doris Roberts
Fall, school, end of summer, sadness, loneliness, leaves turning—but here in Los Angeles the only birds I see fly south have feathers made by machine.

54. An Unusual Friendship

Win Rockefeller

An unusual friendship? You mean besides the fact I'm a meat-eating predator married to a vegetarian animal rights activist? By the time it becomes friendship, it's not unusual.

Vince Spezzano

When we bought a group of publications in the Virgin Islands, the magazine *The Virgin Islander* came as part of the package. Maureen O'Hara had owned it and sold it with the proviso that she would continue to write a monthly column. She did not concern herself much about deadlines, but somehow her columns would always show up—special mail, dictated over the phone, somehow. And I would pay her $1,000 each month, not as the publisher but as a writer. That really appealed to her. I loved to remind her that she was the reporter and I the publisher. But one day she said that she felt $1,000 was not sufficient.

"Why?" I said.

"Well, in my business," she said, "the amount of money that you're given for what you do has status. It would seem more appropriate if I made more than $1,000."

I said, "What I think would be even more appropriate and visible would be to do it for nothing."

She looked at me and said, "Are you Irish?"

We became good friends. We often had breakfast meetings, and even early in the morning she was always immaculately dressed and made up. I was there the morning after the day John Wayne died, and for three hours she told me anecdotes about Wayne and her husband and the three of them.

Julie Rogers

Jim Dickerson. He's a crazy man, raised in Arkansas, who's the minister of a small grass-roots church here and also a very sophisticated developer of nonprofit housing. He has lots of demons and sticking points in his life—he's a recovering alcoholic—which he is very public about. Exercising is one of the things that helps to keep him centered, and he also takes Friday afternoons to go to a nearby monastery to just chill out a little bit.

Jim loves me and I love him and it's pure as the driven snow. It was difficult for Jim's family to put the money together for him to go to the Key West Conchathon. It was also extremely difficult for Jim to allow himself to go on a vacation without his family. So several of us decided to give Jim a birthday party to help raise the money for the trip. It was a major shift in his life to accept the money for himself. He came and he ran a damn good race and had a wonderful time.

Richard Duke

I like to go backpacking, but I hate going with large groups—that seems the antithesis of getting close to nature. I met Art through a third party who knew Art felt the same way about backpacking.

Somehow we fitted perfectly as hiking companions, though we are very different. He's a pianist. I'm a mathematician. I'm certainly illiterate when it comes to classical music. Art claimed to have no scientific bent at all. So we couldn't talk much about such things, but we fitted beautifully in other ways.

In hiking we wanted to go equally far or equally hard at the same speed. The strain of trying to go a hundred miles with someone who goes a little faster or slower can destroy the whole pleasure of the trek. So that clicked from the beginning.

The friendship started there but grew.

Kurt Vonnegut

The carpenter who gave me a new roof here. I work out here alone a lot in the summer, and so he and I have talked a whole lot. He's a fundamentalist preacher on the side and I'm an atheist and we have a lot of fun talking back and forth.

Timothy Sultan

My friendship with Boris Babic, a Yugoslavian, is unusual because it's endured although we haven't seen each other in over four years and then only briefly. Through his letters I see his life as immediately as if he still lived here in the city. When he was in the Yugoslav conscript army, he wrote to me while on guard duty at night, tales of sneaking past the other guards at night, climbing over a wall and scurrying through a fence to see this girl he liked, his sense of displacement at being forced into the army. He sent a black-and-white picture of himself in front of his squad—a picture that looked as though it were taken fifty years ago.

55. *Burying a Friend: Martin Hoose, a Portrait*

John Emery

Martin Hoose wasn't someone I was extremely close to all my life, but he was someone who helped me be who I am, who gave me the freedom to be me without any pretense or playing or anything. He was just completely open about who he was.

He was such a handsome, magnificent human being, one of those larger-than-life persons. His hands were wonderful drawing machines. Just to watch him draw was an adventure.

Martin died of AIDS in 1991.

I took my twelve-year-old son, Anthony, to see him before he died. I wanted my son to meet him at least once, though Martin by then was in such bad condition. I wanted my son to see Martin's art and, more important, to understand courage. Martin was never afraid. Not much later he decided he just didn't want to deal with it anymore. He'd had a catheter inserted directly in his heart to pump in chemicals, and he just pulled it out.

Several hundred people came to his funeral at the Surfside Theatre in Cocoa Beach. I'd filled the entire lobby with his artwork. There were magnificent flowers everywhere. I was one of his friends who spoke. I equated Martin Hoose's life to the Australian pines that used to line this county from one end to the other. The one thing I remember as a child is running through those Australian pines at Sebastian Inlet. The wind through them gave you a sense of great freedom, of being very alive. When Martin Hoose walked up to you, the wind blowing through his long blond hair, you had that same sense of the human spirit and freedom.

Many people spoke at the funeral, one of them a young girl in a wheelchair, so sick she could barely speak. Even after Martin was sick, he had gone to her school to speak about the power of art, the gift of art. That talk had given her the courage to unleash her own creative spirit.

Not long ago, a deep freeze killed off most of the great stands of Australian pines in our county, an enormous loss. The dead stands were cut down, and we all thought that was the end of them. But just last week, I noticed that a lot of seedlings are coming up around those big old roots.

56. *Burying a Friend*

Paul Mockler

My favorite uncle Ozzie really loved the sea. In World War II he spent all his time on corvettes, the Canadian wooden boats used to hunt German subs. My uncle always wanted to be buried at sea, too. Just before he died, he told my sister this again, told her to give his ashes to me.

So, on my last trip here to Grand Bahama, I brought my uncle along in this little plastic container provided by the crematorium. Ozzie absolutely wasn't religious at all, but he did like to tip the glass and have fun. So, I called a couple of friends, and we started out that afternoon drinking daiquiris. Then we got in the Boston Whaler and took Uncle Ozzie right out to the deep water just beyond the reef. One of my friends knew my uncle. The other didn't, but we kept telling him stories about Ozzie, toasting Ozzie, and then finally we threw Ozzie overboard. It was fabulous! The perfect funeral!

Zar Rochelle

Harry was my absolute best all-time friend. All his doctors told him he got throat cancer from Agent Orange in Vietnam. He'd had his larynx removed and learned to talk again using a muscle in the throat. According to his therapist, he learned to talk faster than anyone who'd had that surgery. They were just amazed at him. Everything was looking good. Then the cancer came back.

For several weeks before he died, he was living with his brother in Savannah, and I went down to stay with him for a week.

I was so shocked when I saw him because he couldn't have weighed a hundred pounds. He couldn't get to the bathroom without help. And all he *could* do was get to the bathroom and back. I tried to make the visit as normal as possible. We talked about friends and old times and current affairs and what have you. I'm glad I got to see him.

Just a little later, I got the call that he was dead. The memorial service was to be in Pennsylvania, but his brother offered to have a memorial service in Savannah if I wanted to come down for one. But I'm not into stuff like that. If a friend moves away, you don't go look at his empty house.

Silvia Munro

My best friend who died of cancer. She was ill for seven years, so we knew it was coming, and it was a blessing for her in the end because life wasn't fun anymore.

But she could talk about her death, and it was a beautiful death actually with her family and friends all around. Her mother and father were together for the first time in twenty-five years.

When we went to see her in hospital after the doctors had given her only a short time to live, she was falling into deep coma and then coming out briefly. It seemed she might be gone any minute. Suddenly, she sat up in bed and said, "God, it takes a long time to snuff it. I want a cigarette and a drink." To be that close to death and to say that: she had fully accepted that she was dying and she had faith. She'd been my friend since I was fifteen or sixteen.

Gerry Cooney

I had a friend who fought bone cancer for many years; he'd lost a leg fighting it. When I had to go out to California to start training camp, I took him out of the hospital and brought him to live with us. But I didn't pull any punches with him. We wouldn't let him be an invalid. If he wanted something in the kitchen, he had to get it. Once when he came out to the pool, I rolled him right in. That made him live, made him feel like one of the guys.

The best thing you can do for someone who's dying is make him feel how much you love him.

Michael Bornn

Scott Sheviski was eighteen, just beginning to mature and blossom, when he died. Scott was the third child in his family like I was in mine. And the Sheviskis and Bornns were neighbors and close friends. I felt like an older brother to Scott.

Typically in St. Thomas, you go to several parties on New Year's Eve. Scott had been to one party with me earlier, then he and a friend left to go to others. Late in the night he turned up at another party I attended. When he was ready to leave, he found my car blocking his and asked me to move it. Like a good friend, I did. Two minutes later, just around the corner from the party, he flipped the car and was killed when the car rolled on him.

I didn't find out until I came home later to find my mother there grieving with his mother. I was the last person to see him alive when I let him out. That was a mark in my life. I said to myself, tomorrow you may not be here so try to live each day to the fullest. You don't live forever.

Phoebe Legere

So, so many. This year we buried Ethel Eichelburger, a great performance artist. It was very, very sad. I loved him. We did a show together called *Moulin Rage*. Ethel was the one who turned me on to the Delsart method. Delsart was married to Ruth St. Denis. This was the school from which Sarah Bernhardt came. I learned so much from him about the spiritual aspect of hair and makeup. Ethel was a drag queen, but not into the type of drag you may imagine, which often has components of malice and caricature. His work was more in the spirit of pretheatrical Greece, where women's roles in tragedy were played by men and the whole performance was a religious offering to the gods.

Ethel never told anyone he had AIDS, which I thought was cruel because I would have liked to say good-bye. He couldn't sustain his performance energy and just went into the bathtub and did the deed. It was too abrupt, I thought. But I understand that he wanted to have control over the time and place of death, and I understand he didn't want to go downhill. I spend a lot of time going through the AIDS wards in New York City, so I know how hideous an AIDS death can become. But still I wish Ethel had given me a chance to tell him how much I loved him.

Lenny Berman

My close friend Shahid Abdullah died of leukemia this past summer. I was sure to the last that a bone-marrow transplant would work, that he would live. But they couldn't get him in remission long enough; he went into cardiac arrest and died.

Shahid was a Muslim and his funeral ceremony was held in a small storefront Muslim funeral home. As people showed up, they brought in more chairs and more chairs. People were standing everywhere—white, black, very religious, not religious—just an outpouring. People came from all over the country—it seemed everyone who'd ever worked on criminal justice reform was there. This incredible draw of people was a real tribute to the man.

Dana Warrington

My brother and sister and I learned about honesty from my mother and father. She and Dad were the two people you never had to lie to, regardless of the subject. They were always up front with us, too, including the day Mom had to tell me she would die soon from an inoperable kidney tumor.

The scary thing about it was she called it almost to the day. Mom spent the last year on severe chemotherapy and made it to my wedding in September. Then she told us she wanted to make it through the Christmas holidays, which were special to us. Our Christmases were right out of a movie.

So we brought her home from the hospital, and the last month was real tough. We were all there most of the time doing round-the-clock shifts with her; that was a scary time because we were basically listening for her breathing. The last three days she really touched close to me. We were able to talk and cry and hold each other, and to the end she wasn't afraid.

My mother died on Christmas Eve, 1981, and except for my wife, I won't have a friend like that again.

Jock Munro

The death of my old nanny was particularly hard for me. When she died I was working on a farm in Denmark, and since my parents did not realize how important coming to her funeral might be to me, I learned of her death only a day before the funeral—too late to make it home. I felt I'd missed something terribly, terribly important for me.

Jerry Preston

Mama taught me to try to be unselfish. After she died, I took pleasure in distributing her things and remembering the gifts I'd brought her. I'd say, "I brought this to her from Italy; I got this for her in France." Once I brought her some fans from Spain, and since the church wasn't air-conditioned, she'd fan herself with these elegant fans, sitting right by the people with those cardboard funeral parlor fans.

Ollie Ferguson

I found out that my grandfather had died late one afternoon when I got back from work and my mom came through the door. I could see the shock and horror on her face. I knew that something was wrong immediately. She said, "Ollie, Boppy has died." I immediately broke down. I remember being in a total, total state of shock. I just could not believe it.

We sat on the couch and just cried. I held her, and she was sobbing so hard her body was shaking. I immediately thought, OK this is it, I have got to be strong and I've got to take her through this.

It was really a hard time. Because he was a leader and a newspaper publisher, everything that my grandfather did was public, even his death. There were a great many people at the funeral. The prime minister of the Bahamas, a lot of people like that were there. Friend and foe alike came out of respect.

The funeral for me was probably the hardest thing I have ever done. I had the honor of carrying my grandfather's ashes and that was extremely hard. I remember walking through those gathered knowing that I had to show everybody the family's strength and dignity. I think that really helped us through. It is not that we don't show emotion, we are a very emotional group, but there is a time for strength just as there is definitely a time for weakness. Being able to be strong at those times where strength is needed was important. But that made probably the greatest demand ever on my inner strength—having all that emotion and respect and love for such a great person and not allowing the great loss to affect my dignity.

Peggy Houliban

While I was training for my first triathlon, my younger brother Tim invited me to visit him in Oregon and go whitewater rafting with him—a sport he really loved. I expressed my concerns about staying in shape on a vacation like that since I was "in training" for the Bahamas. Tim laughed and assured me that it would not adversely affect my fitness level. During that vacation, we climbed mountains and battled the waters of the Snake and Payette rivers—it was the most active vacation I had ever had. And it was a wonderful experience visiting with my brother after not seeing each other for four years.

Then tragedy struck—just one week after I returned home to the East Coast, Tim died in a freak rafting accident.

The whole family was devastated. I didn't feel like doing anything—let alone training for a triathlon. My friend Pat, who was also training for the minitriathlon in D.C. and in the Bahamas, helped and encouraged me by reminding me what a sports nut my brother was and how proud he was of my getting out of the Washington rut of working too hard and not working out enough. But I still couldn't work through the sadness and grief.

When I went home to Pennsylvania for Tim's funeral, I took my bicycle without even thinking. By that time, it had become a habit to take my bike wherever I went. The next day I convinced my dad, who's a great biker, to go out for a ride with me. We rode and rode for hours. It took some of the edge from the stress we were under. My dad and I shared a special experience that day. Two weeks later, I did the D.C. triathlon, my first one, and I dedicated it to Tim. I knew he would have been proud of me.

Myrtis Brown

When Florry Little, the granddaughter of the Littles who owned the plantation where I was born, got real sick with cancer, I went out and took care of her. I'd stay with her every night. When she was out of her head, near the end, she'd ask for my mother, though my mother was gone. I would sit and look at her and pray. I'd hold her in my arms. She was so sick one night, I called the doctor and he said, "Myrtis, I've been out to see her and it's just a matter of hours."

It touched me to be in the room with her by myself. She would look up at me—she couldn't say anything—and I would wet her tongue with a little wet rag—she couldn't drink anything—and she would sort of grip me. She knew I cared; I knew she did.

I wanted to cry but I couldn't cry and let her see me. So I went and got her niece and mother and said, "You come in the room, I think she's passing." And they told me no, they didn't want to.

Finally I sat there, and I said, "Lord, will you help me do this." When she passed, I laid her down and I went in the room and I told her mother, "Miss Lois, Miss Florry's gone." Then her niece came in and we did what we could.

57. *Your Greatest Fear*

Phoebe Legere

I always fear that I will play a wrong note, and my life has been a process of overcoming that fear.

Margaret Mason

Becoming dull-eyed would be my greatest fear. Not delighting in the world, not seeing the joy and the wonder, not maintaining a sense of adventure.

Win Rockefeller

I'm afraid I'll die before my kids have the opportunity to begin to communicate with me so that I can share some of my knowledge with them. Looking back, there's been time and time again when I've said, "Damn, Dad, why did you go and do that? You know, I wanted to ask you about something in this situation, and you're not here to tell me about it."

Cliff Robertson

My greatest fear is that I will run out of time. I am not afraid to die, but there's so much to do. Maybe that's why I never rest.

Desy Campbell

Losing my mobility.

A. J. Hiers

Even more than health, I think I had rather be dead than fail. I don't mean the economy going sour or losing the business, but becoming complacent, or a lush of some sort, and losing and failing. I'd rather be dead. I would fear that over death.

David Prowse

My greatest fear is financial destruction, not being able to provide. One of the worst things that ever happened to me was that I had a company once that went into liquidation. I'd gotten myself into debt and couldn't get out. I was working at Harrods at the time, too, and the phone would ring. "Hopkins here," the funny-looking accountant from the liquidation house would say, and it really put the fear up me.

We used to sit down at a table together, and he'd say, "Have a read of this"—promise to tell the truth and all this sort of business.

"I read it the last time."

"Well, I do like you to read it every time," Mr. Hopkins would say.

I had nothing to fear or hide. But I used to live in fear and dread of this guy.

Egbert Donovan

I have a big fear about this island right now. Because I know Tortola is growing and there are problems like drugs, I feel the island's gonna ruin in time to come. I'm afraid because it's very serious in St. John, St. Thomas, and those places now. Right now you can go anywhere, leave your home open, leave your keys in your car and no one will be a problem to you. But I see lots of things that make me think it's gonna be a problem in time to come.

Lyn Lear

My greatest fear is that I grow old and don't live up to my ideal of who I would like to be as a human being. It would be a tremendous hurt to look back on my life and say, *Boy, you really blew it; you had so much, and you did nothing with most of it.*

It's less and less a fear now that my life is becoming more and more of what I feel good about.

Eric Jensen

I worry about my medical career. What if I have devoted so much of my life and energy to medicine and I get to the end and find out I don't like it or aren't good at it? What then? What a terrifying thought!

Michael Bornn

My greatest fear is being injured and not dying, being a vegetable. My grandfather was a horse, as strong mentally and physically as anyone ever was. Then one day he had a stroke and lived for a year and a half as a vegetable. He died when he had that stroke, but we had to see this other person in his body for that year and a half. Living is something more than just breathing. I don't want that to happen to me.

Edward Colquhoun

To die in pain, I guess. I write about cancer a great deal, and I know that cancer's pain is undertreated throughout the world. Dying in pain is most people's greatest fear.

Mary Lou Retton

Death. I've talked to a lot of older people who aren't afraid to die, but they've experienced a lot of things in their lives. But I'm really afraid to die. I'm very fortunate, but there is so much more I want to do, and having a family is so important to me. So, I worry about death for everyone I love: the people who are hurt when you go, everyone. I hope sometime in my life I'll feel content about the prospect, but I'm not now.

The Supper Club

Mary Costigan: Yes, I think there is a great deal of fear in older people but it's not fear of being old . . .

Mildred Sutton: It's fear of not being able to look after yourself.

Bill Peck: I think that's a much stronger fear than dying.

Henry Kemp: Death is inevitable, we know that.

Rose Wing: The main fear is that you'll lose your independence.

Mildred Sutton: But we do have each other for support.

Others: Oh, yes!

58. No Grieving for Peyton, Please: A Portrait

Patrick Goddard

Our daughter Peyton's birth seemed normal, and she certainly was a good-looking baby. But at about ten months, my wife Dianne began to notice that some of the things you look for in a baby— reaction to repetitive sounds, a head turned when someone came in the room—weren't happening. There was no recognition.

And so the tests began. At first we thought she might be deaf. Many tests later, they told us Peyton had multiple learning disabilities. Something happened—they didn't know what—which kept her from communicating fully with the outside world. She observes it but very seldom comments on it with gesture or word.

Even after we knew that, the realization that something was wrong took some time to come clear. There was no painful phone call in the middle of the night saying your son had been killed in a wreck. Instead, there was more of a sense of trying to understand what was going on with our daughter and then saying, "OK, now that we know, what's the best way to handle it?" So there was a lot of mental evolution and growth on *our* part. There was no grieving, but a lot of sadness imposed on us by people around us. People saw difficulties ahead and wanted to be comforting.

But we didn't need comforting. We decided to raise our daughter as a normal child, to treat her with love and comfort rather than treating her as handicapped. It's an odd situation, but Peyton taught us real quickly that *everyone*, including our son Patrick, had special needs. But Patrick's needs were masked by normal growth. Peyton also made us aware that we all have disabilities.

That realization made us much more attuned to compassion than to judgment when it comes to others. Raising our daughter has given a depth to our lives and understanding you can't get unless you've experienced her life. Now it's hard for me to look at a homeless person without thinking of her. At one point, that person might have been like my daughter.

Peyton has also given our son, I believe, a greater understanding of goodness. Peyton has such a primitive innocence, even at seventeen. She's untainted. She could walk out of the house nude to the middle of the freeway and not feel threatened. Patrick has therefore lovingly learned to protect—and enjoy—his sister. We all just took a trip to Disney World, where Dianne and I watched the two of them getting on the rides together and laughing. Do you know how wonderful that felt?

Our family has a friend, Barbara Buchan, who was on the American Women's Cycling Team. Barbara was in a terrible biking accident once—terrible brain damage. They actually thought she was brain dead, but her parents wouldn't let the doctors pull the plug even though she would supposedly be a vegetable. Barbara is very close to us now, very close to Peyton. Because she says, "I know what Peyton's going through. Because during all that time they thought I was a vegetable, *I knew what was going on.*" Barbara is a living example for us of a heroic comeback through the will to live a productive life. We have similar expectations for Peyton.

I believe in my heart that Peyton knows what's going on. It's just like a Rubik's Cube. If she can just move it one more notch, the right notch, it will all fall in place. I can't tell you the elation my family feels knowing that we can help Peyton uncover that last move herself.

We're very upbeat about that thought, because we know it's coming.

59. A Fear for Your Children

Win Rockefeller

How much paper do you have? My fears: That despite all the best, all the things that we try to do for them, and all of our mistakes, stupidities, and inanities not withstanding, that they won't end up achieving their objectives. That they'll have problems, that they'll be unhappy, miserable. Or that I'll lose them, whatever way that might occur. I suppose one of the fears would be that somebody would try to hurt them, and that thought comes back to that animal instinct in me that you don't mess with my children.

Jim Swann

That something will happen to my kids. When my parents used to worry about me when I was a kid, I'd go, "Sure, nothing's going to happen to me. You don't need to worry about me; I'm indestructible." Then you see that that's what your kids think. Yet you have to let them learn to fly. If they don't try, they can't learn. So what a horrible paradox—I don't know the right word, but it's a pushmi-pullyu. You know what I mean? You've got to let them do stuff but if you let them do stuff, they'll end up like some of my friends' kids, wrapped around trees in their automobiles.

I've already told my kids they're going to have pickup trucks when they get cars. All their friends may be driving sports cars, but they are going to have something that is as close to a *tank* as I can afford to buy. If their friends laugh at them, I say, "Just tell 'em it's because your dad is afraid you'll wrap yourselves around a tree, and he'd rather kill the tree than you."

A. J. Hiers

The biggest fear I have for my daughter is that she won't turn out all right. I see so many families that have three or four children, and there's always one that isn't quite on dead center. I have this one little girl now, and we're going to have another child in about three months. I hope they turn out good. I'll give them the education they deserve and the start in life that I didn't quite have. But I still worry.

Mary Costigan, Wednesday Bridge Club

I've always hoped that my daughter Kay will never have to live through a depression like we had to live through. That was a most painful time. They don't know what it was like; you can't tell them what it was like. And some of our generation still have that depression mentality—taking advantage of saving or making do at every opportunity.

Gerry Cooney

I have a little baby boy, and he's just unbelievable. I want my son to learn everything that I never had a chance to learn. I want him to have as much as he can have. A fear for my son is that he won't be able to find that.

John Emery

That they will die before I do.

Emily Cook

It's easier to tell you what I hope for my daughter than what I hope not. I want her to be comfortable with who she is. I want her to have a secure home where, no matter what happens outside in the world, she has a place to come home to, to talk, to be safe. I want her to be able to fall apart and express her feelings, whatever they are, and have that be OK. Obviously, I'm worried about drinking and the genetics of that kind of stuff. When she's old enough to have the discussion, I'll tell her my story. I think the best I can do is tell her what I've been through and hope that I can help guide her to be a strong person and make her own decisions based on her choices rather than peer pressure. This is idealistic, but it is my hope.

Mimi Taufer

I have realized how very important it is for our son that both Ed and I take care of ourselves, that we survive. I had never thought so much about that before. But knowing and feeling how much a child needs his parents and craves his parents at his age, four, I would fear for him terribly if he lost us. He's one of the reasons why I tell Ed to go to the doctor and have a complete checkup.

Barbara Bailey

I fear AIDS for them, but perhaps worse, I'm afraid they might be in an awful accident and lie in a vegetable state for years. That I think is worse than AIDS. At least there is a timespan to AIDS, but there is no timespan to vegetative states.

Marla Hanson

Life can be really tough and difficult, and I'm a little fearful of bringing children into that. I want to protect them, teach them enough to get through it all as a decent human being.

Edward Colquhoun

We have a very unusual situation in that we are older parents—I was forty-nine when we adopted David—and while racially he is Brazilian Indian, African, and some sort of European, when people see brown skin then their perception stops right there. From then on, they judge by surfaces. So when you read it's been proven that the banks turn down more brown-skinned people regardless of education, when you have people being turned down for jobs because they have brown skin—all of these things—you worry. We know the sort of educational opportunity that David will have and how well spoken he will be, for instance, but he is still going to have a hard life, and we won't be there. Even if we were twenty, it would be a hard life that we couldn't fix. There's no way we can control what happens beyond a certain point.

This has always been a concern for brown people in general, but now it is very close to home. It needs a solution—for the world.

60. What Makes You Feel Young? A Portrait
The Wednesday Bridge Club

Ever since they retired, these four ladies have gathered most Wednesdays for sandwiches and bridge. The laughter wafting from the porch reveals their enjoyment. We asked this lively group, most of them over eighty, What makes you feel young?

Mildred: When somebody tells you that you look nice or that you've done something well, it lifts your spirits whether it makes you feel young or not. It's kind of hard to feel young at this age.

Peggy: But some days you feel a lot better than you do other days, and you enjoy them more, too.

Mary: Doing yard work makes me feel young—that I'm still able to do it. I got out and cut down that big old bush beside my house. I didn't get it completed, but I had a huge pile of brush to put out for the trash collector. I felt so good.

Mildred: Then, when you see children that you've taught and they say something about school, it makes you think about those days and you can't realize it's been as long ago as it was.

Peggy: I think it makes you feel a little younger when you're with the young people.

Mildred: Their enthusiasm rubs off on you a little bit.

Mary: I feel surprise when you go in a store and someone says— I bought some fabric the other day—and they say, "You get your senior citizen's discount." They knew it without asking—surely that's not possible.

61. What Makes You Feel Young?

Win Rockefeller
Driving. I've been known to drive fast on occasion.

Jonathan Peter
The fact that everything still amazes me. Like a child, I'm still impressed by what people are doing. We also decided not to have children—for us that is the most responsible act because most of the world's problems seem to me caused by too many people—and that, too, helps keep me young.

Foxy Callwood
Watching my last two kids. I'm fifty-two. I got one seven and one eight. And my not living a hard life anymore—all that drinking and partying—that makes me feel young.

Nancy Edmondson
A few weeks ago I spent the afternoon helping my niece Kelley get ready for her big prom. I helped her get her date's boutonniere and paint her nails. I took her to get her makeup done. We had fun being silly. It was more like I was a sixteen year-old buddy, not her thirty-five-year-old aunt.

Marge Spezzano
There is a lot of laughter in our lives and our marriage.

Margaret Mason

Running. I started running at fifty. I started by walking around the track, then running a little bit. First one time, then two. It was hard to believe when I could go a third of a mile around the track. Then a mile. Now I've done two marathons—the Marine Corps in Washington. I hope to keep doing them forever.

I do it for my mind and spirit as much as anything, not for the workout. The act of running is so freeing.

Kim Litton

When it rains those big cold drops and you want to take off your shoes and splash—that makes me feel like a kid.

Nan Thomas

The attitude of the people of Tortola about age. They attach absolutely no numbers to anybody. I'm certain a great many don't know their own ages. For instance, my neighbor Teresa across the street thinks she's in her nineties, but she's not sure. And you see couples together who have vast age differences—men older than women, women older than men—and nobody thinks anything of it. Or of any other combination—black and black, white and black. The man I live with is twelve years younger than I am and he's black. As far as I know, that's always been accepted here.

John Emery

When somebody younger than I am wants me.

Barbara Bailey

To say yes when people suggest I do things. I've learned to travel alone across the Atlantic, doing all the things I do, because I've decided to stay an active person.

Vince Spezzano

I had a goal that I was going to retire at sixty-five, and then my life was to begin, to become my own. So I never thought of being old really. My dad died at ninety-six and he was married for sixty-seven years. Marge's family has a lot of longevity also. So I never thought of either one of us getting old.

Michael Bornn

My mother. She's seventy, but no one believes it. People think I have a high energy level, but my mother says, "You're the laziest bum in the world." As long as she's around, I'll have quite a benchmark to keep me active.

Myrtis Brown

I'm still able to go. My marbles upstairs are pretty clever yet. And I'm able to do things. I'm able to help out my kids. I can do for others that can't do for themselves.

I went to the beauty shop; the girls walked in, "Oh, Mrs. Brown, you got a pony tail." I said, "Oh yes, I'm still young and foxy 'round here." When my daughter Vera said, "This lady was eighty on the third," everybody in every chair in the beauty shop jumped up and said, "No! Not Mrs. Brown."

I said, "Oh, yeah, but I feel like I'm sixteen." It makes me feel good to get eighty and be in good health. I've only been to the hospital one time and that was to have one baby—the last one.

My life has brought me joy in my eightieth year and I hope that I will continue on. Because I'm not going to sit like a lot of people.

A lot of people retire to that rocking chair. And they get where they have to push up on the arms to get out and get a stick to help them go. But I've got to get active, I've got to get that hoe.

Why just the week before last, a pecan limb fell out and hit my schefflera. So I got my ax and cut that big limb up. And everybody who passed saw me handling that ax and said, "Miss Myrtis, you shouldn't do that." I said, "I don't have nobody to do it for me. Miss Myrtis got to get the limb out of her yard." So I put it on the street. The trashmen asked me, "Who put this here limb out here?"

I said, "Who you think? The boss here on E Street did it."

"I know you, Myrtis Brown, you did it."

I said, "Shore did." And they laughed at me about that limb. I cut my grass, I rake—don't need nobody to do nothing for me now. I got to do it myself and that's what makes me young at eighty.

Sonya Friedman

Everything. I am young, though I'm fifty-four. I think being young has to do with having absolute delight in the world and its adventures and experiences and in trying new things. I also feel young when I wake up and nothing hurts—in any sense.

62. Regrets

Richard Duke

A minor regret? It has to do with a snowshoe. I was hiking and traveling in southeast Alaska and in the Yukon territory, and one day I was walking outside of Whitehorse in the woods when I saw an old snowshoe. A beautiful thing. Handmade. It had been there a long time, clearly forgotten by the person who'd lost it. And I thought, that would be really nice to have to look at; I'll take it with me. But then I said, no, I'm going to be traveling for more weeks; it'd be very hard to deal with, too much trouble. So I left it there. And I've regretted it ever since. I think the next day I knew better. I could have gotten it out of there and now when I run into a situation where something's a little inconvenient I say to myself, *snowshoe.*

John Marston

I regret not having gone up to Alaska ten years ago—before I started putting on the monkey suit and tie and fighting the traffic in Los Angeles.

Foxy Callwood

I regret they got automobiles on the island.

Mary Lou Retton

My biggest regret, and I'm still working on it, is not finishing college. I'm still a freshman.

Eric Jensen

Never learning how to play an instrument. I wanted to play the saxophone. It may never be too late; now I'm thinking about things like learning to fly.

Campion Platt

I don't have regrets. I really look at life as a series of experiences. To get a grasp and a sense of its essence, you have to understand that every experience, good or bad, adds to the overall wealth of your life. I look at regrets on a much more personal level. For instance, if you say something to a person that hurts them, that's a mistake, a slip-up. You correct it. If you have a bad day, it goes away at sunset. But larger-than-life problems? I may not like them, but I've never found one yet that doesn't teach me a lot.

Sonya Friedman

Though I wish my mother were not too ill to see what a good life I have and to know her grandchildren, I have to tell you, I've made peace with myself, which has taken a very long time. And my life has turned out so splendidly with my family and my career I don't really have any minor regrets.

Damian Miller

I regret not really being able to come to grips with things with my father and having to just leave it behind without letting him know why.

David Prowse

A lifetime regret is that I really didn't look after Mother well enough toward the end. I used to go see her occasionally, used to give her money. But Mother had a hard life, and now I look back and think I could have been a lot more helpful, been with her more, especially toward the end.

Peggy Houlihan

That my younger brother is not here to grow old with me, to be there for me and me for him. He was real special.

Princess Pamela Strobel

Because Beauty, my mama, was away working all the time, supporting us, I never got to be with her much. Even when she came home to visit, I couldn't be with her enough because everybody wanted to be with her, and it looked like they were pushing me away.

Even when Beauty got sick in Boston when I was twelve and came home to die, I couldn't be with her enough. She was only twenty-eight. And she had been getting ready to bring me up there. Beauty wanted me to be a concert pianist or a doctor!

I can tell you something. Beauty was on her deathbed, and she called us all in there. And pretty soon she asked for some food. Well, I was a little thing and I didn't do any cooking. But I went in the kitchen and boiled some water and put some cauliflower in, and brought it to my mother.

Then she said to my uncles and all, "I have taken care of you all, all these years. But now I want to rest, and now I want you to take care of my child."

I never got the chance to say the things I really wanted to say to Beauty—all by myself, without any interference or anybody around me. I never got a chance to say them one-to-one.

63. A Legacy to Pass On

Campion Platt

The best gift for your children is a sense of space, the ability to find out for themselves.

Torre Andrews

The way my grandmother lived taught me independence—making the best out of whatever situation comes along, not using your own personal situation or interests to justify treating other people in ways you wouldn't want to be treated.

Peggy Hackman

My parents didn't say it in words, but they taught us always to be open-minded and fair. My father always encouraged my brother and me. For instance, he never said to me, "You can't do this because you're a girl." My brother was never treated differently from me. My parents never said we have to save money so *he* can go to college. I was always in on it. Though both my parents were first generation and came from an ethnic group that has much male chauvinism, my father and mother were always encouraging and giving.

Nancy Perkins

Back around 1900, my father's family owned a large, prosperous farm outside Postville, Iowa. They lived modestly on the farm but had plenty. Each summer they used to order about $500 worth of fireworks to put on a spectacular display for the county. And my dad's grandfather never went around without at least a couple of thousand dollars in his overalls.

When tractors first came out, my great-grandfather went to town to look at one; he planned to buy. Of course, he looked awful in his dirty old overalls, old boots, and scruffy old straw hat. The salesman, all dressed up in a suit, never spoke to him, never asked what he wanted, because he looked like he couldn't afford to buy anything. So great-grandfather went home and later talked to the tractor store's owner. He bought his tractor and the salesman lost his job. That became a family lesson: never judge by appearances.

Mimi Taufer

The fact that my parents came from different traditions was special to me. My father was Catholic and my mother Jewish. My father followed his religion without question. My mother's grandfather was a card-carrying atheist, quite literally a member of the club, and my grandmother was against any sort of organized religion. Nor was my grandfather devout in any sense. When my mother had to undergo six months of religious instruction in order to marry my father, she fought relentlessly with the young priest who instructed her.

So it was an unspoken conviction in our family that there was more than one way of doing things. Though they didn't talk about it, they left me open for exploring different possibilities. It was a subtle example, but important. And they preached equality, really preached that everybody was the same, with the same rights, same potential. That was very important to me.

Eric Edmondson

My grandmother, my mother's mother, Mamie, had a universal acceptance of people. Since she worked at Russell High School for thirty-five years when it was one of the few high schools in Atlanta, she knew all kinds of people. Everywhere we went, she knew rich people and poor people, blacks and whites. She seemed to take everybody at face value. Although she was very old school, fairly conservative, never drove, never drank in her life, went to church all the time, she was very tolerant. She taught me there's some good in just about everybody out there.

Phoebe Legere

What I got from my grandmother was moral and what I got from my parents was aesthetic. My grandmother had the most uncanny ability to see the best in everyone. She never uttered a word of criticism about anyone. If other women criticized someone's looks, my grandmother would say, "Oh, but she has beautiful hands!" She saw something wonderful in every moment and every person. My mother and father are pretty much that way about nature. They infused me with a profound love and respect for beauty in natural form, the light of a living, growing thing.

Hamilton Fish

My father has every reason to think he is somehow different from the rest of the people who walk in the world. He is a man with a big name and a big family heritage and a background of privilege. He is the ranking member of the Judiciary Committee of the U.S. House of Representatives—and he didn't bounce any checks. Yet he has absolutely no sense of his own importance. He's not manipulative, either with his family or in his job. And he is utterly principled. Any thoughts on my father's legacy certainly center on my own aspirations to develop these qualities.

Chris Keefe

Do things the honest way and nothing can come down on you too hard. My dad worked for the city once, and everyone around him was being brought in for embezzlement. He was completely clean, above it all, and that sticks in my mind so strongly.

Emily Cook

The thought that has been passed down in my family, particularly to the men, is "Leave the world a better place than you found it." It was really emphasized. Even today if I take a nap in the middle of the afternoon because I'm exhausted, I feel guilty. I have to be accomplishing and contributing.

I'd like to pass on to our daughter English the thought that you should take care and concern for what's going on around you, that you should reach out to others, but do it without making it such an expectation to live up to. It needs to come out of what she wants to do, out of her sense of herself.

Carolyn Abrams

My belief in God came from my mother. She set that foundation from the earliest time. We said our prayers and grace at meals, and she took us to church. When things got really rough and food was scarce, she'd always sing, "I know the Lord will make a way somehow." She planted a seed, and I believed in this God that she talked about who was going to make a way and who has always seemed to make that way.

So when I think about her I do have some resentment about her leaving us, but I cherish what she gave me. She had patience with me as a child, and she taught us to take care of others.

We lived near the railroad track during the time when hobos would still ride the train. If anyone knocked at our door, she would always speak to them because she said, "Turn away a stranger, you might be turning away angels unawares."

And she taught us to work. I used to think she'd work me to death. If a neighbor needed help, she'd send me or a sister. I washed more diapers by hand. I went to the store for anyone who needed it. We were taught to do things for people. And even if offered money, we were to say, "No, thank you." These things, she taught us, you do out of kindness and love.

Bunny Johnson

My grandmother used to think anywhere you went you ought to either wear hat and gloves or carry an apron. When you went to other people's houses, you were either going to be dressed up or you were going to help them. She told me that when I was a very little girl.

Edward Colquhoun

My grandmother was a very generous, thoughtful person. For instance, for years she anonymously paid the utility bills for two elderly, crippled sisters she knew. One day they just stopped getting gas and electric bills. It didn't occur to them what had happened. She never came on as the grande dame; she'd visit them and bring cake but never let them know. And she had other one-on-one charities. I certainly want David to know about that, to learn from that example.

John Emery

More than any moral or mental or philosophical thing, my stepmother gave me the feeling of *belonging* somewhere, and I'd never really had that.

Kate Learson

My magical grandfather gave me something that I have given my kids that I hope they give to their kids. He wasn't a brilliant man, wasn't well read or well educated, but he always said to me, "Learn something every day. When you go to bed think of it again. It might be something you witnessed or something that was said or something else you didn't know. Think of it as a gift." Grandpa would be happy today that my kids and I are the same way—we always want to *know* something new.

Buck Johnson

Mama had a saying she used when I wanted something. She'd say, "Well, honey, you can't get that. Like it says in the Bible, 'Blessed are they that want not, for they shall not be disappointed.'" Of course, it wasn't from the Bible at all; she made it up.

James Royce

To get me here, to get my brothers and sister where they are, my mother has made great sacrifices. All along the way, she's tried to teach us what is important. She's got these phrases, and she always gets them wrong: "Don't break the egg of the golden goose," for instance.

Mom was always there to take care of me, to pick me up when I was down. And that wasn't easy, either: I was resentful a lot.

When I was young, it was easy for me to get down on myself, but I'd hide it from everybody. Mother would see, though. "Just keep your perspective, honey," she'd say. "It's easy to get down on yourself, but the important parts of life are always there: your family, your health, a good education, being around people who care about you." My mother is an extremely classy lady, but more important, she never let me lose faith in my future.

Marla Hanson

My stepmother was quite wise. Back then, of course, I used to hate her. I called her not long ago after breaking up with someone, and she said, "Marla, you can change your mood like you can change your clothes. Feel bad for yourself for a day, and then get on with it."

When I was in high school, I used to have these violent mood swings. One morning, I got up in a really foul mood and started off to school when my stepmother stopped me.

"You're not going to school today," she said. "You're going to spend some time putting yourself in a better mood."

Well, I blew up. "You can't keep me from school!

"Marla," she said, "you spend all this time getting your outside ready for school, but what are you doing for the inside? You spend an hour putting on your face, but you haven't prepared for the day. Now, go upstairs and work on yourself."

It was the smartest thing anyone ever said to me, and I thought, she's right. Why didn't I think of that?

Stuart Perkins

How to set an absolutely beautiful table for a dinner party. My parents were very stuffy people who gave a lot of formal dinner parties. Though I was never allowed to go to them—I don't think I wanted to either—I learned at sixteen or seventeen how to do them. I gave a lot of parties myself when I was in my twenties.

Stephanie Beacham

"Good, better, best—never it let it rest, till the good is better, and the better best." That early adage has always been in my brain, but I'm not sure the route of perfectionism is best. I get the greatest joy often from my painting and drawing—things I have no standards for. Perhaps Have I used today to the fullest? would be a better question than Did I do my best?

Robert Abrams

As I look back at his life, I know my daddy is a greater man than I could ever be. He was a restaurant cook and he taught me how to work. He was a strong black man in a time in Hattiesburg when the black man got no respect. He was tough.

I went to work in the restaurant when I was thirteen. Dad taught me to wash dishes. I'd wash the pots and he'd run his hand around the pot to see if there was any grease. If there was, I did them again.

He taught me little things you don't think about. For instance, he and I were sitting down in the kitchen one day, and the boss walked in. My first reflex was to jump up. He snatched me back down. He said, "Let me tell you, whatever you're doing, I don't care who it is walks in, you keep doing it. You're a man and you got the right to do what you're doing."

He taught me to fight, then got mad because I got good at it. Then he looked for somebody to whip me. But he always taught me to be the best. He said, "Bobby, if it's worth doing, it's worth doing right. Do it right the first time so you don't have to do it again."

He taught me to get it right the first time by making me do everything twice. If it was right, he found something wrong. If there was nothing wrong, he made it wrong. But he ingrained this in me: he taught me to work and he taught me that work was the only way I could make it.

He taught me not to be afraid of anything. He taught me to tackle everything head on. For a long time, Daddy had a problem with alcohol; drinking was a way of easing the anger of not being able to be a man the way he wanted. But ten years ago, he quit drinking. Just stopped. That's strong.

My daddy made it rough on me. But he loved me. He showed me the way. I've finished everything I ever started.

George Plimpton

The importance of self-discipline. My father was a corporate lawyer, an expert particularly in mortgage indentures, a kind of legal science, which is the most taxing thing in the world. It is a part of legal training that young lawyers most despise. But father loved it because it was a huge challenge to put down absolutely precise language that could not be challenged. A mistake can cost millions. It's a very different exercise than, say, writing a novel, where someone like Thomas Wolfe or Theodore Dreiser can make a host of mistakes. For father, self-discipline was almost a tonic.

He carried this wonderful little notebook with him. Maybe one page would read "Tennis." Or "Golf." Most people go out to a golf course and just hack around. But before Father would play, he'd read his fifteen rules that made him hit a better golf shot—all having to do with performance, all having to do with the right frame of mind to do one's best.

When I got into trouble in school, which was almost all the time, Father would write me letters about the marvelous things which came with a disciplined mind. He thought of the mind as a machine. You should therefore oil it, you should take care of it, add bigger flywheels to it. And if the mind worked properly, there was nothing that gave greater pleasure in life. Nothing. And don't waste time. My father never read, for example, the sports pages. He thought it was a waste.

I think Father was right, but I don't have that kind of discipline. I'd give anything if I had. I'd have written at least twenty more books. I'd have planned my life more sensibly. I would have steered clear of Bohemia! I probably wouldn't have done *The Paris Review*. I don't know, maybe it's best *not* to have a plan!

Dana Warrington

My father, who loves life as my mother did, has told me that there's always plenty of time, just make sure you use it wisely.

Amy Holloway

I was over at Freddy Houchin's house and I was standing on the edge of a porch with a huge drop-off. "Don't stand on the edge of the porch, Amy," my father said. I didn't move. And Freddy walked out and pushed me off. Since then, "Don't stand on the edge of the porch" has been one of Dad's admonitions anytime I'm taking on something new. Yet I'm always standing on the edge—taking risks.

Perhaps in part because of something else he has always said: "Look out the window." If you don't look out the window, you might miss something—like the new snow.

John Emmerling

There's an attitude I would very much like to pass down to my children: Do anything you can to live life optimistically. You will have a more rewarding life if you assume that things will work out than if you assume they won't. If you live by this principle, you always have something to look forward to. I'm always thinking four steps down the line: If this happens, then this can happen. For instance, I've just figured out what my next book will be, and I'm already thinking how I'm going to promote it and what I'm going to say in the talk shows and what the cover of the paperbacks going to be. Some people have an idea and think, *Well, that probably won't work out.* I have an enormous advantage over that person because I think my idea will work and I've already projected what the next steps need to be.

You have to be willing to fail once in a while. I fail all the time. I'll get down for maybe a day; then there will be another challenge and I'll move on. There are enough successes that I live well and I'm always excited about the next opportunity. If I can pass that quality on to my children, that would be the greatest gift.

Ollie Ferguson

My family didn't sit down and philosophize, but through example they taught me tenacity. Quitting simply was not part of our vocabulary; no matter what the difficulties or opposition, it was not an option.

Mary Lou Retton

It may sound corny, but I'm the perfect example it works: Believe in yourself and you can do it.

64. Something You Want to Do

Mary Lou Retton

I'd love to go to space, to be weightless. I know about flying through the air, but I would like to do it for a long time! Once in Nevada all the gymnasts were invited to the astronaut training center for a "ride" in a room where they simulate weightlessness with an airstream. Everybody got to go, but my coach, Bela, wouldn't let us, and was I mad!

Buck Johnson

I want to be a good songwriter. And I want to learn to clog and to play the guitar. I'd like to be able to put on a show clogging, playing the guitar, and singing a hit song that I wrote. And I'd love getting paid for it.

Tommy Sammons

Ride my motorcycle in the Canadian Rockies. I'm going to do it one day.

Jean Dorrance

Learn to read and write because it will help me. I've had a blackboard quite a few years. And on the weekend or when I have the time—there's never much—I write the ABCs and practice. My husband helps me when he's home; sometimes my daughter does. I haven't read any books yet. I don't know if I could manage that—I'd have to have more spare time.

Foxy Callwood

Get the Island Preservation Society going well here on Jost Van Dyke. About four years ago, I came up with the idea when I see how things are working around here and what "progress" looks like to me. The only thing the people in charge seem to care about is money. They don't care about preserving the land.

I said, well I could go into real estate but what good will that do? That only helps me, and my kids will sell it anyway. What we need is something like a national park. So I say if Rockefeller could come all the way from the States to do something for St. John, then at the least some of the people from here ought to be able to do something.

So as I was talking about it, a guy picked my hat off my head and passed it around, and it came back with fifty dollars in it. So I said, well, I have to do something. So we threw a big party on Valentine's Day—we do raffle and sell T-shirts and all like that. Now there is a bank account of over $5,000. And people are beginning to talk about it and write about it in magazines. And now we're working on a corporation.

I'd like to see what is beautiful saved for the people. What's happening now isn't meant for me. See, we have such a lovely beach and then all of a sudden they give us a public works department and they come with a backhoe and haul away sand off the beach to build roads. We don't need that—that destroys. We need a nucleus of people who'll start working. I'd rather see fruit trees and pasture than condominiums.

Princess Pamela Strobel

To walk into my little restaurant and find things just right—and to know that one morning I could wake up and the wolf wouldn't be waiting outside the door.

Edward Colquhoun

Play the classical guitar. I took lessons until we adopted David but didn't make tremendous progress, but I still like the idea.

Stuart Perkins

I would like to succeed Lee Iacocca.

Mildred Sutton

I've accomplished more things than I ever thought I would. I wish I thought I was young enough to go to Ireland, something I'd really like to do. I don't. But I've done a lot more than I ever thought I could, so there I am.

Torre Andrews

Live to be 117. It's a promise I made to myself when I was sixteen. That year they were ramming the bicentennial celebration down everyone's throat. So I said, I'll live to the tricentennial so I can say, "Yes, I was at both of them and I remember . . ."

65. Things Are Going to Be Better: A Portrait

Jean Dorrance

I was born in Jamaica. When I was coming up in life, I have life very hard because my father did not own me. My mother have it very hard to rear me up. My mother was a seamstress, and sometime after work she don't reach home in time, don't get dinner real early and sometimes she go to work and she don't get paid and then she don't have any food for us. So you know we had to go to bed with nothing to eat. She'd read her Bible and she'd pray and she'd say, "One day, things are going to be better." That didn't happen every night. Maybe sometime in the month, things may be harder, when she had to pay rent and such. Later, she married someone who was more able to take care of her.

But for my come-up I help myself. I start very early working, like baby-sitting. I iron shirts for a lawyer, and have the energy to always work. We didn't have time to play sports when I was young, always working. We had to go to the ground and dig food—my parents had their own garden. We bring the food home and then we go look for wood to cook and we go get water from the reservoir about two miles from the house. So we didn't play sports but we learned to work.

When I was eleven, my father take me away from my mother and carry me to his house late at night. He just tell me he going to take me to a nice home and not to worry. He were happy then, but I were unhappy because I didn't like my stepmother. She treat her kids good and treat me bad. She always want me to stay home and work, wash her kids' clothes, cook for them and she didn't send me to school. That were one of the worst things she did for me.

So when I was small, a kid you know, it was tough. But from growing up, when I started getting children, it wasn't bad. I met my husband in Kingston. He's a chef. I was baby-sitting for a lady and my husband used to come there near to the tailor shop. And we used to talk about life. Things have been good since then. I enjoy my work.

Things worth waiting for: A house.

An unexpected special moment: Moving into our own house in Jamaica. It was so much quieter. That house was a three-bedroom house, nice lawn, front porch. You could arrange your yard outside like you want to. We had all kinds of flowers—carnation, hibiscus, a lot of others. You could lock up the house and go when you want, come when you want. You don't have fears somebody is going to break in like when you live in the project.

Simple things that give you pleasure: Looking after the baby, you know. Wash their clothes, feed them, put them to bed, stuff like that. Take care of my house, stuff like that.

A treasured possession: My kids, my husband. He's a very loving man.

Your lowest moment, one that made you feel like quitting: My son died five years ago. He and a friend went swimming, diving, at the beach and almost drowned. So he was in a coma three years and seven months. I take him to the States, to Puerto Rico. They could not do anything because he was hemorrhaging in his brain. But the doctors said he lived so long because he was very strong. He died when he was twenty-one.

What gives you courage to go on? I keep working on because of one thing—I may get a house before I die. We have a piece of land from a long time ago, from before when my son die. We had planned to build on it but when he had his accident we had to spend all the savings to take him to the States, to Puerto Rico, and back here. But one day.

An unexpected treat: My husband bring me a nice basket of flowers on my anniversary last month—all different kinds of roses. He know it was our anniversary but I didn't expect flowers.

What holding hands makes you feel like: Feels like I believe I'm going to get something. I believe I'm going to get a house.

66. Something Worth Waiting For

Kurt Vonnegut

Brief epiphanies. When you suddenly find yourself dancing very well, with the right person. Or a marvelous piece of music. Those moments are what keeps us going. It's not the things that we are doing for hours. Magical moments. At least, those are what keep me putting one foot in front of the other. I know they're going to come along, unexpectedly and not sought by me.

Patrick Goddard

The ability to understand what is really important and to sort it out and the ability to be patient and make hard decisions—balance seems to be very important to me.

Phoebe Legere

That moment when you suddenly realize that you don't give a damn about anyone else's opinion and that the work itself is good enough. Critics don't matter, what jealous women say doesn't matter, the work is strong enough to be satisfaction in itself.

George Plimpton

A surprise. My father used to say that life was worth living for the surprises around the corner. As long as you believe life is filled with things like that, you continue to go on, and you peek around the bend.

Nan Thomas

Solvency. It's terribly expensive to live on an island—a quart of milk is $3.55. The only thing you don't need is seasonal clothes.

Kathy Bater Brackett

Money. Why? Because I'm always waiting for it. I've supported myself since I left home when I was sixteen.

John Marston

Fifteen percent interest on a savings account.

Jonathan Peter

Good weather. Most important to a sailor.

Stephanie Beacham

I don't know if I like the word *waiting*. I think there are things worth working for—anything you want. But don't wait for it, work for it.

Jane Burke

Until two years ago, I was extremely obese. Being so overweight gave me the feeling that my life hadn't yet started—oh, I'll lose weight and then my life will begin. I always felt like I was trapped in this body that was not Jane Burke.

But being fat was also a great excuse—when I didn't get a part I had auditioned for, I could blame it on my weight. When I didn't excel at this or that or the other, I could say, "Oh, I'm being discriminated against because I'm fat." So it was a great catchall excuse for anything that didn't go right for me.

I was so overweight that I thought there was no way I would ever be anything but fat. I had these wild dreams of being thin and feeling normal. I never felt normal when I was fat. I felt like a freak. And I think the decision to quit waiting and finally do something was one of the scariest I've ever had to make.

I made that decision and I stuck with it. I changed a lifetime of eating patterns and inactivity patterns and even the way I think.

After thirty-four years of having obesity color practically every thought, making that change in my basic thinking was the hardest part. It's still a struggle.

But the changes have made a difference. Daily I notice the little changes that reflect the big changes. For instance, I turned sideways to go through a door one day fairly early in my weight-loss program and realized I didn't have to anymore. Then my ribs showed up. I walked five miles in a stretch for the first time since I was a child. Or there's the day I cut up my credit card for the fat store because I can buy clothes anywhere now. I fit into an airplane seat and can go swimming without embarrassment. But I still can't walk into a Blimpie's.

Most important, I've been able to lift some of the limitations I put on myself and accept the risks and the happiness of having a life.

John Englander

Success. Off the cuff, I'd say that means having a lifestyle you find comfortable and feeling fulfilled in having achieved an accomplishment, which for me has been making several businesses work in the diving industry. The challenge is to make something self-sustaining. I like being the architect of something that stands in place without me. And I've done it a couple of times.

Egbert Donovan

For the people to find out what their culture is all about. I do something like my shell museum and am waiting and hoping that a lot of people will follow up on it.

In these days, people don't really have the money to advertise these things. We just have to wait. Since I've had the museum going, a lot of people have passed it, but they didn't come in. After a while, people started coming. They said, "Oh, I didn't know it was something like this." More, I know, will come.

Vince Spezzano

What I'm waiting for is to be totally in charge of my own agenda. Somebody—my boss or the public—has always decided for me. I keep waiting for the day when I don't have to do anything I don't want to. I'll probably get bored.

Silvia Munro

A brief time when I can think—*I'm doing nothing tomorrow, nothing the day after, nothing the day after.* I can just do something fun with my children or go and play with my flowers. That's what I pray for—to be happy one day just to be left content and quiet.

Nancy Perkins

Happiness has been worth waiting for. I began to learn that in 1974 when I had Guillain-Barré syndrome, a disease that paralyzes you. That's when I determined that nothing was going to beat me as I began literally to learn to crawl and then to walk. In the hospital I would wear a large dog harness and a big orderly would take me out to walk; when I began to fall, he would yank me up.

My life began again. I had been through a lot of adversity. I began to realize my own self-worth. I learned to stand on my own two feet and not be totally dependent on somebody else to be happy. When you're alone in the world and you learn to like and respect yourself, then other people like and respect you in return. It was a long time coming, but worth it.

John Emmerling and Kate Learson

John: A wonderful fulfilling relationship with another human being. I feel that I have gotten that with Kate. Kate and I dated and knew each other for ten years before we got married. Being married after going together that long is different; it's very special and very much worth waiting for.

Kate: I agree with him on that, but I'd like to give a wider answer. If there is something you really want—whether it's something material like a trip or something like a personal goal—it is better to wait until you can do it right. Whatever you envision, wait until you can either afford it or you have enough experience to do it right. It was a while before we knew that being together was going to be worth it.

John: We basically hated each other during our first date.

Kate: John was so obnoxious, so full of himself. Right?

John: I was horrible. I saw myself as this newly divorced man who owned an advertising agency, was a skier, a pilot, made enough money to take advantage of New York—I had it all.

Kate: And that's all he talked about on our first date—all the things in his life, his kids, his apartment, his plane, his company, other women in New York—he made the hairs on the back of my neck stand up. I thought, *Oh, this man is so dreadful.* So when he hailed a cab for me and bent down to give me a quick kiss goodnight, I said to myself, *I'm going to kiss this jerk so well he's never going to forget me and then I'm never going to go out with him again.* And I did.

John: I was intrigued—particularly when she didn't call. Typically back in the early eighties, if you went out with a woman she called for the second date.

Kate: I left the next morning to go to Cleveland to see my grandmother, who was dying of cancer, and had no intention of seeing him again.

John: I did all the calling. I don't know why she did agree, but we had another date a month later and started over. The fulfilling relationship we now have has been well worth working toward and waiting for.

Amy Holloway

Some days I think I'll get married. I'd want to get married to have someone at night, just as I'm going to sleep, tell me a joke. That would be worth waiting for.

Anne Brunson

I think children. Though I've always been a baby person, it wasn't until I was pregnant that I really realized that. I loved every minute of it. It was so neat to have a life inside of you; it was like you were never alone. To me it was fantastic; I loved the labor, I loved the delivery. I loved everything about it.

And I've liked every stage they have gone through. They have all been different.

Peggy Hackman

I decided to quit smoking on my forty-fourth birthday. I was coughing and not feeling good, and I suddenly thought, I'm not going to make it to forty-five because of these things. My children are going to grow up and be productive citizens, I hope. My oldest son will probably get married soon and have his own children, and I'm going to miss it all. So I quit. Seeing your children grow up and be productive is worth waiting for.

Alvis Waite

Getting our own house. We were born in Methodist parsonages and have lived in Methodist parsonages all our lives. We always enjoyed the challenge of each parsonage and made it home. Still it has been wonderful to get a house of our own. Marynell said on the conference floor that she'd be able to drive as many nails in the walls as she wanted and hang as many pictures.

And one afternoon just after the new carpet had been installed and our new family room chairs delivered, she and I sat in the chairs, put our feet up on the footrests, admired the walls she'd just finished painting, and said, "Our rug, our chairs, and our house!"

Jerry Preston

Maturity. Most people say, "Gee, I want to be young again." I look back when I was young, and I was always apprehensive about growing up. A lot of kids couldn't wait till they were teenagers. I remember when I turned thirteen I was depressed; I felt like I wasn't a kid anymore. And then through life, a lot of things bothered me. Well, *nothing* bothers me that much anymore. You begin to realize things you thought were terribly important weren't important at all. Maturing is not all that bad.

Myrtis Brown

Just before my birthday, I stood up in church on Sunday and told them I'd be eighty and was in perfectly good health and I knew I was a foxy lady. There's still something in store for me.

One thing worth waiting for is things we've never had. I worked hard to be able to give my kids things I never had growing up.

Another thing I have waited for is opportunities to get out and help someone.

And what I wait for most—to be loved by people. There's not a person 'round here in my neighborhood in Greene County that something goes wrong doesn't say, *Let's go get Aunt Myrtis. Let's go tell Nanny. Let's see what she says.* It's the same way at church: *Let's get Myrtis; let's see can we get this program going.* And I've got some famous kids that love me—four boys and a girl.

Being loved—that's what I wait for. It's not money. All I want is somebody to hold me under their wings and love me. That's what I want.

How We Met

We thought you might like to learn a little about the storytellers in this book. Each person first tells you how they met us—from hitchhiking to fanning mosquitos. We then retaliate with a brief look at what each friend does. Of course, you'll really get to know them through the stories they share in *Common Ground*.

Robert Abrams, 42
Carolyn Abrams, 42

"We met Mary Abbott as volunteers at a Breakfast Club for homeless people. She hasn't got the grits right yet, but we've been friends ever since."

Robert and Carolyn Abrams are United Methodist ministers from Mississippi. They just graduated from Candler School of Theology, Emory University, where Carolyn held the Woodruff Fellowship and Robert the United Methodist Minority Scholarship. Both are active in human rights and justice issues.

Torre Andrews, 31

"I went to college to be a doctor, spent a year there, decided it sucked, and decided I wasn't ever going back to college again. I became a scuba instructor and guide. On Grand Bahama Island, I lived in Remar's house while he was in England. A month after he came back, he came into UNEXSO, where I worked, and someone said 'that's the guy whose place you were staying at.' "

That was six years ago. Torre Andrews went back to school and is now a physician specializing in radiology in Los Angeles, California.

Barbara Bailey, 82

"Remar and I met at dinner at the home of good friends on Grand Bahama."

Dr. Barbara Bailey, formerly of London, is a retired physician living on Grand Bahama Island.

Alastair Barbour, 39
Helen Barbour, 37

Helen: "Remar's flat on Grand Bahama Island was next to ours. We shared an interest in scuba diving."

Alastair: "And then Remar had us stop and visit him in New York when we moved to Bermuda. I remember champagne in the car, and George Plimpton at dinner."

Helen: "And then out of the blue, George Plimpton called us when he was visiting Bermuda and said, 'Bubba said let's go for cocktails.' "

Alastair: "I remember champagne and Plimpton and his other guest, Gary Hart. We didn't talk about the *Monkey Business,* though."

Alastair and Helen Barbour now live in Edinburgh, Scotland, where Alastair is a partner in KPMG Peat Marwick. They have two children.

Stephanie Beacham, 40

"I was on Grand Bahama to do a television show, and Remar asked me to dinner. We cooked spaghetti and then watched 'The Colbys' on TV."

Stephanie Beacham was Sable Colby on that show, then Sister Kate on the NBC series of that name. Before she moved to California, she was acting with the National Theatre in London. Stephanie lives in Malibu and Beverly Hills, California, and doesn't watch television much, particularly soaps.

Leonard Berman, 45

"I was training for Remar's Conchathon in Key West, jogging at night so no one would see me. Then Julie introduced me to Remar, and I got to watch him jog. From then on, I wasn't afraid for anybody to see me."

Leonard Berman is a program officer at the Public Welfare Foundation in Washington, D.C., and is married to Julie Rogers.

Edith Bornn, 70

"I met Mary Abbott and Remar through the Atlantic Blue Marlin Tournament directed by my son Michael."

Edith Bornn is an attorney in St. Thomas, the United States Virgin Islands. Her family traces its roots there to the 1700s.

Michael Bornn, 34

"Remar and Mary Abbott put together a nonprofit foundation here to sponsor minitriathlons, but Hurricane Hugo blew that idea away. Remar stayed, anyway, to fish for marlin."

Michael Bornn is president of the Boy Scout Council of the Virgin Islands, directs the Atlantic Blue Marlin Tournament, which benefits the Scouts, and manages family businesses throughout the Virgin Islands. Says Michael, "My family has its fingers in so many pies we should open a bakery."

Kathy Bater Brackett, 40

"Back then, I dated Remar's best friend. One day I challenged him and Mary Abbott to enter the minitriathlon on Grand Bahama, called the Conch Man. I didn't know they would bring along about 500 of Remar's readers from the *Washington Post*."

Kathy Bater Brackett lives on Grand Bahama Island and owns the Lake View Manor time-share resort.

Myrtis Brown, 81

"Mary Abbott and I met at her niece Katherine's christening on St. Simons Island. And then a bit later, I met Bubba in Atlanta after he moved back from the Virgin Islands."

Myrtis Brown is a professional baby nurse and nanny who lives in Greensboro, Georgia. She's also everybody's grandmother.

Don Brunson, 45
Anne Brunson, 45

Don: "BuBa (rhymes with *pooh bah*) was the senior resident counselor in my dorm at Emory in 1966. He lived in a cavernous, refrigerator-equipped basement suite. The room's "luxury" appointments—it had *real* furniture—and BuBa himself became really popular. I remember Tom Brokow (then a local newsman) came by to interview BuBa once."

Anne: "A friend got a group of Agnes Scott girls together to go over to Emory to help with this project. I didn't know what the project was but she said boys were involved, so I went. I met Remar first, and then Don."

Don Brunson is executive vice president of Jimmy Dean Foods, a division of the Sara Lee Corporation in Memphis, Tennessee. Anne Brunson is a homemaker, math tutor, and part-time math teacher. Anne and Don with their three children, Bobby, Becky, and Scott, enjoy camping, tennis, golf, scuba diving, and church and community activities.

Daniel A. Buettner, 28

"I was eighteen and had won a trip to St. Thomas in the Virgin Islands by selling lots of newspaper subscriptions to the Minneapolis *Star Tribune*. My brother and I were hitchhiking to town, and Bubba picked us up. A year later, I was working as his intern and driving Peter Jennings around during our NPR Croquet Benefit. Bubba believes in serendipity, and I do too.

"I met Mary Abbott when I was Bubba's intern and now write books with her."

Author and adventurer Dan Buettner lectures regularly around America about his bicycle treks. He has biked from Alaska to the tip of South America and around the world, setting world records. AfricaTrek is next. His home base is Minneapolis, Minnesota.

Jane Burke, 36

"I was hired as a ringer soprano angel for St. Mark's memorable rendition of 'The Holy City' and found myself sitting next to Mary

Abbott, an alto in the heavenly choir. You can still catch our act weekly at the corner of Fifth and Peachtree.

"I met Remar when Mary Abbott enticed him to my birthday dinner by promising he'd be the only male at a table of charming women."

A singer and actress, Jane Burke pays the rent by running her own business and research services company. She sings with the Atlanta Symphony Orchestra Chorus and Chamber Chorus and with the Robert Shaw Festival Singers.

Foxy Callwood, 52

"I met Remar one Labor Day weekend during the Wooden Boat Regatta, but he won't remember 'cause of the rum punch."

Foxy Callwood has lived on the island of Jost Van Dyke, population 200, all his life. He owns Foxy's Tamarind Beach Bar, founded Foxy's Wooden Boat Regatta (the Caribbean's wildest Labor Day bash), started the island's preservation society, and composes songs about his bar patrons.

Desy Campbell, 41

"I finished number 148 in the Bahamas Conch Man with Remar. He always thinks I came in last, but I have the certificate on my icebox to prove him wrong. I was midfield!"

Desy Campbell lives and works on her family's farm outside Culpeper, Virgina, where she also writes for a farming newspaper. Recently, she's been active in starting the League of Women Voters in Culpeper.

Edward Colquhoun, 53

"Mary Abbott and I used to flea market with friends around Massachusetts and Pennsylvania on weekend outings from New York. We've also parsed a sentence or two together over the years and were original partners in the Me-and-Thee Trucking Company whenever a friend's furniture needed moving. I met Remar when she took up writing books with him."

Edward Colquhoun is a medical writer with an international pharmaceutical company. He's married to Mimi Taufer.

Emily Cook, 33

"Mary Abbott and I were both bridesmaids when her brother married my aunt. I was nine then. All my life, I'd heard about Bubba from the family and what a vagabond he is. He started my vagabond career by sending me off to learn to scuba-dive in the Bahamas."

Emily Cook sits on the board of the Fernbank Planetarium and is very involved in raising funds for the new Fernbank Museum of Natural History in Atlanta.

Rodney Cook, 35

"I accompanied Emily to a family Easter dinner and spotted Mary Abbott in the shrubbery—helping niece Rhodes find an egg, she said. I met Bubba at dinner at our farm. Two weeks later I listened as Princess Pamela Strobel and he sang duets at a dinner in New York."

Rodney Cook is a design consultant and developer who is now designing the Cropsey Museum in Hastings-on-Hudson, New York. He also serves as president of WPBA, TV 30, and WABE FM 90, public broadcasting stations in Atlanta.

Gerry Cooney, 35

"I knew a friend of Remar's and first met him at a concert in East Hampton, Long Island. We now fish blue marlin together occasionally."

Gerry Cooney is a retired heavyweight boxer living on Long Island, New York.

Mary Costigan, 83

"I've known Bubba (can I call him that?) since he was born, and Mary Abbott since they met."

Mary Costigan is an expert on Shakespeare, a serious bridge player, and a member of Remar's parents' supper club, which met for over forty-five years. She lives in Marietta, Georgia.

Dorothy Cross, 68

"I first met Remar in Key West at the *Washington Post*'s mini-triathlon—which I finished!"

Dorothy Cross is a retired librarian living in Alexandria, Virginia.

Dave DeGrandpre, 22

"Erik and Aubrey Peterson were going to visit Bubba over spring break 1991 in the Bahamas, and they dragged me along. We were expecting to camp out on the deck of a sailboat, but Bubba was staying on a yacht filled with Persian rugs and antique army helmets. Medora Plimpton was there, too, as was her mother. But we had lots of room and lots of fun and I'm waiting to be asked back."

Dave DeGrandpre is a junior at the University of Montana.

Jean Dorrance, 47

"Dan Buettner, a friend of theirs, used to come here to eat breakfast, and he brought Remar once. And then Remar started staying here."

Jean Dorrance is the housekeeper for a private estate on St. Thomas and cooks up extraordinary island food. A tip from Jean about picking mangoes or sapodillas from the trees: "Pick from the sunny side, 'cause they're the sweet ones."

Egbert Donovan, 38

"I was mixing soursop daiquiris when this beautiful girl, Marla Hanson, and this bald old guy, Remar, walked up to my shell museum. I talked history to them and before long we all were singing scratch band together. Marla played washtub."

Egbert Donovan is a master chef and proprietor and historian of the North Shore Shell Museum on Tortola.

Richard Duke, 53

"Apartment life in a busy city like Atlanta doesn't sound like a good basis for lasting friendships, but somehow about ten years ago just about everyone in the eight units in two neighboring old houses in Ansley Park became close friends. Mary Abbott was one of those people; I was another. Those still in Atlanta now have their own homes and others are spread across the U.S., with one in England, but all keep in touch."

Richard Duke is professor of mathematics at Georgia Institute of Technology and a specialist in combinatorics.

Eric Edmondson, 38

"Soon after Mary Abbott moved next door, Richard Duke soon had us all enjoying Friday night pizza together and late afternoons and evenings on the patio. Remar dropped in from his jaunts to stir things up."

Eric Edmondson is an insurance agent for MAG Mutual Insurance Company in Atlanta and a formidable threat on the tennis court as well as our resident science fiction expert.

Nancy Edmondson, 35

"Zar Rochelle must have introduced Mary Abbott and me shortly after we both moved to Peachtree Circle; we were probably standing in the driveway chatting. Remar was a master at pulling everyone into his projects. On one memorable occasion he took me in a limo to the airport to greet George Plimpton. Mary Abbott and the rest of us later used the limo to pick up our dry cleaning."

Nancy Edmondson is a legal secretary for Allen & Peters in Atlanta. Her chocolate amaretto terrine keeps Richard Duke and Mary Abbott longing for their birthdays to arrive.

John Emery, 42

"My partner in the stained-glass business is Jerry Preston, so I met Bubba and Mary Abbott through him. The first time Bubba brought George Plimpton to dinner, I tried to honor them both by cooking up a very fancy dish. I'd invented it. Absolutely filled with meats and sauces and the like, and decided to ask George to name it since he'd eaten at every fancy place on the planet. Something elegant, you know. He named it 'John's Goulash.' I guess it wasn't that good after all.''

John Emery is a partner in Preston Stained Glass Studios in Melbourne, Florida, where he is also very active in the Artists' Forum of the Brevard Art Center and Museum.

John Emmerling, 53

"I can tell you exactly when I met Remar: September 4, 1969, at Young & Rubicam in New York. That's when he was assigned as an account executive on our project to build a park in Harlem. I met Mary Abbott shortly after that.''

John Emmerling owns an advertising agency in New York City and is the author of a recent book on creative ideas, *It Only Takes One*. He is married to Kate Learson.

John Englander, 42

"Bubba and I became great dive buddies on Grand Bahama, and pretty soon he had me proofreading manuscripts for his books. And, incidentally, I'm *not* the model for the Englander character in his novel *Long Lines*. That guy's too old. I met Mary Abbott many times here on the island.''

John Englander is president of the Underwater Explorer's Society (UNEXSO) on Grand Bahama Island and a former president of the National Association of Underwater Instructors.

Ollie Ferguson, 33

"Remar came waltzing into the Underwater Explorer's Society with a *bodyguard*. His book about the automobile business was out then, and there had been threats. Since I was a scuba guide, we began to dive a lot together. And then I taught Mary Abbott how to dive.''

Ollie Ferguson is vice president for dive operations at the Underwater Explorer's Society on Grand Bahama Island. Ollie's grandfather was Sir Etienne Dupuch, founder of the *Nassau Tribune* and a topic of Remar's *Washington Post* column.

Hamilton Fish III, 36

"I first met Remar when I was a freshman at Harvard cleaning dormitories during summer break. Remar was on the board of the Student Vote. We next saw each other in Bermuda when he picked us up at the airport in a dinghy and took us through choppy seas in the rain back to his villa to a lunch of cold duck."

Hamilton Fish was the publisher of *The Nation* for a time and later an unsuccessful congressional candidate. He was the producer of the Academy Award-winning film *Hotel Terminus* and is now the managing director of Human Rights Watch in New York City. Ham's father, Congressman Hamilton Fish, Jr., supported his son's bid for Congress. His grandfather was vehemently opposed to it.

Sonya Friedman, 54

"I first met Remar in 1985 when he was on my show about his car book. Then he was on about his body book. And then about his novels and Conchathons. Lately, we've been going to watch fireworks together on the East River in New York."

Sonya Friedman holds a Ph.D. in clinical psychology from Wayne State University. She is the host of "Sonya Live" on CNN and the author of several books, including *Men Are Just Dessert, Smart Cookies Don't Crumble,* and *A Hero Is More Than Just a Sandwich.*

Patrick Goddard, 50

"I met BuBa, as we called him, when we went around the world together as kids on the University of the Seven Seas. I didn't particularly like the cut of his jib. As a matter of fact, I spoke against him when he ran for president of the student body. But he won and unexpectedly invited me to take a train with him from Singapore to Kuala Lumpur, Malaysia, where the entire student body was to have Christmas Eve dinner with the prime minister. BuBa and I made the arrangements. And then we went to see *My Fair Lady* with Malaysian subtitles. We became best friends. I remember two years after the Seven Seas, I turned on television, and there was BuBa with Bob Hope! I've never been surprised: that's the kind of stuff I've come to expect from my good friend."

Patrick Goddard is staff commodore of the San Diego Yacht Club and executive vice president of the Chart House Restaurants. He is a trustee of the San Diego Maritime Museum and a board member of the San Diego Visitor and Convention Bureau. For the last twenty-six years, many Chart House executive meetings "have been held as we're jogging on the way to Swammies surf beach to catch a wave or two," says Pat.

Peggy Hackman, 48

"Remar wrote the funniest letter to the *Post* about doing a column on his Body Worry project. Our only concern when he started was that something might happen to him—heat stroke, perhaps—and throw the exercise industry back a hundred years. He lived, but I still think he set the industry back at least fifty!"

Peggy Hackman is editor of the Style Plus section of the *Washington Post*. She lives in Rockville, Maryland, with her husband Bob, children Andrea and Nicole, and mother Bea. Son Zack is off on his own.

Carol Boyd Hallett, 54

"Remar met me at a party on Grand Bahama Island and asked if he could take a power walk with Jim and me the next morning. We did, at 6:00 A.M., and then promptly signed up for the Conch Man minitriathlon. I met Mary Abbott at the event. Remar then wrote about us in his column, where he said I had an 'awfully good set of gams.' Despite that, we became friends. Or maybe because of that."

When we met, Carol Hallett was ambassador to the Bahamas. She is now United States commissioner of customs in Washington, D.C.

Jim Hallett, 55

"Remar stayed at the ambassador's residence in Nassau once and ate every single chocolate chip cookie. We didn't have him back."

Jim Hallett is assistant to the administrator for agricultural stabilization and conservation services (whew) in Washington, D.C.

Kathryn Hames, 74

"We knew Bubba's family since he was born and met Mary Abbott in 1980."

Kathryn Hames is a homemaker in Marietta, Georgia. She and her husband, Judge Luther Hames, were original members of the Supper Club.

Marla Hanson, 31

"I met Remar on a ferry boat one night in New York during a *Paris Review* fireworks party. That summer, we shared a house in Little Apple Bay, Tortola. We sang a duet, too, at the shell museum there."

Marla Hanson is a film producer who lives in New York City.

A. J. Hiers, 38

"A long time ago Remar hired me as a salesman at the Lincoln-Mercury dealership in Melbourne, Florida."

A. J. Hiers is now a dealer and partner in several Florida automobile dealerships.

Amy Holloway, 42

"We met on Jane Burke's birthday. I breezed in telling a tale about Apple Day at the TV station and I've been recounting my adventures since."

Amy Holloway is administrative assistant to the president and general manager at WXIA, Channel 11, Atlanta. A talented songwriter, pianist, and singer, she sings with the Sentimental Journey Orchestra. She formerly taught at the Northside High School for the Performing Arts.

Peggy Houlihan, 42

"I was one of the 500 people from Washington who participated in the Grand Bahama Island Conch Man minitriathlon and met Mary Abbott and Remar there."

Peggy Houlihan is a lobbyist. More important, she's the president of the Conch Out Club of America, a group of enthusiastic, perhaps slightly over-the-hill, but determined athletes. We both belong to the club. Peggy lives in Virginia.

John Jaxhiemer, 16

"Bubba was staying at Taylor Plimpton's house in Sagaponack, Long Island, and I was spending the night there, making entirely too much noise. He told us to cool it, but in a nice way."

John Jaxhiemer is one of Taylor Plimpton's best friends and is a student in New York City.

Eric Jensen, 25

"My dad was chairman of Remar's Body Worry Committee, and I met Remar at our house for dinner by the pool one May. Remar needed a summer intern. I ended up working fifteen months in the Bahamas—as his trainer and in charge of his Dolphin Research project. I spent a lot of my time working with Mary Abbott trying to keep Remar on the straight and narrow. He wandered often."

Eric Jensen is a third-year medical student at Southwestern University in Dallas, Texas.

Bunny Johnson, 57
Grady "Buck" Johnson, 59

"Buck and I were the Pine Tree Festival King and Queen here in Swainsboro when Bubba was ten. He rode on the fire engine right behind us in the parade. Then later he peeked when Buck and I were courting on my grandmother's front porch." Bunny, Remar's first cousin, has "a perfectly beautiful name—Sarah Marian—but no one has ever used it because I was born on Easter Sunday."

Grady "Buck" Johnson has been senior aide for the congressman from Georgia's First District for twenty years. He writes and sings country music. Bunny Johnson is a columnist for the Swainsboro *Forest Blade* and a civic leader.

Virginia Kahl, 71

"We met at the Key West Conchathon, where I finished last but finished nevertheless."

Virginia Kahl is the author of sixteen children's books published by Scribner's and is a librarian. She lives in Virginia.

Chris Keefe, 27

"My brother Bill was an instructor at the Underwater Explorer's Society on Grand Bahama, and for a couple of years he had lived in Remar's apartment while Remar was traveling. Then, one weekend I was on Grand Bahama when Remar was there with George Plimpton. I'll never forget: George didn't know me from Adam, but he talked to me a lot and then bought me dinner!"

Chris Keefe taught high school for a time and then taught diving. He's now a model who works regularly in Paris, Italy, Switzerland, Greece, Tokyo, and Spain.

Shannon Kelly, 26

"I first met Remar at George Plimpton's apartment. He and Jamie Royce, Remar's former intern, took us out on the town. Boy, did they! I avoided Remar for two years."

Shannon Kelly is an investment counselor and TV talk show host in Houston, Texas.

Henry Kemp, 80

"I was principal of Bubba's elementary school and used to see him quite regularly. He was usually sent to the principal's office for talking too much in class. I've known Mary Abbott for about twelve years and am happy someone can finally keep him in line."

Henry Kemp is the retired superintendent of the Marietta City School system. He and his wife were founding members of Remar's parents' supper club.

Peggy Kemp, 78

"Mary Abbott, according to Bubba's mother, changed his life much to the better, so I was glad to meet her in 1980."

Peggy Kemp has played bridge with Remar's mother every week since 1948. She's a member of the Daughters of the American Revolution, a woman who makes Marietta civic life click, and a homemaker—her cheese straws are famous throughout the South.

Lyn Lear, 45

"I met Remar at dinner with Norman before we were married. They talked a lot about lifting weights and turning into hunks . . ."

Lyn Lear holds a Ph.D in psychology from the Professional School of Psychological Studies in San Diego and also holds a license in marriage, family, and child counseling. For a time she taught psychology and philosophy at the private Brentwood School in Los Angeles.

Norman Lear, 70

"Remar's 'Body Worry' column was in the *Los Angeles Times*. I thought anyone crazy enough to remake himself in front of millions of people might be an interesting person to know. We began to exchange letters."

Norman Lear conceived and produced two of the most successful series in television, "All in the Family" and "Maude." While he continues to produce series and movies, he spends an increasing amount of time working on human rights and justice issues. He is founder of People for the American Way.

Kate Learson, 49

"Bubba has been this Renaissance character in my husband's [John Emmerling's] life from way back. I just marvel at all of Bubba's energy and interests."

Kate Learson is a painter who also advises corporations on art purchases for their collections. She volunteers as a caregiver for the boarder babies at a large urban public hospital. She is married to John Emmerling.

Phoebe Legere, 31

"Remar had heard me perform and asked me to perform at George Plimpton's birthday party. I said yes if he'd sing with me. 'But I don't sing!' he said. 'But you will!' I said. He was very good, actually. Then, that summer we biked quite frequently through the potato fields of Sagaponack together. Remar sent me to paint a perfectly straight row of corn bordering a field of low, green potato vines. I sat in his favorite oak to do the painting."

Phoebe Legere is a composer and a multiple instrumentalist who is attempting to synthesize the arts of painting, theater, music, dance, and science. She attended the Concord Academy, the New England Conservatory of Music, and the Stockbridge School, and graduated from Vassar College. She is a candidate for a master's degree in music composition at New York University and has studied with John Lewis of the Modern Jazz Quartet.

The Librarians

Dorothy Cross, Virginia Kahl, and Mary Randolph were friends and librarians who decided to train together for a Conchathon. "That was Virginia's mistake," says Mary. "She was turning seventy and wanted to do something big." None could swim when they started, but all finished a minitriathlon. That's how Remar met them, and they were featured in his *Washington Post* column. They also did the *Common Ground* interview together—all for one and one for all.

Kim Litton, 34

"I was the next-to-last finisher in the 1988 Grand Bahama Conch Man that Remar invited his readers to. I finished and Remar didn't—but he came out and rode the last mile with me on his bike, encouraging me all the way. I sweated, but Remar didn't."

Kim Litton is a critical clinical nurse specialist at the Osteopathic Medical Center of Texas in Fort Worth.

John Marston, 31

"I met Remar when I visited Torre Andrews on Grand Bahama Island. Three years later, when he visited Torre in San Diego, I saw him there, too. We became good friends and now dive together."

John Marston is an artist and works on an Alaskan fishing boat six months of the year.

Margaret Mason, 57

"When I was Style Plus editor at the *Washington Post*, I opened a letter one day that stated, 'I'm a forty-five-year-old bald man without muscles.' This unlikely candidate (photo enclosed) went on to say he planned to remake himself into a hunk and would I be interested in a column tracking his progress. How could I not be? I figured whatever happened, it would be a good column. It was; a lot of people got caught up in his Body Worry project, and Remar did become a hunk. Plus, he inspired hundreds of people to remember their bodies and get moving. Remar's a great person to walk and talk with. And he's still a hunk."

Margaret Mason is now a free-lance writer for the *Washington Post*, but her interest in Remar's writing sparked the national press's interest in his Body Worry project.

Will McIntyre, 38
Deni McIntyre, 36

Will: "At a Hemingway seminar on Key West, where I was photographing George Plimpton for *People* magazine, Remar stood out from everyone else because in the midst of all the literati and would-be illuminati he was a genuinely funny person and a gentleman and one of the few people who knew he didn't look like Ernest Hemingway. I met Mary Abbott when Deni and I joined Remar and her in the North Carolina mountains one weekend to start worrying about bodies."

Deni: "In one of our first social interactions Remar asked me for my underwear—because he thought it would make less of a line under his cheery red leotard. We were doing the before shots for *Body Worry*. At that moment I knew it wouldn't be a run-of-the-mill relationship. Then Mary Abbott and I got the giggles as we measured his biceps because both of ours looked bigger. But his weight training paid off, and matters are reversed now."

Will and Deni McIntyre are corporate and editorial photographers who work on location around the world. Occasionally they may be found at their home, Loose Ends, in Winston-Salem, North Carolina. They shot the photographs for *Remar Sutton's Body Worry*.

Damian Miller, 23

"My mother and I are neighbors of George Plimpton, and I met Remar at his apartment when I was a kid. One summer I lived at the Plimpton's country home and spent a month working out with Remar at the gym."

Damian Miller is a student at the London School of Economics.

Paul Mockler, 47

"I met Remar at the Underwater Explorer's Society on Grand Bahama Island, where we're both on the board of governors. Then he went to Mexico with us to catch dolphins for our open release program. Then we got in a lot of mischief together—which I can't tell you about—and finally he modeled the character Jon Rumble in his novel *Boiling Rock* after me. The village I live in is a model in the book, too. I liked being in the novel, but I don't really drink that much rum. Do I?"

Paul Mockler is a Canadian cinematographer now living full time in the village of Smith's Point, an original island settlement, on Grand Bahama Island. In 1987, the Academy of Canadian Motion Picture Arts and Sciences awarded him the Gemini Award—its equivalent of an Emmy—for the best cinematography in a series or special on Canadian television.

John Munro of Foulis, 33

"We met Mary Abbott and Remar at a party on Grand Bahama Island. At Remar's halloween party, I also played the bagpipes. Remar was dressed as a Martian sex pervert."

Jock Munro's family has lived on their ancestral lands in Scotland for 951 years; their home is Foulis Castle. His father, Capt. Patrick Munro of Foulis, is chief of the Clan Munro. Jock is manager of the Ledreborg Estates in Lejre, Denmark, where he lives with his wife and children. Three hundred sixty-five years ago, by sheer coincidence, Jock's ancestors brought 3,000 high-landers to Denmark to fight for King Frederik IX. They camped, according to a document from that time, near where Jock and Silvia now live.

Countess Sylvia Munro, 34

"Remar became my scuba-diving companion on Grand Bahama, and Mary Abbott a favorite dinner companion."

Silvia Munro's family has lived at Ledreborg Palace since 1739. Her grandmother was the grand duchess of Luxembourg. Silvia works directly with Jock in managing their estate. She likes to feed the chickens, too.

Bill Peck, 66

"Bubba was balding for as long as I can remember, and I've known him since he was six. I met Mary Abbott in 1980, when she and Remar were guests of the Supper Club."

Bill Peck owns a printing company in Marietta, Georgia.

Doris Peck, 64

"Mildred, Bubba's mother, always kept us up on Bubba, and she was thrilled when Mary Abbott became his friend."

Doris Peck is a homemaker; she and Bill are members of the Supper Club.

Nancy Daugenberg Sutton Perkins, 50

"I am Bubba's former sister-in-law and current very good friend. As a matter of fact, I met him a *long* time ago in high school before I met his brother. Now *that* would be a book, believe me. But we're all good friends now. I've met Mary Abbott many times at dinner at Mrs. Sutton's."

Nancy Perkins is office manager of an accounting firm in Atlanta. She tends a "very small" rose garden at their home, "since my husband won't help."

Stuart Perkins, 65

"I met Bubba and Mary Abbott at Mrs. Sutton's when Nancy and I came to Atlanta so Nancy could meet her kids again for the first time in seventeen years. I will never forget the love and under-standing the Sutton family gave Nancy on that traumatic weekend."

Stuart Perkins is a turnaround and crisis manager and an avid polo player. His great-grandfather founded the Jackson & Perkins Nurseries, and the Dorothy Perkins rose is named for his mother. This accounts for his total aversion to any form of yard work. Long before Stuart had heard of a Sutton, he and Remar's friend George Plimpton were runners-up in the 1964 bottle pool tournament at the New York Racquet and Tennis Club. "I blew the championship in the finals—twice," Stuart says, "but George was his usual gentlemanly self."

Jonathan Peter, 46

"My sailboat was anchored in Maho Bay on St. John in the Virgin Islands, and I was going boat to boat in my dinghy selling postcards of my drawings. Remar was on a trawler and had me aboard for a drink."

Jonathan Peter lives on his boat and travels the world with a companion. He "makes enough selling the cards to serve up a pleasant meal or two every day," and since he owns his boat, that's about all the money he needs. But he reports he's expanding.

Aubrey Peterson, 22

"When I was seventeen, I was dating Medora Plimpton, George's daughter, and took a spring break with Medora visiting Bubba on Grand Bahama Island. One day he caught us making out and said, 'I think we need to have a talk.' We've been honest since then, and we hug each other, too."

Aubrey Peterson is a NAUI-certified scuba instructor and a junior at the University of Montana majoring in social work and minoring in African-American studies. He lives with his father in East Hampton, New York.

Erik Peterson, 21

"When I was nineteen, I was attending a summer pool party at Medora Plimpton's house in Sagaponack. I didn't know Bubba but knew of him from my brother. And I saw this bald old guy across the pool having fun and thought, that's the guy. The next month my brother and Scott Smith and I were diving with Bubba on his rented trawler about a mile from Jost Van Dyke in the British Virgin Islands. An awesome shark was checking us out, and I noticed that Bubba got on the boat first."

Erik Peterson is a junior studying liberal arts at the University of Montana and lives with his mother in Southhampton, Long Island. He works each summer as an independent landscaping contractor in East Hampton.

Campion Platt, 33

"I met Remar through my good friend Jay McInerney, the writer. I can remember all of us bumbling around on the *Paris Review* boat at the mouth of the East River struggling to view the July Fourth fireworks. George Plimpton was screaming at the captain to constantly reposition the old ferryboat while he gave a splendid running commentary describing each of the colorful explosions. Remar had his hands full, literally, dealing with all the eccentric personalities on the boat but spent the time to chat me up. We've been friends since."

Campion Platt is an architect and developer. He is the owner of the Mercer Hotel and a Soho gallery in New York.

George Plimpton, 64

"I first heard about Bubba through a mutual friend, Coach Bill Curry. Bubba was staging a professional football game in Paris at that time. Soon, we were sharing hot-air balloon rides over Florida cow pastures with a man named Thunder Chicken."

George Plimpton is editor of *The Paris Review*, editor of the *Paris Review* Writers at Work series of interviews, and author of numerous books.

Medora Plimpton, 21

"I first really remember Bubba at our house in Boca Raton when I was eleven. He was there when my brother and I caught a big barracuda in the canal and put it in the jacuzzi. He was there when we buried it, too."

Medora Plimpton is the daughter of Freddy Plimpton and George Plimpton. Recently she helped her dad host a tour of Africa and spends the summers working as an independent landscaping contractor in East Hampton, Long island. Medora is a student at Hampshire College in Amherst, Massachusetts.

Taylor Plimpton, 16

"Bubba used to let me sit in his lap and steer his dune buggy on Grand Bahama Island when I was eight."

Taylor Plimpton, the son of Freddy Plimpton and George Plimpton, is a serious tennis player and a student at St. Paul's School in Concord, New Hampshire.

Jerry Preston, 56

"Bubba leased the beach house I'd lived in for years in Satellite Beach, Florida, and we met when he moved in. Pretty soon, he found out I loved to scuba-dive. The next month, I was in Cozumel diving; the *next* month I was in New York watching fireworks with George Plimpton. We call him Never-boring Bubba. I've met Mary Abbott dozens of times with him, including in Atlanta."

Jerry Preston's stained-glass works of art, featuring mainly nature settings, are in many permanent collections around the world and grace hundreds of custom homes. His latest animal-training project is to teach a pileated woodpecker to eat from his hand. He lives in the midst of his personal wildlife preserve (his yard) in the middle of Melbourne, Florida.

Joy Melton Prickett, 31

"Mary Abbott gave a dinner party to celebrate our friend Jane Burke's birthday. Remar was there, too. We had so many talkers and storytellers at the table we almost never finished eating for laughing."

While she lived in Atlanta, Joy Melton Prickett was commercial sales manager for the John H. Harland Company. She also sang with the Atlanta Symphony Orchestra Chorus and Chamber Chorus. She is now married to Larry Prickett, and they live in Richmond, Virginia, with their dog Lester and cat Sybil.

David Prowse, 57

"Remar decided that Darth Vader would be a good weight coach in his search for hunkdom, so he came to London to learn serious weight training with me. Mary Abbott and his mother came along as nurses, I think."

David Prowse played Darth Vader in the *Star Wars* movies, the bodyguard in *A Clockwork Orange*, and now works full time promoting his gym in London and nearly full time as a volunteer raising funds for British and American children's charities.

Mary Randolph, 52

"We met at the Key West minitriathlon."

Mary Randolph is a librarian systems analyst with the Alexandria Libraries. She is one of the three librarians and lives in Lorton, Virginia.

Mary Lou Retton, 24

"Remar's intern Jamie Royce was one of my best friends and was lifelong best friend of my (then) fiancé, Shannon Kelly. Jamie had moved to New York to attend graduate school and was living at George Plimpton's apartment in the city as a big brother to George's son. One weekend Jamie invited us up, and there was Remar! He gave us a *very* unusual tour of New York. By the next morning, Remar and I were in the kitchen cooking pancakes for the crew. We washed the dishes, too."

Olympic champion Mary Lou Retton lives in Houston, Texas, with her husband Shannon Kelly.

Doris Roberts, 61

"Remar and I met on Grand Bahama Island, where I ate lunch under a large banyan tree at his house and then went out on an afternoon dart-throwing date."

Doris Roberts won an Emmy for her portrayal of a homeless person on the television series "St. Elsewhere" and the Outer Critics Circle Award for her role in *Bad Habits*. Her late husband was the noted American author William Goyen, who was interviewed in the *Paris Review* Writers at Work series.

Cliff Robertson, 63

"I met Remar at a party on Grand Bahama Island and soon found out we had a mutual friend, George Plimpton, and shortly after found myself swimming with dolphins with him. One year I went blue marlin fishing with him in St. Thomas."

Cliff Robertson's latest film, *Wind*, produced by Frances Ford Coppola and directed by Carol Ballard, is about the America's Cup. He won an Oscar for best actor in the movie *Charlie*. He lives in Water Mill, Long Island.

Zar Rochelle, 44

"Mary Abbott and I were backdoor neighbors on Peachtree Circle, and we spent many evenings on the patio watching the sun go down, fanning the mosquitos. I met Remar on the patio. Through the years, these two have gotten me in more trouble than the money's worth."

Zar Rochelle is an Atlanta artist. He illustrated Remar's novel *Boiling Rock* and *Inside Grand Bahama,* by Mary Abbott and Dan Buettner.

Winthrop Rockefeller, 43

"Remar and I met at the Atlantic Blue Marlin Tournament in St. Thomas, went to dinner on my boat with George Plimpton and others, and now run into each other on islands. We didn't get off to a good start, because the first year we met he caught three marlin and I caught none."

Win Rockefeller is founder of the Billfish Foundation, a rancher, and a businessman. He's also a working commissioner of the Arkansas State Police.

Julie Rogers, 41

"I met Remar and Mary Abbott at Remar's first Conchathon in the Bahamas. About 500 readers of his *Washington Post* column were there for that minitriathlon. Remar chickened out of the event, though. 'Too stressed,' he said. Unhuh."

Julie is president of the Meyer Foundation in Washington, D.C., and is married to Leonard Berman.

Ben Rose, 51

"Remar was upside-down on a scuba dive when I first saw him: standing on his head on the bottom of the ocean. Shortly thereafter, he studied underwater marine identification with me, where he did the same thing a lot. Does he do that with other friends?"

Ben Rose is an expert in marine biology and a painter. Ben's discovery of an inland cave on Grand Bahama Island that connected with the ocean helped establish scuba diving in the world's largest underwater cave system.

Judy Rose, 51

"When Bubba was doing his Body Worry project, I enrolled in the aerobics class at his house, and I'll tell you a secret: his idea of aerobic dancing consists entirely of doing the twist! And not a very good one, at that. Most of the class got more exercise laughing at his aerobic technique than we did dancing."

Judy Rose manages the restaurant at a health spa on Grand Bahama Island and is one of the island's most noted chefs.

James Royce, 26

"Remar was on campus in February interviewing interns, but I wasn't one of them. By accident, we worked out together in the gym and talked casually. At the end of the workout he said, 'How would you like to have your life turned upside down?' Within a month I was in Washington, D.C., helping organize minitriathlons; by summer I was living in the Bahamas; and a year later, I was living in the Virgin Islands and then Key West. It pays to work out at gyms. Somewhere along the way I met Mary Abbott."

James Royce was Remar's intern for a year and then director of Remar's Conchathon foundation in the Virgin Islands. For two years, he lived with the George Plimpton family in New York as he completed his MBA at New York University. Jamie is now a broker on Wall Street and lives in Manhasset, New York.

Peggy Sammons, 66

"I'm Bubba's youngest aunt. My claim to fame is teaching Bubba a love of English."

Peggy Sammons is the retired registrar and director of admissions of Emmanual County Junior College in Swainsboro, Georgia.

Tommy Sammons, 66

"When Peggy and I were dating, Bubba always wanted to tag along, particularly to the pool. Though we certainly didn't need it, he always acted like Peggy's lifeguard. He was only ten."

Tommy Sammons is a pharmacist in Swainsboro, Georgia. After Tommy's comments in this interview about wanting to motorcycle through the Rockies, he left the house and five minutes later had a serious motorcycle accident when a truck swerved into him. He still plans to make the trip.

Muriel Sichveland, 73

"I met Remar and Mary Abbott when they popped in to say hello while we were playing bridge."

Muriel Sichveland is a member of the Wednesday Bridge Club with Remar's mother. Natives of western Montana, she and her husband, an engineer, moved to Atlanta in 1951 when he joined the Lockheed Company.

Scott Smith, 22

"I met Bubba at a pool party at Medora Plimpton's house when I was twenty. I've seen him more in Montana than anywhere."

Scott Smith is a junior studying liberal arts at the University of Montana. He lives in East Hampton with his father and works in the summer with Erik Peterson as an independent landscaping contractor.

Vince Spezzano, 66
Marge Spezzano, 65

"I was the publisher of *Florida Today*, and Bubba asked me to serve on his secret M3 Committee—the Madcap Mischief Makers."

He wanted to promote Brevard County, but in unorthodox ways. I remember we couldn't wear shoes to our meetings, and once we met in a round boat. I think it sank. Marge met Bubba at one of those meetings.''

Vince Spezzano is the retired president of *USA Today* and publisher of *Florida Today* and other Gannett newspapers. Marge Spezzano is a master calligrapher and homemaker.

Princess Pamela Mary Elizabeth Martha Strobel

"Bubba had a party at my club with all these fancy people, and then he sang with me and gave me a big kiss, and now I'm afraid he's going to give me an apple.''

Princess Pamela Strobel is a well-known jazz singer and proprietor of Princess' Southern Touch, a take-your-own-booze, postage-stamp-size private restaurant on New York's lower East Side—78 East First Street, to be exact. But don't go without calling and "tell whoever answers the phone that Bubba said call, and I mean that,'' adds Princess. Telephone (212) 477-4460 after 5:00 P.M.

Timothy Sultan, 24

"I met Bubba at *The Paris Review* and can recommend his spaghetti sauce, but not his pool.''

Timothy Sultan is an editorial assistant for *The Paris Review* and managing editor of *Translation* magazine at the Translation Center at Columbia University's School of the Arts. He was born in Bangkok; grew up in Laos, Germany, and the Ivory Coast; and now lives in New York City.

The Supper Club

The Supper Club, of which Remar's parents were founding members, started as a couple's bridge club over thirty years ago in Marietta, Georgia. Says Mildred Sutton, "We'd bring supper and play bridge, but then it got where the men didn't want to play bridge so we just ate and talked.'' The Supper Club from time to time invited us "youngsters" to join them, and we had such a good time and so enjoyed the club's enduring friendships that we asked them to do a joint interview for *Common Ground*.

Mary Costigan, Mildred Sutton, Peggy and Henry Kemp, Kathryn Hames, Bill and Doris Peck, and Rose and Steve Wing are Supper Club members.

Mildred Sutton, 82

"I am Bubba's mother. I'm happy to say I'm also the model for Evelyn Wade in his novels *Long Lines* and *Boiling Rock*. But whatever he says in those books, I'm not getting married again."

A retired schoolteacher, a teacher of an adult ladies' Bible class at First Baptist Church, and a teacher of English to foreign students, Mildred Sutton is a student of Shakespeare and bridge and likes to entertain at her home in Marietta, Georgia.

Jim Swann, 43

"I met Bubba the night we stole a motor home together during Plimpton World Record Week here in Brevard County, Florida. That's when we got 65,000 people to hold hands in one line along the beach (Bubba's idea). I remember that night we roasted armadillo on my ranch for Bubba and George Plimpton and the others in that crew."

Jim Swann is a developer with his stepfather Jack Eckerd. With his wife Jonnie, his latest project is getting 20,000 people together to build a zoo in a week in Brevard County, Florida.

Mimi Taufer, 50

"I met Mary Abbott sometime in early 1973. Ed took me to Brooklyn to dinner at her home. I will always remember the large, warm apartment filled with plants and antiques. Mary Abbott introduced us to Bubba (I had never heard that name before) shortly after they began working together."

Mimi Taufer is a graphic artist in New York City. She's married to Ed Colquhoun.

Nan Thomas, 59

"Remar and his friends each day would walk by my art stand in Little Apple Bay, Tortola, just down from Sebastian's. We just started talking one day."

Nan Thomas is an artist living in the village of Little Apple Bay on Tortola, the British Virgin Islands. If you wish to obtain a copy of her children's books about Toby the Sea Turtle, you may do so by sending $15 (check or money order) and indicating whether you want Toby I or Toby II to Nan Thomas, Carrot Bay Post Office, Tortola, British Virgin Islands. It takes a while for the mail to get there, but Nan will be delighted to hear from you.

Kurt Vonnegut, 64

"I met Remar at the Plimptons' and other places here in Sagaponack."

Kurt's house is a literal stone's throw from the Plimpton country home. He is the author of numerous books, including *Slaughterhouse-Five* and *Hocus Pocus*.

Alvis A. Waite, Jr., 71
Marynell S. Waite, 73

"We're Mary Abbott's parents, so we claim proud first acquaintance. We met Remar as a college friend of our son Jay."

Alvis Waite is a retired United Methodist minister who served as pastor, district superintendent, and director of the South Georgia Conference Council on Ministries.

Marynell Waite, an active church historian, edits *Historical Highlights* and has served on the United Methodist General Commission on Archives and History.

Dana Warrington, 39

"My mother served on Bubba's M3 Committee. One day she said, 'Oh, what are you doing this afternoon?' By three, I was on the way to Disney World in a German World War II staff plane serving drinks to an astronaut; to Martin Cadin, author of *The Six Million Dollar Man*; to Bubba; and to an Arab who had bought the liner

France. Bubba thought we should anchor it in Brevard County. That night, Disney gave the Arab a key to the laundry room rather than a suite. We didn't get the liner, but I became a regular on the M3 circuit and Bubba's first intern. I met Mary Abbott in Atlanta in 1982. I think she's a little more normal than Bubba.''

Dana Warrington is a marketing consultant living in Alexandria, Virginia, with his wife and two children.

The Wednesday Bridge Clue

Every Wednesday on Mildred Sutton's porch or in Peggy Kemp's den or at Mary Costigan's or Muriel Sichveland's you can find these four ladies enjoying a brown-bag lunch, lots of good bridge, and great conversation. More important than the bridge, though, is the friendship of many years. That's why we made an extrafancy lunch (no brown bag that day) and put our tape recorder in the centerpiece and tossed out our questions to the group. The resulting conversation was as rich as we expected it would be.

Rose Wing, 74

"I've known Mary Abbott since 1980, and Bubba forever.''

A retired schoolteacher, Rose Wing and her husband are founding members of the Supper Club and live in Marietta, Georgia.

Steve Wing, 75

"Once Mary Abbott and Bubba cooked for us, and I'll tell you, Mary Abbott is far and away the better cook.''

Steve Wing is a retired probation officer in the Cobb County Division of the Georgia Superior Court.

Springboards for Discussions with Your Own Friends

Skip the movie this weekend, gather a group of friends, and throw out as many of these conversation starters as you like to the group. Give anyone who wants to a chance to answer. The questions roughly match the chronological order of events in our lifetimes. You'll find some people will answer very few, but their answers will be extraordinary.

Here's a tip: Don't ask just the "deep" questions; ask the fun ones, too.

We prefaced our interviews with this question: What memory or thought do these topics bring to mind? Your response can be a word, a phrase, an anecdote, or a story; or it may be nothing at all.

1. What's your very first memory?
2. What's your first memory with a parent?
3. Did you have a special childhood friend?
4. Did you have a pet? What do you remember about it?
5. Do you remember a special moment with one of your parents?
6. Tell me about an awkward moment with a parent.
7. Who's someone other than your parents who really made an impact on your life? Why?
8. Tell me a discovery about yourself—at any time in your life—that surprised you.

9. When was the first time you felt like an adult with your parents?
10. What is a legacy you'll pass on from your parents to others?
11. A summer job
12. An unusual vacation
13. Tell me about your first date.
14. Your greatest moment of glory in sports (It might have happened in practice or a backyard badminton game, but if you think about it, you probably have one.)
15. Friends or family at their funniest
16. A famous family story
17. What's something worth waiting for in life?
18. A simple thing that brings you pleasure
19. A moment of real loneliness
20. What makes you feel young?
21. How has serendipity affected your life?.
22. A special moment to you (perhaps one that no one else knew about at the time)
23. What takes your breath away?
24. Burying a friend
25. Something that shines
26. A fear for your children
27. Instructions misunderstood
28. A treasured possession (if the house were on fire, what, other than people and pets, would you grab first?)
29. Your lowest point
30. An unexpected moment provoking compassion
31. What makes you want to give up?
32. What gives you the courage to go on?
33. Name a vile thing.
34. When I say *holding hands,* what comes to mind?
35. Your first intimation of mortality. When did you first realize that we don't live forever?
36. A minor regret
37. If I say money, what comes to mind?
38. Once on a rainy afternoon . . .

39. Failing
40. A unexpected treat
41. An unexpected threat
42. Your greatest regret
43. An unusual friendship
44. Your greatest fear
45. A relationship that is meaningful to you
46. What is art without merit?
47. What is art with merit?
48. What comes to mind when I say *birds flying south?*
49. Name something that's sweet.
50. A moment of real fear
51. A vivid dream
52. Something you've always wanted to do

Acknowledgments

The Common Ground Book would never have become a reality without the insight, energy, and just plain hard work of a number of people. We haven't room to name everyone, but we'd like to express our thanks to these in particular:

— All the friends who opened their doors to us, though it meant facing microphones and a number of impertinent questions.

— Lori Krise, Jane Burke, and Zar Rochelle, who variously transcribed dozens of interviews and spent hours at the computer helping us pull thousands of pieces into a final manuscript.

— Reid Boates, as much a literary man as a good agent.

— Elizabeth Coccio, whose outstanding copy editing and collegial way of work helped us get the little and big things right, and Amy Griffin, British American's intern.

— Ultimately, Kathleen Murphy, managing editor at British American, who inspired and supported our efforts.

Index

A CHRISTMAS CAROL, Mason, 239
ABDULLAH, SHAHID, Berman, 346
ABRAMS, ROBERT, first memory, 14; summer job, 158; glory in sports, 194; treat, 234; a legacy to pass on, 373;
ABRAMS, CAROLYN, first memory, 17; special moment with parent, 36; special private moment, 242; Letting Veronica Go, a portrait, 249; rainy afternoon, 263; a legacy to pass on, 370;
ACCEPTING THE INEVITABLE, rats as example of, Thomas, 184
ACCIDENT
    as teacher of mortality, Colquhoun, 87
    dead woman on street, Jaxhiemer, 292
    drowning death prevented by porno films, Plimpton 299
    finding dead woman in ocean, T. Plimpton, 292
    funny airplane incident, Johnson, 294
    funny ones driving a tractor, McIntyre, 159
    losing a brother, Houlihan, 348
    losing a grandfather, Lear, 7
    losing a son, Brown, 224
    mother's death changes family roles, Fish, 143
    on wedding day, Colquhoun, 87
    ski ropes imperil, Litton, 305
    terrifying fire, Kahl, 300
ACCIDENT, AUTO
    in Cyprus, Peter, 87

    with new jeep, M. Plimpton, 95
    losing a friend, Bornn, 345
    wrecking father's car, Colquhoun, 44
ACCIDENT, BICYCLE
    broken bike teaches ingenuity, Buettner, 219
    repeated accidents frustrating, Buettner, 228
ACCIDENT, CHILDHOOD
    accident leads to life's work, Andrews, 169
    releasing car brake, Englander, 13
    runaway horse teaches a lesson, Peck 196
    stuck to a railing, McIntyre, 17
    tumbles, Brunson, 12; Peck, 17
ACCIDENT, DIVING,
    diving death impacts rescuer, Ferguson, 291
    overconfidence threatens diver, Englander, 306
    stuck in a submarine at 1,000 feet, Mockler, 296
ACCORDION, Preston's mother plays, 10
ACHIEVEMENT OF POTENTIAL, a wish for one's children, Cooney, 356; Hiers, 356; Rockefeller, 355
ACHIEVEMENT, Sutton, 379
ACTING
    determination can get you there, Burke, 211
    dying fish lead to TV stardom, Beacham, 215

how a career began, Roberts, 42;
Beacham, 167; Burke, 331
a good way to judge talent, Roberts,
281
if you're speeding, playing a nun is
smart, Burke 232
learning to love as child, Roberts, 42
ACTING INSTRUCTOR, as a powerful
influence, Roberts, 120
ACTORS, see Beacham, Burke, Holloway,
Prowse, Roberts, Robertson
ADDICTION, a young drug addict takes
control of life, Marston 225
ADOPTING A CHILD, first moments,
Colquhoun, 238
ADOPTION, DeGrandpre's thought as
adoptive child, 318
ADULTHOOD, see also "The Time You
First Felt Like an Adult with Your
Parents," chapter 20, p. 138
adult feeling when mistaken for wife,
Bornn, 141
being called sir means you're on way,
Emery, 145
comes slowly, Cooney, 88; Rose, 148
complexity of reaching with parents,
Beacham, 147
farm chores teach, Cross, 139
helping family changes children's
role, Colquhoun, 146
illness of father helps establish,
Learson, 148
marriage and moving makes you feel
like, Hames, 145; Ferguson, 145;
Brunson, 332
supporting parents brings on, Lear,
153
tackling adults, McIntyre, 319
traditions for kids in the Virgin
Islands, Donovan, 145
ADVENTURE
bicycle treks around world, Buettner,
195, 219, 228, 251, 264, 284, 292, 298

childhood train trip, Plimpton, 25
deep ocean, big whales, Jensen 303
discovering cave systems, Rose, 247
diving on the *Titanic*, Mockler, 285
dogsled riding, Mockler, 248
ice diving in the Arctic, Englander,
248
a night walk, Sultan, 308
stuck 1,000 feet underwater, Mockler,
296
ADVERSITY
a grandmother overcomes, Andrews,
110
break big problems into little pieces,
M. Plimpton, 212
business problems test you,
Englander, 226
confronting an upside-down life,
Hanson, 210
courage to confront, Prowse, 206
dealing with, Friedman, 319
getting over drugs teaches lesson,
Keefe, 209
librarian faces danger in Vietnam,
Randolph, 296
obstacles as opportunities, Robertson,
208
Russian spirit overcomes, Roberts, 212
a test from God, Brown, 210
AFGHANISTAN, stranded in, Barbour, 317
AFRICA
childhood memories, Barbour, 7; 80
a trip together, M. Plimpton, 48; G.
Plimpton, 48
AFRICAN AMERICANS
as important influences, Waite, 81;
Johnson, 116; Colquhoun, 116;
Cook, 259; Thomas, 326, 361;
influence of strong parents, C.
Abrams, 36, 370; R. Abrams, 373;
Bornn, 40, 362; Brown, 23;
influence of strong grandparents,
Strobel, 164; Ferguson, 114

AGE
lying about, T. Plimpton, 96
refreshing attitudes on Tortola,
Thomas, 361
AGING, see also ADULTHOOD
activity keeps you young, Brown, 362
fear of, Royce, 87
importance of financial freedom,
Sichveland, 162
parents' changing roles, Rose, 148;
Spezzano, 148
requires determination, Sutton, 201,
334
Supper Club on independence, 352
thoughts on, Mockler, 323; Vonnegut,
334
Wednesday Bridge Club on feeling
young, 359
what's ahead at eighty, Brown, 389
AIDS
affects friends, Sultan, 120
death of a friend, Edmondson, 117;
Emery, 341; Legere, 345
fear for children, Bailey, 357
tragedy of babies with, Learson, 185
AIMLESSNESS, a boxer confronts,
Cooney, 203
AIR CONDITIONER, what size do you
need? Johnson, 272
AIR RAID WARNING, during war, Rose, 13
AIRPLANE, see also GLIDER
AIRPLANE
dawn flight, Emmerling, 71
in dreams, Berman, 102
AIRPLANES, A Portrait, Johnson, 294
ALABAMA, Midfield, Brunson, 12
ALASKA
hiking in, Duke, 364
a new life there, Marston, 364
Petersburg, Marston, 175
ALCOHOL, see also COCKTAILS
a boarding school treat, DeGrandpre,
233

a day in a bar changes life to better,
Brackett, 214
and father, Johnson, 93
first drink is with parents, Hallett, 143
impact on family, Hanson, 227
loneliness, drinking and doing drugs,
Keefe, 260
penalties of drinking too much,
Sultan, 225
ALCOHOLISM, road to recovery, Perkins,
135; Cook, 320
ALLOWANCES, CLOTHING, makes you
feel like an adult, Thomas, 142
AMAZEMENT, a childlike quality, Peter,
360
AMAZEMENT, provoked by birds, Sutton,
336
AMBITION, a young man's motivating
force, Miller, 209
AMBULANCE, mean bad news, Hiers,
222
ANALYSIS OF SELF, can be unsettling,
Robertson, 230
ANDREWS, TORRE, first memory, 15; things
that shine, 20; treasured possession,
103; Someone You Could Talk To, a
portrait, 110; finding work, 169; simple
pleasures, 184; loneliness, 258; funny
story, 273; compassionate moment,
285; self-discovery, 321; legacy, 367;
something you want to do, 379.
ANDREWS, EVELYN MAY THOMPSON,
Andrews, 110
ANDREWS, FRANK, Andrews, 20
ANGER
as animal instinct, Rockefeller, 322
child toward siblings, Andrews, 321;
Kahl, 13
effect on children, Hanson, 227
in childhood, Bailey, 12; Learson, 258
indifference is worse, McIntyre, 204
makes you give up, Vonnegut, 201

ANIMALS, see also by species
being with any brings pleasure,
Preston, 185
cruelty to them is worse, Sultan, 290
various, as friends, Preston, 63
ANIMALS, see "Mutual Respect, a
portrait," Preston, 63
ANNABELL, the actress, Lear, 34
ANSWERING MACHINE
a grandmother loves, Prickett, 276
a message from Olivier, Roberts, 236
ANTHROPOLOGY, as a gut course,
Plimpton, 176
ANTICIPATION
a good trait for a sailor, Peter, 231
looking ahead at eighty, Brown, 389
makes life interesting, Houlihan, 209
ANXIETY
has funny physical impact, Berman,
86, 325
about weight, Taufer, 301; Burke, 384
stage fright, Burke, 73
APARTMENTS, start a friendship, Peck,
216
APPEARANCES, no basis for judgment,
Perkins, 367
APPLE
can make you pregnant, Strobel, 264
the consequences of eating green,
Rose, 55
ARDULLIE LODGE, Munro, 7
ARGUMENTS, witnessing them made
Lear feel adult, 138
ARMITRAJ, VIJAY, winning a trophy
with, Plimpton, 106
AROMA, see ODOR
ART, see also "Art With and Without
Merit," Chapter 27, p. 179
ability to move us, Learson, 73;
Taufer, 73; Prowse, 181
anything you can get away with,
Marston 179
good intentions define art, Learson, 181

takes breath away, Taufer, 73
turtles and making a living, Thomas,
215
ART WITH MERIT
gives pleasure, Emmerling, 180
moves you in some way, Plimpton,
179
ART WITHOUT MERIT
doesn't exist, Hanson, 179
inaccessible art, examples, Duke, 180
is pervasive, Legere, 179
ARTHRITIS
a miracle with a child, Prowse, 287
grandmother overcoming, Andrews, 110
ARTISTS, see also R. Cook, Emery,
Emmerling, Learson, Legere, Preston,
Rochelle, Taufer
being a cartoonist, Emmerling, 166
beginning a career, Taufer, 123
drawing on napkins boosts career,
Cook, 216
Martin Hoose, Emery, 341
painters for parents, Legere, 43
Rembrandt's ability to manage light,
Learson, 73
role models of independent thinking,
Beacham, 113
talented grandfathers as, Learson, 121
ATHEISM
atheist and fundamentalist as friends,
Vonnegut, 339
grandfather carries the card, Taufer,
368
shock value of in small towns,
Rochelle, 158
makes a Boy Scout think, Peter, 220
ATHLETIC ABILITY, see also "Your
Moment of Glory in Sports," chapter
30, p. 192
a natural skier, Rochelle, 197
a personal discovery, Berman, 325;
Hackman, 326; Learson, 325;
Mason, 326, 361

ATTITUDE
fix your mood as well as face, Hanson, 372
optimism the best approach, Emmerling, 375
a positive one turns adversity around, Prowse, 206
thinking young, Friedman, 363
ATTORNEY, see LAWYER
AU PAIR, see NANNY
AUCTION, winning a trip at, Friedman, 197
AUNT
and birthdays, Abrams, 14
Aunt Maude, ever the same, Edmondson, 274
a major influence, Sutton, 124
AUSTRALIA, a miracle at an arthritis camp, Prowse, 287
AUTHORITY, a hard hat a symbol of, Duke, 156
AUTHORS, see WRITERS
AUTOMOBILE ACCIDENT, see ACCIDENT, AUTO
AUTOMOBILES, see CARS or TRUCKS or make
AUTUMN, images of, Colquhoun, 336; Legere, 335; Miller, 336; Roberts, 337; Sultan, 187
AWAY WENT WOLFCANG, the book, Kahl, 174
AWKWARD MOMENTS, see "An Awkward Moment with a Parent," chapter 14, p. 91
feeling of never belonging as a child, Roberts, 253
finding out son is married, Sutton, 135

BABIES
critical illness of, Johnson, 222
father's joy of holding, Platt, 238
in dreams, Legere, 100
holding them a simple pleasure, Learson, 185
lonely moment helped by them, Beacham, 256
a nap in front of the fire, Cook, 239
sixty years a baby nurse, Brown, 169
BACKACHE, an unusual solution to mother's, Johnson, 27
BACKPACKING, Duke, 339
BACKYARD, Waite, 11; Colquhoun, 15; Edmondson, 55
BAGPIPES
in the Arkansas wilderness, Rockefeller, 237
playing them as a summer job, Munro, 150
treasured possession, Munro, 103
BAHAMAS, GRAND BAHAMA ISLAND, see also Bailey, Brackett, Englander, Ferguson, Rose
discovering cavern system, Rose, 247
moving to, Bailey, 263; Brackett, 214
starting a diving business, Englander, 173; 226
BAHAMAS, NASSAU, childhood memories, Ferguson, 24
BAILEY, Dr. Barbara, first memory, 12; early memories, 28; mortality, 82; adult with parents, 140; work, 170; loneliness, 255; rainy afternoon, 263; a self-discovery, 334; fear for children, 357; feel young, 361
BAKING, with grandmother, Hackman, 8
BALDNESS, as something that shines, Rochelle, 19
BAMBOO, hiding under saves Laotian, Sultan, 28
BANANAS, smoking them isn't recommended, Thomas, 262
BARBADOS, M. Plimpton's memory of, 14
BARBECUE, a picnic on the Maui coast, Hallett, 235

BARBOUR, ALASTAIR, first memory, 14; mortality, 81; summer job, 154; special private moment, 237; a self-discovery, 317; funny story, 280

BARBOUR, HELEN, first memory, 7; early memory, 29; a pet, 66; mortality, 80; summer job, 154; simple pleasures, 188; special private moment, 237

BARKER, a summer job, Lear, 153

BARS, see also PUBS
a day with Dad, Brackett, 214
drinking at with grandfather, Perkins, 44
penalties of drinking too much, Sultan, 225
sitting outside of with smelly fish, Swann, 25

BASEBALL CARDS, as treasured possessions, DeGrandpre, 107

BASEBALL
played as a child, Bornn, 14; DeGrandpre, 58
played with parents, Edith Bornn, 15
Rochester Red Wings, Spezzano, 16

BATHROOM
a first memory, Plimpton, 6
locking self in, Lear, 11; Cook, 27

BATHTUB
early memories of, Buettner, 36
hiding a person in, Sultan, 28

BAVARIA, and a special honeymoon, Munro, 266

BEACHAM, STEPHANIE, first memory, 14; early memories, 29; holding hands, 32; special moment with parent, 45; mortality, 76; person who influenced, 113; adult with parents, 147; finding work, 167; serendipity, 215; unexpected threats, 230; loneliness, 256; a legacy, 372; something worth waiting for, 384

BEACH
discovery of dead person, Plimpton, 292
a natural moment, Platt, 25
walking on with mother, Callwood, 8

BEARS, Asian brown bears as pets, Sultan, 68

BEATERS, working a hunt on a Scottish estate, Barhour, 154

BEAUTY, Princess Strobel's mother, 67

BEAUTY, PHYSICAL
as a breathtaking power, Vonnegut, 74
in old age, Preston, 19

BEAUTY PARLOR
going to with mother, Retton, 27
still foxy at eighty, Brown, 362

BEDSPREAD, memory of, Rose, 13

BEES
on Jost Van Dyke, Callwood, 8
terrifying experience, Houlihan, 307

BEETHOVEN
singing the Ninth in East Berlin, Burke, 246
studying, McIntyre, 115

BELL, RICKY, Burke, 56

BELONGING
stepmother's gift, Emery, 371
universal need, Duke, 287

BEN'S CAVE, discovering, Rose, 247

BERLIN
Beethoven's Ninth and connecting, Burke, 246
desolation creates lonely moment, Kahl, 259

BERMAN, LEONARD, early friendship, 57; mortality, 86; dream, 102; person who influenced, 130; adult with parents, 144; give up, 202; loneliness, 254; a self-discovery, 325; burying a friend, 346

BICYCLE
as an adventure, Buettner, 121
Alaska to South America, Buettner, 195

biking in strange locations, Buettner, 72
childhood in the Hamptons, Hanging
Together, 50
first rides on, Buettner, 27
hand-me-down from sisters, Munro, 56
in St. Thomas, Bornn, 40
learning to ride, Beacham, 45
riding to work, Abrams, 158
riding with father, Prowse, 26;
Houlihan, 348
Russian teaches ingenuity to American,
Buettner, 219
BICYCLIST, as a career influence,
Buettner, 121
BIGOTRY, see also "Vile Things," chapter
46, p. 283
Aryan Nation, DeGrandpre, 202
BIKING
best treat on a trip is, Buettner, 235
treks, see Buettner, 195, 219, 228,
251, 264, 284, 292, 298
BIRD, David, Johnson, 54
BIRDS AND BEES, see SEX EDUCATION
BIRDS, see, "Birds Flying South,"
chapter 53, p. 335
BIRTH DEFECTS
can be a blessing, Johnson, 222
teenager deals with, DeGrandpre, 225
BIRTHDAY
celebrating eighty, Brown, 362
unexpected treat, Abrams, 14, 234
BITING, a sweet outcome, Munro, 6
BLOND HAIR, Legere, 11
BLUEBERRIES, picking with father,
Legere, 43
BOARDING SCHOOL
a lonely experience in Scotland,
Munro, 252
a treat, DeGrandpre, 233
BODYBUILDING, see also WEIGHT
LIFTING
a disappointing start, Prowse, 206
BODYSURFING, in Nassau, Ferguson, 24

BOER WAR, Munro, 103
BOOKS
buying first, Prowse, 37
counting them on a rainy day,
Rochelle, 266
father reads to sons, Emmerling, 46
Great Books series, Peter, 119
learning how to build staircase,
Vonnegut, 242
simple pleasure or not? Duke, 187
surrounded by, Beacham, 113
take them with you when you retreat,
Robertson, 264
treasured possession, Rockefeller, 104;
Peter, 107
an uninterrupted read, Abrams, 263
writing first book, Kahl, 174
You Can't Go Home becomes WW II
symbol, Kahl, 259
BORING PEOPLE, to be avoided, Mason,
201
BORNN, EDITH, first memory, 36;
things that shine, 20; special moment
with parent, 40; breath away, 74;
mortality, 82; adult with parents, 141;
simple pleasure, 189; special private
moment, 246; vile thing, 283; something
sweet, 312; a self-discovery, 329;
BORNN, MICHAEL, first memory, 14;
special moment with parent, 40;
early friendship, 56; dream, 98;
failing, 177; simple pleasure, 186;
glory in sports, 194; a compassionate
moment, 288; burying a friend, 345;
greatest fear, 352; what makes you
feel young, 362;
BORNN, STEVE, E. Bornn, 20
BORNN, DAVID, E. Bornn, 20
BOURJAILY, VANCE, Roberts, 86
BOWLING, on a rainy day, Jaxhiemer, 262
BOWL, as treasured possessions, Sutton,
108

BOXING
  losing a big fight, Cooney, 178
  million-dollar payday, Cooney, 195
  with best friend, Royce, 59
  with brother, M. Plimpton, 321
BOY SCOUTS
  an example of courage, Bornn, 288
  leader as good influence, Colquhoun,
    116
  Scout learns an uncomfortable lesson,
    Peter, 220
BRACKETT, KATHY BATER, special
  moment with parent, 34; serendipity,
  214; treasured possession, 107; adult
  with parents, 139; summer job, 154;
  what makes you give up, 204; going
  on, 210; vile thing, 284; real fear,
  304; a self-discovery, 330; something
  worth waiting for, 384
BRAZIL, escape to, McIntyre, 335
BREATHING, as a metaphor for life,
  Mason, 213
BREATHING UNDERWATER, in dreams,
  Hallett, 101
BRIDGE (card game)
  a lifetime enjoyment, Kemp, 197
  parties and marijuana, Andrews, 273
BRIDGE
  falling off, Brunson, 12
  rising water, Wing, 304
  swinging rope bridge, Hanson, 12
BRITISH VIRGIN ISLANDS, see
  TORTOLA, JOST VAN DYKE
BRITISH COLUMBIA, Duke, 105
BROOKLYN DODGERS, DeGrandpre, 107
BROOK, see STREAM
BROOM, sweeping in St. Thomas, Bornn,
  312
BROTHEL, a family's fortune starts with,
  Cook, 281
BROTHERS
  death of, Brunson, 223; Edmondson,
    254; Houlihan, 348; Litton, 222

as friends, M. Plimpton, 321
  hitting over head, Kahl, 13
  jealousy of, Beacham, 14
  sister's desire to be with, Lear, 54
  taking a brother to a drug center,
    Keefe, 260
  teaching one to swim, Cooney, 239
BROTHERS AND SISTERS, sticking
  together, Hiers, 222
BROWN, MYRTIS, early memories, 23;
  finding work, 169; give up, 205;
  courage to go on, 210; lowest
  moment, 224; something sweet, 311;
  burying a friend, 349; what makes
  you feel young, 362; something
  worth waiting for, 389
BRUNSON, ANNE, adult with parents,
  143; lowest moment, 226; special
  private moment, 238; funny story,
  275; a self-discovery, 324; something
  worth waiting for, 387
BRUNSON, DON, first memory, 12;
  summer job, 153; simple pleasure,
  190; serendipity, 218; lowest moment,
  223; treat, 235; a self-discovery, 332
BUCHAN, BARBARA, inspiring friend,
  Goddard, 353
BUDDHA, Sultan, 18
BUETTNER, DAN, things that shine, 20;
  early memories, 27; holding hands,
  32; special moment with parent, 36;
  a pet, 70; breath away, 72; person
  who influenced, 121; glory in sports,
  195; courage to go on, 211; serendipity,
  219; lowest moment, 228; treat, 235;
  special private moment, 240;
  loneliness, 251; rainy afternoon, 264;
  vile thing, 284; a compassionate
  moment, 292; real fear, 298; a self-
  discovery, 324
BUGS, as vile things, Brackett, 284
BUILDING A STAIRCASE, a private
  moment, Vonnegut, 242

BULIMIA, overcoming, Brunson, 226
BULLDOGS, Edmondson, 69
BULLS, in dreams, Marston, 100
BURKE, JANE, holding hands, 32; early
friendship, 56; pet, 69; breath away,
73; treasured possession, 104; person
who influenced, 125; summer job,
155; courage to go on, 211; threats,
232; special private moment, 246;
funny story, 277; a self-discovery, 331;
something worth waiting for, 384
BURKITTS LYMPHOMA, Royce, 89
BURYING A FRIEND, a portrait, John
Emery, 341
BUSH MEDICINE, Callwood, 35
BUSINESS PROBLEMS, dealing with,
Englander, 226
BYLINES, Plimpton's at school, 166

CADAVER, as symbol of mortality,
Marston, 82
CAKE, GERMAN CHOCOLATE, Abrams, 14
CALIFORNIA
Carmel, early memories, Hallett, 23, 118
Catalina Island, early memories,
Brackett, 34, 154
La Jolla, early memories, Robertson, 77
Palm Springs, Lear, 11
CALLIGRAPHY, as a learning discipline,
Spezzano, 123
CALLWOOD, FOXY, first memory, 8;
special moment with parent, 35;
money, 161; glory in sports, 197;
treat, 234; a special relationship, 270;
real fear, 303; feel young, 360;
regrets, 364; something you want to
do, 378
CAMBODIA, a brother is killed in action,
Brunson, 223
CAMP, SUMMER, loneliness of first time,
Swann, 251
CAMPBELL, DESY, courage to go on,
212; loneliness, 253; real fear, 302;
greatest fear, 350

CAMPERDOWN ESTATE, in Nassau,
Ferguson, 24
CAMPING
counselor takes charge, Brunson, 143
listening to bagpipes on Arkansas
creek, Rockefeller, 237
nature sights, Cross, 336
with family a special pleasure,
Brunson, 190; Sammons, 40
with father, Rockefeller, 39; Buettner,
240
CANCER
a childhood mentor lives with, Platt,
117
losing a friend to, Berman, 346;
Brown, 349; Cooney, 344; Munro,
344; Platt, 117; Rochelle, 343
mistaken case of, Bornn, 82
teaching value of life, Cross, 83
as threat, Rockefeller, 231
CANOEING, with father, Buettner, 240
CAPE COD, Platt, 25
CAREERS, see VOCATIONS
CARS
first rides in, Callwood, 35
Ford Model A, Lear, 34
Ford Sedans, Emmerling, 140
Hudsons, Lear, 34
making a convertible, Marston, 21
a regret on Jost Van Dyke, Callwood,
364
riding with sister, Sammons, 124
rolling over leg, Englander, 13
Oldsmobile with speed, Kemp, 19
problems with on islands, Thomas,
201
as something that shines, Prickett, 21
as a success symbol, Rochelle, 158
wrecking father's, Colquhoun, 44
CARTOONIST, impact of Charles Addams
on budding, Emmerling, 166
CASH REGISTER, good for storing Sugar
Babies, Prickett, 158

CASKET, first sight of, Hiers, 76
CASTLE
Bonskeid, Barbour family home, 280
buying your own, Taufer, 218
Foulis, Munro, 150
CATALINA ISLAND, CALIFORNIA,
Brackett, 34, 154
CATS
eighteen in a will, Kahl, 209
lost in household fire, Kahl, 300
no more than nine lives, Thomas, 78
nuzzling, Edmondson, 312
raised as dogs, M. Plimpton, 289
at a palace, Munro, 67
watching Plimpton shave, 69
CAVE, the discovery of a cave system,
Rose, 247
CELEBRITIES, unexpectedly meeting
Fellini, Roberts, 233
CENTRAL PARK, skating in, Royce, 33
CHAIR, as treasured possession,
McIntyre, 107
CHALLENGES
conquering fear of water, Hallett, 245
as incentive, McIntyre, 209
losing weight, Burke, 384
rebuilding a business, Prowse, 206;
Englander, 173, 226
CHANGE
of plans leads to discovery, Rose, 247
a teacher's ability to change her
ideas, Peter, 119
thoughts on, Cooney, 335
CHEATING, getting caught, Jaxhiemer, 44
CHECKBOOK, heaven is not having to
balance one, Sutton 163
CHEERLEADERS, don't try too hard to
be one, Lear, 193
CHICAGO, ILLINOIS
Andrews, 110
a southern nanny leaves for, Brown, 169
CHICKEN POX, Waite, 11; Perkins, 12

CHICKENS
Brown, 23; see also COCKERELS
CHILDHOOD ACCIDENTS, see
ACCIDENTS, CHILDHOOD
CHILDHOOD ADVENTURES, see
ADVENTURE
CHILDHOOD HANGOUTS
gas stations, Hallett, 118
police stations, McIntyre, 118
CHILDHOOD ILLNESSES see also
specific ailment
bedridden for a year, Prowse, 206
chicken pox, Waite, 11; Perkins, 12
measles, Emmerling, 13
mumps and a treat, Mason, 239
rheumatic fever means school by
phone, Holloway, 60
CHILDHOOD INFLUENCES
policeman, McIntyre, 118
teachers, Kelly, 119
CHILDHOOD INTERESTS, as a precursor
to livelihood, Cook, 133
CHILDHOOD LEARNING EXPERIENCES
all ideas aren't good ideas, Waite, 61
admiration for a classmate can change
life, Plimpton, 122
baking with grandmother, Hackman, 8
curiosity causes accident, Rochelle, 6
dignity and hand-me-down clothes,
Holloway, 289
don't release car brakes, Englander 13
eating dirt, Marston, 7
families can cause fear, Hanson, 12
families stick together, Bornn, 20
family tragedy observed, Lear, 7
father more understanding than you
think, Prickett, 94
father teaches daughter to be self-
sufficient, Learson, 38
fishing not for kids, Beacham, 14
grandmothers as energetic teachers,
Burke, 125
grandmother's strictness, Strobel, 9

impulse is a dangerous childhood
trait, Rochelle, 60

intelligent people can change their
position, Peter, 119

limited expectations, Friedman, 11

memory of smells affects the present,
Roberts, 12

miracle of electric lights, Johnson, 22

mother as a comforter, Brunson, 12

playing in the makeup, Lear, 11

radio is a new miracle, Sutton, 28

Santa arrives in helicopter, Sultan, 18

stepsisters can be as close as real
sisters, Hallett, 23

summer camp, loneliness of first time,
Swann, 251

threats that work with children,
Callwood, 8

trying the unknown, Mason, 131

you can't trust everybody, Munro, 252

CHILDREN, see chapters 2, 4, 6, and 8
in particular

adopting, first moments with,
Colquhoun, 238

as best friends, Robertson, 270

birth defects seen in positive vein,
Johnson, 222

a cure for loneliness, Beacham, 256

fantasy life gets Roberts through sad
childhood, 253

father's joy in watching grow, Platt 238

going off to camp, Swann, 251

impact of war, Lear, 291

importance of sharing with, Rockefeller,
350

make you feel young, Callwood, 360;
Bridge Club, 359

physically impaired child responds,
Prowse, 287

reunion with after years, Perkins, 135

protection from violence important,
Colquhoun, 291

safety counseling, Prowse, 323

as simple pleasure, Cooney, 186

worth waiting for, Brunson, 387

CHOCOLATE COOKIES, Duke remembers,
9

CHRISTIANITY, as an exclusionary force,
Peter, 220

CHRISTMAS

can lead to lonely time, Campbell,
253

drug addiction acknowledged at,
Marston, 225

family sadness during, Warrington, 346

grandmother teaches lessons at,
Goddard, 128

a nanny makes special, Munro, 127

putting "ointments" on the tree,
Johnson, 274

a special North Dakota snowy Christmas,
Mason, 239

tree as family project, Prickett, 186

unusual job at, Brunson, 153

CHURCH

do you need one to be religious?
Peter, 220

Holy Rollers, Preston, 63

CHURCH WORKERS, the influence of,
Waite, 127

CHUTZPA

a good quality in acting, Beacham, 167

who's afraid of the big boys? Emmerling,
166

CIGARETTES

Rockefeller, 72

the cop missed the cigarette, Burke, 232

quitting, Hackman, 388

CITY FATHERS, a portrait, Peter, 220

CIVIL WAR, THE

family fortune start in, Cook, 281

family skeletons come out, Cook, 280

CIVIL RIGHTS MOVEMENT, fear in,
Colquhoun, 301

CLAMMING, with grandfather, Learson,
121

CLOCK TOWER, as hiding place, Silvia Munro, 30

CLOSENESS
death of brother disrupts family, Edmondson, 254
death of spouse removes, Bailey, 255; Sutton, 255
of a mother and father, Plimpton, 270
of grandparents, Ferguson, 271

CLOTHES
a dress for mother, Costigan, 140
hand-me-downs, Munro, 56; Holloway, 289
not wool for the islands, Brackett, 214
picking out college wardrobe, Sichveland, 140

CNN, Friedman, 217

COACHES, as influence on life, Retton, 117

COCA-COLA, crates make good steps, Strobel, 164

COCAINE
an addict takes control of his life, Marston, 225
loneliness during use, Keefe, 260
recognizing a problem, Keefe, 320
telling parents about use, Keefe, 94

COCKEREL, as pet, Munro, 67

COCKTAILS
first drink is with parents, Hallett, 143
martini's *cachong*, Vonnegut, 188
special island drinks a specialty, Donovan, 242

COCO, JIMMY, and food, Roberts, 281

COINCIDENCE, see "Serendipity," chapter 34, p. 214

COLBYS, THE, dying goldfish lead to a starring role, Beacham, 215

COLEMAN, REVEREND, Strobel, 9

COLLEGE COURSES, see also GUT COURSES

COLLEGE
consequences of cutting class, Plimpton, 176

a professor's impact, Randolph, 265
still trying, Retton, 364

COLLOQUIALISMS, southern, Johnson, 116

COLQUHOUN, EDWARD, first memory, 15; special moment with parent, 44; mortality, 87; dream, 101; person who influenced, 116; adult with parents, 146; finding work, 172; threat, 230; treat, 234; special private moment, 238; funny story, 275; a compassionate moment, 291; real fear, 301; something sweet, 311; a self-discovery, 324; birds flying south, 336; greatest fear, 352; fear for children, 357; legacy, 370; something you want to do, 378

COMANECI, NADIA, watching, Retton, 43

COMFORT
a boulder provides it to a lonely child, Learson, 258
hugs provide, Brunson, 12; Waite, 81
giving to a dying person, Roberts, 85; Brown, 349

COMICS, Preston, 10

COMMITMENT, sometimes circumstances control us, Rockefeller, 209

COMPASSION, see "An Unexpected Moment Provoking Compassion," chapter 47, p. 285

COMPETITION, see "Your Moment of Glory in Sports," chapter 30, p. 192

COMPETITIVENESS, impact of, Retton, 174

CONCH SHELLS, cleaning, Donovan, 72

CONEY ISLAND, a summer job on, Lear, 153

CONFIDENCE, see also SELF-CONFIDENCE
optimistic outlook builds, Emmerling, 375
a teacher helps instill, Holloway, 132

CONFUSION, when did you say you were coming? Costigan, 257

CONNECTICUT, WESTPORT, Lear, 34

CONTRIBUTING, as a sign of adulthood, Colquhoun, 146

CONVERSATION
exchange of ideas with Russian women, Bornn, 246
importance of, Andrews, 109
COOK, EMILY, early friendship, 57; pet, 68; breath away, 73; person who influenced, 133; serendipity, 216; funny story, 281; a self-discovery, 320; fear for children, 356; legacy, 369
COOK, RODNEY, early memories, 27; early friendship, 62; person who influenced, 133; special private moment, 239; loneliness, 259; funny story, 280; something sweet, 311
COOKE, HARRY HUTCHESON, Perkins, 44
COOKIE JAR, really caught with hand in, Costigan, 92
COOKIES, as a cause of accidents, Peck, 17
COOKING, see also FOOD
over fireplaces, Hallett, 120
potatoes, Fish, 29
a simple pleasure, McIntyre, 190
COONEY, GERRY, breath away, 75; mortality, 88; treasured possession, 106; adult with parents, 142; money, 161; failing, 178; simple pleasure, 186; glory in sports, 195; give up, 203; special private moment, 239; rainy afternoon 263; real fear, 296; birds flying south, 335; burying a friend, 344; fear for children, 356
COONEY, GERRY, watching on TV, Andrews, 109
COOPERATION, birds an example, Colquhoun, 336
CORNERSTONE, at Majority Baptist Church, 9
COSTIGAN, MARY, early friendship, 61; awkward with a parent, 92; treasured possession, 108; adult with parents, 140; on friendship, 191; simple pleasures, 191; loneliness, 257; funny story, 273; fear for children, 356; greatest fear, 352

COUNSELORS, as major influence, Berman, 130
COUNTRY MUSIC, funny stories about, Buck Johnson, 241
COURAGE, see "What Gives You Courage to Go On?" chapter 33, p. 208
Boy Scout learns courage on a mountain, Bornn, 288
dying people need to be touched, Roberts, 85
equated to dancing, Roberts, 212
faith in God gives it to you, Sutton, 210
feeding cats can even give it to you, Kahl, 209
finding good in potential tragedy, Johnson, 222
a friend faces death, Emery, 341; Munro, 344
a friend lives with cancer, Platt, 117
getting over drugs teaches lesson, Keefe, 260
librarian faces real danger in Vietnam, Randolph, 296
a mother teaches, Mason, 213
multiple hardships can't stop you, Prowse, 206
not wanting to know is courage, Roberts, 236
old age takes it, Sutton, 201
a parentless child faces life, Strobel, 164
sometimes we have no choice, Rockefeller, 209
standing up for beliefs, Brunson, 324
surviving an attack, Hanson, 314
Tiananmen Square example, Miller, 288
woman faces fighter pilot underwater test, Hallett 245
COURTING, see also DATING
a fire truck is nice, Roberts, 266
under the preacher's eye, Wing, 30
COUSINS
how big an air conditioner, Johnson, 272
staying with Cousin Myrtis, Sutton, 10

COVETING, brother's toys, Kahl, 13
COWS
  escaping, Wing, 92
  milking, Kemp, 30
CRACK, SEE COCAINE
CREATIVITY
  aided by loneliness, Legere, 254
  composing music, Preston, 330
CRIB, Zar Rochelle remembers, 6
CRICKET CLUB, drinking at, Perkins, 44
CRIME, see MUGGING
CROSS, DOROTHY, first memory, 7; special
  moment with parent, 48; early friendship, 59; mortality, 83; treasured
  possession, 104; adult with parent, 139;
  vile thing, 284; real fear, 300; a self-
  discovery, 328; birds flying south, 336
CROSS-COUNTRY, a thirteen-year-old's
  triumph, Miller, 199
CROWN, wearing to school, Munro, 56
CRUELTY TO ANIMALS, worse than to
  people, Sultan, 290
CRUELTY, potential for, T. Plimpton, 322
CRUSHES, see SWEETHEARTS
CRYING
  at birth of son, Swann, 322
  as a child, Beacham, 14; Friedman, 35
  at the death of a brother, Brunson,
  223
  loneliness of boarding school, Munro,
  252
  on way home, Callwood, 8
  over realization of death, Plimpton,
  79; Waite, 81; Lear, 82
  when mentor dies, Buettner, 121
CURIOSITY, the importance of in life,
  McIntyre, 115
CURSING, SEE PROFANITY

DANCING
  at Disney World job, Emery, 172
  special college dance, Sutton, 37

  memories of as child, Burke, 32
  as a metaphor for courage, Roberts, 212
  with hula hoops, Brunson, 153
DANGER, see also "A Moment of Real
  Fear," chapter 49, p. 296
  a cobra attack in Laos, Sultan, 230
DARTS, throwing at a sister's back, Lear, 54
DATEBOOKS, treasuring a grandmother's,
  Andrews, 20
DATING
  apples and men, a dangerous combo,
  · Strobel, 264
  at ice-skating rink, Buettner, 32
  can be a real fear, Miller, 302
  a fire truck is nice, Roberts, 266
  a first meeting, Cook, 133
  grownups do it this way, Emmerling
  and Learson, 386
  memories of first dates, Wing, 30
  and misrepresenting age, T. Plimpton, 96
DAUGHTER, see also chapters 6, 14, 20;
  FATHER and MOTHER
  caring for ill father, Learson, 148
  hunting with dad, Hallett, 41
  Peyton's special, Goddard, 353
  riding with mother, Sammons, 186
  wanting to be close to father, Legere, 91
DEADLINES, it's good to have them,
  Rochelle, 209
DEAFNESS, a young girl overcomes,
  Beacham, 167
DEATH, see "Your First Intimation of
  Mortality," chapter 12, p. 76, and
  "Burying a Friend," chapter 56, p.
  343
  accepting it because of accident,
  Peter, 87
  baby's death brings grief, healing,
  Abrams, 249
  brings radical change, Platt, 79
  child's innocent questions, Emery, 84
  child's responsibility for, Emmerling,
  77

comforting a dying person you love,
  Roberts, 85
crying over, Plimpton, 79; Lear, 82
daughter dies, Spezzano, 84
father dies, Platt, 79; Abrams, 36
father's sense of humor in face of,
  Rochelle, 277
fear that goodness will bring an early,
  Learson, 80
fear of, Retton, 352
fish by the thousands makes you
  think, Marston, 290
funny story, Perkins, 44
grandmother's, Prowse, 80
how to handle impending, Roberts, 85
hunting teaches about, Barbour, 81
ignoring, Cooney, 88; Swann, 88
lifetime relationship rises from,
  Brunson, 218
lightning kills, Sutton, 78
mother is told good-bye, Emery, 84
mother's conversation about, Mason, 78
of mother, Prowse, 255; Berman, 254
of brother, Litton, 222; Brunson, 223;
  Edmondson, 254; Houlihan, 348
of a son, how to accept it, Brown,
  224; Dorrance, 380
of a spouse, facing first night alone,
  Sutton, 255
of a spouse, missing his touch, Bailey,
  255
pet sheep, Munro, 81
pets teaching about, Keefe, 68
realization of depresses as child,
  Rochelle, 79
relationship to food, Waite, 81
scuba death impacts rescuer,
  Ferguson, 291
several lead to uneasy realization,
  Edmondson, 146
Uncle Ozzie's sea burial, Mockler, 343
young doctor's inability to stop it,
  Andrews, 285

DEBUTANTE BALL, meeting spouse at,
  Cook, 133
DECISION MAKING
  learning how, Barbour, 317
  Retton, 317
  makes you an adult, Kelly, 143
DEER, hunting with father, Hallett, 41
DEGRANDPRE, DAVE, first memory, 18;
  special moment with parent, 47; early
  friendship, 58; awkward with a
  parent, 93; treasured possession, 107;
  a person who influenced, 131; money,
  161; simple pleasure, 185; give up,
  202; lowest moment, 225; treat, 233;
  loneliness, 258; rainy afternoon, 263;
  real fear, 305; a self-discovery, 318
DENMARK, see MUNRO, SILVIA
DEPRESSION
  a famous boxer handles, Cooney, 203
  learning there are choices, Hanson, 210
DEPRESSION, THE
  a fear, Costigan, 356
  a vivid summary, McIntyre, 190
DESK, a grandmother's brings back
  memories, Andrews, 103
DETENTION HALL, a cow sends him to
  one, Wing, 92
DETERMINATION
  accepting what's happening,
    Robertson, 208
  active at eighty, Brown, 362
  at times we have no choice,
    Rockefeller, 209
  better than talent, Buettner, 211
  big dreams help you keep it, Burke, 211
  a boxer takes control of his life,
    Cooney, 203
  brother raises brothers and sisters,
    Hiers 222
  child raises self, Berman, 254
  conquering weight problem, Burke, 384
  a daughter learns the value of, M.
    Plimpton, 212

faith keeps an island museum going, Donovan 204

getting over drugs teaches lesson, Keefe, 209

how to get through the day, Emery, 208

making yourself enjoy life, Swann, 208

mother wins parking battle, Rochelle, 277

overcoming a problem, Cook 320

a portrait of a man's lifelong, Prowse, 206

prevents mugging, Platt, 301

a Russian metaphor, Roberts, 212

setbacks on bike trek require, Buettner, 228

to keep going, Sutton, 334

to live fully in face of death, Emery, 341

winning the gold after failing, Retton, 229

a woman voices hers, Brown, 205

DETROIT, MICHIGAN

Emmerling, 13; 98

Johnson, 38

DICKERSON, JIM, Rogers, 339

DIET BOOKS, as treasured possessions, 104

DIETING, Jimmy Coco's diet plan, Roberts, 281

DIGGING HOLES, Edmondson, 55

DIGNITY

a grandmother teaches, Goddard, 128

hand-me-down clothes teach, Holloway, 289

in face of grief, Ferguson, 347

memory of father's, Abrams, 36

DINGHIES, Callwood, 35

DINNER PARTIES

how to give, Perkins, 372

table mate boosts career, Cook, 216

DIRECTORS, THEATER, as major influence, Holloway, 132

DIRT

eating as a child, Marston, 7

playing in mud, Peck, 264

DISAPPROVAL, parental, Legere, 91

DISCIPLINE

father as a disciplinarian, Colquhoun, 44

harsh, Callwood, 35

remembered, Strobel, 9

DISCOVERY, of an island cave system, Rose, 247

DISEASE, see ILLNESS and specific diseases

DISGUSTING THINGS, see "Vile Things," chapter 46, p. 283

DISILLUSIONMENT

a child's friends leave her, Campbell, 253

for a Scout, Peter, 220

going nowhere, Cooney, 203

DISNEY WORLD, where dancing irons work hard, Emery, 172

DIVING

for quarters, an unusual job, Brackett, 154

into a pool, a simple pleasure, Vonnegut, 188

Keefe wins championship, 47

DIVING, SCUBA-

compassionate moment on wreck of *Titanic,* Mockler, 285

dramatic under ice experience, Englander, 248

a scuba death brings mortality eye-to-eye, Ferguson, 291

stuck in a submarine at 1,000 feet, Mockler, 296

DIVORCE

calming anger unusually, Perkins, 256

dealing with loneliness it brings, Beacham, 256

as failure, Thomas, 178

impact on children, "Hanging Together," 50; Andrews, 258

retreating to woods to deal with, Robertson, 264

starting over, Rose, 319; Perkins, 333

unexpected, Emmerling, 226

DOCTORS
  grandfather seldom saw, Perkins, 44
  grief for a patient, Andrews, 277
  son of, Kemp, 38
  wanting to be, Bailey, 170
DOGS
  any old dog brings pleasure, Marston, 185
  at tea parties, Randolph, 14
  death of, Hanson, 67; Beacham, 76; Robertson, 77
  gets child in trouble, Emery, 69
  Gordon Setters, Hallett, 41
  Labrador raises cats, Plimpton, 289
  treasured possessions, Randolph, 104
  wire-haired terrier, a gift, Strobel, 67
DOGSLEDS, riding in, Mockler, 248
DOLLS
  as first gift, Johnson, 38
  playing with as child, Johnson, 115
DOMINOES, Preston, 10
DONOVAN, EGBERT, breath away, 72; adult with parents, 145; simple pleasure, 189; give up, 204; special private moment, 242; greatest fear, 351; something worth waiting for, 385
DORRANCE, JEAN, birds flying south, 337; "Things Are Going to Be Better," a portrait, 380; something you want to do, 377
DR. SEUSS, meeting as a special moment, Kahl, 242
DRAGONS, in dreams, Emmerling, 98
DREAMING
  can give you courage, Burke, 211
  fantasy life gets Roberts through sad childhood, 253
  why not be a writer? Kahl, 174
DREAMS, see also "A Vivid Dream," chapter 15, p. 98
  coming true, Rockefeller, 101
  enjoying them, Platt, 99

sleeping position brings back same dream, Swann, 100
understanding father because of them, Lear, 47
DRESSAGE, an amateur wins a national championship, Houlihan 196
DRINKING
  and driving, M. Plimpton, 95
  boarding school treat, DeGrandpre, 233
  chef makes special drinks, Donovan, 242
  effect on son, Johnson, 93
  teenage drinking bout embarrasses, Sultan, 225
  unexpectedly changes life to better, Brackett, 214
DRIVING
  beware of tractor driver, McIntyre, 159
  early memories of, Lear, 34
  a father's fears, Swann, 355
  first long trip by self, Waite, 144
  learning as sixth-grader, Kemp, 38
  makes you feel young, Rockefeller, 360
  produces fear on Tortola, Thomas, 302
  a rite of passage, P. and T. Sammons, 141; Emmerling, 140; Waite, 142
  special time with mother, Sammons, 186
DRUG ADDICTION, a young man takes control of life, Marston, 225
DRUGS, see also ALCOHOL, COCAINE
  loneliness of dependency, Keefe, 260
  overcoming addiction, Marston, 225; Keefe, 209
  smoking banana peels isn't recommended, Thomas, 262
  tragic effect of abuse on babies, Learson, 185
DUCK HUNTING
  with family, Brunson, 190
  with popgun, Mockler, 26
DUCKS, as pets, Jensen, 66
DUKE, RICHARD, first memory, 9; treasured possession, 105; summer job, 156; art, 180; simple pleasure,

187; a compassionate moment, 287;
unusual friendship, 339; regrets, 364

EAST BERLIN, a powerful, symbolic
moment in, Burke, 246
EASTER
memories of in Florida, Plimpton, 25
a perfect time for a funeral,
Edmondson, 117
singing hymn comforts, Waite, 81
ECCENTRICITY, seeing the value of,
Beacham, 113
ECOLOGY
gliding ecologically sound, Robertson,
194
goal to preserve island life, Callwood,
161
ECOSYSTEMS, is that tank really self-
sustaining? Jensen, 188
EDMONDSON, NANCY, early friendship,
55; person who influenced, 117; adult
with parents, 146; special private
moment, 244; funny story, 274; vile
thing, 284; feel young, 360
EDMONDSON, ERIC, early friendship,
55; pet, 69; person who influenced,
117; adult with parents, 146;
loneliness, 254; vile thing, 284;
something sweet, 312; legacy, 368
EGGS, worse than eating fish on Friday,
Kahl, 272
EGYPT, riding horses in the desert of,
McIntyre, 244
EICHELBURGER, ETHEL, Legere, 345
ELEVATORS
good place to meet future wife,
Warrington, 216
insight strikes in, Cooney, 75
ELIZABETH I, studying, McIntyre, 115
EMBARRASSMENT, see ''An Awkward
Moment with a Parent,'' chapter 14,
p. 91
caused by death of pet, Robertson, 77

EMBRACING, at time of tragedy, Lear, 7
EMERY, JOHN, pet, 69; mortality, 84;
dream, 101; adult with parents, 145;
work, 172; give up, 204; courage to
go on, 208; something sweet, 311;
Burying a Friend: Martin Hoose, a
portrait, 341; fear for children, 356;
feel young, 361; legacy, 371
EMMERLING, JOHN, first memory, 13;
special moment with parent, 46;
breath away, 71; mortality, 77; dream,
98; person who influenced, 114; adult
with parents, 140; work, 166; art,
180; lowest moment, 226; loneliness,
260; rainy afternoon, 267; legacy,
375; something worth waiting for, 386
EMOTION
father finally shows some, Keefe, 47
father's at birth of child, Swann, 322
music and thoughts of freedom bring,
Burke, 246
ENCAMPMENTS, see FORTS
ENCOURAGEMENT
important in child's growth, Andrews,
110
teachers give, Kelly, 119; Waite, 119;
Sultan, 120; Kahl, 123; Houlihan, 131
ENDURANCE
discovering your own, Plimpton, 212
a surprise, Mason, 326
ENGLAND, see also WORLD WAR II,
MEMORIES OF
early memories, Rose, 13; Bailey, 28
ENGLANDER, JOHN, first memory, 13;
work, 173; serendipity, 217; lowest
moment, 226; special private moment,
248; real fear, 306; something worth
waiting for, 385
ENJOYING LIFE
do it or die, Swann, 208
never dull-eyed, Mason, 350
ENNUI, as an attitude, Swann, 74

ENTERTAINING
first party makes feel like adult, Edmundson, 146
a parental legacy, Perkins, 372
ENTREPRENEURSHIP
busking with bagpipes, Munro, 150
pine cones up in smoke, Johnson, 153
starting a lawn-maintenance company, Royce, 156
EPIPHANIES, worth waiting for, Vonnegut, 383
EQUALITY
desire for one's child, Colquhoun, 357
don't ignore this female soccer ace, McIntyre, 198
family sets the standard, Hackman, 367
a family value, Taufer, 368
in Tortola society, Thomas, 326
mother is a good mechanic, Colquhoun, 275
ESKIMOS
as friend, Hiers, 59
peering through ice hole, Englander, 248
ESSAYS, winning a contest, Bunny Johnson, 240
EXETER, see Phillips Exeter Academy
EXPECTATIONS
as challenge, McIntyre, 209
limited, Friedman, 11

FAILING, see chapter 26, p. 176; see also GIVING UP
accepting it and going on, Robertson, 208
attitude for handling, Prowse, 206
avoiding, Rogers, 202
getting over drugs teaches lesson, Keefe, 209
is OK, Friedman, 178
learning from, Platt, 203
no big deal, Munro, 178
there's no such thing, Marston, 178
winning after failure, Retton, 229

worse than death, Hiers, 350
yourself, T. Plimpton, 176
FAIRS, memory of, Sultan, 18
FAITH
at times it doesn't appear to work, Andrews, 285
close-minded is dangerous, DeGrandpre, 202
death of baby tests, Abrams, 249
father's in a daughter, Cross, 48
gives you courage to go on, Sutton, 210
God controls the life and budget, Brown, 210
in yourself, Retton, 376
island museum stays open because of owner's, Donovan 204
planting seeds, Abrams, 370
role in accepting son's death, Brown, 224
FALL, see AUTUMN
FALLING FROM BRIDGE, Brunson, 12
FAMILY
adults visiting parents brings out kid, Holloway, 147
a brother raises his brothers and sisters, Hiers, 222
couple spends unusual time together, McIntyre, 244
impact of illness on, Royce, 89
importance of love, Dorrance, 380
importance of caring for, Brown, 311
importance of pride in, Duke, 287
its love keeps you going, Sutton, 210
mother's life sets daughter's milestone, Abrams, 242
phones calls from a simple pleasure, Sutton, 186
teaches about the world, Bornn, 186
unexpected divorce breaks up, Emmerling, 226
loneliness being away from on exotic trip, Buettner, 251

learning the importance of, Perkins, 135

a special child strengthens, Goddard, 353

FAMILY PICTURE, as treasured possession, Royce, 104

FAMILY TRADITIONS

attending the same school, Waite, 41

children at their own table, Randolph, 39

FARMING

childhood memories of, Cross, 7; Rockefeller, 8; Brown, 23

funny childhood memories, McIntyre, 159

great-grandfather buys a tractor, Perkins, 367

makes a child an adult, Cross, 139

FATALISM, a librarian learns about it in Vietnam, Randolph, 296

FATHER

as role model, Abrams, 36; Abrams, 373; Fish, 369; Keefe, 369

as protector, Fish, 35

awkward moments with, DeGrandpre, 93; G. Plimpton, 96; Royce, 89

communicating with, Berman, 144; Degrandpre, 47; M.Plimpton, 48

death of wife changes role, Fish, 143

disappointment and hero, Lear, 34

domino player, Preston, 10

emotion in for the first time, Keefe, 47

friends would be nice dual role, Royce, 89

holding first baby, Swann, 322

holding hands with, Beacham, 32

illness gives daughter bigger role, Learson, 148

job well done impresses, Edmundson, 146

larger than life, Lear, 7

Lear wished he'd been a better one; 178

living without, Royce, 89

model of self-discipline, Plimpton, 374

never knowing, Friedman, 11; Roberts, 253

punished by, Callwood, 35

special moment camping with, Buettner, 240

special hike with a son, Goddard, 245

standing up to, Cooney, 142

sympathetic, Prickett, 94

teach daughters, Beacham, 45

teacher of unusual talents for a girl, Learson, 38

thoughts on, Miller, 365

trip with, Sutton, 10; Waite, 15

FAUCETS, Buettner, 36

FEAR, see "A Moment of Real Fear," chapter 49, p. 296; "Your Greatest Fear," chapter 57, p. 350; and "A Fear for Your Children," chapter 59, p. 355

comes from the unknown, Cooney, 296

dealing with it, Campbell, 212

deep ocean, big whales, their world, Jensen, 303

as a drive on a pretty island, Thomas, 302

equated with sexual feelings, Legere, 307

faucets can drown a kid, Buettner, 36

girls bring it, Miller, 302

gunfire in Vietnam, Randolph, 296

nearly drowning on a bridge, Wing, 304

none in civil rights march, Colquhoun, 301

of discovery saves life, Plimpton, 299

of fire, Hackman, 299

of being weighed, Taufer, 301

of dangerous surgery as a child, Campbell, 302

quick thinking prevents mugging, Platt, 301

river blocks streetcar, Hames, 304

singing a solo, Burke, 73

strangled by ski ropes, Litton, 305

stuck in a submarine at 1,000 feet, Mockler, 296

stuck on a pyramid, Brackett, 304
terror on a Russian river, Buettner, 298
tough moments in a glider,
Robertson, 309
troops desert soldier in World War II,
Peck, 297
what's that knocking outside?
Johnson 307
FEELINGS, brothers talk at drug
treatment center, Keefe, 260
FELLINI, an expected meeting with,
Roberts, 233
FEMININITY, doesn't equate with frailty,
McIntyre, 198
FERGUSON, OLLIE, early memories, 24;
holding hands, 33; dream, 100;
person who influenced, 114; adult
with parents, 145; special private
moment, 243; a special relationship,
271; a compassionate moment, 291;
with the whales and Jensen, 303;
burying a friend, 347; legacy, 375
FERRIS WHEELS, Sultan, 18
FIANCÉE, holding hands with, Royce, 98
FINANCIAL INDEPENDENCE, the need for
in old age, Sichveland 162
FINANCIAL SECURITY
fear of losing, Prowse, 351
as something that shines, Sichveland, 21
wish for one's child, Costigan, 356
FINDLEY, JOHNNY, Edmondson, 55
FIRE
fear of, Hackman, 299
near-death in darkened house, Kahl, 300
a tragic war story, Cross, 284
FIREPLACES, father and baby sleep
before, Cook, 239
FIRE TRUCKS, nice way to meet future
husband, Roberts, 266
FIREWORKS
grandfather uses shotgun as,
Emmerling, 13
a treat with grandfather, Waite, 243

FISH, HAMILTON, early memories, 29;
special moment with parent, 35;
early friendship, 57; adult with
parents, 143; simple pleasure, 184; a
compassionate moment, 286; a self-
discovery, 317; legacy, 369
FISH
fear of dying goldfish starts Hollywood
career, Beacham, 215
fried, an awful smell, Roberts, 12
interest in leads to important discovery,
Rose, 247
lizard fish, Bornn, 40
memories of sitting in car with dead fish,
Swann, 25
FISHERMAN, watching, Jost Van Dyke,
Hanson, 19
FISHING, COMMERCIAL
death on a large scale, Marston, 290
as vocation, Marston, 146; Marston, 175
FISHING
catching first, Litton, 39
lifelong fisherman catches first
marlin, Callwood, 197
not going because of age, Beacham, 14
sign of independence, Marston, 175
with strong-minded daughter,
Robertson, 275
with parents, but never catching,
Sammons, 40
with a hand line, Bornn, 40
FISHTANK, as a simple pleasure, Jensen,
188
FITZGERALD, ELLA, memories of
listening to, Legere, 43
FIXING THINGS, as a simple pleasure,
Andrews, 184
FLEXIBLE FLYER, Lear, 7
FLORIDA
Boca Raton, starting life again,
Perkins, 256
Cocoa Beach, pines grow again,
Emery, 340

Ormond Beach, Plimpton, 25
Tampa Bay, Swann, 25
Winter Park, Emery, 69
FLOWERS
buying for mother, Emmerling, 46
lead to marriage proposal, H. Barbour,
237
roses help Beacham's loneliness,
Beacham, 256
FLYING
dawn flight, Emmerling, 71
in dreams, Colquhoun, 101
thunderstorm nightmares, McIntyre, 231
plane lands, community turns out,
Johnson, 294
a fearful moment, Hallett, 308;
Rockefeller, 309; Robertson, 309
FOLK MEDICINE, Callwood, 35
FOOD, see also individual items
Aunt Hazel's pie, Preston, 311
baking with grandmother, Hackman, 8
double-chocolate cookies, Duke, 9
famed crepes, Sultan, 312
fixing for the preacher, a tradition,
Strobel, 9
hot cakes in the wild, Marston, 312
Jimmy Coco's diet plan, Roberts, 281
learning to be a good cook, Strobel, 164
old woman eats garbage, Buettner, 292
smell of grandmother's leads to
conversation, Cook, 133
unexpected treat, Miller, 235
unusual Peruvian lunch, Buettner, 284
FOOTBALL
a hero who wasn't there, Bornn, 194
heros, horrors, McIntyre, 193
in dreams, Marston, 100
they think you're better than you are,
Lear, 192
twenty seconds to go, Kelly, 193
FOREIGN SERVICE, Fish, 29
FORTS
digging, Edmondson, 55

large planters as, Cook, 62
a sister's housekeeping chores in one,
Retton, 54
FOXES
in the hen house (really), Munro, 67
as pet, Sultan, 68
FOXHOLES, digging, Edmondson, 55
FRANCE
early memories of Paris, Plimpton, 6
a surprising time, Miller, 47
FREEDOM
American woman talks with Russian
women, 246
first drive in car gives sense of,
Emmerling, 140
mother's attitude about, Platt, 42
powerful moment in East Berlin,
Burke, 246
FRIEDMAN, SONYA, first memory, 11;
things that shine, 19; special moment
with parent, 35; breath away, 74;
mortality, 83; treasured possession,
109; person who influenced, 129;
failing, 178; glory in sports, 197;
serendipity, 217; loneliness, 256; a
self-discovery, 319; feel young, 363;
regrets, 365
FRIEDMAN, DR. LEAH HECHT-, 129
FRIENDS, see "An Early Friendship,"
chapter 8, p. 54, and "An Unusual
Friendship," chapter 54, p. 337
hide one from bad times at home,
Hanson, 59, 227
parents as, McIntyre, 43
unexpected visits with on a boat,
Peter, 233
watching television together in the
yard, Hames, 234
your children are the best, Robertson,
270
FRIENDSHIP, see chapters 8 and 54
demonstrated by fellow pilots,
Hallett, 308

efforts to be together, Cross, 59
grandmother's, Legere, 271
grandparents' special, Ferguson, 271
in marriage, Rockefeller, 338
last days with Harry, Rochelle, 343
the last service, Brown, 349
lifelong friends, a dialogue, Bridge
    Club, 191
lifetime friendships, Roberts, 281
long distance with Yugoslavian,
    Sultan, 340
long-term, "Hanging Together," 50
making new friends, Rockefeller, 233
mother and father's special, Plimpton,
    270
phone home, don't hold hands,
    Hallett, 268
and rainy days, Randolph, 265
upstairs/downstairs beginning, Peck, 216
FROG WALLOW WADDLE contest,
    Prickett, 199
FUNERALS, see "Burying a Friend,"
    chapter 56, p. 343
    mother's, HIERS, 76
FUNNY STORIES, see "Friends and Family
    at Their Funniest," chapter 45, p. 272
ace the exam, flunk the course,
    Plimpton, 176
are you Irish? Spezzano, 337
aunt's routine stays the same,
    Edmondson 274
backing that tricycle, Johnson, 16
beating the bees home, Callwood, 8
busking with bagpipes leads to jail,
    Munro, 150
a call from Olivier, Roberts, 236
dying to drive the tractor, McIntyre, 159
dying with humor, Rochelle, 277
eggs are worse than fish on Fridays
    Kahl, 272
famous last words, Perkins, 44
fire engine substitutes for doorbell,
    Roberts, 266

get a haircut! Plimpton, 96
grandmother at the opera, Burke, 277
grandmother pours milk in camera,
    Prickett, 276
grandmothers and answering
    machines, Prickett, 276
a hand in the cookie jar, Costigan, 92
hiking an interception, McIntyre, 193
a human dart board, Lear, 54
importance of positive attitudes,
    Robertson 275
Jimmy Coco's diet plan, Roberts, 281
jump, Charlie! Rochelle, 60
jury duty isn't like television,
    Holloway, 279
just how old did you say? T.
    Plimpton, 96
making your own convertible,
    Marston, 21
malapropistic friends, Johnson, 274
Mama's back trouble, Johnson, 27
marijuana and grandmother, Andrews,
    273
mother as mechanic, Colquhoun, 275
a preacher who hollered big,
    Johnson, 54
problem of mistaken identity,
    Costigan, 273
put the baby in an adult size
    fourteen, Brunson, 275
Sardis Frog Wallow Waddle, Prickett,
    199
sleepwalking and the dog, Munro, 276
they've killed Gail with that plane,
    Johnson, 294
an unforgettable debut, Cook, 133
volunteering for a spanking, Goddard,
    276
waiting with the fish, Swann, 25
walking-tall tomcat, Burke, 69
woman as big as an air conditioner,
    Johnson 272
you're older than you think, Wing, 273

FURNITURE
grandmother's desk, Andrews, 103
world's best chair, McIntyre, 107
FURNITURE POLISH, O-Cedar, Johnson,
27
FUTURE, THE, knowing it's there gives
courage, Keefe, 209

GAMANS, ERIK, DeGrandpre, 58
GAMES, with children, Swann, 32
GARAGES, Englander, 13
GARBAGE, young American biker
watches old woman eat, Buettner 292
GARBAGE MEN, Colquhoun, talking
with, 15
GARDENERS, in Laos, Sultan, 28
GARDENING
as a simple pleasure, Callwood, 161;
Bornn, 189; Vonnegut, 188
at eighty, Brown, 362
GAS STATION, as childhood hangout,
Hallett, 16
GAY FRIENDS, as a positive influence,
Sultan, 120
GEESE
a lame goose, Sulton, 335
observed, Colquhoun, 336; Librarians,
336; Miller, 336
GENEROSITY
a powerful lesson in sharing,
Holloway, 289
thoughts on, Roberts, 323
GEORGIA
Athens, Brunson, 332
Brunswick, Waite, 41
Egypt, Waite, 61
Green County, Brown, 23
Lake Allatoona, Sammons, 40
Mableton, Prickett, 59
Marietta, dating memories of, Wing, 30
Marietta, learning to drive a Model T
in, Kemp, 38
Midland, Waite, 15

Midville, trip by buggy, Sutton, 10
Milledgeville, Sutton, 37
Sardis, Frog Wallow Waddle, Prickett,
199
Swainsboro, Johnson, 38, see also
Sammons, Johnson entries
Twin City, Johnson, 16
Waynesboro, taking father lunch,
Sammons, 39
GERBILS, as pets, Buettner, 70
GERMANY, penalties of drinking too
much, Sultan, 225
GHOSTS, Johnson, 116
GIFTS
first present from a trip, Johnson, 38
as important symbols, Jensen, 240
a special dog, Strobel, 67
GIRLS
can bring fear, Miller, 302
can't play with boys, Beacham, 14;
can play with boys, Retton, 54
as a simple pleasure, Jaxhiemer, 187
GIVING UP, see "What Makes You Give
Up?" chapter 31, p. 201
comes hard, Lear, 202
do it fast if you're sure to fail,
Swann, 203
it's OK, Lear, 202
it's a choice, Brackett, 210
learn from it, Platt, 203
you can't do it when you're old,
Sutton, 201
GLIDERS
silent beauty in the air, Robertson, 194
teaching self-reliance, Robertson, 309
GOALS, see "Something You Want To
Do," chapter 64, p. 377
doing nothing, Munro, 386
living until the tricentennial,
Andrews, 379
making marriage work, Hallett, 268
something that shines, Buettner, 20
GOD AND FAMILY, all you need,
Callwood, 270

GODDARD, PAT, person who influenced, 128; special private moment, 245; rainy afternoon, 267; funny story, 276; "No Grieving for Peyton, Please," a portrait, 352; something worth waiting for, 383

GOLDFISH
a metaphor for life, Cooney, 75
a simple pleasure, Rochelle, 185

GOOD LUCK, see also "Serendipity," chapter 34, p. 214

GOODNESS, the danger of being good, Learson, 80

GOVERNESSES, see also NANNIES
raised by, Perkins, 44

GOVERNMENT, the failure of it, Berman, 202

GOYEN, WILLIAM, Roberts, 281, 323

GRAND BAHAMA ISLAND, see BAHAMAS

GRAND OLE OPRY, Buck Johnson, 241

GRAND DUCHESS CHARLOTTE, as a grandmother, Munro, 125

GRANDDAUGHTER, a sweet miracle, Brown, 311

GRANDFATHER
best friend, Keefe, 57
death of, Lear, 7; Ferguson, 347
great and unusual friend, Perkins, 44
magical gift, Learson, 371
major influence, Ferguson, 114; Learson, 121
negative influence, Fish, 35
unusual and funny death of, Perkins, 44
a V-E day treat, Emmerling, 13

GRANDMOTHER
as major influence, Andrews, 110; Hallett, 120; Burke, 125; Munro, 125; Goddard, 128; Cook, 133
as role model, Edmondson, 368; Colquhoun, 371
as something sweet, Cook, 311
as special friends, Legere, 271
baking with, Hackman, 8

bearer of bad news, Edmondson, 254
death of, Andrews, 109
disciplinarian, Strobel, 9
example of independence, Andrews, 367
and food, Miller, 235
funny story involving grandson, Johnson, 241
funny night at the opera, Burke, 277
good teacher, Robertson, 44
loves answering machine, Prickett, 276
and marijuana, Andrews, 273
matriarchal figure, Barbour, 14
a person you can talk to, Andrews, 109
planting tree with, Ferguson, 24
remembered, Lear, 11
says apples make you pregnant, Strobel, 264
says live together before marriage, Barbour, 237
the smell of talcum reminds Andrews of, 103
tea and TV at the palace, Munro, 237

GRANDPARENTS
early mornings with, Rockefeller, 8
fear with, Hanson, 12
holding hands with, Ferguson, 33
special closeness, Ferguson, 271
special moments with, Waite, 243
as supporters, Legere, 329

GRASS, newly cut, Colquhoun, 311

GREAT BOOKS, studying them, Peter, 119

GREED, an artist hates it, Legere, 284

GREEK, speaking with grandmother, Hackman, 8

GRIEF
handling privately, Brunson, 223; Brown, 224
loneliness over the death of a baby, Abrams, 249
trauma of brother's death, Edmondson, 254

GROUND HOGS, as pets, Cook, 68

GROWING UP, see also ADULTHOOD
in Indiana, Rockefeller, 8
in Scotland, Barbour, 14
who'd want to, Preston, 388
never with parents, Strobel, 149
GUARDS, H. Barbour remembers, 29
GUILLAIN-BARRÉ SYNDROME, Perkins,
135, 386
GUITAR
plays only in C, Callwood, 270
wish to play, Colquhoun, 378
GUM, soldiers give gum to kids, Rose, 13
GUT COURSES
anthropology, Plimpton, 176
family living, Rochelle, 177
GUTSY, see COURAGE, DETERMINATION,
PERSEVERANCE, INDEPENDENCE
GYMNASTICS, Retton, 43, 95, 117

HACKMAN, PEGGY, first memory, 8;
awkward with a parent, 95; real fear,
299; a self-discovery, 326; legacy, 367;
something worth waiting for, 388
HAD I A HUNDRED MOUTHS, Roberts, 85
HAINTS, Johnson, 116
HAIR
dyed many colors, Rochelle, 41
father washing gently, Buettner, 36
long hair leads to humiliation, G.
Plimpton, 96
HAIRCUTS
fear of, Retton, 27
hiding to avoid, Munro, 30
HALLETT, CAROL, early memories, 23;
special moment with parent, 41;
person who influenced, 120; adult
with parents, 143; special private
moment, 245; "Holding Hands," a
portrait, 268; real fear, 308
HALLETT, JIM, first memory, 16; dream,
101; person who influenced, 118;
threats, 231; treat, 235; "Holding
Hands," a portrait, 268

HAMES, KATHRYN, early memories, 26;
adult with parents, 145; treat, 234;
real fear, 304
HAMSTERS, a Peruvian delicacy,
Buettner, 284
HAND-ME-DOWNS
for a countess, Munro, 56
lesson in sharing, Holloway, 289
HANDICAP
physically impaired person inspires,
Retton, 288
physically impaired man and child
meet, Prowse, 287
HANDS, see Holding Hands, chapter 5, p. 32
seeing mortality in a mother's hands,
Roberts, 85
HANDYMAN, learning how to be, Learson,
38
HANGING OUT WITH KIDS, a simple
pleasure, Cooney, 186
HANGOVER, just where am I? Brackett, 214
HANSON, MARLA, first memory, 12;
things that shine, 19; early friendship,
59; pet, 67; awkward with a parent,
91; art, 179; courage to go on, 210;
lowest moment, 227; "Discovering
Courage," a portrait, 314; fear for
children, 357; legacy, 372
HAPPINESS
has four ingredients, Peter, 187
in life, Lear, 320
money doesn't bring, Cooney, 161
worth waiting for, Perkins, 386
you may lose some as an adult,
Edmondson, 146
HARD HAT, as a symbol of authority,
Duke, 156
HARD WORK
it's better than talent, Abrams, 194
key to success, Strobel, 164
a lifetime philosophy, Prowse, 206
HARDSHIP, as a learning experience,
Platt, 203

HARVARD UNIVERSITY
don't miss classes, Plimpton, 176
a teacher friend, Platt, 117
HATE, facing the Ku Klux Klan as a
white child, Cook, 259
HAWAII, Hallett, 235
HEALTH
a physical saves a life, Hallett, 231
importance of, Taufer, 357
HEART ATTACK, as reminder of
mortality, Bailey, 82
HEART-TO-HEART TALKS, a doctor saves
a life, Hallett, 231
HEAT, the effects of on dancing irons,
Emery, 172
HEDGES
as place to hide, Munro, 30
father jumping over, Lear, 7
a shortcut through, Cook, 27
HELPING AROUND THE HOUSE,
Learson, 38
HERO, FATHER AS, Lear, 34
HIDING PLACES
clock towers, Munro, 30
giant urns, Cook, 62
hedges, Jock Munro, 30
HIERS, A. J., early friendship, 59;
mortality, 76; treasured possession,
104; lowest moment, 222; special
private moment, 242; greatest fear,
350; fear for children, 356
HIGH SCHOOL REUNION, what people
really thought of you, Lear, 192
HIGH SCHOOL
detention threatened, Wing, 92
rewarding moment for hard work,
Abrams, 194
HIKING
Maachu Pichu in the moonlight with
a son, Goddard, 245
a test of friendship, Duke, 339
HISTORY
as an important influence on a chile,
McIntyre, 115
as a personal pleasure, Donovan, 189

HODGKINS DISEASE, kills mother,
Berman, 254
HOLDING HANDS, see chapter 4, p. 23
children and parents, Swann, 32
don't do it, Hallett, 268
grandparents and grandchildren,
Ferguson, 33
ice skating, Buettner, 32; Royce, 33
intimate act, Vonnegut, 33
nervously, Thomas, 33
tall and short people, Retton, 33
HOLLOWAY, AMY, things that shine, 22;
early friendship, 60; treasured
possessions, 104; person who
influenced, 132; adult with parents,
147; rainy afternoon, 262; funny
story, 279; a compassionate moment,
289; real fear, 305; legacy, 374;
something worth waiting for, 387
HOLLYWOOD, hungary goldfish start a
hollywood career, Beacham 215
HOLMES, LARRY, Cooney, 178
HOME
birds flying south, Strobel, 335
losing in a fire, Cross, 105
of one's own, Dorrance, 380, Waite, 388
as a treasured possission, Kemp, 108
visiting parents brings out the child,
Holloway, 147
HOMELESS PEOPLE, an encounter,
Vonnegut, 292
HOMESTEADING
in California, Hallett, 23
island traditions include, Donovan, 145
HONDURAS, growing papayas, Munro, 327
HONESTY, learning the importance of,
DeGrandpre, 131
HOOSE, MARTIN, a portrait, Emery, 341
HOPKINS, a poem by, Kahl, 123
HORMED TOADS, Colquhoun, 15
HORSE AND BUGGY, trip by, Sutton, 10
HORSES
amateur wins a national championship,
Houlihan, 196

breath-taking ride in Arabian desert, McIntyre, 244

brothers compete in horse show, Bornn, 20

first jump, McIntyre, 312

in dreams, Ferguson, 100

in Nassau, Ferguson, 24

playing horse show, Edmondson, 55

playing polo, Perkins, 196

riding workhorses, Costigan, 61

a runaway, Peck, 196

HOSPITALS

site for summer job, Colquhoun, 172

stay in leads to life's work, Andrews, 169

staying with ill husband, Roberts, 85

a young doctor and a husband face death, Andrews, 285

HOSTILITY

facing the KKK, Cook, 259

feeling it as a child, Learson, 258

hoping no one will yell at you, Andrews, 258

HOTELS

aunt thinks home is still hotel, Edmondson, 274

running a small one, Brackett, 34

working as a desk clerk, Sammons, 157

HOULIHAN, PEGGY, person who influenced, 131; glory in sports, 196; courage to go on, 209; real fear, 307; burying a friend, 348; regrets, 365

HOUSES, MINIATURE, as dog houses, Strobel, 67

HOUSTON, TEXAS, Retton, 117

HUGGING

babies, a simple pleasure, Learson, 185

critically ill person needs, Roberts, 85

memories of mother holding on rainy day, DeGrandpre, 263

secure men do it, too, DeGrandpre, 185

HULA HOOPS, dancing with on oil rigs, Brunson, 153

HUMILITY, the importance of taught by grand duchess, Munro, 125

HUMMINGBIRDS, in Barbados, Plimpton, 14

HUMOR, see also FUNNY STORIES

difficulty of writing, Plimpton, 329

falling hemlines—on men, Barbour, 280

the importance of, Waite, 127

HUNGER, young American biker sees vivid example, Buettner, 292

HUNTING

daughter hunts with her father, Hallett, 41

pet ducks need protecting, Jensen, 66

South Georgia, Sammons, 157

teaches about death, Barbour, 81

thoughts on, Marston, 290; Retton, 337

with popgun, Mockler, 26

working at hunts on an estate, Barbours, 154

HURT, HENRY AND CLAUDIE, Brown, 23

HUSBAND, Lear wished he'd been a better one, 178

HUSBAND-AND-WIFE TEAMS, a wife looks at, McIntyre, 171

HYMNS, concerts with mother, Preston, 10

"I LEFT MY HEART IN SAN FRANCISCO" and loneliness, Emmerling, 260

IACOCCA, LEE, Perkins, 379

ICE CREAM

memories of, Hallett, 118

as special treat, Brunson, 235

ICE SKATING

childhood memory, Barbour, 14

childhood escape from family problems, Cook, 57

dating excuse, Buettner, 32

holding hands excuse, Royce, 33

IDAHO, Sun Valley, Cook, 57

IGNORANCE, it's frustrating, DeGrandpre, 202

ILLINOIS, Chicago, Brown, 169;
Andrews, 306
ILLNESS
bulimia, Brunson, 226
child's miracle at an arthritis camp,
Prowse, 287
childhood rheumatic fever, Holloway, 60
courage and 3 sick children, Johnson,
222
father's illness prepares son for
adulthood, McIntyre, 139
father's illness means son supports
family, Lear, 153
father's illness changes a daughter's
role, Learson, 148
handling terminal illness, Roberts, 85
strain on the family, Royce, 89
teenager deals with serious,
DeGrandpre, 225
threat, Colquhoun, 230
unexplained one defeats young doctor,
Andrews, 285
IMAGINATION, seeing importance of,
Beacham, 113
IMMORTALITY
child's belief in, Emmerling, 77
childhood feeling, Ferguson, 24
thinking about, Swann, 88
IMPROVISATION, a philosophy to get
through life, Emery, 208
INCARCERATION, bagpipes lead to jail,
Munro, 150
INDECISION, learning to deal with it,
Hanson, 210
INDEPENDENCE
brother raises siblings, Hiers, 222
child strikes out on her own, Strobel,
164
commercial fishing teaches, Marston,
175
fear of losing when aging, Supper
Club, 352
fighting for in a family, Retton, 174

financial independence needed in old
age, Sichveland, 162
first drive in car gives sense of,
Emmerling, 140
a gift to a child, Andrews, 367; Platt,
367
as goal, Spezzano, 386
grandmother teaches, Andrews, 306
a hard lesson well learned, Plimpton,
212
kids given independence, Swann, 355
learning from teachers, Beacham, 113
mother as mechanics, Colquhoun, 275
parents teaching, McIntyre, 140
personal discovery, Retton, 317
raising self at death of mother, Berman,
254; Strobel, 164
single father instills in children, Fish, 143
staying active, Bailey, 361; Brown, 362
wanting to know who wants you,
Roberts, 236
INDIAN ARTIFACT, treasured Haida
blanket box, Duke, 105
INDIANA, early memories, Rockefeller, 8
INEVITABILITY
accepting it, Thomas, 184
sometimes we have no choice,
Rockefeller, 209
INFLATION, the impact of, Wing, 162
INGENUITY, a Russian teaches an
American, Buettner, 219
INJURY, fear of debilitating, Bornn, 352
INNOCENCE, losing it at boarding
school, Munro, 252
INSECURITY, a teacher helps overcome,
Holloway, 132
INSOMNIA, depression leads a person to,
Hanson, 210
INTEGRITY, a parental role model, Fish,
369; Keefe, 369
INTELLECTUAL CURIOSITY
being raised with, McIntyre, 115
learn every-day, Learson, 371

INTERNATIONAL STUDIES, as a family pleasure, Bornn, 186

INTROSPECTION, at times an unsettling act, Robertson, 230

IRONY, know the facts before you leap, McIntyre, 156

IRREVERENCE, a grandmother's, Andrews, 307

ISLAND MEMORIES, Callwood, 35

ISLAND LIFE
age unimportant on Tortola, Thomas, 361
discovering an island cave system, Rose, 247
expensive, Thomas, 384
Jost Van Dyke Preservation Society, Callwood, 378
museum to preserve culture, Donovan, 189, 385
Smith's Point, Mockler, 182
traditions endangered, Donovan, 351

ISLAND, an unusual job on, Brackett, 154

ISRAEL, Friedman, 83

ITALY,
buying a castle in, Taufer, 218
Venice, making love in the rain, Emmerling, 682

JAIL
sleeping in for fun as a child, McIntyre, 118
bagpipes sent me to jail, Munro, 150

JAMAICA, childhood memories, Dorrance, 380

JAXHIEMER, JOHN, a discovery about myself, 322; rainy afternoon, 262; takes my breath away, 71; thoughts on money, 161; compassionate moment, 292; simple things that bring pleasure, 187; special moment with parent, 44

JAYCEES, winning their contest, Bunny Johnson, 240

JEALOUSY, with brother, Beacham, 14

JENSEN, ERIC, greatest fear, 352; moment of real fear, 303; regrets, 365; private moment, 240; a pet, 66

"JESUS KNOWS," Preston sings, 10

JEWELRY, a special piece of, Friedman, 109

JOAN OF ARC, studying, McIntyre, 115

JOBS, SUMMER, see "A Summer Job," chapter 22, p. 153

JOBS, see VOCATIONS and "Finding Work," chapter 25, p. 166

JOGGING, see RUNNING

JOHNSON, GRADY "BUCK," first memory, 16; things that shine, 22; early memories, 27; awkward with a parent, 93; person who influenced, 116; adult with parents, 142; summer job, 153; special private moment, 241; funny story, 272; "Airplanes," a portrait, 294; legacy, 371; something you want to do, 377

JOHNSON, BUNNY, things that shine, 22; special moment with parent, 38; early friendship, 54; person who influenced, 115; adult with parents, 141; lowest moment, 222; special private moment, 240; funny story, 274; real fear, 307; legacy, 370

JOHNSON, TOM, Spezzano, 84

JOST VAN DYKE, BVI
father punishes on, Callwood, 35
Hanson visits, 19
preserving a way of life, Callwood, 378

JOURNALISM
start in, Mason, 132; Plimpton, 166
start in leads to another career, W. McIntyre, 171

JUMPING, horses, McIntyre, 312

JUNGLE, childhood memories, Barbour, 7

JUNGLE GYMS, in dreams, Litton, 99

JURY DUTY, not like television, Holloway, 279

KAHL, VIRGINIA, first memory, 13; mortality, 83; treasured possession, 104; person who influenced, 123; adult with parents, 138; work, 174; courage to go on, 209; special private moment, 242; loneliness, 259; funny story, 272; real fear, 300; a self-discovery, 328; birds flying south, 336

KARATE, fifty-year-old woman learns, Randolph, 501

KAROLYI, BELA, coaches Mary Lou Retton, 43, 117, 377

KEEFE, CHRIS, early memories, 26; special moment with parent, 47; early friendship, 57; pet, 68; awkward with a parent, 94; courage to go on, 209; loneliness, 260; a self-discovery, 320; legacy, 369

KELLY, SHANNON, things that shine, 20; dream, 99; person who influenced, 119; adult with parents, 143; glory in sports, 193; birds flying south, 337

KELLY, SHANNON, as friend, Royce, 59

KEMP, PEGGY, things that shine, 21; treasured possession, 108; adult with parents, 140; money, 162; on friendship, 191; simple pleasure, 191; glory in sports, 197; rainy afternoon, 263

KEMP, HENRY, things that shine, 19; early memories, 30; special moment with parent, 38; greatest fear, 352

KENNEDY, BOBBY, rafting trip turns terrifying, Plimpton, 299

KICKING, a fit of anger, Bailey, 12

KILTS
a safer hemline, Barbour, 280
not always safe for busking, Munro, 150

KINDERGARTEN
nearly deserted, Warrington, 17
embarrassing moment, Costigan, 273

KINDNESS
breathtaking act, Bornn, 74

physically impaired man helps sick child, Prowse, 287
remembering to thank a teacher, Roberts, 120

KING, DON, Cooney, 178

KISSING, as an awkward moment, Hanson, 91

KKK, see KU KLUX KLAN

KNIGHTHOOD, a grandfather's, Ferguson, 114

KOUFAX, SANDY, DeGrandpre, 107

KU KLUX KLAN, Cook remembers fearful moment, Cook, 259

LAKE
childhood gathering place, Beacham, 29
floating in is moment of nice loneliness, Sultan, 257
lame goose in Virginia, Sulton, 335
last time with parent, Sammons, 40
quiet moment on Polly Lake, Buettner, 240
working at Lake Geneva, Duke, 287

LAMP, as treasured possession, Costigan, 108

LANGUAGES, trouble with changes degree goals, Sutton, 177

LAOS
childhood memories, Sultan, 18
playing in the rain, a memory, Sultan, 264
unusual pets in, Sultan, 68

THE LAST OF THE MOHICANS, Emmerling, 46

LAUGHING, AT YOURSELF, the importance of, Burke, 125; Waite, 127; Perkins, 333

LAUGHTER
couple laughs together, Spezzano, 360
mother and daughter get lost together, Sammons, 186
simple pleasure, Plimpton, 187

LAURELS, not resting on, Prowse, 195

LAWN, as scene of family gathering, 7

LAWRENCE, T. E., studying, McIntyre, 115
LAWYERS
American woman works with Russian
women, Bornn, 246
Plimpton's father, 374
start of career, Bornn, 329
watching them in action, Jaxhiemer,
71; Holloway, 279
LAZINESS, Rose, 91
LEAGUE OF WOMEN VOTERS, Bornn, 246
LEAR, NORMAN, first memory, 7; special
moment with parent, 34; breath away,
71; mortality, 82; adult with parents,
138; summer job, 153; failing, 178;
glory in sports, 192; give up, 202;
loneliness, 255; a compassionate
moment, 291; a self-discovery, 328
LEAR, LYN, first memory, 11; special
moment with parent, 47; early friendship, 54; mortality, 82; glory in
sports, 193; give up, 202; loneliness,
255; a compassionate moment, 291; a
self-discovery, 320; greatest fear, 351
LEARNING, LOVE OF, a grandfather's
gift, Learson, 371
LEARNING DISABILITIES, portrait of
Peyton, Goddard, 353
LEARSON, KATE, special moment with
parent, 115; breath away, 73;
mortality, 80; dream, 282; person
who influenced, 121; adult with
parents, 148; art, 181; simple
pleasure, 185; loneliness, 258; a self-
discovery, 325; legacy, 371; something
worth waiting for, 386
LEDREBORG, surprise move to, Munro, 327
LEGERE, PHOEBE, first memory, 11;
special moment with parent, 43;
mortality, 80; awkward with a parent,
91; dream, 100; art, 179; loneliness,
254; rainy afternoon, 265; a special
relationship, 271; vile thing, 284; a
compassionate moment, 290; real

fear, 307; a self-discovery, 329; birds
flying south, 335; burying a friend,
345; greatest fear, 350; legacy, 369;
something worth waiting for, 383
LETTERS, kept as mementos, Prowse, 26;
Andrews, 103
LEUKEMIA, denying, Roberts 85
LIBRARIANS, surprising career, 328
LIBRARIES
in Berlin, Kahl, 259
napping by, Legere, 11
teaches Vonnegut how to build
staircase, 242
wonderful environment, Beacham, 113
LIFE, see MORTALITY
LIGHT
column of, in dreams, Peter, 101
on dawn flight, Emmerling, 71
quality in painting, Learson, 73
standing in spotlight, Holloway, 22
wartime searchlights, Johnson, 22
LIGHTNING
as a killer, Sutton, 78
terrifying moment, M. Plimpton, 300
LILLIOM, the play, Lear, 34
LIMITED EXPECTATIONS, from father,
Friedman, 11
LINDELL'S RESTAURANT, Hackman, 11
LINOLEUM, grandparent's, Rockefeller, 8
LIPS, memories of mother's, Hanson, 91
LIPSTICK
playing with, Lear, 11
sign of growing up, Kemp, 140
LITTLE, IDA AND WATT, Brown, 23
LITTLE APPLE BAY, TORTOLA
something beautiful, Thomas, 19
sunsets, Hanson, 19
LITTON, KIM, special moment with
parent, 39; dream, 99; glory in
sports, 199; lowest moment, 222; real
fear, 305; feel young, 361
LIVING TOGETHER, grandmother gives
her approval, A. Barbour, 237

LIZARDS
active curly tail, Preston, 63
as simple pleasure, Thomas, 184
LOBSTERS, as pets, Barbour, 66
LOG CABINS, being raised in, Hallett, 120
LONELINESS, see "A Moment of Loneliness," chapter 41, p. 251; see also
UNHAPPINESS
abandoned at airport, Costigan, 257
bad relationship better than none, N.
Lear, 255
biking can be lonely, Buettner, 251
boarding school in Scotland brings,
Munro, 252
caused by lack of self worth,
Beacham, 256
child raises self, Berman, 254
child protects women in danger,
Cook, 259
childhood friends desert after illness,
Campbell 253
child's, Roberts, 253
death of a brother, Edmondson, 254
desolation of WW II Berlin, Kahl,
259
drug use builds it, Keefe, 260
ex-wife's name on polo balls, Perkins,
256
father/daughter share camp memories,
Swann, 251
first memory, Friedman, 11
good feeling of self-awareness, Sultan,
257
grandmother handles with courage,
Goddard, 128
grief over the death of a baby,
Abrams, 629
happens in crowds, Rockefeller, 257
leaving parents for career, Legere, 254
missing a spouses human touch,
Bailey, 255
spiritual void brings it, N. Lear, 255
surrounded by people, Friedman, 256

traveling alone feels good,
DeGrandpre, 258
traveling alone causes it, Emmerling,
260
violence helps a model understand it,
Hanson, 210
whales and deep ocean brings,
Jensen, 303
widow faces first night alone, Sutton,
255
LONGEVITY, Spezzano, 361
LOS ANGELES TIMES, Spezzano, 84
LOU GEHRIG'S DISEASE, Colquhoun, 146
LOVE
brothers talk at a drug treatment center,
Keefe, 260
father and mother's special, Plimpton,
270
grandmother's special love, Legere, 271
grandparents' special love, Ferguson, 271
horse named Love, Ferguson, 24
making love in the rain in Venice,
Emmerling, 267
off on the wrong foot, Emmerling
and Learson, 386
saying without reservation to father,
DeGrandpre, 47
something that shines, Andrews, 20;
Sutton, 20
what we all want, Brown, 389
young man and big brother explore,
Jensen, 240
LOVE STORY, Bornn, 56
LOYALTY
family always remains loyal, Perkins, 135
something that shines, Mockler, 19
LUCAYAN NATIONAL PARK, Ben's Cave
discovered, Rose, 247
LUCK, see "Serendipity," chapter 34, p. 214
birds as sign of, Dorrance, 337
LUNCH
playing hooky with mother, McIntyre, 43
taking to father, Sammons, 39
teacher treats, Mason, 131

MACHU PICCHU, Goddard, 245
MADAME BOVARY, unusual reading for a
  child, Beacham, 307
MADISON SQUARE GARDEN, Cooney
  remembers special fight, 195
MAIDS, Chinese, Sultan, 68
MAIDSTONE GOLF CLUB, Hanging
  Together, 50
MAILMEN, as good influence on child,
  Colquhoun, 116
MALLARD DUCKS, as pets, Jensen, 66
MAMA FLO, Mockler, 182
MARACICH, MARIA, Cook, 57
MARIJUANA
  beats smoking banana peels, Thomas,
    262
  boarding school treat, DeGrandpre, 233
  grandmother's humor with, Andrews,
    273
  talking to parents about, Hanging
    Together, 53
  teenage highjinks, Cook, 57
MARION, MARTY, baseball player,
  Spezzano, 16
MARITAL PROBLEMS, impact on kids,
  Hanging Together, 50; Hanson, 59,
  227; Peter, 93; Andrews, 258
MARLIN FISHING, a lifetime fisherman
  catches first, Callwood, 197
MARRIAGE
  fire trucks build a relationship,
    Roberts, 266
  flowers on roof lead to, H. Barbour, 237
  grandmother says live together first,
    A. Barbour, 237
  making marriage work, Hallett, 268
  making love in a Venice rain,
    Emmerling, 682
  marriage means you move from
    home, Ferguson, 145
  mother sets a milestone for, Abrams,
    242
  why it might be worth it, Holloway, 387

MARSTON, JOHN, first memory, 7; things
  that shine, 21; holding hands, 33;
  mortality, 82; dream, 100; adult with
  parents, 383; work, 175; failing, 178;
  art, 179; simple pleasure, 185; lowest
  moment, 225; a compassionate moment,
  290; real fear, 312; regrets, 364;
  something worth waiting for, 384
MARTINIS, a fond memory, Vonnegut, 188
MASON, MARGARET, early friendship,
  61; mortality, 78; person who
  influenced, 131; simple pleasure, 188;
  give up, 201; courage to go on, 213;
  lowest moment, 224; special private
  moment, 239; something sweet, 311;
  a self-discovery, 326; greatest fear,
  350; feel young, 361
MASSACHUSETTS,
  Cambridge, Hames, 145
  Nantasket, Learson, 121
  where mother worked, Strobel, 9, 67
MATURITY
  discovering, Perkins, 333
  worth waiting for, Preston, 388
MCINTYRE, DENI, first memory, 17;
  special moment with parent, 43;
  treasured possession, 107; person
  who influenced, 115; adult with parents,
  140; summer job, 156; work, 171;
  glory in sports, 198; courage to go
  on, 209; threats, 231; a self-discovery,
  332; birds flying south, 335
MCINTYRE, WILL, person who
  influenced, 118; adult with parents,
  139; summer job, 159; work, 171;
  simple pleasure, 190; glory in sport,
  193; give up, 204; special private
  moment, 244; something sweet, 312;
  a self-discovery, 319; birds flying
  south, 335
MEASLES, Waite, 11, Emmerling, 13
MECHANICS, mother becomes one,
  Colquhoun, 275

MEDICINE
  baking soda as medicine, Perkins, 12
  black physic-nut bushes are best,
    Callwood, 35
  doesn't work sometime, Andrews, 285
  right career? Jensen, 352
MEDITATION, playing bagpipes to
  meditate, Munro, 103
MEISNER, SANDY, Roberts, 120
MEMORIES, see "A First Memory,"
  chapter 2, p. 6 and "Early
  Memories," chapter 4, p. 23
  treasured possession, Cross, 104
MENIAL LABOR, performing with
  dignity, Abrams, 36
MENTORS, see also TEACHERS
  bicycler, Buettner, 121
  remembering to thank, Roberts, 120
MICHIGAN
  Detroit, Emmerling remembers, 13, 46
  parents bring doll from, Johnson, 38
  Upper Peninsula, Hackman, 8
MIDLIFE CRISIS, handling, Rockefeller, 86
MILESTONES, finishing gth grade,
  Abrams, 242
MILITARY SERVICE
  bad news at sea, Brunson, 322
  nearly left by outfit, Peck, 297
MILLER, DAMIAN, special moment with
  parent, 47; breath away, 73; glory in
  sports, 199; courage to go on, 209;
  treat, 235; vile thing, 283; a compassionate moment, 288; real fear, 302;
  birds flying south, 336; regrets, 365
MINISTERS, see C. Abrams, R. Abrams, Waite
  fundamentalist friend, Vonnegut, 339
  keeping an eye out, Wing, 30
  one who hollers big, Johnson, 54
  Rogers' friend Dickerson, 339
MINNESOTA
  biking Minneapolis at night, Buettner,
    121
  canoeing with father, Buettner, 240

MINNOWS, Brunson, 12
MISSIONARIES
  car trouble leads to important
    discovery, Rose, 247
  original goal, Bailey, 170
MISSISSIPPI, HATTIESBURG, Abrams, 36
MOBILITY, Campbell, 350
MOCKLER, PAUL, things that shine, 19;
  early memories, 78; Village Life, a
  portrait, 182; treasured possession,
  106; special private moment, 248; a
  compassionate moment, 285; real
  fear, 296; a self-discovery, 323;
  burying a friend, 343
MODEL T FORD
  grandparents', Waite, 243
  remembered, Hames, 26; Waite, 15
  learning to drive, Kemp, 38
MODESTY, a man's hemline, Barbour, 280
MONEY, see also chapter 23, 161
  dreams of aren't good, Prowse, 99
  gives independence in old age,
    Sichveland, 162
  God makes the payments, Brown, 210
  happiness isn't bought with, Cooney, 161
  impact of inflation, Wing, 162
  mountain man's wise words about,
    McIntyre, 190
  not understanding, Peter, 162
  opportunity-maker, DeGrandpre, 161
  simply a tool, Rockefeller, 161
  solvency a treat, Thomas, 384
  worrisome thing, Peter, 162
  worth waiting for, Brackett, 384;
    Marston, 384
MONGOLIA, bicycling in, Buettner, 219
MONKEY, childhood African memory,
  Barbour, 7
MORTALITY, see also "Your First Intimation
  of Mortality," chapter 12, p. 76
  aged hands show, Roberts, 85
  brother's death in Cambodia,
    Brunson, 223

brother's death, Litton, 222
death of a son teaches courage,
   Brown, 224
death of a father reminds son,
   Rockefeller, 231
doctor's warning changes life, Hallett,
   231
librarian faces in Vietnam, Randolph,
   296
life ends quickly, like this, Plimpton, 79
mugging incident scares young man,
   Platt, 301
parent's kindness scares daughter,
   Campbell, 302
pet brings first glimpse, Beacham, 76;
   Keefe, 68
realization of at Israeli memorial,
   Friedman, 83
restaurant as metaphor for, Lear, 82
scuba death impacts a rescuer,
   Ferguson, 291
understanding finally, Emmerling, 77
young doctor faces it, Andrews, 285
MOTHER, see particular chapters 6, 14,
   and 20
active at an old age, Roberts, 85
bites back, Munro, 6
cared for by daughters, Spezzano, 148
courage facing cancer, Warrington, 346
death of brings regrets, Prowse, 255, 365
looking at as a child, Legere, 11
milestones set in daughter's life,
   Abrams, 242
no chance to talk to, Strobel, 366
optimism and stoicism taught by,
   Mason, 213
optimistic, Brackett, 105
remembered, Lear, 11; Strobel, 9
role model, Abrams, 370
saves from accident, Rochelle, 6
savior in dream, Ferguson, 100
search for his natural, DeGrandpre, 318
singing with, Preston, 10

spanking by mistake, Goddard 276
unconventional, Rochelle 41
unusual skill, Colquhoun, 275
violent, Hanson, 227
waiting for in the rain, Goddard, 267
walking on beach with, Callwood, 8
MOTHER-IN-LAW, as major influence,
   Friedman, 129; Perkins, 135
MOTORCYCLING, someday through the
   Rockies, Sammons, 377
MOTTOES, family, Ferguson, 114
MOUNTAIN SAYINGS, McIntyre, 190
MOUNTAIN CLIMBING
   with Scout, Bornn, 288
   with son, Goddard, 245
MOVIES
   playing Darth Vader, Prowse, 323
   roles in, Roberts, 236, 282
   The Sound of Music scares before
      surgery, Campbell, 302
   source for *Divorce American Style*,
      Lear, 138
   talking to Fellini, Roberts, 233
MOVING
   Catalina Island as new home,
      Brackett, 105
   effect on children, Andrews, 110
   getting married means you move,
      Ferguson, 145
   means adulthood, Hames, 145
MUD HUTS, as home, Barbour, 29
MUGGING
   father attacked, Callwood, 303
   makes person stronger, Mason, 224
   model attacked, Marla Hanson, 314
   a young man talks his way out of,
      Platt, 301
MUMPS, special time with mother,
   Mason, 239
MUNRO, SILVIA, first memory, 6; early
   memories, 30; early friendship, 56; a
   pet, 67; dream, 98; person who
   influenced, 125; special private

moment, 237; rainy afternoon, 266; funny story, 276; burying a friend, 344; something worth waiting for, 386

MUNRO, JOCK, first memory, 7; early memories, 30; mortality, 81; treasured possession, 103; person who influenced, 127; Busking, a portrait, 150; failing, 178; simple pleasure, 184; glory in sports, 198; loneliness, 252; a self-discovery, 327; burying a friend, 347

MUSEUMS
building your own, Donovan, 189
a serendipitous commission, Cook, 216

MUSHROOMS, wild fried, Costigan, 61

MUSIC, see also SINGING
composing, Preston, 330
fear of wrong notes, Legere, 350
plays only in C, Callwood, 270
power of, an East Berlin example, Burker 246
rainy days and divorce, good time to play, Vonnegut, 265

MUSICAL INSTRUMENTS, see individual instruments

NANNIES
best friends as child, Fish, 57
death of a special friend, Munro, 347
major influence, Munro, 127
Scottish memories of, Munro, 7
special southern, Brown, 169
threaten sometime, Beacham, 230

NASHVILLE, a son's country music rise, Buck Johnson, 241

NASSAU, see BAHAMAS

NAZIS, and thoughts of mortality, Friedman, 83

NECKLACE, as treasured possession, Friedman, 109

NEIGHBORS, watching television together, a treat, Hames, 234

NEUHARTH, AL, as a personal influence, Spezzano, 130, 328

NEW YORK
The Bronx, Roberts, 12
early memories of, Plimpton, 6
Rochester, Spezzano, 16

NEW YORKER, THE, effect on future cartoonist, Emmerling, 166

NEW HAMPSHIRE, DeGrandpre, 93

NEW MEXICO, PHILMONT, a Boy Scout learns courage, Bornn, 288

NEWSPAPERS
island publishing leads to friendship, Spezzano, 338
publishing, gave many opportunities, Spezzano, 328
selling subscriptions changes life, Buettner, 121

NICARAGUA, biking through, Buettner, 251

NO, NO NANETTE, Holloway, 22

"No. 55, Spring and Fall," Hopkins's poem, Kahl, 123

NORTH DAKOTA, MINOT, Christmas memories of, Mason, 239

NORTH CAROLINA, WINSTON-SALEM, Strobel, 164

NORTON, KEN, Cooney fights, 195

NUDITY, Platt, 25

NUNS
school run by, McIntyre, 39
smoking and speeding nun wins out, Burke, 232
as teachers, Houlihan, 131; McIntyre, 332

O'HARA, MAUREEN, in the Virgin Islands, Spezzano, 338

OAK TREES, memories of playing in, Colquhoun, 15; Beacham, 29

OBEDIENCE, dangers of disobeying, M. Plimpton, 95; Peck, 196

OBESITY
a fear, Taufer, 301
moving beyond, Burke, 384

OCEAN
fearful and beautiful object, Jensen, 303

getting stuck on, Hames, 26
pleasure of, Barbour, 188
stuck in a sub at 1,000 feet, Mockler, 296
ODOR, of talcum powder and memory, Andrews, 103
OIL RIGS, working on, Brunson, 153
OLD AGE, see also AGING
beauty comes for some then, Preston, 19
being active in, Roberts, 85
need for financial independence, Sichveland, 162
OLDSMOBILES, as something that shines, Kemp, 19
OLIVIER, LAURENCE, Roberts, 236
OLYMPICS
training for, Retton, 43
watching, Kelly, 20
ON THE LOOSE, a treasured book, Peter, 107
OPEN-MINDEDNESS, family legacy, Hackman, 367; Taufer, 368; Edmondson, 368
OPENNESS, learning the importance of, DeGrandpre, 131
OPERA, a night at *Lucia* with Granny, Burke, 277
OPTIMISM
funny story about, Robertson, 275
legacy to pass on, Emmerling, 375
mother teaches, Mason, 213
mother has lots, Brackett, 105
positive thoughts at tough times, Johnson, 222
seeing good in a funny tractor accident, McIntyre, 161
OUTWARD BOUND, Learson, 325; M. Plimpton, 212
OVERCONFIDENCE, of scuba expert, Englander, 306
OWLS, PRAIRIE DOG, Preston, 63
OXFORD UNIVERSITY, in dreams, Rockefeller, 101

PAIN
fear of, Colquhoun, 352
helping another's, Roberts, 85
PAINTINGS
as treasured possessions, Vonnegut, 108; Holloway, 104
of turtles, Thomas, 215
PALERMO, IRENE, Buettner, 27
PALOMINO, night watchman, Barbour, 29
PARAKEETS
good luck, Dorrance, 337
pet, Emmerling, 77
PARENTS, see particularly chapters 6, 14, and 20
admired by childhood friends, Rochelle, 41
children as equal with means you're an adult, Spezzano, 148
children's best friend, Robertson, 270
cursing in front of means you're an adult, Preston, 148
daughter's visit makes her adult, Beacham, 147
drifting away from brings regret, Prowse, 255
early memories of, Plimpton, 6; Lear 7; Callwood, 8; Preston, 10; Sutton, 10; Legere, 11; Bornn, 15; Waite, 15; Spezzano, 16
as equals, McIntyre, 43
mother's little talks, Rose, 91
other people's as refuge, Cook, 57
son's unusual job finally accepted by, Marston, 383
strong relationship develops slowly, DeGrandpre, 318
taking care of means you're an adulthood, Rose, 148
unexpectedly understanding problems, Jaxhiemer, 44
visiting brings out the child, Holloway, 147

PARKER, CHARLIE, memories of
listening to, Legere, 43
PARKS
Paris park, early memory, Plimpton, 6
park with a swinging bridge, Hanson, 12
PARSONAGES
as home, Waite, 15, 388
walking by on way to date, Wing, 30
PARTIES
learning to give, Perkins, 372
meeting a mate at, Rose, 218
a success, Edmondson, 146
PASSION, intellectual, McIntyre, 115
PATIENCE
building a business, Englander, 173
don't give up too quickly, Donovan, 204
setbacks on bike trek require,
Buettner, 228
PAVEMENT, a treat for a biker, Buettner, 235
PEA SHOOTERS, Andrews, 15
PEACEFULNESS
feeling with family, Cook, 73
worth waiting for, Munro, 386
PECK, DORIS, glory in sports, 196;
serendipity, 216; rainy afternoon, 264
PECK, BILL, first memory, 16; serendipity,
216; real fear, 297; greatest fear, 352
PENTECOSTALS, Preston, 10
PERFECTIONISM, a questionable legacy,
Beacham, 372
PERFORMANCE ART
beginning a career, Legere, 329
knowing Ethel Eichelburger, Legere, 345
PERKINS, NANCY, first memory, 12;
"The Ex-Mother-in-Law," a portrait,
135; legacy, 367; something worth
waiting for, 386
PERKINS, STUART, special moment with
parent, 44; glory in sports, 196;
loneliness, 256; a self-discovery, 333;
legacy, 372; something you want to
do, 379

PERSEVERANCE
better than talent, Abrams, 194;
Buettner, 211
cats can give it to you, Kahl, 209
child raises self, Berman, 254
conquering drugs teaches lesson,
Keefe, 209
doing it right, Abrams, 373
exploring ideas for work, Emmerling,
166
getting through the day, Emery, 208
importance of in life, Goddard, 128
in those facing death, Roberts, 85;
Edmondson, 117;Emery, 340;
Rochelle, 343
lifetime philosophy, Prowse, 206
long-distance biking teaches, Buettner,
195
old age requires it, Sutton, 201
prolongs uncle's life, Colquhoun, 146
Russian friend teaches an American,
Buettner, 219
setbacks on bike trek require,
Buettner, 228
taking control of one's life, Perkins,
135, 386; Cooney, 203
triathlon changes a life, Litton, 199
winning the gold after failing, Retton,
229
PERSISTENCE, see PERSEVERANCE
PERSPECTIVE, worth waiting for,
Goddard, 383
PETER, JONATHAN, mortality, 87;
awkward with a parent, 93; dream,
101; treasured possession, 107; person
who influenced, 119; money, 162;
simple pleasure, 187; City Fathers, a
portrait, 220; threats, 231; treat, 233;
vile thing, 283; feel young, 360;
something worth waiting for, 384
PETERSON, AUBREY, Hanging Together,
a portrait, 50
PETERSON, ERIK, Hanging Together, a
portrait, 50

PETERSON, AUBREY AND ERIK,
DeGrandpre, 131
PETS, see also individual species
accidental death, Plimpton, 289
bird teaches mortality, Emmerling, 77
bulldog poisoned, Hanson, 67
bulldogs, Edmondson, 69
cat watches shaving, Plimpton, 69
cat walks tall, Burke, 69
cats sip water, Sammons, 185
cockerels and countesses, Munro, 67
dog leads boy astray, Emery, 69
dog lives in special house, Strobel, 67
dog teaches mortality, Keefe, 68
ducks as pets and breakfast, Jensen, 66
family members, Hanson, 67
friends, Preston, 63
gerbil as baseball, Buettner, 70
good for the nerves, Preston, 185
ground hogs at boarding school,
Cook, 68
lobsters makes good friends, Barbour, 66
mortality teachers, Keefe, 68;
Beacham, 76
Sultan's unusual Asian, 68
PHILLIPS EXETER ACADEMY, G.
Plimpton, 96, 122, 166
PHOBIAS
learning to ski conquers some,
Friedman, 197
rats are OK, but keep the snakes
away, Thomas, 184
swimming fear conquered, Randolph,
198
terrifying way to overcome fear of
water, Hallett, 245
vertigo at top of a pyramid, Brackett,
308
PHONE CALLS, see also TELEPHONES
from exotic places, Hallett, 268
from family a simple pleasure, Sutton,
186
from Olivier, Roberts, 236

grandmother's always there, Andrews,
110
PHOTOGRAPHY
career evolves, D. McIntyre, 171
grandmother's world, Prickett, 277
unusual professional start, W.
McIntyre, 171
PHYSIC-NUT BUSH, as medicine,
Callwood, 35
PHYSICALS, a physical saves a life,
Hallett, 231
PIANO
childhood wish, Preston, 37
kids playing in bars, Keefe, 26
no accompanying this time, Burke, 330
PICNICS, mai tais, pork & beans on
Kona, Hallett, 235
PIE, Preston's aunt's, 311
PINE CONES, collecting for lots of
money, Johnson, 153
PINES, AUSTRALIAN, symbol of life,
Emery, 341
PITLOCHRY, SCOTLAND, Barbour, 14
PLANTATION, as home, Brown, 23
PLATT, CAMPION, early memories, 25;
special moment with parent, 42;
mortality, 79; dream, 99; person who
influenced, 117; adult with parents,
139; give up, 203; special private
moment, 238; rainy afternoon, 266;
real fear, 301; a self-discovery, 321;
regrets, 365; legacy, 367
PLAY MAMAS, in childhood, Strobel, 9
PLAYING
digging holes, Edmondson, 55
gerbils don't make good baseballs,
Buettner, 70
huge planters make good hiding
places, Cook, 62
marriage at 8, Bornn, 56
mud can't be beat, Peck, 264
Paula wants to be a horse,
Edmondson, 55

playing hooky with mother's help, McIntyre, 43

playing hooky sends Plimpton to summer session, 176

rainy days in Laos, Sultan, 264

PLAYS, see also THEATER

conducting *No, No Nanette*, Holloway, 22

going to theater with date, Lear, 34

Ubu Le Roi with Olivier, Roberts, 236

PLIMPTON, GEORGE, first memory, 6; early memories 25; special moment with parent, 48; a pet, 69; mortality, 79; awkward with a parent, 96; dream, 102; treasured possession, 106; person who influenced, 122; work, 166; failing, 176; art, 179; rainy afternoon, 266; special relationship, 270; real fear, 299; a self-discovery, 329; legacy, 374; something worth waiting for, 383

PLIMPTON, MEDORA, first memory, 14; special moment with parent, 48; awkward with a parent, 95; glory in sports, 198; give up, 204; courage to go on, 212; a compassionate moment, 289; real fear, 300; a self-discovery, 321

PLIMPTON, TAYLOR, awkward with a parent, 96; dream, 98; failing, 176; rainy afternoon, 262; a compassionate moment, 292; a self-discovery, 322

PLIMPTON, GEORGE

daughter talks of, 48; 95

son talks of, 264

with Preston, 63

PLIMPTON, FRANCIS T. P., 96

PLOWRIGHT, JOAN, friendship with, Roberts, 236

PLUMBING, noisy, Brackett, 105

POISONING, of a dog, Hanson, 67; Robertson, 77

POLAND, URUBASHOV, Friedman, 83

POLICE

childhood influences, McIntyre, 118

dreams of, Kelly, 99

only a warning, Prickett, 94

smoking, speeding nun saved by habit, Burke, 232

vite, vite, said the gendarme, Munro, 150

POLIO, learning to help a child with, Brown, 169

POLITICIANS, as major influence, Rogers, 130

POLITICS

problems with cause concern, Berman, 202

surprising interest in for an older woman, Sichveland, 334

POLO

learning to play at fifty-seven, Perkins, 196

wife's name on polo balls calms aggression, Perkins, 256

PONIES, learning to ride, Beacham, 45

POPE, THE, meeting him, Ferguson, 243

POPGUNS, hunting with, Mockler, 26

PORCHES

child sleeps on, Sutton, 10; Waite, 243

child sleeps on after school, Warrington, 17

falling off earns cookie, Peck, 17

rainy days good times to sit on one and hug, DeGrandpre, 263

tongue sticks to railing, McIntyre, 17

too near the edge, Holloway, 374

tractor demolishes, McIntyre, 159

PORNO FILMS prevent fatal rafting accident, Plimpton, 299

PORTRAITS, in *Common Ground*

"Airplanes," Johnson, 294

"Burying a Friend," Martin Hoose, Emery, 341

"City Fathers," Peter, 220

"Discovering Courage," Hanson, 314

"Hanging Together," 50

"Holding Hands," Hallett, 268

"Letting Veronica Go," Abrams, 249
"Life without Father," Royce, 89
"Mutual Respect," Preston, 63
"No Grieving for Peyton, Please,"
Goddard, 353
"Overcoming Adversity," Prowse, 206
"Somebody You Could Talk To,"
Andrews, 110
"Standing Tall on the Coca-Cola
Crates," Strobel, 164
"The Ex-Mother-in-Law," Perkins, 135
"Things Are Going to Be Better,"
Dorrance, 380
"Village Life," Mockler, 182
"What Makes You Feel Young?"
Bridge Club, 359
POSITIVE ATTITUDE
lifetime philosophy, Prowse, 206
tragedy notwithstanding, Johnson, 222
POT, see MARIJUANA
POTATOES, ordering too many, Fish, 29
POVERTY
biker Sees terrible example, Buettner,
292
dignity and poverty can go hand-in-
hand, Holloway, 289
encounter with a homeless woman,
Vonnegut, 292
first realization of, Barbour, 80
mountain man's wise words about,
McIntyre, 190
POWER, TYRONE, Lear, 34
PRAGMATISM, as an important trait,
Rogers, 130
PRAMS, tipped over in Scotland, Munro, 7
PRAYER
camping trip replaces, Buettner, 240
gets you on right track, Brown, 210
PREACHERS, see MINISTERS
PREGNANCY
ends skiing career, Thomas, 196
special feeling, Brunson, 238
PRESSURE, it's good at work, Rochelle, 209

PRESTON, JERRY, first memory, 10; things
that shine, 19; special moment with
parent, 37; Mutual Respect, a portrait,
63; awkward with a parent, 93; adult
with parents, 148; simple pleasure,
185; something sweet, 311; a self-
discovery, 330; burying a friend, 347;
something worth waiting for, 388
PRICKETT, JOY MELTON, things that shine,
21; early friendship, 59; awkward
with a parent, 94; summer job, 158;
simple pleasure, 186; glory in sports,
199; rainy afternoon, 264; funny
story, 276
PRIDE
don't bask, go to work, Prowse, 195
thoughts on, Duke, 287
PRINCE CHARLES, in dreams, Rockefeller,
101
PRINCESS PAMELA, see Strobel
PRINCESS ANNE, in dreams, Rockefeller,
101
PRINCIPALS, talking with, Waite, 41;
Wing, 92
PRISONERS, a memory of a Laotian,
Sultan, 28
PRIVACY, an unexpected treat, Rose, 235
PROBLEMS
learning experience, Platt, 203
marital, impact on kids, "Hanging
Together," 50; Hanson, 59, 227;
Peter, 93; Andrews, 258
siblings create, Munro, 6
PROCRASTINATION, Fish, 317
PROFANITY
better ways to tell people off than
that, Bornn, 283
cussing in front of parents means
you're adult, Preston, 148
PROMS, helping a niece, Edmondson, 360
PROWSE, DAVID, early memories, 26;
special moment with parent, 37; early
friendship, 62; mortality, 80; dream, 99;

art, 181; glory in sports, 195;
Overcoming Adversity, a portrait,
206; loneliness, 255; a compassionate
moment, 287; a self-discovery, 323;
greatest fear, 351; regrets, 365
PUBS, going to with dad, Keefe, 26
PUERTO RICO
taking an injured son to doctor,
Dorrance, 380
traveling to call children, Bornn, 40
PUNCH AND JUDY SHOW, in Paris park,
Plimpton, 6
PYRAMIDS, stuck at the top, Brackett, 304

QUAIL PRESERVES, Sammons, 157
QUILTS, treasured possession, Burke, 104
QUITTING, see "What Makes You Give
Up?" chapter 31, p. 201
not an option, Brown, 205; Ferguson,
375
QUOTATIONS, learning in class, Kahl, 123

RACCOONS, Preston, 63
RACISM
effect on adopted son, Colquhoun, 357
learning about, Colquhoun, 116; Abrams,
924
RADIO
first hearing, Sutton, 28
listening to "Inner Sanctum" as child,
Johnson, 115
treasured possession, Hiers, 104
RAFFLES, winning leads to new sport and
husband, Rose, 218
RAFTING
father knows best, Rockefeller, 39
last trip with brother, Houlihan, 348
porno films save drowning Plimpton,
299
terrifying trip in Russia, Buettner, 298
RAIN, see "Once on a Rainy Afternoon,"
chapter 42, p. 262
adult films with mother, Plimpton, 266

college days remembered, Randolph,
265
deluge nearly drowns, Wing, 304
fire trucks and fiancées, Roberts, 266
great time to hug mom, DeGrandpre,
263
honeymoon in Bavaria, Munro, 266
how wonderful, Holloway, 262
learning about birds and bees in it,
Strobel, 264
listening to music while it rains,
Vonnegut, 265
magazine ad on rainy day changes
life, Bailey, 263
playing in the mud, Peck, 264
rafting trip and umbrellas, Rockefeller,
39
something to do on rainy day,
Rochelle, 266
Soviet biking trip in mud, Buettner, 264
splashing in, Litton, 361
takes guilt away from bridge games,
Kemp, 263
tin roofs in the Ivory Coast, Sultan, 264
walks in the woods, Legere, 265
wonderful childhood memories of,
Goddard, 267
RANDOLPH, MARY, first memory, 14;
special moment with parent, 117;
early friendship, 56; mortality, 831
treasured possession, 104; glory in
sports, 198; rainy afternoon, 265; vile
thing, 283; real fear, 296; a self-
discovery, 328; birds flying south, 336
RATS, a simple pleasure, Thomas, 184
READING
father reading books to, Emmerling, 46
first memory, Abrams, 17
on a rainy afternoon, Cooney, 263
pastime with friend, Mason, 61
personal goal, Dorrance, 377
pleasure, Munro, 184; Duke, 187;
Abrams, 263; Lear, 328

REGRETS, see chapter 62, p. 363
  Lear wishes he'd been a better
    father/husband, 178
  none just experiences, Platt, 365
RELATIONSHIPS, see "A Special
  Relationship," chapter 44, p.
  270
  bad one is better than none, Lear, 255
  building one with father, Royce, 89
  friendship better than sex, Mockler, 323
  lead to self-knowledge, Platt, 32
  working for the right one, Emmerling
    and Learson, 386
RELIGION
  interest in diversity, Lear, 328
  Pentecostal, Preston, 10
  Scouts require, Peter, 220
  shock value of atheism, Rochelle, 158
RESOURCEFULNESS, grandmother's gift,
  Burke, 125
RESPECT
  family legacy, Hackman, 367; Taufer,
    368; Edmondson, 368; Legere, 369
  mother treated with, Brackett, 139
  strangers giving is sign of adulthood,
    Emery, 145
RESPONSIBILITY, the importance of,
  Goddard, 128
RESTAURANTS,
  metaphor for life, Lear, 82
  Strobel runs a special one, 378
RETIREMENT
  goal, Spezzano, 361
  nice treat, Colquhoun, 234
RETTON, MARY LOU, early memories,
  27; holding hands, 33; special
  moment with parent, 43; early
  friendship, 54; awkward with a
  parent, 95; person who influenced,
  117; work, 174; lowest moment, 229;
  loneliness, 257; a compassionate
  moment, 288; a self-discovery, 317;
  birds flying south, 337; greatest fear,
  352; legacy, 376; something you want
  to do, 377; regrets, 364

REUNION, HIGH SCHOOL, what they
  really thought of you, Lear, 192
REVENGE, rugby bad guy gets just
  reward, Munro, 198
RHEUMATIC FEVER, as a child,
  Holloway, 60
RISK TAKING
  losing weight, Burke, 384
  pushed to a new view, Holloway, 374
RITES OF PASSAGE
  adulthood equals land in islands,
    Donovan, 145
  breaking down big problems,
    Plimpton, 212
  can't go back home, Retton, 95
  conversation between son and mom,
    Miller, 47
  conversation with dad, DeGrandpre, 47
  daughter hunts with her father,
    Hallett, 41
  discovering your best talent,
    Emmerling, 166
  driving again after a wreck,
    Colquhoun, 44
  driving father, Kemp, 38
  father sees daughter in new light,
    Plimpton 48
  father spends time with daughter
    Learson, 34
  first time called "Sir," Emery, 145
  kid sees the effect of authority, Duke,
    156
  learning we must go on, Hanson, 210
  life goes on regardless, Keefe, 631
  mother encourages freedom, Platt, 42
  moving away from home as a kid,
    Retton, 43
  moving to the big table, Randolph, 39
  parentless child faces life, Strobel, 164
  riding a bike, Beacham, 45
  travelling alone for first time,
    Robertson, 44

triathlon changes a life, Litton, 199
young boy accepts big brother,
   Jensen, 240
RIVERA, DIEGO, power of art, Taufer, 73
RIVERS
   fair on Mekong, Sultan, 18
   fishing on the Ohoopee, fishing on,
      Sammons, 40
   rafting Buffalo with father,
      Rockefeller, 39
   rafting accident nearly drowns, porno
      saves, Plimpton 299
   rafting with brother, Houlihan, 348
   terrifying episode on a Russian river,
      Buettner, 298
ROBBERY, see MUGGING
ROBERTS, DORIS, first memory, 12;
   special moment with parent, 42;
   mortality, 85; person who influenced,
   120; courage to go on, 212; treat,
   233; special private moment, 236;
   loneliness, 253; rainy afternoon, 266;
   funny story, 281; a self-discovery,
   323; birds flying south, 337
ROBERTSON, CLIFF, special moment
   with parent, 44; mortality, 77; glory
   in sports, 194; courage to go on, 208;
   threats, 230; rainy afternoon, 264; a
   special relationship, 270; funny story,
   275; real fear, 309; greatest fear, 350
ROCHELLE, ZAR, first memory, 6; things
   that shine, 19; special moment with
   parent, 41; early friendship, 60;
   breath away, 71; mortality, 79;
   summer job, 158; failing, 177; simple
   pleasure, 185; glory in sports, 197;
   courage to go on, 209; rainy
   afternoon, 266; funny story, 277; vile
   thing, 283; birds flying south, 337;
   burying a friend, 343
ROCHESTER RED WINGS BASEBALL
   TEAM, Spezzano, 16

ROCKEFELLER, WIN, first memory, 8;
   special moment with parent, 39;
   breath away, 72; mortality, 86; dream,
   101; treasured possession, 104;
   money, 161; courage to go on, 209;
   threats, 231; treat, 233; special private
   moment, 237; loneliness, 257; real
   fear, 309; a self-discovery, 322;
   unusual friendship, 338; greatest fear,
   350; fear for children, 355; feel
   young, 360
ROCKS
   boulders give a place to hide from
      hostility, Learson, 258
   hitting head on, Brunson, 12
ROGERS, JULIE, person who influenced,
   130; what makes you give up, 202;
   unusual friendship, 339
ROLE MODEL, see FATHER,
   GRANDPARENTS, MOTHERS and
   "Someone Other Than a Parent Who
   Had a Major Influence on You,"
   chapter 18, p. 113
ROLLINS COLLEGE, Emery, 69
ROOMMATES, in college, Mildred Sutton, 57
ROOSTER, countess and cockerel,
   Munro, 67
ROOTLESSNESS, the effect of on children,
   Friedman, 12; Andrews, 110; Roberts,
   253
ROOTS, importance of, DeGrandpre, 318
ROSE, JUDY, first memory, 13; awkward
   moment with a parent, 91; adult with
   parents, 148; serendipity, 218; treat,
   235; a self-discovery, 319
ROSE, BEN, first memory, 13; early
   friendship, 55; serendipity, 218; treat,
   235; special private moment, 247; a
   self-discovery, 330
ROSE BEDS, childhood memories of,
   Marston, 7
ROSES
   barometer of life, Mason, 311

family gardening tradition, Bornn, 189

help Beacham deal with loneliness, Beacham, 256

something sweet, Mason, 311

ROTHSCHILDE, PHILIPPE, doing story on, McIntyre, 171

ROWAN TREES, Munro, 30

ROYCE, JAMES, holding hands, 33; early friendship, 59; mortality, 86; "Life without Father," a portrait, 89; treasured possession, 104; adult with parents, 144; summer job, 156; real fear, 302; legacy, 371

RUGBY, dirty player gets just reward, Munro, 198

RUM, smell of Mount Gay, Thomas, 72

RUNNING

cross-country triumph of thirteen year-old, Miller, 199

minitriathlons build confidence, Berman, 325; Litton, 199

new start at fifty, Mason, 361

Sardis Frog Wallow Waddle, Prickett, 199

surprise pleasure, Hackman, 326

RUNNING AWAY FROM HOME, dealing with violence, Hanson, 227

RURAL ELECTRIC ASSOCIATION, Johnson, 22

RUSSIA

bike wheel made from Russian jet, Buettner, 219

bitterness on Russian biking trip, Buettner, 228

mud nearly defeats biker in Russia, Buettner, 264

Russian spirit as a metaphor, Roberts, 212

terrifying trip down Russian river, Buettner, 298

women exchange ideas in, Bornn, 246

SADNESS, as childhood memory, Friedman, 35

SAFETY COUNSELING, Green Cross Code Man, Prowse, 323

SAILING

just finishing was a victory, Plimpton, 198

way of life, Peter, 384

SALUTATIONS, being called sir feels like adulthood, Emery, 145

SAMMONS, PEGGY, special moment with parent, 40; pet, 69; person who influenced, 124; adult with parents, 141; simple pleasure, 186

SAMMONS, TOMMY, special moment with parent, 39; adult with parents, 141; summer job, 157; something you want to do, 377

SANTA CLAUS

Laotian surprise, Sultan, 18

not believing in, DeGrandpre, 18

SANTA GIULIANA, ITALY, Taufer, 218

SAUNDERS, ADA, Goddard, 128

SAVINGS, a nice treat, Colquhoun, 234

SAXOPHONE,

a treasured possession, Cooney, 106

a wish to play, Jensen, 365

SAYINGS, mixed up, Johnson, 371; Royce, 371

SCHOOL, see also HIGH SCHOOL, COLLEGE

cow causes detention problem, Wing, 92

driving the teachers, Waite, 142

lunch with teacher, Mason, 131

remembering first day as a young countess, Munro, 56

a rough start to, McIntyre, 17

SCISSORS, fear of, Retton, 27

SCORPIONS, Preston, 63

SCOTLAND, see also J. Munro, H. & A. Barbour

SCOTLAND

hunting in, Barbour, 81, 154

memories of being raised in, Munro, 7, 127

Pitlochry, Barbour, 14

SCUBA-DIVING
  death impacts rescuer, Ferguson, 291
  expert's near-death experience,
    Englander, 306
  unexpected life in, Englander, 173
  win lessons, find husband, Rose, 218
SCYTHES, mowing ski trails with,
  Sultan, 72
SEACOMBER, mother's hotel, Brackett, 105
SEARCHLIGHTS, as something that shines,
  Johnson, 22
SEASONS, see AUTUMN, SUMMER,
  WINTER
SECRETS, see "An Unexpected Special
  Moment," chapter 39, p. 236
SECURITY, for one's children, Hanson,
  357; Swann, 355; Taufer, 357
SELF-ANALYSIS, can be unsettling,
  Robertson, 230
SELF-CONFIDENCE, see also CONFIDENCE
  gaining, Berman, 130
  running builds, Berman, 325
  worth waiting for, Legere, 383
SELF-DISCIPLINE, a father's legacy,
  Plimpton, 374
SELF-ESTEEM
  athletic event gives, Litton, 199
  wrapped up in success, Rogers, 202
SELF-IMAGE, thoughts on, Hanson, 314;
  Colquhoun, 324
SELF-REALIZATION, a goal, Lear, 351
SELF-RELIANCE, flying a glider teaches,
  Robertson, 309
SELF-RESPECT, a father's legacy, Abrams,
  373
SELF-SUFFICIENCY
  sometimes not what it seems, Jensen,
    188
  going on alone, Bailey, 334
SERENDIPITY, see chapter 34, p. 214
  meeting Fellini, Roberts, 233
  nun's habit saves a smoking speeder,
    Burke, 232

rainy day leads to famous cave
  discovery, Rose, 247
rainy day read changes life, Bailey, 263
SERMONS, as something that shines,
  Waite, 20
SERVICE TO OTHERS, a family legacy,
  Cook, 369; Abrams, 370; Johnson,
  370; Colquhoun, 370
SEWING, makes you feel like an adult,
  Costigan, 140
SEX
  awkward moments around parents,
    Sultan, 91
  in dreams, Emery, 101
SEX EDUCATION
  apples make you pregnant, Strobel, 264
  too late to find out, Thomas, 95
  what are they doing in that film?
    Plimpton, 266
  where does he plant that seed?
    Preston, 93
SHARECROPPERS, Brown, 23
SHARING
  a fan after the funeral, Preston, 347
  hand-me-downs and dignity,
    Holloway, 289
  hand-me-downs at the palace, Munro,
    56
  parents really shared, Plimpton, 270
SHELLS, see CONCH
SHIPS
  early memory of the *Bremen*,
    Plimpton, 6
  sinking in dreams, Plimpton, 102
SHOCK THERAPY, assisting on summer
  job, Colquhoun, 172
SHOES
  the Pope's red velvet, Ferguson, 243
  touching sight at wreck of the Titanic,
    Mockler, 285
SHOPPING, father and daughter buy a
  bathing suit, Brunson, 275

SHOTGUNS
  as fireworks, Emmerling, 13
  hunting with father, Mockler, 26
SHOW BUSINESS, as something that
  shines, Holloway, 22
SIBLINGS, see BROTHERS and SISTERS
SICHVELAND, MURIEL, things that
  shine, 21; adult with parents, 140;
  money, 162; simple pleasure, 191; a
  self-discovery, 334
SICKNESS, see ILLNESS and specific diseases
SIERRA LEONE, Barbour, 29
SIMPLE PLEASURES, see chapter 29, p.
  184
SIMPLICITY, not as simple as it sounds,
  Jensen, 188
SINGING
  "Old MacDonald" moves a crippled
    child, Prowse, 287
  so you think you can? McIntyre, 332
  terrifying act, Burke, 73
  with mother, Preston, 10
SINN, JULIE, Hanson, 59
SIRENS, during war, Rose, 13
SISTERS
  ally in tough times, Hanson, 227
  as biters, Munro, 6
  as dart boards, Lear, 54
  happy visit with parents, Holloway, 147
  major influence, Sammons, 124
  raising them makes you feel like
    adult, Johnson, 141
  when did you say you were coming?
    Costigan, 257
SIX FLAGS OVER GEORGIA, a summer
  job, Prickett, 158
SKELETONS, in an old family closet,
  Cook, 280
SKI TRAILS, mowing with scythe, Sultan, 72
SKIING, SNOW
  learning was a snap, Rochelle, 197
  making the pro team, Thomas, 196

skiing trip alone is satisfying,
  DeGrandpre, 258
winning a trip to learn, Friedman, 197
SKIN, as something that shines,
  Friedman, 19
SKY DIVING, DeGrandpre, 305
SLEDDING, on grass, Lear, 7
SLEEP WALKING, Munro, 276
SLEEPING through danger, Cross, 300
SLIPPERY ROCK, UTAH, bicycling in,
  Buettner, 72
SMALL TOWN LIFE, problems with,
  Rochelle, 158
SMALL-TOWN VIRTUES, a look at an
  island village, Mockler, 182
SMALL-TOWN ATTITUDES, an example
  in south Georgia, Johnson, 116
SMELL, see ODOR
SMELTS, Roberts, 12
SMILES
  coaxing smiles from ill babies,
    Learson, 185
  something that shines, Kelly, 20
SMITH, SCOTT, "Hanging Together," a
  portrait, 50
SMITH, SCOTT, DeGrandpre, 131
SMITH'S POINT, Mockler, 182
SMOKING
  a nun smokes and speeds, Burke, 232
  quitting, Hackman, 388
SMUGNESS, no time for it in a champion,
  Prowse, 195
SNAILS, as metaphor for life, Learson, 282
SNAKES
  cobra attack in Laos, Sultan, 230
  young counselor kills one, Brunson, 143
  pet, Preston, 63
  a threat, Thomas, 184
SNOWSHOES, an Alaskan regret, Duke, 363
SOARING, silent beauty in the air,
  Robertson, 194
  a woman beats a man, McIntyre, 198
SOCIABILITY, Buettner, 324

SOLDIERS
    nearly left by outfit, Peck, 297
    prisoners, Sultan, 28
SOLITUDE
    time out in woods, Robertson, 264
    wish for a mother, Abrams, 263
SONGWRITING, a goal, Johnson, 377
SONS, see also FATHERS and MOTHERS,
    chapters 6, 14, and 20
    drifting from parents brings regret,
        Prowse, 255
    father's joy in, Platt, 238
    killed in accident, Brown, 224;
        Dorrance, 379
    relationship to father, DeGrandpre,
        47; Abrams, 373; Lear, 34
    a shining moment with, Bornn, 20
    special trip with, Goddard, 245
SOUTH AMERICA, biking through,
    Buettner, 251
SOUTH CAROLINA
    Aiken, Sutton, 10, 124
    Spartanburg, Strobel, 9
SOVIETREK, Buettner, 219, 228, 264, 298
SPAGNOLA, NICHOLAS, Keefe, 57
SPANKING, getting one by mistake,
    Goddard, 276
SPEECHES
    fearful object, Royce, 302
    make you feel like adult, Johnson, 142
SPEEDING, consequences of, Prickett, 94
SPELLING, learning to, Abrams, 36
SPEZZANO, MARGE, mortality, 84;
    person who influenced, 123; adult
    with parents, 148; feel young, 360
SPEZZANO, VINCE, first memory, 16;
    mortality, 84; person who influenced,
    130; a self-discovery, 328; unusual
    friendship, 338; feel young, 361;
    something worth waiting for, 386
SPONTANEITY, as a goal in life, Cooney, 75
SPORTS, see also "Your Moment of
    Glory in Sports," chapter 30, p. 192,
    and individual categories

baseball cards, DeGrandpre, 58
horse riding in the Arabian desert,
    McIntyre, 244
next-to-last, hut a victory anyway,
    Prickett, 199
polo at 57, Perkins, 196
rugby bad guy gets just reward,
    Munro, 198
snow skiing at 57 is exciting,
    Friedman, 197
woman teaches man a thing or two,
    McIntyre, 198
SPOUSES, a treat to be with alone, Waite,
    190; Rose, 235
SQUIRRELS, Preston, 63
ST. THOMAS, USVI, see also E. and M.
    Bornn
    taking father to hospital there,
        Callwood, 35
STABLES
    as children's rooms, Munro, 67
    tack room nuptials, Bornn, 56
STAGE FRIGHT, anticipating a solo,
    Burke, 73
STAYING IN TOUCH, twenty-eight years
    later, a friend again, Randolph, 265
STENOGRAPHY SERVICE, mother
    owning, Roberts, 42
STEPBROTHERS AND SISTERS,
    loneliness around, Andrews, 258
STEPMOTHERS, special gifts, Emery, 371;
    Hanson, 372
STICKS, as a metaphor for life, Plimpton, 79
STOICISM, a mother's attitude, Mason, 213
STORIES, importance of listening to
    grandmothers, Hallett, 120
STORMS
    small plane excitement, McIntyre,
        231; 308
    terrifying moments, Warrington, 263
    wonderful childhood memories of,
        Goddard, 267

STORYTELLING, made her feel like an adult, Kahl, 138

STREAMS
jumping in takes your breath away, Miller, 72
swimming in as a child Rose, 55

STRENGTH
coming back from a vicious attack, Hanson, 314
physical, Prowse, 195

STRICKLAND, CHARLIE, Rochelle, 60

STRICTNESS, from grandmother, Strobel, 9

STROBEL, PRINCESS PAMELA, first memory, 9; a pet, 67; person who influenced, 126; adult with parents, 149; "Standing Tall on the Coca-Cola Crates," a portrait, 164; rainy afternoon, 264; birds flying south, 335; regrets, 366; something you want to do, 378

STROKES, death of grandfather, Perkins, 44

STUBBORNNESS, not listening to parents is dangerous, Peck, 196

SUBMARINES, stuck in one at 1000 brings fear, Mockler, 296

SUCCESS
don't rest on laurels, Prowse, 195
a special moment, Hiers, 242
worth waiting for, Englander, 385
a young man's motivating force, Miller, 209

SUICIDE, contemplating, Legere, 80

SUITCASES, mistaking caskets for, Hiers, 76

SULTAN, TIMOTHY, first memory, 18; pet, 68; breath away, 72; awkward with a parent, 91; person who influenced, 120; simple pleasure, 187; lowest moment, 225; threats, 230; loneliness, 257; rainy afternoon, 264; vile thing, 283; a compassionate moment, 290; real fear, 308; something sweet, 312; birds flying south, 335; unusual friendship, 340

SUMMER SCHOOL, Plimpton, 176

SUMMER JOBS, see chapter 22, p. 153

SUMMER CAMP, loneliness of first time, Swann, 631

SUMMER
beach idyll, Platt, 25; Hames, 26
effect of summer heat on dancing irons, Emery, 172
holidays with best friend, Cook, 57
playing summer stock, Holloway, 132
surfing with grandmother, Goddard, 128

SURF BOARDS, Marston, 33

SURFING
grandmother teaches, Goddard, 128
Nassau memories of, Ferguson, 24

SURGERY, young girl fears, Campbell, 212, 302

SURPRISES, keep you going, Plimpton, 383

SUTTON, MILDRED, first memory, 10; things that shine, 20; early memories, 28; special moment with parent, 37; early friendship, 57; breath away, 74; mortality, 78; treasured possession, 108; person who influenced, 124; money, 162; failing, 177; simple pleasure, 186; on friendship, 191; give up, 201; courage to go on, 210; loneliness, 255; a self-discovery, 334; birds flying south, 336; greatest fear, 352; something you want to do, 379

SUTTON, REMAR "Bubba", with Jensen and whales, 303; in Perkins's portrait, 135; awkward moment with T. Plimpton, 96; in Bahamas with Preston, 63

SUTTON, GEORGE, Perkins, 135

SUTTON, SUE, Perkins, 135

SUTTON, DAWN, Perkins, 135

SWANN, JIM, early memories, 25; holding hands, 32; breath away, 74; mortality, 88; dream, 100; give up, 203; courage to go on, 208; loneliness, 251; a self-discovery, 322; fear for children, 355;

SWEEPING
  brother's fort, Retton, 54
  in St. Thomas, Bornn, 312
SWEETHEARTS, childhood, Burke, 56;
  Randolph, 56
SWIMMING
  childhood swims in streams, Rose, 55
  deep ocean with big whales, Jensen, 303
  drowning brother (nearly), Cooney, 239
  learning is accomplishment,
    Randolph, 198
SWINGS, Sutton, 10
SYMBOLS, the power of, Duke, 156

TALCUM POWDER, the smell of brings
  back memories, Andrews, 103
TALENT,
  a natural skier, Rochelle, 197
  determination is better, Buettner, 211
TALKING IN SLEEP, Lear, 47
TALKING IN CHURCH, the consequences
  of, Johnson, 54
TAMPA BAY, FLORIDA, Swann, 25
TAUFER, MIMI, breath away, 73; person
  who influenced, 123; serendipity,
  218; vile thing, 283; real fear, 301;
  fear for children, 357; legacy, 368
TAXI, being hit by, Colquhoun, 87
TEA PARTIES, WITH A DOG, Randolph, 14
TEACHERS, see A. Brunson, Costigan,
  Duke, Holloway, B. Rose, Sutton, M.
  Waite
  adult influences, Kahl,123; Spezzano, 123
  childhood influences, Houlihan, 131;
    Kelly, 119; Sultan, 120; Waite, 119
  courage required to be one, Brunson,
    324
  influence on future profession,
    Mason, 131
  remembering to thank, Roberts, 120
TEACHING, discovering a talent, B. Rose,
  330
TELEPHONES, see also PHONE CALLS

  fire trucks recommended instead,
    Roberts, 266
  traveling to another island to use,
    Bornn, 40
  a way to attend school, Holloway, 60
TELEVISION
  dying goldfish lead to a starring
    role, Beacham, 215
  no good without stations, Johnson, 240
  unexpected treat in the yard, Hames, 234
  watching at the palace, Munro, 237
TENACITY, a family trait, Ferguson, 375
TENNESSEE, NASHVILLE, Johnson, 241
TENNIS TROPHY, as treasured possession,
  Plimpton, 106
TEXACO gas station, as a hangout,
  Hallett, 40, 118
TEXAS
  Brownsville, Preston, 10
  childhood memories, Colquhoun, 15;
    Preston, 37
  Houston, Retton, 117
THANKS, remembering to thank a
  mentor, Roberts, 120
THANKSGIVING, a vivid scene to
  remember on that day, Buettner, 292
THEATER
  director as major influence, Holloway,
    132
  Fellini encounter, Roberts, 233
  going to as a child, Roberts, 42
  writing a musical, Legere, 329
THERAPY, listening helps, Berman, 130;
  Perkins, 256
THINKING FOR YOURSELF, the
  importance of, McIntyre, 140
THOMAS, NAN, things that shine, 19;
  holding hands, 33; breath away, 72;
  mortality, 78; awkward with a parent,
  95; adult with parents, 142; failing,
  178; simple pleasure, 184; glory in
  sports, 196; give up, 201; courage to
  go on, 208; serendipity, 215; rainy

afternoon, 262; real fear, 302; a self-discovery, 326; feel young, 361; something worth waiting for, 384
THOMPSON, HILARY, Bornn, 56
THOUGHTFULNESS, as a breathtaking act, Bornn, 74
THREATS, see chapter 37, 230
TIANANMEN SQUARE, Miller, 288
TICKETS, SPEEDING, smoking nun saved by habit, Burke, 232
TIME
running out is a worry, Robertson, 350
using it wisely, Warrington, 374
TIMING IS EVERYTHING, Englander, 217; Friedman, 217
TIPPING, as an example of style, Emmerling, 114
TITANIC
diving on it brings moment of compassion, Mockler, 285
a piece of, as treasured possession, Mockler, 106
TOBY THE SEA TURTLE, Thomas, 215
TOGETHERNESS, a simple pleasure, Waite, 190; McIntyre, 190
TOLERANCE, grandmother's legacy, Edmondson, 368
TOMBOY, trying to be, Legere, 91
TONGUES, frozen to railings, McIntyre, 17
TORNADO, nearly hits, Cross, 300
TORTOLA
attitudes about age, Thomas, 361
Donovan, 351, 385
Little Apple Bay, Thomas, 19, 326
museum preserves its history, Donovan, 189
TOTEM POLES, father carving for son, DeGrandpre, 93
TOUCH
memory of a teacher's comforting hand, Kelly, 119
missing a spouse's, Bailey, 255
TOW TRUCKS, Hallett, 118

TRACTORS
first drive causes a disaster, McIntyre, 161
great-grandfather's instructive tale, Perkins, 367
TRADITION
island traditions preserved, Donovan, 189
preserving Jost Van Dyke, Callwood, 378
TRAGEDY, see also chapters 36 and 41
baby's death brings grief, loneliness, Abrams, 249
death of a brother, Brunson, 223; Edmondson, 254
lifetime relationship rises from, Brunson, 218
young doctor learn mortality, Andrews, 285
TRAIL BIKES, in Nassau, Ferguson, 24
TRAINS
extra ride on a kid's train, Edmondson, 244
first trip on by self, Robertson, 44
riding on with mother, Preston, 10
spring trip to Florida, Plimpton, 25
TRANQUILITY, feeling with family, Cook, 73
TRAVEL, see also TRIPS
Brazil, McIntyre, 335
buying your own castle, Taufer, 218
first trip as a kid, Johnson, 240
London to Delhi by bus, Barbour, 317
Model T with grandparents, Waite, 243
month early and abandoned at airport, Costigan, 257
Puerto Rico to use the telephone, Bornn, 40
sign of a young person's freedom, Robertson, 44
solo trip makes lonely, Emmerling, 260
summer camp by bus, Swann, 251

with grandparents, special times, Ferguson, 243
with father, Edmondson, 244
TREASURES, see "A Treasured Possession," chapter 16, p. 103
TREATS, see chapter 38, 233
anniversary roses, Dorrance, 380
TREES
climbing for money, Johnson, 153
memories of playing in, Ferguson, 24
TREKKING, an unforgettable sports moment, Buettner, 195
TRICYCLES, Peck, 17; Johnson, 16
TRIPS
by Model T Ford, Hames, 26
in red wagons, Waite, 11
on trains to Florida, Plimpton, 25
on trains, Preston, 10
with mother, to get first haircut, Retton, 27
with father to bar, Keefe, 26; Swann, 25
with father, Sutton, 10; Waite, 15
TROPHY, a tennis trophy as treasured possession, Plimpton, 106
TROPICAL FRUITS, Ferguson, 24
TRUCKS, driving as a summer job, Lear, 153
TRUST
boarding school experience shows danger of, Munro, 252
how it makes us loyal, Spezzano, 130
stranger shows to a pilot, Hallett, 308
TURTLES, lead to a book, Thomas, 215
TUTORS, a grandmother's special humor as, Andrews, 273

ULCER, David Prowse's father dies of, 26
UMBRELLAS, on rafting trips, Rockefeller, 39
UNCLE
major influence, DeGrandpre, 94; Emmerling, 114; Strobel, 126
UNDERHILL, FATHER, Rose, 247

UNEXSO
a business challenge, Englander, 173, 226
teaching marine life, Rose, 330
UNHAPPINESS
as childhood memory, Friedman, 35
as early memory, Johnson, 38
as a child, Roberts, 253
may be sign of adulthood, Edmondson, 146
UNITED NATIONS, private signal of friendship, Plimpton, 270
UNIVERSITY OF MONTANA, DeGrandpre, 131
UNORTHODOXY
busking as a summer job, Munro, 150
commercial fishing as a job, Marston, 175
finally accepted by parents, Marston, 383
oil rigs, as a summer job, Brunson, 153
URUBASHOV, POLAND, Friedman, 83
UTAH, SLIPPERY ROCK, bicycling in, Buettner, 72

VACATIONS
college student's solo trip feels good, Degrandpre, 258
unexpected treat for island man, Callwood, 234
with grandmother, Andrews, 110
VALUES, moral and aesthetic legacy, Legere, 369
VAN MORRISON, on a rainy day, Platt, 266
V-E DAY, Emmerling remembers as a child, 13
THE VELVETEEN RABBIT, Cooney is read to, 263
VENICE, ITALY, making love in the rain, Emmerling, 682
VERMONT, Sugarbush, Thomas, 326
VERONICA, her death tests faith, Abrams, 249

VERTIGO, stuck on top of a pyramid, Brackett, 308

VICTORY, no time to rest when you're winning, Prowse, 195

VIDAL, GORE, influence on Plimpton, 166

VIENTIANE, LAOS, Sultan, 18, 28

VIETNAM, a librarian's moment of real fear, Randolph, 296

VILE THINGS, see chapter 46, p. 283

VILLAGES,
   buying your own in Italy, Taufer, 218
   portrait of a Bahamian village, Mockler, 182

VIOLENCE
   against children, Colquhoun, 291
   leads a person to loneliness, Hanson, 210
   learning to live with, Hanson, 227
   made person stronger, Mason, 224

VIRGIN ISLANDS, playing baseball with parents, Bornn, 14

VISIONARIES, preserving an island's history, Donovan, 189

VOCATIONS, see also "Finding Work," chapter 25, p. 166
   husband and wife together, McIntyre, 171
   mother never understood, Prowse, 255
   parent's look at son's in new light, Colquhoun, 146
   playing bagpipes for dinner, Munro, 150
   restaurateur remembers her start, Strobel, 164
   serendipitous route, Munro, 327
   start in, Plimpton, 166
   supporting your parents, Lear, 153
   unorthodox job finally wins over parents, Marston, 383

VONNEGUT, KURT, holding hands, 33; breath away, 74; treasured possession, 108; failing, 176; simple pleasure, 188; give up, 201; treat, 235; special private moment, 242; rainy afternoon, 265; a compassionate moment, 292; a self-discovery, 334; unusual friendship, 339; something worth waiting for, 383

WAITE, MARYNELL, first memory, 11; early friendship, 61; mortality, 81; person who influenced, 127; adult with parents, 142; simple pleasure, 190; something worth waiting for, 388

WAITE, ALVIS, first memory, 15; things that shine, 20; special moment with parent, 41; person who influenced, 119; adult with parents, 144; simple pleasure, 190; special private moment, 243

WAITE, JAMES THOMAS HAMILTON, 41

WAITE, MARY ABBOTT, 41

WAITING, work, don't wait, Beacham, 384

WALKING
   simple pleasures, Mason, 188
   with grandfather, Learson, 121

WALLPAPER, makes for fun and games, Beacham, 256

WAR, see also WORLD WAR I, WORLD WAR II
   death of a brother, Brunson, 223
   impact on children, Lear, 291
   librarian learns about courage in Vietnam, Randolph, 296
   tragic story, Cross, 284
   tragic effects of on father, Lear, 47
   troops desert you, Peck, 297

WARRINGTON, DANA, first memory, 17; serendipity, 216; rainy afternoon, 263; burying a friend, 346; legacy, 374

WARTS, memories of child's hands with, Burke, 32

WASHING MACHINE, in Plimpton bathtub, 6

WASTE. as a breathtaking act, Sutton, 74

WATCHMEN, Barbour remembers, 29

WATER,
  fear of sticking head under, Buettner, 36
  floating in lake brings self-aware
    moment, Sultan, 257
  in dreams, Platt, 99
  playing in the rain in Laos, Sultan,
    264
  unexpected moment diving on the
    Titanic, Mockler, 285
WEATHER
  bad weather leads to historic
    discovery, Rose, 247
  brings fear in small plane, Hallett, 308
  importance to a sailor, Peter, 187
  tornado near hit, Cross, 300
  wonderful memories of storms,
    Goddard, 267
WEDDING
  accident on day of, Colquhoun, 87
  anxiety approaching, Berman, 86
WEIGHTLESSNESS, a desired experience,
  Retton, 377
WEIGHTLIFTING, becoming a champ,
  Prowse, 195
WEST INDIES COMPANY, fishing on
  docks of, Bornn, 40
WHALES, swimming with then in deep
  ocean, Jensen, 303
WHEELCHAIR, spending life in,
  Andrews, 307
WHERRY, TOBY, Plimpton, 122
WIDOWHOOD, the lonliness of,
  Goddard, 128, Sutton, 255; Bailey
  255
WILLIAMSBURG, a kids special trip to,
  Johnson, 240
WILSDEN, MELANIE, Prickett, 59
WINE, a simple pleasure, McIntyre, 190
WING, ROSE, early memories, 30; awkward
  with a parent, 92; money, 162; funny
  story, 273; greatest fear, 304
WING, STEVE, awkward with a parent,
  92; real fear, 304

WINNING, see also "Your Moment of
  Glory in Sports," chapter 30, p. 192
  gold medal after failing three times,
    Retton, 229
  raffle leads to new avocation and
    husband, Rose, 218
WINTER, see also CHRISTMAS
  frozen to a railing, McIntyre, 17
  Indiana mornings, Rockefeller, 8
  learning to ski, Rochelle, 197
  North Dakota blizzard, Mason, 239
WISCONSIN, McIntyre, 17
WITCHES, in dreams, Munro, 98
WOMEN
  alone, builds creativity, Legere, 254
  breathtaking power, Vonnegut, 74
  changing self-image, Learson, 325
  competitive as men, McIntyre, 244, 198
  conversations with Russian, Bornn, 246
  taught as men, Hallett, 245
WOOD BOXES, filling, Wing, 92
WOOD STOVES, Rockefeller, 8
WOODPECKERS, a scary sound for kid
  at night, Johnson, 307
WORK, see "Finding Work," chapter 25,
  p. 166; VOCATIONS: and individual jobs
  cure to fear, Campbell, 212
  hard work a lifetime philosophy,
    Prowse, 206
  importance of, Goddard, 128
  makes an adult, Cross, 139
WORLD WAR I, memories of in London,
  Bailey, 28
WORLD WAR II
  childhood memories, Georgia,
    Johnson, 22
  childhood memories, Detroit,
    Emmerling, 13
  childhood memories, England, Rose, 13
  isolates daughter from parents, Bornn,
    40
  soldier's terror when deserted, Peck, 297
  tragic effects on father, Lear, 47

WORRY, a good trait for a sailor, Peter, 231

WRECKS, wrecking father's car, Colquhoun, 44

WRESTLING ON TELEVISION, an unexpected treat, Hames, 234

WRIGHT, FRANK LLOYD, Rochelle, 71

WRITERS, see Buettner, Colquhoun, Emmerling, Friedman, G. Plimpton, Hackman, Kahl, Lear, Mason, Spezzano, Thomas, Vonnegut

WRITING
    beginning a career, Kahl, 328; Plimpton, 329
    first experience, Kahl, 174
    turtle leads to a new career, Thomas, 215

YAMACRAW, a horse, Ferguson, 24

YANKEE SYMPATHIZERS, come out of family closet, Cook, 280

YANKEES, a determined lot, Thomas, 208

YARD WORK, as a summer job, Royce, 156

YOU CAN'T GO HOME AGAIN, book disappears in Berlin, Kahl, 259

YOUTH, see "What Makes You Feel Young?" chapter 61, p. 360

YOUTH AT THE ZOO, the book, Prowse, 37

YOUTHFULNESS
    adult feeling when mistaken for wife, Bornn, 141
    attitude makes difference, Friedman, 363
    being called sir gives adult feeling, Emery, 145